Bureaucratic
Power in
National
Policy Making

Bureaucratic Power in National Policy Making

Fourth Edition

Readings Edited by

Francis E. Rourke
The Johns Hopkins University

Little, Brown and Company
Boston   Toronto

Library of Congress Cataloging in Publication Data
Main entry under title:

Bureaucratic power in national policy making.

Rev. ed. of: Bureaucratic power in national politics.
3rd ed. c1978.
1. Administrative agencies—United States—Addresses,
essays, lectures. 2. United States—Executive depart-
ments—Addresses, essays, lectures. 3. Bureaucracy—
United States—Addresses, essays, lectures. I. Rourke,
Francis E. (Francis Edward), 1922–   . II. Title:
Bureaucratic power in national politics.
JK421.B86 1985   353.01   85–12910
ISBN 0–316–75973–2

Library of Congress Catalog Card No. 85–12910

ISBN 0-316-75973-2

9 8 7 6 5 4 3 2 1

MV

Published simultaneously in Canada
by Little, Brown & Company (Canada) Limited

Printed in the United States of America

Contents

v

VII
Implementing Public Policy: Bureaucratic Problems   405

VIII
Improving Bureaucratic Performance: The Politics of Reform   485

Editor's Introduction

Bureaucratic power and public policy are the central topics of this book. These readings focus on the power of bureaucratic organizations, the sources from which this power is derived, and the ways in which it is used to shape the direction and development of public policy. But behind this analytical focus there lies also a normative concern: Has the power of bureaucracy in modern democratic states grown so great as to threaten the ability of the public and its elected representatives to control the government's decisions? Is bureaucracy, in short, a danger to democracy?

This is an old question, but it has been given new urgency in modern times by the growing role of government in every sector of society, and the resulting expansion in both the number of bureaucratic organizations and the powers they exercise. In democratic theory, at least, bureaucrats are expected to defer to the preferences of the public. These preferences are expressed in the United States through an election system, which empowers both a president and Congress to translate the popular will into public policy directives that bureaucrats are charged with carrying out.

As these readings show, however, the actual role of bureaucrats may deviate widely from their theoretical role as servants of policy. Bureaucrats may help to create as well as to carry out the public will by generating new policy initiatives which the public accepts. In some areas of policy their expertise may even entitle them to act at their own discretion, limited only by the vaguest set of guidelines laid down by the White House or Congress. So, as is often the case with the master-servant relationship, the activities of some bureaucratic servants may very much resemble those of a master.

It is strongly believed in many quarters that bureaucrats have far too much power in U.S. government today. This conviction has helped give rise to widespread pressure from citizen organizations at the grass roots level to reduce the tax base on which public bureaucracies depend for financial support. Within the national government, the president, Congress, and the courts have all sought in various ways to curb the power of bureaucracy: the president by expanding his White House staff, Congress by establishing new oversight mechanisms to monitor bureaucratic behavior, and the courts by intervening more vigorously in behalf of citizens and organizations aggrieved by administrative actions.

In all recent national administrations—from Kennedy to Reagan—there has been an antagonistic relationship between national politicians and the bureaucracy. Kennedy sought to isolate the bureaucracy from major governmental policy and to vest power in his own appointees, the so-called "best and the brightest." Through citizen participation the Johnson administration tried to shift control over decision making from the bureaucracy to the people. Nixon centered executive power in the White House staff, and sought through his "New Federalism" to downgrade the national bureaucracy by giving states and localities greater control over major domestic programs.

Reforming the bureaucracy was also a major theme in the Carter administration—a goal the White House zealously pursued through reorganization, zero-based budgeting, and the Civil Service Reform Act of 1978. The political movement that brought Ronald Reagan to the presidency in 1980 was hostile to bureaucracy in its heart and soul, and the Reagan administration has been firmer and more vigorous than any of its predecessors in asserting an anti-bureaucratic attitude.

Despite the strong animus against bureaucracy in modern American politics, dependence has continued to characterize the relationship of each new administration to the bureaucratic apparatus. The Reagan presidency is no exception. The estate of the domestic bureaucracy has sunk to a new low, largely because the administration does not seek to achieve many social or economic objectives through governmental action. It prefers governmental inaction in the domestic sphere, on the assumption that private initiatives rather than government intervention contribute most strongly to domestic prosperity. And yet at the same time, the Reagan administration has lavishly praised and generously financed that huge sector of the bureaucracy commonly known as the national security establishment. Like all previous administrations, the Reagan administration has found that attaining some of its major objectives required a strengthening rather than a weakening of bureaucracy. One of the primary goals the Reagan presidency set for itself was that of enhancing the influence of U.S. military power around the world, and this goal could not be attained without a strengthening of bureaucratic capabilities in the national security sector.

So as the power of bureaucracy declines in one area, it increases in another. As the Reagan administration has shown, the goals of conservatives as well as of liberals require the presence and power of an effective bureaucracy in modern government. In the case of the Reagan administration, this has been most notably true in the international arena, but it has been visible in the domestic sector too. The administration's efforts to strengthen domestic law enforcement have inevitably required a beefing up of that portion of the bureaucratic apparatus.

The picture presented in these readings is that of a bureaucracy that plays a highly influential role in policy making through its ability to shape the design and basic character of government policies, and its responsibility for putting these policies into effect once they have been devised. At the same time, however, these readings try to put such bureaucratic power into proper perspective—as a formidable but not unlimited kind of influence. No executive agency in the national government exercises monopolistic power. It shares influence over policy making with other organizations, both public and private—pressure groups, legislative committees, or in some instances other executive institutions including the White House. Of course, as the readings in section IV show, bureaucracy may greatly transform these other institutions with which it interacts, even if it does not actually overpower them.

Acknowledgments

A number of anonymous readers reviewed the previous edition of this book and made many helpful suggestions for its improvement. Kenneth Kato helped in a great many inventive ways in putting this collection together, and Hiroko Takayanagi and Richard Smith did their best to keep the text error-free. Evelyn Scheulen typed the editorial portions of the manuscript with her customary skill and patience. At Little, Brown, Jayna Pike and John Covell helped greatly in the book's development. Sally Lifland guided it through the production process. I would like to thank all of these kind people for their generous assistance.

Last but not least, I want to express my gratitude to the authors who allowed us to reprint the selections included in this volume. Without their work, this book would not exist.

Bureaucratic
Power in
National
Policy Making

I

Administrative Agencies and Their Constituencies

Executive agencies in the United States derive their power from essentially two sources: their ability to create and nurse constituencies and the technical skills that they command and can focus on complicated issues of public policy. This first section centers on how agencies build their influence by cultivating public support; the next section, "The Power of Bureaucratic Expertise," emphasizes the professional or technical skills that are so important in shaping bureaucratic power in all societies.

I

In Norton E. Long's analysis, "Power and Administration," the influence of bureaucratic organizations is seen to rest primarily on their capacity for "public relations and the mobilization of political support." A legal mandate conferring specific statutory authority by itself is not enough. "Agencies and bureaus more or less perforce are in the business of building, maintaining, and increasing their political support. They lead and in large part are led by the diverse groups whose influence sustains them."

Viewed from the perspective of Long's essay, the bureaucrat's power is very much like the politician's. The bureaucrat's success, like the elected official's, depends on mobilizing a political following. According to Long, this kind of politicized bureaucracy springs from the decentralized character of the United States' political system. In the absence of centrally organized and

1

disciplined political parties, or of a presidential cabinet backed by a cohesive legislative majority, each executive agency must fend for itself in the political arena. Executive officials cannot assume that the programs they administer will have political backing, as would ordinarily be the case in a parliamentary democracy. Instead, each agency must constantly create a climate of acceptance for its activities and negotiate alliances with powerful legislative and community groups to sustain its position. It must, in short, master the art of politics as well as the science of administration. It does so primarily by working through channels of interest-group politics rather than through party politics.

It must be remembered that the bureaucratic apparatus in the United States emerged in an environment of a vigorously functioning system of democratic politics during the late nineteenth and early twentieth centuries. In Western Europe the bureaucrat's authority was originally derived from membership in the king's household, and thus the bureaucrat received a share of the awe and deference usually accorded the monarch in traditional European society. In this country, on the other hand, legitimate political power came from the consent of the governed. Hence, as executive agencies moved toward positions of power in the political system, they could greatly strengthen their authority by showing that it rested on popular support. The drive for constituency support by administrative agencies in the United States can thus be interpreted as a quest for political legitimacy in a highly egalitarian democratic society.

II

In "The Struggle for Organizational Survival," Herbert A. Simon, Donald W. Smithburg, and Victor A. Thompson trace the efforts of executive agencies to build outside support to their need to survive as organizations. Powerful legislators must be won over because they control resources vital to an agency's continued existence, and similar considerations dictate the negotiation of alliances with outside publics. The interaction resulting from this activity, however, may modify an agency's power even as it ensures its survival. As happened when the Tennessee Valley Authority was established in the 1930s, an agency may be forced to abandon some of its basic goals in order to gather outside support. The bargain thus struck may not always be advantageous for the agency.[1]

One important way agencies can maximize their strength and ensure their survival is by seeking to expand the size and strength of the private groups whose interests they serve and from whom they derive so much of their power. But in doing so they also serve other unintended goals as well—most notably, helping outside groups gain access to executive agencies and an opportunity to influence those agencies' policies.

Matthew Holden, Jr.'s essay, "Imperialism in Bureacracy," demonstrates how the needs of administrative agencies and private sector groups can dovetail in this way. He compares government agencies to nation-states and, using this metaphor, describes their efforts to expand their constituencies as a form of "imperialist" expansion. As Holden notes, this expansion may occur at the expense of other agencies from whom group support can be detached, or it may take the form of an agency's taking over a previously unattached constituency group.

New organizations are particularly prone to engage in such imperialist behavior and may seek missions to perform in order to bring additional groups within their political orbit. An administrator, Holden writes, "must have the jurisdiction out of which he can tease the suitable combinations of constituency support." Older and more established organizations may be oriented primarily toward maintaining rather than expanding their jurisdiction, especially when extending their authority may disturb well-established patterns of constituency support.

But at its best, an agency's search for public support can make bureaucracy more representative of the community as a whole, because it is in the interest of administrative agencies to welcome and serve outside groups that are not presently part of any agency's constituency. In Holden's words, "Agency initiative in a competitive political atmosphere permits the dissatisfied to 'shop around' until they find somewhere in the administrative system agencies responsive to their claims." Of course, it is also true that one of the chief factors giving rise to the establishment of new

---

[1]See Philip Selznick, *TVA and the Grass Roots* (Berkeley: University of California Press, 1949).

organizations is the need to satisfy the demands of a group for which the existing administrative system has failed to provide adequate representation.

It should be noted that not all agencies have imperialist ambitions. They may in fact fail to exploit opportunities for expansion that are open to them. Witness, for example, the case of the U.S. Department of State, which has always rather narrowly defined its appropriate role in international affairs. Since World War II, the national security activities of the executive branch have multiplied, but the jurisdiction of the State Department has remained relatively stable. The department has allowed other agencies to encroach upon its domain and, in the view of many observers, has yielded primacy in the national security area to the Department of Defense.[2]

An agency's ability to broaden its support may also be hampered by its single-minded attachment to a group that demands its exclusive attention. A study of the Interstate Commerce Commission by Samuel P. Huntington points up this problem very graphically. Huntington shows that the ICC's dedication to the group it originally served—the railroad industry—prevented it from reaching out to new segments of the transportation industry as they emerged in the wake of technological change.[3]

III

In most discussions of the subject, the term *administrative constituency* refers to private groups with which agencies have close and mutually rewarding relationships. It is important to remember, however, that many of the organizations with which national agencies deal are in the public rather than the private sector—state and local agencies that depend on the national government for financial and other forms of assistance. Given the fact that so many domestic programs of the national government

[2]For an explanation of some of the factors involved in this failure, see Andrew M. Scott, "Environmental Change and Organizational Adaptation: The Problem of the State Department," *International Studies Quarterly* 14 (March 1970): 85–94.

[3]Samuel P. Huntington, "The Marasmus of the I.C.C.: The Commissions, the Railroads, and the Public Interest," *Yale Law Journal* 61 (April 1952): 467–509.

are carried on through intergovernmental arrangements, it is fair to say that the concept of constituency applies as much to the public sector as it does to the private sector.

Samuel Beer analyzes the political relationships that prevail in the program areas where intergovernmental constituencies have a major impact on policymaking. He sees national, state, and local agencies as increasingly joined together in what he describes as "professional-bureaucratic complexes." Within these complexes new programs spring up not in response to pressures or demands from outside groups, but as a result of initiatives undertaken by public-sector officials and organizations.

The distribution of power within these bureaucratic complexes is surprisingly decentralized. The intergovernmental lobby of state and local officials and their organizations has a great deal of influence over the character of the programs that national agencies nominally direct. As Beer writes: "In intergovernmental relations, the flow of power was not unidirectional, but complex and interactive. The lesser jurisdictions acquired an ability to negotiate and bargain with the federal government."

Thus, when the various federal grant-in-aid programs were established, a bilateral system of dependence was created. The state and local agencies in various program areas became dependent on their counterpart organizations at the national level for financial assistance. At the same time, each national agency had to rely on state and local units for the actual delivery of services to the public, and on the help of the intergovernmental lobby in maintaining the support of the White House, Congress, and the public for the activities being carried on. This was true not only of the General Revenue Sharing program on which Beer's analysis is mainly focused, but also of a host of other national programs in the domestic arena that are administered through a state and local agency network.

What analysis of the intergovernmental area reveals is that administrative agencies may be drawn into a constituency role by becoming consumers as well as producers of government services. This phenomenon occurs within as well as between different levels of government. Intelligence agencies in the national government provide information to a great variety of public organizations that regard themselves as having a need for this service. During the period of domestic unrest in the 1960s, many of the agencies that were customers for this information became, in effect, "intelligence junkies" and exerted pressure to have the activity continued long past the time when the intelligence organizations themselves were prepared to close it out.

1
Power and Administration

NORTON E. LONG

I

There is no more forlorn spectacle in the administrative world than an agency and a program possessed of statutory life, armed with executive orders, sustained in the courts, yet stricken with paralysis and deprived of power. An object of contempt to its enemies and of despair to its friends.

The lifeblood of administration is power. Its attainment, maintenance, increase, dissipation, and loss are subjects the practitioner and student can ill afford to neglect. Loss of realism and failure are almost certain consequences. This is not to deny that important parts of public administration are so deeply entrenched in the habits of the community, so firmly supported by the public, or so clearly necessary as to be able to take their power base for granted and concentrate on the purely professional side of their problems. But even these islands of the blessed are not immune from the plague of politics. . . . To stay healthy one needs to recognize that health is a fruit, not a birthright. Power is only one of the considerations that must be weighed in administration, but of all it is the most overlooked in theory and the most dangerous to overlook in practice.

The power resources of an administrator or an agency are not disclosed by a legal search of titles and court decisions or by examining appropriations or budgetary allotments. Legal authority and a treasury balance are necessary but politically insufficient bases of administration. Administrative rationality requires a critical evaluation of the whole range of complex and shifting forces on whose support, acquiescence, or temporary impotence the power to act depends.

Reprinted with permission from *Public Administration Review* (Autumn 1949). Copyright 1949 by The American Society for Public Administration, 1120 G Street, N.W., Washington, D.C. 20005. All rights reserved.

Analysis of the sources from which power is derived and the limitations they impose is as much a dictate of prudent administration as sound budgetary procedure. The bankruptcy that comes from an unbalanced power budget has consequences far more disastrous than the necessity of seeking a deficiency appropriation. The budgeting of power is a basic subject matter of a realistic science of administration.

It may be urged that for all but the top hierarchy of the administrative structure the question of power is irrelevant. Legislative authority and administrative orders suffice. Power adequate to the function to be performed flows down the chain of command. Neither statute nor executive order, however, confers more than legal authority to act. Whether Congress or President can impart the substance of power as well as the form depends upon the line-up of forces in the particular case. A price control law wrung from a reluctant Congress by an amorphous and unstable combination of consumer and labor groups is formally the same as a law enacting a support price program for agriculture backed by the disciplined organizations of farmers and their Congressmen. The differences for the scope and effectiveness of administration are obvious. The presidency, like Congress, responds to and translates the pressures that play upon it. The real mandate contained in an executive order varies with the political strength of the group demand embodied in it, and in the context of other group demands.

Both Congress and President do focus the general political energies of the community and so are considerably more than mere means for transmitting organized pressures. Yet power is not concentrated by the structure of government or politics into the hands of a leadership with a capacity to budget it among a diverse set of administrative activities. A picture of the presidency as a reservoir of authority from which the lower echelons of administration draw life and vigor is an idealized distortion of reality.

A similar criticism applies to any like claim for an agency head in his agency. Only in varying degrees can the powers of subordinate officials be explained as resulting from the chain of command. Rarely is such an explanation a satisfactory account of the sources of power.

To deny that power is derived exclusively from superiors in the hierarchy is to assert that subordinates stand in a feudal relation in which to a degree they fend for themselves and acquire support peculiarly their own. A structure of interests friendly or hostile, vague and general or compact and well-defined, encloses each significant center of administrative discretion. This structure is an important determinant of the scope of possible action. As a source of power and authority it is a competitor of the formal hierarchy.

Not only does political power flow in from the sides of an organization, as it were; it also flows up the organization to the center from the constituent parts. When the staff of the Office of War Mobilization and Reconversion advised a hard-pressed agency to go out and get itself some popular support so that the President could afford to support it, their action reflected the realities of power rather than political cynicism.

It is clear that the American system of politics does not generate enough power at any focal point of leadership to provide the conditions for an even partially successful divorce of politics from administration. Subordinates cannot depend on the formal chain of command to deliver enough political power to permit them to do their jobs. Accordingly they must supplement the resources available through the hierarchy with those they can muster on their own, or accept the consequences in frustration—a course itself not without danger. Administrative rationality demands that objectives be determined and sights set in conformity with a realistic appraisal of power position and potential.

II

The theory of administration has neglected the problem of the sources and adequacy of power, in all probability because of a distaste for the disorderliness of American political life and a belief that this disorderliness is transitory. An idealized picture of the British parliamentary system as a Platonic form to be realized or approximated has exerted a baneful fascination in the field. The majority party with a mandate at the polls and a firmly seated leadership in the cabinets seems to solve adequately the problem of the supply of power necessary to permit administration to concentrate on the fulfillment of accepted objectives. It is a commonplace that the American party system provides neither a mandate for a platform nor a mandate for a leadership.

Accordingly, the election over, its political meaning must be explored by the diverse leaders in the executive and legislative branches. Since the parties have failed to discuss issues, mobilize majorities in their terms, and create a working political consensus on measures to be carried out, the task is left for others—most prominently the agencies concerned. Legislation passed and powers granted are frequently politically premature. Thus the Council of Economic Advisors was given legislative birth before political acceptance of its functions existed. The agencies to which tasks are assigned must devote themselves to the creation of an adequate consensus to permit administration. The mandate that the parties do not supply must be attained through public relations and the mobilization of group support. Pendleton Herring and others have shown just how vital this support is for agency action.

The theory that agencies should confine themselves to communicating policy suggestions to executive and legislature, and refrain from appealing to their clientele and the public, neglects the failure of the parties to provide either a clear-cut decision as to what they should do or an adequately mobilized political support for a course of action. The bureaucracy under the American political system has a large share of responsibility for the public promotion of policy and even more in organizing the political basis for its survival and growth. It is generally recognized that the agencies have a special competence in the technical aspects of their fields which of necessity gives them a rightful policy initiative. In addition, they have or develop a shrewd understanding of the politically feasible in the group structure within which they work. Above all, in the eyes of their supporters and their enemies they represent the institutionalized embodiment of policy, an enduring organization actually or potentially capable of mobilizing power behind policy. The survival interests and creative drives of administrative organizations combine with clientele pressures to compel such mobilization. The party system provides no enduring institutional representation for group interest at all comparable to that of the bureaus of the Department of Agriculture. Even the subject matter committees of Congress function in the shadow of agency permanency.

The bureaucracy is recognized by all interested groups as a major channel of representation to such an extent that Congress rightly feels the competition of a rival. The weakness in party structure both permits and makes necessary the present dimensions of the political activities of the administrative branch—permits because it fails to protect administration from pressures and fails to provide adequate direction and support, makes necessary because it fails to develop a consensus on a leadership and a program that makes possible administration on the basis of accepted decisional premises.

Agencies and bureaus more or less perforce are in the business of building, maintaining, and increasing their political support. They lead and in large part are led by the diverse groups whose influence sustains them. Frequently they lead and are themselves led in conflicting directions. This is not due to a dull-witted incapacity to see the contradictions in their behavior but is an almost inevitable result of the contradictory nature of their support.

Herbert Simon has shown that administrative rationality depends on the establishment of uniform value premises in the decisional centers of organization. Unfortunately, the value premises of those forming vital elements of political support are often far from uniform. These elements are in Barnard's and Simon's sense "customers" of the organization and therefore parts of the organization whose wishes are clothed with a very real authority. A major and most time-consuming aspect of administration consists of the wide range of activities designed to secure enough "customer" acceptance to survive and, if fortunate, develop a consensus adequate to program formulation and execution.

To varying degrees, dependent on the breadth of acceptance of their programs, officials at every level of significant discretion must make their estimates of the situation, take stock of their resources, and plan accordingly. A keen appreciation of the real components of their organization is the beginning of wisdom. These components will be found to stretch far beyond the government payroll. Within the government they will encompass Congress, Congressmen, committees, courts, other agencies, presidential advisors, and the President. The Aristotelian analysis of constitutions is equally applicable and equally necessary to an understanding of administrative organization.

The broad alliance of conflicting groups that makes up presidential majorities scarcely coheres about any definite pattern of objectives, nor has it by the alchemy of the party system had its collective power concentrated in an accepted leadership with a personal mandate. The conciliation and maintenance of this support is a necessary condition of the attainment and retention of office involving, as Madison so well saw, "the spirit of party and faction in the necessary and ordinary operations of government." The President must in large part be, if not all things to all men, at least many things to many men. As a consequence, the contradictions in his power base invade administration. The often criticized apparent cross-purposes of the Roosevelt regime cannot be put down to inept administration until the political facts are weighed. Were these apparently self-defeating measures reasonably related to the general maintenance of the composite majority of the administration? The first objective—ultimate patriotism apart—of the administrator is the attainment and retention of the power on which his tenure of office depends. This is the necessary pre-condition for the accomplishment of all other objectives.

The same ambiguities that arouse the scorn of the naive in the electoral campaigns of the parties are equally inevitable in administration and for the same reasons. Victory at the polls does not yield either a clear-cut grant of power or a unified majority support for a coherent program. The task of the presidency lies in feeling out the alternatives of policy which are consistent with the retention and increase of the group support on which the administration rests. The lack of a budgetary theory (so frequently deplored) is not due to any incapacity to apply rational analysis to the comparative contribution of the various activities of government to a determinate hierarchy of purposes. It more probably stems from a fastidious distaste for the frank recognition of the budget as a politically expedient allocation of resources. Appraisal in terms of their political contribution to the administration provides almost a sole common denominator between the Forest Service and the Bureau of Engraving.

Integration of the administrative structure through an overall purpose in terms of which tasks and priorities can be established is an emergency phenomenon. Its realization, only partial at best, has been limited to war and the extremity of depression. Even in wartime the Farm Bureau Federation, the American Federation of Labor, the Congress of Industrial Organizations, the National Association of Manufacturers, the Chamber of Commerce, and a host of lesser interests resisted coordination of themselves and the agencies concerned with their interests. A presidency temporarily empowered by intense mass popular support acting in behalf of a generally accepted and simplified purpose can, with great difficulty, bribe, cajole, and coerce a real measure of joint action. . . . Only in crises are the powers of the executive nearly adequate to impose a common plan of action on the executive branch, let alone the economy.

In ordinary times the manifold pressures of our pluralistic society work themselves out in accordance with the balance of forces prevailing in Congress and the agencies. Only to a limited degree is the process subject to responsible direction or review by President or party leadership. . . .

III

The difficulty of coordinating government agencies lies not only in the fact that bureaucratic organizations are institutions having survival interests which may conflict with their rational adaptation to overall purpose, but even more in their having roots in society. Coordination of the varied activities of a modern government almost of necessity involves a substantial degree of coordination of the economy. Coordination of government agencies involves far more than changing the behavior and offices of officials in Washington and the field. It involves the publics that are implicated in their normal functioning. To coordinate fiscal policy, agricultural policy, labor policy, foreign policy, and military policy, to name a few major areas, moves beyond the range of government charts and the habitat of the bureaucrats to the marketplace and to where the people live and work. This suggests that the reason why government reorganization is so difficult is that far more than government in the formal sense is involved in reorganization. One could overlook this in the limited government of the nineteenth century but the multi-billion dollar government of the mid-twentieth permits no facile dichotomy between government and economy. Economy and efficiency are the two objectives a laissez faire society can prescribe in peacetime as overall government objectives. Their inadequacy as either motivation or standards has long been obvious. A planned economy clearly requires a planned government. But, if one can afford an unplanned economy, apart from gross extravagance, there seems no compelling and therefore, perhaps, no sufficiently powerful reason for a planned government.

Basic to the problem of administrative rationality is that of organizational identification and point of view. To whom is one loyal— unit, section, branch, division, bureau, department, administration, government, country, people, world history, or what? Administrative analysis frequently assumes that organizational identification should occur in such a way as to merge primary organization loyalty in a larger synthesis. The good of the part is to give way to the reasoned good of the whole. This is most frequently illustrated in the rationalizations used to counter self-centered demands of primary groups for funds and personnel. Actually the competition between governmental power centers, rather than the rationalizations, is the effective instrument of coordination.

Where there is a clear common product on whose successful production the subgroups depend for the attainment of their own satisfaction, it is possible to demonstrate to almost all participants the desirability of cooperation. The shoe factory produces shoes, or else, for all concerned. But the government as a whole and many of its component parts have no such identifiable common product on which all depend. Like the proverbial Heinz, there are fifty-seven or more varieties unified, if at all, by a common political profit and loss account.

Administration is faced by somewhat the same dilemma as economics. There are propositions about the behavior pattern conducive to full employment—welfare economics. On the other hand, there are propositions about the economics of the individual firm—the counsel of the business schools. It is possible to show with considerable persuasiveness that sound considerations for the individual firm may lead to a depression if generally adopted, a result desired by none of the participants. However, no single firm can afford by itself to adopt the course of collective wisdom; in the absence of a common power capable of enforcing decisions premised on the supremacy of the collective interest, *sauve qui peut* is common sense.

The position of administrative organizations is not unlike the position of particular firms. Just as the decisions of the firms could be coordinated by the imposition of a planned economy so could those of the component parts of the government. But just as it is possible to operate a formally unplanned economy by the loose coordination of the market, in the same fashion it is possible to operate a government by the loose coordination of the play of political forces through its institutions.

The unseen hand of Adam Smith may be little in evidence in either case. One need not believe in a doctrine of social or administrative harmony to believe that formal centralized planning—while perhaps desirable and in some cases necessary—is not a must. The complicated logistics of supplying the city of New York runs smoothly down the grooves of millions of well-adapted habits projected from a distant past. It seems naive on the one hand to believe in the possibility of a vast, intricate, and delicate economy operating with a minimum of formal overall direction, and on the other to doubt that a relatively simple mechanism such as the government can be controlled largely by the same play of forces. . . .

IV

It is highly appropriate to consider how administrators should behave to meet the test of efficiency in a planned polity; but in the absence of such a polity and while, if we like, struggling to get it, a realistic science of administration will teach administrative behavior appropriate to the existing political system.

A close examination of the presidential system may well bring one to conclude that administrative rationality in it is a different matter from that applicable to the British ideal. The American presidency is an office that has significant monarchical characteristics despite its limited term and elective nature. The literature on court and palace has many an insight applicable to the White House. Access to the President, reigning favorites, even the court jester, are topics that show the continuity of institutions. The maxims of La Rochefoucauld and the memoirs of the Duc de Saint Simon have a refreshing realism for the operator on the Potomac.

The problem of rival factions in the President's family is as old as the famous struggle between Jefferson and Hamilton. . . . Experience seems to show that this personal and factional struggle for the President's favor is a vital part of the process of representation. The vanity, personal ambition, or patriotism of the contestants soon clothes itself in the generalities of principle and the clique aligns itself with groups beyond the capital. Subordinate rivalry is tolerated if not encouraged by so many able executives that it can scarcely be attributed to administrative ineptitude. The wrangling tests opinion, uncovers information that would otherwise never rise to the top, and provides effective opportunity for decision rather than mere ratification of prearranged plans. Like most judges, the executive needs to hear argument for his own instruction. The alternatives presented by subordinates in large part determine the freedom and the creative opportunity of their superiors. The danger of becoming a Merovingian is a powerful incentive to the maintenance of fluidity in the structure of power.

The fixed character of presidential tenure makes it necessary that subordinates be politically expendable. The President's men must be willing to accept the blame for failures not their own. Machiavelli's teaching on how princes must keep the faith bears rereading. Collective responsibility is incompatible with a fixed term of office. As it tests the currents of public opinion, the situation on the Hill, and the varying strength of the organized pressures, the White House alters and adapts the complexion of the administration. Loyalties to programs or to groups and personal pride and interest frequently conflict with whole-souled devotion to the presidency. In fact, since such devotion is not made mandatory by custom, institutions, or the facts of power, the problem is perpetually perplexing to those who must choose.

The balance of power between executive and legislature is constantly subject to the shifts of public and group support. The latent tendency of the American Congress is to follow the age-old parliamentary precedents and to try to reduce the President to the role of constitutional monarch. Against this threat and to secure his own initiative, the President's resources are primarily demagogic, with the weaknesses and strengths that dependence on mass popular appeal implies. The unanswered question of American government—"who is boss?"—constantly plagues administration. . . .

2

The Struggle for Organizational Survival

HERBERT A. SIMON, DONALD W. SMITHBURG, AND VICTOR A. THOMPSON

It is now necessary to see how organizations adjust themselves to the world about them; their relations with other and competing organizations, with Congress, and with the general public. These adjustments and relations are essentially of a political character, and indeed, the topics we are about to discuss are sometimes referred to as "the politics of administration."

Which organizational relations are "internal" and which "external" depends on the standpoint. From the standpoint of the Chief of the Forest Service, his relations with the Secretary of Agriculture are external; from the standpoint of the Secretary, these same relations are internal. We will be concerned largely with relations that are external to major organizational units—departments and bureaus. . . .

Kinds of External Support Needed

Among the participants, other than employees, with whom we shall be concerned are the legislature, the chief executive, other govern-

Adapted from *Public Administration*, by Herbert A. Simon, Donald W. Smithburg, and Victor A. Thompson, pp. 381, 383–388, 392–393, 395–397, 399–401. Copyright 1950 by Herbert A. Simon, Donald W. Smithburg, and Victor A. Thompson. Reprinted by permission of the authors.

The Post Office Department mentioned here became the U.S. Postal Service in 1970.

mental organizations, groups regulated or served by the organization ("clientele" groups), and the general public.

Legislative Support

No administrative organization in this country can come into being or long exist without the support of the legislature and usually the chief executive. The legislature provides the legal authority and the funds for the organization. The legal basis of the organization includes not only the definition of its goal or objective, but very often also a rather detailed description of the organizational structure. The legislative body also passes many laws that stipulate how the organization may carry out its objective—laws relating to the management of personnel, accounting for funds, expenditures, procurement, the rights of the citizen as against the organization, and many others. In most cases these laws or statutes, which provide the legal basis for administration, must be approved by the chief executive before they go into effect.

In addition to laws of this kind, the legislature and the executive pass appropriation bills which allow the organization to spend money for personnel and for other purposes and without which it could spend no money. In some cases the chief executive has various kinds of legal authority, either in his own right under the Constitution or by delegation from the legislature, that he may redelegate to an administrative organization. Given this legal framework, it is clear that an administrative organization must have the support of the legislature or the executive—and usually both—if it is to come into existence and continue to exist.

Support of Other Organizations

From this ultimate dependence of administrative organizations on the legislature and the chief executive there develops in a democracy a dependence upon many other persons and groups in a society. In the first place, other governmental organizations, such as a central budget agency or a civil service commission, will have considerable power to hinder or aid any administrative organization in the accomplishment of its goals. Thus the support of these other governmental organizations also becomes necessary.

Clientele Support

In the second place, the backing of groups or individuals that can influence the behavior of the legislature and the executive must also be sought. For some administrative organizations there are groups within society whose support, working through their representatives in the legislature, can guarantee the survival of the organization against almost any odds and whose opposition, in like fashion, is tantamount to the death of the organization or at least considerable modification of its objective and methods. Thus farmer organizations working through the farm bloc in the Federal Congress can often make or unmake agriculture programs and the agencies that administer them.

The group within society that is most immediately interested in an organization's program may be called its *clientele*. Thus, organized labor is more directly concerned with the activities of the Department of Labor than is any other segment of the community. American business is more directly concerned with the activities of the Department of Commerce than is any other segment of the community. The railroads and the shippers are directly concerned with the activities of the Interstate Commerce Commission, and so forth. If the clientele group is large, united in interest, and well organized, it can have an impact on the legislature that makes its support or at least acquiescence important, if not necessary, to the existence of the administrative agency in question.

There is another reason why the support of outside groups must be sought. The administrative organization plans and carries out programs that require the cooperation of segments of the public or even the whole public. If the required amount of cooperation is not forthcoming, the organization will fail to accomplish its objectives and hence to satisfy its supporters. Those who are regulated must generally approve of, or at least accede to, these programs. Administrative regulations can not be enforced against a generally hostile public. The reader can appreciate this point if he will try to imagine an attempt to enforce a draft law toward which most of the people were actively hostile. Even in dictatorships administrative organizations must cultivate some general feeling of support or acquiescence in their programs or they will not be able to carry them out.

The General Public

Finally, the general public through its vote may become a source of support or opposition to an administrative organization. The party in power may come to feel that the activities of a particular agency are so affecting general public opinion that it must interfere with the operations or objectives (or even the existence) of that agency.

Since public opinion concerning any particular governmental

agency is generally rather vague, groups with specific interests in an agency's activities will usually have more effect than an incoherent general public. Thus it sometimes happens that opinion polls will show a majority of the people in favor of some activity which nevertheless is abolished or greatly modified by the legislature or the executive or both. . . .

Although public opinion is usually not as influential as are pressure groups in affecting an agency's programs, still an enthusiastic general public support could probably not be negated by any pressure group. Likewise a general public hostility would probably result in abolition or substantial modification of any governmental program. . . .

The Motives for External Support

In general, the inducements to external supporters come from the goals and objectives of governmental organizations or the values created by them. Even as the customer of a commercial organization is interested in its product, so the "customers" of governmental organizations are interested in the products of governmental action. They give their support, their contribution to the organization, in return for the satisfactions they derive from the values created by the organization, whether these be increased educational opportunity or national defense.

When a group of people in a society becomes aware of an opportunity to achieve certain of the values that it holds either by supporting or opposing a governmental program, we call this set of values an *interest*, and the group that is organized around the promotion of the values an *interest group*. The activities of any particular governmental organization promote certain interests that have developed in society, are irrelevant to many interests, and are antagonistic to still others. Thus, for every administrative organization there are groups whose interests are promoted by the organization's activities, and who give in return their political support (e.g., the support of the American Legion for the Veterans' Administration). Other people and groups will be indifferent to the organization because it does not affect their interests (e.g., the Bureau of Foreign and Domestic Commerce has generally received neither support nor opposition from farm groups). Still others may develop an interest in its abolition or the modification of its activities because these activities challenge or destroy some of the values of the groups in question (e.g., a rent control agency becomes a target for landlord groups; pacifist groups oppose appropriations to the military departments).

The Changing Environment

Since the structure of interests in society is dependent upon the physical and social environment, when these environmental conditions change, the pattern of interests in society changes with them. A change in environment may create a new group of interests; it may intensify or diminish old ones; it may cause an interest to disappear. An environmental change may greatly increase or decrease the number of persons sharing an interest; or it may shift the interest to an entirely new group of people.

As fire hazards increase, the fire department receives more support. As good land runs out, an interest in public irrigation appears. As floods become worse, an interest in flood control intensifies. When depressions occur, interest in relief becomes much stronger. As employment rises, the support of relief agencies and unemployment insurance agencies wanes. As the dependence of business upon technical knowledge increases, an interest in cheap technical education appears. As war becomes total and more terrible and imminent, an interest in the health of young men and the development of skills in the labor force begins to appear. As the economic situation of the railroad industry deteriorates, hostility toward the Interstate Commerce Commission decreases.

Conflicts of Interests

For most goals in society there are antithetical or conflicting interests. Hence programs that satisfy one group of people often reduce satisfactions of other groups. Regulating prices in the interest of consumers decreases profits of producers and sellers. Protecting and strengthening the collective bargaining interest of unions destroys the advantages many employers derive from weak unions or from power over working conditions. Protecting the interests of shippers in fair and uniform rates reduces earnings of railroad companies derived from the ability to impose high and discriminatory rates. Protecting the broadcasting industry (and the listening public) by licensing broadcasters interferes with people who would like to enter the industry but are not allowed to by the Federal Communications Commission.

Which interest will be protected and which sacrificed is determined by the political process. In fact, many political scientists would take this as the very definition of politics—in the words of Harold Lasswell, politics determines "who gets what, when, how."

When one interest is politically strong and well organized and its opponents are weak and unorganized, the answer is simple—as witness the defeat of the public housing program in the Eightieth Congress. Sometimes, however, the conflicting interests are of roughly the same strength, and the conflict resolves itself in some sort of compromise. Subsequent shifts in the relative strengths of conflicting groups then are reflected, from time to time, in program changes. Thus, successive changes in labor legislation over the past generation have reflected changes in the strength and degree of organization of labor and employer groups.

Few, indeed, are the administrative agencies that have all friends and no enemies. There is almost certain to be some hostility toward any administrative organization and its program. To survive with any given program of activities, an agency must find friendly groups whose political support is strong enough to overcome the opposition of hostile groups. To preserve its friends, it must to some degree adapt its program to their interests. To neutralize its enemies, it must sometimes sacrifice elements in its program that attract the most effective political opposition. Hence, organizations are in a continual process of adjustment to the political environment that surrounds them—an adjustment that seeks to keep a favorable balance of political support over political opposition. . . .

Resistance to Adjustment

We find among organizational members, then, three sets of motives that tend to make the organization adapt to the demands of external forces, if these demands are sufficiently strong. The first is a tactical opportunism which arises out of a desire to preserve the organization as an effective means of goal accomplishment, even at the cost of a partial modification of goals and program. The second is an opportunism that seeks to preserve the organization as an object of the pride of membership. The third is a self-protective opportunism which arises out of a desire of the individual to protect his position, power, prestige, and salary.

On the other side of the picture, we find two forces within organizations that resist adjustment to external pressures. The first of these—goal attachment—may countenance adjustment, but only grudgingly and with minimum sacrifice of goals, as we have just seen. The second may be described as "inertia"—resistance due to the painfulness of altering habitual and accustomed ways of doing things. This inertia is derived from a number of psychological forces, including the disinclination to admit that the old ways are not the best ways and the personal cost of thinking out and trying new ways.

A good illustration of the inertia factor is the appeal made to the Congress in 1903 by General Miles, Commanding General of the Army, in opposition to the establishment of the General Staff.

> More than 100 years ago our Army was organized by the genius of Washington, Steuben, Hamilton, and others. In all the wars in which we have been engaged it has in the end been victorious. It has withstood intrigue and contaminating influence from without and has absorbed the injurious elements that have been forced upon it, sustaining the honor of the Nation, and the glory of American arms in every campaign and in its present organization is best adapted to our great Republic. In my judgement a system that is the fruit of the best thought of the most eminent patriots and ablest military men that this country has produced should not be destroyed by substituting one that is more adapted to the monarchies of the Old World. . . .[1]

The Executive and Organizational Adjustment

The principal organ of adjustment within an organization is the executive hierarchy. There are several reasons why the executives (increasingly so as we mount the hierarchy) are normally more adjustive, more compromising, than the bulk of the organization's members.

"Natural Selection"

In the first place, a sort of natural selection brings about this phenomenon. The executive hierarchy has a much greater influence on the organization than the bulk of its members, and so, if that hierarchy were incapable of adjustment, the organization would cease to exist. In other words, if an organization continues to exist it is a safe conclusion that its hierarchy is adjustable.

[1]Quoted in [Otto L.] Nelson, [Jr.,] *National Security and the General Staff* [Washington, D.C.: Infantry Journal Press, 1946], pp. 53–54.

Mobility of Executives

Highly mobile individuals—individuals with very strong personal ambitions—gravitate into positions of power. In order to mount the ladder of hierarchical success it is often necessary to take actions or make decisions of a somewhat cold-blooded kind. One must "go to lunch with the right people." Sometimes friends must be by-passed. Occasionally someone must be fired who badly needs his job. Yearnings and aspirations of incapable people must sometimes be disregarded. Most persons, except those who have strong personal ambitions or unusually strong attachments to a goal, find such behavior difficult. Consequently, many highly mobile people climb upward in organizational hierarchies by a kind of self-selection.

Identifications of Executives

There is yet another reason why the executive hierarchy is usually increasingly adjustable or compromising as we go up toward the highest levels. The head of an agency, if he identifies with anything, is likely to identify with the whole agency, with its total program rather than with any of its parts. If it is necessary to sacrifice one branch or the program it administers to obtain the necessary support for the whole agency, that sacrifice may appear to the top executive merely a means to an end—and not the sacrifice of the end itself, as it may appear to the branch personnel. This difference in the breadth of identification between the executive and the people below him will usually be evident from the lowest supervisory level to the highest.

External Contacts of Executives

A final reason for executive adaptability is that the executive is less insulated from the rest of the world than those below him. He must answer questions and justify the operations of his staff to his superiors. Higher-level executives must often justify the operations of their agencies or bureaus to legislative committees. Interested groups and individuals and other administrative agencies will usually make their demands known through the executives; and it is the executives who are often singled out for criticism by the press. This wide range of interests and influences that play upon the executives sharpens their awareness of other points of view, and the political consequences of the agency's decisions will have a special impact on them. It is easy to be firm and uncompromising only when one is remote from the political consequences of his own actions.

The executive hierarchy has a particularly important role to play both in adjustment and in resistance to adjustment. Both because of the expectations of their staffs and because of their own desires, executives will play a leading part in warding off external dangers. Because of position and prestige they will have influence with external groups and individuals, be they the Civil Service Commission, the chief executive, or a legislative committee. A good deal of their attention will usually be given to preventing actions within the organization that might stimulate the antagonism of external individuals and groups. Frequently the very top executive of an administrative organization, whether he is elected or appointed, is a representative of an important political constituency.

The importance of the opportunistic or compromising element in the satisfactions of the executive hierarchy is that it renders the executive more flexible and adjustable; it enables him to see the importance of, and to act on the principle of, "doing a little wrong to do a great right." Through his efforts persons interested in the organization's goals, both within and without the organization, may accomplish part of their desires whereas otherwise they might accomplish nothing. . . .

The Conditions of Survival

We have seen that various groups and individuals, both within and outside of administrative organizations, make contributions to them in return for satisfactions derived from them. Groups and individuals outside contribute political support in return for satisfactions derived from the accomplishment of the organization's goal. Members of the organization contribute time, skills, and knowledge in return for the satisfaction of personal and organizational goals to which they are attached.

Survival for Whom?

However, as we have also seen, the satisfaction-contribution equilibria of various organizational members may not all be the same, so that a readjustment to the external world which is desired by some may not be acceptable to others. Even as some individuals and groups outside the organization gain at the expense of others, so within an organization the survival of one set of satisfactions may be at the expense of another. Prestige and power may not survive unless goals are modified; but goal modifications may be impossible unless some accustomed ways of doing and thinking are sacrificed. For organizations to survive there must be a continuous and delicate adjustment of several different sets of satisfactions and contributions to the conditions that determine the shifting interests within society.

Adjustment to What?

The problems of survival are not the same for all administrative organizations. Some promote or protect newly recognized interests that have struggled long for recognition, such as the interest of labor unions in worker organization and collective bargaining. Here the external support is enthusiastic and the external opposition bitterly hostile. Here also strong goal attachments within the organization are likely. Such organizations are quite insecure because a shift in the political tide may bring the organization's enemies into political power. In the 1946 elections, the enemies of the National Labor Relations Board secured political power and vastly modified its program (through the Taft-Hartley Act), turning it to some extent into an enemy of organized labor. Many employees of the Board found it difficult to accept the new orientation and resigned or were shunted into positions of relative unimportance.

Other organizations promote interests so thoroughly accepted that no one questions the organization's goals any longer. Such is the case with fire and police departments, the Post Office Department, and many others. Here, strong goal attachments are more difficult, though not impossible, to maintain. External "dangers" are more likely to consist in demands for better, more courteous, or more efficient service.

Some interests are obviously and admittedly short-lived, and it is expected that the organizations established to promote them will disappear when their objectives are completed. Here, although organizational members may wistfully wish that their agency could be continued, the fact that it cannot is so absolute as to be acceptable. Organizations in this class include emergency agencies dealing with floods, wars, and the like. Even in this kind of agency there may sometimes be a struggle for continuance. An example is the difficulty of disarming after a war—a difficulty not ascribable solely to the "dangers of the international situation."

Whereas some organizational goals represent a clear triumph of one interest over conflicting ones, many represent compromises among conflicting interests. In this category we would include much governmental regulatory activity. For example, railroad regulation is always a shifting compromise among the interests of the road managements, the shippers, the passengers, railroad labor, the small stockholders, railroad suppliers, and railroad financial control groups.[2] In this kind of organization, the attempts of the conflicting external interests to get complete control are constant, and the organizational members are, for this reason, constantly embroiled in the politics of survival.

Whether or not there are external conflicts of interest in an organization's goals, the problem of survival is continuous. A new high executive may have ideas about reorganizing or "improving operations"; or a citizens' group may demand a "shakeup"; or some executive, agency, or bureau may begin to acquire more power within the whole government or the whole organization. Any of these may threaten the survival of satisfactions derived from accustomed methods, from prestige and other personal opportunities, and even from the values reflected by the organization's operations.

Conclusion

The material set forth in this chapter gives considerable credence to the charge often made by critics of government that government agencies are exceedingly hardy and long-lived. But our analysis does not lend support to the doctrine that this longevity is due to some bureaucratic "will to survive." To be sure, there are many strong motivations at work within organizations that lead these organizations to adapt their activities to the requirements of survival. But government agencies cannot exist without appropriations or enabling statutes. They can survive only so long as they can continue to secure the support of politically effective groups in the community and continue through these groups to secure legislative and executive support. "Bureaucrats" can wish to survive, but they do not determine the conditions of survival.

[2]See Merle Fainsod and Lincoln Gordon, *Government and the American Economy* (New York, 1941), chap. 9.

3

"Imperialism" in Bureaucracy

MATTHEW HOLDEN, JR.

I. Constituency, Jurisdiction, and Power

If an important part of the political scientist's mission is to anticipate and explain "the critical problems that generate turbulence"[1] in that part of the world which attracts his attention, then, in the study of administration, bureaucratic "imperialism"[2] must be of compelling interest. If systematic data directly assembled for the purpose are lacking, and if there are some signal problems of theory which have been little investigated,[3] there is still enough evidence from studies of other political problems[4] that it seems worthwhile to set out some trial-run ideas in the hope that they will elicit further discussion.

From Matthew Holden, Jr., " 'Imperialism' in Bureaucracy," reprinted by permission of the author and the American Political Science Association from *The American Political Science Review* 60 (December 1966): 943–951.

[1]Albert B. Martin, *Personal Communication.*

[2]Cf., Gordon Tullock, *The Politics of Bureaucracy* (Washington, D.C.: Public Affairs Press, 1965), pp. 134–136; and Bela Gold, *Wartime Economic Planning in Agriculture* (New York: Columbia University Press, 1949), pp. 530–535.

[3]Cf., Philip Selznick, *Leadership in Administration* (Evanston: Row, Peterson and Company, 1957), p. 11.

[4]Herbert Emmerick, *Essays on Federal Reorganization* (University, Ala.: University of Alabama Press, 1950), chap. 2; Irving K. Fox and Isabel Picken, *The Upstream-Downstream Controversy in the Arkansas-White-Red Basins Survey (ICP, #55)* (University, Ala.: University of Alabama Press, 1960); Samuel P. Huntington, *The Common Defense: Strategic Programs in National Politics* (New York: Columbia University Press, 1961); James Miller Leake, "Conflict over Coordination," [*The American Political Science Review*] 12 (August 1918):365–380; Sidney I. Ploss, *Conflict and Decision-Making in Soviet Russia* (Princeton: Princeton University Press, 1965); F. F. Ridley, "French Technocracy and Comparative Government," *Political Studies* 14 (February 1966):41; Ashley L. Schiff, *Fire and Water: Scientific Heresy in the Forest Service* (Cambridge: Harvard University Press, 1962), chap. 5; Warner R.

Bureaucratic imperialism seems preeminently a matter of interagency conflict in which two or more agencies try to assert permanent control over the same jurisdiction, or in which one agency actually seeks to take over another agency[5] as well as the jurisdiction of that agency. We are thus primarily concerned with the politics of allocation[6] and shall, except incidentally, bypass some other interesting aspects of interagency politics[7] such as cooperation between agencies sharing missions, competition for favorable "one-time-only" decisions which do not involve jurisdictional reallocation, or the critical problems of the "holding company" administrative organization and its internal politics.[8] For the moment, our concern with the politics of allocation leads to a focus on what would appear to be the likely behaviors of those decisionmakers who have both inclination and opportunity to look after the institutional well-being of agencies. Administrators at this level are really "administrative politicians," and the genesis of their problem is the necessity to increase power if the agency is to survive and flourish in an administrative habitat crowded with other agencies:[9] agencies embryonic or decaying, nascent, adolescent or mature.

This by no means implies that administrative politicians are pirates out for plunder. But it does imply that the most saintly idealist (if a saintly idealist ever could arise to such a high post) could not function if he abandoned the maxim of "my agency, right or

Schilling, *Strategy, Politics, and Defense Budgets* (New York: Columbia University Press, 1962), pp. 22–24; and Herman M. Somers, *Presidential Agency: The Office of War Mobilization and Reconversion* (Cambridge: Harvard University Press, 1950), particularly chaps. 1 and 2.

[5]The well-known case of Interior Secretary Ickes's effort to acquire control over the Forest Service is in point: Harold L. Ickes, *The Secret Diary of Harold L. Ickes: The First Thousand Days*, 1933–36 (New York: Simon and Schuster, 1953).

[6]Emmette S. Redford, "Perspectives for the Study of Government Regulation," *Midwest Journal of Political Science* 6 (February 1962):8–9; and Marshall Dimock, "Expanding Jurisdictions: A Case Study in Bureaucratic Conflict," in Robert K. Merton, *et al.*, *Reader in Bureaucracy* (Glencoe, Ill.: Free Press, 1952), pp. 282–291.

[7]For a pertinent contribution, see William M. Evan, "Toward a Theory of Inter-Organizational Behavior," *Management Science* 11 (August 1965):B217–230.

[8]Health, Education and Welfare, and Housing and Urban Development are, at the federal level, particularly good examples of "holding company" organizations lacking an integrating goal or mythology.

[9]Norton E. Long, *The Polity* (edited by Charles Press) (Chicago: Rand McNally and Company, 1960), chap. 4, remains the best statement on this point; also Herbert Kaufman, "Organization Theory and Political Theory," [*The American Political Science Review*] 58 (March 1964):12 and note 9 at the same page.

wrong!" The condition of power is a favorable balance of constituencies. Constituency means any group, body or interest to which the administrative politician looks for aid and guidance, or which seeks to establish itself as so important (in his judgment) that he "had better" take account of its preferences even if he finds himself averse to those preferences. The constituency of the agency, like the legislative constituency, includes not only those with whom the politician has a stable *and friendly* relationship, but those who support his ends, those who oppose his ends, and those who wish to intervene for what he regards as "irrelevant" purposes. Moreover, the term "constituency," although only customarily applied to the external groups which make claims upon the administration, is equally applicable to subordinates, employees, and colleagues who constitute internal constituencies.

To achieve a favorable balance of constituencies, in other words, administrative politicians must discover, identify, or manufacture suitable combinations of means and ends to yield effective incentives for the constituents [they desire]. This is the signal importance of jurisdiction. The goods the administrative politician can deliver, and the penalties he can impose, are a function of jurisdiction. Hence, he must have the jurisdiction (or competence)[10] over those policy issues out of which he can tease the suitable combinations of constituency support.

II. Strategies in Bureaucratic Imperialism

It would be unreasonable to assume that the incentives of agency power always lead to imperialistic behavior.[11] Yet the evidence of such behavior occurs often enough that we can believe it is not rare or trivial. Hence, we have to reach for some greater clarity about agency strategies. By strategy we mean calculation by some "broad" or "general" set of partially explicit, partially implicit "decision rules" which provide clues to action in unforeseen—and often unforeseeable—contingencies.

Strategic patterns will naturally reflect such idiosyncratic fea-

[10]We recall that the "sphere of competence" is an essential criterion of the "administrative organ" as defined in Max Weber, *Theory of Social and Economic Organization* (Glencoe, Ill.: Free Press and Falcon's Wing Press, 1947), p. 330.
[11]Victor A. Thompson, *The Regulatory Process in OPA Rationing* (New York: King's Crown Press, 1950), makes this point by noting the *indisposition* of the OPA's Gasoline Eligibility Committee to grab jurisdiction.

tures as the disposition of the individual decisionmaker, his sense of purpose, or his sense of agency capability to perform in the area where opportunity exists. But if the basic criterion of agency strategy is power achieved through constituency organized around jurisdiction, then we suggest that the administrative politician tends to adopt the impact on *existing* constituencies as the criterion by which to respond to each potential reallocation of jurisdiction. In this regard, there are at least three major considerations which will govern strategic choice: agency disposition, available occasions for allocation issues, and modes of resolution.

Agency Disposition

Some agencies rather clearly have a greater disposition to take on new jobs than do others which might, in principle, take on the same jobs. One of the critical factors here is the nature of the internal constituency. Administrative empire-building may, of course, be little more than a self-promotion strategy for an agency head to build a reputation and move on. This is somewhat unlikely, it would seem, for administrative empire-building also requires signs of successful performance or evidence that successful performance is likely. If this is to be achieved, the internal constituents have to make a serious decision to produce: the agency and its enterprises must engage their loyalties and enthusiasm. The boss's orders won't be enough!

While the energizing mythology which sustains a disposition to take on new jobs may be found in many different kinds of agencies, it may be suggested that it is most likely in the new organization. A new organization will exist only because someone thought there was something to be "reformed," "improved," or "developed" and this is likely to carry over into the selection of personnel. But there is a vital collective incentive. In the nature of government, there is an almost inevitable mixture of missions between agencies (e.g., a labor department, a commerce department, and a development department). If the old agencies have somewhat come to terms with the mixture of missions, the new agency can vindicate itself only if it finds a substantial share which it can control by itself. This requires energetic pursuit of opportunities and, necessarily, imposes conflicts with previously existent agencies. (Witness OEO in relation to HEW, Labor, etc.) But the very novelty of the situation means that the organization will have on board people who see brilliant opportunities if only they can so extend their reach as to bring all the relevant program fragments under their own agency's control. They lack commitment to existing programs, slots, routines, and schedules and therefore have great mobility.

In the first stages, at any rate, the novel organization is also likely to benefit from the interest of those external constituencies which provided support for its very creation. These constituencies will be inclined to think of all resistance from existing agencies as "old fogeyism" and, equally, will, having just gone through the process of creating the agency, be much on the alert for possible external threats. Defense politics since World War II would be acutely relevant, since it is *the* best (and *the* test) case of effective reorganization. The military needs of the Cold War were perceived as great enough and specific enough that the most important constituent—the President—had a vested interest in supporting reorganization. These same needs, plus the awareness of presidential support, activated the doctrines of obedience and inhibited potential resisters.

Each time the expanding agency acquires a new constituency, that constituency co-opts[12] part of the agency's money, people, time, skill and working doctrine. If the agency then seeks to shift those resources, it may find itself constrained by the demands of the co-opting constituency which has, so to speak, now acquired a first mortgage on those resources. From this arises a disposition toward maintenance rather than basic expansion. When this process first manifests itself, the agency officials may find it regrettable, and may even console themselves that the lapse from expansion into maintenance is purely temporary. But the fact is that it is difficult to shift funds once committed, to get personnel to interest themselves in new jobs, or even to find the time. Even more, it is virtually impossible to change these commitments without offending or injuring powerful constituencies, so that "temporary" maintenance becomes "permanent" maintenance.

When maintenance-minded agencies are challenged, one common response is to attempt to prove that what it is doing is all that could be done in the area (witness the Triborough Bridge Authority contra Mayor Lindsay) or that it is doing all the new things now desired.

Perhaps the most neglected cases are those in which there is a

---

[12]Philip Selznick, *TVA and the Grass Roots* (Berkeley: University of California Press, 1949).

clear agency disposition toward retrenchment or self-limitation. It is not merely that the agency adopts kid-glove tactics in order to maintain a cooperative relationship with a constituency, but that it actually denies its powers. The history of the Natural Gas Act of 1938, as interpreted by the Federal Power Commission, provides one fairly clear example.[13] The FPC has several times seemed to be faced with a cleavage between the preference of the industry (little or no regulation) and the preferences of others (greater regulation). Recurrently, the Commission chose the strategy of denying (by quasi-judicial interpretation) that the Act conferred those powers which the proregulatory forces desired it to exercise. (The Federal Courts tended to assert exactly the contrary.)

Retrenching agencies may be forced to reorient themselves in order merely to maintain the status quo. This special case of reluctant running just to keep in place seems to be an interpretation one may impose upon the recent responses of the Texas Railroad Commission—an agency regulating oil and gas production[14]—to legislation establishing the Texas Water Pollution Control Board. The new statute (1961) apparently consolidates powers formerly vested in several agencies (not including the Commission).[15] Prior to this legislation, the Commission had disclaimed the power to regulate the discharge of oilfield brines (saline wastes) into water-courses, although it did describe such discharges as a necessary incident to production. By this disclaimer, the Commission was freed of any responsibility to impose penalties upon the producing constituency, with which it had a long-standing and protective relationship.

The Commission pursued its policy of self-limitation in a slightly different form when the new legislation first became effective. In administrative conferences to set up the Control Board machinery, Commission spokesmen agreed that (1) the Board had authority to

[13]The interpretation is my own, but the evidence is presented in Edith T. Carper, "Lobbying and the Natural Gas Bill," in Edwin A. Bock and Alan K. Campbell (Eds.), *Case Studies in American Government* (Englewood Cliffs, N.J.: Prentice-Hall, Inc., 1962), pp. 178–184.

[14]York Y. Willbern, "Administrative Control of Petroleum Production," in Emmette S. Redford (Ed.), *Public Administration and Policy Development* (Austin: University of Texas Press, 1956), pp. 3–50.

[15]The statute is H.B. No. 24 of the 57th Legislature, First-Called Session, codified as Article 7621d, *Vernon's Annotated Civil Statutes*. It is reprinted in: U.S. House of Representatives, Committee on Government Operations, Subcommittee on National Resources and Power, *Hearings on Water Pollution Control and Abatement* (Washington, D.C.: Government Printing Office, 1965), Part 6, p. 3579 *et seq.*

issue or withhold permits for discharges into water-courses, (2) the Commission itself lacked such authority, and (3) "the Commission would depend upon the Board in regard to the decisions regarding quality to be maintained in the waters of the State in line with the Board's responsibility as the coordinating agency in pollution matters."[16] This administrative treaty, subsequently sanctioned by an Opinion of the Attorney General,[17] became the basis for the Board's new permit system. However, when a producing firm challenged the Board's new permit system, arguing that authority in oilfield matters lay exclusively with the Commission, the Commission intervened on the producer side, thus negating its acceptance of the earlier agreement.

How can this change-about be explained? If we accept the constituency hypothesis of this paper, the following interpretation would appear to be consistent with the facts. In the absence of a competing agency, no problem existed for the Commission, but it could hardly oppose some kind of permit system once the new statute was effective. Nor could it easily accept the controlling role for itself, in view of its previous position. If this were so, then the administrative treaty would seem a reasonable settlement. Once the Board actually began to operate, however, its course seriously disturbed the equilibrium of the Commission-producer relationship by a highly restrictive interpretation of one aspect of the problem. "Grandfather" permits were, under the statute, to be available to producers already in business, but when the Board began to operate, it actually issued "grandfather" permits to only 45 percent of the existing producers. Almost inevitably, one producer brought the lawsuit mentioned and the Commission's choices became much more constricted. It could sustain the original agreement, and violate the basic reciprocity owed its primary constituency, or it could join that constituency. It chose the latter course claiming, in effect, powers broader than any which it had exercised previously. It won the suit in the trial courts, but the legal issue was soon moot, for the legislature amended the law (before the appeal could be heard), making the primacy of the Commission with respect to oilfield matters unmistakable.

[16]This recitation of the facts is based upon Board briefs filed in litigation. Since it is of considerable importance and apparently nowhere rebutted, we assume its accuracy.
[17]Opinion No. WW-1465, October 31, 1962, as reprinted in House Committee on Government Operations, *op. cit.*, p. 3586 *et seq.*

This shift from retrenchment indicates what we suspect is a more persistent factor. The disposition toward retrenchment would seem to depend upon the extent to which there is one critical constituency which cannot be changed or which has substantially inflexible ends. When there is at least one such, and the administrative politician does not perceive possibilities for a favorable constituency balance with diverse constituencies, he will tend to seek ways for self-limitation. This is particuarly important in agencies where the internal constituency is a relatively homogeneous professional or skill group. For the agency head is more immediately jeopardized by the demoralization or silent sabotage of this internal group than by external criticism.

If the phenomenon of retrenchment is little noted in formal discussion, it is nonetheless apparent in many familiar situations. Political scientists need only consider some of their departmental problems. If, for example, there is a legal requirement that students be taught a course in "the Government of North State," a chairman is very likely to experience difficulty reconciling this with faculty desires to work in an atmosphere of academic high fashion. If the professional constituency is to be satisfied, therefore, it makes sense for a chairman to try to get rid of the requirement. In contemporary urban politics, the relationship between the police departments and the civil rights groups raises this problem. Police departments tend to be highly cohesive bodies in which the normative rules acceptable to the internal constituency are defined primarily from the inside,[18] so that the more responsive the police commissioner is to those who allege "police brutality," the more he will find himself forced to fight his internal constituency. The more responsive he is to his men, the more he must try to get an allocation of responsibility which permits him to ignore the outside. In federal administration, the recent signal example has been the Public Health Service which never wanted serious *police* power over environmental pollution—a power largely inconsistent with the developed tradition of PHS.

---

[18]Wallace S. Sayre and Herbert Kaufman, *Governing New York City* (New York: W. W. Norton & Company, 1965), pp. 285–292; William Westley, "Secrecy and the Police," *Social Forces* 34 (March 1956):254–257; Westley, "Violence and the Police," *American Journal of Sociology* 59 (July 1953):34–41; William Kephart, *Radical Factors in Urban Law Enforcement* (Philadelphia: University of Pennsylvania Press, 1959); and Murray Kempton, "The Cop as Idealist: The Case of Stephen P. Kennedy," *Harper's Magazine* (March 1962):66–71.

Occasions for Allocation Decisions

The administrative politician's strategies must go, of course, far beyond the estimate which he can make of the agency disposition to act. One of the primary considerations must be the "ecology"[19] within which action is to take place, and an important component of this ecology is the state of the competition. What are the alternatives open to those on whom he is dependent if he does not move? What are the alternatives if he does move? If he refuses to take on a new task, will he cut his own throat because some other agency will be given the task to the eventual detriment of his own agency? If his subordinates do not like the course he follows and resign, are there really places they can go, or do they have to stay with him?

Even more, however, he must consider the extent to which there is a consensus about policy or the extent to which there is uncertainty. (1) If we may agree that the ultimate limitation is some arbitrary criterion which makes some possible claims patently "ridiculous," then one critical occasion for making agency claims exists when policies are in their infancy. Doubt and confusion about policy ends lead to similar doubt and confusion about appropriate instruments. There is likely to be an almost primitive uncertainty[20] such that the decisionmaker does not "know what he wants," nor how "to make things turn out right," nor possibly even what "right" is. (2) Fluidity and confusion in a policy area, where there are some major fixed points of substance, but where connecting "threads" of policy have not been worked out so that the area is stable, also permit disputes about allocation. For who gets the job will do much to determine the eventual policy fabric. (3) The commonest situation appears to be that in which policy norms appear to be agreed upon, but in which there is dissatisfaction *superficially* directed to the forms and techniques of administration. When this occurs, the ambitious administrative

---

[19]John M. Gaus, *Reflections on Public Administration* (University, Ala.: University of Alabama Press, 1947), chap. 1; Kaufman, *op. cit.*; Long, *op. cit.*, chap. 10; Fred W. Riggs, *The Ecology of Administration* (London: Asia Publishing House, 1961); and Redford, "Perspectives for the Study of Government Regulation," *op. cit.*, pp. 4–5, all embody literary formulations of the idea of ecology in administration. Evan, *op. cit.*, has contributed a more precise statement in the notion of the "organization-set."

[20]On levels of uncertainty, see Mattew Holden, Jr., "Committee Politics under Primitive Uncertainty," *Midwest Journal of Political Science* 9 (August 1965):236–237.

politician may put forth his agency as the "natural" or "logical" candidate to do the job efficiently.

Under primitive uncertainty, maintenance may be feasible for very strong organizations, but few such are actually likely to exist. Retrenchment, on the other hand, is almost a sure recipe for disaster, for the disposition to retrench actually protects the agency only so long as the constituency which loses thereby does not secure opportunities by other channels to achieve the same ends. Primitive uncertainty gives the freest play to dispositions to expand and this is most likely to be manifest when the governmental system is yet evolving[21] or, even more, when the very basic frame of social order is unsure.[22] But this may be fundamentally akin to the problem of administrative coordination whenever policy problems are severe enough that the existing system, if continued in its dominant mode, cannot accommodate to them. Even in highly stable countries, particular administrative units, whether mature or embryonic, find these seasons of crisis and confusion favorable to attempts to satisfy their most elemental power requirements.[23]

When uncertainties depend mainly upon the fluidity of policy, but where a few major points are more or less fixed, or where there is a presumption of policy consensus so that only administrative technique is overly disputable, the problem of acting on one or another agency disposition is even more complex. In these instances, retrenchment can be successfully pursued only by very strong organizations which jettison what they regard as irritating trivialities,[24] or by weak organizations which can afford only the least measure of turbulence. Organizations which do not tower over all their competitors, but which are still strong enough to be in the competition, have the problem that jettisoning any area of responsibility for which there is support opens the door for other agencies to appeal to the

---

[21]Leonard D. White, *The Federalists* (New York: The Macmillan Company, 1956), particularly chap. 18.

[22]Lucian W. Pye, *Politics, Personality, and Nation-Building* (New Haven: Yale University Press, 1962), chaps. 15, 16.

[23]This seems to me the conclusion supportable by Somers, *op. cit.*, on economic administration during World War II.

[24]See, for example, Leslie Goldner, "Air Pollution Control in the Metropolitan Boston Area: A Case Study in Public-Policy Formulation," in Harold Wolozin (Ed.), *The Economics of Air Pollution* (New York: W. W. Norton and Company, Inc., 1966), p. 137, n. 11.

pertinent constituencies. This is particularly important in public as against private administration where the constituency is likely to entertain a presumption that the agency has a responsibility to look after its welfare.[25] (Imagine the fate of a Secretary of Labor who concluded that the major international unions really did not deserve his attention any more and tried to redefine "labor" to mean people largely outside the union movement.) The administrative politician thus has the complicated problem, if he really prefers to act on the retrenchment disposition, of trying to do as little as possible while not vacating the jurisdiction to possible competitors.

On the other hand, situations other than primitive uncertainty impose constraints on *explicit* self-aggrandizement because of the normative doctrine that all governmental agencies are "really" directed to a common purpose. Political ritual thus precludes, as a usual procedure, an open display of ambition or an explicit attack on the opposition. Consequently, the administrative politician is more likely to cooperate with, and sometimes to generate, surrogate or third-party claims in his own behalf, as in the Texas law suit or the well-known practice of leaking criticism through a friendly newspaper or legislator. But, in any event, he is likely to appeal to the pertinent constituencies by setting up a straw man. Thus, a limited area of authority may be expanded if it can successfully be argued that "the problem is *really* not X [which is what the competitor presumably can handle] but Y [which is what the claimant can handle]."

Again, water pollution control provides an illustration beyond those equally applicable cases (e.g., defense reorganization) with which there is such common familiarity that the basic process may be missed. Pennsylvania is, for example, a state in which this issue has recently come to be of considerable political value. The main agency contestants are the Health Department and the Mines Department. The rule-making Sanitary Water Board characteristically exercises its authority through, or at the recommendation of, its "enforcement agent": the Department of Health.

Over the years, the more obvious dangers of bacterial pollution which Health has emphasized have receded, and the relevant external constituency ("the conservationists") has looked more toward

---

[25]In this respect, the idea that there is "ordinarily little or no limit to the amount of inaction an organization can 'undertake' [because] inaction does not absorb resources" seems in error. See James G. March and Herbert A. Simon, *Organizations* (New York: John Wiley, 1958), p. 175.

ending chemical pollution, mainly associated with the drainage of toxic acids from coal mines, a matter of less importance to the sanitary engineers. Meantime, the Mines Department has had some recent successes with controlling pollution from highly visible bituminous surface (strip) mines. Legislators and newspapers have tended to praise the good faith and efficiency of the Mines Department, while viewing the Health Department with skepticism, if not hostility, for "not enforcing the law."

The Secretary of Mines did not miss the opportunity to advise the legislature that acid drainage was necessarily incident to the mining business, was as repugnant to the mine firms as to anyone else, and was actually "a mine problem" and "not a water problem." Having thus established this rationale, the Secretary then proposed to remove the matter from the Sanitary Water Board into an entirely new Mine Drainage Board. The particular proposal failed, but the door was opened. The Sanitary Water Board retained its regulatory power but a Mine Drainage Research Commission was created and, in the normal course of administrative politics, one would expect future efforts to expand its jurisdiction at the expense of the Sanitary Water Board.

For all the effort to place the issue in the perspective of proper administrative techniques to do an agreed job, the opportunity to seek a reallocation existed in 1965 and not some other time precisely because there was a general mystique supporting "clean streams" and considerable dissatisfaction with existing administration.

Modes of Resolution

The third consideration in the strategies of administrative politicians is that they know that issues of jurisdiction can seldom long be resolved, except in very broad terms. This is a point which appears rather obvious, yet is largely missed in existing administrative theory because the latter is largely a theory of kingship, i.e., how the executive-ruler may compel subordinates to do his will ("achieve organizational goals") and no more. If one adopts the regio-centric perspective, autonomous or contradictory agency action is pathological or, as Selznick says, "adventitious and subversive."[26] This is an important consideration in the tendency to pursue what Clawson appropriately describes as "the mirage of reorganization,"[27] or the effort to give internally consistent settlements of jurisdictional issues.

[26]Selznick, *Leadership in Administration*, p. 11.
[27]Marion Clawson, *The Public Lands* (Washington, D.C.: Resources for the Future, Inc., and American Forestry Association, 1965), Part 5.

Unless one could imagine simple free enterprise in the bureaucratic system, there could be only two ways to settle questions of boundaries. One would be some form of interagency bargaining such as the process by which the Corps of Engineers and the Bureau of Reclamation merged their conflicting downstream-flood control and upstream-irrigation interests, thus forestalling deadlock among their respective congressional supporters and obstructing effective presidential advocacy of a "basin authority" for the Missouri basin.[28]

As a general rule, it would seem doubtful that agencies have any great ability to make such deals explicitly. Since each party aims at its own continuance, it is apparent that bargains will not be accepted unless parties consider themselves advantaged by the deals. If Party A enters a deal, A must be able to protect itself against such of its followers as are disaffected, or the deal cannot stand. Similarly, A and B must be able jointly to maintain the integrity of their deal by jointly protecting themselves against third-party attack. If the effective deal depends upon the ability of each to assure the other that the deal will more likely be kept than not, the issues at stake must be issues which can have reasonably clear termination points. The division of interests in the Missouri basin permitted this to some degree by the sheer physical nature of the two areas of activity. Most jurisdictional issues do not lend themselves to specific termination points, simply because of the continued intermixture of missions.

Moreover, differences in agency power become extremely relevant. Given the intermixture of missions, there is a variety of constituency interests often "shopping" from one agency to the next, providing ambitious agencies with incentives to break their deals and defensive agencies with much ground for uncertainty about the consequences of such broken deals. The more firmly an agency is bound to a previous deal, the less opportunity it will have to ward off new challenges or to respond to new opportunities provided by the incidence of constituency "shopping." Accordingly, the resolution of agency jurisdictional conflicts must much more often be tacit than explicit, and accordingly much more uncertain of future stability.

The limitations of bargaining must often mean some kind of central decision or arbitration by a third official party—presumably "above" the contending agencies—as to which agency shall occupy a particular jurisdiction. Litigation is the clearest form of arbitra-

---

[28]Henry C. Hart, *The Dark Missouri* (Madison: University of Wisconsin Press, 1957), chap. 7.

tion, leading to a decision by a court which says (as in the Texas case) that "this matter lies within the jurisdiction of this agency rather than that." But most of the arbitration lies with other officials, e.g., the President, the Governor, the Congress or the legislature. Insofar as each administrative agency has, or will seek to have, its autonomous base of power, it is evident that such arbitration is not likely to have lasting effect. The resolution of jurisdictional disputes tends to become more like mediation or conciliation in which the disputes are tentatively settled, on incremental terms. In making claims before third parties, agencies may exploit all the ordinary techniques of politics. The extent to which they do so determines whether the third-party officials making the allocation decisions can or cannot be coercive in forcing settlements upon the agencies.

The point now takes on considerable practical relevance because there is a mood in American politics—appropriately symbolized by the idea of systems analysis or the more startling notion of "goals research"[29]—suitable to the idea of "modernization" or "rationalization."[30] One of its manifestations is a revival of the regiocentric notion that bureaucratic imperialism is a form of pathology to be dealt with appropriately by institutional design which eliminates the conflicts and cross-purposes.

Since so much of the rationalization case is based on DOD experience, we have to note how consistent that experience appears to be with the idea that success in reorganization also requires time to wear down the centers of resistance. . . . The Defense experience is highly consistent with the view that reorganization which denies powerful parties' access to the internal decision process of the new organization will itself precipitate a new round of jurisdictional controversies, including new efforts to change the boundaries of the organization. Its product is reality rather than mirage if, and only if, the side being "attacked" can be deprived of alternative channels of influence or if powerful marginal constituents can be brought to the side of the "attacker." Even then, there is no guarantee that the process will stop, nor is it evident that even if, by some criteria, there are critical substantive problems to which appropriate responses are

---

[29]See the "Introduction" by Gerhard Colm in Leonard A. Lecht (Ed.), *Goals, Priorities, and Dollars* (New York: The Free Press, 1966), pp. 1–16.

[30]Cf. Paul Y. Hammond, "Foreign Policy-Making and Administrative Politics," *World Politics* 17 (July 1965):656–671; and Charles J. Hitch, *Decision-Making for Defense* (Berkeley: University of California Press, 1965).

not forthcoming, . . . institutional reorganization is necessarily likely to produce those responses.[31]

Finally, the pressure toward reorganization involves a normative issue to which a postscript reply may be made. It would be improper for us to conclude that bureaucratic imperialism never involves irrationalities. But what we know of administration in an imperfect world suggests two considerations in terms of which bureaucratic imperialism may also have highly rational[32] effects in the policy process.

1. The administrative world in reality is a place of confusion and uncertainty, with false signals strewn about like dandelion seeds in an open meadow. Bureaucratic imperialism is a part of the process of clarification. Decisionmakers need some guides to the needs, preferences, ambitions and hopes of the various and constantly changing constituencies. Competition between agencies, engendered by competition between constituencies, is a vital part of the process of clarification.

2. Since administrative agencies tend to be co-opted by particular constituencies, other constituencies whose interests are affected have difficulty entering the process as agency boundaries are stabilized and, indeed, ossified. This is the source of pathological disinclinations to adapt to new circumstances. The idea that "higher authority" alone could either know enough of all the relevant situations or afford to make continuous readjustments of agency missions simply ignores the complex reality.[33] There must be numerous means of readjustment of missions including agency initiative. Agency initiative in a competitive political atmosphere permits the dissatisfied to "shop around" until they find somewhere in the administrative system agencies responsive to their claims.

[31]For a case demonstration, see Francis E. Rourke, "The Politics of Administrative Organization," *Journal of Politics* 19 (August 1957):461–478.

[32]For a sympathetic reconsideration by an economist–systems analyst, see Roland N. McKean, "The Unseen Hand in Government," *American Economic Review* 60 (June 1965):496–506; and McKean, "Limitations, Risks, and Problems," in David G. Novick (Ed.), *Program Budgeting* (Cambridge: Harvard University Press, 1965), pp. 295–296.

[33]The practical irrelevance of regio-centric approaches is evident when one reviews discussions of the problems of the President—indubitably the public figure most like a king. Richard E. Neustadt, *Presidential Power: The Politics of Leadership* (New York: John Wiley, 1960); and Theodore Sorensen, *Decision-Making in the White House* (New York: Columbia University Press, 1963).

Competition through self-aggrandizement may thus enhance the sense of reality and maintain the fluidity of choice which prevents serious error. This phenomenon may be deemed "irrational" or "pathological" if, but only if, one has assumed that there is at some point a central policy mechanism capable of articulating a single "public interest" and that those interests not so articulated ought not to be permitted avenues of realization. Those who advocate this may describe it as "rational planning," but gamblers have a more honest name: they call it stacking the deck.

III. Summary and Comments

Bureaucratic imperialism arises, it is argued here, from the simple fact that, whatever the purpose of the administrative politician, his first necessity is to maintain sufficient power for his agency. Power is organized around constituency and constituency around jurisdiction. Hence the conflicts over the allocation of jurisdiction. Since it is obvious that not all administrative politicians move their agencies with the same frequency into efforts to claim jurisdiction, we have to look for clues to their strategies. Among the manifold considerations which may be pertinent, three seem of permanent relevance: agency disposition, occasions for allocation, and modes of resolution.

1. Agencies may have dispositions toward expansion, maintenance, or retrenchment. The disposition to expand is likely to be greatest when the agency is relatively new because the novel organization has (a) the necessity to establish a secure place for itself in relation to other agencies, (b) internal constituencies with little commitment to existing programs, slots, routines, and schedule, and (c) external constituencies still energized, from the effort to get the agency created, to support its claims against the threatening resistance of older agencies which may otherwise obstruct realization of the desirable results which people had in mind when they sponsored the new agency.
2. Dispositions toward maintenance are a function of the "first mortgage" expectations which constituencies develop toward agency resources—money, people, skill, time, working doctrine— as the agency goes through the process of exploiting jurisdiction to build up support.
3. Retrenchment dispositions—dispositions actually to deny agency powers—develop when administrative politicians perceive no op-

portunity to create favorable constituency balances out of existing jurisdiction and when they possess some critical constituency which cannot be changed and for which the critical incentives are flexible.

4. Administrative politicians' choices of strategies are further determined by the critical occasions for decision. Dispositions toward expansion may most freely be pursued under primitive uncertainty. Under the same condition, very strong organizations may, in principle, pursue a disposition toward retrenchment because the very meaning of primitive uncertainty makes such a disposition trivial. Retrenchment, always dangerous because of the room it leaves for competing organizations, is under these conditions an invitation to organizational disaster.

5. Resolution of interagency jurisdictional conflict would tend to be highly problematical whether the method of resolution were bargaining or central decision (arbitration). Explicit bargaining is feasible mainly when the relevant agencies can fix physical limits to the areas of contention (e.g., the Pick-Sloan Plan). Tacit bargaining will normally be more relevant because the intermixture of agency missions is continual and because agencies will wish to leave open options for reassessing their power relations by future competition for constituencies as circumstances change. The existence of constituencies "shopping around" for places to get satisfaction also constitutes the critical limit on the durability and coerciveness of central decisions.

6. The normative case for reorganization—manifest both in administrative theory as usually known and in the more common version of systems analysis—is not necessarily to be rejected, but it is at least open to doubt. For, assuming that the criteria of judgment are clear, it may also be argued that bureaucratic "imperialism" may also clarify constituency preferences and disrupt stale or archaic bureaucracies through the emergence of competitors. Moreover, it is open to doubt whether there is any specific relationship between systematic reorganization and improved substantive outputs, beyond the fact that stale and archaic routines are disrupted—a result equally accomplished by the self-aggrandizement of ambitious agencies. . . .

4

Bureaucracies as Constituencies: The Adoption of General Revenue Sharing

SAMUEL H. BEER

. . . The intergovernmental lobby played a crucial role in the adoption of general revenue sharing. But if we are to understand how this lobby and its constituent organizations acquired an interest in such a measure and the political influence to promote it effectively before Congress, we must look first at another new type of political formation within the public sector, the professional-bureaucratic complex. The term is singular, but the examples are many. The "military-industrial complex" was one of the first such collocations of power to be perceived, and I have adapted the name from it. But other similar formations have developed in other specialized fields of policy, such as the "welfare establishment," and the "health syndicate."

The Professional-Bureaucratic Complex

The new character of the bureaucratic component of the public sector derives from the rise of what Mosher calls "the Professional State."[1] In the evolution of the federal civil service, as he sees it, the

From Samuel H. Beer, "The Adaptation of General Revenue Sharing: A Case Study in Public Sector Politics," *Public Policy*, Vol. 24 (1976), pp. 157–169. Reprinted by permission of the Kennedy School of Government, Harvard University. Footnotes and tables are renumbered.

[1]Frederick C. Mosher, *Democracy and the Public Service* (New York: Oxford University Press, 1968).

change dates from the mid-fifties, when the "government by administrators" that had arisen with the New Deal began to be superseded by "government by professionals." Thanks to the growth of specialized sciences and fields of technology and their application to public policy, "professional specialisms" gained a larger influence in policy-making.[2] The influence of science on public policy and its administrators was not something new, but goes back to the earliest days of the American polity and of other modern states.[3] It has been the vastly increased rate of scientific advance in the past generation that has been the ground for the transformation of the Professional State.

Stripped of its apocalyptic overtones, the term "technocracy" characterizes the political tendency of the change, which consists in a certain shifting of initiative and influence from the private sector to the public sector. The growing complexity of the knowledge that is used in identifying and solving contemporary problems means that there must be a greater dependence upon experts in policy-making. The familiar models of the polity that find the origin of government action in demands arising outside government and in the developing environment of the polity do not fit well with the new realities. In technocratic politics, the pressures and proposals tend to arise *within* government and its associated circles of professionals and technically trained cadres. To be sure, science has a life of its own that is in some degree independent of government. Yet its current advances in the United States not only depend very greatly upon government finance but also are often shaped by the goals of agencies in the public sector. A professional-bureaucratic complex may have a hand in the acquisition of new knowledge which it then translates into policy.

The growing influence of professionalism in government is familiar. But it will clarify and give point to the discussion to have an example. The development and enactment of the Community Mental Health Facilities Act of 1963 brings out the features that need emphasis. A recent study of this legislation shows how federal officials identified an important problem, promoted the research necessary for a solution, attracted a coalition united in its goals and successful in its lobbying, and finally administered the resulting program of federal-state cooperation.[4] The central figure was Dr. Rob-

[2]Ibid., p. 105.
[3]Abundantly illustrated in Don K. Price, *The Scientific Estate* (Cambridge, Mass.: Harvard University Press, 1965).
[4]Henry A. Foley, *Community Mental Health Legislation: The Formative Process* (Lexington, Mass.: Lexington Books–D.C. Heath, 1975).

ert Felix, of the National Institute of Mental Health, who from his early days as a resident was committed to abolishing the state mental hospital in favor of some form of community care. But the compassion of Dr. Felix and his associates would have been ineffectual without the advances in medical technology promoted by the NIMH and its National Advisory Mental Health Council. In Congress these bureaucratic professionals had powerful allies and partners in Senator Lister Hill and Representative John Fogarty, chairmen of the respective subcommittees that handled appropriations for the National Institutes of Health. The cause was promoted before the interested publics by a conglomerate of professional organizations, the Joint Commission on Mental Illness and Health. Lobbying of Congress was conducted by the National Committee Against Mental Illness. Kennedy's election finally gave the program a sympathetic listener in the White House who proposed it in his State of the Union Message of 1963.

As this example suggests, there are several components in such a political formation. The bureaucratic professionals usually work in conjunction—often in close cooperation—with the relevant specialized committees and subcommittees of Congress, especially their chairmen, who like Hill and Fogarty may make their legislative achievements in such a specialized field the crown of their political careers. The bureaucrats and politicians may also be associated with special interest groups of beneficiaries, or with those who claim to speak for the beneficiaries, of the programs. In the hyperbole of American political comment, these three elements are sometimes termed "the triple alliance" or "the iron triangle."[5] Insofar as the technocratic tendency prevails, however, it is the first two elements—Congressmen can develop considerable expertise—rather than the groups from the private sector that are the initiating influence. Lobbies with an interest in particular programs do arise and use their influence to maintain and expand programs. But in a professional-bureaucratic complex, in contrast with the older responsive models of policy-making, the initial sequence of causality is reversed: it is the program that creates the lobby, not the lobby that creates the program.

Probably the most noteworthy examples of the new professionalism have consisted in the application of science and technology to public policy in the fields of defense and space. For the student of

[5]Harold Seidman, *Politics, Position, and Power* (New York: 1970), p. 37.

federalism, however, the most interesting role of the professional-bureaucratic complex has been its part in producing the programs of the Great Society. To a pronounced degree there was a "professionalization of reform." In the fields of health, housing, urban renewal, highways, welfare, education, and poverty the new programs drew heavily upon specialized and technical knowledge in and around the federal bureaucracy for conception and execution. Building on the old system of cooperative federalism dating from the New Deal, the new programs depended upon conditional grants to state and local governments for administration.[6] But the enhanced importance of scientifically and professionally trained civil servants at all levels of government tended, to a greater extent than in the past, to create strong vertical connections among bureaucratic cadres in specialized functional fields. In this manner the professional-bureaucratic complex reshaped the intergovernmental system along the lines of what in the sixties came to be called "functional federalism."[7]

The programs of the Great Society were expensive, and between 1964 and 1969, in spite of Vietnam, the domestic, that is non-defense, portion of federal spending grew substantially—from 8.4 to 10 percent of GNP.[8] But the point of interest to the present study is the way that that money was spent. There was, of course, an increase in the absolute amount of direct federal expenditure, which, incidentally, included substantial sums for "private federalism,"[9] that is, grants to universities, hospitals, and other private nonprofit institutions. But relative to total domestic expenditure, direct spending

---

[6]The term "cooperative federalism" was coined by Jane Perry Clark in her pioneering book, *The Rise of a New Federalism: Federal-State Cooperation in the United States* (New York: Russell, 1938). In contrast with the older "dual federalism," in which federal and state governments carried on largely different and separate activities, cooperative federalism referred to the increasing cooperation between the two levels of government and gave emphasis to the greater use under the New Deal of conditional grants to secure certain kinds of action by the states in response to "the need for a minimum of uniform national policy" (p. 7).

[7]I do not know when the term "functional federalism" was first used. The concept and the stress on the term "functionalism," however, were pronounced in a perceptive report of the Muskie subcommittee as early as 1965. Committee on Government Operations, Subcommittee on Intergovernmental Relations (89th Congress, 1st Session), *The Federal System: As Seen by Federal Aid Officials* (Washington, D.C.: GPO, 1965), esp. chapter 6, "Bureaucracy and Federalism: Some Observations and Proposals."

[8]ACIR, *Trends in Fiscal Federalism, 1954–1974*, Table 3.

[9]Charles E. Gilbert and David G. Smith, "The Modernization of American Federalism," in Murray Stedman (ed.), *Modernizing American Government: The Demands of Social Change* (Englewood Cliffs, N.J.: Prentice-Hall, 1968), p. 145.

declined. As Table 1 shows, the two growing dimensions were Social Security payments and federal aid to state and local governments. What is particularly important for this study, however, is the fact that federal aid grew even more rapidly than Social Security—in 5 years rising by 4.4 percentage points as compared with an increase of 2.3 percentage points. In the crucial period of the Great Society, 1963–1968, it leaped up as a fraction both of federal domestic outlays and of state and local revenues. One may also impute much of its continuing growth under Nixon to the momentum established in the Great Society years. No less important than the increase in the absolute and relative sums that were distributed was the rise in the number of programs. Although an accurate count for the period is not yet available, it is probably right to say that between 1962 and 1967 the number of categorical programs, including both project and formula grants, rose from 160 to 379.[10] No one doubts that there was great "proliferation," to use a favorite term of critics.

In spending for social purposes the Great Society was in the tradition of the New Deal. But a major field of New Deal activity had also been direct federal action: securities regulation, the Wagner Act, the TVA, the Wage-Hour Act, the AAA, and other measures of "countervailing power." Only one major program of the Great Society was a direct act of federal regulation: the Voting Rights Act of

TABLE 1 *Growth of Federal Aid to State and Local Governments, 1960–1972 (%)*

	1960	*1963*	*1968*	*1972*
Social Security as % federal domestic outlays	27.0	30.2	32.5	33.4
Federal aid as % federal domestic outlays	16.4	16.5	20.9	24.5
Federal aid as % state and local revenues	11.7	11.5	15.8	21.1

Source: Adapted from Deil Wright, "Understanding Intergovernmental Relations: Historical Patterns, Fiscal Impacts and Citizen Perspectives" (Chapel Hill, 1974, mimeo.), p. 36a.

[10]David B. Walker, "The New System of Intergovernmental Assistance: Some Initial Notes" (paper presented at 1975 ASPA National Conference, April 1–4, 1975).

1964. Otherwise, it built on the spending foundations laid by the New Deal in the form of the Social Security system and especially of cooperative federalism. Within this tradition, however, the Great Society acquired a special character by its emphasis upon spending for services provided largely by state and local governments.

This services strategy has been attacked by critics who say that greater use should have been made of the incomes strategy. The choice of the services strategy, however, was strongly related to the new professionalism, which presumably was being equipped by advances in the natural and social sciences to design programs that would combat heart disease, lessen mental illness, reduce pollution, develop backward areas, train manpower, raise reading scores, cut down juvenile delinquency, and perhaps even cure poverty. If the new professionalism led naturally to the services strategy, this strategy in turn made it virtually inevitable that there would be a wide use of state and local governments, whose bureaucracies were already engaged in the delivery of services in such fields of policy.

Functional federalism was criticized for its centralizing and fragmenting effects.[11] Conservative critics in particular made much of the need to protect the generalists of state and local government against narrow bureaucratic functionalists, and the polemic against the Great Society emphasized attacks upon "balkanized bureaucracies," "vertical functional autocracies," and "feudal functional federalisms."[12] Indeed the reversal of these tendencies of the categorical system became the main ground for the conservatives' essentially political case for general revenue sharing.[13]

Yet a paradoxical and quite unanticipated consequence of this new phase of centralizing federalism was to create powerful countervailing forces. The Great Society programs did impose federal policies upon subnational governments. By the same token they greatly heightened the concern and increased the contacts of subnational governments with federal policy-making and administration. Project

---

[11]These criticisms of the categorical system can be found as early as the mid-fifties. See, for instance, Commission on Intergovernmental Relations (Kestnbaum Commission) *Report* (Washington, D.C.: GPO, 1955), esp. the section "The Uses and Limitations of the Grant-in-Aid," pp. 124–142.

[12]See Deil Wright, "Policy Control: The Hidden Issue in Revenue Sharing," in F. M. Carney and H. F. Way (eds.), *Politics 1972: Trends in Federalism* (Belmont, Calif.: Wadsworth, 1972).

[13]See Edward Banfield, "Revenue Sharing in Theory and Practice," *The Public Interest* (Spring 1971), pp. 38–46.

grants are surely the leading examples of how this happened. Increasing in number from 100 in 1962 to 280 in 1966,[14] programs of this sort provided the spoils for some spectacular grantsmanship as energetic mayors took to commuting to Washington. Fiscally much more significant, formula grants also made a difference to the finances and activities of state and local governments.

Moreover, even though subnational governments were given ever greater reason and opportunity to concern themselves with federal action, they were also endowed with new means of influence on the federal government. As the federal government in the Great Society period extended its responsibilities by means of state and local governments, it also became dependent upon them for the successful discharge of these responsibilities. Functional federalism increased the concern of subnational governments with federal policy and drew them into frequent contact with its formulation. Less tangible but not less important was the way functional federalism also created a new and wider responsibility on the part of the federal government in both its executive and legislative branches toward these communities and their welfare. In intergovernmental relations, the flow of power was not unidirectional, but complex and interactive. The lesser jurisdictions acquired an ability to negotiate and bargain with the federal government. As Allen Pritchard of the National League of Cities could write at the height of the struggle over general revenue sharing: "intergovernmental 'relations' are in fact intergovernmental 'negotiations,' in which the parties are negotiating in dead earnest for power, money and problem solving responsibility."[15]

This dependence of the controller upon the controlled is a familiar paradox of the corporatistic arrangements of modern democratic states (the authoritarian states have means of countering it). In a free country, as government extends its powers over the society, it must at the same time so act as to win a substantial degree of consent and cooperation from the organizations being controlled. "The greater the degree of detailed and technical control the gov-

[14]David Walker, ftn. 10, p. 7.

[15]Allen Pritchard, Editorial, *Nation's Cities*, 10 (8) (June 1972): 12. Quoted in Jeremy Plant, *The Big Seven: The Role of Public Official Associations in the American Political System* (unpublished Ph.D. dissertation, University of Virginia, 1975). See also Deil Wright on the bargaining-exchange model as applying to intergovernmental relations in the United States in his *Understanding Intergovernmental Relations: Historical Patterns, Fiscal Impacts and Citizens Perspectives* (Chapel Hill, N.C., 1974, mimeo.), pp. 9–11.

ernment seeks to exert over industrial and commercial interests,"
E. P. Herring wrote more than a generation ago, "the greater must
be their degree of consent and active participation."[16] In the United
States the familiar phenomenon of "cooptation" of the regulatory
agency by the interest being regulated results in part from this necessity of seeking advice and winning cooperation. On this condition
much of the power of organized producers in the managed economies
of the contemporary world is based. Indeed, one of the reasons that
producers organize is to mobilize this power for the purpose of serving interests in part created by the extension of government control.
The history of trade associations illustrates the process. Service functions such as market information are a reason for their formation, as
are economic functions relating to labor relations. But to a very great
extent the incentive and pressure to organize and to affiliate more
widely come from government intervention and the concerns and
opportunities it presents.

This familiar evolution of the relations between the public and
private sectors is paralleled by a similar development among different levels of government in the growth of the intergovernmental
lobby. The pluralizing tendencies that arise in the managed economy
because of interactions within the control relationship are analogous
to the tendencies toward decentralization produced by the initially
centralizing measures of the welfare state. In their influence on public policy, certain producers of public goods, namely, the subnational
governments, moved into positions of influence rather like those occupied by producers of private goods. The successful drive for general revenue sharing in great degree arose out of these essentially
political developments. In terms of American experience, one might
think of general revenue sharing as the cooptation phase of functional federalism.

To speak of "cooptation" in this connection is, of course, to exaggerate. I do so as a rhetorical help in breaking away from the conventional perspective on the relations of the professional bureaucratic
complex and the intergovernmental lobby. Commonly, these relations are viewed as one more instance of the antagonism of "functionalists" and "generalists,"[17] the passage of the Act of 1972

[16]E. P. Herring, *Public Administration and the Public Interest* (New York: McGraw-Hill, 1936), p. 192.
[17]See, for instance, Donald H. Haider, *When Governments Come to Washington: Governors, Mayors and Intergovernmental Lobbying* (New York: The Free Press, 1974), passim.

constituting a victory of the latter over the former. I agree to a great extent and indeed find this antagonism a major dimension of the cleavage of forces in the passage of the act. This conventional view, however, is too static. It neglects the interactive nature of power in these relations, and specifically what David Walker calls "the reciprocal character of creative federalism."[18] A critic of an earlier draft of this paper put the point succinctly: "If these federal technicians, linked to committees in Congress and clienteles outside, were so powerful, how did they lose on revenue sharing? The answer seems to be that the creation of government clienteles outside Washington to administer the programs [of the Great Society] planted the seed of organized interests with their own values, minds, and clout."[19]

A look at the growth of the intergovernmental lobby in the sixties will throw further light on this paradoxical, not to say dialectical, process.

The Intergovernmental Lobby

By the intergovernmental lobby I mean organizations of public officials, elected or appointed, exercising general responsibilities in subnational governments. Table 2 gives some of the basic facts about the seven main organizations, which are distinguished here from associations of public officials based on specialized functions, such as the highway engineers or social workers, the National Association of State Budget Officers, or the National Association of Housing and Redevelopment Officials.[20] The constituent organizations of the intergovernmental lobby perform functions other than lobbying. They do a great deal of research, largely financed by federal grants, and they make themselves useful to their members by service functions such as help with personnel systems, budgeting methods, and so on. The key to their growth, however, was federal action. The nature of the connection is indicated in a communication from Allen Pritchard, a member of the staff of the American Municipal Association (shortly to become the National League of Cities) to its executive

[18]David Walker, in a private letter. "Creative federalism" was, of course, President Johnson's term for the Great Society approach to intergovernmental relations.
[19]Prof. Jay Goodman of Wheaton College in a private letter.
[20]If a single term is wanted to refer to this group, it could be called "the interbureaucratic lobby." In the term "the intergovernmental lobby" the term "government," as in British usage, refers to persons or offices charged with the general powers and obligations of political rule.

TABLE 2   *The Intergovernmental Lobby*

Association	Date Founded	Basis of Membership
Council of State Governments	1933	Direct membership by all states and territories. Umbrella organization for 9 affiliated and 25 cooperating associations
National Governors' Conference	1908	Incumbent governors of all states and territories
National Legislative Conference	1948	State legislative officials, members, and staff of legislative service agencies
National Association of Counties	1937	Direct membership by counties and statewide leagues. Umbrella organization for 11 affiliated associations
National League of Cities (Name changed from American Municipal Association in 1964)	1924	Direct membership by municipal units and statewide municipal leagues
United States Conference of Mayors	1933	Direct membership by 469 cities over 30,000 population
International City Management Association	1915	Direct membership by professional city and county managers

From Jeremy F. Plant, "National Associations of State, City, and County Officials," *The University of Virginia News Letter* (published by Institute of Government, University of Virginia), Vol. 50, No. 6 (Feb. 15, 1974), p. 22. Reprinted by permission.

director, Patrick Healy, early in the Kennedy administration. Foreseeing the creation in the near future of such an agency as HUD, Pritchard observed that the mayors and the cities would then need a strong lobbying capacity in order to assist with program development by the new agency and that therefore their association should take immediate steps to expand its resources and prepare itself for this role.[21] At this time the AMA, like the USCM, had a staff of three and a budget of about $100,000.[22] Table 3, which sets out the ex-

[21]Quoted from interviews with Pritchard (February 18, 1975) in David Grizzle, *The Intergovernmental Lobby: A Response to Changing Federalism* (unpublished Senior Honors Essay, Harvard College, 1975), p. 94.
[22]Grizzle, ftn. 21, p. 30.

penses of the USCM, will serve as a rough index of the increase in its staff, service functions, and lobbying activity.

Generally in the postwar years, the mayors responded to whatever Washington had to offer. In the late fifties, usually operating on an individual basis, they fought hard for urban renewal money. But although suburbanization was in full spate, and in the cities, as Patrick Moynihan has observed, "the signs of social morbidity were obvious to anyone who cared to look,"[23] the city organizations, like the rest of the intergovernmental lobby, took no new initiatives. When, however, the Kennedy and Johnson administrations launched their programmatic approach to urban problems, the mayors again responded and now, as organizations, sent their representatives to meet with White House planners to help develop the new proposals.[24] When trying to design a workable Model Cities law the White House itself took the initiative in soliciting the formation of the urban coalition, a group of public and private organizations centered around the USCM, to consult with federal officials.[25]

Like the mayors, the organizations enjoyed a sharp increase in staff, budgets, and lobbying from the mid-sixties.[26] Although the National Association of Counties had been founded during the New Deal it was little more than a letterhead organization as late as 1957, when it was run on a part-time basis by two Washington lawyers on an annual budget of $18,000. Between 1963 and 1973 the counties represented increased from 400 to 820 to include 60 percent of the U.S.

TABLE 3 *Expenses of the U.S. Conference of Mayors*

Date	Amount	
1950	$ 85,000	
1960	88,000	
1962	108,000	
1964	175,000	
1968	338,000	
1972	550,000	(Includes joint operations with the National League of Cities)

Source: NLC–USCM.

[23]Patrick Moynihan, "Poverty and Progress," *The American Scholar*, 33 (Autumn 1964): 594–606. Quoted in Grizzle, ftn. 21.

[24]Grizzle, ftn. 21, p. 96; interviews with John Gunther and Patrick Healy.

[25]Plant, ftn. 15, interview with John Gunther, Oct. 18, 1973.

[26]See Haider, ftn. 17, chapter I, "The Government Interest Groups."

population, and in the latter year its executive director could claim a staff of 100, of whom 70 were in the field and 30 were in the Washington office.[27] Slower to respond, the National Governors' Conference depended for its staff on the Council of State Governments, which has its headquarters at Lexington, Kentucky. Finally in 1966 the NGC set up a Washington office with a separate staff and in 1974 it acquired an independent research facility. The International City Management Association likewise grew rapidly after its move to Washington in 1964.

Conceivably, the intergovernmental lobby might have developed in the sixties in response to pressures from the private sector of the polity, which in turn had been stimulated by changes in the economic and social environments. For instance, the increase in activity of the mayors could have taken place because certain growing problems, such as the decay of the central city and the plight of the urban poor, led affected groups in the city to press their needs on mayors, who then turned to Washington with a shopping list of demands for which they asked federal assistance in the form of Great Society programs. That is not the way things happened. The initiative came when the federal government launched the Great Society programs, which then provided the opportunity and occasion for the rapid and vast development of the intergovernmental lobby. . . .

[27]Interview with Bernard Hillenbrand, Executive Director, NACO, March 29, 1974.

II

The Power of Bureaucratic Expertise

Max Weber's "Essay on Bureaucracy" is the classic analysis of the way in which bureaucrats draw power from the expertise they bring to government decision-making. Without the technical and professional skills of bureaucrats, government today would not be able to cope with the difficult social and economic problems it confronts. This bureaucratic expertise comes essentially from two sources. First, government agencies are major employers of skilled professionals in various fields. Second, these organizations operate through a division of labor that enables even unskilled workers to achieve results as a group that they could never attain while working as individuals. Thus, the expertise of bureaucratic organizations comes from both the proficiency of the people they employ and the skills that an organizational setting itself engenders.

"Under normal conditions," Weber writes, "the power position of a fully developed bureaucracy is always overpowering. The 'political master' finds himself in the position of the 'dilettante' who stands opposite the 'expert', facing the trained official who stands within the management of administration." From an American perspective, Weber's words may seem to overstate somewhat the superior resources of bureaucrats in policy discussions. Political officials in both the executive and the legislative branch are not without skills of their own, and they can always call on experts from the private sector to help equalize their power in dealing with bureaucracy.

In Congress, for example, the continuity in office of the

heads of legislative committees often exceeds that of the bureaucrats with whom they deal. So it is sometimes a moot point as to
who is the "dilettante" and who the "expert" in confrontations between Congress and the bureaucracy. But Weber is certainly correct in identifying expertise as a central factor underlying the
influence that bureaucrats exert on government decision-making in
all areas of public policy.

In Section I, bureaucratic power was attributed in large part
to the ability of bureaucrats to mobilize public support through
constituency-building activities. But the power of any bureaucracy
is most secure when it is also buttressed by public deference to the
professional skills that an agency commands. The influence that
health-agency professionals have long exerted over the development of health-care policy in the United States does not rest exclusively on their ability to mobilize public support. It also stems
from the enormous prestige that medical practitioners enjoy in
American society. Of course these two factors interact. An agency
is best equipped to build a strong political following if it commands widespread public respect for its professional skill.

I

In "The Professional State," Frederick C. Mosher
demonstrates how thoroughly bureaucracy in the United States is
honeycombed with a wide variety of professional groups. As he
notes, the percentage of government employees who have
professional status is far higher than the percentage of
professionals in the private sector. Both the private and the public
sector employ some types of professionals, such as lawyers and
doctors. Others, like military and foreign service officers, work
only for the government. In government agencies in which such
professionals play a prominent role, Mosher writes, "the 'climate'
of an organization as well as its view of mission and its
effectiveness in carrying it out are in considerable part a product
of its professional structure and professional value system." The
expertise of bureaucracy is thus very much a product of the ability
of government agencies to recruit highly trained people as career
employees.

One of the principal roles that professional employees play in
any government organization is to give advice to political

officeholders on what course of action to follow in dealing with problems that come before the agency. Professionals at high levels within bureaucracy shape political officeholders' views of the world by providing the information on which these officeholders rely in making decisions on the myriad questions that come before them. It often takes such experts to determine what a particular piece of information means. No less important is their ability to inform policymakers of remedies that may be available to deal with the problems revealed to them by the information at their disposal.

In "The Power of Bureaucratic Routines: The Cuban Missile Crisis," Graham Allison focuses on an aspect of bureaucratic expertise quite distinct from the professional skill of individual employees. He demonstrates that government organizations themselves develop routines or standard operating procedures that are essential for achieving the objectives that elected officials commonly seek. Such organizational capabilities supplement the professional training of individual employees as a source of bureaucratic power. They represent a way in which a bureaucratic organization can create as well as exploit its members' expertise.

Allison's analysis deals with the routines that military organizations long ago developed to attain their objectives. He shows that the standard operating procedures of the military limit the policy options of elected officials to the courses of action that the organizations themselves are prepared to carry out. On occasion the inflexibility of such routines may produce consequences that the elected official might prefer to avoid, or that prove very difficult to reverse or turn off once they have been launched in particular directions. And of course the worst fear is that these routines may spin out of control altogether, leading—in the case of the military, at least—to catastrophic results.

II

Concern over the rising power of bureaucratic expertise in the development of public policy has led in recent years to increased attempts to reestablish or reinforce political controls over the bureaucracy. Some of this fear of bureaucracy is based on the belief that it will use its power excessively. This has certainly been the predominant view among conservative groups in the United

States as the country has moved from a laissez-faire economy to a society in which government agencies are empowered to intervene in a pervasive way in social and economic life.

As bureaucracy has become securely established as part of the governmental apparatus in democratic societies, another kind of concern has begun to surface on the liberal side of the political spectrum: the complaint that government agencies suffer not from excessive zeal in using their powers but from inadequate enthusiasm in seeking the goals for which they were originally created. Groups looking to executive agencies for services and assistance often feel that the agencies are mainly interested in safeguarding the career interests and working conditions of their own employees and, in the case of regulatory organizations, are unduly deferential toward the industries they are supposed to be monitoring.

The goal of attaining better control over the power of bureaucracy has been pursued through various avenues in the United States during recent years. Perhaps the most significant effort to bring bureaucracy under closer and more continual control has come from the presidency itself. One of the chief means through which presidents have sought to achieve this goal is by extending their capacity to make executive appointments so as to ensure that the policies being pursued within the bureaucracy are in accord with the president's own objectives.

This development reverses a long-standing effort in the United States, beginning with the enactment of the Pendleton Act in 1883, to depoliticize the bureaucracy. In "OMB and the Presidency—The Problem of Neutral Competence," Hugh Heclo examines what this trend has meant for one agency, the executive budget office (OMB), and he attempts to measure the costs of repoliticizing an agency that has long symbolized the power and value of independent bureaucratic expertise within the councils of government.

What Heclo is essentially arguing is that, although political control over bureaucracy is indispensable for the conduct of democratic government, bureaucratic competence is no less essential. It can provide political officials with a detached and impartial evaluation of the feasibility of a pending course of action which may save an officeholder from political grief. It also provides continuity from one administration to another, making it unnecessary for each new administration to "reinvent the wheel" and making employment in the career sectors attractive to those young people whose talents the government badly needs.

So, although repoliticizing the bureaucracy has the indisputable advantage of making government more responsive to the public or at least to its elected representatives, it may also have a negative impact on the skill and efficiency with which the governmental apparatus performs its assigned tasks in a democracy. Like most other reforms, the current effort to strengthen political control over the bureaucracy has damaging consequences that are no less significant for being unintended.

5

Essay on Bureaucracy

MAX WEBER

Characteristics of Bureaucracy

Modern officialdom functions in the following specific manner.

I. There is the principle of fixed and official jurisdictional areas, which are generally ordered by rules, that is, by laws or administrative regulations.

1. The regular activities required for the purposes of the bureaucratically governed structure are distributed in a fixed way as official duties.
2. The authority to give the commands required for the discharge of these duties is distributed in a stable way and is strictly delimited by rules concerning the coercive means, physical, sacerdotal, or otherwise, which may be placed at the disposal of officials.
3. Methodical provision is made for the regular and continuous fulfillment of these duties and for the execution of the corresponding rights; only persons who have the generally regulated qualifications to serve are employed.

In public and lawful government these three elements constitute "bureaucratic authority." In private economic domination, they constitute bureaucratic "management." Bureaucracy, thus understood, is fully developed in political and ecclesiastical communities only in the modern state, and, in the private economy, only in the most advanced institutions of capitalism. Permanent and public office authority, with fixed jurisdiction, is not the historical rule but

Abridged from *From Max Weber: Essays in Sociology*, edited and translated by H. H. Gerth and C. Wright Mills, pp. 196–198, 214–216, 228–230, 232–235. Copyright 1946 by Oxford University Press, Inc., renewed © by Dr. Hans H. Gerth. Reprinted by permission.

rather the exception. This is so even in large political structures such as those of the ancient Orient, the Germanic and Mongolian empires of conquest, or of many feudal structures of state. In all these cases, the ruler executes the most important measures through personal trustees, table-companions, or court-servants. Their commissions and authority are not precisely delimited and are temporarily called into being for each case.

II. The principles of office hierarchy and of levels of graded authority mean a firmly ordered system of super- and subordination in which there is a supervision of the lower offices by the higher ones. Such a system offers the governed the possibility of appealing the decision of a lower office to its higher authority, in a definitely regulated manner. With the full development of the bureaucratic type, the office hierarchy is monocratically organized. The principle of hierarchical office authority is found in all bureaucratic structures: in state and ecclesiastical structures as well as in large party organizations and private enterprises. It does not matter for the character of bureaucracy whether its authority is called "private" or "public."

When the principle of jurisdictional "competency" is fully carried through, hierarchical subordination—at least in public office—does not mean that the "higher" authority is simply authorized to take over the business of the "lower." Indeed, the opposite is the rule. Once established and having fulfilled its task, an office tends to continue in existence and be held by another incumbent.

III. The management of the modern office is based upon written documents ("the files"), which are preserved in their original or draught form. There is, therefore, a staff of subaltern officials and scribes of all sorts. The body of officials actively engaged in a "public" office, along with the respective apparatus of material implements and the files, make up a "bureau." In private enterprise, "the bureau" is often called "the office."

In principle, the modern organization of the civil service separates the bureau from the private domicile of the official, and, in general, bureaucracy segregates official activity as something distinct from the sphere of private life. Public monies and equipment are divorced from the private property of the official. This condition is everywhere the product of a long development. Nowadays, it is found in public as well as in private enterprises; in the latter, the principle extends even to the leading entrepreneur. In principle, the executive office is separated from the household, business from private correspondence, and business assets from private fortunes. The more consistently the modern type of business management has been carried through, the more are these separations the case. The beginnings of this process are to be found as early as the Middle Ages.

It is the peculiarity of the modern entrepreneur that he conducts himself as the "first official" of his enterprise, in the very same way in which the ruler of a specifically modern bureaucratic state spoke of himself as "the first servant" of the state. The idea that the bureau activities of the state are intrinsically different in character from the management of private economic offices is a continental European notion and, by way of contrast, is totally foreign to the American way.

IV. Office management, at least all specialized office management—and such management is distinctly modern—usually presupposes thorough and expert training. This increasingly holds for the modern executive and employee of private enterprises, in the same manner as it holds for the state official.

V. When the office is fully developed, official activity demands the full working capacity of the official, irrespective of the fact that his obligatory time in the bureau may be firmly delimited. In the normal case, this is only the product of a long development, in the public as well as in the private office. Formerly, in all cases, the normal state of affairs was reversed: official business was discharged as a secondary activity.

VI. The management of the office follows general rules, which are more or less stable, more or less exhaustive, and which can be learned. Knowledge of these rules represents a special technical learning which the officials possess. It involves jurisprudence, or administrative or business management.

The reduction of modern office management to rules is deeply embedded in its very nature. The theory of modern public administration, for instance, assumes that the authority to order certain matters by decree—which has been legally granted to public authorities—does not entitle the bureau to regulate the matter by commands given for each case, but only to regulate the matter abstractly. This stands in extreme contrast to the regulation of all relationships through individual privileges and bestowals of favor, which is absolutely dominant in patrimonialism, at least in so far as such relationships are not fixed by sacred tradition. . . .

Technical Advantages
of Bureaucratic Organization

The decisive reason for the advance of bureaucratic organization has always been its purely technical superiority over any other form of organization. The fully developed bureaucratic mechanism compares with other organizations exactly as does the machine with the nonmechanical modes of production.

Precision, speed, unambiguity, knowledge of the files, continuity, discretion, unity, strict subordination, reduction of friction and of material and personal costs—these are raised to the optimum point in the strictly bureaucratic administration, and especially in its monocratic form. As compared with all collegiate, honorific, and avocational forms of administration, trained bureaucracy is superior on all these points. And as far as complicated tasks are concerned, paid bureaucratic work is not only more precise but, in the last analysis, it is often cheaper than even formally unremunerated honorific service.

Honorific arrangements make administrative work an avocation and, for this reason alone, honorific service normally functions more slowly, being less bound to schemata and being more formless. Hence it is less precise and less unified than bureaucratic work because it is less dependent upon superiors and because the establishment and exploitation of the apparatus of subordinate officials and filing services are almost unavoidably less economical. Honorific service is less continuous than bureaucratic and frequently quite expensive. This is especially the case if one thinks not only of the money costs to the public treasury—costs which bureaucratic administration, in comparison with administration by notables, usually substantially increases—but also of the frequent economic losses of the governed caused by delays and lack of precision. The possibility of administration by notables normally and permanently exists only where official management can be satisfactorily discharged as an avocation. With the qualitative increase of tasks the administration has to face, administration by notables reaches its limits—today, even, in England. Work organized by collegiate bodies causes friction and delay and requires compromises between colliding interests and views. The administration, therefore, runs less precisely and is more independent of superiors; hence, it is less unified and slower. All advances of the Prussian administrative organization have been and will in the future be advances of the bureaucratic, and especially of the monocratic, principle.

Today, it is primarily the capitalist market economy which demands that the official business of the administration be discharged precisely, unambiguously, continuously, and with as much speed as possible. Normally, the very large, modern capitalist enterprises are themselves unequalled models of strict bureaucratic organization. Business management throughout rests on increasing precision, steadiness, and, above all, the speed of operations. This, in turn, is determined by the peculiar nature of the modern means of communication, including, among other things, the news service of the press. The extraordinary increase in the speed by which public announcements, as well as economic and political facts, are transmitted exerts a steady and sharp pressure in the direction of speeding up the tempo of administrative reaction towards various situations. The optimum of such reaction time is normally attained only by a strictly bureaucratic organization.[1]

Bureaucratization offers above all the optimum possibility for carrying through the principle of specializing administrative functions according to purely objective considerations. Individual performances are allocated to functionaries who have specialized training and who by constant practice learn more and more. The "objective" discharge of business primarily means a discharge of business according to *calculable rules* and "without regard for persons."

"Without regard for persons" is also the watchword of the "market" and, in general, of all pursuits of naked economic interests.
. . .

The second element mentioned, "calculable rules," also is of paramount importance for modern bureaucracy. The peculiarity of modern culture, and specifically of its technical and economic basis, demands this very "calculability" of results. When fully developed, bureaucracy also stands, in a specific sense, under the principle of *sine ira ac studio*. Its specific nature, which is welcomed by capitalism, develops the more perfectly the more the bureaucracy is "dehumanized," the more completely it succeeds in eliminating from official business love, hatred, and all purely personal, irrational, and

---

[1]Here we cannot discuss in detail how the bureaucratic apparatus may, and actually does, produce definite obstacles to the discharge of business in a manner suitable for the single case.

emotional elements which escape calculation. This is the specific nature of bureaucracy and it is appraised as its special virtue.

The more complicated and specialized modern culture becomes, the more its external supporting apparatus demands the personally detached and strictly "objective" *expert*, in lieu of the master of old social structures, who was moved by personal sympathy and favor, by grace and gratitude. Bureaucracy offers the attitudes demanded by the external apparatus of modern culture in the most favorable combination. As a rule, only bureaucracy has established the foundation for the administration of a rational law conceptually systematized on the basis of such enactments as the latter Roman imperial period first created with a high degree of technical perfection. During the Middle Ages, this law was received along with the bureaucratization of legal administration, that is to say, with the displacement of the old trial procedure which was bound to tradition or to irrational presuppositions, by the rationally trained and specialized expert. . . .

The Permanent Character of the Bureaucratic Machine

Once it is fully established, bureaucracy is among those social structures which are the hardest to destroy. . . . [B]ureaucracy has been and is a power instrument of the first order—for the one who controls the bureaucratic apparatus.

Under otherwise equal conditions, a "societal action," which is methodically ordered and led, is superior to every resistance of "mass" or even of "communal action." And where the bureaucratization of administration has been completely carried through, a form of power relation is established that is practically unshatterable.

The individual bureaucrat cannot squirm out of the apparatus in which he is harnessed. In contrast to the honorific or avocational "notable," the professional bureaucrat is chained to his activity by his entire material and ideal existence. In the great majority of cases, he is only a single cog in an ever-moving mechanism which prescribes to him an essentially fixed route of march. The official is entrusted with specialized tasks and normally the mechanism cannot be put into motion or arrested by him, but only from the very top. The individual bureaucrat is thus forged to the community of all the functionaries who are integrated into the mechanism. They have a common interest in seeing that the mechanism continues its functions and that the societally exercised authority carries on.

The ruled, for their part, cannot dispense with or replace the bureaucratic apparatus of authority once it exists. For this bureaucracy rests upon expert training, a functional specialization of work, and an attitude set for habitual and virtuoso-like mastery of single yet methodically integrated functions. If the official stops working, or if his work is forcefully interrupted, chaos results, and it is difficult to improvise replacements from among the governed who are fit to master such chaos. This holds for public administration as well as for private economic management. More and more the material fate of the masses depends upon the steady and correct functioning of the increasingly bureaucratic organizations of private capitalism. The idea of eliminating these organizations becomes more and more utopian.

The discipline of officialdom refers to the attitude-set of the official for precise obedience within his *habitual* activity, in public as well as in private organizations. This discipline increasingly becomes the basis of all order, however great the practical importance of administration on the basis of the filed documents may be. The naive idea of Bakuninism of destroying the basis of "acquired rights" and "domination" by destroying public documents overlooks the settled orientation of *man* for keeping to the habitual rules and regulations that continue to exist independently of the documents. Every reorganization of beaten or dissolved troops, as well as the restoration of administrative orders destroyed by revolt, panic, or other catastrophes, is realized by appealing to the trained orientation of obedient compliance to such orders. Such compliance has been conditioned into the officials, on the one hand, and, on the other hand, into the governed. If such an appeal is successful it brings, as it were, the disturbed mechanism into gear again.

The objective indispensability of the once-existing apparatus, with its peculiar, "impersonal" character, means that the mechanism—in contrast to feudal orders based upon personal piety—is easily made to work for anybody who knows how to gain control over it. A rationally ordered system of officials continues to function smoothly after the enemy has occupied the area; he merely needs to change the top officials. This body of officials continues to operate because it is to the vital interest of everyone concerned, including above all the enemy.

During the course of his long years in power, Bismarck brought his ministerial colleagues into unconditional bureaucratic dependence by eliminating all independent statesmen. Upon his retirement, he saw to his surprise that they continued to manage their offices unconcerned and undismayed, as if he had not been the mastermind and creator of these creatures, but rather as if some single figure had been exchanged for some other figure in the bureaucratic machine. With all the changes of masters in France since the time of the First Empire, the power machine has remained essentially the same. Such a machine makes "revolution," in the sense of the forceful creation of entirely new formations of authority, technically more and more impossible, especially when the apparatus controls the modern means of communication (telegraph, et cetera) and also by virtue of its internal rationalized structure. In classic fashion, France has demonstrated how this process has substituted coups d'état for "revolutions": all successul transformations in France have amounted to coups d'état. . . .

The Power Position of Bureaucracy

Everywhere the modern state is undergoing bureaucratization. But whether the *power* of bureaucracy within the polity is universally increasing must here remain an open question.

The fact that bureaucratic organization is technically the most highly developed means of power in the hands of the man who controls it does not determine the weight that bureaucracy as such is capable of having in a particular social structure. The ever-increasing "indispensability" of the officialdom, swollen to millions, is no more decisive for this question than is the view of some representatives of the proletarian movement that the economic indispensability of the proletarians is decisive for the measure of their social and political power position. If "indispensability" were decisive, then where slave labor prevailed and where freemen usually abhor work as a dishonor, the "indispensable" slaves ought to have held the positions of power, for they were at least as indispensable as officials and proletarians are today. Whether the power of bureaucracy as such increases cannot be decided a priori from such reasons. The drawing in of economic interest groups or other nonofficial experts, or the drawing in of nonexpert lay representatives, the establishment of local, interlocal, or central parliamentary or other representative bodies, or of occupational associations—these *seem* to run directly against the bureaucratic tendency. How far this appearance is from the truth must be discussed in another chapter rather than in this purely formal and typological discussion. In general, only the following can be said here:

Under normal conditions, the power position of a fully developed bureaucracy is always overpowering. The "political master" finds himself in the position of the "dilettante" who stands opposite the "expert," facing the trained official who stands within the management of administration. This holds whether the "master" whom the bureaucracy serves is a "people," equipped with the weapons of "legislative initiative," the "referendum," and the right to remove officials, or a parliament, elected on a more aristocratic or more "democratic" basis and equipped with the right to vote a lack of confidence, or with the actual authority to vote it. It holds whether the master is an aristocratic, collegiate body, legally or actually based on self-recruitment, or whether he is a popularly elected president, a hereditary and "absolute" or a "constitutional" monarch.

Every bureaucracy seeks to increase the superiority of the professionally informed by keeping their knowledge and intentions secret. Bureaucratic administration always tends to be an administration of "secret sessions": in so far as it can, it hides its knowledge and action from criticism. Prussian church authorities now threaten to use disciplinary measures against pastors who make reprimands or other admonitory measures in any way accessible to third parties. They do this because the pastor, in making such criticism available, is "guilty" of facilitating a possible criticism of the church authorities. The treasury officials of the Persian shah have made a secret doctrine of their budgetary art and even use secret script. The official statistics of Prussia, in general, make public only what cannot do any harm to the intentions of the power-wielding bureaucracy. The tendency toward secrecy in certain administrative fields follows their material nature: everywhere that the power interests of the domination structure toward *the outside* are at stake, whether it is an economic competitor of a private enterprise, or a foreign, potentially hostile polity, we find secrecy. If it is to be successful, the management of diplomacy can only be publicly controlled to a very limited extent. The military administration must insist on the concealment of its most important measures; with the increasing significance of purely technical aspects, this is all the more the case. Political parties do not proceed differently, in spite of all the ostensible publicity of Catholic congresses and party conventions. With the increasing bureaucratization of party organizations, this secrecy will prevail even more. Commercial policy, in Germany for instance, brings about a concealment of production statistics. Every fighting posture of a social structure toward the outside tends to buttress the position of the group in power.

The pure interest of the bureaucracy in power, however, is efficacious far beyond those areas where purely functional interests make for secrecy. The concept of the "official secret" is the specific invention of bureaucracy, and nothing is so fanatically defended by the bureaucracy as this attitude, which cannot be substantially justified beyond these specifically qualified areas. In facing a parliament, the bureaucracy, out of a sure power instinct, fights every attempt of the parliament to gain knowledge by means of its own experts or from interest groups. The so-called right of parliamentary investigation is one of the means by which parliament seeks such knowledge. Bureaucracy naturally welcomes a poorly informed and hence a powerless parliament—at least in so far as ignorance somehow agrees with the bureaucracy's interests.

The absolute monarch is powerless opposite the superior knowledge of the bureaucratic expert—in a certain sense more powerless than any other political head. All the scornful decrees of Frederick the Great concerning the "abolition of serfdom" were derailed, as it were, in the course of their realization because the official mechanism simply ignored them as the occasional ideas of a dilettante. When a constitutional king agrees with a socially important part of the governed, he very frequently exerts a greater influence upon the course of administration than does the absolute monarch. The constitutional king can control these experts better because of what is, at least relatively, the public character of criticism, whereas the absolute monarch is dependent for information solely upon the bureaucracy. The Russian czar of the old regime was seldom able to accomplish permanently anything that displeased his bureaucracy and hurt the power interests of the bureaucrats. His ministerial departments, placed directly under him as the autocrat, represented a conglomerate of satrapies, as was correctly noted by Leroy-Beaulieu. These satrapies constantly fought against one another by all the means of personal intrigue, and, especially, they bombarded one another with voluminous "memorials," in the face of which, the monarch, as a dilettante, was helpless.

With the transition to constitutional government, the concentration of the power of the central bureaucracy in one head became unavoidable. Officialdom was placed under a monocratic head, the prime minister, through whose hands everything had to go before it got to the monarch. This put the latter, to a large extent, under the tutelage of the chief of the bureaucracy. Wilhelm II, in his well known conflict with Bismarck, fought against this principle, but he had to withdraw his attack very soon. Under the rule of expert knowledge, the actual influence of the monarch can attain steadiness only by a continuous communication with the bureaucratic chiefs; this intercourse must be methodically planned and directed by the head of the bureaucracy.

At the same time, constitutionalism binds the bureaucracy and the ruler into a community of interests against the desires of party chiefs for power in the parliamentary bodies. And if he cannot find support in parliament the constitutional monarch is powerless against the bureaucracy. The desertion of the "Great of the Reich," the Prussian ministers and top officials of the Reich in November, 1918, brought a monarch into approximately the same situation as existed in the feudal state in 1056. However, this is an exception, for, on the whole, the power position of a monarch opposite bureaucratic officials is far stronger than it was in any feudal state or in the "stereotyped" patrimonial state. This is because of the constant presence of aspirants for promotion, with whom the monarch can easily replace inconvenient and independent officials. Other circumstances being equal, only economically independent officials, that is, officials who belong to the propertied strata, can permit themselves to risk the loss of their offices. Today as always, the recruitment of officials from among propertyless strata increases the power of the rulers. Only officials who belong to a socially influential stratum, whom the monarch believes he must take into account as personal supporters, like the so-called *Kanalrebellen* in Prussia, can permanently and completely paralyze the substance of his will.

Only the expert knowledge of private economic interest groups in the field of "business" is superior to the expert knowledge of the bureaucracy. This is so because the exact knowledge of facts in their field is vital to the economic existence of businessmen. Errors in official statistics do not have direct economic consequences for the guilty official, but errors in the calculation of a capitalist enterprise are paid for by losses, perhaps by its existence. The "secret," as a means of power, is, after all, more safely hidden in the books of an enterpriser than it is in the files of public authorities. For this reason alone authorities are held within narrow barriers when they seek to influence economic life in the capitalist epoch. Very frequently the measures of the state in the field of capitalism take unforeseen and unintended courses, or they are made illusory by the superior expert knowledge of interest groups. . . .

6

The Professional State

FREDERICK C. MOSHER

. . . In the 1960s, Daniel Bell wrote of an emerging new society in which old values and social power associated with property, wealth, production, and industry are giving way to knowledge, education, and intellect.

> To speak rashly: if the dominant figures of the past hundred years have been the entrepreneur, the businessman, and the industrial executive, the "new men" are the scientists, the mathematicians, the economists, and the engineers of the new computer technology. And the dominant institutions of the new society—in the sense that they will provide the most creative challenges and enlist the richest talents—will be the intellectual institutions. The leadership of the new society will rest, not with businessmen or corporations as we know them . . . but with the research corporation, the industrial laboratories, the experimental stations, and the universities.[1]

Viewed broadly, the professions are social mechanisms, whereby knowledge, particularly new knowledge, is translated into action and service. They provide the means whereby intellectual achievement becomes operational. . . .

The Professions and Government

The prominent role of American governments in the development and utilization of professions went largely unnoticed for a long time. Governments are the principal employers of professionals. According to estimates of the Bureau of Labor Statistics, about two of every

[1]"Notes on the Post-Industrial Society," I *The Public Interest*, 6 (Winter, 1967), p. 27.

five workers classified as "professional, technical, and kindred" (39.4%) were employed by governments in 1978, a proportion which has been stable since 1970.[2] This category does not include the multitude of engineers, scientists, and others on private rolls who are actually paid from government contracts, subsidies, and grants. Looked at another way, more than one third (36.7%) of all government employees were engaged in professional or technical pursuits, more than three times the comparable proportion in the private sector (10.9%). The governmental proportion is swollen by the education professions, especially elementary and secondary school teachers. But even if education is removed from both sides of the ledger, the percentage of professional and technical personnel in government (21.2%) is nearly double the comparable percentage in the private sector (11.6%).

Leaving aside the political appointees at or near the top of our public agencies and jurisdictions, the administrative leadership of government became increasingly professional in terms of educational and experiential backgrounds. This is not to say that public leadership as such is an administrative profession, rather that it consists of a very wide variety of professions and professionals in diverse fields, most of them related to the missions of the organizations in which they lead.

In government, the professions are the conveyor belts between knowledge and theory on the one hand, and public purpose on the other. The interdependencies of the professions and government are many. Governments are, or have been:

the creators of many professions;

the *de jure* legitimizers of most of those which have been legitimized;

protectors of the autonomy, integrity, monopoly, and standards of those which have such protections;

the principal supporters of their research and of that of the sciences upon which they depend;

[2]Data in this paragraph are drawn from "The 1978 Class of Worker Matrix for the United States," an unpublished table furnished by the Bureau of Labor Statistics. The definition of "professional, technical, and kindred" includes occupations that some might not construe as professional, such as applied scientists, athletic coaches, embalmers, writers, artists, and entertainers. On the other hand, it excludes others that might be considered professional, including all of those who describe themselves as "managers, officials, proprietors" (of whom governments employed some 1,170,000 in 1978), military officers, and police.

subsidizers of much of their education;

among their principal employers and the nearly exclusive employers of some of them; which means also

among the principal utilizers of their knowledge and skills.

For their part, the professions:

contribute to government a very substantial proportion of public servants;

provide most of the leadership in a considerable number of public agencies;

through their educational programs, examinations, accreditation, and licensing, largely determine what the content of each profession is in terms of knowledge, skills, and work;

influence public policy and the definition of public purpose in those many fields within which they operate;

in varying degree and in different ways provide or control the recruitment, selection, and other personnel actions for their members;

shape the structure as well as the social organization of many public agencies.

There is nothing very new about professionalism in government. The principal spawning period for educational programs for many of the professions . . . was the first quarter of this century, and the U.S. Classification Act of 1923 established as the most distinguished segment a professional and scientific service. In all probability the number of professionally educated personnel in all American governments has been rising for the past century. Yet there appears to have been very little recognition of, or concern about, the significance of professionalism in the public service and its leadership until quite recently. For example, the Brownlow report and those of the two Hoover commissions, for all of their emphasis upon administrative management, paid scant attention to professionals in fields other than management as such.

The degree to which individual professional specialisms have come to dominate public agencies is suggested by the small table here. The right hand column indicates both the primary professional field in the agency and the normal professional source of its career leadership.

Federal

All military agencies	military officers
Department of State	foreign service officers
Public Health Service	public health doctors
Forest Service	foresters
Bureau of Reclamation	civil engineers
Geological Survey	geologists
Department of Justice	lawyers
Department of Education	educators
Bureau of Standards	natural scientists

State and Local

Highways and other public works agencies	civil engineers
Welfare agencies	social workers
Mental hygiene agencies	psychiatrists
Public health agencies	public health doctors
Elementary and secondary education offices and schools	educators
Higher education institutions	professors
Attorneys general, district attorneys, legal counsel	lawyers

I define the word "profession" liberally as 1. a reasonably clearcut occupational field, 2. which ordinarily requires higher education at least through the bachelor's level, and 3. which offers a lifetime career to its members.[3] The professions in government may conveniently be divided into two classes: first, those in fields employed in the public *and* the private sectors and for whom the government must compete in both recruitment and retention. This category, which I shall call "general professions," includes most of the callings com-

---

[3]The definition is unquestionably too loose to satisfy many students of occupations, who would like to add other requisites, such as: professional organization; or eleemosynary or service orientation; or legal establishment; or individual autonomy in performance of work; or code of ethics. In terms of governmental consequences, the liberal usage is more appropriate. For example, in terms of their group behavior in government, the officers of the U.S. Navy are at least as "professionalized" as are lawyers.

monly understood as professions: law, medicine, engineering, archi-tecture, and many others. I also include among them applied scientists in general and college professors. Second are those em-ployed predominantly and sometimes exclusively by governmental agencies, which I shall call "public service professions." Most of these were generated within government in response to the needs of public programs, and although there has been a tendency in the direction of increased private employment for many of them, governments are still the predominant employers. They consist of two groups: first, those who are employed exclusively by a single agency such as mil-itary officers, Foreign Service officers, and Coast Guard officers; and, second, those employed by a number of different governmental jur-isdictions, such as school teachers, educational administrators, social workers, public health officers, foresters, agricultural scientists, and librarians.

Most of those listed above in both categories may be described as "established professions" in the sense that they are widely recog-nized as professions, and with only a few exceptions their status has been legitimized by formal state action through licensing, creden-tialing, commissioning, recognizing educational accreditation, or a combination of these.

In addition to these professions, there are many "emergent professions" which have not been so recognized and legitimized but which are valiantly and hopefully pulling themselves up by their vo-cational bootstraps to full professional status. In this group are in-cluded specialists in personnel, public relations, computer technology, and purchasing. Emergent in the "public service" category are gov-ernmental subdivisions of all of these and some which are more exclusively governmental: e.g., assessors, police, penologists, em-ployment security officers, air pollution specialists.

The professions—whether general or public service, whether established or emergent—display common characteristics which are significant for democracy and the public service. One of these is the continuing drive of each of them to elevate its stature and strengthen its public image as a profession. In a very few highly esteemed fields, such as law and medicine, the word "maintain" is perhaps more ap-propriate than "elevate." A prominent device for furthering this goal is the establishment of the clear and (where possible) expanding boundaries of work within which members of the profession have *exclusive* prerogatives to operate. Other means include: the assurance and protection of career opportunities for professionals; the establishment and continuous elevation of standards of education and entrance into the profession; the upgrading of rewards (pay) for professionals; and the improvement of their prestige before their associates and before the public in general.

A second common denominator of the professions is their concentration upon the *work substance* of their field, both in preparatory education and in journeyman activities, and the differentiation of that field from other kinds of work (including other professions) and from work at a lower or subprofessional level in the same field. Accompanying this emphasis upon work substance has been a growing concentration, particularly in preprofessional education, upon the sciences, which are considered foundational for the profession in question, whether they be natural or biological or social (behavioral). This emphasis is an inevitable consequence of the explosive developments of science in the last several decades, and unquestionably it has contributed to the betterment of professional performance in the technical sense. . . .

Each profession brings to an organization its own particularized view of the world and of the agency's role and mission in it. The perspective and motivation of each professional are shaped, at least to some extent, by the lens provided by professional education, prior professional experience, and professional colleagues. These distinctive views are further molded and strengthened through training and experience in the agency itself; and where the professional corps within the agency is one of long standing, where it operates through a well-entrenched career system, and where there is a vigorously defended stratification between the professional elite and others in the organization, these post-entry forces can be very strong indeed.

The analysis of different public organizations in terms of their professional structure and intraprofessional and interprofessional systems of relationships is basic to a true understanding of how they work. Important decisions are likely to be the product of intraprofessional deliberation, representing the group views of the elite profession in the agency, compromised in some cases to satisfy the demands of other professions and nonprofessionals. Social relationships outside the office usually parallel professional relationships within. Members of the same profession in an agency are "colleagues," like professors in a university; and the flavor of their work is similarly collegial. Toward members of other professions, their behavior is likely to be more formal, sometimes suspicious or even hostile. Toward paraprofessionals and other workers, the relationship may more frequently be paternalistic, patronizing, or dictatorial. Members of the elite profession identify their own work and that of the agency with their profession; the others are a little "outside," they are supplementary or supporting. The "climate" of an organization as well as its view of mission and its effectiveness in carrying it out are in considerable part a product of its professional structure and professional value system.

The Public Employment of Professionals

As the professional composition of public agencies has substantially revolutionized their internal anatomy, physiology, and nervous systems, so has the emergence of professions revolutionized the precepts and practices of public employment. Both revolutions continue with the development and solidification of new fields and new subspecialties. Although there are large differences in precepts and practices among different jurisdictions of government, the basic directions in public service employment are clear. They also are probably inevitable. They apply to virtually all professional fields, whether or not under civil service laws. They are often at odds with the most central—and most cherished—principles associated with civil service reform in this country: equal opportunity to apply and compete for jobs; competitive examinations for selection and (sometimes) promotion; equal pay for equal work; neutral and objective direction and control of the personnel system.

The most important of the changes is the last one, which involves the direction of personnel activities; it underlies the others. In general, what has happened (and is happening) is a *delegation* of real personnel authority, formal and/or informal, from a central personnel office or civil service commission to the professions and the professionals themselves.[4]

A basic drive of every profession, established or emergent, is *self-government* in deciding policies, criteria, and standards for employment and advancement, and in deciding individual personnel

---

[4]The word "delegation" is not precisely accurate in a good many fields, since many developed independently of any central personnel office, and there was no real *process* of delegation. But delegation is a reasonably accurate description of the product, whatever the nature of the evolution which preceded it.

matters. The underlying argument for such professional hegemony is that no one outside—no amateur—is equipped to judge or even to understand the true content of the profession or the ingredients of merit in its practice. This thesis is difficult to challenge, particularly in highly developed, specialized, and scientized fields with which an amateur—or a professional in personnel administration—can have only a passing acquaintance.

The means whereby the professionals assert their control over personnel policies and actions are many and diverse. Some are specified and required by law or regulation; others grow out of gentlemen's agreements within—or in spite of—civil service laws; some reflect a silent abdication by the civil service agencies or a failure to assume an effective role; and some are unintended (or mayhap intended) consequences of others. I shall discuss them under three headings: influence and control by the professional elites within governmental agencies; influence and control by "outside" professions and their organizations; and influence and control by institutions of professional education.

Professional Elites

The extreme examples of professional control within agencies are provided by the various commissioned corps in the federal government which have never been under a general civil service system. Here one finds the most consolidated mechanisms of internal control by the elite group and particularly by senior members—the *elite cadre*, as Janowitz termed it. They determine the standards and criteria for entrance; the policies and procedures of assignment; the appropriate work content of elite corps positions; the criteria for promotion. They also set up the machinery for personnel operations, usually including boards, all or a majority of whose members are drawn from the corps itself. They also superintend the policies and operations of personnel management for other employees, including other professionals, who are not in the elite, yielding as little as they must to civil service requirements, to other employee groups, to outside professional interests, and to political pressures.

Much of this personnel control is sanctioned by law. It is significant that personnel matters in the various corps carry such preeminent weight and importance. Historically in the Army the handling of personnel was long entrusted to the staff division known as G-1 (A-1 in the Air Force); today the officers in charge of personnel are first deputy chiefs of staff. In the State Department the Board of Foreign Service has, since its founding, been essentially a personnel board, as the Director General of the Foreign Service has been primarily concerned with matters of personnel. It may be noted too that in these cases the professional elites have assumed control over the administration of agency personnel who are not in the corps: reserve officers, enlisted personnel (or Foreign Service staff), and civil servants.

Among the agencies not dominated by a commissioned corps, professional control over personnel matters has been less conspicuous but still effective. In many cases it is carried out under the canopy of civil service laws and regulations. The professional elites normally have the most influential voice in determining personnel policies, standards, and criteria within broad prescriptions of civil service law. The recent trend toward decentralization, both at the federal level and in other large jurisdictions, has of course facilitated this development. Personnel selection for professionals is in many places left to boards, which are usually dominated by agency professionals. . . . [C]ompetitive written and performance examinations in most of the established professional fields have largely been abandoned in favor of evidences of qualification determined outside the agency and indeed outside the civil service system. What is left—normally an "unassembled" examination of the candidates' records and/or an oral examination—is conducted by boards composed principally of members of the agency's elite profession. The same situation pertains to other personnel actions: assignments, promotions, disciplinary actions. In most cases the central influence is that of the agency; and if it is controlled by a professional elite, the basic control lies with that elite. The civil service or personnel agency provides assistance in recruitment, a certain amount of professional personnel guidance, certain procedural requisites, and participation and perhaps inspection to ensure conformance with regulations. The substance of personnel policy and decision rests, however, in the professional elite.

Our studies conducted some years ago of employment practices of federal, state, and local jurisdictions in California in general confirmed the tendency toward professional elite control of policies, standards, and actions within the agencies in which there was a professional elite. There were, of course, variations in the degree of control and in the techniques whereby it was made effective. In general, these variations seemed responsive to two factors: first, the degree to which the professional group had established itself as truly elite within a given agency; and second, the degree to which demand exceeded supply for professionals in the field in question. The better established, more recognized professions had greater control, as did those in which supply was scarcest. In our California studies, we found this to be true at all levels of government in the employment of lawyers, natural scientists, engineers, doctors, social workers, and health professionals. In the federal government, we found it true also for foresters, architects, and some others. In the state of California, it applied to psychiatrists in mental hygiene; among local governments, it applied in varying degrees to recreation workers, city planners, librarians, and some others.

The Professionals and Their Organizations

Among the established general professions, the practice of licensing practitioners is an old one. Indeed, it is a common index of whether or not a profession is truly "established," and many of the aspiring newer fields are seeking it to give them official and legal sanction. The licensing of professionals, as of craftsmen, is normally accomplished by the legal delegation of state powers to a board, itself composed exclusively or predominantly of members of the profession. It normally requires the passing of an examination, drafted and graded by the board or other professional group. In all of this, the public personnel organization usually plays no part, and the examinations themselves are directed almost exclusively to the knowledge and skills required for private practice, not to governmental policy and managerial problems, nor to those of large organizations of any kind. In well-established fields, such as law, medicine, dentistry, architecture, some kinds of engineering, and school teaching, licensing is normally requisite to practice at the journeyman level. In others, it is essential to advancement to higher levels of responsibility and supervision: accounting and nursing, for example.

Governmental agencies, other than the licensing boards themselves, play little part in the licensing process and have little influence upon or even interest in the content and standards of the examinations. Very probably, the finding of James W. Fesler in his 1942 study *The Independence of State Regulatory Agencies* is still accurate: "Professional licensing boards are virtually the creatures of the professional societies. . . . "[5] Yet it is clear that these examinations significantly affect the education and the qualifications which make for a professional man or woman. The governments by and large accept those qualifications as gospel in their own employment. In some fields (e.g., law, medicine) a license is an absolute requisite to employment at any professional level. In others, while not required, it may be sufficient evidence for hiring—without further evidence of qualification—and a basis for preferential treatment for advancement as well. Professionals who have gained their credentials in most fields are likely to escape any further tests of competence and knowledge if they aspire to enter government employ. For them the governments have abandoned to the professions the testing of merit insofar as it can be determined by examinations of knowledge and skill. Further, the licensing tests are noncompetitive among the candidates. Qualifications are measured only in terms of passing a minimum standard—which may of course be a high one.

But perhaps most important is the effect of the licensing structure upon the content, the dimensions, and the boundaries of the individual professions. As Corinne Lathrop Gilb has observed: "Public administrators generally fail to acknowledge *the extent to which the structure and composition of regulatory boards affect the division of labor and authority in the work world.*"[6] And the "work world" of course includes the administration of government itself.

Professional Education

Over the long pull, the most profound impact upon the professional public services is that of the universities—their professional schools, their departments in the physical and social sciences which produce professionals, and their faculties in general. Higher education produces the bulk of future professionals. By their images, and by their impressions upon students, the schools have a great influence upon who opts for what fields and what kinds of young people—of what quality, what interests, what values—go where. It is clear too that they influence the choices by students among employers— whether government or other, and which jurisdictions and agencies of government. By their curricula, their faculties, their teaching, they

---

[5]Chicago, Public Administration Service, pp. 60–61.
[6]*Hidden Hierarchies: The Professions and Government* (New York, Harper & Row, 1966), p. 194. (Author's emphasis.)

define the content of each different specialism and the expectations and aspirations of the students in each. These students will of course include the principal operators in government tomorrow and the principal leaders the day after tomorrow.

In most professional fields, governments have accepted, without much question or knowledge, the academic definition of content and the academic criteria of qualification and merit. Most governments, like other employers, rely heavily upon credentials; possession of the sheepskin from an accredited institution is enough. Accreditation itself is normally based upon a review and approval of a given school's program by a committee of a larger organization composed of, or dominated by, professional educators in the same field. It reflects a consensus among academics as to the minimal curricular and faculty requirements necessary to produce qualified practitioners. In some fields accreditation and high academic standing (grade point average) are more important to governmental employers than professional licenses. In fields for which licensing has been provided in only a few states (or in none)—like social work, city planning, or librarianship—accreditation and grades become almost the sole criteria. Accreditation moreover is sometimes a requirement for licensing. Where government employers have any significant choice among candidates for jobs in the recognized professions, their reliance is placed upon 1. whether they come from accredited schools, 2. their grade point averages, and 3. the recommendations of professors. All three are of course academic determinants.

In the main, governments have yielded to the universities and professional educators the significant influences, the criteria, and the choices about public employment. Few of our larger governmental units give any competitive examinations on substance—that is, knowledge and skill—for candidates in professional fields. They leave it largely to the universities to determine what knowledges and skills are appropriate, and who among the graduating students are deserving of appointment. In a few fields, they also rely upon licensing examinations, themselves controlled by practitioners and educators outside of government. Among the agencies dominated by an elite professional corps, personnel decisions are largely dictated by the corps. . . .

. . . As knowledge has grown and as occupations have been increasingly professionalized, the public services have become more dependent upon the founts of knowledge, the universities. In their own organizations, governments have both reflected and influenced the occupational structure of the society. In so doing they have benefited tremendously through the advancement in the level of knowledge and skill in every field. They may also have suffered in the degree to which the central governments could control and direct operations in the general interest. For in the process, they have yielded a great deal of influence over *who* will conduct and direct individual programs, and how the content of programs will be defined as well.

For better or worse—or better *and* worse—much of our government is now in the hands of professionals (including scientists). The choice of these professionals, the determination of their skills, and the content of their work are now principally determined, not by general governmental agencies, but by their own professional elites, professional organizations, and the institutions and faculties of higher education. It is unlikely that the trend toward professionalism in or outside of government will soon be reversed. . . .

7

The Power of Bureaucratic Routines: The Cuban Missile Crisis

GRAHAM T. ALLISON

For some purposes, governmental behavior can be usefully summarized as action chosen by a unitary, rational decision-maker: centrally controlled, completely informed, and value maximizing. But this simplification must not be allowed to conceal the fact that a "government" consists of a conglomerate of semi-feudal, loosely allied organizations, each with a substantial life of its own. Government leaders do sit formally, and to some extent in fact, on top of this conglomerate. But governments perceive problems through organizational sensors. Governments define alternatives and estimate consequences as organizations process information. Governments act as these organizations enact routines. Government behavior can therefore be understood . . . less as deliberate choices of leaders and more as *outputs* of large organizations functioning according to standard patterns of behavior.

To be responsive to a broad spectrum of problems, governments consist of large organizations among which primary responsibility for particular areas is divided. Each organization attends to a special set of problems and acts in quasi-independence on these problems. But few important problems fall exclusively within the domain of a single organization. Thus government behavior relevant to any im-

From Graham T. Allison, "Conceptual Models and the Cuban Missile Crisis," reprinted by permission of the author and The American Political Science Association from *The American Political Science Review* 63 (September 1969): 689–718. This extract covers pp. 698–707; footnotes are renumbered.

An expanded version of this article appears in Graham T. Allison, *Essence of Decision: Explaining the Cuban Missile Crisis* (Boston: Little, Brown and Co., 1971).

portant problem reflects the independent output of several organizations, partially coordinated by government leaders. Government leaders can substantially disturb, but not substantially control, the behavior of these organizations.

To perform complex routines, the behavior of large numbers of individuals must be coordinated. Coordination requires standard operating procedures: rules according to which things are done. Assured capability for reliable performance of action that depends upon the behavior of hundreds of persons requires established "programs." Indeed, if the eleven members of a football team are to perform adequately on any particular down, each player must not "do what he thinks needs to be done" or "do what the quarterback tells him to do." Rather, each player must perform the maneuvers specified by a previously established play which the quarterback has simply called in this situation.

At any given time, a government consists of *existing* organizations, each with a *fixed* set of standard operating procedures and programs. The behavior of these organizations—and consequently of the government—relevant to an issue in any particular instance is, therefore, determined primarily by routines established in these organizations prior to that instance. But organizations do change. Learning occurs gradually, over time. Dramatic organizational change occurs in response to major crises. Both learning and change are influenced by existing organizational capabilities. . . .

Organizational Process Paradigm[1]

I. Basic Unit of Analysis: Policy as Organizational Output

The happenings of international politics are, in three critical senses, outputs of organizational processes. First, the actual occurrences are organizational outputs. For example, Chinese entry into the Korean War—that is, the fact that Chinese soldiers were firing at United Nations' soldiers south of the Yalu in 1950—is an organizational action: the action of men who are soldiers in platoons which are in companies, which in turn are in armies, responding as privates

---

[1]The formulation of this paradigm is indebted both to the orientation and insights of Herbert Simon and to the behavioral model of the firm stated by Richard Cyert and James March, *A Behavioral Theory of the Firm* (Englewood Cliffs, 1963). Here, however, one is forced to grapple with the less routine, less quantified functions of the less differentiated elements in government organizations.

to lieutenants who are responsible to captains and so on to the commander, moving into Korea, advancing against enemy troops, and firing according to fixed routines of the Chinese army. Government leaders' decisions trigger organizational routines. Government leaders can trim the edges of this output and exercise some choice in combining outputs. But the mass of behavior is determined by previously established procedures. Second, existing organizational routines for employing present physical capabilities constitute the effective options open to government leaders confronted with any problem. Only the existence of men, equipped and trained as armies and capable of being transported to North Korea, made entry into the Korean War a live option for the Chinese leaders. The fact that fixed programs (equipment, men, and routines which exist at the particular time) exhaust the range of buttons that leaders can push is not always perceived by these leaders. But in every case it is critical for an understanding of what is actually done. Third, organizational outputs structure the situation within the narrow constraints of which leaders must contribute their "decision" concerning an issue. Outputs raise the problem, provide the information, and make the initial moves that color the face of the issue that is turned to the leaders. As Theodore Sorensen has observed: "Presidents rarely, if ever, make decisions—particularly in foreign affairs—in the sense of writing their conclusions on a clean slate. . . . The basic decisions, which confine their choices, have all too often been previously made."[2] If one understands the structure of the situation and the face of the issue—which are determined by the organizational outputs—the formal choice of the leaders is frequently anti-climactic.

II. Organizing Concepts
A. Organizational Actors The actor [in international politics] is not a monolithic "nation" or "government" but rather a constellation of loosely allied organizations on top of which government leaders sit. This constellation acts only as component organizations perform routines.[3]

[2]Theodore Sorenson, "You Get to Walk to Work," *New York Times Magazine*, March 19, 1967.

[3]Organizations are not monolithic. The proper level of disaggregation depends upon the objectives of a piece of analysis. This paradigm is formulated with reference to the major organizations that constitute the United States government. Generalization to the major components of each department and agency should be relatively straightforward.

B. Factored Problems and Fractionated Power   Surveillance of the multiple facets of foreign affairs requires that problems be cut up and parcelled out to various organizations. To avoid paralysis, primary power must accompany primary responsibility. But if organizations are permitted to do anything, a large part of what they do will be determined within the organization. Thus each organization perceives problems, processes information, and performs a range of actions in quasi-independence (within broad guidelines of national policy). Factored problems and fractionated power are two edges of the same sword. Factoring permits more specialized attention to particular facets of problems than would be possible if government leaders tried to cope with these problems by themselves. But this additional attention must be paid for in the coin of discretion for *what* an organization attends to, and *how* organizational responses are programmed.

C. Parochial Priorities, Perceptions, and Issues   Primary responsibility for a narrow set of problems encourages organizational parochialism. These tendencies are enhanced by a number of additional factors: (1) selective information available to the organization, (2) recruitment of personnel into the organization, (3) tenure of individuals in the organization, (4) small group pressures within the organization, and (5) distribution of rewards by the organization. Clients (e.g., interest groups), government allies (e.g., congressional committees), and extra-national counterparts (e.g., the British Ministry of Defense for the Department of Defense, ISA, or the British Foreign Office for the Department of State, EUR) galvanize this parochialism. Thus organizations develop relatively stable propensities concerning operational priorities, perceptions, and issues.

D. Action as Organizational Output   The preeminent feature of organizational activity is its programmed character: the extent to which behavior in any particular case is an enactment of preestablished routines. In producing outputs, the activity of each organization is characterized by:

1. *Goals: Constraints Defining Acceptable Performance.* The operational goals of an organization are seldom revealed by formal mandates. Rather, each organization's operational goals emerge as a set of constraints defining acceptable performance. Central among these constraints is organizational health, defined usually

in terms of bodies assigned and dollars appropriated. The set of constraints emerges from a mix of expectations and demands of other organizations in the government, statutory authority, demands from citizens and special interest groups, and bargaining within the organization. These constraints represent a quasi-resolution of conflict—the constraints are relatively stable, so there is some resolution. But conflict among alternative goals is always latent; hence, it is a quasi-resolution. Typically, the constraints are formulated as imperatives to avoid roughly specified discomforts and disasters.[4]

2. *Sequential Attention to Goals.* The existence of conflict among operational constraints is resolved by the device of sequential attention. As a problem arises, the subunits of the organization most concerned with that problem deal with it in terms of the constraints they take to be most important. When the next problem arises, another cluster of subunits deals with it, focusing on a different set of constraints.

3. *Standard Operating Procedures.* Organizations perform their "higher" functions, such as attending to problem areas, monitoring information, and preparing relevant responses for likely contingencies, by doing "lower" tasks, for example, preparing budgets, producing reports, and developing hardware. Reliable performance of these tasks requires standard operating procedures (hereafter SOPs). Since procedures are "standard" they do not change quickly or easily. Without these standard procedures, it would not be possible to perform certain concerted tasks. But because of standard procedures, organizational behavior in particular instances often appears unduly formalized, sluggish, or inappropriate.

4. *Programs and Repertoires.* Organizations must be capable of performing actions in which the behavior of large numbers of individuals is carefully coordinated. Assured performance requires clusters of rehearsed SOPs for producing specific actions, e.g., fighting enemy units or answering an embassy's cable. Each cluster comprises a "program" (in the terms both of drama and of computers) which the organization has available for dealing with a situation. The list of programs relevant to a type of activity,

---

[4]The stability of these constraints is dependent on such factors as rules for promotion and reward, budgeting and accounting procedures, and mundane operating procedures.

e.g., fighting, constitutes an organizational repertoire. The number of programs in a repertoire is always quite limited. When properly triggered, organizations execute programs; programs cannot be substantially changed in a particular situation. The more complex the action and the greater the number of individuals involved, the more important are programs and repertoires as determinants of organizational behavior.

5. *Uncertainty Avoidance.* Organizations do not attempt to estimate the probability distribution of future occurrences. Rather, organizations avoid uncertainty. By arranging a *negotiated environment*, organizations regularize the reactions of other actors with whom they have to deal. The primary environment, relations with other organizations that comprise the government, is stabilized by such arrangements as agreed budgetary splits, accepted areas of responsibility, and established conventional practices. The secondary environment, relations with the international world, is stabilized between allies by the establishment of contracts (alliances) and "club relations" (United States State Department and United Kingdom Foreign Office or United States Treasury and United Kingdom Treasury). Between enemies, contracts and accepted conventional practices perform a similar function, for example, the rules of the "precarious status quo" which President Kennedy referred to in the missile crisis. Where the international environment cannot be negotiated, organizations deal with remaining uncertainties by establishing a set of *standard scenarios* that constitute the contingencies for which they prepare. For example, the standard scenario for Tactical Air Command of the United States air force involves combat with enemy aircraft. Planes are designed and pilots trained to meet this problem. That these preparations are less relevant to more probable contingencies, e.g., provision of close-in ground support in limited wars like Vietnam, has had little impact on the scenario.

6. *Problem-directed Search.* Where situations cannot be construed as standard, organizations engage in search. The style of search and the solution are largely determined by existing routines. Organizational search for alternative courses of action is problem-oriented: it focuses on the atypical discomfort that must be avoided. It is simple-minded: the neighborhood of the symptom is searched first; then, the neighborhood of the current alternative. Patterns of search reveal biases which in turn reflect such

factors as specialized training or experience and patterns of communication.

7. *Organizational Learning and Change.* The parameters of organizational behavior mostly persist. In response to nonstandard problems, organizations search and routines evolve, assimilating new situations. Thus learning and change follow in large part from existing procedures. But marked changes in organizations do sometimes occur. Conditions in which dramatic changes are more likely include: (1) Periods of budgetary feast. Typically, organizations devour budgetary feasts by purchasing additional items on the existing shopping list. Nevertheless, if committed to change, leaders who control the budget can use extra funds to effect changes. (2) Periods of prolonged budgetary famine. Though a single year's famine typically results in few changes in organizational structure but a loss of effectiveness in performing some programs, prolonged famine forces major retrenchment. (3) Dramatic performance failures. Dramatic change occurs (mostly) in response to major disasters. Confronted with an undeniable failure of procedures and repertoires, authorities outside the organization demand change, existing personnel are less resistant to change, and critical members of the organization are replaced by individuals committed to change.

E. Central Coordination and Control   Action requires decentralization of responsiblity and power. But problems lap over the jurisdictions of several organizations. Thus the necessity for decentralization runs headlong into the requirement for coordination. (Advocates of one horn or the other of this dilemma—responsive action entails decentralized power vs. coordinated action requires central control—account for a considerable part of the persistent demand for government reorganization.) Both the necessity for coordination and the centrality of foreign policy to national welfare guarantee the involvement of government leaders in the procedures of the organizations among which problems are divided and power shared. Each organization's propensities and routines can be disturbed by government leaders' intervention. Central direction and persistent control of organizational activity, however, is not possible. The relation among organizations, and between organizations and the government leaders, depends critically on a number of structural variables including: (1) the nature of the job, (2) the measures and information available to government leaders, (3) the system of rewards and punishments for organizational members, and (4) the procedures by which human and material resources get committed. For example, to the extent that rewards and punishments for the members of an organization are distributed by higher authorities, these authorities can exercise some control by specifying criteria in terms of which organizational output is to be evaluated. These criteria become constraints within which organizational activity proceeds. But constraint is a crude instrument of control.

Intervention by government leaders does sometimes change the activity of an organization in an intended direction. But instances are fewer than might be expected. As Franklin Roosevelt, the master manipulator of government organizations, remarked:

> The Treasury is so large and far-flung and ingrained in its practices that I find it is almost impossible to get the action and results I want. . . . But the Treasury is not to be compared with the State Department. You should go through the experience of trying to get any changes in the thinking, policy, and action of the career diplomats and then you'd know what a real problem was. But the Treasury and the State Department put together are nothing compared with the Na-a-vy. . . . To change anything in the Na-a-vy is like punching a feather bed. You punch it with your right and you punch it with your left until you are finally exhausted, and then you find the damn bed just as it was before you started punching.[5]

John Kennedy's experience seems to have been similar: "The State Department," he asserted, "is a bowl full of jelly."[6] And lest the McNamara revolution in the Defense Department seem too striking a counter-example, the navy's recent rejection of McNamara's major intervention in naval weapons procurement, the F-111B, should be studied as an antidote.

F. Decisions of Government Leaders   Organizational persistence does not exclude shifts in governmental behavior. For government leaders sit atop the conglomerate of organizations. Many important issues of governmental action require that these leaders decide what organizations will play out which programs where. Thus stability in the parochialisms and SOPs of individual organizations is consistent with

[5]Marriner Eccles, *Beckoning Frontiers* (New York, 1951), p. 336.
[6]Arthur M. Schlesinger, Jr., *A Thousand Days* (Boston, 1965), p. 406.

some important shifts in the behavior of governments. The range of these shifts is defined by existing organizational programs.

III. Dominant Inference Pattern

If a nation performs an action of this type today, its organizational components must yesterday have been performing (or have had established routines for performing) an action only marginally different from this action. At any specific point in time, a government consists of an established conglomerate of organizations, each with existing goals, programs, and repertoires. The characteristics of a government's action in any instance follows from those established routines, and from the choice of government leaders—on the basis of information and estimates provided by existing routines—among existing programs. The best explanation of an organization's behavior at t is $t - 1$; the prediction of $t + 1$ is t. . . .

IV. General Propositions

A number of general propositions have been stated above. . . . This section formulates several more precisely.

A. Organizational Action   Activity according to SOPs and programs does not constitute farsighted, flexible adaptation to "the issue" (as it is conceived by the analyst). Detail and nuance of actions by organizations are determined predominantly by organizational routines, not government leaders' directions.

1. SOPs constitute routines for dealing with *standard* situations. Routines allow large numbers of ordinary individuals to deal with numerous instances, day after day, without considerable thought, by responding to basic stimuli. But this regularized capability for adequate performance is purchased at the price of standardization. If the SOPs are appropriate, average performance, i.e., performance averaged over the range of cases, is better than it would be if each instance were approached individually (given fixed talent, timing, and resource constraints). But specific instances, particularly critical instances that typically do not have "standard" characteristics, are often handled sluggishly or inappropriately.

2. A program, i.e., a complex action chosen from a short list of programs in a repertoire, is rarely tailored to the specific situation in which it is executed. Rather, the program is (at best) the most appropriate of the programs in a previously developed repertoire.

3. Since repertoires are developed by paraochial organizations for standard scenarios defined by that organization, programs available for dealing with a particular situation are often ill-suited.

B. Limited Flexibility and Incremental Change   Major lines of organizational action are straight, i.e., behavior at one time is marginally different from that behavior at $t - 1$. Simple-minded predictions work best: Behavior at $t + 1$ will be marginally different from behavior at the present time.

1. Organizational budgets change incrementally—both with respect to totals and with respect to intraorganizational splits. Though organizations could divide the money available each year by carving up the pie anew (in the light of changes in objectives or environment), in practice, organizations take last year's budget as a base and adjust incrementally. Predictions that require large budgetary shifts in a single year between organizations or between units within an organization should be hedged.
2. Once undertaken, an organizational investment is not dropped at the point where "objective" costs outweigh benefits. Organizational stakes in adopted projects carry them quite beyond the loss point.

C. Administrative Feasibility   Adequate explanation, analysis, and prediction must include administrative feasibility as a major dimension. A considerable gap separates what leaders choose (or might rationally have chosen) and what organizations implement.

1. Organizations are blunt instruments. Projects that require several organizations to act with high degrees of precision and coordination are not likely to succeed.
2. Projects that demand that existing organizational units depart from their accustomed functions and perform previously unprogrammed tasks are rarely accomplished in their designed form.
3. Government leaders can expect that each organization will do its "part" in terms of what the organization knows how to do.
4. Government leaders can expect incomplete and distorted information from each organization concerning its part of the problem.
5. Where an assigned piece of a problem is contrary to the existing

goals of an organization, resistance to implementation of that piece will be encountered.

V. Specific Propositions

1. *Deterrence.* The probability of nuclear attack is less sensitive to balance and imbalance, or stability and instability . . . than it is to a number of organizational factors. Except for the special case in which the Soviet Union acquires a credible capability to destroy the United States with a disarming blow, United States superiority or inferiority affects the probability of a nuclear attack less than do a number of organizational factors.

First, if a nuclear attack occurs, it will result from organizational activity: the firing of rockets by members of a missile group. The enemy's *control system*, i.e., physical mechanisms and standard procedures which determine who can launch rockets when, is critical. Second, the enemy's programs for bringing his strategic forces to *alert status* determine probabilities of accidental firing and momentum. At the outbreak of World War I, if the Russian Czar had understood the organizational processes which his order of full mobilization triggered, he would have realized that he had chosen war. Third, organizational repertoires fix the range of effective choice open to enemy leaders. The menu available to Czar Nicholas in 1914 had two entrees: full mobilization and no mobilization. Partial mobilization was not an organizational option. Fourth, since organizational routines set the chessboard, the training and deployment of troops and nuclear weapons is crucial. Given that the outbreak of hostilities in Berlin is more probable than most scenarios for nuclear war, facts about deployment, training, and tactical nuclear equipment of Soviet troops stationed in East Germany—which will influence the face of the issue seen by Soviet leaders at the outbreak of hostilities and the manner in which choice is implemented—are as critical as the question of "balance."

2. *Soviet Force Posture.* Soviet force posture, i.e., the fact that certain weapons rather than others are procured and deployed, is determined by organizational factors such as the goals and procedures of existing military services and the goals and processes of research and design laboratories, within budgetary contraints

that emerge from the government leader's choices. The frailty of the Soviet air force within the Soviet military establishment seems to have been a crucial element in the Soviet failure to acquire a large bomber force in the 1950s (thereby faulting American intelligence predictions of a "bomber gap"). The fact that missiles were controlled until 1960 in the Soviet Union by the Soviet ground forces, whose goals and procedures reflected no interest in an intercontinential mission, was not irrelevant to the slow Soviet build-up of ICBMs (thereby faulting United States intelligence predictions of a "missile gap"). These organizational factors (Soviet ground forces' control of missiles and that service's fixation with European scenarios) make the Soviet deployment of so many MRBMs that European targets could be destroyed three times over, more understandable. Recent weapon developments, e.g., the testing of a Fractional Orbital Bombardment System (FOBS) and multiple warheads for the SS-9, very likely reflect the activity and interests of a cluster of Soviet research and development organizations, rather than a decision by Soviet leaders to acquire a first strike weapon system. Careful attention to the organizational components of the Soviet military establishment (strategic rocket forces, navy, air force, ground forces, and national air defense), the missions and weapons systems to which each component is wedded (an independent weapon system assists survival as an independent service), and existing budgetary splits (which probably are relatively stable in the Soviet Union as they tend to be everywhere) offer potential improvements in medium and longer term predictions.

The United States Blockade of Cuba . . .

Organizational Intelligence

At 7:00 P.M. on October 22, 1962, President Kennedy disclosed the American discovery of the presence of Soviet strategic missiles in Cuba, declared a "strict quarantine on all offensive military equipment under shipment to Cuba," and demanded that "Chairman Khrushchev halt and eliminate this clandestine, reckless, and provocative threat to world peace."[7] This decision was reached at the pinnacle of the United States government after a critical week of

[7]U.S. Department of State, *Bulletin* 47:715–720.

deliberation. What initiated that precious week were photographs of Soviet missile sites in Cuba taken on October 14. These pictures might not have been taken until a week later. In that case, the President speculated, "I don't think probably we would have chosen as prudently as we finally did."[8] United States leaders might have received this information three weeks earlier—if a U-2 had flown over San Cristobal in the last week of September.[9] What determined the context in which American leaders came to choose the blockade was the discovery of missiles on October 14.

There has been considerable debate over alleged American "intelligence failures" in the Cuban missile crisis.[10] But what both critics and defenders have neglected is the fact that the discovery took place on October 14, rather than three weeks earlier or a week later, as a consequence of the established routines and procedures of the organizations which constitute the United States intelligence community. These organizations were neither more nor less successful than they had been the previous month or were to be in the months to follow.[11]

The notorious "September estimate," approved by the United States Intelligence Board (USIB) on September 19, concluded that the Soviet Union would not introduce offensive missiles into Cuba.[12] No U-2 flight was directed over the western end of Cuba (after September 5) before October 4.[13] No U-2 flew over the western end of Cuba until the flight that discovered the Soviet missiles on October 14.[14] Can these "failures" be accounted for in organizational terms?

On September 19 when USIB met to consider the question of Cuba, the "system" contained the following information: (1) shipping intelligence had noted the arrival in Cuba of two large-hatch Soviet lumber ships, which were riding high in the water; (2) refugee

[8]Schlesinger, *op. cit.*, p. 803.

[9]Theodore Sorensen, *Kennedy* (New York, 1965), p. 675.

[10]See U.S. Congress, Senate, Committee on Armed Services, Preparedness Investigation Subcommittee, *Interim Report on Cuban Military Build-up*, 88th Congress, 1st Session, 1963, p. 2; Hanson Baldwin, "Growing Risks of Bureaucratic Intelligence," *The Reporter* (August 15, 1963), pp. 48–50; Roberta Wohlstetter, "Cuba and Pearl Harbor," *Foreign Affairs* [43] (July 1965): 706.

[11]U.S. Congress, House of Representatives, Committee on Appropriations, Subcommittee on Department of Defense Appropriations, *Hearings*, 88th Congress, 1st Session, 1963, p. 25ff.

[12]R. Hilsman, *To Move a Nation* (New York, 1967), pp. 172–173.

[13]Department of Defense Appropriations, *Hearings*, p. 67.

[14]*Ibid.*, pp. 66–67.

reports of countless sightings of missiles, but also a report that Castro's private pilot, after a night of drinking in Havana, had boasted: "We will fight to the death and perhaps we can win because we have everything, including atomic weapons"; (3) a sighting by a CIA agent of the rear profile of a strategic missile; (4) U-2 photos produced by flights of August 29, September 5 and 17 showing the construction of a number of SAM sites and other defensive missiles.[15] Not all of this information was on the desk of the estimators, however. Shipping intelligence experts noted the fact that large-hatch ships were riding high in the water and spelled out the inference: the ships must be carrying "space consuming" cargo.[16] These facts were carefully included in the catalogue of intelligence concerning shipping. For experts sensitive to the Soviets' shortage of ships, however, these facts carried no special signal. The refugee report of Castro's private pilot's remark had been received at Opa Locka, Florida, along with vast reams of inaccurate reports generated by the refugee community. This report and a thousand others had to be checked and compared before being sent to Washington. The two weeks required for initial processing could have been shortened by a large increase in resources, but the yield of this source was already quite marginal. The CIA agent's sighting of the rear profile of a strategic missile had occurred on September 12; transmission time from agent sighting to arrival in Washington typically took 9 to 12 days. Shortening this transmission time would impose severe cost in terms of danger to subagents, agents, and communication networks.

On the information available, the intelligence chiefs who predicted that the Soviet Union would not introduce offensive missiles into Cuba made a reasonable and defensible judgment.[17] Moreover, in the light of the fact that these organizations were gathering intelligence not only about Cuba but about potential occurrences in all parts of the world, the informational base available to the estimators involved nothing out of the ordinary. Nor, from an organi-

[15]For (1) Hilsman, *op cit.*, p. 186; (2) [Elie] Abel [*The Missile Crisis* (Philadelphia, 1966)], p. 24; (3) Department of Defense Appropriations, *Hearings*, p. 64; Abel, *op. cit.*, p. 24; (4) Department of Defense Appropriations, *Hearings*, pp. 1–30.
[16]The facts here are not entirely clear. This assertion is based on information from (1) "Department of Defense Briefing by the Honorable R. S. McNamara, Secretary of Defense, State Department Auditorium, 5:00 P.M., February 6, 1963," a verbatim transcript of a presentation actually made by General Carroll's assistant, John Hughes; and (2) Hilsman's statement, *op. cit.*, p. 186. But see R. Wohlstetter's interpretation, "Cuba and Pearl Harbor," *op. cit.*, p. 700.
[17]See Hilsman, *op. cit.*, pp. 172–174.

zational perspective, is there anything startling about the gradual accumulation of evidence that led to the formulation of the hypothesis that the Soviets were installing missiles in Cuba and the decision on October 4 to direct a special flight over western Cuba.

The ten-day delay between that decision and the flight is another organizational story.[18] At the October 4 meeting, the Defense Department took the opportunity to raise an issue important to its concerns. Given the increased danger that a U-2 would be downed, it would be better if the pilot were an officer in uniform rather than a CIA agent. Thus the air force should assume responsibility for U-2 flights over Cuba. To the contrary, the CIA argued that this was an intelligence operation and thus within the CIA's jurisdiction. Moreover, CIA U-2s had been modified in certain ways which gave them advantages over air force U-2s in averting Soviet SAMs. Five days passed while the State Department pressed for less risky alternatives such as drones and the air force (in Department of Defense guise) and CIA engaged in territorial disputes. On October 9 a flight plan over San Cristobal was approved by COMOR [Committee on Overhead Reconnaissance], but to the CIA's dismay, air force pilots rather than CIA agents would take charge of the mission. At this point details become sketchy, but several members of the intelligence community have speculated that an air force pilot in an air force U-2 attempted a high altitude overflight on October 9 that "flamed out," i.e., lost power, and thus had to descend in order to restart its engine. A second round between air force and CIA followed, as a result of which air force pilots were trained to fly CIA U-2s. A successful overflight took place on October 14.

This ten-day delay constitutes some form of "failure." In the face of well-founded suspicions concerning offensive Soviet missiles in Cuba that posed a critical threat to the United States' most vital interest, squabbling between organizations whose job it is to produce this information seems entirely inappropriate. But for each of these organizations, the question involved the issue: "*Whose* job was it to be?" Moreover, the issue was not simply, which organization would control U-2 flights over Cuba, but rather the broader issue of ownership of U-2 intelligence activities—a very long standing territorial dispute. Thus though this delay was in one sense a "failure," it was

---

[18]Abel, *op. cit.*, pp. 26 ff.; Weintal and Bartlett, *Facing the Brink* (New York, 1967), pp. 62 ff.; *Cuban Military Build-up*; J. Daniel and J. Hubbell, *Strike in the West* (New York, 1963), pp. 15 ff.

also a nearly inevitable consequence of two facts: many jobs do not fall neatly into precisely defined organizational jurisdictions; and vigorous organizations are imperialistic.

Organizational Options

Deliberations of leaders in ExCom meetings produced broad outlines of alternatives. Details of these alternatives and blueprints for their implementation had to be specified by the organizations that would perform these tasks. These organizational outputs answered the question: What, specifically, *could* be done?

Discussion in the ExCom quickly narrowed the live options to two: an air strike and a blockade. The choice of the blockade instead of the air strike turned on two points: (1) the argument from morality and tradition that the United States could not perpetrate a "Pearl Harbor in reverse"; (2) the belief that a "surgical" air strike was impossible.[19] Whether the United States *might* strike first was a question not of capability but of morality. Whether the United States *could* perform the surgical strike was a factual question concerning capabilities. The majority of the members of the ExCom, including the President, initially preferred the air strike.[20] What effectively foreclosed this option, however, was the fact that the air strike they wanted could not be chosen with high confidence of success.[21] After having tentatively chosen the course of prudence—given that the surgical air strike was not an option—Kennedy reconsidered. On Sunday morning, October 21, he called the air force experts to a special meeting in his living quarters where he probed once more for the option of a *"surgical"* air strike.[22] General Walter C. Sweeny, Commander of Tactical Air Forces, asserted again that the air force could guarantee no higher than 90 percent effectiveness in a surgical air strike.[23] That "fact" was false.

The air strike alternative provides a classic case of military estimates. One of the alternatives outlined by the ExCom was named "air strike." Specification of the details of this alternative was delegated to the air force. Starting from an existing plan for massive United States military action against Cuba (prepared for contingen-

[19]Schlesinger, *op. cit.*, p. 804.
[20]Sorensen, *Kennedy*, p. 684.
[21]*Ibid.*, pp. 684 ff.
[22]*Ibid.*, pp. 694–697.
[23]*Ibid.*, p. 697; Abel, *op. cit.*, pp. 100–101.

cies like a response to a Soviet Berlin grab), air force estimators produced an attack to guarantee success.[24] This plan called for extensive bombardment of all missile sites, storage depots, airports, and, in deference to the navy, the artillery batteries opposite the naval base at Guantanamo.[25] Members of the ExCom repeatedly expressed bewilderment at military estimates of the number of sorties required, likely casualties, and collateral damage. But the "surgical" air strike that the political leaders had in mind was never carefully examined during the first week of the crisis. Rather, this option was simply excluded on the grounds that since the Soviet MRBMs in Cuba were classified "mobile" in United States manuals, extensive bombing was required. During the second week of the crisis, careful examination revealed that the missiles were mobile, in the sense that small houses are mobile: that is, they could be moved and reassembled in six days. After the missiles were reclassified "movable" and detailed plans for surgical air strikes specified, this action was added to the list of live options for the end of the second week.

Organizational Implementation

ExCom members separated several types of blockade: offensive weapons only, all armaments, and all strategic goods including POL (petroleum, oil, and lubricants). But the *"details"* of the operation were left to the navy. Before the President announced the blockade on Monday evening, the first stage of the navy's blueprint was in motion, and a problem loomed on the horizon.[26] The navy had a detailed plan for the blockade. The President had several less precise but equally determined notions concerning what should be done, when, and how. For the navy the issue was one of effective implementation of the navy's blockade—without the meddling and interference of political leaders. For the President, the problem was to pace and manage events in such a way that the Soviet leaders would have time to see, think, and blink.

A careful reading of available sources uncovers an instructive incident. On Tuesday the British Ambassador, Ormsby-Gore, after having attended a briefing on the details of the blockade, suggested to the President that the plan for intercepting Soviet ships far out of

[24]Sorensen, *Kennedy*, p. 669.
[25]Hilsman, *op. cit.*, p. 204.
[26]See Abel, *op. cit.*, pp. 97 ff.

reach of Cuban jets did not facilitate Khrushchev's hard decision.[27] Why not make the interception much closer to Cuba and thus give the Russian leader more time? According to the public account and the recollection of a number of individuals involved, Kennedy "agreed immediately, called McNamara, and over emotional navy protest, issued the appropriate instructions."[28] As Sorensen records, "in a sharp clash with the navy, he made certain his will prevailed."[29] The navy's plan for the blockade was thus changed by drawing the blockade much closer to Cuba.

A serious organizational orientation makes one suspicious of this account. More careful examination of the available evidence confirms these suspicions, though alternative accounts must be somewhat speculative. According to the public chronology, a quarantine drawn close to Cuba became effective on Wednesday morning, the first Soviet ship was contacted on Thursday morning, and the first boarding of a ship occurred on Friday. According to the statement by the Department of Defense, boarding of the *Marcula* by a party from the *John R. Pierce* "took place at 7:50 A.M., E.D.T., 180 miles northeast of Nassau."[30] The *Marcula* had been trailed since about 10:30 the previous evening.[31] Simple calculations suggest that the *Pierce* must have been stationed along the navy's original arc which extended 500 miles out to sea from Cape Magsi, Cuba's easternmost tip.[32] The blockade line was *not* moved as the President ordered and the accounts report. . . .

This attempt to leash the navy's blockade had a price. On Wednesday morning, October 24, what the President had been awaiting occurred. The 18 dry cargo ships heading towards the quarantine stopped dead in the water. This was the occasion of Dean Rusk's remark, "We are eyeball to eyeball and I think the other fellow just blinked."[33] But the navy had another interpretation. The ships had simply stopped to pick up Soviet submarine escorts. The President became quite concerned lest the navy—already riled because of presidential meddling in its affairs—blunder into an incident. Sensing the President's fears, McNamara became suspicious of

[27]Schlesinger, *op. cit.*, p. 818.
[28]*Ibid.*
[29]Sorensen, *Kennedy*, p. 710.
[30]*The New York Times*, October 27, 1962.
[31]Abel, *op. cit.*, p. 171.
[32]For the location of the original arc see Abel, *op. cit.*, p. 141.
[33]Abel, *op. cit.*, p. 153.

the navy's procedures and routines for making the first interception. Calling on the Chief of Naval Operations in the navy's inner sanctum, the Navy Flag Plot, McNamara put his questions harshly.[34] Who would make the first interception? Were Russian-speaking officers on board? How would submarines be dealt with? At one point McNamara asked Anderson what he would do if a Soviet ship's captain refused to answer questions about his cargo. Picking up the Manual of Navy Regulations the navy man waved it in McNamara's face and shouted, "It's all in there." To which McNamara replied, "I don't give a damn what John Paul Jones would have done; I want to know what you are going to do, now."[35] The encounter ended on Anderson's remark: "Now, Mr. Secretary, if you and your Deputy will go back to your office the navy will run the blockade."[36]

[34]See *ibid.*, pp. 154 ff.
[35]*Ibid.*, p. 156.
[36]*Ibid.*

8

OMB and the Presidency— The Problem of "Neutral Competence"

HUGH HECLO

In 1970 the Bureau of the Budget (BOB) officially died and the Office of Management and Budget (OMB) was born. Subsequent years have not been kind to the organization. Renaming the agency was supposed to signal a new era in which the traditional job of budget-making would be augmented by a new emphasis on government management, but the management side of OMB has been in disarray throughout most of the organization's short life. An agency which traditionally valued its heritage of anonymity and quiet diplomacy inside government has found itself slugging it out in nasty public fights on issues such as impoundment. From now on, every OMB director and deputy director will have to be confirmed by the Senate—a blow to the special Presidential status which the old Bureau of the Budget enjoyed. . . . All in all, it has been a tough childhood for the young OMB.

The Idea of Neutral Competence

. . . In the Anglo-American democracies, neutral competence is a relatively recent growth and corresponds roughly with the appearance of a higher civil service about a century ago. It envisions a continuous, uncommitted facility at the disposal of, and for the support of, political leadership. It is not a prescription for sainthood. Neu-

Reprinted with permission of the author from: *The Public Interest*, No. 38 (Winter 1975), pp. 80–98. © 1975 by National Affairs, Inc.

trality does not mean the possession of a direct-dial line to some over-arching, non-partisan sense of the public interest. Rather it consists of giving one's cooperation and best independent judgment of the issues to partisan bosses—and of being sufficiently uncommitted to be able to do so for a succession of partisan leaders. The independence entailed in neutral competence does not exist for its own sake; it exists precisely in order to serve the aims of elected partisan leadership. Nor is neutral competence merely the capacity to deliver good staff work to a political superior, for a major part of this competence lies in its ability to gain compliance from lower-level officials. The competence in question entails not just following orders but having the practical knowledge of government and the broker's skills of the governmental marketplace that makes one's advice worthy of attention. Thus neutral competence is a strange amalgam of loyalty that argues back, partisanship that shifts with the changing partisans, independence that depends on others. Its motto is "Speak out, shut up, carry up, carry out."

As a performance standard, neutral competence is valuable in a number of ways. For one thing, it smooths communication and thus improves the capacity of elected leadership to get what it wants out of the government machine. Officials with neutral competence can help bring along the more committed specialists elsewhere who are easily antagonized by outsiders ignorant of their ways. When fights become necessary, aid from those with neutral competence can help political leaders chastise others in a way that encourages them to go along rather than fight further. Equally important, neutral competence accumulates informal sources of information within the bureaucracy, sources which can be the key to governing the sprawling executive machinery and which are otherwise unavailable to transient political appointees. Neutral competence, therefore, helps to avoid gratuitous conflicts that would use up resources and relations needed for more important issues, prejudice cooperation the next time around, and risk the ultimate disaster—a complete close-down of information from the offended party.

Another virtue of neutral competence is that it has a vested interest in continuity. Agencies and officials with this attribute have a highly developed institutional memory and a special concern that initiatives be capable of being sustained for the period ahead. They temper boldness with the recognition that they will have to live with the consequences of misplaced boldness. They worry about administrative feasibility because they do not want to have to deal later with problems of administrative breakdown.

Finally, neutral competence contributes a quality of impartiality to be set against other, more sectional appeals in government. Its viewpoint is no more pure or unbiased than anyone else's, but the axes it has to grind are broader than most. Its analysis is less concerned with the short-term political ramifications of who believes what how strongly, and more concerned with the substance of the policy issues themselves. Moreover, because it has an interest in continuity, it is likely to be more concerned with the brokerage process in general than with any particular issue or case. It cares about good form and the use of discretionary authority in a more even-handed way than might be preferred by individual contending parties. Thus its advice and analysis provide a useful counterweight to those more interested in a given subject matter or immediate advantage and less interested in brokerage, continuity, and staying around to pick up the pieces.

If all of this sounds too good to be true, it is. Even when achieved, each blessing of neutral competence imposes its own curse. Communication and bringing people along can promote delays, timidity, and debilitating compromise. Concern with continuity not only can have all these vices but can frustrate any mandate for fundamental change. Officials raised by the norm of impartiality and speaking their mind can generate more trouble, more unanswerable questions, more reasons for not doing something. No one would want a government composed only of neutral competents. Yet their services are invaluable in the play of power and advice. They survive by keeping the government mechanism well-oiled and in working order. . . .

From BOB to OMB

Neutral competence has always been a somewhat fragile growth in American government, and the old (post-1939) Bureau of the Budget was one of the few places where it was nourished and took root. Talk with veterans of that institution and they harken back to a golden age when "the old Bureau really was something special." The Bureau was a place where the "generalist ethic was admired and defended," a place where "you were both a representative for the President's particular view and the top objective resource for the continuous institution of the Presidency."

Of course, the pristine golden age never existed except in retrospect. Not all directors consulted as virtual equals with young examiners, and the Eisenhower years did not inspire outstanding feats of innovative policy analysis. An unpublished poll of staff attitudes in 1959 confirmed complaints about the immobility of personnel and inadequate promotion opportunities. But the nostalgic memories do contain an important core of truth. At the end of the Eisenhower years, the surveys did find that the vast majority of BOB staff felt they were kept well informed by superiors, that they had adequate opportunity to defend their recommendations before decisions were made, that they would recommend the Bureau to friends as a place to work, that they expected to remain with the organization indefinitely, and that they were "proud" when telling people they worked for the Bureau.

Today's Office of Management and Budget is by no means falling apart, nor is it a resting place for political hacks. The changes that have occurred are more subtle shifts in the nature of the organization, its premises, and its climate of activity. Taken together, however, these changing norms and relationships call into question the possibility of preserving the institution as a source of impartial continuity for the Presidency. There is a real and growing danger that as demands on government performance are growing, and as the need for continuity, executive branch coordination, and independent analysis is increasing, the standards of neutral competence are being eroded.

Numbers tell a small part of the story of these changes at the level of the career staff. In the last 20 years, the number of professional staff at BOB/OMB has grown by about one half, to 430; but the top layer of this civil service staff (supergrades GS 16–18) has grown over five times, to 75 persons. While this growth rate is roughly in line with the changes in the executive branch as a whole, it has made coordination and communication more difficult in an agency which has always prided itself on letting each of its many hands know what the others are doing.

At the same time, the turnover of this permanent staff is up. Compared to a rate in the 'teens or lower in the 1960's, over one quarter of the professional full-time staff (GS 9 and above) separated from the agency for one reason or another during Fiscal Year 1973.

Those who remained were relatively inexperienced in government compared with their counterparts of former years. In 1960, of the heads of major offices (budget review, legislative reference, and management) and examining divisions, nearly three quarters had six or more years' experience in BOB, and nearly half had been in their current posts for six or more years. In 1974, however, of the same group, only a quarter had six or more year's experience in BOB/OMB (while nearly two thirds had one years' experience or less), and only 13 per cent had been in their current posts for six or more years. A similar trend took place among key subordinates (i.e., staff down to the budget examiner level), so that by 1974 almost two thirds had been in their current jobs for one year or less. Experience elsewhere in the executive branch among top OMB staff likewise declined dramatically. . . .

The Rise of the PADs

One reason for the decreasing continuity among major office heads has been the establishment in OMB of a new category of politically appointed staff. In 1960 the Bureau of the Budget had, basically, five political officers—director, deputy director (himself a former BOB civil servant), and three assistant directors. These assistant directors served largely as staff assistants to the director, assembling *ad hoc* teams of civil servants for whatever particular projects came their way. The 1970 OMB reorganization has added four program associate directors as well as a new assistant director to head the management division. PADs, as the program associate directors have become known, are political appointees. Unlike the old assistant directors working on *ad hoc* assignments, PADs head the examining divisions, exercise continuous operating responsibility for given areas, and have permanent staffs directly under them. The change is important because the examining divisions in BOB and OMB have always been a key locus of enduring power at the government center; they control a process—budget-making—that is of vital interest to almost all other agencies, and they thereby possess sanctions and access to information which few other actors can match. Whereas career division chiefs headed these examining groups in BOB, now it is a layer of political line officers who are in charge, with the civil service division chiefs serving as their deputies.

In essence, a new layer of political line control has been introduced, and to it has gravitated not only leadership of the powerful examining divisions, but other responsibilities as well. Legislative proposals by the departments, for instance, have to be cleared through BOB/OMB, and throughout the postwar period this has been handled through the Legislative Reference Section, a unit co-equal with the examining divisions and headed by a succession of powerful civil servants. Now this section is much less important, and the academic literature on "central legislative clearance" is seriously out of date. No longer does the Office of Legislative Reference deal directly with the White House staff or the departments; now it usually deals through the PADs. Having less information to trade, Legislative Reference gets called to fewer meetings and has more trouble getting in on things. In effect, the institutional role and government-wide perspective in legislative clearance has been ceded to the PADs and their particular policy bailiwicks. . . .

OMB and the Presidency

Just as important as these changes within the organization itself have been the changes in the agency's relationship with its chief client, the President. A number of postwar BOB directors saw more of the President than their recent counterparts can claim, but these earlier directors typically had access in their capacity as heads of a Presidential staff agency. By contrast, the last three Nixon directors— George Shultz, Caspar Weinberger, and Roy Ash—showed a stronger tendency to position themselves as personal advisors to the President, with a new office in the West Wing of the White House to symbolize the fact. The result was to identify OMB more as a member of the President's own political family and less as a broker supplying an independent analytic service to every President. A milestone of sorts was reached in September 1974 when the director of the supposedly economy-minded OMB testified to Congress in favor of an $850,000 transition expense account for the departed President. . . .

It would be unfair and wrongheaded to imagine that these changes have constituted anything like a full-scale raid by political partisans on OMB. For one thing, the PADs appointed to date have not had any special interest or background in party politics. For another, the interposition of this new layer of political appointees was a response to what some in the White House and BOB itself perceived as increasingly clear institutional deficiencies and coordination needs.

As early as 1959, a self-evaluation by senior civil servants decided by only a narrow vote against recommending the use of political appointees in line guidance over the various offices and divisions. By 1967 more painful experience had accumulated: OMB staff was heavily involved in Presidential task forces to create major new policies; the new Planning, Programming, Budgeting System was causing headaches for the director and everyone else; Great Society programs were proliferating and creating who-knew-what demands on administrative machinery and future economic resources. To a 1967 BOB study group composed of the institution's political and career leadership, it was clear that things needed to be tightened up.

. . . Quite apart from any dissatisfaction that BOB staffers themselves felt with the old situation, there were good policy reasons for increasing political control over the agency and agency identification with the President. Increasingly interventionist policies—with civil servants dealing in questions of birth control, consumerism, medical care, environment, energy, transportation, civil rights, and so on—provide a legitimate justification for a much greater political interest in civil service decisions. Moreover, the Nixon Administration, intent on reversing this interventionist trend but frustrated by an opposition Congress, began emphasizing administrative actions that could be taken independently by the executive branch. In the eyes of the White House, administration policy faced not only an opposition Congress but also an opposition executive, a collection of agencies and departments with a vested interest in the ways of the past. Dependence on the normal run of departmental political appointees was unreliable, given their tendency to "go native." Attempts were made at direct intervention by the White House staff but they proved cumbersome, unsustained, and vulnerable to outmaneuvering due to a lack of coordination among the staff itself.

This distrust of many operating agencies was paralleled by the Nixon Administration's growing awareness that it could rely on OMB as its chosen agent in the executive branch. Since responsiveness to the President is the one quality which BOB/OMB has always needed in order to survive, a beleaguered White House often found itself pushing against an open door. Lacking any outside clientele in Congress or interest groups, OMB can resist only through inactivity; its choice is to be of use to the President of the day or to atrophy. OMB preferred to be of use.

A Shifting Role

Although the internal shakeup at OMB aimed at making it more responsive to the White House, it was not intended to allow the organization to provide policy leadership in the Executive Office of the President. For this function, the Domestic Council was created. As the slogan of the time had it, the Domestic Council would concern itself with what to do, the OMB with how to do it and how well it was being done. The Domestic Council would be the antipode of everything the traditional Bureau of the Budget had been. Its virtue would be not institutional routine but policy innovation, not continuity but personnel turnover, not professional detachment but loyalty to "the man."

It was an ill-starred division of tasks. Thinking about what to do turned out to be difficult without having the people around who could tell you how to do it. Since they had a great deal of the necessary experience and expertise, OMB staff were increasingly drafted into Domestic Council operations—and even directed by Council leaders not to inform OMB colleagues of their work (a secrecy which, predictably enough, was rarely pledged and even more rarely maintained). . . .

From the convulsions of the last few years, then, the OMB has emerged stronger than ever. The question is: a strong what? Has OMB balanced the demands placed on it for policy advocacy outside and for quiet diplomacy within government? Has it succeeded in being a close member of the President's political family yet maintaining itself as a detached staff for the ongoing President? In short, what has happened to the idea of neutral competence as a result of all these changes?

Well, one thing that has happened is that there has been a fundamental shift in OMB's role away from wholesaling advice to the Presidency and toward retailing policy to outsiders. The Bureau of the Budget had carefully shunned public visibility and served as an administration spokesman only infrequently and in specialized areas. Similarly, most public comment on BOB was second-hand, via the well-worn ploy by which spending departments found it convenient to blame BOB for frustrating the demands of the departments' clients. Since 1971, however, the director and his associates have sought more prominence, at least in part because of adverse Congressional reactions to Presidential impoundment. More OMB officials can now be found going to Capitol Hill to negotiate with Congressmen. Orders have come down to OMB career staff to do more liaison work with Congressional staff and provide more intelligence on what they learn. There is more OMB lobbying with agencies and the press in order to sell administration policy.

However well-intentioned some of these efforts have been, the fact remains that the easiest way for an organization to become politicized and lose neutral competence is to become visibly identified with a given political bargain or piece of public advocacy. As one experienced official put it:

> The organization is becoming more vulnerable the more it gets associated with particular public positions. By doing things for this and not that group, selling this and not that deal, we become more politically identified with one administration.

Another OMB official observed:

> One of the hardest things to do is to disassociate yourself from a stance taken before large audiences and it's becoming harder and harder to avoid doing that. Frankly it tends to make this agency an extension of the party in power. . . . I guess we've always been that, but we're also supposed to be more than that. It's hard to achieve in practice, but there's something of value in the idea of serving the Presidency, as well as each particular President.

As OMB's visibility has grown, it is understandable if others fail to make the distinction between OMB's governmental authority as an institution of the Presidency and its political power as the President's personal staff. Spending agencies find it more tempting to justify themselves to their clients by complaining not just about the normal BOB/OMB penny-pinching but about its arbitrary power as a political partisan of a given administration. Decreasing the rate of growth in scientific research spending, for example, becomes less a question of value for money and more a question of one particular political administration's anti-science attitude. Those seeking to maintain independence from a President's personal difficulties naturally think of holding OMB at arm's length as well. When Elliot Richardson became Attorney General, OMB staff were shaken to hear that he had instructed his subordinates to have no dealings with White House or OMB staff; it took later clarification of these orders to reestablish the distinction and proscribe only White House personnel.

Even more threatening than problems with outsiders is the fact that members of the Executive Office of the President themselves may become less able to distinguish service to the President from service to the Presidency. The aim of lodging the director in the West Wing, of creating a powerful layer of line political officers, and of projecting a visible OMB profile of administration advocacy has been to increase responsiveness to the President's policy. But what happens when the authoritative Presidential aide, laying down the political overview which is to guide OMB budget-makers, instructs that only capital projects in certain politically rewarding districts are to be approved? Such questions have indeed come forth, and the answer to the question "What happens?" is that in this case nothing happened, besides a collective shiver of disgust throughout all levels of OMB. But there is no escaping the final implication. If OMB is to be the administration's loyal advocate and lead agency, then there are likely to be people in the White House who expect it to follow with a minimum of questioning.

Dilemmas of the Civil Servant

The change from BOB to OMB expressed a legitimate concern for the political responsibility and responsiveness of the people making important decisions. No one should be surprised by the visibility which goes with this avowed political responsibility, nor is it necessarily a bad thing if the organization itself is held more publicly accountable for what it does. But there are also the legitimate claims of neutral competence in government, and if the organization moves toward increased external political identification, the need for understanding and protecting its internal capacities for impartial continuity becomes even greater, particularly in the relations between transient political appointees and more permanent career staff. Here, too, the traditional performance standards have come under strain and may be even more problematic in the future. Political appointees have too often lacked the experience, time, or inclination to care that abstract boundaries for civil service roles be maintained or to be concerned that, once lost, a tradition of neutral competence can be almost impossible to re-establish.

Experienced civil servants worry both when they are too far from political power and when they are too near, when they are suspected by their political bosses and when they are treated so familiarly that the political/civil service distinction disappears. Many senior officials who were once held at arm's length now find that they are being drawn into a closer political embrace at OMB. The PAD is supposed to be the political person, but in the nature of things he cannot go to all the meetings or engage in all the negotiations that come his way. Civil service staff often substitute, partly out of physical necessity and partly as a result of prodding by some political appointees. And as the officials have become more involved politically, they have found it more difficult to maintain that neutral identity which would allow them to be of service to succeeding administrations.

Most career officials are trying hard to avoid political identification, though a few of the less experienced or more politically ambitious among them are not inclined to send for instructions to cover themselves. One senior official contrasted the current situation with the BOB he had joined in the late 1950's:

> Of course, you've always had to bargain, but now I run around town and people assume I am acting in [the PAD's] stead. But in fact I'm a career man and I'm not being paid to become an advocate. I don't have the perquisites, the power, or the status to go with that job. I try and do an honest job of analysis, and the danger is you'll lose your standing as objective. But I'm getting stuck and having to take more and more public positions.

A much younger man at the examiner level commented on the perils of "getting stuck":

> I got sucked in. I guess you could say I was politicized. You get wrapped up in the crisis and pressures of the administration's mission and don't ask the questions or draw the distinctions you might have done in calmer times. . . . The White House wanted to make decisions and you were supposed to give them the reasons.

In some cases, such as the heavy-handed use of impoundment or the dismantling of OEO, for example, independent OMB advice was unduly compromised by close and ingratiating ties between White House and OMB staff.

Increased pressure to deal with Congress has proven an additional source of difficulty. As one middle-aged examiner put it:

We like to think of ourselves as a bureaucracy existing over time. Recently word has come down from the head office that we're supposed to find out more about what is going on up on the Hill. I guess we're supposed to be talking about the status of legislation and lobbying for certain things. That should be the political guys' job. When those people can't do it, they ask us to.

Some who do try to keep on the proper side of the political line are then criticized for providing poor service. One supergrade official commented:

When I am told to go to meetings with Congressional staff, I keep my damn mouth shut. A question of fact I supply, but if they ask for opinion or judgment I look to the guy from the White House or send back for instructions. . . . Then when he's sent me with minimal instructions, [a PAD] has the gall to ask why I can't carry the ball.

Obviously, a good civil servant should be expected to look out for himself, to know his proper role and keep to it. But circumstances can help or hinder his efforts, and the trend at OMB has been to make the protection of neutral competence much more difficult. When both the agency and careerists are unshielded from politicization, then communication, impartiality, and continuity all suffer. . . .

The Future of OMB

The threat to neutral competence was not initiated by the Nixon Administration. Both the Eisenhower and the Kennedy Administrations came to Washington vowing vengeance against a Bureau of the Budget suspected of disloyalty to the new President; in both cases the new BOB directors went to the barricades to protect the agency, and other political appointees soon came to appreciate the asset they had acquired. Nor were senior White House staff in the Johnson Administration particularly interested in the niceties of neutral competence. Events of more recent years, though, raise more serious questions than ever before about the norms of impartial continuity. The same threat can be found in other agencies, but BOB/OMB is the one place at the government center where impartial continuity has traditionally been cherished and had a chance to grow. Its disappearance there would be a change of special consequence. OMB has not yet been thoroughly politicized, but enough inroads have been made for there to be cause for concern and for serious rethinking about the direction in which developments are taking us.

The use made of OMB depends heavily on what the President wants to do. Eisenhower relegated BOB to a secondary role in making policy. As he was not interested in initiating very much on his own, he preferred to use BOB mainly to help keep the government machine ticking. Another possible option arises at the other extreme, and was utilized by the Nixon Administration in its attempt to mobilize the executive branch in a given direction. Since OMB sits astride the budget, management, and legislative coordination processes, it can be used with one or two layers of additional political appointees as the chosen agent of this leadership. The costs in terms of losing the assets of neutral competence are likely to be great for the President, but he can decide to pay them. . . .

In the absence of more serious concern for the uses of OMB, the Ford Administration [slipped] into another approach which emphasizes coordination almost to the point of Presidential abdication. Problems of energy, the economy, and the environment put a premium on coordinating overlapping jurisdictions within the executive branch. Presidential inclination to appoint czars over these areas is an attempt to redefine the jurisdictions at a stroke and mandate coordination. The problem is that the czars were elected by a vote of one to nothing. Unless the responsibility implied by popular election of the President is to be abandoned, the President cannot allow himself to be in the hands of his czars, or his cabinet officers, or his best friends, or some combination of all three. He needs to know things that even (and especially) his best friends will not or cannot tell him. He needs his own lines into the agencies and his own independent source of advice. Presidential openness is itself no answer and may easily, by overloading the President with entreaties and unverifiable information, become part of the problem.

A System Where Everyone Loses?

In present circumstances the most useful course is to begin by returning to first principles. OMB can be valuable to Presidents in many ways, but its most appropriate use is as an independent source of analytic advice and governmental coordination in line with expressed Presidential desires. In terms of advice, OMB should be the place to look for analysis with a minimum of political body English—that is, a place with a fine disregard for the political bearing of who believes what at a given time. This is not to say that OMB staff should be politically insensitive and fail to make such marginal notes; but assessing political trade-offs should not be the main focus of OMB work.

But if this is to be the case, then OMB is not enough. There is an important truth in the comment of a leading Nixon participant in the 1970 reorganization who said, "BOB we figured was the kind of place that could make a one-term President out of anybody." If the traditional strength of BOB was its independent analytic view of pros and cons, that was also its weakness. By paying less attention to the political trade-offs involved in acting on the results of its work, BOB was in a poor position to give the political man in the Oval Office all the service he needed. . . . The need is not for bright and incisive analysts calling themselves political appointees, but for real pols on the White House staff with the wit and understanding to use analysis. A group of political appointees is needed to politicize the White House analysis of issues, not to politicize OMB. . . .

What is at stake for any President or OMB director is not the conventional question of whether White House staff or OMB is too strong or too weak. The events of recent years suggest that it is possible for them to be both, and thus to produce the worst of both worlds. OMB can prove so effective a lead agency in administration advocacy that it prejudices its chance of acceptance by a successor administration. Civil servants may simultaneously become too suspect to, and too intimate with, political leadership. Appointees and "their" careerists may provide more temporary political responsiveness but at the price of a lessened long-term capacity to respond, as career staff who are not politically identified are kept further from events and rendered less knowledgeable than they should be to service a new administration. There can be more intermediaries and less mediation. Political power may become more competitive with bureaucratic power at the same time as the net experience and continuity of the government machine as a whole declines. Bureaucracy can become more politicized and more difficult to control. All of which is to say that the way things are going, we can easily create a system in which everyone loses.

III

American Bureaucracy: Historical Development

It is fair to say that, however they may differ in other respects, all modern political systems have very similar bureaucratic institutions that pose much the same problems for each of the societies in which they are located. For example, the United States and the Soviet Union are very far apart in their political orientation, and yet in the two political systems the public expresses nearly identical complaints against bureaucracy, and political leaders experience the same kind of frustration with its performance.

But in spite of this universal resemblance among bureaucracies, the history and culture of various countries have shaped bureaucratic development somewhat differently, and differences in the roles of today's bureaucracies in policymaking reflect these variations in their historical experience. In the United States, for example, the contemporary role of bureaucrats in policymaking is very much a product of the late start bureaucracy had in this country and of the fact that administrative institutions came into being in a society already highly impregnated with democratic ideology and practice. As a result, the unelected bureaucracy has had a great deal more difficulty in establishing itself as a legitimate part of the governmental apparatus in America's democratic culture than has been the case elsewhere.

In "The Rise of the Bureaucratic State," James Q. Wilson points up the singular role of pressure groups in bringing about the establishment of new administrative agencies in the United States.

In earlier days these groups took the lead in trying to gain a seat at the bureaucratic table, hoping in this way to influence government policymaking in their own favor. More recently, Wilson argues, the bureaucracy itself has begun to play a prominent part in mobilizing its own network of group support. As Wilson puts it: "Whereas federal money was once spent in response to the claims of distinct and organized clients, public or private, in the contemporary period federal money has increasingly been spent in ways that have created such clients."

From a policy perspective the high degree of interaction between agency and outside group that characterizes U.S. bureaucracy has one very pronounced result. It narrows the perspective of agencies on policy issues to the point where they may become incapable of taking any broader view of the public good than that reflected by the demands of their own clients. This is precisely the criticism public interest groups commonly advance with respect to the policies and decisions of many regulatory bodies.

I

The history of U.S. bureaucracy has been largely a history of reform. In his article on this topic, Herbert Storing contends that the initial step taken in this direction in 1883, civil service reform, was designed not so much to enhance the efficiency of the public service as to purify the political parties and to protect them from the unseemly temptation to parcel out the administrative offices at their disposal in corrupt ways.

However, after the principle that public employees would be recruited on the basis of merit rather than patronage was accepted, the enduring problem was that of building a bureaucracy that was both politically responsive and administratively efficient. Finding the right balance between these two imperatives has drawn the attention of many of the leading students of U.S. political institutions, most especially Woodrow Wilson in a pioneering essay published in 1887, "The Study of Public Administration."

Storing is especially good at spelling out how political officeholders and career bureaucrats can fruitfully interact in the development of public policy. Differing with those who see bureaucrats as merely unimaginative "paper-shufflers," he notes that bureaucrats not only "exercise discretion in interpreting and applying the commands of their political superiors; they participate intimately in the formation of those commands. . . . They make a vital contribution to the process of deciding what is to be done." At its best, Storing concludes, public policy develops in the executive branch through a judicious melding of political and bureaucratic perspectives.

Michael Nelson also examines the recurring efforts to reform bureaucracy in the United States. He emphasizes the element of irony that is so often present at critical points in the history of bureaucratic reform—the disparity between what was intended and what is achieved. For example, when the bureaucracy came under the simultaneous supervision of both the president and Congress in the nineteenth century, this dual system of control enabled administrators to increase their own independence by playing off each of these institutions against the other.

An ultimate conclusion that can be drawn from Nelson's essay—a "grand" irony, as he puts it—is that the power of bureaucracy has grown not in spite of, but to some degree because of, the efforts that have been made to limit it. What this proposition suggests is that the political system cannot really operate without a strongly functioning bureaucratic apparatus— that something resembling a bureaucratic imperative has been at work in the entire sequence of events that Nelson so skillfully analyzes. Bureaucracy has managed to persevere even in the most inhospitable of political environments. This historical record raises a question about the ultimate effects of many of the attempts now being made to trim the power of bureaucracy, including deregulation, civil service reform, and cutbacks in governmental expenditures that seek to remove the financial underpinning from a wide range of bureaucratic activities: Will these efforts in the end also reinforce rather than weaken the power of bureaucracy?

II

There are wide variations not only among bureaucracies in different societies but also within the bureaucratic apparatus in any single society. In "A Cabinet of Unequals," Thomas E. Cronin examines the chief characteristic of the major executive departments in the United States. He divides these departments into two groups. One group, made up of the Defense, Justice,

State and Treasury departments, he characterizes as the "inner" cabinet. These inner departments carry on functions that are inclusive in nature; that is to say, they are meant to be of benefit to the entire population. They are also oriented toward the White House, and their chief executives commonly serve as major advisers of the president.

The other nine executive departments in the United States are part of what Cronin calls the "outer" cabinet. They are more specialized in function; their activities are, for the most part, designed to benefit particular segments of the population rather than the country as a whole. Much to the dismay and sometimes the anger of White House aides, these departments are not as presidentially oriented as are the inner cabinet departments. Outer cabinet departments expend a good deal of effort staying on good terms with Congress, on which they depend for financial and other forms of support. They are also closely tied to the domestic constituencies they serve. The heads of these departments commonly become strong advocates of their clientele groups. In time they may come to give more attention to the needs of this constituency than to White House requests or directives.

In light of the cross-pressures that play upon the heads of these executive departments, it should not be surprising that the career of a cabinet member in the U.S. political system can be "nasty, brutish, and short." In recent years, at least, more cabinet members have been fired by presidents for disloyalty than have ever been sacked for incompetence. All four of our most recent presidents (Nixon, Ford, Carter, and Reagan) replaced cabinet members for this reason. In the turbulent cross-currents of national politics, the head of an executive department must employ administrative statecraft of the highest order to avoid being capsized.

9

The Rise of the Bureaucratic State

JAMES Q. WILSON

During its first 150 years, the American republic was not thought to have a "bureaucracy," and thus it would have been meaningless to refer to the "problems" of a "bureaucratic state." There were, of course, appointed civilian officials: Though only about 3,000 at the end of the Federalist period, there were about 95,000 by the time Grover Cleveland assumed office in 1881, and nearly half a million by 1925. Some aspects of these numerous officials were regarded as problems—notably, the standards by which they were appointed and the political loyalties to which they were held—but these were thought to be matters of proper character and good management. The great political and constitutional struggles were not over the power of the administrative apparatus, but over the power of the President, of Congress, and of the states.

The Founding Fathers had little to say about the nature or function of the executive branch of the new government. The Constitution is virtually silent on the subject and the debates in the Constitutional Convention are almost devoid of reference to an administrative apparatus. This reflected no lack of concern about the matter, however. Indeed, it was in part because of the Founders' depressing experience with chaotic and inefficient management under the Continental Congress and the Articles of Confederation that they had assembled in Philadelphia. Management by committees composed of part-time amateurs had cost the colonies dearly in the War of Independence and few, if any, of the Founders wished to return to that system. The argument was only over how the heads

Reprinted with permission of the author from: *The Public Interest*, No. 41 (Fall 1975), pp. 77–103. © 1975 by National Affairs, Inc.

of the necessary departments of government were to be selected, and whether these heads should be wholly subordinate to the President or whether instead they should form some sort of council that would advise the President and perhaps share in his authority. In the end, the Founders left it up to Congress to decide the matter.

There was no dispute in Congress that there should be executive departments, headed by single appointed officials, and, of course, the Constitution specified that these would be appointed by the President with the advice and consent of the Senate. The only issue was how such officials might be removed. After prolonged debate and by the narrowest of majorities, Congress agreed that the President should have the sole right of removal, thus confirming that the infant administrative system would be wholly subordinate—in law at least—to the President. Had not Vice President John Adams, presiding over a Senate equally divided on the issue, cast the deciding vote in favor of Presidential removal, the administrative departments might conceivably have become legal dependencies of the legislature, with incalculable consequences for the development of the embryonic government.

The "Bureaucracy Problem"

The original departments were small and had limited duties. The State Department, the first to be created, had but nine employees in addition to the Secretary. The War Department did not reach 80 civilian employees until 1801; it commanded only a few thousand soldiers. Only the Treasury Department had substantial powers—it collected taxes, managed the public debt, ran the national bank, conducted land surveys, and purchased military supplies. Because of this, Congress gave the closest scrutiny to its structure and its activities.

The number of administrative agencies and employees grew slowly but steadily during the 19th and 20th centuries and then increased explosively on the occasions of World War I, the Depression, and World War II. It is difficult to say at what point in this process the administrative system became a distinct locus of power or an independent source of political initiatives and problems. What is clear is that the emphasis on the sheer *size* of the administrative establishment—conventional in many treatments of the subject—is misleading. . . .

Political Authority

There are at least three ways in which political power may be gathered undeniably into bureaucratic hands: by the growth of an administrative apparatus so large as to be immune from popular control, by placing power over a governmental bureaucracy of any size in private rather than public hands, or by vesting discretionary authority in the hands of a public agency so that the exercise of that power is not responsive to the public good. These are not the only problems that arise because of bureaucratic organization. From the point of view of their members, bureaucracies are sometimes uncaring, ponderous, or unfair; from the point of view of their political superiors, they are sometimes unimaginative or inefficient; from the point of view of their clients, they are sometimes slow or unjust. No single account can possibly treat of all that is problematic in bureaucracy; even the part I discuss here—the extent to which political authority has been transferred undesirably to an unaccountable administrative realm—is itself too large for a single essay. But it is, if not the most important problem, then surely the one that would most have troubled our Revolutionary leaders, especially those that went on to produce the Constitution. It was, after all, the question of power that chiefly concerned them, both in redefining our relationship with England and in finding a new basis for political authority in the Colonies.

To some, following in the tradition of Weber, bureaucracy is the inevitable consequence and perhaps necessary concomitant of modernity. A money economy, the division of labor, and the evolution of legal-rational norms to justify organizational authority require the efficient adaptation of means to ends and a high degree of predictability in the behavior of rulers. To this, Georg Simmel added the view that organizations tend to acquire the characteristics of those institutions with which they are in conflict, so that as government becomes more bureaucratic, private organizations—political parties, trade unions, voluntary associations—will have an additional reason to become bureaucratic as well.

By viewing bureaucracy as an inevitable (or, as some would put it, "functional") aspect of society, we find ourselves attracted to theories that explain the growth of bureaucracy in terms of some inner dynamic to which all agencies respond and which makes all barely governable and scarcely tolerable. Bureaucracies grow, we are told, because of Parkinson's Law: Work and personnel expand to consume the available resources. Bureaucracies behave, we believe, in accord with various other maxims, such as the Peter Principle: In hierarchical organizations, personnel are promoted up to that point at which their incompetence becomes manifest—hence, all important positions are held by incompetents. More elegant, if not essentially different, theories have been propounded by scholars. The tendency of all bureaus to expand is explained by William A. Niskanen by the assumption, derived from the theory of the firm, that "bureaucrats maximize the total budget of their bureau during their tenure"— hence, "all bureaus are too large." What keeps them from being not merely too large but all-consuming is the fact that a bureau must deliver to some degree on its promised output, and if it consistently underdelivers, its budget will be cut by unhappy legislators. But since measuring the output of a bureau is often difficult—indeed, even *conceptualizing* the output of the State Department is mind-boggling—the bureau has a great deal of freedom within which to seek the largest possible budget.

Such theories, both the popular and the scholarly, assign little importance to the nature of the tasks an agency performs, the constitutional framework in which it is embedded, or the preferences and attitudes of citizens and legislators. Our approach will be quite different: Different agencies will be examined in historical perspective to discover the kinds of problems, if any, to which their operation gave rise, and how those problems were affected—perhaps determined—by the tasks which they were assigned, the political system in which they operated, and the preferences they were required to consult. What follows will be far from a systematic treatment of such matters, and even farther from a rigorous testing of any theory of bureaucratization: Our knowledge of agency history and behavior is too sketchy to permit that.

Bureaucracy and Size

During the first half of the 19th century, the growth in the size of the federal bureaucracy can be explained, not by the assumption of new tasks by the government or by the imperialistic designs of the managers of existing tasks, but by the addition to existing bureaus of personnel performing essentially routine, repetitive tasks for which the public demand was great and unavoidable. The principal problem facing a bureaucracy thus enlarged was how best to coordinate its activities toward given and noncontroversial ends.

The increase in the size of the executive branch of the federal government at this time was almost entirely the result of the increase in the size of the Post Office. From 1816 to 1861, federal civilian employment in the executive branch increased nearly eightfold (from 4,837 to 36,672), but 86 per cent of this growth was the result of additions to the postal service. The Post Office Department was expanding as population and commerce expanded. By 1869 there were 27,000 post offices scattered around the nation; by 1901, nearly 77,000. In New York alone, by 1894 there were nearly 3,000 postal employees, the same number required to run the entire federal government at the beginning of that century.

The organizational shape of the Post Office was more or less fixed in the administration of Andrew Jackson. The Postmaster General, almost always appointed because of his partisan position, was aided by three (later four) assistant postmaster generals dealing with appointments, mail-carrying contracts, operations, and finance. There is no reason in theory why such an organization could not deliver the mails efficiently and honestly: The task is routine, its performance is measurable, and its value is monitored by millions of customers. Yet the Post Office, from the earliest years of the 19th century, was an organization marred by inefficiency and corruption. The reason is often thought to be found in the making of political appointments to the Post Office. "Political hacks," so the theory goes, would inevitably combine dishonesty and incompetence to the disservice of the nation; thus, by cleansing the department of such persons these difficulties could be avoided. Indeed, some have argued that it was the advent of the "spoils system" under Jackson that contributed to the later inefficiencies of the public bureaucracy.

The opposite is more nearly the case. The Jacksonians did not seek to make the administrative apparatus a mere tool of the Democratic party advantage, but to purify that apparatus not only of what they took to be Federalist subversion but also of personal decadence. The government was becoming not just large, but lax. Integrity and diligence were absent, not merely from government, but from social institutions generally. The Jacksonians were in many cases concerned about the decline in what the Founders had called "republican virtue," but what their successors were more likely to call simplicity and decency. As Matthew Crenson has recently observed in his book *The Federal Machine*, Jacksonian administrators wanted to "guarantee the good behavior of civil servants" as well as to cope with bigness, and to do this they sought both to place their own followers in office and—what is more important—to create a system of depersonalized, specialized bureaucratic rule. Far from being the enemies of bureaucracy, the Jacksonians were among its principal architects.

Impersonal administrative systems, like the spoils system, were "devices for strengthening the government's authority over its own civil servants"; these bureaucratic methods were, in turn, intended to "compensate for a decline in the disciplinary power of social institutions" such as the community, the professions, and business. If public servants, like men generally in a rapidly growing and diversifying society, could no longer be relied upon "to have a delicate regard for their reputations," accurate bookkeeping, close inspections, and regularized procedures would accomplish what character could not.

Amos Kendall, Postmaster General under President Jackson, set about to achieve this goal with a remarkable series of administrative innovations. To prevent corruption, Kendall embarked on two contradictory courses of action: He sought to bring every detail of the department's affairs under his personal scrutiny and he began to reduce and divide the authority on which that scrutiny depended. Virtually every important document and many unimportant ones had to be signed by Kendall himself. At the same time, he gave to the Treasury Department the power to audit his accounts and obtained from Congress a law requiring that the revenues of the department be paid into the Treasury rather than retained by the Post Office. The duties of his subordinates were carefully defined and arranged so that the authority of one assistant would tend to check that of another. What was installed was not simply a specialized management system, but a concept of the administrative separation of powers.

Few subsequent postmasters were of Kendall's ability. The result was predictable. Endless details flowed to Washington for decision but no one in Washington other than the Postmaster General had the authority to decide. Meanwhile, the size of the postal establishment grew by leaps and bounds. Quickly the department began to operate on the basis of habit and local custom: Since everybody reported to Washington, in effect no one did. As Leonard D. White was later to remark, "the system could work only because it was a vast, repetitive, fixed, and generally routine operation." John Wanamaker, an able businessman who became Postmaster General under President Cleveland, proposed decentralizing the department under 26 regional supervisors. But Wanamaker's own assistants in Washington were unenthusiastic about such a diminution in their authority and, in any event, Congress steadfastly refused to endorse decentralization.

Civil service reform was not strongly resisted in the Post Office; from 1883 on, the number of its employees covered by the merit system expanded. Big-city postmasters were often delighted to be relieved of the burden of dealing with hundreds of place-seekers. Employees welcomed the job protection that civil service provided. In time, the merit system came to govern Post Office personnel almost completely, yet the problems of the department became, if anything, worse. By the mid-20th century, slow and inadequate service, an inability technologically to cope with the mounting flood of mail, and the inequities of its pricing system became all too evident. The problem with the Post Office, however, was not omnipotence but impotence. It was a government monopoly. Being a monopoly, it had little incentive to find the most efficient means to manage its services; being a government monopoly, it was not free to adopt such means even when found—communities, Congressmen, and special-interest groups saw to that.

The Military Establishment

Not all large bureaucracies grow in response to demands for service. The Department of Defense, since 1941 the largest employer of federal civilian officials, has become, as the governmental keystone of the "military-industrial complex," the very archetype of an administrative entity that is thought to be so vast and so well entrenched that it can virtually ignore the political branches of government, growing and even acting on the basis of its own inner imperatives. In fact, until recently the military services were a major economic and political force only during wartime. In the late 18th and early 19th centuries, America was a neutral nation with only a tiny standing army. During the Civil War, over two million men served on the Union side alone and the War Department expanded enormously, but demobilization after the war was virtually complete, except for a small Indian-fighting force. Its peacetime authorized strength was only 25,000 enlisted men and 2,161 officers, and its actual strength for the rest of the century was often less. Congress authorized the purchase and installation of over 2,000 coastal defense guns, but barely six per cent of these were put in place.

When war with Spain broke out, the army was almost totally unprepared. Over 300,000 men eventually served in that brief conflict, and though almost all were again demobilized, the War Department under Elihu Root was reorganized and put on a more professionalized basis with a greater capacity for unified central control. Since the United States had become an imperial power with important possessions in the Caribbean and the Far East, the need for a larger military establishment was clear; even so, the average size of the army until World War I was only about 250,000.

The First World War again witnessed a vast mobilization—nearly five million men in all—and again an almost complete demobilization after the war. The Second World War involved over 16 million military personnel. The demobilization that followed was less complete than after previous engagements, owing to the development of the Cold War, but it was substantial nonetheless—the Army fell in size from over eight million men to only half a million. Military spending declined from $91 billion in the first quarter of 1945 to only slightly more than $10 billion in the second quarter of 1947. For the next three years it remained relatively flat. It began to rise rapidly in 1950, partly to finance our involvement in the Korean conflict and partly to begin the construction of a military force that could counterbalance the Soviet Union, especially in Europe.

In sum, from the Revolutionary War to 1950, a period of over 170 years, the size and deployment of the military establishment in this country was governed entirely by decisions made by political leaders on political grounds. The military did not expand autonomously, a large standing army did not find wars to fight, and its officers did not play a significant potential role except in wartime and occasionally as Presidential candidates. No bureaucracy proved easier to control, at least insofar as its size and purposes were concerned.

A "Military-Industrial Complex"?

The argument for the existence of an autonomous, bureaucratically led military-industrial complex is supported primarily by events since 1950. Not only has the United States assumed during this period world-wide commitments that necessitate a larger military establishment, but the advent of new, high-technology weapons has created a vast industrial machine with an interest in sustaining a high level of military expenditures, especially on weapons research, development, and acquisition. This machine, so the argument goes, is allied with the Pentagon in ways that dominate the political officials nominally in charge of the armed forces. There is some truth in all this. We have become a world military force, though that decision was made by elected officials in 1949–1950 and not dictated by a (then nonexistent) military-industrial complex. High-cost, high-technology weapons have become important and a number of industrial concerns will prosper or perish depending on how contracts for those weapons are let. The development and purchase of weapons is sometimes made in a wasteful, even irrational, manner. And the allocation of funds among the several armed services is often dictated as much by inter-service rivalry as by strategic or political decisions.

But despite all this, the military has not been able to sustain itself at its preferred size, to keep its strength constant or growing, or to retain for its use a fixed or growing portion of the Gross National Product. . . . [T]he total budget, and thus the total force level, of the military has been decided primarily by the President and not in any serious sense forced upon him by subordinates. (For example, President Truman decided to allocate one third of the federal budget to defense, President Eisenhower chose to spend no more than 10 per cent of the Gross National Product on it, and President Kennedy strongly supported Robert McNamara's radical and controversial budget revisions.) . . .

The principal source of growth in the military budget in recent years has arisen from Congressionally determined pay provisions. The legislature has voted for more or less automatic pay increases for military personnel with the result that the military budget has gone up even when the number of personnel in the military establishment has gone down.

The bureaucratic problems associated with the military establishment arise mostly from its internal management and are functions of its complexity, the uncertainty surrounding its future deployment, conflicts among its constituent services over mission and role, and the need to purchase expensive equipment without the benefit of a market economy that can control costs. Complexity, uncertainty, rivalry, and monopsony are inherent (and frustrating) aspects of the military as a bureaucracy, but they are very different problems from those typically associated with the phrase, "the military-industrial complex." The size and budget of the military are matters wholly within the power of civilian authorities to decide—indeed, the military budget contains the largest discretionary items in the entire federal budget.

If the Founding Fathers were to return to review their handiwork, they would no doubt be staggered by the size of both the Post Office and the Defense Department, and in the case of the latter, be worried about the implications of our commitments to various foreign powers. They surely would be amazed at the technological accomplishments but depressed by the cost and inefficiency of both departments; but they would not, I suspect, think that our Constitutional arrangements for managing these enterprises have proved defective or that there had occurred, as a result of the creation of these vast bureaus, an important shift in the locus of political authority.

They would observe that there have continued to operate strong localistic pressures in both systems—offices are operated, often uneconomically, in some small communities because small communities have influential Congressmen; military bases are maintained in many states because states have powerful Senators. But a national government with localistic biases is precisely the system they believed they had designed in 1787, and though they surely could not have then imagined the costs of it, they just as surely would have said (Hamilton possibly excepted) that these costs were the defects of the system's virtues.

Bureaucracy and Clientelism

After 1861, the growth in the federal administrative system could no longer be explained primarily by an expansion of the postal service and other traditional bureaus. Though these continued to expand, new departments were added that reflected a new (or at least greater) emphasis on the enlargement of the scope of government. Between 1861 and 1901, over 200,000 civilian employees were added to the federal service, only 52 per cent of whom were postal workers. Some of these, of course, staffed a larger military and naval establishment stimulated by the Civil War and the Spanish-American War. By 1901 there were over 44,000 civilian defense employees, mostly workers in government-owned arsenals and shipyards. But even these could account for less than one fourth of the increase in employment during the preceding 40 years.

What was striking about the period after 1861 was that the government began to give formal, bureaucratic recognition to the emergence of distinctive interests in a diversifying economy. As Richard L. Schott has written, "whereas earlier federal departments had been formed around specialized governmental functions (foreign affairs, war, finance, and the like), the new departments of this period—Agriculture, Labor, and Commerce—were devoted to the interests and aspirations of particular economic groups."

The original purpose behind these clientele-oriented departments was neither to subsidize nor to regulate, but to promote, chiefly by gathering and publishing statistics and (especially in the case of agriculture) by research. The formation of the Department of Agriculture in 1862 was to become a model, for better or worse, for later political campaigns for government recognition. A private association representing an interest—in this case the United States Agricultural Society—was formed. It made every President from Fillmore to Lincoln an honorary member, it enrolled key Congressmen, and it began to lobby for a new department. The precedent was followed by labor groups, especially the Knights of Labor, to secure creation in 1888 of a Department of Labor. It was broadened in 1903 to be a Department of Commerce and Labor, but 10 years later, at the insistence of the American Federation of Labor, the parts were separated and the two departments we now know were formed.

There was an early 19th-century precedent for the creation of these client-serving departments: the Pension Office, then in the Department of the Interior. Begun in 1833 and regularized in 1849, the Office became one of the largest bureaus of the government in the aftermath of the Civil War, as hundreds of thousands of Union Army veterans were made eligible for pensions if they had incurred a permanent disability or injury while on military duty; dependent widows were also eligible if their husbands had died in service or of service-connected injuries. The Grand Army of the Republic (GAR), the leading veterans' organization, was quick to exert pressure for more generous pension laws and for more liberal administration of such laws as already existed. In 1879 Congressmen, noting the number of ex-servicemen living (and voting) in their states, made veterans eligible for pensions retroactively to the date of their discharge from the service, thus enabling thousands who had been late in filing applications to be rewarded for their dilatoriness. In 1890 the law was changed again to make it unnecessary to have been injured in the service—all that was necessary was to have served and then to have acquired a permanent disability by any means other than through "their own vicious habits." And whenever cases not qualifying under existing law came to the attention of Congress, it promptly passed a special act making those persons eligible by name.

So far as is known, the Pension Office was remarkably free of corruption in the administration of this windfall—and why not, since anything an administrator might deny, a legislator was only too pleased to grant. By 1891 the Commissioner of Pensions observed that his was "the largest executive bureau in the world." There were over 6,000 officials supplemented by thousands of local physicians paid on a fee basis. In 1900 alone, the Office had to process 477,000 cases. Fraud was rampant as thousands of persons brought false or exaggerated claims; as Leonard D. White was later to write, "pensioners and their attorneys seemed to have been engaged in a gigantic conspiracy to defraud their own government." Though the Office struggled to be honest, Congress was indifferent—or more accurately, complaisant: The GAR was a powerful electoral force and it was ably and lucratively assisted by thousands of private pension attorneys. The pattern of bureaucratic clientelism was set in a way later to become a familiar feature of the governmental landscape— a subsidy was initially provided, because it was either popular or unnoticed, to a group that was powerfully benefited and had few or disorganized opponents; the beneficiaries were organized to supervise the administration and ensure the funding of the program; the law authorizing the program, first passed because it seemed the right thing to do, was left intact or even expanded because politically it became the only thing to do. A benefit once bestowed cannot easily be withdrawn.

Public Power and Private Interests

It was at the state level, however, that client-oriented bureaucracies proliferated in the 19th century. Chief among these were the occupational licensing agencies. At the time of Independence, professions and occupations either could be freely entered (in which case the consumer had to judge the quality of service for himself) or entry was informally controlled by the existing members of the profession or occupation by personal tutelage and the management of reputations. The latter part of the 19th century, however, witnessed the increased use of law and bureaucracy to control entry into a line of work. The state courts generally allowed this on the grounds that it was a proper exercise of the "police power" of the state, but as Morton Keller has observed, "when state courts approved the licensing of barbers and blacksmiths, but not of horseshoers, it was evident that the principles governing certification were—to put it charitably—elusive ones." By 1952, there were more than 75 different occupations in the United States for which one needed a license to practice, and the awarding of these licenses was typically in the hands of persons already in the occupation, who could act under color of law. These licensing boards—for plumbers, dry cleaners, beauticians, attorneys, undertakers, and the like—frequently have been criticized as particularly flagrant examples of the excesses of a bureaucratic state. But the problems they create—of restricted entry, higher prices, and lengthy and complex initiation procedures—are not primarily the result of some bureaucratic pathology but of the possession of public power by persons who use it for private purposes. Or more accurately, they are the result of using public power in ways that benefited those in the profession in the sincere but unsubstantiated conviction that doing so would benefit the public generally.

The New Deal was perhaps the high water mark of at least the theory of bureaucratic clientelism. Not only did various sectors of society, notably agriculture, begin receiving massive subsidies, but the government proposed, through the National Industrial Recovery Act (NRA), to cloak with public power a vast number of industrial groupings and trade associations so that they might control production and prices in ways that would end the depression. The NRA's Blue Eagle fell before the Supreme Court—the wholesale delegation of public power to private interests was declared unconstitutional. But the piecemeal delegation was not, as the continued growth of specialized promotional agencies attests. The Civil Aeronautics Board, for example, erroneously thought to be exclusively a regulatory agency, was formed in 1938 "to promote" as well as to regulate civil aviation and it has done so by restricting entry and maintaining above-market rate fares.

Agriculture, of course, provides the leading case of clientelism. Theodore J. Lowi finds "at least 10 separate, autonomous, local self-governing systems" located in or closely associated with the Department of Agriculture that control to some significant degree the flow of billions of dollars in expenditures and loans. Local committees of farmers, private farm organizations, agency heads, and committee chairmen in Congress dominate policy-making in this area—not, perhaps, to the exclusion of the concerns of other publics, but certainly in ways not powerfully constrained by them.

"Cooperative Federalism"

The growing edge of client-oriented bureaucracy can be found, however, not in government relations with private groups, but in the relations among governmental units. In dollar volume, the chief clients of federal domestic expenditures are state and local government agencies. To some degree, federal involvement in local affairs by the cooperative funding or management of local enterprises has always existed. The Northwest Ordinance of 1784 made public land available to finance local schools and the Morrill Act of 1862 gave land to support state colleges, but what Morton Grodzins and Daniel Elazar have called "cooperative federalism," though it always existed, did not begin in earnest until the passage in 1913 of the 16th Amendment to the Constitution allowed the federal government to levy an income tax on citizens and thereby to acquire access to vast sources of revenue. Between 1914 and 1917, federal aid to states and localities increased a thousandfold. By 1948 it amounted to over one tenth of all state and local spending; by 1970, to over one sixth.

The degree to which such grants, and the federal agencies that administer them, constrain or even direct state and local bureaucracies is a matter of dispute. No general answer can be given—federal support of welfare programs has left considerable discretion in the hands of the states over the size of benefits and some discretion over eligibility rules, whereas federal support of highway construction carries with it specific requirements as to design, safety, and (since 1968) environmental and social impact.

A few generalizations are possible, however. The first is that the states and not the cities have been from the first, and remain today, the principal client group for grants-in-aid. It was not until the Housing Act of 1937 that money was given in any substantial amount directly to local governments, and though many additional programs of this kind were later added, as late as 1970 less than 12 per cent of all federal aid went directly to cities and towns. The second general observation is that the 1960's mark a major watershed in the way in which the purposes of federal aid are determined. Before that time, most grants were for purposes initially defined by the states—to build highways and airports, to fund unemployment insurance programs, and the like. Beginning in the 1960's, the federal government, at the initiative of the President and his advisors, increasingly came to define the purposes of these grants—not necessarily over the objection of the states, but often without any initiative from them. Federal money was to be spent on poverty, ecology, planning, and other "national" goals for which, until the laws were passed, there were few, if any, well-organized and influential constituencies. Whereas federal money was once spent in response to the claims of distinct and organized clients, public or private, in the contemporary period federal money has increasingly been spent in ways that have *created* such clients.

And once rewarded or created, they are rarely penalized or abolished. What David Stockman has called the "social pork barrel" grows more or less steadily. Between 1950 and 1970, the number of farms declined from about 5.6 million to fewer than three million, but government payments to farmers rose from $283 million to $3.2 billion. In the public sector, even controversial programs have grown. Urban renewal programs have been sharply criticized, but federal support for the program rose from $281 million in 1965 to about $1 billion in 1972. Public housing has been enmeshed in controversy, but federal support for it rose from $206 million in 1965 to $845 million in 1972. . . .

Self-Perpetuating Agencies

If the Founding Fathers were to return to examine bureaucratic clientelism, they would, I suspect, be deeply discouraged. James Madison clearly foresaw that American society would be "broken into many parts, interests and classes of citizens" and that this "multiplicity of interests" would help ensure against "the tyranny of the majority," especially in a federal regime with separate branches of government. Positive action would require a "coalition of a majority"; in the process of forming this coalition, the rights of all would be protected, not merely by self-interested bargains, but because in a free society such a coalition "could seldom take place on any other principles than those of justice and the general good." To those who wrongly believed that Madison thought of men as acting only out of base motives, the phrase is instructive: Persuading men who disagree to compromise their differences can rarely be achieved solely by the parceling out of relative advantage; the belief is also required that what is being agreed to is right, proper, and defensible before public opinion.

Most of the major new social programs of the United States, whether for the good of the few or the many, were initially adopted by broad coalitions appealing to general standards of justice or to conceptions of the public weal. This is certainly the case with most of the New Deal legislation—notably such programs as Social Security—and with most Great Society legislation—notably Medicare and aid to education; it was also conspicuously the case with respect to post-Great Society legislation pertaining to consumer and environmental concerns. State occupational licensing laws were supported by majorities interested in, among other things, the contribution of these statutes to public safety and health.

But when a program supplies particular benefits to an existing or newly created interest, public or private, it creates a set of political relationships that make exceptionally difficult further alteration of that program by coalitions of the majority. What was created in the name of the common good is sustained in the name of the particular interest. Bureaucratic clientelism becomes self-perpetuating, in the absence of some crisis or scandal, because a single interest group to which the program matters greatly is highly motivated and well-situated to ward off the criticisms of other groups that have a broad but weak interest in the policy.

In short, a regime of separated powers makes it difficult to overcome objections and contrary interests sufficiently to permit the enactment of a new program or the creation of a new agency. Unless the legislation can be made to pass either with little notice or at a time of crisis or extraordinary majorities—and sometimes even then—the initiation of new programs requires public interest arguments. But the same regime works to protect agencies, once created, from unwelcome change because a major change is, in effect, new legislation that must overcome the same hurdles as the original law, but this time with one of the hurdles—the wishes of the agency and its client—raised much higher. As a result, the Madisonian system makes it relatively easy for the delegation of public power to private groups to go unchallenged and, therefore, for factional interests that have acquired a supportive public bureaucracy to rule without submitting their interests to the effective scrutiny and modification of other interests.

Bureaucracy and Discretion

For many decades, the Supreme Court denied to the federal government any general "police power" over occupations and businesses, and thus most such regulation occurred at the state level and even there under the constraint that it must not violate the notion of "substantive due process"—that is, the view that there were sharp limits to the power of any government to take (and therefore to regulate) property. What clearly was within the regulatory province of the federal government was interstate commerce, and thus it is not surprising that the first major federal regulatory body should be the Interstate Commerce Commission (ICC), created in 1887. . . .

The true significance of the Commerce Act is not that it allowed public power to be used to make secure private wealth but that it created a federal commission with broadly delegated powers that would have to reconcile conflicting goals (the desire for higher or lower prices) in a political environment characterized by a struggle among organized interests and rapidly changing technology. In short, the Commerce Act brought forth a new dimension to the problem of bureaucracy: not those problems, as with the Post Office, that resulted from size and political constraints, but those that were caused by the need to make binding choices without any clear standards for choice.

The ICC was not, of course, the first federal agency with substantial discretionary powers over important matters. The Office of Indian Affairs, for a while in the War Department but after 1849 in the Interior Department, coped for the better part of a century with the Indian problem equipped with no clear policy, beset on all sides by passionate and opposing arguments, and infected with a level of fraud and corruption that seemed impossible to eliminate. There were many causes of the problem, but at root was the fact that the government was determined to control the Indians but could not decide toward what end that control should be exercised (extermination, relocation, and assimilation all had their advocates) and, to the extent the goal was assimilation, could find no method by which to achieve it. By the end of the century, a policy of relocation had been adopted *de facto* and the worst abuses of the Indian service had been eliminated—if not by administrative skill, then by the exhaustion of things in Indian possession worth stealing. By the turn of the century, the management of the Indian question had become the more or less routine administration of Indian schools and the allocation of reservation land among Indian claimants.

Regulation versus Promotion

It was the ICC and agencies and commissions for which it was the precedent that became the principal example of federal discretionary authority. It is important, however, to be clear about just what this precedent was. Not everything we now call a regulatory agency was in fact intended to be one. The ICC, the Antitrust Division of the Justice Department, the Federal Trade Commission (FTC), the Food and Drug Administration (FDA), the National Labor Relations Board (NRLB)—all these *were* intended to be genuinely regulatory bodies created to handle under public auspices matters once left to private arrangements. The techniques they were to employ varied: approving rates (ICC), issuing cease-and-desist orders (FTC), bringing civil or criminal actions in the courts (the Antitrust Division), defining after a hearing an appropriate standard of conduct (NRLB), or testing a product for safety (FDA). In each case, however, Congress clearly intended that the agency either define its own standards (a safe drug, a conspiracy in restraint of trade, a fair labor practice) or choose among competing claims (a higher or lower rate for shipping grain).

Other agencies often grouped with these regulatory bodies— the Civil Aeronautics Board, the Federal Communications Commission, the Maritime Commission—were designed, however, not primarily to regulate, but to *promote* the development of various infant or threatened industries. However, unlike fostering agriculture or commerce, fostering civil aviation or radio broadcasting was thought to require limiting entry (to prevent "unsafe" aviation or broadcast interference); but at the time these laws were passed few believed that the restrictions on entry would be many, or that the choices would be made on any but technical or otherwise noncontroversial criteria. We smile now at their naïveté, but we continue to share it—today we sometimes suppose that choosing an approved exhaust emission control system or a water pollution control system can be done on the basis of technical criteria and without affecting production and employment.

Majoritarian Politics

The creation of regulatory bureaucracies has occurred, as is often remarked, in waves. The first was the period between 1887 and 1890 (the Commerce Act and the Antitrust Act), the second between 1906 and 1915 (the Pure Food and Drug Act, the Meat Inspection Act, the Federal Trade Commission Act, the Clayton Act), the third during the 1930's (the Food, Drug, and Cosmetic Act, the Public Utility Holding Company Act, the Securities Exchange Act, the Natural Gas Act, the National Labor Relations Act), and the fourth during the latter part of the 1960's (the Water Quality Act, the Truth in Lending Act, the National Traffic and Motor Vehicle Safety Act, various amendments to the drug laws, the Motor Vehicle Pollution Control Act, and many others).

Each of these periods was characterized by progressive or liberal Presidents in office (Cleveland, T. R. Roosevelt, Wilson, F. D. Roosevelt, Johnson); one was a period of national crisis (the 1930's); three were periods when the President enjoyed extraordinary majorities of his own party in both houses of Congress (1914–1916, 1932–1940, and 1964–1968); and only the first period preceded the emergence of the national mass media of communication. These facts are important because of the special difficulty of passing any genuinely regulatory legislation: A single interest, the regulated party, sees itself seriously threatened by a law proposed by a policy entrepreneur who must appeal to an unorganized majority, the members of which may not expect to be substantially or directly benefited by the law. Without special political circumstances—a crisis, a scandal, extraordinary majorities, an especially vigorous President, the support of media—the normal barriers to legislative innovation (i.e., to the formation of a "coalition of the majority") may prove insuperable.

Stated another way, the initiation of regulatory programs tends to take the form of majoritarian rather than coalitional politics. The Madisonian system is placed in temporary suspense: Exceptional majorities propelled by a public mood and led by a skillful policy entrepreneur take action that might not be possible under ordinary circumstances (closely divided parties, legislative-executive checks and balances, popular indifference). The consequence of majoritarian politics for the administration of regulatory bureaucracies is great. To initiate and sustain the necessary legislative mood, strong, moralistic, and sometimes ideological appeals are necessary—leading, in turn, to the granting of broad mandates of power to the new agency (a modest delegation of authority would obviously be inadequate if the problem to be resolved is of crisis proportions), or to the specifying of exacting standards to be enforced (e.g., *no* carcinogenic products may be sold, 95 per cent of the pollutants must be eliminated), or to both.

Either in applying a vague but broad rule ("the public interest, convenience, and necessity") or in enforcing a clear and strict standard, the regulatory agency will tend to broaden the range and domain of its authority, to lag behind technological and economic change, to resist deregulation, to stimulate corruption, and to contribute to the bureaucratization of private institutions.

It will broaden its regulatory reach out of a variety of motives: to satisfy the demand of the regulated enterprise that it be protected from competition, to make effective the initial regulatory action by attending to the unanticipated side effects of that action, to discover or stretch the meaning of vague statutory language, or to respond to new constituencies induced by the existence of the agency to convert what were once private demands into public pressures. For example, the Civil Aeronautics Board, out of a desire both to promote aviation and to protect the regulated price structure of the industry, will resist the entry into the industry of new carriers. If a Public Utilities Commission sets rates too low for a certain class of customers, the utility will allow service to those customers to decline in quality, leading in turn to a demand that the Commission also regulate the quality of service. If the Federal Communications Commission cannot decide who should receive a broadcast license by applying the "public interest" standard, it will be powerfully tempted to invest that phrase with whatever preferences the majority of the Commission then entertains, leading in turn to the exercise of control over many more aspects of broadcasting than merely signal interference—all in the name of deciding what the standard for entry shall be. If the Antitrust Division can prosecute conspiracies in restraint of trade, it will attract to itself the complaints of various firms about business practices that are neither conspiratorial nor restraining but merely competitive, and a "vigorous" antitrust lawyer may conclude that these practices warrant prosecution.

Bureaucratic Inertia

Regulatory agencies are slow to respond to change for the same reason all organizations with an assured existence are slow: There is no incentive to respond. Furthermore, the requirements of due process and of political conciliation will make any response time consuming. For example, owing to the complexity of the matter and the money at stake, any comprehensive review of the long-distance rates of the telephone company will take years, and possibly may take decades.

Deregulation, when warranted by changed economic circumstances or undesired regulatory results, will be resisted. Any organization, and *a fortiori* any public organization, develops a genuine belief in the rightness of its mission that is expressed as a commitment to regulation as a process. This happened to the ICC in the early decades of this century as it steadily sought both enlarged powers (setting minimum as well as maximum rates) and a broader jurisdiction (over trucks, barges, and pipelines as well as railroads). It even urged incorporation into the Transportation Act of 1920 language directing it to prepare a comprehensive transportation plan for the nation. Furthermore, any regulatory agency will confer benefits on some group or interest, whether intended or not; those beneficiaries will stoutly resist deregulation. . . .

The operation of regulatory bureaus may tend to bureaucratize the private sector. The costs of conforming to many regulations can be met most easily—often, *only*—by large firms and institutions with specialized bureaucracies of their own. Smaller firms and groups often must choose between unacceptably high overhead costs, violating the law, or going out of business. A small bakery producing limited runs of a high-quality product literally may not be able to meet the safety and health standards for equipment, or to keep track of and administer fairly its obligations to its two employees; but unless the bakery is willing to break the law, it must sell out to a big bakery that can afford to do these things, but may not be inclined to make and sell good bread. I am not aware of any data that measure private bureaucratization or industrial concentration as a function of the economies of scale produced by the need to cope with the regulatory environment, but I see no reason why such data could not be found.

Finally, regulatory agencies that control entry, fix prices, or substantially affect the profitability of an industry create a powerful stimulus for direct or indirect forms of corruption. The revelations about campaign finance in the 1972 presidential election show dramatically that there will be a response to that stimulus. Many corporations, disproportionately those in regulated industries (airlines, milk producers, oil companies), made illegal or hard to justify campaign contributions involving very large sums. . . .

The Bureaucratic State and the Revolution

The American Revolution was not only a struggle for independence but a fundamental rethinking of the nature of political authority. Indeed, until that reformulation was completed the Revolution was not finished. What made political authority problematic for the colonists was the extent to which they believed Mother England had subverted their liberties despite the protection of the British constitution, until then widely regarded in America as the most perfect set of governing arrangements yet devised. The evidence of usurpation is now familiar: unjust taxation, the weakening of the independence of the judiciary, the stationing of standing armies, and the extensive use of royal patronage to reward office-seekers at colonial expense. Except for the issue of taxation, which raised for the colonists major questions of representation, almost all of their complaints involved the abuse of *administrative* powers.

The first solution proposed by Americans to remedy this abuse was the vesting of most (or, in the case of Pennsylvania and a few other states, virtually all) powers in the legislature. But the events after 1776 in many colonies, notably Pennsylvania, convinced the most thoughtful citizens that legislative abuses were as likely as administrative ones: In the extreme case, citizens would suffer from the "tyranny of the majority." Their solution to this problem was, of course, the theory of the separation of powers by which, as brilliantly argued in *The Federalist* papers, each branch of government would check the likely usurpations of the other.

This formulation went essentially unchallenged in theory and unmodified by practice for over a century. Though a sizeable administrative apparatus had come into being by the end of the 19th century, it constituted no serious threat to the existing distribution of political power because it either performed routine tasks (the Post Office) or dealt with temporary crises (the military). Some agencies wielding discretionary authority existed, but either they dealt with groups whose liberties were not of much concern (the Indian Office) or their exercise of discretion was minutely scrutinized by Congress (the Land Office, the Pension Office, the Customs Office). The major discretionary agencies of the 19th century flourished at the very period of greatest Congressional domination of the political process—the decades after the Civil War—and thus, though their supervision was typically inefficient and sometimes corrupt, these agencies were for most practical purposes direct dependencies of Congress. In short, their existence did not call into question the theory of the separation of powers.

But with the growth of client-serving and regulatory agencies, grave questions began to be raised—usually implicitly—about that theory. A client-serving bureau, because of its relations with some source of private power, could become partially independent of both the executive and legislative branches—or in the case of the latter, dependent upon certain committees and independent of others and of the views of the Congress as a whole. A regulatory agency (that is to say, a truly regulatory one and not a clientelist or promotional agency hiding behind a regulatory fig leaf) was, in the typical case, placed formally outside the existing branches of government. Indeed, they were called "independent" or "quasi-judicial" agencies (they might as well have been called "quasi-executive" or "quasi-legislative") and thus the special status that clientelist bureaus achieved *de facto*, the regulatory ones achieved *de jure*.

It is, of course, inadequate and misleading to criticize these agencies, as has often been done, merely because they raise questions about the problem of sovereignty. The crucial test of their value is their behavior, and that can be judged only by applying economic and welfare criteria to the policies they produce. But if such judgments should prove damning, as increasingly has been the case, then the problem of finding the authority with which to alter or abolish such organizations becomes acute. In this regard the theory of the separation of powers has proved unhelpful.

The separation of powers makes difficult, in ordinary times, the extension of public power over private conduct—as a nation, we came more slowly to the welfare state than almost any European nation, and we still engage in less central planning and operate fewer nationalized industries than other democratic regimes. But we have extended the regulatory sway of our national government as far or farther than that of most other liberal regimes (our environmental and safety codes are now models for much of Europe), and the bureaus wielding these discretionary powers are, once created, harder to change or redirect than would be the case if authority were more centralized.

The shift of power toward the bureaucracy was not inevitable. It did not result simply from increased specialization, the growth of industry, or the imperialistic designs of the bureaus themselves. Before the second decade of this century, there was no federal bureaucracy wielding substantial discretionary powers. That we have one now is the result of political decisions made by elected representatives. Fifty years ago, the people often wanted more of government than it was willing to provide—it was, in that sense, a republican government in which representatives moderated popular demands. Today, not only does political action follow quickly upon the stimulus of public interest, but government itself creates that stimulus and sometimes acts in advance of it.

All democratic regimes tend to shift resources from the private to the public sector and to enlarge the size of the administrative component of government. The particularistic and localistic nature of American democracy has created a particularistic and client-serving administration. If our bureaucracy often serves special interests and is subject to no central direction, it is because our legislature often serves special interests and is subject to no central leadership. For Congress to complain of what it has created and it maintains is, to be charitable, misleading. Congress could change what it has devised, but there is little reason to suppose it will.

10

Reforming
the Bureaucracy

HERBERT J. STORING

I

. . . [The] exclusion of the political party from the vast majority of
federal offices . . . resulted from a deliberate reform of the American
political system which found expression primarily in the Pendleton
Act of 1883. As is well known, this Act established a bipartisan Civil
Service Commission charged, among other things, to provide open
competitive examinations for entry into the "classified" federal service. Originally only about 10 per cent of the 140,000 positions in
the federal service were covered, but provision was made for exten-
sions by executive order. Except for the provision that no person
should be removed for failure to contribute time or money to a political party, the Act imposed no limitations on removal from office;
but limitations were imposed later, especially with respect to veterans. Later legislation also sought to complete the "neutralization"
of the public administration by severely limiting the political activities of civil servants.

The post–Civil War reform movement which led to this legislation was directed immediately at the civil service, but its more fundamental objective was the reform of political parties. While the
reformers did not seek to eradicate parties, they were, like the American Founders, keenly aware that "party spirit, from the first, has

From Herbert J. Storing, "Political Parties and the Bureaucracy" in Robert A. Gold-
win, ed., *Political Parties U.S.A.* (Skokie, IL: Rand McNally, 1961). Reprinted by
permission of Rand McNally & Company. Footnotes and sections are renumbered.

been the terror of republics."[1] It is, George Curtis said, "the one fire that needs no fanning. The first duty of patriotism is to keep that fire low."[2] Specifically, the reformers were trying to rid the country of the spoils system, in which they saw three evils:

1. By distributing public office as the booty of party warfare, the spoils system introduced gross inefficiency and corruption into the public administration.
2. By basing political parties on a network of selfish private relationships, the spoils system distorted and frustrated the expression of the popular will.
3. By channelling men's minds along the lines of private and narrow group interest and away from a concern with the public interest, the spoils system corrupted American political life and character.

Unlike their successors, the early reformers—such men as George Curtis, Dorman Eaton, and Carl Schurz—thought that administrative inefficiency was the least of these evils. "[T]he question whether the Departments at Washington are managed well or badly," said Carl Schurz, "is, in proportion to the whole problem, an insignificant question after all. . . . The most important point to my mind is, how we can remove that element of demoralization which the now prevailing mode of distributing office has introduced into the body-politic."[3] Similarly Dorman Eaton wrote that "civil service reform is not merely a mode of procedure and an economy, but has become a vital question of principle and public morality, involving the counterpoise and in no small degree the stability of the government itself."[4] In an important statement of the object of civil service reform in an editorial for *Harper's Weekly* Schurz conceded that one aim was "an improved conduct of the public business."

> But the ultimate end of civil service reform is something far more important than a mere improvement in the machinery of administration. It is to elevate the character of our political life by eliminating from it as much as possible the demoralizing elements of favoritism

[1]"The Relation Between Morals and Politics," in *Orations and Addresses of George William Curtis*, ed. Charles E. Norton (New York: Harper & Brothers, 1894), II, 124.

[2]"The Reason and the Result of Civil Service Reform," *ibid.*, II, 387.

[3]Speech in the Senate, January 27, 1871, in *Speeches, Correspondence and Political Papers of Carl Schurz*, ed. Frederic Bancroft (New York: G. P. Putnam's Sons, 1913), II, 123.

[4]*Civil Service in Great Britain* (New York: Harper & Brothers, 1880), p. 438.

and of mercenary motives which under the spoils system have become the moving powers in our politics. It is to rescue our political parties, and in a great measure the management of our public affairs, from the control of men whose whole statesmanship consists in the low arts of office-mongering, and many of whom would never have risen to power had not the spoils system furnished them the means and opportunities for organizing gangs of political followers as mercenary as themselves. It is to restore ability, high character, and true public spirit once more to their legitimate spheres in our public life, and to make active politics once more attractive to men of self-respect and high patriotic aspirations.[5]

Many of the reformers were Abolitionists in the controversy over slavery and regarded civil service reform as an extension of the same movement. Having freed the Negro slaves, they argued, it was time to free the civil service from its slavery to political parties. Like the system of chattel slavery, the spoils system corrupts slave, master, and the community that gives it countenance. The reformers' righteous indignation was founded on their conviction that the only two political questions of their time about which reasonable and patriotic men could not differ were Negro slavery and civil service reform. "Since the movement against personal slavery there has been nothing more truly American than this absolutely unselfish and patriotic demand for the emancipation of the Civil Service."[6] In consequence of their abundant and rather rigid morality, the civil service reformers were often scorned as idealistic dreamers, blind to the realities of American politics. But they did more than preach that good government is good. They had a specific, hard-headed program by means of which they proposed to purify American parties and elevate American politics.

This program and the reasoning on which it was based were given remarkably clear expression by William Dudley Foulke, who

---

[5]XXXVII (July 1, 1893), 614.

[6]"The Administration and Reform," in *Orations and Addresses of George William Curtis*, II, 359. Another reformer asserted, "no other public issue since the agitation against slavery has been so clearly and incontestably proved as Civil Service Reform. Every other question has two sides and a conclusion must be formed by balancing the advantages and disadvantages of each. . . . But the necessity of abolishing the evils which have accompanied the spoils system seems so clear and the methods proposed so perfectly adapted to the purpose that I find it hard to understand how any unprejudiced mind, after careful study of the subject, can oppose the competitive system." William Dudley Foulke, *Fighting the Spoilsmen* (New York: G. P. Putnam's Sons, 1919), p. 3. Copyright 1919 by G. P. Putnam's Sons.

was active in the reform movement both nationally and in his own state of Indiana. Foulke explained that there are three major remedies that can be applied to corruption: penal legislation, which is necessary but effective only for the graver crimes; appeal to the moral sense of the community, which is desirable but often ineffective; and removal of the temptation, which is the principle of civil service reform.

> The great purpose of [civil service reform] is not so much to provide an efficient civil service (although it does this) as to remove the temptation to use the offices of the government for personal or party ends, in other words, to remove the incentive to that kind of political corruption which is nourished by the hope of office. It does this by something akin to a mechanical contrivance, making it automatically impossible for the politician seeking the control of patronage to appoint the particular man he wants. It was the concurrence of personal discretion with party government which brought in the spoils system, and rules requiring appointments by competitive examinations destroy this personal discretion.[7]

Thus while the problem was fundamentally a moral and political one, the solution was found in "something akin to a mechanical contrivance." Without attempting to plumb philosophical depths, the reformers reasoned that the immediate cause of political corruption was the spoils system; the spoils system, in turn, depended upon the discretion of appointing officers in choosing their subordinates. Abolish that discretion and you abolish the spoils system and the corruption flowing from it.

Although this chain of reasoning is not simply wrong, it is certainly insufficient. Civil service reform was not so efficacious as the reformers had expected in purifying politics and raising the moral tone of the community, and it brought new and unanticipated problems. Yet corruption *was* very considerably reduced, and politics *did* become less a matter of sheer self-seeking; most people would regard these as gains. One might imagine a moderate reformer asking us to imagine a situation where, not half, but all of the people were moved by nothing but selfish interests and where the political system positively fostered this tendency. Conceive the utter degradation and disaster to which such a system must inevitably lead. These are the

[7]*Ibid.*, pp. 9–10.

results which, but for civil service reform, the spoils system might well have produced.

It is undeniable, however, that the reformers grossly oversimplified the problem of popular government. They were inclined to think that, once the spoils system was out of the way, citizens would become pure, leaders noble, and politics patriotic. "[B]y making election, not a fight for plunder, but a contest of principle," civil service reform would make "the honest will of the people the actual government of the country."[8] Although the reformers often described their movement as a return to the original principles of the American republic, they paid too little heed to the Founders' warning that a government fit for angels is not fit for men. Confronted with the need to rid American politics of selfishness run riot, they underestimated the enduring force of selfish interests, and consequently they failed to recognize sufficiently the permanent need to take account of such interests. They forgot the wisdom that lay in the Founders' "policy of supplying by opposite and rival interests, the defect of better motives. . . . " It is an indication of the extent to which the reformers' ideas still dominate our political thinking that we have to rediscover the lesson that political stability may be found in a politics of interests. And it is ironical that this primary principle of the first American planners and reformers, the Founding Fathers, should now appear in the guise of an argument against planning and reform.

II

With the passage of the Pendleton Act and the steady extension of the merit system in the federal service, the immediate objectives of the reformers were largely accomplished. Although the question of civil service reform erupted periodically, it ceased to be a major political issue. The reform movement did not die, but it moved from the political arena to the universities. The men associated with the second phase of reform were not primarily agitators, pamphleteers, and politicians, like Schurz and Curtis, but university professors, like Frank Goodnow, or professor-politicians, like Woodrow Wilson.

This second generation of reformer–political scientists sought to state systematically the theory of government implicit in the re-

---

[8]"The Administration and Reform," in *Orations and Addresses of George William Curtis*, II, 359.

form movement and to elaborate in more detail its practical consequences. In so doing they established the main lines from which most contemporary thinking about political parties and public administration derives. The key words are "responsible parties" and "efficient administration." As these men generally saw it, the ideal democracy consists, as it were, of two pyramids joined at the top. The will of the people flows up through the pyramid of politics where it is collected by political parties and formed into programs of legislation. The programs of the majority party then flow down through the administrative pyramid where they are implemented in the most efficient manner. According to this theory the prime requisites of a civil service are political neutrality and technical competence. The civil servant is not supposed to make policy. He decides, according to scientifically established technical criteria, the best, that is, most efficient, way to accomplish any given ends. Those ends are set by his political superiors who are responsible through the party to the people.

In spite of some fairly obvious difficulties, this theory proved to be extremely durable, because it seems to state simply and clearly the whole problem of democratic government: to ensure the free expression and the efficient implementation of the popular will. With customary diligence and thoroughness the academicians set about investigating and explaining how the pyramid of politics and the pyramid of administration ought to be governed, each according to its proper principle. . . . [I]t is significant that . . . proposals [for the reform of political parties] have fared much worse than proposals for the reform of administration. Thus while the report of the American Political Science Association on *A More Responsible Two-Party System* has produced little but mild academic controversy, its predecessor and intellectual companion, the 1937 report of the President's Committee on Administrative Management, was widely accepted and largely implemented. A new and vigorous discipline of administration has grown up within the universities, and it trains and fosters a huge corps of professional administrators. Public administration today is subjected to continuous and exhaustive analysis, and a stream of proposals for improvement flows out of universities, research bureaus, and government offices. Administrative theorists and practitioners seem to have moved steadily forward in their understanding, improvement, and conduct of public administration.

So successful is this movement that there has been a tendency to ignore the crucial question of the proper *connection* between administration and politics. The stock answer is that of course the political master gives the orders, but he should not meddle in the activities of his administrative servants; if he does he will only get in the way of the efficient implementation of his own orders. "Administrative questions are not political questions," Wilson said. "Although politics sets the tasks for administration, it should not be suffered to manipulate its offices."[9] It is true that even the most ardent proponents of a neutral civil service rarely went so far as to assert that the intermediate and lower levels of public administration could be altogether free of direct political influence. There were even some doubts whether political control at the top could ever be sufficient to keep the administration politically responsible; but generally students and reformers of administration were too busy extending the merit system, neutralizing the civil service, and devising principles of administration to concern themselves much with the "external" problem of political control. In any case, the logic of the two pyramids, joined somehow at their respective peaks, seemed to settle the question in principle, whatever the practical difficulties.

In addition to its beguiling symmetry, this theory of government seemed to find powerful support in that country to which Americans have always looked for political instruction. One of the first shots in the early battle for civil service reform was Dorman Eaton's book on the civil service in Britain; and later Woodrow Wilson saw in the British system "perfected party government."[10] In Britain, the reformers explained, responsible, disciplined, centralized, programmatic parties compete for public favor. In Parliament the party programs are formed into legislation which is then handed to an efficient, unbiased, politically neutral civil service for execution. The link between the political and the administrative pyramids is provided by the Cabinet and, above all, the Prime Minister: leader of the House of Commons, chief of his political party, and head of the administration. . . .

[9] Woodrow Wilson, "The Study of Administration," *Political Science Quarterly,* LVI (December 1941), 494.

[10] Woodrow Wilson, *Congressional Government* (New York: Meridian Books, 1956), p. 91.

III

One manifestation of the basic problem of government by political parties is the fact that politicians who run for office in their capacity as leaders of organized parts, or parties, of the body politic are expected to assume a responsibility for the government of the whole. This formulation is obviously incomplete. American political parties themselves undertake to form particular individuals, groups, interests, and opinions into some kind of whole. This is not the place to discuss this broad responsibility or the various means by which American parties discharge it. It may be observed, however, that one means is the appointment of men who are not distinctively party men to fill even high political positions, to say nothing of the appointment of members of the opposite party. . . . Yet in spite of this and other qualifications, the fact remains that in a very important sense our system of government gives to a part the responsibility for governing the whole.

It is notorious that party politicians tend to learn moderation and responsibility when in office; but it is perhaps less generally recognized that one of their main teachers is the civil service. The common contrast between the politician, as the "practical man" experienced in "real life" and in touch with the wants and needs of the people, and the bureaucrat, as the remote, paper-shuffling office boy, is grossly overdrawn. In the first place, many civil servants have, in their particular fields, a kind of direct contact with the people and experience of the problems of government which even the politician whose ear never leaves the ground cannot possibly match. Moreover, modern government is to a large extent conducted by "shuffling papers," and it is of vital importance that they be shuffled well. Finally, a large part of the proposals for new policies and legislation come up through the civil service. Not only do civil servants exercise discretion in interpreting and applying the commands of their political superiors; they participate intimately in the formulation of those commands. They make proposals of their own and fight for them; they comment on the proposals of their political superiors—and may fight against them. They make a vital contribution to the process of deciding what is to be done. Government would come to a standstill if our "closet statesmen" in the civil service suddenly started doing only what they were told.

In the United States, of course, due partly to the constitutional system of checks and balances, the civil servant does not and perhaps cannot be expected to confine his statesmanship to the closet. Indeed, one of the peculiarities of American public administration is the fact that the civil servant may have more political knowledge and skill, even in the rather narrow sense, than his "political" superior. And he is almost certain to have, at least at first, more familiarity with the politics involved in actually running the government. A new Secretary or Assistant Secretary will normally find himself heavily dependent upon his experienced civil servants to facilitate not only the internal management of the agency but also its relations with Congress, interested organizations, other agencies of government, and even the White House itself. Compared with his counterpart in England, the American political executive has, generally speaking, to steer through political waters that are more cloudy and turbulent and to do it with less training and experience. Little wonder that he has to place extensive trust in the political judgment of experienced pilots in the civil service.

It is true that much of the contribution of the civil service to the art of government, even in the United States, is of a restraining and even negative kind. The civil servant, especially at the higher levels, has seen many programs tried, and many failures; even the successful innovations have usually fallen short of their makers' hopes. His experience has caused him to be sensitive to difficulties; he is an expert in seeking out unanticipated consequences. Even after a new policy has been decided upon, the civil servant is likely to explain, perhaps at exasperating length, why it cannot possibly be carried out the way his political chief wants. The civil servant is full of procedures, rules, and regulations, and he will (if he is performing properly) instruct his chief in the reasons for them. Orderly administration is not the most important quality of good government and it may sometimes have to be sacrificed to higher ends, but it is, generally speaking, indispensable. The cautious prudence and orderliness which tend to characterize the civil service are precisely that part of practical wisdom in which the party politician is likely to be deficient. The political leader in the United States is at least as much in need of the "prudent counsel and efficient aid" of "able and judicious men" as was the English statesman of the nineteenth century addressed by Sir Henry Taylor;[11] and he will find many of them in the civil service.

[11] *The Statesman* (New York: Mentor Books, 1958), p. 108.

The special kind of practical wisdom that characterizes the civil servant points to a more fundamental political function of the bureaucracy, namely to bring to bear on public policy its distinctive view of the common good or its way of looking at questions about the common good. The preoccupation of the civil service with rules and regulations, for example, is not aimed merely at orderly administration, important as that is. The rules and regulations, and the principle that there should *be* rules and regulations, represent a certain principle of justice, if only the principle of treating equals equally. Similar considerations apply to the civil servant's predilection for the way things have been done in the past. Generally speaking, to follow precedents is orderly, reasonable, and fair. One of the basic principles of American government is that governmental action should ordinarily be taken on the basis of established rules, however irritating that may sometimes be to a politician with a substantive program to put through. Like judges, civil servants have a special responsibility to preserve the rule of law.

Civil servants also bear a similarity to judges in their possession of what is, for most practical purposes, permanent tenure in office. Of course, like judges, they are influenced by the election returns— and it would be dangerous if they were not; but they have a degree of insulation from shifting political breezes. The rhythm of their official lives and thoughts is not governed so strictly as is that of the political executive by periodic elections. Their position enables them to mitigate the partisanship of party politics, and it gives them some protection from the powerful temptation, to which the party politician is always subject, to serve the people's inclinations rather than their interests.

Clement Attlee described the higher civil servant in Britain as having, in addition to long personal experience, "that mysterious tradition of the office wherein is somehow embalmed the wisdom of past generations."[12] The civil service in the Unites States is of course far less time-encrusted, but here too the higher civil servant will ordinarily have long experience in government, nearly always longer than his political chiefs. Moreover the duties of the civil servant and the way he works—his concern for written records, for example— tend to make him conscious of the "long-termness" of political decisions to a degree that is unusual for transient party politicians. At

[12]In Robson (ed.), *The Civil Service in Britain and France*, p. 17.

its best, the civil service is a kind of democratic approximation to an hereditary aristocracy whose members are conscious of representing an institution of government which extends into the past and into the future beyond the life of any individual member. In our mobile democracy, the civil service is one of the few institutions we have for bringing the accumulated wisdom of the past to bear upon political decisions.

Perhaps the most important political contribution that a civil service can make is, of all those we have considered, the one the American civil service makes least. Neither the bureaucracy nor political parties merely "represents" or reflects the American polity; they also help to shape and guide that polity, and they perform this function by what they are as well as by what they do. The character of a country's public servants is one of the determinants of the character of its people. When George Washington sought honest, honorable, and loyal gentlemen to fill the public offices of the new country, he was concerned not only with getting the work of government done but also with distributing the patronage of government in such a way as to set the public stamp of approval on certain human qualities. When Andrew Jackson established the system of rotation in public office, he had the same broad objective in mind, but he sought to elevate the common man in the place of the gentleman. And what the civil service reformers feared most about the spoils system was the effect on the political character of the people of the example set by the kind of men which the spoils system tended to elevate. "Politics cannot be made a mere trade," George Curtis argued, "without dangerously relaxing the moral character of the country."[13] In the words of Dorman Eaton,

> It is in the struggles for office, and the opportunities for gain in the exercise of official power, that selfishness, deception, and partisan zeal have their everlasting contest with virtue, patriotism, and duty. It is in that contest that statesmen and demagogues, patriots and intriguers, the good citizen and the venal office seeker, all the high and all the low influences of political life, meet face to face, and by the balance of power, for good or for evil, give character to politics and determine the morality of nations.[14]

---

[13]"The Reform of the Civil Service," in *Orations and Addresses*, II, 43.
[14]*Civil Service in Great Britain*, pp. 423–24.

Except for the removal of corruption, however, the reformers gave little thought to the kind of character and morality which their neutral, merely technical civil service would exemplify. One indication of the result is the fact that American civil servants themselves, though they may be thoroughly devoted to serving the common good, ordinarily prefer to identify themselves by their profession or occupation or "job" rather than by their public service. It is thought more respectable to be an agricultural economist or a personnel specialist than to be a civil servant. Not the least of the merits of the Hoover Commission proposal for a senior civil service is the influence such a corps of public servants might have on American life and character by restoring to a place of honor and respect the title of "civil servant."

The civil service is, then, in possession of certain institutional qualities which give it a title to share with elected officials in rule. It has a distinctive competence in the art of government and a unique knowledge of the problems of government, without which stable and intelligent government under modern conditions would be literally impossible. It has, moreover, a distinctive view of the common good which can guide and supplement the view likely to be taken by elected party politicians. On the foundation of its procedures, its rules, its institutional memory and foresight, its traditions, its skepticism of political panaceas, and its protection from the whims of popularity, the civil service stands for the continuity and wholeness of American government.

IV

It is not to be denied that bureaucracy suffers characteristic limitations and defects. Neither the party politician nor the bureaucrat has an unqualified claim to rule; neither is unqualifiedly competent or entitled to act on behalf of the whole people. Under ordinary circumstances the actual conduct of American government is in the charge of a partnership between them. We have emphasized the contributions of the bureaucratic part of this partnership, because they are less generally understood. But as the civil servant teaches, so also he is taught by the party politician. The civil servant is likely, for example, to overdo his concern with procedures and rules. He may be blind to the fact that procedural justice can do substantive injustice. It may be necessary for his political chief to show him that procedures have become so complex as to defeat their purpose or that the original reason for a rule has disappeared. While the civil servant may take a longer view of the common good, his view may also be distorted by a preoccupation with one program or a rather narrow range of programs. The broader range of responsibilities of the political chief may provide a corrective.[15] Moreover, although the civil servant bears the immediate responsibility for government because he does (or is closer to) the actual governing, he does not bear the final responsibility. He may instruct his political chief, he may advise him, guide him, even manage him—but he does not have the last word. This means that he may be overruled, for good reasons or bad; but it also means that his way of thinking and acting is molded in part by the fact of his formal subordination. Even at his best he is not a political captain but a faithful, wise, and influential counsellor and servant.[16]

This is connected with a final limitation of bureaucracy. Although a good civil service is one of the guardians of the traditional political wisdom of a regime, "sometimes it is necessary," as Attlee says, "to react violently against the tradition which was formed for a different state of society."[17] . . . The very tradition which it is the responsibility of the bureaucrat to carry forward may require fundamental redefinition, and that is a task for which his duties, train-

[15]As one civil service bureau chief explained, "The assistant secretary and I deal with the same people and do many of the same sorts of things, but the task of the assistant secretary is to keep me from losing touch with the mass of the people, from becoming too ingrown. The political executive provides that sensitivity to the public pulse. He and I approach our similar jobs from different angles. If we can learn to talk each other's language, we make a good team." Marver H. Bernstein, *The Job of the Federal Executive* (Washington: The Brookings Institution, 1958), p. 49.

[16]"I remember that I went to my new secretary and said: 'I think a man coming into your job should have his own men around him. I am a career employee, but if you should decide to have your own man in this job, I hope you will first give me a trial because I think I can help you. But if you decide to have your own man, there will be no difficulty about it. All you need to do is tell me. If you want to try me first, I will attempt to give you all the facts bearing on your particular problem, and I will give them to you as accurately and impartially as I can. You will have to have faith in me until you learn to know me better. If you want me to make a recommendation, I will do so. If we get to the point where I cannot live with your decisions, I will get out. I will fight you outside the government, but I won't do so in the government. I won't make any end runs on you. Now, you don't know me from Adam, and you never heard of me before in all likelihood. You don't know whether I am going to live up to that statement or not. You will have to take it on faith.' The secretary really needed me, but he didn't know it yet. As it turned out, we got along very well." *Ibid.*, p. 191.

[17]In Robson (ed.), *The Civil Service in Britain and France*, p. 17.

ing, and experience disqualify him. During such times of crisis, "administration" does become radically subordinate to "politics"; the institution of the civil service does become to a much greater extent than usual an instrument of the man who is President. The peak of the spoils system is generally regarded as having come during Lincoln's first administration, and Lincoln removed the incumbents of almost all offices under his immediate control. He used the spoils of office to help bind together the Republican Party, the North, and thereby the Union. So much was this the paramount aim that, according to one historian, Lincoln "made no attempt to obtain the men best fitted to perform the functions of the various offices, except in case of the very highest; for minor places he did not even insist that a man be fit."[18] The Civil War is an extreme example, but it is not the only one. The transformation which the civil service underwent at the hands of Franklin Roosevelt is well known. Roosevelt gave a new meaning to the civil service and to the Democratic Party in the course of giving a new meaning to American political life as a whole. During such critical times, the question of bureaucracy as such is almost entirely subordinated to the more fundamental question of political reconstruction. It is not unfair to say of the bureaucracy (and perhaps of political parties too) that it contributes least to government in the most important cases, provided it is remembered that a government requires a capacity for everyday competence, prudence, and public-spiritedness, as well as a capacity for greatness.

---

[18]Carl Russell Fish, *The Civil Service and the Patronage* (Cambridge: Harvard University Press, 1920), p. 170.

11

The Irony of American Bureaucracy

MICHAEL NELSON

The history of American national bureaucracy, if not untold, certainly is unsung. Political scientists seem to have assumed that for most purposes the federal bureaucracy became a subject worth studying only with the coming of the New Deal, and then only in its contemporary form.[1] Historian Morton Keller notes that his profession has not done much better.[2] Nor have American sociologists, who,

From Michael Nelson, "A Short, Ironic History of American National Bureaucracy," *The Journal of Politics* 44 (August 1982). Reprinted by permission. Footnotes are renumbered.

Author's note: I would like to thank Thomas Tillman of Johns Hopkins University for assistance in the research for this article. My thanks also go to Cullen Murphy (*The Wilson Quarterly*) and Charles Peters (*The Washington Monthly*) for their encouragement; to Elizabeth McKee and Mildred Tyler for their help in preparing the manuscript; to Robert M. Kaus (*American Lawyer*), David Kling and Francis Rourke (both of Johns Hopkins); William Morrow (College of William and Mary); Kenneth Betsalel, Robert Birkby, George Graham, Erwin Hargrove, William Havard, Avery Leiserson, and Jack Matlock (all of Vanderbilt University); and two anonymous referees for their helpful criticisms. An earlier version of this paper was presented at the 1981 Annual Meeting of the American Political Science Association, Washington, D.C.

[1]Herbert Kaufman, "Fear of Bureaucracy: A Raging Pandemic," *Public Administration Review*, XLI (January/February 1981), 1. For two important exceptions, see Woodrow Wilson, "The Study of Administration," *Political Science Quarterly*, II (June 1887), 197–222; and Frank Goodnow, *Politics and Administration: A Study in Government* (New York: Macmillan, 1900).

[2]Morton A. Keller, *Affairs of State: Public Life in Late Nineteenth Century America* (Cambridge: Harvard University Press, 1977), 318. For an excellent review of the extensive literature on British bureaucratic development, see Roy M. MacLeod, "Statesmen Undisguised," *American Historical Review*, LXXVIII (December 1973), 1386–1405.

unlike European colleagues as early as Mosca, Michels, and Weber, have left their own country's bureaucratic development largely unexplored.[3] . . .

Recently, however, the argument has been made that, for American bureaucracy, the present really is the sum of the past. Stephen Skowronek contends that one must return to the 1877–1920 period to find the "systemic changes in long-established political and institutional arrangements which first had to be negotiated in order to begin to accommodate an expansion of national administrative capacities in American government."[4] Matthew Crenson goes further, suggesting that the roots of modern bureaucracy are to be found in the Jackson administration, "when . . . bureaucratic forms of organization were superimposed upon the business of the national government."[5] Leonard White's tetralogy on pre-twentieth-century national administration takes us all the way to 1789: "Washington, Hamilton, Jefferson, . . . and many others dealt with most of the administrative problems that presidents and department heads face today" and developed an approach "to public management that is untouched by time and valid even on the scale of modern administration."[6]

In a chronological sense, at least, White is closest to the mark.[7] Although American national bureaucracy did not spring full-grown from the head of the First Continental Congress in 1775, its fundamental nature and structure began to develop then and substantially were formed well before the New Deal. Further, at almost every critical turn in American bureaucratic history, the efforts of public officials and organized political groups to enhance popular

[3]A notable exception is Sidney H. Aronson, *Status and Kinship Ties in the Higher Civil Service: Standards of Selection in the Administrations of John Adams, Thomas Jefferson, and Andrew Jackson* (Cambridge: Harvard University Press, 1964).

[4]Stephen Skowronek, *Building a New American State: The Expansion of National Administrative Capacities, 1877–1920* (New York: Cambridge University Press, 1982), x.

[5]Matthew A. Crenson, *The Federal Machine: Beginnings of Bureaucracy in Jacksonian America* (Baltimore: Johns Hopkins University Press, 1975), ix.

[6]Leonard D. White, *The Federalists* (New York: Macmillan, 1948), vii, viii. The other three volumes of his "Study in Administrative History" series, all published by Macmillan, are *The Jeffersonians* (1951); *The Jacksonians* (1954); and *The Republican Era* (1958).

[7]White's notion of "modern administration" seems concerned more with executive leadership of administration by the president and department heads than with bureaucracy as a form of organization or a force in society. Weber, for example, is nowhere cited.

control of government inadvertently planted the seeds of modern bureaucratic power. This is grand irony in the sense that Reinhold Niebuhr uses the word: an "apparently fortuitous incongruit[y]" between what one intends and what one actually achieves that is not fortuitous at all, but rather is caused by a "hidden relationship" that experience reveals.[8]

Seven particular ironies of pre-1933 American bureaucratic history—ironies of "Revolution," of "Jacksonian Democracy," of "Reform," and of "Representation"—form the heart of this essay. The concluding section offers some notes toward a theory of the "hidden relationship" that underlies the grand irony of American bureaucracy.

Ironies of Revolution: 1775–1828

The country was conceived as much in anger as in liberty, with much of that anger directed at perceived abuses by the British administration.[9] As James Q. Wilson has observed, even a cursory review of the particulars of the revolutionaries' indictment of British colonial rule, for "the weakening of the independence of the judiciary, the stationing of standing armies, and the extensive use of royal patronage to reward office-seekers at colonial expense," reveals that "almost all of their complaints involved the abuse of *administrative* powers."[10] "He [King George] has erected a multitude of new offices," charged the Declaration of Independence, "and sent hither swarms of officers to harass our people and eat out their subsistence."

The colonies' distasteful experience with British executive power caused many Americans to reject all executive forms as potentially tyrannical. Thus, though the sole task of the provisional government established by the First Continental Congress in 1775 was an executive one—to raise, support, and direct an army of revolution—it was made purely legislative in structure. Not only did Congress omit a chief executive, it followed the recommendation of what Francis

[8]Reinhold Niebuhr, *The Irony of History* (New York: Charles Scribner's Sons, 1952), viii.

[9]Lawrence Henry Gibson, *The Triumphant Empire: British Sails Into the Storm 1770–1776* (New York: Alfred A. Knopf, 1965); A. F. Pollard, *Factors in American History* (New York: Macmillan, 1925).

[10]James Q. Wilson, "The Rise of the Bureaucratic State," in *The American Commonwealth*, eds. Nathan Glazer and Irving Kristol (New York: Basic Books, 1976), 101.

Wharton called the "liberative-expulsive" school, led by Sam Adams, and determined that there would be no departments to serve as adjuncts of Congress.[11] Congress instead created committees from its members to make administrative decisions, however minor, by itself. John Adams, who originally had supported his cousin's proposal for legislative government, found himself working eighteen-hour days just to keep up with the business of the ninety committees on which he served. In one typical case, Congress formed a three-member committee "to prepare a plan for intercepting two [enemy supply] vessels" that were en route to America.[12]

This form of decisionmaking doubtless comforted British sea captains, but it exasperated almost everyone else. "Inefficiency and waste, if not downright peculation and corruption" were the rule, writes Charles Thach; General George Washington complained that ". . . there is a vital and inherent Principle of Delay incompatible with military service in transacting business thro' such numerous and different channels."[13] After much debate, Congress first created boards, embryonic departments made up of congressmen, such as the Board of War and Ordnance; later, it added outside officials to the boards; and finally, in 1781 it established separate departments of Foreign Affairs, War, Marine, and Finance (later Treasury).[14] They were headed by single executives, elected by and accountable to Congress, but otherwise in full control of their jurisdictions, at least until war's end.[15] One historian argues that Robert Morris, the country's first Superintendent of Finance, "wielded more power in the United States than any man had yet done."[16]

In creating the departments, following a pattern which would become typical, Congress inaugurated the First Irony of American bureaucratic history, by which *the revolt against the old adminis-*

[11]Francis Wharton, *The Revolutionary Diplomatic Correspondence of the United States* (1889), I, 252. For a fuller discussion of the creation of the departments, see Lloyd M. Short, *The Development of National Administrative Organization in the United States* (Baltimore: Johns Hopkins University Press, 1923), ch. 2; and Jennings B. Sanders, *Evolution of Executive Departments of the Continental Congress* (Chapel Hill: University of North Carolina Press, 1935).

[12]John T. Morse, *John Adams* (Boston: Houghton Mifflin, 1898), 142; Charles C. Thach, Jr., *The Creation of the Presidency, 1775–1789* (Baltimore: Johns Hopkins University Press, 1923), 59.

[13]Thach, *Creation*, 62, 63.

[14]*Ibid.*, 67.

[15]Short, *Development*.

[16]Merrill Jensen, *The New Nation: A History of the United States During the Confederation, 1781–1789* (New York: Vintage, 1950), 56.

trative order planted the seeds of a new administrative order. The political goal of securing American independence from British administrative power led Congress to give to the new country administrative institutions of its own. This was done "without very much conscious attempt to pattern after foreign systems";[17] indeed, writes Lloyd Short, "the adoption of a system of single-headed executive departments was a step distinctly in advance of formal English [administrative] development."[18]

To be sure, this first irony was an irony of necessity. State administration of some sort is virtually inherent to societies more complex than the agricultural village.[19] Certainly, too, the executive departments were, as had been hoped, vastly more efficient than the boards and committees that had preceded them.[20] Their examples, as well as George Washington's model of "energy, probity, disinterestedness, and a magnificent tactfulness" in his career as the country's chief military executive, and the bitter experiences of those states that continued through the mid-1780s to experiment with almost purely legislative government, helped to allay popular doubts about executive powers.[21] But they did not end those doubts; memories of the royal governors and their agents were too fresh.

Inevitably, the Constitutional Convention of 1787 took this popular ambivalence into account. The framers' purpose, after all, was to write a plan of government that was sellable as well as workable. They had no desire to wave red flags at the still-powerful champions of legislative supremacy. That there would be departments headed by single officials appointed by the president with the advice and consent of the Senate was desired by the framers and allowed by precedent. But the convention debates were almost silent on the issue of who would control the government's administrative apparatus. Not surprisingly, the Constitution produced by those debates is equally unhelpful.

It never has been clear to whom the administrative agencies

[17]H. B. Learned, *The President's Cabinet* (New Haven: Yale University Press, 1912), 55.
[18]Short, *Development*, 75.
[19]Morton H. Fried, *The Evolution of Political Society* (New York: Random House, 1967), chs. 5–6.
[20]Louis Fisher, *President and Congress: Power and Policy* (New York: Free Press, 1972), ch. 1.
[21]Thach, *Creation*, 65. Washington's role is assessed in Seymour Martin Lipset, *The First New Nation: The United States in Historical and Comparative Perspective* (New York: Basic Books, 1963), ch. 1.

are to be constitutionally accountable. Presidential scholars have made much of *Federalist* No. 72, which refers to civil servants as "assistants or deputies of the chief magistrate, . . . subject to his superintendence," and of the First Congress's decision in 1789, when it re-created the State, War, and Treasury departments, to vest the president with the power to remove administrative officials unilaterally. They argue that the presence in that Congress of so many of the framers indicates that the Convention's real, though unstated, intent was to place government agencies under presidential control.[22] . . .

Through the committee system, Congress used its clear constitutional powers, such as investigation, to dominate administration, and claimed near-monopolistic control over the statute-writing and appropriations powers shared with the president. Even the president's specific constitutional authority was undercut by Congress in this period. Jefferson found that only 600 of the federal government's 2,700 civilian positions were his alone to fill—Congress had entrusted the Postmaster-General with more appointees than the president. Given the number of applications per job, applications that sometimes were sent in anticipation of the incumbent office holder's death, each appointment he made *"me donne un ingrat, et cent enemis."*[23] The best jobs, department heads, United States attorneys, territorial governors, and ambassadors, required Senate confirmation, which meant realistically that most diplomatic and secretarial appointments went to congressmen or ex-congressmen, and the others usually were awarded to their friends. Once, after Monroe expressed reservations about some of Crawford's nominations for customs officers, the secretary raised his cane and called him a "damned infernal old scoundrel," causing Monroe to grab the fireplace tongs in self-defense and order him out, the last time the two men met.[24] When Monroe invoked his constitutional power to "require the opinion, in writing" of his department heads and asked a cabinet meeting not to send departmental messages to Capitol Hill before clearing them with him, he was greeted with general silence, then told by a secretary that the practice had existed "ever since the

[22]See, for example, Thach, *Creation*, ch. 6.
[23]James S. Young, *The Washington Community 1800–1828* (New York: Columbia University Press, 1966); White, *Jeffersonians*, 366.
[24]John Quincy Adams, *Memoirs*, ed. Charles F. Adams (Philadelphia: J. B. Lippincott, 1874–75), VII, 81.

establishment of Government" and presumably would continue.[25] Secretary of War Calhoun, for one, continued to urge internal improvements legislation that Monroe opposed.

Yet Henry Clay, whose "American System" would explicitly have strengthened national administration under congressional control, ultimately was as unsuccessful as Hamilton, who would have done so under the direction of the president. Agencies, forced to live with the ambiguities of control from both elected branches, set about developing power resources of their own. The "secretarial salons" were born—lavish entertainments (in an entertainment-starved city) at which the host cabinet member would woo congressmen with good wine, attractive if decorous women, and fine music. In all this, there was a Second Irony: *the system of dual control of administration became one of limited control.* The Constitutional Convention, in loosing the agencies from their old legislative moorings (politically necessary if the support of executive power adherents was to be won) without tying them securely to the presidency (equally politic if antifederalist support was to be kept)[26] forced agencies to find and exercise relatively independent power. Agencies began to learn to play one branch off against the other; if neither president nor Congress was supreme, then law was, and the agencies interpreted and implemented the law.

The status of administration as a locus of political power in national government was, of course, still nascent in the early nineteenth century. Though the government of this period was responsive to the limited demands placed upon it—as Skowronek notes, it ". . . maintained an integrated legal order on a continental scale; it fought wars, expropriated Indians, secured new territories, carried on relations with other states, and aided economic development"[27]— the "runaway bureaucracy" of pre-Jacksonian America was small and its functions were modest, essentially to collect customs and excise taxes and to deliver the mail. (The Post Office was created in 1792.) A Navy Department was added to War in 1793, the last new department until well into the nineteenth century, but national defense was entrusted primarily to the state militia. The tiny regular army

[25]*Ibid.*, IV, 217–18.

[26]John P. Roche, "The Founding Fathers: A Reform Caucus in Action," *American Political Science Review*, LV (December 1961), 799–816; Michael Nelson, "Holding Bureaucracy Accountable: The Search for a Model," in *Accountability in the American Policy Process*, ed. George J. Graham (forthcoming).

[27]Skowronek, *Building*, 19.

consisted of the corps of engineers and a few frontier patrols. Congressmen outnumbered civil servants in Washington until the 1820s; the Attorney-General (there was no Justice Department) was a private lawyer for whom the government was one client. The president had no staff at all; Washington was known to call department heads in for dictation, which made them secretaries in both senses of the word.[28]

Equally important, administrative agencies at this time were not organized bureaucratically. Crenson observes that in:

> . . . the semiaristocratic society of pre-Jackson days, the federal establishment was fashioned to the tastes of men who were born to rule. Management was a mystery, not reducible to rational and explicit techniques, a fitting vocation for men who were supposed to carry the knack for governance in their blood and breeding. The operation of federal offices during this period tended to be idiosyncratic, reflecting the personal tastes and intuitions of highborn administrative chieftains.[29]

In other words, congressional or presidential interference aside, the idea was that agencies were to be run in the same way as the law firms, small businesses, plantations, and military units that agency chieftains came from. The standard rule of management was that the boss should direct the show as he saw fit: choose his subordinates for their personal loyalty and "fitness of character," tell them what to do, and keep an eye out to see that it was done.[30] As Jeffersonian America was a country of shopkeepers, so was its government a collection of shops. But, due inadvertently to the efforts of political leaders to forge a new government, they were distinct shops and on the way to becoming independent ones.

Ironies of Jacksonian Democracy: 1829–1860

The mass political movement that raised Andrew Jackson to the presidency was fueled by popular resentment of the emerging administrative independence, specifically of the social privilege associated

[28]*Ibid.*, 23; Young, *Washington*, 31; Short, *Development*, 184–95; White, *Federalists*, 497.
[29]Crenson, *Federal*, 5.
[30]*Ibid.*, Introduction, ch. 3.

with agency staffing and the corruption that were by-products of this independence. Both of these ills spurred remedial action by the Jackson administration to enhance political branch control of the departments. Yet both sets of remedies planted seeds of irony that later would contribute to the rise of bureaucratic power in America.

Privilege

Toward the end of his volume on *The Jeffersonians,* White accurately describes the civil service of the pre-Jackson period as "a solid and unchanged official substructure" whose members ". . . tended to come from an identifiable section of the population; they were not infrequently succeeded by their sons, . . . and they grew old in office."[31] Certainly, this had been no one's intention. The United States, in fact, was the envy of Great Britain because it had an opportunity to staff its administration on the basis of competence rather than peerage and tenure.[32] Washington clearly regarded good appointments as a fundamental task of his presidency. "Perfectly convinced I am," he wrote Samuel Vaughan just before leaving Mt. Vernon to be sworn into office, "that, if injudicious or unpopular measures should be taken by the Executive under the New Government with regards to appointments, the Government itself would be in the utmost danger of being utterly subverted." His "primary object" was to appoint men imbued with "fitness of character."[33]

"Of course," writes Kaufman, Washington's "standards of fitness, his measures of ability and criteria of competence, were not precisely what ours are today."[34] "Expertise" counted for little (not a single appointee to the State Department, for example, other than Secretary Jefferson, had any training or experience in foreign affairs); standing in "the gentry" counted for much.[35] Adams continued and defended this policy: "The proposition that [the people] are the best keepers of their liberties is not true. They are the worst keepers; they are no keepers at all. They can neither act, judge, think,

---

[31]White, *Jeffersonians,* 548, 555–56.
[32]Skowronek, *Building,* 31.
[33]Franklin P. Kilpatrick, *et al., The Image of the Federal Executive* (Washington: Brookings Institution, 1964), 28; George Washington, *The Writings of George Washington,* ed. John Fitzpatrick (Washington: Government Printing Office, 1931), XXX, 469.
[34]Herbert Kaufman, "The Growth of the Federal Personnel System," in *The Federal Government Service: Its Character, Prestige, and Problems,* ed. Wallace S. Sayre (New York: American Assembly, 1954), 22.
[35]White, *Federalists,* 128; Kaufman, "Growth," 22.

or will."[36] Even President Jefferson and his Republican successors tended to equate fitness of character with fitness of family; if 70 percent of Adams's higher civil service appointments had been to men whose fathers had high-status occupations and 92 percent to men who held such occupations themselves, the comparable figures for the Jefferson administration were 60 percent and 93 percent, respectively. Though of a different party, "the basic outlook, predispositions, habits, and ways of life of men in the [Republican] public service were unchanged," concludes White.[37]

Kinship as well as class helped to assure the elite character of the early civil service. No fewer than sixteen members of the Livingston/Clinton family held positions in the federal government of 1804. Forty percent of Adams's high-level appointees were relatives of other high-level appointees in his or Washington's administration, and though Jefferson made a point of selecting Republicans, so were 34 percent of his, including 22 percent who shared common kinship with earlier Federalist appointees. Some subsecretarial American civil servants, like their British counterparts, asserted not only a property right to their offices, but a right of inheritance as well.[38] Henry Dearborn, William Ellery, Abraham Bishop, and John Page were among those succeeded in office by their sons, a practice so widespread that John C. Calhoun wrote President Monroe to note its cause and warn of its effects: "It is certainly painful to do an act, which may leave the family of the late collector in want, yet the tendency to hereditary principle from this very cause in the inferior offices of our country merits great consideration. What is humanity now, may in the course of one or two generations ripen into a claim on the government."[39] Decades of administrative stalemate between president and Congress meant that few appointees ever were removed.

None of these sources of administrative privilege—the narrow definition of character rooted in an electorate that was property based until the 1820s, the sympathetic attitude toward patrician office

---

[36]Quoted in Aronson, *Status*, 5.

[37]Crenson, *Federal*, 13; White, *Jeffersonians*, 548.

[38]Carl Russell Fish, *The Civil Service and the Patronage* (New York: Longmans, Green, 1905), 87; Aronson, *Status*, 141–42; David H. Rosenbloom, *Federal Service and the Constitution: The Development of the Public Employee Relationship* (Ithaca, N.Y.: Cornell University Press, 1971), chs. 1–2.

[39]Quoted in White, *Jeffersonians*, 357.

holders and their orphaned sons, or the inter-branch stalemate over appointments and removals (such that almost a third of the cabinet members serving [in] the Jeffersonian era were holdovers from previous administrations)—were very persuasive to the socially, geographically, and economically diverse voters of 1828.[40] If the answer of disgruntled and newly enfranchised western farmers, eastern workers, and rising entrepreneurs of both regions was Jackson's election, Jackson's own answer was equally blunt. In his first annual message to Congress, the president attacked the "corruption," "perversion," and "indifference" of an administrative system in which ". . . office is considered a species of property, and government . . . a means of promoting individual interests," then made his fabled argument that, "The duties of all public officers are, or at least admit of being made, so plain and simple that men of intelligence may readily qualify themselves for their performance; and I cannot but believe that much more is lost by the long continuance of men in office than is generally to be gained by their experience."[41]

Rotation in office was the elevated description of this philosophy, one which Jeremy Bentham told Jackson that he subscribed to as well.[42] "To the victor belong the spoils of the enemy" was Democratic Senator William Marcy's blunt corollary.[43] In eight years, Jackson removed 252 "presidential officers," more than his six predecessors combined had in forty years, even though the pool of offices so designated had dropped from 824 in 1816 to 610 in 1829.[44] Although no more than 20 percent of the total civil service were fired during the Jackson years, almost half of those firings took place in the first 18 months, thus setting the tone for the administration.[45] Many more resigned in anticipation of removal, and spoils were the

---

[40]Young, *Washington*, 242; Kaufman, "Growth," 24–27.

[41]Quoted in Rosenbloom, *Federal*, 49. As Aronson points out (*Status*, 243), there is a striking similarity between the last sentence of Jackson as quoted above, and the following one by Lenin: "The majority of functions of the old 'state power' have become so simplified and can be reduced to such simple operations of registration, filing, and checking that they will be quite within the reach of every literate person."

[42]Arthur M. Schlesinger, Jr., *The Age of Jackson* (Boston: Little, Brown, 1946), 46.

[43]William Safire, *Safire's Political Dictionary* (New York: Random House, 1978), 679.

[44]Rosenbloom, *Federal*, 65.

[45]Erik M. Eriksson, "The Federal Civil Service under President Jackson," *Mississippi Valley Historical Review*, XIII (March 1927), 528–29.

formula for filling new posts created while Jackson was president.[46]
More important, concludes Skowronek, ". . . while some managed
to escape rotation, the new organization men now defined the character of . . . administration."[47]

What was that new character of administration? The conventional wisdom, familiar to every schoolchild, is that rotation represented the ultimate politicization of administration, the opposite of
modern technocratic bureaucracy. Nothing could be less accurate;
indeed, it is the Third Irony of American bureaucratic history that
spoils bred bureaucracy: Jackson's patronage system helped to hasten
the reorganization of federal administrative agencies along bureaucratic lines.

One source of this ironic bureaucratization was the changing
nature of party politics. As historian Lynn Marshall points out, Jackson's Democrats were the world's first mass-based political party.
Their "whole structure was firmly cemented by the award of federal
offices," especially local postmasterships.[48] But government jobs,
though less technical then than now, still were not so simple that any
backwoods party stalwart could perform them at a moment's notice.
Thus, the Democrats' dilemma: satisfaction of the party faithful
seemed to require the appointment of incompetent officials whose
poor performance eventually might bring on a popular backlash fa-
tal to the party. After all, more voters send mail than deliver it.

Jackson's remedy lay in the key phrase of his message to Congress: federal jobs "admit of being made" so simple that any intelligent person could do them. "The Jacksonians proposed to organize
the executive department as a rationalized complex of offices," writes
Marshall, "ordered by function, and defined by rules and regulations." Labor was to be divided, tasks defined, jobs simplified. "In
this system, individuals could be placed or replaced [after an elec-
tion] without upsetting the integrity of the whole. . . . It was the
administrative counterpart of the interchangeability of machine

---

[46]Similarly, President James K. Polk filled nearly 10,000 postmasterships va-
cated by resignation. Thus, he had to remove only 1,600 in order to effect an almost
85 percent turnover during his four-year term. White, *Jacksonians*, 312.

[47]Skowronek, *Building*, 32.

[48]Lynn Marshall, "The Strange Stillbirth of the Whig Party," *American Historical Review*, LXXII (January 1967), 450.

parts."⁴⁹ Consequently, it also was an impetus, however inadvertent, to bureaucratic organization in American government.⁵⁰

Corruption

The second source of the bureaucratization of administration that took place under Andrew Jackson also was the second of his supporters' expressly governmental concerns: rampant corruption in the executive agencies. Westward expansion in the 1820s and the new temptations it had spawned for land and currency speculation had subverted occupational morality in almost every sector of society, including government.⁵¹ The extension of agency branch officers, particularly those of the Post Office and the Treasury Department's General Land Office, into new and distant states and territories made administrators' efforts to supervise field agents precatory at best.

Jackson tried at first to infuse the existing "personal organization" mode of administration with new life. Its unity-of-command principle fit nicely with his military background and, for that matter, with the experience of his department heads running civilian enterprises.⁵² But for the agency chief to run a clean shop required that one of two conditions pertain: either he and his employees all were able and honest men who could be left on their own, or, if the chief alone was honest, his employees were few enough in number and compact enough in location so that he could monitor their actions personally. Neither of these conditions existed any longer in the rapidly and raucously expanding United States of the mid-nineteenth century. Jackson learned this the hard way, as, for example, when his customs collector in New York City, Samuel Swartwout, sailed off to Europe with $1.25 million in his satchel—a sum equal to more than five percent of the federal budget!—leaving "swartwouting" to the national vocabulary as a synonym for embezzlement. (Joshua

⁴⁹*Ibid.*, 455–56.
⁵⁰This is the view of Marshall, *ibid.*, 468. The more traditional theory is that government is best conceived of as society's "brain," whose development follows rather than precedes the social organism's own developing complexity. See Emile Durkheim, *Professional Ethics and Civil Morals* (Glencoe: Free Press, 1958). With regard to business, see Alfred D. Chandler, "The United States," in *Managerial Hierarchies*, ed. Chandler and Herman Daems (Cambridge: Harvard University Press, 1980), 35–39.
⁵¹Crenson, *Federal*, ch. 2.
⁵²Albert Somit, "Andrew Jackson as an Administrative Reformer," *Tennessee Historical Quarterly*, XIII (September 1954), 204–23.

Phillips, a customs house employee, had known of Swartwout's activities, but being a good personal organization man, told a House committee that "I was Mr. Swartwout's clerk, and would not betray the secrets of my employer.") When Amos Kendall, Jackson's political adviser and Postmaster-General, sent memorandums to branch office employees about "sauntering about the streets . . . in office hours" and the like, they were filed and forgotten.[53]

Kendall was the first to see what had to be done to restrain official thievery. He reorganized the Post Office into an elaborate system of administrative checks and balances among newly organized offices of Accounts, Appointment, Contract, and Inspection, each watchful of the others. Lower-level jobs were redefined strictly to remove temptation; no longer would those who handed out mail contracts, for example, be the ones to oversee their fulfillment, an arrangement that had been an invitation to shady dealing. Carefully kept records of every official action were required of employees, and auditors were hired to pore over them. In the new system, the locals spoke only to the auditors, and the auditors spoke only to Kendall. In contrast to the personal organization mode that had preceded it, Crenson concludes in his study of *The Federal Machine*, that Kendall's "administrative organization did not embody the personalities of its members; it counteracted them." His innovations spread to the other departments.[54]

The decision to shape federal offices for the purpose of preventing corruption did not come without cost. Form follows function in bureaucracy; agencies designed to prevent internal fraud look and act differently from those designed to promote efficiency, coordination, responsiveness, or some other value. All those internal checks and balances took time. For example, when the House Ways and Means Committee convened in 1836 to investigate complaints about the Treasury Department's excruciating slowness in releasing funds, it found that in order to prevent embezzlement five internal clearances had to be made prior to any departmental financial transaction[55]—hence, the Fourth Irony: *agencies organized to avoid evil become that much less able to do good.* The popular political demand for honest bureaucracy restricted the possibility for efficient

[53]Crenson, *Federal*, 80–84.
[54]*Ibid.*, 136–39.
[55]*Ibid.*

and responsive bureaucracy that could satisfactorily meet other, later popular political demands. . . .

An Irony of Reform: 1861–1932

The lessons of the Fourth Irony were not immediately apparent. Indeed, mid-nineteenth-century advocates of a merit-selected civil service sold their proposal with the argument that honest administration and efficient, politically responsive administration were one and the same. Their case, according to Herbert Kaufman, rested on a view of "policy and administration as distinct and separate, though related, activities, and they wanted to restrict partisanship to the policy-makers in order to provide a superlative mechanism by which the voters' mandates could be carried out. They perfected the instrument; let the people put it to what use they would."[56] In short, reformers seemed to feel, a bureaucracy devoid of political appointees would be like a royal guard of eunuchs—an agency with no distracting wants of its own to impede the execution of its assigned tasks. Or, in Kaufman's more subdued analogy, ". . . the civil service was like a hammer or a saw; it would do nothing at all by itself, but it would serve any purpose, wise or unwise, good or bad, to which any user put it."

Admittedly, spoils had become an easy target in the years after Jackson. Rapid turnover made continuity in government difficult to maintain. As the House Committee on Retrenchment noted in 1842, ". . . it very often happens that individuals are brought from a distance, perfect strangers to the duties and details of their offices, installed in bureaus or clerkships with which they never become familiar until in their turn they have to give place to others equally ignorant with themselves." Also, despite the success of the new bureaucratic checks and balances at reducing internal peculation, there was wide corruption at the hiring stage. The "Wanted-Situations" columns of Washington newspapers sometimes carried advertisements like this one from the *Star:* "$100 Cash and 10 per cent of

[56]Kaufman, "Growth," 36. Ari Hoogenboom, among others, suggests that civil service reformers were a displaced patrician New England elite whose motive was to regain power from the professional politicians. "An Analysis of Civil Service Reformers," *The Historian*, XXIII (November 1960), 54–78. Be that as it may, their cause was sold to—and presumably bought by—the voters in democratic terms.

salary for one year, will be given for a Position in any of the Departments." And some political leaders were known to featherbed agencies in order to free employees' time for party labors. Gideon G. Westcott's half-year paid "leave of absence" from his position as an appraiser in the Philadelphia customhouse to serve on Pennsylvania's Democratic Central Committee during the 1856 election campaign was not wholly atypical.[57]

But these reasonable criticisms barely broached the reformers' indictment of spoils. One civil service advocate wailed that:

> Some young women in despair, losing hope at the loss of their jobs, went wrong on the town. . . . Oh! the pity of it . . . [T]he amiable madam's [sic] of the oldest trade in the world hospitally [sic] extended a welcome to these unfortunate recruits, and the folks back home unknowingly continued to enjoy the wages of an erring daughter whom of course they still thought a Government employee.[58]

More serious was the argument that blood was on the hands of the spoilsmen. Meritless employees, reformers argued, had so prolonged the Civil War by their incompetence that thousands of soldiers had died needlessly.

In hindsight, the case for spoils is a powerful one. By democratizing the public service, it helped to legitimate the national government among the new classes of Jacksonian America and assimilate those that emerged later. "There was value," as White puts it, "in the sense of union between common folk on the one hand and their public officers on the other."[59] The actual proportion of swindlers probably was not much higher than it had been before spoils, however conspicuous the exceptions. For very sound electoral reasons, "neither party welcomed scoundrels or irresponsibles in public office"; President John Tyler, for example, reported as he left office that during the preceding four years only two cases of embezzlement had been found.[60] As for the Civil War, spoils had no greater triumph. Without patronage to bargain with, Abraham Lincoln—

---

[57]White, *Jacksonians*, 328, 339. U.S. Civil Service Commission, *Biography of an Ideal: A History of the Federal Civil Service* (Washington: Government Printing Office, 1975), 20.

[58]Quoted in Kaufman, "Growth," 32.

[59]White, *Jacksonians*, 344.

[60]*Ibid.*, 344, 430.

no president ever used spoils more extensively than he—would have been hard-pressed to keep sullen northern congressmen on board through the military setbacks of 1861 and 1862. And had federal agencies been staffed by tenure-protected employees before secession, the government might have had to prosecute the war half-full of southern sympathizers, a house divided in the most literal sense.[61]

But whatever its retrospective value, spoils' fate was sealed during the administration of James Garfield. Garfield let it be known that he had little liking for the distribution of patronage. Shortly after he entered the White House he complained to James G. Blaine: "All these years I have been dealing with ideas, and here I am . . . considering all day whether A or B should be appointed to this or that office."[62] It was, however, the deceased Garfield, assassinated in 1881 by Charles Guiteau, the campaign worker since immortalized as a "disappointed office seeker," who did the cause of civil service reform the most good. Shortly after the assassination, it was revealed that in one of his many letters to Garfield, Guiteau had written: "The men that did the business last fall are the ones to be remembered." The shock value of this remark, then and now, is evidenced by this dark, decades-later assessment in the Civil Service Commission's official history: "No more revealing description of the spoils system had ever been penned."[63] The Pendleton Act passed soon after, in 1883, giving birth to the modern civil service.

In the half-century that followed, a Fifth Irony emerged: *reformers' efforts to make the civil service more responsive to the political branches made it less responsive.* This was true in part because, as Richard Schott states, the new civil service's "emphasis on merit in hiring promoted the development of a professional, specialized bureaucracy whose expertise [could] not be matched either by president or Congress. Its emphasis on tenure and permanence in office built into this bureaucracy an insensitivity toward and protection from direct overhead political control."[64] . . .

[61]Lincoln replaced 1,457 of 1,639 presidential officers. Kilpatrick, *Image*, 33.
[62]Quoted in Keller, *Affairs*, 298.
[63]Civil Service Commission, *Biography*, 39. The official history of the Civil Service Commission also attributes the death of President William Henry Harrison to the spoils system, in the form of job-seekers who insisted on visiting the President while he was attempting to recover from pneumonia.
[64]Lawrence C. Dodd and Richard L. Schott, *Congress and the Administrative State* (New York: John Wiley & Sons, 1979), 25.

Ironies of Representation: 1861–1932

Though the size of the federal government grew through the early and middle decades of the nineteenth century, its functions really did not. The only new department created in this period was Interior in 1849, and it consisted almost entirely of already-existing agencies such as the Patent Office and the Office of Indian Affairs that were grouped together because their previous departmental custodians "had grown tired of them."[65] Of the almost eight-fold increase in federal employment between 1816 and 1861, 86 percent were in the Post Office, which simply had a larger country to serve.[66]

The next seventy years were different. New agencies proliferated, seemingly without pattern. By 1887, Woodrow Wilson reasonably could compare American administration to a "lusty child" that "has expanded in nature and grown great in stature, but has also become awkward in movement. The vigor and increase of its life has been altogether out of proportion to its skill in living."[67] The President's Committee on Administrative Management, the oft-cited Brownlow Commission, concluded a half-century later that bureaucracy in this period grew like a farm: a wing added to the house now, a barn put up later, a shed built at some other time, a silo at one stage, a corn crib at another, until it was spread over the landscape in a haphazard and thoroughly confusing way.

But as with most farms, there was an underlying order to bureaucracy's apparent chaos. The United States had been changing rapidly, from a rural society, individualist in its values yet rather homogeneous in composition, to one that was urban, industrial, and highly diverse. The rise of a national market economy produced new demands on government for "clientele" agencies that would represent and support society's increasingly distinct economic groups. It also generated a second set of demands for regulation, in part to protect weak, albeit large, groups from more powerful ones.

None of this came easily, not in a political system invested with all the qualities of Newton's First Law of Motion. American government at rest tends to stay at rest; except in unusual times, its inertial resistance is overcome only when a powerful group is able to press the kind of claim on government that other powerful groups do not

---

[65]Dodd and Schott, *Congress*, 20.
[66]J. Wilson, "Rise," 81–82.
[67]W. Wilson, "Study," 203.

strenuously oppose. Such was the birth of the federal government's first important clientele agency, the Agriculture Department, in 1862.[68] Farmers had organized a lobby, the United States Agricultural Society, to press for the creation of a department that would represent their interests in the administrative realm. Powerful congressmen, mindful of the farm vote, and President Lincoln and former presidents back to Millard Fillmore were enrolled as honorary members. The specific proposal the Society advanced seemed modest—a new department that merely would sponsor agricultural research and collect useful data. Who could object?

The story of what happened will sound familiar to observers of modern bureaucracy, but it doubtless astonished the political Newtonians of the day. For, once in motion, the new Department of Agriculture not only stayed in motion but accelerated, snowballing in size and eventually in function. By 1901 it had added divisions of Forestry, Animal Husbandry, Entomology, Pomology, Ornithology and Mammalogy, and Plant Industry, as well as the Weather Bureau and an Office of Experiment Stations. The politics of this process were as follows: the new department was staffed, for obvious and entirely innocent reasons, by friends of agriculture. The legislative committees with jurisdiction over the department attracted sympathetic congressmen from farm districts, eager to advance their constituents' and thus the department's interests. The agriculture lobby grew in influence; its new power in Washington made it more powerful with the folks back home; the latter's support made it even more influential in Washington, and so on. Keller notes that during this period, "an agricultural establishment consisting of the department, land grant colleges, and agricultural experiment stations took form."[69]

Other groups followed agriculture's lead and demanded agencies of their own.[70] In 1869, education interests obtained the establishment by Congress of a Bureau of Education, the forerunner of the Office of Education and later the Department of Education, in the Interior Department. The Knights of Labor and other unions persuaded Congress to begin a Bureau of Labor in Interior in 1884, and, as union power grew, a full-fledged Labor department in 1913.

---

[68]This discussion of the Agriculture Department is based largely on J. Wilson, "Rise," and Keller, *Affairs*, ch. 8.

[69]Keller, *Affairs*, 314.

[70]Theodore Lowi, *The End of Liberalism* (New York: W.W. Norton, 1969).

Samuel Gompers, president of the American Federation of Labor, may have been embarrassingly blunt when he hailed the new department as "Labor's Voice in the Cabinet," but the department's legal definition of purpose was not much different: to "foster, promote, and develop the welfare of wage earners of the United States, to improve their working conditions, and to advance their opportunities for profitable employment." . . .

The largest clientele agency of the period, however, was the Bureau of Pensions, precursor to the modern Veterans Administration. Originally created in 1833, its clients as the nineteenth century wore on were civil war veterans and the Grand Army of the Republic, the largest of the interest groups that represented them. As the GAR grew in size from 60,678 to 427,981 and, correspondingly, in political influence, Congress responded by loosening the terms of eligibility for veterans' benefits. The original idea had been to give pensions to those who had been injured on the battlefield. "The Pension Act of 1890," observes Keller, "made almost every northern Civil war veteran and his dependents eligible." In 1891, the Pension Office spent 34 percent of the federal budget.[71]

A century ago, the creation of client agencies must have seemed like democracy at its best—worthy groups in society demanding, government responding—but once again things turned out less than happily. The Sixth Irony of American bureaucratic history, in fact, is that *client agencies, created to enhance political representation in government, often became almost independent from general political branch control.* "Subgovernments" consisting of constituencies, agencies, and committees grew secure from the direction of either distracted presidents or apathetic majorities of congressmen, whose districts directed their attention to the advancement of other interests, perhaps through subgovernments of their own.[72]

The other set of demands born of the rise of a national industrial economy was for the restriction of economic power; it resulted in the creation of the first independent regulatory agencies. Railroads, which not only were the fastest growing enterprise in the new interregional commerce but its very foundation, also were the first

---

[71]Keller, *Affairs*, 311–12.

[72]The term is Douglass Cater's. *Power in Washington* (New York: Random House, 1964). But the concept is J. Leiper Freeman's. See *The Political Process: Executive Bureau-Legislative Committee Relations* (New York: Doubleday, 1955).

objects of federal regulation. The politics of the Interstate Commerce Act of 1887 and of the Interstate Commerce Commission it established set the pattern for the regulatory explosion that followed.

The railroad system that emerged in the post–Civil War period operated on two planes. The five great trunk lines, the Grand Trunk, New York Central, Erie, Pennsylvania, and Baltimore and Ohio, competed on longhaul runs, but they and their affiliates each enjoyed monopoly control within some region or state. The railroads' correspondingly two-pronged economic strategy, first, was to charge high rates at the local level to make up for the lower rates competition occasionally forced them to charge on the longhaul runs; and, second, to try to keep longhaul rates high by means of cartel-style "pooling," that is, by informally agreeing among themselves not to compete on the basis of price.

Both these practices enraged the Grange-represented dirt farmers, western merchants, Pennsylvania independent oil producers and refiners, New York businessmen, and others who shipped their products by rail.[73] Each group's protests have been singled out by one scholar or another as the reason Congress eventually passed regulatory legislation. In truth, writes Edward Purcell, ". . . It was neither 'the people,' nor 'the farmers,' nor even 'the businessmen' who were responsible for the government's regulation of the railroads. Rather it was many diverse economic groups in combination throughout the nation who felt threatened by the new national economy and sought to protect their interests through the federal government."[74]

To mute these mass protests, Congress created the ICC and charged it to block pooling and to regulate rates. Then, in the familiar manner of "majoritarian politics," the triumphant small shippers, rendered "quiescent" by their legislative victory in Murray Edelman's phrase, happily abandoned political affairs and went on

---

[73]Solon Buck, *The Granger Movement: A Study of Agricultural Organization and Its Political, Economic and Social Manifestations, 1870–1880* (Lincoln: University of Nebraska Press, 1913); George Miller, *Railroads and the Granger Laws* (Madison: University of Wisconsin Press, 1971); Gerald D. Nash, "Origins of the Interstate Commerce Act of 1887," *Pennsylvania History*, XXIV (1957); Lee Benson, *Merchants, Farmers and Railroads: Railroad Regulation and New York Politics* (Cambridge: Harvard University Press, 1955).

[74]Edward Purcell, Jr., "Ideas and Interests: Business and the Interstate Commerce Act," *Journal of American History* (December 1967), 578.

about their business.[75] Who was left to provide the new commission with the political support it needed to survive? Who was to influence its staffing and monitor its activities? Who, aided by a sympathetic Supreme Court, was to dominate its legalistic rate-setting proceedings? The railroad lobby that had "lost" the war found the peace that followed to be its for the asking. By the time of its second annual report, the Commission already was saying—the Commerce Act and the new Sherman Anti-Trust Act notwithstanding—that pooling was permissible in its eyes. The annual report for 1898 went even further, asking Congress to recognize the railroad industry as a natural monopoly.[76] In 1920, Congress succumbed; the Transportation Act passed that year authorized the ICC to approve such proposals for railroad pooling as it deemed desirable. As for rates, the Commission now was authorized to set minimum as well as maximum limits.

Thus, the Seventh, and familiar, Irony is *regulatory agencies created in response to popular political movements often became, in effect, client agencies of the regulated.* The Food and Drug Administration, established (under a different name) in 1906 to protect customers from unsafe "medicines," soon became highly lenient in approving new drug applications from pharmaceutical companies. The other major regulatory creation of this period, the Federal Trade Commission (1914), became "noted for its hit-and-miss attacks on many relatively small firms involved in deceptive advertising or unfair trade practices while it continued to overlook much of the really significant activity it [was] ostensibly established to regulate: monopoly, interlocking directorates, and so on."[77]

Grand Irony, Unintended Consequences, and the "Hidden Relationship"

Sorting out the relative importance of historical influences on contemporary bureaucracy from newer ones is no easy task. . . .

Yet, in at least one area of surpassing modern concern, the past seems to speak convincingly. "Unintended consequences" are the bane

[75]Wilson, "Rise," 96–97; Murray Edelman, "Symbols and Political Quiescence," *American Political Science Review*, LIV (September 1960), 695–704.
[76]Skowronek, *Building*, 159.
[77]Edelman, "Symbols," 72. But cf. Robert A. Katzman, *Regulatory Bureaucracy: The Federal Trade Commission and Antitrust Policy* (Cambridge: MIT Press, 1980).

of the modern policy process: programs are established by law with certain purposes in mind; their actual effects, however, are not (or are not only) those that were intended. Welfare programs that subvert family life, school integration plans that lead to greater segregation, technologically advanced weapons systems that reduce national security are among the familiar examples. The prevalence of unintended consequences concerns not just policy theorists but democratic theorists as well. After all, even a strong connection between the electorate and its representatives is inconsequential if the demands made by the former and enacted into law by the latter still are not satisfied.

Most efforts to account for these breakdowns in the policy process come in two parts: first, the self-interest of implementing agencies, which adds goals of organizational preservation and growth to those provided by the program statute: and second, the lack of care and specificity characteristic of many such statutes themselves. But the questions again are why? Why is the organizational self-interest of bureaucratic agencies such a powerful force in the American policy process? Why are American legislators and political executives so inattentive to program design?

It is possible that history offers the answers to these questions. If nothing else, history shows that unintended consequences are nothing new; the evolution of American bureaucracy has been marked by one ironic failure after another, the "grand irony" of which is that repeated efforts to bring government under political branch control have enhanced the power of bureaucracy. In particular, I would argue that clues to the nature of the "hidden relationship" discussed in the introduction to this essay that causes this irony are to be found in historical *sequence*, the order in which things happened in the country's political development.

The importance of historical sequence becomes apparent through comparison. In Western Europe, a monarchical past meant that the democratization of national political systems occurred long after their bureaucratization. Because the legitimate presence and power of bureaucratic organizations were given by the time democracy came along, the primary democratic task was to control and direct their activities to popular ends. One of the reasons that European political parties developed as programmatic, disciplined organizations was to provide the kind of clear, sustained external direction that bureaucratic agencies need if their organizational goals are to be overcome. The strict internal hierarchy of these agencies, a carry-over from pre-democratic days, facilitated this effort: to appoint or control the agency heads was a giant step toward controlling the agency.

In the United States, however, the establishment of democratic political institutions *preceded* the establishment of administrative ones. The latter, which were resisted strenuously in the Continental Congress and scarcely mentioned in the Constitution, have remained somewhat illegitimate in American political culture ever since.[78] From the start, this has forced bureaucratic agencies to build independent political bases to provide sustenance to their pursuit of organizational goals, an endeavor encouraged by the constitutional system of divided political control. "The development of political skills," writes Rourke, "was part of the process by which executive agencies adapted to their environment in order to survive in the egalitarian democratic society in which they found themselves."[79]

The order of American political development (democracy before bureaucracy) also affected the country's political parties (which, in turn, affected the later development of national bureaucracy which, in turn, affected the parties, and so on). Early American parties, quite understandably, had little of the European concern for curbing and directing bureaucratic power. To them, administrative agencies were sources of bounty (pork and patronage), not loci of power in need of control; indeed, Jackson's Democrats fostered the process of bureaucratization in order to reap the harvest of spoils such organizational changes allowed. In part, because bureaucracy was looked at this way, parties also had no incentive to develop as programmatic organizations. This meant, for example, that unlike Great Britain where civil service reform followed the establishment of central party leadership and really did turn British bureaucracy into a "hammer and saw" for the elected government, the American civil service took shape with no vision at all from the parties as to what policy purposes it should serve. This made it a good deal easier for it to foster purposes of its own.

In recent years, as the size and complexity of governmental tasks have increased, the technical expertise to handle them has become

---

[78]Nelson, "Holding Bureaucracy Accountable"; "Power to the People: The Crusade for Direct Democracy," *Saturday Review* (November 24, 1979), 12–17.

[79]Francis E. Rourke, *Bureaucracy, Politics, and Public Policy,* 2nd ed. (Boston: Little, Brown, 1976), 73.

an added source of power for bureaucratic agencies. The challenge to party control thus has become more formidable even if a) the party organizations were strong, and b) the will was there. Actually, neither of these conditions obtain. Parties are unprecedentedly weak, in no small measure because bureaucracy now distributes the jobs and welfare that once were the parties' main appeals to their members. Legislators, interested as never before in Congress as a vocation, pay less attention to the politically unrewarding task of writing clear, careful legislation and more to its symbolic and distributive aspects.[80] Presidents, observes Erwin Hargrove, also neglect program implementation because their desire for re-election and a place in history leads them to emphasize the "dramatic achievement" of "dramatic goals."[81] Without clear policy direction from the parties or their elected officials, organizational self-interest has been able to thrive. And so have unintended consequences. . . .

[80]Morris P. Fiorina, *Congress: Keystone of the Washington Establishment* (New Haven: Yale University Press, 1977).

[81]Erwin C. Hargrove, *The Missing Link: The Study of the Implementation of Social Policy* (Washington: Urban Institute, 1975), 111. This may be changing; see Michael Nelson, "The White House, Bureaucracy and Foreign Policy: Lessons from Cambodia," *The Virginia Quarterly Review*, LVI (Spring 1980), 193–215.

12

A Cabinet of Unequals

THOMAS E. CRONIN

Cabinet roles and influence with the White House differ mark-edly according to personalities, the department, and the times. Each cabinet usually has one or two members who become the dominant personalities. Herbert Hoover's performance as secretary of commerce under Harding was of this type. George Marshall's performance in both State and Defense under Truman was similar. George Humphrey of the Treasury and John Foster Dulles of State clearly towered over others in the Eisenhower cabinet. Robert McNamara enjoyed especially close ties with both Kennedy and Johnson. His reputation as manager of a large, complex organization and his performance in a similar capacity at Defense virtually mesmerized both presidents and most of the White House staff, few of whom had ever managed any organization except temporary campaign staffs. Both Kennedy and Johnson repeatedly pointed to McNamara and the Defense Department as models for other departments to imitate, conspicuously congratulating their Planning, Programming and Budgeting System (PPBS), cost reduction, and cost-effectiveness operations. McNamara's capacity to present his own case before the presidents seemingly made it unnecessary for White House aides to serve as intermediaries; for example, he personally carried his annual budgetary requests directly to the president, and the president granted the budget director the opportunity for selective appeals or disagreements. George Shultz's early influence with President Nixon substantially exceeded the power inherent in the Labor Department, leading to his reassignment, first as director of the Office of Management and Budget, then as secretary of the treasury.

Certain departments and their secretaries gained prominence in recent decades because every president has been deeply involved with their priorities and missions—Defense and State in the cold war as well as in the so-called détente years, for example. The Acheson-Dulles-Rusk-Kissinger-Vance tradition of close and cordial ties with their presidents were founded in an era of continuous international tension during which diplomatic and alliance strategy loomed large. Other departments may become important temporarily in the president's eyes, sometimes because of a prominent cabinet secretary who is working in an area in which the president wants to effect breakthroughs: for example, John Kennedy's Justice Department headed by his brother Robert. HEW sometimes was thought to be developing into a presidential department during the mid-1960s when under John W. Gardner it was growing rapidly in order to manage Johnson's major educational and health programs. The Department of Energy enjoyed special considerations in the early Carter years for similar reasons.

Much White House–cabinet estrangement undoubtedly arises because presidents simply lack the time to spend with all cabinet officers, let alone the leaders of independent agencies or major bureau chiefs. Most of a president's schedule is consumed with national-security and foreign-policy matters. One recent cabinet member complained: "In retrospect, all of the past three presidents have spent too much time on foreign affairs. They all felt that's where the action is and that's how they would be judged in the history books!"

Vast differences exist in the scope and importance of cabinet-level departments. The three million-person Defense Department and the sixteen-thousand-person or so departments of Labor or Housing and Urban Development are not similar. Certain agencies not of cabinet rank—the Central Intelligence Agency, the National Space and Aeronautics Administration, the Veterans Administration, and the Environmental Protection Agency—may be more important, at least for certain periods of time, than cabinet-level departments. Conventional rankings of the departments are based on their longevity, annual expenditures, and number of personnel. Rankings according to these indicators can be seen in the first three columns of Table 1(A). Even a casual comparison of these columns reveals unexpected characteristics. Thus, although the State Department is about 190 years older than some of the newer departments, its expenditures are the lowest of all. On the other hand, the Department of Human Services,

TABLE 1 *Ways of Looking at the Executive Departments*

A. By Rank-Order

Seniority	Expenditures (1980)	Personnel (1980)	Real Political Power and Impact (Alsop's assessment) (1968)
1. State	1. HHS	1. Defense	1. Defense
2. Treasury	2. Defense	2. HHS	2. State
3. War/Defense	3. Treasury	3. Treasury	3. Treasury
4. Interior	4. Labor	4. Agriculture	4. Justice
5. Justice	5. Agriculture	5. Transportation	5. Interior
6. Agriculture	6. Transportation	6. Justice	6. HEW
7. Commerce	7. Education	7. Interior	7. Labor
8. Labor	8. HUD	8. Commerce	8. Agriculture
9. HHS	9. Energy	9. State	9. Commerce
10. HUD	10. Interior	10. Labor	10. HUD
11. Transportation	11. Commerce	11. Energy	11. Transportation
12. Energy	12. Justice	12. Education	
13. Education	13. State	13. HUD	

B. By Organization

Inner and Outer Clusterings[a]	Nixon's 1971 Proposals	Carter Staff Suggestions 1979[b]	Supercabinet Plan A[c]
Inner:	State	State	National Security
State	Defense	Defense	Economic stability
Defense	Treasury	Treasury	and growth
Treasury	Justice	Justice	Domestic policy
Justice	Human resources	HEW	
Outer:	Natural resources	Energy	
Agriculture	Economic devel-	Transportation	
Interior	opment	Labor	
Transportation	Community	Natural Resources	
HHS	development	Development	
HUD		Assistance	
Labor		Food and Nutrition	
Commerce		Trade,	
Energy		Technology	
Education		and Industry	
		Education	

[a]Genetic clustering made according to counseling-advocacy department.

[b]A cabinet consolidation plan proposed by some of President Carter's re-organization staff in 1979.

[c]The way some White House aides view aggregate departmental concerns, and the apparent priority of these concerns as viewed by recent presidents.

Source: Expenditures from estimated budget outlays of the executive departments in 1980; personnel from *The Budget of the United States Government, Fiscal Year*

formerly the Department of Health, Education and Welfare, officially only about thirty years old, ranks first in expenditures and second only to Defense in personnel.

The contemporary cabinet can be differentiated also into inner and outer cabinets, as shown in Table 1(B). This classification, derived from extensive interviews, indicates how White House aides and cabinet officers view the departments and their access to the president. The inner cabinet includes the secretaries of state, defense, and treasury and the attorney general. The occupants of these cabinet positions generally have maintained a role as counselor to the president; the departments all include broad-ranging, multiple interests. The explicitly domestic-policy departments with the exception of justice, have made up the outer cabinet. By custom, if not by designation, these cabinet officers assume a relatively straightforward advocacy orientation that overshadows their counseling role.

The Inner Cabinet

A pattern in the past few administrations suggests strongly that the inner, or counseling, cabinet positions are vested with high-priority responsibilities that bring their occupants into close and collaborative relationships with presidents and their top staff. Certain White House staff counselors also have been included in the inner cabinet with increasing frequency. The secretary of defense was one of the most prominent cabinet officers during all recent administrations, for each president recognized the priority of national-security issues. Then, too, the defense budget and the DOD personnel, the latter ranging from 3 to 4 million (including the military), makes it impossible for a president to ignore a secretary of defense for very long. Despite the inclination of recent presidents to serve as "their own secretary of state," the top man at the Department of State has nevertheless had a direct and continuous relationship with contemporary presidents. Recent treasury secretaries—George Humphrey, Robert Anderson, Douglas Dillon, John Connally, George Shultz, William Simon—also have played impressive roles in presidential deliberations on financial, business, and economic policy. The position of

1980, pp. 524 and 529 respectively; Alsop's assessment from Stewart Alsop, *The Center* (Harper & Row, 1968), p. 254; Nixon's proposals from the State of the Union Message, January 22, 1971. Carter proposals from Carter press conferences and from Rochelle L. Stanfield, "The Best Laid Reorganization Plans Sometimes Go Astray," *National Journal,* 20 January 1979, pp. 84–91.

attorney general often, though not always, has been one of the most influential in the cabinet.

The inner cabinet, as classified here, corresponds to George Washington's original foursome and to most memoirs of the Eisenhower through Carter period. Note that these inner-cabinet departments alone were immune to President Nixon's proposed overhaul of the executive branch in 1971; all others were nominated for merger. The status accorded these cabinet roles is, of course, subject to ebb and flow, for the status is rooted in a cabinet officer's performance as well as in the crises and the fashions of the day.

A National-Security Cabinet

The seemingly endless series of recent international crises—Berlin, Cuba, the Congo, the Dominican Republic, Vietnam, the Middle East, and continuing strains with the USSR—have made it mandatory for recent presidents to maintain close relations with the two national-security cabinet heads. Just as George Washington met almost every day with his four cabinet members during the French crisis of 1793, so also all of our recent presidents have been likely to meet at least weekly and be in daily telephone communication with their inner cabinet of national-security advisers. One Johnson aide said it was his belief that President Johnson personally trusted only two members of his cabinet, Rusk and McNamara. Kennedy aides quote their president to the effect that his "regional assistant secretaries of state were more important officers of the government than most of the cabinet." Carter aides said Harold Brown and Cyrus Vance were probably President Carter's best appointments as well as two of his closest counselors.

Throughout recent administrations, more than a little disquiet has been engendered in the White House by the operational lethargy of the State Department. Although the secretary of state is customarily considered by the White House to be a member of the president's inner cabinet, the department itself was regarded as one of the most difficult to deal with. More than 25 percent of the White House staff interviewed cited the State Department to illustrate White House–department conflicts. They scorned the narrowness and timidity of the encrusted foreign service and complained of the custodial conservatism reflected in State Department working papers.

Some of State's problems may stem from the threats of the Joe

McCarthy era of the early 1950s, which intimidated State Department careerists into holding only the most puristic interpretations of the received policies of the day and inhibited imaginative and inventive policy. In State, more than in the other departments, the method and style of personnel, the special selection and promotion processes, and the protocol consciousness all seem farther removed from the political thinking at the White House. Although they often may be gifted and cultured, State's personnel invariably become stereotyped by White House aides as overly cautious and tradition bound.

Another source of the department's problems is the way in which recent secretaries, especially John Foster Dulles, Dean Rusk, and Henry Kissinger, have defined their job. The demands on Rusk personally were such that departmental management was hardly his major priority. John Leacacos has surmised that the priorities appeared to have been: "First, the President and his immediate desires; second, the top operations problems of the current crisis; third, public opinion as reflected in the press, radio and TV and in the vast inflow of letters from the public; fourth, Congressional opinion; fifth, Rusk's need to be aware, at least, of everything that was going on in the world; and only sixth and last, the routine of the State Department itself."[1] That the secretary of state so often serves as the president's representative abroad or before Congress is another reason so few secretaries have had the time or energy necessary for managing the department's widely scattered staff. Moreover, more than fifty federal departments, agencies, and committees are involved in some way in the administration or evaluation of United States foreign policy.

Legal and Economic Counsel

The Justice Department is often identified as a counseling department, and its chiefs usually are associated with the inner circle of presidential advisers. That Kennedy appointed his brother, Nixon appointed his trusted campaign manager and law partner, and Carter appointed a close personal friend to be attorneys general indicates the importance of this position, although extensive politicization of the department has a long history. The Justice Department tradi-

[1]John Leacacos, *Fires in the In-Basket* (World, 1968), p. 110.

tionally serves as the president's attorney and law office, a special obligation that brings about continuous and close professional relations between White House domestic-policy lawyers and Justice Department lawyers. The White House depends heavily and constantly on the department's lawyers for counsel on civil-rights developments, presidential veto procedures, tax prosecutions, antitrust controversies, routine presidential pardons, and the overseeing of regulatory agencies and for a continuous overview of the congressional judiciary committees. That these exchanges involve lawyers working with lawyers may explain in some measure why White House aides generally are more satisfied with transactions with Justice than with other departments. Attorney General Griffin Bell in the late 1970s was especially close to Jimmy Carter. White House aides said Bell "is powerful because he has immediate and frequent access to the President. He also has a lot of self-confidence; like many former judges he thinks pretty highly of his decisions."

The secretary of the treasury continues to be a critical presidential adviser on both domestic and international fiscal and monetary policy, but he also plays somewhat of an advocate's role as an interpreter of the nation's leading financial interests. At one time the Treasury Department included the Bureau of the Budget. With budget staff and numerous economists, particularly within the Council of Economic Advisers, now attached to the White House, however, Treasury has become a department with major institutional authority and responsibility for income and corporate tax administration, currency control, public borrowing, and counseling of the president on such questions as the price of gold and the balance of payments, the federal debt, and international trade, development, and monetary matters. In addition, Treasury's special clientele of major and central bankers has unusual influence. Although the Council of Economic Advisers and the Federal Reserve Board may enjoy greater prestige in certain economic deliberations, they are less effective as counterweights in international commerce and currency issues, in which Treasury participation is most important. The latter connection helps to draw the department's secretary into the inner circle of foreign-policy counselors to the president. Also, the treasury secretary is almost always a pivotal figure on key cabinet-level committees, such as the Cabinet Committee for Economic Growth, the Cabinet Commitee on Balance of Payments, the Cabinet Committee on Economic Policy, and the Cabinet Committee on Price Stability.

The importance of the treasury secretary as a presidential counselor derives in part from the intelligence and personality of the incumbent. Dillon and Connally, for example, were influential in great part because of their self-assuredness and personal magnetism. President Eisenhower found himself responding in a similar manner to George M. Humphrey: "In Cabinet meetings, I always wait for George Humphrey to speak. I sit back and listen to the others talk while he doesn't say anything. But I know that when he speaks, he will say just what I was thinking."[2] Leonard Silk has suggested, however: "Formally, the Treasury Secretary had a mystique and power potential fully comparable to those of the Chancellor of the Exchequer in Britain or the Minister of Finance in France. The mystique may not be all that mysterious to explain; it derives from money. Power over money, in the hands of the right man, can enable a Secretary of the Treasury to move into every definite action of government—in military and foreign affairs as well as in domestic economic and social affairs."[3]

President Carter's first treasury secretary, W. Michael Blumenthal, described his cabinet role this way:

> A department like the Treasury is a conglomeration of different activities, operating under set laws about hiring and firing and the seniority system and the Civil Service employment rights. So the top man coming in has very few tools with which to influence who's hired, who's fired, and who's moved where, except for the very top. So, even though I'm technically the chief executive of the Treasury, I have little real power, effective power, to influence how the thing functions.
>
> . . . As in any organization, you have to decide where to put your energies. You learn very quickly that you do not go down in history as a good or bad Secretary in terms of how well you run the place, whether you are a good administrator or not. You're perceived to be a good Secretary in terms of whether the policies for which you are responsible are adjudged successful or not: what happens to the economy, to the budget, to inflation, and to the dollar, how well you run debt financing and international economic relations, and what the

[2]Quoted in Richard H. Rovere, "Eisenhower: A Trial Balance," *The Reporter*, 21 April 1955, pp. 19–20.
[3]Leonard Silk, *Nixonomics* (Praeger, 1972), p. 81.

bankers and the financial community think of you. Those are the things that determine whether you are a successful Secretary.[4]

Inner Circles

The inner-circle cabinet members have been noticeably more interchangeable than those of the outer cabinet. Henry Stimson, for example, alternated from Taft's secretary of war to Hoover's secretary of state and then back once more to war under FDR. Dean Acheson was undersecretary of the treasury for FDR and later secretary of state for Truman. Dillon reversed this pattern by being an Eisenhower undersecretary of state and later a Kennedy secretary of the treasury. When Kennedy was trying to lure McNamara to his new cabinet, he offered him his choice between Defense and Treasury. Attorney General Nicholas Katzenbach left Justice to become an undersecretary of state; Eisenhower's attorney general William Rogers became Nixon's first secretary of state; and John Connally, once a secretary of the Navy under Kennedy, became Nixon's secretary of the treasury. Within a mere four and a half years, Elliot Richardson, sometimes called "our only professional cabinet member," moved from undersecretary of state to HEW secretary to defense secretary to attorney general. He became, his unexpectedly short tenure notwithstanding, the fourteenth head of the Justice Department to have served also in another inner-cabinet position. Cyrus Vance, who had served as deputy secretary of defense for LBJ, became Carter's secretary of state. Harold Brown, LBJ's secretary of the Air Force, became Carter's secretary of defense. Occasional shifts have occurred from inner to outer cabinet, but these have been exceptions to the general pattern.

This interchangeability may result from the broad-ranging interests of the inner-cabinet positions, from the counseling style and relationship that develop in the course of an inner-cabinet secretary's tenure, or from the already close personal friendship that has often existed with the president. It may be easier for inner-cabinet than for outer-cabinet secretaries to maintain the presidential perspective;

[4]W. Michael Blumenthal, "Candid Reflections of a Businessman in Washington," *Fortune*, 29 January 1978, p. 31. For the on-the-job views of an earlier Treasury Secretary see Lawrence C. Pierce, *The Politics of Fiscal Policy Formation* (Goodyear, 1971), p. 100.

presidents certainly try to choose men they know and respect for these intimate positions.

In recent years several members of the White House staff have performed cabinet-level counselor roles. Eisenhower, for example, explicitly designated Sherman Adams to be a member of his cabinet ex officio. Kennedy looked upon Theodore Sorensen, McGeorge Bundy, and some of his economic advisers as perhaps even more vital to his decision making than most of his cabinet members. Johnson and Nixon also assigned many of their staff to cabinet-type counseling responsibilities. Carter advisor Robert Strauss performed several cabinet-level responsibilities in the late 1970's, ranging from anti-inflation matters to diplomatic negotiations.

The people to whom presidents turn for overview presentations to congressmen and cabinet gatherings are another indicator of inner-counselor status. When Kennedy wanted to brief his cabinet on his major priorities, typically he would ask Secretary Rusk to review foreign affairs, chairman of the Council of Economic Advisers Walter Heller to review questions about the economy, and Sorensen to give a status report on the domestic legislative program. When Lyndon Johnson held special seminars for gatherings of congressmen and their staffs, he would invariably call upon the secretaries of state and defense to explain national-security matters and then ask his budget director and his chairman of the Council of Economic Advisers to comment upon economic, budgetary, and domestic program matters. Nixon and Ford usually called upon Henry Kissinger, the director of the Office of Management and Budget, and one of their chief White House domestic-policy counselors.

The Outer Cabinet

The outer-cabinet positions deal with strongly organized and more particularistic clientele, an involvement that helps to produce an advocate relationship to the White House. These departments—Health and Human Services, HUD, Labor, Commerce, Interior, Agriculture, Transportation, Energy, and Education—are the outer-cabinet departments. Because most of the president's controllable expenditures, with the exception of defense, lie in their jurisdictions, they take part in the most intensive and competitive exchanges with the White House and the Office of Management and Budget. These departments experience heavy and often conflicting pressures from clientele groups, from congressional interests, and from state and local governments, pressures that often run counter to presidential priorities. Whereas three of the four inner-cabinet departments preside over policies that usually, though often imprudently, are perceived to be largely nonpartisan or bipartisan—national security, foreign policy, and the economy—the domestic departments almost always are subject to intense crossfire between partisan and domestic interest groups.

White House aides and inner-cabinet members may be selected primarily on the basis of personal loyalty to the president; outer-cabinet members often are selected, as already mentioned, to achieve a better political, geographical, ethnic, or racial balance. In addition to owing loyalty to their president, these people must develop loyalties to the congressional committees that approved them or to those that finance their programs, to the laws and programs they administer, and to the clientele and career civil servants who serve as their most immediate jury. Johnson's HEW secretary Wilbur Cohen describes the cross-pressures vividly: "If you're the secretary of HEW, you're responsible really, in the end, to the Ways and Means Committee and the House Education and Labor Committee. And, boy, they can tell you in the White House, they can tell you in the Office of Management and Budget, and they can tell you everywhere, do this, that and the other thing. But if you come back next time to Capitol Hill, and you've violated what is their standard for their delivery system, you're not going to get what you're asking for."[5]

Advocacy Conflicts

White House aides generally view outer-cabinet executives as special pleaders for vested clientele interests over the priorities of the president. One of Franklin Roosevelt's commerce secretaries frankly acknowledged his representational and advocacy obligations when he explained: "If the Department of Commerce means anything, it means as I understand it the representation of business in the councils of the administration, at the Cabinet table, and so forth."[6] Few White House aides speak of the virtue of having a cabinet member reflect

[5]Wilbur Cohen, former secretary of HEW under Lyndon Johnson, quoted in *National Journal*, 16 December 1972, p. 1921.
[6]Jesse Jones, quoted in Richard Fenno, "President-Cabinet Relations and a Pattern and a Case Study," *American Political Science Review*, March 1958, p. 394.

his or her constituency and how this helps, or could help, educate a president. Most White House aides speak of the cabinet as a burden and an ordeal for presidents rather than as a chance to forge coalitions and exercise leadership. For example, as one Carter aide put it: "Nobody expects Ray Marshall at Labor to be a spokesman for anything other than big labor. You just have to live with this, although Marshall does seem to be making the best out of a bad situation." Advocacy usually, though not always, is viewed in negative terms.

Because presidents have less and less time to spend with the outer-cabinet members, the advocate role becomes less flexible and more narrowly defined. Unlike senior White House aides who enjoy greater access to the president, outer-cabinet members find they have little chance to discuss new policy ideas or administrative problems with the president. They must make the most of their limited meetings:

> One basic problem lies in the fact that domestic cabinet members are so rarely with the president that when they do have a chance to see him, they have to advocate and plug their departmental program in an almost emotional style, trying to make a plea for expanded appropriations or some new departmental proposal. But precisely at such times, the senior White House aide present can adopt or strike a pose as the more objective, rational statesman taking a non-advocate and more "presidential" position—all of which leaves the domestic cabinet members appearing like a salesman or lobbyist rather than part of the president's team. But the cabinet member seldom has a chance to make his points or his case. The White House aide knows, on the other hand, that he can see the president later that day or the next, and so can afford to play a more reasonable and restrained role in such meetings. Such role-casting clearly favors the staff man while placing the cabinet member in a most uneasy position.

The interpretation of the advocate role by both the outer-cabinet member and the president may vary. It is much easier to listen to an advocate whose point of view fits with the White House philosophy than to one who continually transmits substantively different arguments or who encroaches upon other policy arenas. As departments have grown and their administration has become more exhausting, fewer of the department heads have had time to be well versed on problems beyond their domain. And as the last three columns in Table 1(B) suggest, White House aides and, to a lesser extent, recent presidents have come to feel that in many ways today's cabinet remains organized around problems of the past far more appropriately than the problems challenging the nation's present or future.

Interior secretary Walter Hickel complained that the performance of the adversary role alienated him from the president. Noting that President Nixon "repeatedly referred to me as an 'adversary,' " he continued:

> Initially I considered that a compliment because, to me, an adversary within an organization is a valuable asset. It was only after the President had used the term many times and with a disapproving inflection that I realized he considered an adversary an enemy. I could not understand why he would consider me an enemy.
>
> As I sensed that the conversation was about to end, I asked, "Mr. President, do you want me to leave the Administration?"
>
> He jumped up from his chair, very hurried and agitated. He said, "That's one option we hadn't considered." He called in Ehrlichman and said: "John, I want you to handle this. Wally asked whether he should leave. That's one option we hadn't considered."[7]

Hickel's advocacy and style both differed from Nixon's and he was fired later that week. Such an occurrence is not inevitable, however: an outer-cabinet member's advocacy and adversary role can and sometimes does fit perfectly with an administration's substantive philosophy.

Outer-Cabinet Isolation

As tension builds around whether, or to what extent, domestic policy leadership rests with the departments or with the Office of Management and Budget or with the White House, and as staff and line distinctions become blurred, the estrangement between the domestic department heads and the White House staff deepens. White House aides believe they possess the more objective understanding of what the president wants to accomplish. At the same time the cabinet heads, day in and day out, must live with the responsibilities for

---

[7]Walter J. Hickel, *Who Owns America?* (Prentice-Hall, 1971), p. 259. In 1978 White House aide Midge Costanza resigned her job, doubtless under pressure to do so, in large part because she too had tried to play an adversarial role. As she noted in her letter of resignation: "My own approach has been largely one of advocacy. . . . There are those who suggest that I should have simply carried out your policies and not voiced my own opinions and ideas openly. But that was not my style. . . ." Margaret Midge Costanza, 31 July 1978, *Weekly Compilation of Presidential Documents*, 2 August 1978, p. 1359.

managing their programs, with the judgment of Congress and with the multiple claims of interest groups. Outer-cabinet members often complain bitterly about the unmanageability of their departments and the many pressures on them.

Interviews with the domestic cabinet members yield abundant evidence that most of them felt removed from the White House in the Kennedy, Johnson, and Nixon years. From a Kennedy-Johnson cabinet-level administrator:

> Recent presidents have let their White House political and personal aides go much too far in pressing administrators to do things they shouldn't. Too many of them are trying to make administrators squirm. There are too many aides at the White House who are just looking for a headline for the president. You have to guard against those types. There is just too much of it and presidents are guilty of letting it continue—they don't sufficiently realize that you have to have confidence in your department administrators. Perhaps it is due to the fact that they have never been administrators—they spent all their time in the Senate.

From Nixon's first secretary of the interior:

> There was an "isolation of thought" developing [in the Nixon presidency]. In early 1970, I was conscious of a deepening malaise inside the Administration—a sense of vague uneasiness. Others in the Cabinet shared my feelings that some of the White House staff were stepping up their efforts to filter contacts between the Cabinet and the President. It appeared that an effort was being made to centralize control of all executive branch activities of the government immediately within the White House, utilizing the various departments—represented by secretaries at the cabinet level—merely as clearing houses for White House policy, rather than as action agencies.
>
> Should a department—for example, Interior—develop policy for those activities under its control, submit those ideas to the White House for approval or disapproval, then follow through at the administrative level? Or, as some of the White House personnel seemed to want it, should a department wait only for marching orders to be issued by the Executive Mansion?[8]

The size of the bureaucracy, distrust, and a penchant for the convenience of secrecy led most recent presidents to rely more heavily on White House staffers. The White House and executive office

---

[8]Hickel, *op. cit.*, pp. 221–22.

aides increasingly became involved not only in gathering legislative ideas but also in getting those ideas translated into laws and those laws into programs. Program coordination and supervision, although often ill managed, also became primary White House interests. To an extent, these additional responsibilities transformed the White House into an administrative rather than a staff agency. Outercabinet departments, understandably, began to lose the capacity to sharpen up their programs, and the department heads felt uneasy about the lack of close working relations with the president.

One of the difficulties of this tendency to pull things into the White House and exclude departmental officials is that excellent ideas or proposals that may exist lower down in the bureaus of the permanent government seldom get the attention they deserve because, according to the departmentalists, nobody asks them. As social psychologists have suggested, one group tends to develop stereotyped perspectives that not only dehumanize the outsiders but also cut off the very communications channels that might provide valuable and even vital information.

In the early 1960s Kennedy and his staff tried to get the domestic departments to come up with proposals for innovative legislation. But, according to White House aides, they usually came up with "interest-group types of claims, very parochial, more-of-the-same types of proposals." Rather than try to strengthen departmental capacities to come up with broader, more innovative proposals, White House aides, impatient for action, instead developed a wide array of advisory committees, commissions, and secret task forces.

IV

Bureaucracy's Impact on United States Government

Not the least important consequence of the growth in the size and the power of the U.S. bureaucracy has been its impact on the three traditional policymaking institutions of U.S. government— the presidency, Congress, and the courts. Because they have been forced to interact with a burgeoning bureaucracy in recent decades, each of these institutions is different in fundamental ways from what it once was. If the bureaucracy has not itself become a fourth branch of government, as many once feared would be the case, it has very much affected the way in which the three already existing branches of U.S. government work.

The presidency, for example, has adapted to the rise of bureaucracy by transforming itself from an office in which power is essentially exercised by a single person to an institution in which a large number of White House aides play a role in executive decision-making. These presidential aides perform varied functions, such as advising the president on how to cope with difficult policy issues and assisting him in his efforts to stay on good terms with the electorate. But the president's staff has no more important job than monitoring and, when necessary, shaping the decisions and actions of the bureaucrats who do the everyday work of government.

Richard Nathan's "The Administrative Presidency" emphasizes the insecurity presidents have long felt in regard to their ability to control the bureaucracy. Both liberal and conservative presidents have feared that bureaucratic obstructionism would frustrate their efforts to achieve their own policy objectives. Like the judiciary before it, the bureaucracy today is often regarded as the dead hand of the past, preserving policies that the voters have repudiated in the most recent presidential election.

Richard Nixon stands out among all recent presidents in terms of the depth of his antipathy for the bureaucracy and his suspicion that it sought to undermine his administration. These views led him to adopt strategies of governance designed to minimize the role of bureaucracy and maximize the power of the White House staff—a course of action that was to account in no small part for his later difficulties in the Watergate affair. More recently, President Reagan has demonstrated that, by the effective use of his power of appointment, the chief executive can in fact ensure that the policies the bureaucracy carries out are—for better or for worse—in harmony with the goals of the White House.

Congress has been affected in much the same way as the presidency by the growth of the bureaucracy. It too has been forced to expand the size of its staff. As a result, the number of staff members serving the legislature has grown by leaps and bounds. Some of these aides work for individual members of Congress, others work for legislative committees, and a third group is employed by the legislative staff institutions that have been established or have been given new life in recent years: the Congressional Research Service, the Congressional Budget Office, the General Accounting Office, and the Office of Technology Assessment. Thus, the contagion effect of bureaucracy has been very visible; the task of dealing with an expanding number of bureaucratic organizations in the executive branch has forced both the White House and Capitol Hill to hire their own bureaucracies.

In the case of Congress, the rise of an executive bureaucracy has had one other interesting consequence: It has made members of the House more secure in their jobs. Morris Fiorina examines this phenomenon in his study "Congress and Bureaucracy: A Profitable Partnership." As he notes, the ability of members of Congress to provide assistance in the many encounters between their constituents and the bureaucracy enables legislators to build a very loyal political following that transcends party affiliation. Intervening with the bureaucracy is a surefire way to make friends in a congressional district, whereas supporting a controversial bill before the House is equally certain to make enemies. As a result, members of Congress have acquired a vested interest in the expansion of the bureaucracy and of the power it exercises. The more agencies there are and the more they do, the greater the opportunity for legislators to ensure their reelection to the House by doing favors for constituents who are having trouble with bureaucrats.

The judicial response to the rise of bureaucracy has been considerably more complex than that of either Congress or the presidency. In their initial dealings with the bureaucracy in the latter part of the nineteenth and the early part of the twentieth century, the courts tended to be very suspicious of this new policymaking institution which acted like a legislature and a court but seemed to lack the procedural safeguards that the Constitution had built into the U.S. political system.

Accordingly, the courts at first construed the powers of these agencies very narrowly and made it very difficult for administrators to accomplish the policy goals that the legislature had set for them. It was not until the New Deal revolutionized the role of government in the United States that the courts shifted their position. They began to accept the fact that bureaucrats knew more in the areas of their special competence than judges did, and that the courts would be wise to defer to the expertise of administrative officials when technical issues were in dispute.

More recently, however, the courts have once again begun to intervene extensively in bureaucratic decision-making. This is the development that David Rosenbloom traces in "The Judicial Response to the Bureaucratic State." Much of the renewed judicial interest in the decisions of administrative agencies has arisen out of a concern for the protection of individual rights, which—from the judicial perspective, at least—the exercise of bureaucratic power often seems to jeopardize. One group that the courts have tried especially hard to protect from the abuse of administrative power is labeled by Rosenbloom "captives of the administrative state." It includes the inmates of prisons, patients confined in mental hospitals, and people living in state facilities for the mentally retarded.

So the courts have been very much affected by the emergence

of administrative power and have responded to this development in different ways at different times. Their intervention in bureaucratic decision-making, like that of Congress and the presidency, has in many cases been prompted by the desire to maintain their own traditional institutional prerogatives. And like Congress and the presidency, the courts themselves have been to some degree bureaucratized by the increasing case loads that the arrival of the bureaucracy has generated. Judges preside over large staffs, they face a wide range of managerial problems, and they increasingly complain that they are no longer able to give sufficient time to the cases that come before them.

13

The Administrative Presidency

RICHARD P. NATHAN

. . . When he was president, John F. Kennedy reportedly once told a caller, "I agree with you, but I don't know if the government will." Whether Kennedy actually said this or not, the remark dramatizes an issue that has been less explored than other aspects of the presidency—the president's relationship to the bureaucracy. Harry Truman is reported to have complained, "I thought I was the president, but when it comes to these bureaucrats, I can't do a damn thing."[1]

Presidential scholar Clinton Rossiter speculated that many presidents would have considered this their hardest job, "not to persuade Congress to support a policy dear to his political heart, but to persuade the pertinent bureau or agency—even when headed by men of his own choosing—to follow his direction faithfully and transform the shadow of the policy into the substance of the program."[2]

Jimmy Carter's experience, perhaps more than others among recent presidents, illustrates the wisdom of Rossiter's remark. In a press conference . . . , Carter said, "Before I became president, I realized and was warned that dealing with the federal bureaucracy would be one of the worst problems I would have to face. *It has been worse than I had anticipated.*"[3]

[1]As quoted in Burt Schorr and Andy Pasztor, "Reaganites Make Sure That the Bureaucracy Toes the Line on Policy," *Wall Street Journal*, February 10, 1982, p. 1.

[2]Clinton Rossiter, *The American Presidency* (New York: New American Library, 1956), p. 42.

[3]As quoted by Haynes Johnson, "Test," *The Washington Post*, April 30, 1978, p. 3. Italics added.

The U.S. Constitution hedges on the role of the president as a manager. Article II, section 1 vests executive power in a president. Yet other provisions assign powers to Congress in ways that water down this assignment. Congress, for example, is empowered to create positions that can be "vested in the heads of department." It has used this power to assign statutory authority to specific officials at or below cabinet rank, instead of to the president. Other powers of the Congress—for instance, those to appropriate funds, conduct investigations, and override vetoes, and that of the Senate to confirm presidential appointees—have also over the years blurred the executive power assigned to the president in Article II.

In his classic study of the presidency, Edward S. Corwin referred to the words "executive power" in Article II as a "term of uncertain content."[4] Each president, he said, gives it his own expression. A president's relationship to the bureaucracy does not depend so much on the law, but on his own strategy, constituencies, and constitutional premises. Presidents have tried different strategies to exert their executive authority.

Three Core Values of American Public Administration

Political scientist Herbert Kaufman has identified three core values of American public administration that have been pursued at different periods of our history. The first, *representativeness*, dates from colonial times and reflects the mistrust of the king and royal governors that was expressed in the denunciation "taxation without representation." It resulted, particularly at the state level, in what Kaufman calls "the enthronement of the legislature."[5] The chief executive was viewed warily, both in his legislative and administrative role. The second period of American public administration for Kaufman is characterized by the value of *neutral competence*. It began in the mid-nineteenth century as a reaction to corruption in government, and is reflected in the civil service movement, which emphasized professionalism and merit. The third period of American public administration is characterized by what Kaufman calls *"the quest for executive leadership."* It began in the early twentieth century and

[4]Edward W. Corwin, *The President: Office and Powers* (New York: New York University Press, 1957), p. 3.
[5]Herbert Kaufman, "Emerging Conflicts in the Doctrines of Public Administration," *American Political Science Review*, vol. 50, no. 4, December 1956, p. 1059.

is reflected in the development of executive budget systems and the strengthening of the office of the presidency under Franklin D. Roosevelt.[6] It is this period that is of greatest interest for our consideration of the role of the president in managing the bureaucracy.[7]

Modern Theories of Presidential Management

In 1936, President Roosevelt appointed a Committee on Administrative Management, headed by management expert Louis Brownlow. The Brownlow committee submitted its report ten months later. The report emphasized the necessity for a strong executive in a democracy, which it said was the unique contribution of the Founding Fathers. It urged changes to carry out this historic design. At points, the Brownlow report became so eloquent on this theme that it was almost embarrassing.

> A weak administration can neither advance nor retreat successfully—it can merely muddle. Those who waver at the sight of needed power are false friends of modern democracy. Strong executive leadership is essential to democratic government today. Our choice is not between power and no power, but between responsible but capable popular government and irresponsible autocracy.[8]

The Brownlow committee called for a basic regrouping of executive agencies. "Just as the hand can cover but a few keys on the piano, so there is for management a limited span of control."[9] The Brownlow committee called for the establishment of "12 great departments directly responsible in administration to the chief executive."[10]

The Brownlow report, however, is not as interesting as what FDR said about it. In submitting the report to Congress and also endorsing all of its recommendations, Roosevelt said:

> The plain fact is that the present organization and equipment of the executive branch of the Government defeats the constitutional intent

[6]*Ibid.*, p. 1062.
[7]The terms "administration" and "management" are used interchangeably in this [article] to refer to the implementation or execution of policy.
[8]*Report of the President's Committee on Administrative Management*, January 1937, p. 53.
[9]*Ibid.*, p. 34.
[10]*Ibid.*

that there be a single responsible Chief Executive to coordinate and manage the departments and activities in accordance with the laws enacted by the Congress. Under these conditions the Government cannot be thoroughly effective in working, under popular control, for the common good.[11]

Some of Roosevelt's proposals that were implemented (notably the creation of the Executive Office of the President) have given the modern presidency management tools used with different degrees of interest and skill since then. But they have not cooled the ardor of those who have followed in this tradition and urged that the president's role as chief executive be further strengthened.

The Brownlow committee's views on presidential management were again expressed in the postwar period in the work of the first Commission on the Organization of the Executive Branch of Government, under former President Herbert Hoover. This commission was appointed by President Harry S. Truman in 1947 and issued its report in March 1949. Its work reflects the same classical management view as that of the more outspoken Brownlow committee a decade earlier. It stressed accountability. The commission called for a "clear line of command from top to bottom." Like the Brownlow committee, the Hoover commission recommended expanding the president's staff and regrouping federal programs according to major functions under the direction of a small group of agency heads who they said should be regarded as "the president's principal assistants."

Besides the Brownlow and Hoover reports, there have been management councils under almost every president since FDR. In characteristic fashion, President Lyndon B. Johnson's council on organization and management operated in secrecy. Its report pulled no punches in diagnosing the problem. The federal government, it said, "is badly organized."

> Top political executives—the President and Cabinet Secretaries—preside over agencies which they never own and only rarely command. Their managerial authority is constantly challenged by powerful legislative committees, well-organized interest groups, entrenched bureau chiefs with narrow program mandates, and the career civil service.[12]

[11]*Ibid.*, p. iv.

[12]President's Task Force on Governmental Organization, "The Organization and Management of Great Society Programs, Final Report of the President's Task Force on Governmental Organization," June 1967, p. 6. "Administratively confidential," unpublished.

The Johnson task force, chaired by railroad executive Ben W. Heineman, was critical of domestic programs. Its conclusion in this area is of particular interest.

> Many domestic social programs are under severe attack. *Some criticism is political.* It comes from those who oppose the goals of these national programs. *Some criticism stems from deflated hopes,* with current funding levels well below ultimate need and demand. *Some criticism arises because of alleged organizational and managerial weaknesses.* After several months of study, we believe the organizational criticism is merited.[13]

The Heineman task force also called for stronger institutional machinery for policymaking and coordination in the White House and urged measures to strengthen agency management structures and reduce the number of domestic agencies.

The steady progression of reports calling for measures to strengthen the management control of the presidency was broken as a result of the Watergate scandal. In a report prepared in 1974 for the special Senate investigative committee headed by Senator Sam J. Ervin, Jr., the National Academy of Public Administration rejected plans that Nixon had developed for his second term to centralize executive management. The authors, breaking sharply with tradition, emphasized "the necessarily pluralistic nature of the federal establishment."[14] Although in many ways the descendants of the authors of the Brownlow and Hoover commissions, the National Academy panel breathed a sigh of relief that Watergate had prevented Nixon from implementing his elaborate plans.

Sandwiched between Nixon and Reagan were Presidents Gerald R. Ford and Jimmy Carter. Neither was strong in terms of exercising control over the bureaucracy. Ford's position is understandable. Coming to office on the heels of Watergate, in which the presidency as an institution had been dealt a hard blow, he was not in a position to exert aggressive leadership over the bureaucracy. Carter's situation is more complicated. His election can be attributed

---

[13]*Ibid.*, p. 1.

[14]Frederick C. Mosher and others, *Implications for Responsible Government,* prepared at the request of the Senate Select Committee on Presidential Campaign Activities by a panel of the National Academy of Public Administration (New York: Basic Books, Inc., 1974), p. 51.

in part to his reputation as a manager and his claim of managerial prowess. Yet his management record as president was unimpressive. Carter's main contribution to the executive management tradition—an ironic one—was his successful effort to create a senior civil service system. The 1978 Civil Service Reform Act created a layer of top-level professionals in the career service with a new status enabling them to win bonuses and prizes for achievement, and also enabling their political superiors to move them around, or even to remove them from the senior service. The irony of this legislation lies in the fact that these new powers have been used aggressively by the Reagan administration to exert greater influence over the federal bureaucracy in order to pursue goals very different from Carter's.

The Role of the Bureaucracy

The American federal bureaucracy, the object of presidential management control strategies, dates from 1883 when Congress passed the Pendleton Act in response to the assassination of President Garfield by a disappointed office seeker. Enactment of the Pendleton Act capped a thirty-year effort to replace the spoils system with a system for appointing career civil servants on the basis of merit.

The essential point of the civil-service reform movement was that elected officials should make policy and that professionals in the career service should carry it out. This notion, which implied that there could be a line of demarcation between policymaking and its execution, dominated theories of public administration, beginning in the 1920s. Although experts in this field have now abandoned the idea that such a line can be drawn to delineate the roles and responsibilities of political and career officials, there is still a strong, almost wistful, feeling on the part of some public administration specialists and old-line career officials that political officials should stay out of administrative processes.

Currently, the predominant view in political science is that the line between making and carrying out policy can never be clearly defined. This position holds that the point at which a political official's influence ends and a civil servant's responsibility begins varies with the issue at hand. It depends on the newness of the issue, the amount of money involved, and the level of public controversy generated. The last factor—*the level of public controversy*—is the most important one. Political scientist Paul H. Appleby observed thirty years ago, "The level at which a decision is made . . . may be shifted downward or upward as evaluations point to more or less controversy, or to more or less 'importance.' "[15] . . .

The Nixon Experience

Richard Nixon stands out among recent presidents for the interest he took in administration. Actually, Nixon took two different approaches to administration in the field of domestic affairs in different periods of his presidency. When he entered office in 1969, Nixon emphasized the development of legislation that would put his stamp on domestic policy. White House working groups were set up to develop legislative initiatives in such fields as welfare, revenue sharing, education, health, urban affairs, the environment, and labor-management relations. In doing this, Nixon followed the pattern of his two immediate predecessors, John F. Kennedy and Lyndon B. Johnson, each of whom had established a variety of legislative task forces.

Nixon also followed the lead of most of his predecessors in the criteria he used to select his cabinet members and the role he asked them to play at the beginning of his presidency. With two exceptions—Robert Finch at the Department of Health, Education, and Welfare and John Mitchell at the Department of Justice—the members of his cabinet were not close to Nixon personally, nor in some cases even politically. They represented a broad range of viewpoints, professions, and geographic areas. Several had gained national reputations before their appointments. This was especially true of the three former governors in Nixon's original cabinet—John Volpe of Massachusetts, secretary of transportation; George Romney of Michigan, secretary of housing and urban development; and Walter Hickel of Alaska, secretary of the interior.

In the first two years of Nixon's presidency, the White House focused on preparing new legislation—sometimes without the advice or even knowledge of the cabinet members whose departments would be affected. The secretaries of the domestic departments were essentially allowed to go their own way in selecting top program officials, supervising these officials, and handling other administrative tasks. For the most part, the White House staff concentrated its attention

[15]Paul H. Appleby, *Policy and Administration* (University, Ala.: University of Alabama Press, 1949), p. 13.

on Congress and its legislative agenda. Cabinet members heard from White House officials mostly in connection with legislative matters. This approach—which had been the traditional one—is called the *legislative strategy.* . . .

Gradually, however, the strategy shifted. The Nixon administration moved toward an administrative strategy. By the end of the first term, plans were made to shift the emphasis to the administrative approach for the second term. The legislative agenda was pared down. No longer was the cabinet to be composed of men with their own national standing disposed to go their own way. Unprecedented changes were made below the cabinet level. Trusted lieutenants who were tied personally to Richard Nixon and had no national reputations of their own were placed in direct charge of the major bureaucracies of domestic government. The goal in 1973, as Nixon's ill-fated second term got underway, was to take over the bureaucracy and by doing so to concentrate much more heavily on achieving policy objectives through administrative action.

The reason for Nixon's switch to an administrative strategy for his second term was the perception that the bureaucracy was a barrier to implementing his policies. This suspicion of the bureaucracy that motivated Nixon and his principal aides in 1972 and 1973 was not new to the political scene. From the very outset, the Nixon administration had been antibureaucracy. In part, this may have been a reflection of the fact that Republicans had been out of office for eight years under Johnson, just before Nixon's presidency. In part it reflected a common attitude of suspicion on the part of conservatives toward big government. Such attitudes were not unfounded. It was true that many newly created social programs of the Johnson period were staffed by career officials with a commitment to the program area in which they worked.[16] Nixon staffers in many of these cases were correct in assuming that this would produce opposition to their more conservative domestic policies and their efforts to achieve decentralization.

The important difference was that, unlike many of its predecessors, the Nixon administration did not come to terms with this initial attitude of mistrust of the bureaucracy or find ways to sub-

---

[16]This point has been documented in Joel D. Aberbach and Bert A. Rockman. See "Clashing Beliefs Within the Executive Bureaucracy: The Nixon Administration Bureaucracy," *The American Political Science Review*, vol. 70, no. 2, June 1976, pp. 456–468.

limate it, as had the Eisenhower administration a decade earlier. On the contrary, these attitudes hardened to the point that an unprecedented reorganization was put into place for Nixon's second term to take control of the domestic bureaucracy.

Nixon's hostility toward the bureaucracy, almost vitriolic in its tone, was apparent in many statements and actions. A White House aide in 1969 referred to "the White House surrounded"—surrounded, that is, by powerful program interests opposed to what the administration was trying to achieve. This attitude was also reflected in a suspicion in the early days of the career staff in the Bureau of the Budget, now the Office of Management and Budget. It was not dispelled until George Shultz replaced Nixon's first budget director, Robert Mayo, who was regarded by the White House as too strong a defender of the bureau's professionism.[17] White House aide Michael Balzano summed up the feelings of many in the Nixon inner circle about the federal bureaucracy.

> President Nixon doesn't run the bureaucracy; the civil service and the unions do. It took him three years to find out what was going on in the bureaucracy. And God forbid if any president is defeated after the first term, because then the bureaucracy has another three years to play games with the next president.[18]

Even though hostility and suspicion underlaid Nixon's moves to trim the power of the bureaucracy, his efforts raise more basic issues.

There are essentially three ways of viewing Nixon's decision in 1973 to adopt an administrative presidency strategy for his second term. One is that he was right. A second is that he was partly right— that in a pluralistic society, many forces can and should influence the bureaucracy, including (but not limited to) the president. The difference between the first and second position is one of degree. The essential question is: What should be the role of the elected chief executive in relation to other power centers in influencing the professional staff of executive branch agencies? One can argue that the

[17]In many respects Robert Mayo performed with wisdom and ability as President Nixon's first budget director. Nevertheless, his lack of experience in political matters made it difficult for him to build confidence in the bureau on the part of the president and the White House at the outset of an administration that followed an eight-year Republican hiatus. Mayo tangled most with John Ehrlichman, who engineered his sudden and, to Mayo, completely unexpected removal in the middle of 1970.

[18]As quoted in the *Wall Street Journal*, June 21, 1972.

Congress, the courts, interest groups, the press, etc., ought to be as influential as the chief executive, or even more.

The argument [here] is that the political chief executives—which includes the president, governors, mayors—should have *the most important role* in this area of modern government. Purely as a practical matter, the chief executive is in a much better position than a large group of people in a legislative body or the courts to give cohesive policy direction and guidance to the work of large public bureaucracies.

There is still a third possible way to view the role of elected officials, which this [article] rejects—that elected chief executives should have a limited role in the administrative process. This position concedes that there is a substantial policy content to many administrative processes, but argues that policymaking in modern government is a proper responsibility of career or professional bureaucrats. Peter Woll, for example, portrays the federal bureaucracy as "an independent force." He says it "cannot be dismissed simply as a part of the executive branch of government controlled by the president or the cabinet."[19] Woll depicts the bureaucracy as "a powerful and viable branch of government, playing a political game to advance its own interest in legislative and judicial, as well as executive matters." Although it is long, it is useful here to include a section of Woll's views on what he calls "the political nature of bureaucracy."

> The political nature of bureaucracy is initially revealed in the behavior of administrative agencies acting as interest groups and in individual behavior within administrative agencies. Administrative agencies come into contact with various external groups both governmental and non-government. To retain their power or to expand all agencies must maintain a balance of political support over opposition. Congress controls finances and has ultimate power over reorganization; thus the agencies always seek political support that can be exerted on Congress. They are responsive to the president, or his coordinating staff agencies such as the Bureau of the Budget, only insofar as they are essential to the maintenance of political support. Agencies that have strong interest group support outside the bureaucracy do not generally have to rely on the president or his staff agencies. On the other hand, some agencies without adequate outside group

---

[19]Peter Woll, *The American Bureaucracy* (New York: W. W. Norton & Co., 1963), p. 3. A similar view of the role of the bureaucracy in contemporary government is expressed in Francis E. Rourke, *Bureaucracy, Politics, and Public Policy* (Boston: Little, Brown, 1969).

support must substitute presidential support in order to survive. One important determinant of presidential control over any particular administrative agency is the extent of the agency's contact with and support from private interest groups. The effectiveness of this control, of course, will vary with the power of the private groups concerned and their ability to influence Congress or the Courts.[20]

An even stronger statement of this point of view has been expressed by Norton Long.[21] Writing thirty years ago, Long argued that we should not only accept the bureaucracy for what it is, but strive to make the bureaucracy independent. This should be so, according to Long, because the bureaucracy represents not just special interests, but the whole nation better than any other of our political institutions. Based on what he calls "our working constitution," Long contends that the bureaucracy has a substantial role as a "representative organ and source of rationality." The bureaucracy is "our great fourth branch of government." There should be, Long argues, a working interaction of the four, not the legal supremacy of any of them.

The Reagan Experience

. . . The lessons of the Nixon period and the frustrations of the Carter presidency have produced a body of experience that the Reagan White House has drawn on skillfully in attempting to push its influence into the administrative processes of government. A *Wall Street Journal* article, written a year after Reagan took office, said his administration "has found a way to reshape the federal government without necessarily changing laws. It is called Reaganizing."[22] The article went on to define Reaganizing as "the transformation of departments and agencies by appointed officials devoted to President Reagan's vow to 'curb the size and influence of the federal establishment.' "

The Reagan administrative strategy is different from Nixon's in a number of respects. It went into effect earlier, right at the beginning of the Reagan presidency. It is less visible and more subtle. It focuses more at the subcabinet level. It is less regimented than the Nixon plan, which was dramatically announced at the outset of the

[20]Woll, *op cit.*, p. 4.
[21]See Norton E. Long, "Bureaucracy and Constitutionalism," *The American Political Science Review*, vol. 46, no. 3, September 1952, p. 808.
[22]Schorr and Pasztor, *op. cit.*, p. 1.

second term as Nixon shifted gears from the conventional legislative approach to an administrative strategy. The biggest difference between Reagan and Nixon is that the Reagan administration has pursued a dual approach to domestic affairs, whereas Nixon started out with one approach (legislative) and then switched to another (administrative). . . .

Basic Issues Examined

Examining Nixon's and Reagan's administrative tactics can help us to understand fundamental issues of American governance. As government in the United States has become larger and more specialized, experts have come to exert growing influence. According to Max Weber, bureaucratic organization involves "the exercise of control on the basis of knowledge."[23] Writing at the turn of the century, Weber viewed bureaucratic control as inevitably increasing as scientific expertise expands. The dilemma of bureaucratic centralization for democratic government is the obvious one. The idea that citizens through their representatives should make governmental decisions is not consistent with a system in which decisions about public policy frequently are made on the basis of technical knowledge.

In the mid-1930s, E. Pendleton Herring wrote about this dilemma in discussing the "increase in administrative discretion." Referring to the role of the administrator, Herring wrote: "The words of the statute delimit his scope, but within the margin of his discretion he must write his interpretation of state purpose." The result, said Herring, is "the transfer from Congress [to the bureaucracy] of much of the direct superintendence of reconciling the conflicting groups within the state."[24]

In this context, the idea of an administrative presidency strategy can be seen as reinforcing democratic theory. The disillusionment with government in the current period should increase the appeal of politicians who have as a major purpose *making government work better.* Doing so requires that *politics penetrate* operations, that the values politicians are elected to advance are reflected

[23]See Max Weber, *The Theory of Social and Economic Organization* (Glencoe, Ill.: The Free Press, 1947).
[24]E. Pendleton Herring, *Public Administration and the Public Interest* (New York: McGraw-Hill Book Co., 1936), p. 8.

in the execution of laws, as well as in their enactment.[25] An important fact that has already been mentioned is critical at this juncture in the argument, specifically, the large and growing amount of administrative discretion contained in the laws of modern governments.

The argument that politics should penetrate operations applies to both liberal and conservative political agendas. . . . [T]he need to adopt an administrative strategy is just as strong, if not stronger in the current period, for liberal chief executives. The 1980s ushered in what undoubtedly will be a long period of austerity in U.S. domestic affairs. If liberals are to respond to this new reality, they must be able to demonstrate that government can work, that rigor and efficiency can be brought to bear to solve social problems. The next liberal agenda has to be one that gives greater weight than in the past to the capability of governmental institutions to carry out social purposes. . . .

[25]This same argument is made, although somewhat wistfully, in a recent book by two writers who worked in the Carter administration. See Ben W. Heineman, Jr., and Curtis A. Hesler, *Memorandum for the President: A Strategic Approach to Domestic Affairs in the 1980s* (New York: Random House, 1980).

14

Congress and Bureaucracy: A Profitable Partnership

MORRIS P. FIORINA

Dramatis Personae

In this chapter, . . . I will set out a theory of the Washington establishment(s). The theory is quite plausible from a commonsense standpoint, and it is consistent with the specialized literature of academic political science. Nevertheless, it is still a theory, not proven fact. Before plunging in let me bring out in the open the basic axiom on which the theory rests: the self-interest axiom.

I assume that most people most of the time act in their own self-interest. This is not to say that human beings seek only to amass tangible wealth but rather to say that human beings seek to achieve their own ends—tangible and intangible—rather than the ends of their fellow men. I do not condemn such behavior nor do I condone it (although I rather sympathize with Thoreau's comment that "if I knew for a certainty that a man was coming to my house with the conscious design of doing me good, I should run for my life.").[1] I only claim that political and economic theories which presume self-interested behavior will prove to be more widely applicable than those which build on more altruistic assumptions.

What does the axiom imply when used in . . . a context peopled by congressmen, bureaucrats, and voters? I assume that the primary

Chapter 5, "The Rise of the Washington Establishment," from Morris P. Fiorina, *Congress: Keystone of the Washington Establishment.* Copyright © 1979 by Yale University. Reprinted by permission of Yale University Press. Footnotes are renumbered.

[1]Henry David Thoreau, *Walden* (London: Walter Scott Publishing Co., no date), p. 72.

goal of the typical congressman is reelection. Over and above the $57,000 salary plus "perks" and outside money, the office of congressman carries with it prestige, excitement, and power. It is a seat in the cockpit of government. But in order to retain the status, excitement, and power (not to mention more tangible things) of office, the congressman must win reelection every two years. Even those congressmen genuinely concerned with good public policy must achieve reelection in order to continue their work. Whether narrowly self-serving or more publicly oriented, the individual congressman finds reelection to be at least a necessary condition for the achievement of his goals.[2]

Moreover, there is a kind of natural selection process at work in the electoral arena. On average, those congressmen who are not primarily interested in reelection will not achieve reelection as often as those who are interested. We, the people, help to weed out congressmen whose primary motivation is not reelection. We admire politicians who courageously adopt the aloof role of the disinterested statesman, but we vote for those politicians who follow our wishes and do us favors.

What about the bureaucrats? A specification of their goals is somewhat more controversial—those who speak of appointed officials as public servants obviously take a more benign view than those who speak of them as bureaucrats. The literature provides ample justification for asserting that most bureaucrats wish to protect and nurture their agencies. The typical bureaucrat can be expected to seek to expand his agency in terms of personnel, budget, and mission. One's status in Washington (again, not to mention more tangible things) is roughly proportional to the importance of the operation one oversees. And the sheer size of the operation is taken to be a measure of importance. As with congressmen, the specified goals apply even to those bureaucrats who genuinely believe in their agency's mission. If they believe in the efficacy of their programs, they naturally wish to expand them and add new ones. All of this requires more money and more people. The genuinely committed bureaucrat is just as likely to seek to expand his agency as the proverbial empire-builder.[3]

[2]For a more extended discussion of the electoral motivation see Fiorina, *Representatives, Roll Calls, and Constituencies*, chap. 2; David R. Mayhew, *Congress: The Electoral Connection* (New Haven: Yale University Press, 1974).

[3]For a discussion of the goals of bureaucrats see William Niskanen, *Bureaucracy and Representative Government* (Chicago: Aldine-Atherton, 1971).

And what of the third element in the equation, us? What do we, the voters who support the Washington system, strive for? Each of us wishes to receive a maximum of benefits from government for the minimum cost. This goal suggests maximum government efficiency, on the one hand, but it also suggests mutual exploitation on the other. Each of us favors an arrangement in which our fellow citizens pay for our benefits.

With these brief descriptions of the cast of characters in hand, let us proceed.

Tammany Hall Goes to Washington

What should we expect from a legislative body composed of individuals whose first priority is their continued tenure in office? We should expect, first, that the normal activities of its members are those calculated to enhance their chances of reelection. And we should expect, second, that the members would devise and maintain institutional arrangements which facilitate their electoral activities. . . .

For most of the twentieth century, congressmen have engaged in a mix of three kinds of activities: lawmaking, pork barreling, and casework. Congress is first and foremost a lawmaking body, at least according to constitutional theory. In every postwar session Congress "considers" thousands of bills and resolutions, many hundreds of which are brought to a record vote (over 500 in each chamber in the 93rd Congress). Naturally the critical consideration in taking a position for the record is the maximization of approval in the home district. If the district is unaffected by and unconcerned with the matter at hand, the congressman may then take into account the general welfare of the country. (This sounds cynical, but remember that "profiles in courage" are sufficiently rare that their occurrence inspires books and articles.) Abetted by political scientists of the pluralist school, politicians have propounded an ideology which maintains that the good of the country on any given issue is simply what is best for a majority of congressional districts. This ideology provides a philosophical justification for what congressmen do while acting in their own self-interest.

A second activity favored by congressmen consists of efforts to bring home the bacon to their districts. Many popular articles have been written about the pork barrel, a term originally applied to rivers and harbors legislation but now generalized to cover all manner of federal largesse.[4] Congressmen consider new dams, federal buildings, sewage treatment plants, urban renewal projects, etc. as sweet plums to be plucked. Federal projects are highly visible, their economic impact is easily detected by constituents, and sometimes they even produce something of value to the district. The average constituent may have some trouble translating his congressman's vote on some civil rights issue into a change in his personal welfare. But the workers hired and supplies purchased in connection with a big federal project provide benefits that are widely appreciated. The historical importance congressmen attach to the pork barrel is reflected in the rules of the House. That body accords certain classes of legislation "privileged" status: they may come directly to the floor without passing through the Rules Committee, a traditional graveyard for legislation. What kinds of legislation are privileged? Taxing and spending bills, for one: the government's power to raise and spend money must be kept relatively unfettered. But in addition, the omnibus rivers and harbors bills of the Public Works Committee and public lands bills from the Interior Committee share privileged status. The House will allow a civil rights or defense procurement or environmental bill to languish in the Rules Committee, but it takes special precautions to insure that nothing slows down the approval of dams and irrigation projects.

A third major activity takes up perhaps as much time as the other two combined. Traditionally, constituents appeal to their congressman for myriad favors and services. Sometimes only information is needed, but often constituents request that their congressman intervene in the internal workings of federal agencies to affect a decision in a favorable way, to reverse an adverse decision, or simply to speed up the glacial bureaucratic process. On the basis of extensive personal interviews with congressmen, Charles Clapp writes:

> Denied a favorable ruling by the bureaucracy on a matter of direct concern to him, puzzled or irked by delays in obtaining a decision, confused by the administrative maze through which he is directed to proceed, or ignorant of whom to write, a constituent may turn to his congressman for help. These letters offer great potential for political

[4]The traditional pork barrel is the subject of an excellent treatment by John Ferejohn. See his *Pork Barrel Politics: Rivers and Harbors Legislation, 1947–1968* (Stanford: Stanford University Press, 1974).

benefit to the congressman since they affect the constituent personally. If the legislator can be of assistance, he may gain a firm ally; if he is indifferent, he may even lose votes.[5]

Actually congressmen are in an almost unique position in our system, a position shared only with high-level members of the executive branch. Congressmen possess the power to expedite and influence bureaucratic decisions. This capability flows directly from congressional control over what bureaucrats value most: higher budgets and new program authorizations. In a very real sense each congressman is a monopoly supplier of bureaucratic unsticking services for his district.

Every year the federal budget passes through the appropriations committees of Congress. Generally these committees make perfunctory cuts. But on occasion they vent displeasure on an agency and leave it bleeding all over the Capitol. The most extreme case of which I am aware came when the House committee took away the entire budget of the Division of Labor Standards in 1947 (some of the budget was restored elsewhere in the appropriations process). Deep and serious cuts are made occasionally, and the threat of such cuts keeps most agencies attentive to congressional wishes. Professors Richard Fenno and Aaron Wildavsky have provided extensive documentary and interview evidence of the great respect (and even terror) federal bureaucrats show for the House Appropriations Committee.[6] Moreover, the bureaucracy must keep coming back to Congress to have its old programs reauthorized and new ones added. Again, most such decisions are perfunctory, but exceptions are sufficiently frequent that bureaucrats do not forget the basis of their agencies' existence. For example, the Law Enforcement Assistance Administration (LEAA) and the Food Stamps Program had no easy time of it this last Congress (94th). The bureaucracy needs congressional approval in order to survive, let alone expand. Thus, when a congressman calls about some minor bureaucratic decision or regulation, the bureaucracy considers his accommodation a small price to pay for the goodwill its cooperation will produce, particularly if he has any connection to the substantive committee or the appropriations subcommittee to which it reports.

[5]Charles Clapp, *The Congressman: His Job As He Sees It* (Washington: Brookings Institution, 1963), p. 84.
[6]Richard Fenno, *The Power of The Purse* (Boston: Little, Brown, 1966); Aaron Wildavsky, *The Politics of the Budgetary Process*, 2d ed. (Boston: Little, Brown, 1974).

From the standpoint of capturing voters, the congressman's lawmaking activities differ in two important respects from his pork-barrel and casework activities. First, programmatic actions are inherently controversial. Unless his district is homogeneous, a congressman will find his district divided on many major issues. Thus when he casts a vote, introduces a piece of nontrivial legislation, or makes a speech with policy content he will displease some elements of his district. Some constituents may applaud the congressman's civil rights record, but others believe integration is going too fast. Some support foreign aid, while others believe it's money poured down a rathole. Some advocate economic equality, others stew over welfare cheaters. On such policy matters the congressman can expect to make friends as well as enemies. Presumably he will behave so as to maximize the excess of the former over the latter, but nevertheless a policy stand will generally make some enemies. ·

In contrast, the pork barrel and casework are relatively less controversial. New federal projects bring jobs, shiny new facilities, and general economic prosperity, or so people believe. Snipping ribbons at the dedication of a new post office or dam is a much more pleasant pursuit than disposing of a constitutional amendment on abortion. Republicans and Democrats, conservatives and liberals, all generally prefer a richer district to a poorer one. Of course, in recent years the river damming and stream-bed straightening activities of the Army Corps of Engineers have aroused some opposition among environmentalists. Congressmen happily reacted by absorbing the opposition and adding environmentalism to the pork barrel: water treatment plants are currently a hot congressional item.

Casework is even less controversial. Some poor, aggrieved constituent becomes enmeshed in the tentacles of an evil bureaucracy and calls upon Congressman St. George to do battle with the dragon. Again Clapp writes:

> A person who has a reasonable complaint or query is regarded as providing an opportunity rather than as adding an extra burden to an already busy office. The party affiliation of the individual even when known to be different from that of the congressman does not normally act as a deterrent to action. Some legislators have built their reputations and their majorities on a program of service to all constituents irrespective of party. Regularly, voters affiliated with the opposition in other contests lend strong support to the lawmaker whose intervention has helped them in their struggle with the bureaucracy.[7]

[7]Clapp, *The Congressman: His Job As He Sees It*, p. 84.

Even following the revelation of sexual improprieties, Wayne Hays won his Ohio Democratic primary by a two-to-one margin. According to a *Los Angeles Times* feature story, Hays's constituency base was built on a foundation of personal service to constituents:

> They receive help in speeding up bureaucratic action on various kinds of federal assistance—black lung benefits to disabled miners and their families, Social Security payments, veterans' benefits and passports.
>
> Some constituents still tell with pleasure of how Hays stormed clear to the seventh floor of the State Department and into Secretary of State Dean Rusk's office to demand, successfully, the quick issuance of a passport to an Ohioan.[8]

Practicing politicians will tell you that word of mouth is still the most effective mode of communication. News of favors to constituents gets around and no doubt is embellished in the process.

In sum, when considering the benefits of his programmatic activities, the congressman must tote up gains and losses to arrive at a net profit. Pork barreling and casework, however, are basically pure profit.

A second way in which programmatic activities differ from casework and the pork barrel is the difficulty of assigning responsibility to the former as compared with the latter. No congressman can seriously claim that he is responsible for the 1964 Civil Rights Act, the ABM, or the 1972 Revenue Sharing Act. Most constituents do have some vague notion that their congressman is only one of hundreds and their senator one of an even hundred. Even committee

---

[8]"Hays Improves Rapidly From Overdose," *Los Angeles Times*, June 12, 1976, part I, p. 19. Similarly, Congressman Robert Leggett (D., Calif.) won reelection in 1976 even amid revelations of a thirteen-year bigamous relationship and rumors of other affairs and improprieties. The *Los Angeles Times* wrote:

> Because of federal spending, times are good here in California's 4th Congressional District, and that is a major reason why local political leaders in both parties, as well as the man on the street, believe that Leggett will still be their congressman next year. . . .
>
> Leggett has concentrated on bringing federal dollars to his district and on acting as an ombudsman for constituents having problems with their military pay or Social Security or GI benefit checks. He sends out form letters to parents of newborn children congratulating them.

Traditionally, personal misbehavior has been one of the few shoals on which incumbent congressmen could founder. But today's incumbents have so entrenched themselves by personal service to constituents that even scandal does not harm them mortally. See David Johnson, "Rep. Leggett Expected to Survive Sex Scandal," *Los Angeles Times*, July 26, 1976, part I, p. 1.

chairmen may have a difficult time claiming credit for a piece of major legislation, let alone a rank-and-file congressman. Ah, but casework, and the pork barrel. In dealing with the bureaucracy, the congressman is not merely one vote of 435. Rather, he is a nonpartisan power, someone whose phone calls snap an office to attention. He is not kept on hold. The constituent who receives aid believes that his congressman and his congressman alone got results. Similarly, congressmen find it easy to claim credit for federal projects awarded their districts. The congressman may have instigated the proposal for the project in the first place, issued regular progress reports, and ultimately announced the award through his office. Maybe he can't claim credit for the 1965 Voting Rights Act, but he can take credit for Littletown's spanking new sewage treatment plant.

Overall then, programmatic activities are dangerous (controversial), on the one hand, and programmatic accomplishments are difficult to claim credit for, on the other. While less exciting, casework and pork barreling are both safe and profitable. For a reelection-oriented congressman the choice is obvious.

The key to the rise of the Washington establishment (and the vanishing marginals)* is the following observation: *the growth of an activist federal government has stimulated a change in the mix of congressional activities.* Specifically, a lesser proportion of congressional effort is now going into programmatic activities and a greater proportion into pork-barrel and casework activities. As a result, today's congressmen make relatively fewer enemies and relatively more friends among the people of their districts.

To elaborate, a basic fact of life in twentieth-century America is the growth of the federal role and its attendant bureaucracy. Bureaucracy is the characteristic mode of delivering public goods and services. Ceteris paribus, the more the government attempts to do for people, the more extensive a bureaucracy it creates. As the scope of government expands, more and more citizens find themselves in direct contact with the federal government. Consider the rise in such contacts upon passage of the Social Security Act, work relief projects and other New Deal programs. Consider the millions of additional citizens touched by the veterans' programs of the postwar period. Consider the untold numbers whom the Great Society and its after-

*Editor's note: Fiorina's theory of the new Washington establishment sprang originally from his desire to unravel the mystery of the "vanishing marginals"—the fact that so many congressional districts are now safe seats for the incumbent.

math brought face to face with the federal government. In 1930 the federal bureaucracy was small and rather distant from the everyday concerns of Americans. By 1975 it was neither small nor distant.

As the years have passed, more and more citizens and groups have found themselves dealing with the federal bureaucracy. They may be seeking positive actions—eligibility for various benefits and awards of government grants. Or they may be seeking relief from the costs imposed by bureaucratic regulations—on working conditions, racial and sexual quotas, market restrictions, and numerous other subjects. While not malevolent, bureaucracies make mistakes, both of commission and omission, and normal attempts at redress often meet with unresponsiveness and inflexibility and sometimes seeming incorrigibility. Whatever the problem, the citizen's congressman is a source of succor. The greater the scope of government activity, the greater the demand for his services.

Private monopolists can regulate the demand for their product by raising or lowering the price. Congressmen have no such (legal) option. When the demand for their services rises, they have no real choice except to meet that demand—to supply more bureaucratic unsticking services—so long as they would rather be elected than unelected. This vulnerability to escalating constituency demands is largely academic, though. I seriously doubt that congressmen resist their gradual transformation from national legislators to errand boy-ombudsmen. As we have noted, casework is all profit. Congressmen have buried proposals to relieve the casework burden by establishing a national ombudsman or Congressman Reuss's proposed Administrative Counsel of the Congress. One of the congressmen interviewed by Clapp stated:

> Before I came to Washington I used to think that it might be nice if the individual states had administrative arms here that would take care of necessary liaison between citizens and the national government. But a congressman running for reelection is interested in building fences by providing personal services. The system is set to reelect incumbents regardless of party, and incumbents wouldn't dream of giving any of this service function away to any subagency. As an elected member I feel the same way.[9]

In fact, it is probable that at least some congressmen deliberately stimulate the demand for their bureaucratic fixit services.

[9]Clapp, *The Congressman: His Job As He Sees It*, p. 94.

. . . Recall that the new Republican in district A travels about his district saying:

> I'm your man in Washington. What are your problems? How can I help you?

And in district B, did the demand for the congressman's services rise so much between 1962 and 1964 that a "regiment" of constituency staff became necessary? Or, having access to the regiment, did the new Democrat stimulate the demand to which he would apply his regiment?*

In addition to greatly increased casework, let us not forget that the growth of the federal role has also greatly expanded the federal pork barrel. The creative pork barreler need not limit himself to dams and post offices—rather old-fashioned interests. Today, creative congressmen can cadge LEAA money for the local police, urban renewal and housing money for local politicians, educational program grants for the local education bureaucracy. And there are sewage treatment plants, worker training and retraining programs, health services, and programs for the elderly. The pork barrel is full to overflowing. The conscientious congressman can stimulate applications for federal assistance (the sheer number of programs makes it difficult for local officials to stay current with the possibilities), put in a good word during consideration, and announce favorable decisions amid great fanfare.

In sum, everyday decisions by a large and growing federal bureaucracy bestow significant tangible benefits and impose significant tangible costs. Congressmen can affect these decisions. Ergo, the more decisions the bureaucracy has the opportunity to make, the more opportunities there are for the congressman to build up credits.

The nature of the Washington system is now quite clear. Congressmen (typically the majority Democrats) earn electoral credits by establishing various federal programs (the minority Republicans typically earn credits by fighting the good fight). The legislation is drafted in very general terms, so some agency, existing or newly established, must translate a vague policy mandate into a functioning program, a process that necessitates the promulgation of numerous rules and regulations and, incidentally, the trampling of numerous toes. At the next stage, aggrieved and/or hopeful constituents petition

---

*Editor's note: Districts A and B are two congressional districts that Fiorina visited and subjected to close study.

their congressman to intervene in the complex (or at least obscure) decision processes of the bureaucracy. The cycle closes when the congressman lends a sympathetic ear, piously denounces the evils of bureaucracy, intervenes in the latter's decisions, and rides a grateful electorate to ever more impressive electoral showings. Congressmen take credit coming and going. They are the alpha and the omega.

The popular frustration with the permanent government in Washington is partly justified, but to a considerable degree it is misplaced resentment. *Congress is the linchpin of the Washington establishment.* The bureaucracy serves as a convenient lightning rod for public frustration and a convenient whipping boy for congressmen. But so long as the bureaucracy accommodates congressmen, the latter will oblige with ever larger budgets and grants of authority. Congress does not just react to big government—it creates it. All of Washington prospers. More and more bureaucrats promulgate more and more regulations and dispense more and more money. Fewer and fewer congressmen suffer electoral defeat. Elements of the electorate benefit from government programs, and all of the electorate is eligible for ombudsman services. But the general, long-term welfare of the United States is no more than an incidental by-product of the system.

15

The Judicial Response to the Bureaucratic State

DAVID H. ROSENBLOOM

The rise of the administrative state has had profound consequences for the nature of politics and citizenship in democratic nations (Wilson, 1975). In the United States, each branch of
government has sought to adjust to the new political conditions posed
by public bureaucracy's growth in size, power, and penetration of
the life of the political community (Nachmias and Rosenbloom,
1980). Considerable attention has been paid to the adjustments made
by Congress (Arnold, 1979; Dodd and Schott, 1979; Fiorina, 1977)
and the presidency (Hess, 1976; Cronin, 1975) but less has been given
to that of the federal judiciary. In part this has been due to a continued research emphasis on traditional questions of administrative
law and the separation of powers, but the diversity of the judicial
response to the rise of the administrative state has also served to obscure the extent to which the courts have moved in a generally coherent fashion to protect individuals against abuses at the hands of
administrative officials and to provide individuals with means of
holding such officials accountable for breaches of their constitutional
rights. This article analyzes the federal courts' response to the administrative state and shows how its current response constitutes a
fundamental effort to assert the rights of individuals in an administrative age.

From David H. Rosenbloom, "The Judicial Response to the Rise of the American
Administrative State," *American Review of Public Administration*, 50 (Spring 1981)
29–51. Reprinted by permission of the author and the publisher.

Judges View Bureaucracy

It is the contention of this essay that in the past three decades the federal judiciary has developed a relatively coherent response to the rise of the administrative state and has thus contributed to a more satisfactory integration of bureaucracy and constitutional government.[1] Yet, this response is not based on a set of doctrines concerning bureaucracy or administrative law. Rather, the cases that comprise the judicial response borrow heavily from legal and constitutional concepts that have been developed generally, as opposed to specifically in the administrative context. For instance, decisions concerning the extent of a public employee's First Amendment rights will often be heavily influenced by doctrines and concepts pertaining to freedom of speech and association generally. At the same time, however, there are enough judicial statements concerning bureaucracy to indicate that there is a widely shared perception among federal judges that the rise of the administrative state has indeed changed the nature of government and citizenship[2] so as to demand a judicial response. . . .

That the federal judiciary continues to react to the rise of the administrative state is indicated by numerous judicial statements placing the issue of public bureaucracy's position in a constitutional democracy in the center of the courts' decision-making. Perhaps Justice Douglas has raised this matter most forcefully. For instance, in dissent in *Wyman v. James* (1971:335), he wrote: "The bureaucracy of modern government is not only slow, lumbering and oppressive; it is omnipresent." Similarly, in *Spady v. Mount Vernon* (1974:985), he asserted that "today's mounting bureaucracy promises to be suffocating and repressive unless it is put into the harness of procedural due process." Douglas also addressed the nature of bureaucracy and constitutional government in *U.S. v. Richardson* (1974), a taxpayer suit seeking information on CIA expenditures under Article I, Section 9, Clause 7 of the Constitution. He stated in dissent that "The sovereign of this Nation is the people, not the bureaucracy. The statement of accounts of public expenditures goes to the heart of the

---

[1]The literature on democracy, constitutionalism, and bureaucracy is too vast to cite. This essay more or less reflects the view taken by Frederick Mosher (1968).

[2]Throughout this essay the word "citizen" is used in the sense of "member of the political community." No effort is made here to distinguish between the constitutional rights of citizens and noncitizens.

problem of sovereignty. If taxpayers may not ask that rudimentary question, their sovereignty becomes an empty symbol and a secret bureaucracy is allowed to run our affairs" (201). A majority of the Supreme Court interpreted Richardson's claim to be that the rise of the administrative state had diminished the quality of his democratic citizenship; "that without detailed information on CIA expenditures—and hence its activities—he cannot intelligently follow the actions of Congress or the Executive, nor can he properly fulfill his obligations as a member of the electorate in voting for candidates seeking national office" (176). However, it held that Richardson lacked standing to bring the suit. Despite the outcome, though, it is evident that both sides on the Court explicitly recognized that the rise of the administrative state had a debilitating impact on the electoral process and the concept of popular sovereignty.

A similar recognition of some of the political realities of the administrative state was evident in *Branti v. Finkel* (1980), a case dealing with the constitutionality of patronage dismissals from the public service. A passage of Justice Powell's dissent, joined by Justice Rehnquist, reads:

> Elected officials depend upon appointees who hold similar views to carry out their policies and administer their programs. Patronage— the right to select key personnel and to regard the party "faithful"— serves the public interest by facilitating the implementation of policies endorsed by the electorate. . . . [T]he Court [i.e., the majority] does not recognize that the implementation of policy often depends upon the cooperation of public employees who do not hold policymaking posts. As one commentator has written, "[w]hat the Court forgets is that, if government is to work, policy implementation is just as important as policymaking. . . . " The growth of the civil service system already has limited the ability of elected politicians to effect political change (9–10).

Nor is the judiciary's concern with the impact of the rise of the administrative state on constitutional government confined to the ranks of the Supreme Court. This is conveniently demonstrated by Judge David Bazelon's article, "The Impact of the Courts on Public Administration" (1976). Bazelon, Chief Judge of the Court of Appeals for the District of Columbia Circuit, believes that the new conditions of government demand a new relationship between courts and administrative agencies:

Administrators are not always happy about judges meddling in their affairs; judges are not always happy with the administrative responses to their meddling. Under the circumstances, a certain amount of disappointment and frustration on both sides is entirely natural. As the Constitutional right to due process of law expands more and more, administrators will find themselves locked into involuntary partnerships with courts. Therefore, efforts should be made to forge a better relationship between the partners (1976:104–5).

In sum, not only have members of the federal judiciary explicitly reacted to the growth of administrative power, but the matter of formulating a coherent response has been placed before them. This being the case, the nature of the emergent response can be analyzed.

Judicial Complicity in the Rise of the Administrative State

Prior to the late 1930s, the federal courts tended to thwart the development of the administrative state by prohibiting delegations of legislative power to bureaucratic agencies. The constitutional issue was defined in terms of the separation of powers. The well-known *Schecter Poultry v. U.S.* (1935) is illustrative. A Live Poultry Code had been promulgated under the National Industrial Recovery Act by an appropriate trade association. The code covered a variety of matters including wages, hours, and general practices. Once approved by the President, such codes had the force of law. Their ultimate purpose was to establish fair competition in various sectors of the economy. The Supreme Court found the scheme to be an unconstitutional delegation of power: "Congress is not permitted to abdicate or to transfer to others the essential legislative functions with which it is . . . vested" (529). Such delegations could only be constitutional if Congress "has itself established the standards of legal obligation, thus performing its essential legislative function" (530), something it had failed to do in the case at hand.

Had the *Schecter* rule been followed faithfully in subsequent cases, rather than been abandoned though not explicitly overturned, it would have presented a very formidable barrier to the rise of the American administrative state. Indeed, Theodore Lowi (1969) argues that "the Court's rule must once again become one of declaring invalid and unconstitutional any delegation of power to an administrative agency that is not accompanied by clear standards of implementation" (298), if the United States government is to escape some of the antidemocratic consequences of the rise of bureaucratic (sub)government. However, *Schecter* has been "universally disregarded" (Lowi, 1969:298) despite some very vague and general congressional delegations to administrative agencies.[3] In the process of ignoring *Schecter*, the federal judiciary has paved the way for increasingly greater administrative power.

The abandonment of *Schecter* is not the only means by which the judiciary nurtured the development of the administrative state. Two additional cases served to assure a measure of constitutional independence for public bureaucrats and some administrative agencies. One was *Humphrey's Executor v. United States* (1935) in which the Supreme Court held that the President did not have the constitutional power to dismiss a Federal Trade Commissioner for reasons of policy preference. Remarkably, the Court held that such an official was beyond the scope of the President's authority under Article II because working in an independent regulatory commission, the official "occupies no place in the executive department and . . . exercises no part of the executive power" (628). A second case was *United States v. Lovett* (1946) in which the Court found a rider on an appropriations act prohibiting the payment of salaries to three named federal employees to be an unconstitutional bill of attainder. Together these cases stand for the general principle that the President lacks the constitutional authority to fire some administrators and Congress lacks the authority to fire others. Thus, administrative power began to slip through the cracks in the separation of powers.

Judicial Acquiescence in the Existence of the Administrative State

Once the constitutional groundwork for the development of the administrative state had been laid, the federal judiciary tended to acquiesce in the exercise of bureaucratic power. In general, this acquiescence was manifested in the form of deference to administrative judgment. As Judge Bazelon summarized the thinking characteristic of this approach, "The court's role was to assure simply that the agency functioned fairly and treated all interests with decency. Agencies were to proceed in a manner designed to ensure that the parties, the public, and the reviewing courts knew the basis of their

---

[3]For instance, see *U.S. v. Southwestern Cable* (1968). There may be some exceptions; see *National Cable TV v. U.S.* (1974).

decision and so that the courts could review their reasoning in light of the evidence" (1976:103). Above all, was the premise that "courts may not substitute their own views for those of the administrators" (1976:103). Consequently, as Martin Shapiro concluded in 1968, "At least during the last twenty years the federal court system has devoted the vast bulk of its energies to simply giving legal approval to agency decisions" (1968:264).

The political ramifications of this approach reduced the incompatibility between bureaucracy and democracy in some respects, but not in others. Thus, this judicial approach and that of the Administrative Procedures Act requiring agencies to engage in a fair procedure enhances procedural justice and accountability, but it does little to assure substantive justice or that bureaucratic power is exercised in a manner responsive to the electorate or the elected. As Shapiro expressed it, "Judicial review of administrative decision making is then marginal in the sense that, at least in the current Washington situation, policy differences are unlikely to arise in most instances in which review is theoretically possible. Thus most of the relations between agencies and courts are relations of acquiescence, consent, or compromise arrived at by anticipation of the other participant's position before even a tremor of conflict arises" (1968:268). Eventually, however, as administrative power was thought to infringe increasingly upon the life of the ordinary citizen this approach was modified in favor of a more forceful judicial response to the rise of the administrative state.

Judicial Restrictions on the Administrative State

The current judicial response to the rise of the administrative state involves a shift away from concerns with the separation of powers and toward the protection of individual rights in the face of administrative action. This is not to say that issues related to the separation of powers no longer arise or that they are not accompanied by continuing legal development. In fact, there is reason to believe that the scope of judicial review of administrative discretion is growing somewhat wider, as Judge Bazelon stated in *Environmental Defense Fund v. Ruckelshaus* (1971):

> We stand on the threshold of a new era in the history of the long and fruitful collaboration of administrative agencies and reviewing courts. For many years, courts have treated administrative policy decisions with great deference, confining judicial attention primarily to matters

of procedure. On matters of substance, the courts regularly upheld agency action, with a nod in the direction of the "substantial evidence" test, and a bow to the mysteries of administrative expertise. Courts occasionally asserted, but less often exercised, the power to set aside agency action on the ground that an impermissible factor had entered into the decision, or a crucial factor had not been considered. Gradually, however, that power has come into more frequent use, and with it, the requirement that administrators articulate the factors on which they base their decisions (597).

Nevertheless, as long as issues are framed in terms of the separation of powers, and broad delegations are deemed acceptable, the judiciary's involvement in the operation of the administrative state is inherently limited. Put simply, judges may lack the technical expertise to substitute effectively their own judgments for those of administrators where matters turn on questions of physical and social science. As Donald Horowitz argues, ". . . it is in the area of requiring affirmative conduct that the Courts' capabilities for forecasting and monitoring are most severely taxed" (1977:266).[4]

Rather, it is in the area of individual rights that judges have their greatest expertise, and it is also here that the administrative state most directly threatens constitutional citizenship. Consequently, once the courts turned away from addressing the administrative state in terms of the traditional separation of powers questions and began confronting it from the perspective of its tendency to erode individual constitutional rights, the impact of the judiciary on public administration expanded immensely. This expansion can be fruitfully discussed by breaking it down into four related categories.

A. The Citizen as Public Bureaucrat   Perhaps the most protracted and complex confrontations between the values of the administrative state and those of the Constitution pertaining to civil rights and liberties have occurred in the area of public employment. In its role as employer, the government not only has extra leverage over the individual citizen-employee, but it also has additional authority. Over the years, governmental employers have often sought to create a kind of bureaucratically desired uniformity among their personnel that poses a serious challenge to the diversity sought by the Constitution.

Bureaucracy is generally thought to value uniformity. Thus,

[4]See the discussion in *Ethyl Corp v. EPA* (1976).

Max Weber referred to "dehumanization" as the "special virtue" of bureaucratic organization (1958:216). He saw the individual bureaucrat as "only a single cog in an ever-moving mechanism which prescribes to him an essentially fixed route of march" (1958:228). Moreover, in this conceptualization, "the individual bureaucrat . . . is forged to the community of all functionaries who are integrated into the mechanism" (1958:228). More recently, Ralph Hummel has argued that "the bureaucrat's personality is devastated. It is no longer possible to easily speak of the individual's personality as 'belonging' to him" (1977:129–130). Such uniformity enhances the ability of superordinates to control their underlings and thus strengthens hierarchy and eliminates employee resistance to the implementation of public policy.

Bureaucracy's emphasis on uniformity is not confined to its own personnel, however; it also extends to clients. As Ralph Hummel observes, often the client ". . . is turned into a case. The bureaucrat has no time and no permission to become involved in the personal problems of clients. From his point of view the more he can depersonalize the client into a thing devoid of unique features the more easily and smoothly he will be able to handle the cases before him" (1977:21).

In the United States there have been several examples of attempts to promote uniformity among bureaucratic personnel. Partisan uniformity was promoted by the spoils system and patronage practices generally. Ideological uniformity was sought through various loyalty-security programs. Uniformity in nonpartisanship was promoted by regulations for political neutrality, such as the Hatch Acts. A measure of social uniformity among bureaucratic personnel was sought through the exclusion by law, official directive, and prevailing practice of women and members of minority groups. Other kinds of uniformity have been promoted by regulations pertaining to morality, personal appearance, and residency.[5]

The Constitution, by contrast, seeks to promote and maintain diversity within the political community and its government. The rationale behind it is, as James Madison wrote in *Federalist No. 10*, that if ". . . you take in a greater variety of parties and interests you make it less probable that a majority of the whole will have a common motive to invade the rights of other citizens; or if such a com-

---

[5]For a review of the development and constitutional questions raised by the practices mentioned in this paragraph, see Rosenbloom (1971).

mon motive exists, it will be more difficult for all who feel it to discover their own strength and to act in unison with each other" (Rossiter, 1961:83). Some measure of diversity in government is assured by the Constitution's provisions for federalism, separation of powers, and bicameralism. Diversity within the society is promoted by the Bill of Rights.

Perhaps the most unequivocal clash between bureaucratic and constitutional perspectives in this context occurred with regard to the loyalty-security program of the late 1940s and early 1950s (Rosenbloom, 1971). It was observed that a code of behavior had developed among bureaucrats in Washington, under which it was deemed, by some, that among other things,

> you should not discuss the admission of Red China to the U.N.; you should not advocate interracial equality; you should not mix with people unless you know them very well; if you want to read *The Nation*, you should not take it to the office; . . . you should take certain books off your private bookshelves (Jahoda, 1955).

As Henry Steele Commager summarized it, the "new loyalty . . . is, above all, conformity" (1947:195). Interrogation of federal employees extended to matters of racial relationships, marriage, sex, literature, and even whether an employee "read the *New York Times*" (Yarmolinsky, 1955; Rosenbloom, 1971). It is clear, then, that the loyalty-security program placed great pressures on the ordinary constitutional rights of public employees as citizens. Initially these were accepted by the courts under the rationale that there is "no prohibition against dismissal of Government employees because of their political beliefs, activities or affiliation . . . The First Amendment guarantees free speech and assembly, but it does not guarantee Government employ . . ." (*Bailey v. Richardson*, 1950:59). Eventually, however, a different set of assumptions prevailed:

> A citizen's right to engage in protected expression or debate is substantially unaffected by the fact that he is also an employee of the government and, as a general rule, he cannot be deprived of his employment merely because he exercises those rights. This is so because dismissal from government employment, like criminal sanctions or damages, may inhibit the propensity of a citizen to exercise his right to freedom of speech and association (*Kiiskila v. Nichols*, 1970:749).

In theoretical terms, therefore, what occurred was a shift from a prevailing judicial approach that allowed public bureaucracy to impose uniformity and conformity upon its personnel to one that promoted the kind of pluralistic diversity anticipated by the Constitution. In doctrinal terms, the distinction between privileges and rights was largely disregarded, thereby enabling the withdrawal of the privilege of public employment to entail constitutional protection. Indeed, in *Board of Regents v. Roth* (1972), the Supreme Court announced that it had "fully and finally rejected the wooden distinction between 'rights' and 'privileges' that once seemed to govern the applicability of procedural due process rights" (571); and in *Sugarman v. Dougall* (1973:644) it reiterated that it had "rejected the concept that constitutional rights turn upon whether a governmental benefit is characterized as a 'right' or as a 'privilege.' "

The demise of the doctrine of privilege led to a series of decisions protecting public employees' freedoms of association, speech, religion, general liberty and their rights to procedural due process in adverse actions under certain circumstances.[6] The applicability of equal protection to public employment was also clearly articulated by the courts for the first time (*Brooks v. School District*, 1959). These decisions have promoted partisan pluralism, social diversity, unionism, political protests, and "whistle-blowing" within the public service. For the most part, the new protections stem from changing concepts of constitutional rights generally, but they are also related to the judiciary's recognition of some of the political consequences of the rise of the administrative state. Two Supreme Court decisions serve to illustrate this point well.

Pickering v. Board of Education (1968) involved the dismissal of a teacher for writing a letter to a local newspaper, in connection with a proposed tax increase, which was critical of the local school authorities' handling of past revenue raising proposals. Upon dismissal, Pickering initiated a suit alleging that his First Amendment rights had been violated. Although certainly concerned with teachers' rights (and by implication, those of other public employees), the Supreme Court also returned to a fundamental question posed by the rise of the administrative state:

> free and open debate is vital to informed decision making by the electorate. Teachers are, as a class, the members of the community most likely to have informed and definite opinions as to how funds allotted

[6]*Ibid.* It should be noted that some Burger Court decisions suggest an approach somewhat less favorable to public employees' rights, though certainly there has been no return to the doctrine of privilege. See Rosenbloom (1978).

to the operation of the schools should be spent. Accordingly, it is essential that they be able to speak out freely on such questions without fear of retaliatory dismissal (571–72).

. . .

A second case also concerns the role of the electorate in the administrative state, but from a different perspective. In *Elrod v. Burns* (1976), the Supreme Court held that patronage dismissals of nonpolicymaking public employees constituted an unconstitutional breach of their First and Fourteenth Amendment rights. The plurality opinion considered the contention that such dismissals could be justified by "the contribution they may make to the democratic process" (369). It went on to reject this possibility:

> Patronage can result in the entrenchment of one or a few parties to the exclusion of others. And most indisputably, . . . patronage is a very effective impediment to the associational and speech freedoms which are essential to a meaningful system of democratic government. Thus, if patronage contributes at all to the elective process, that contribution is diminished by the practice's impairment of the same (369–370).

Thus, whatever the historical accuracy of its interpretation, it is indisputable that in holding "unconstitutional a practice as old as the Republic" (376), the plurality's concerns extended well beyond the rights of public employees to the impact of the administrative state on the electoral process.

B. The Citizen as Client of the Administrative State Citizens' interaction with public bureaucracy is not, of course, confined to government employment. Individuals are also clients of the administrative state, and increasingly full-fledged citizenship requires the individual to take advantage of various kinds of benefits bestowed by bureaucratic agencies. Under the administrative state, as Charles Reich observes:

> One of the most important developments in the United States during the past decade [1950s] has been the emergence of government as a major source of wealth. Government is a gigantic syphon. It draws in revenue and power, and pours forth wealth: money, benefits, services, contracts, franchises, and licenses. Government has always had this function. But while in early times it was minor, today's distribution of largess is on a vast, imperial scale.
>   The valuables dispensed by government take many forms, but

they all share one characteristic. They are steadily taking the place of traditional forms of wealth—forms which are held as private property. Social insurance substitutes for savings; a government contract replaces a businessman's customers and good will; the wealth of more and more Americans depends upon a relationship to government. Increasingly, Americans live on government largess . . . (1964:733).

Among the largess to which Reich refers are income, benefits, jobs, occupational licenses (extending well beyond jobs requiring much education or training), franchises, contracts, subsidies, use of public resources, use of governmental services, and drivers' licenses. Thus, the individual citizen, as client of the administrative state, becomes heavily dependent upon government for his/her well-being.

It is commonplace of American politics that dependence upon government extracts a heavy political price. Thus, as Reich notes, "When government—national, state, or local—hands out something of value, whether a relief check or a television license, government's power grows forthwith; it automatically gains such power as is necessary and proper to supervise its largess. It obtains new rights to investigate, to regulate, and to punish" (Reich, 1964:746). Moreover,

Broad as is the power derived from largess, it is magnified by many administrative factors when it is brought to bear on a recipient. First, the agency granting government largess generally has a wide measure of discretion to interpret its own power. Second, the nature of administrative agencies, the functions they combine, and the sanctions they possess, give them additional power. Third, the circumstances in which the recipients find themselves sometimes make them abettors, rather than resisters, of further growth of power (Reich, 1964:749).

This power can be used to assault both substantive and procedural constitutional rights.

Examples by which individuals' rights have been attacked through the allotment of largess include efforts to exclude the "disloyal" from welfare and public housing; from various occupations, including law, radio-telegraph workers, and port workers, from unemployment compensation, and the receipt of various licenses (Reich, 1964:747). Government has also sought to intrude into questions of individual morality through the allotment of largess, including welfare benefits and government pensions (Reich, 1964:747). Procedurally, under the traditional view, as William Van Alstyne points out:

A public housing tenant summarily evicted without a hearing or any stated reason should have no basis for complaint; surely one no more has a right to public housing than to public employment; in either case he simply takes the benefits on the terms offered him. . . . And certainly public university students summarily expelled or suspended should have no constitutional grounds for reinstatement, for it must be equally clear that while petitioners may have a right to procedural due process, they have no right to be educated at the public expense (1968:1441–1442).

By and large, the traditional approach that might allow such developments to occur was the doctrine of privilege, which was not confined to largess involving public employment. As in the latter area, it was rejected by the Supreme Court precisely for its inability to protect the citizen in the bureaucratized polity. Two cases are illustrative of the judiciary's response to the rise of the administrative state in this context.

Sherbert v. Verner (1963) concerned a citizen-client's substantive constitutional rights. Sherbert, a Seventh Day Adventist, lost her private sector job when she refused to work on Saturday. Not being able to find other suitable work, she filed a claim for unemployment compensation under the South Carolina Unemployment Compensation Act. However, the ". . . Employment Security Commission . . . found that [Sherbert's] restriction upon her availability for Saturday work brought her within provision disqualifying for benefits insured workers who fail, without good cause, to accept 'suitable work when offered' . . ." (401). This administrative ruling was sustained by the South Carolina Supreme Court. The U.S. Supreme Court rejected the doctrine of privilege and ruled in favor of Sherbert:

> Nor may the South Carolina court's construction of the statute be saved from constitutional infirmity on the ground that unemployment compensation benefits are not appellant's "right" but merely a "privilege." It is too late in the day to doubt that the liberties of religion and expression may be infringed by the denial or placing of conditions upon a benefit or privilege. . . . [T]o condition the availability of benefits upon [Sherbert's] willingness to violate a cardinal principle of her religious faith effectively penalizes the free exercise of her constitutional liberties . . . (404–406).

In sum, *Sherbert* stands for the principle that the allocation of largess cannot constitutionally be used to restrict the citizen-client's constitutional rights except where such restrictions are necessary to serve "some compelling state interest" (406).[7] Even under those circumstances, however, more than perfunctory judicial review of the merits could be obtained and the burden of proof would fall upon the government.

The citizen-client of the administrative state has also been afforded procedural protection by the federal judiciary. In *Goldberg v. Kelly* (1970), the Supreme Court was confronted with the question of whether New York City's termination of welfare payments to an individual without affording him the opportunity for a *prior* evidentiary hearing violated the due process clause of the Fourteenth Amendment. The Court's decision was not only important for the precedent it set, but also for its direct recognition of the extent of individuals' dependence on the largess allotted by the administrative state. In the course of ruling that Kelly was entitled to a prior hearing, the Court stated: "The extent to which procedural due process must be afforded the recipient is influenced by the extent to which he may be 'condemned to suffer grievous loss' . . . and depends upon whether the recipient's interest in avoiding that loss outweighs the governmental interest in summary adjudication" (262–63). Under the circumstances, in which Kelly might be deprived of "the very means by which to live while he waits" (264) for the opportunity for a post-terminated hearing, the Court considered his interests in a prior hearing to outweigh the government's alleged interests in not affording one. Thus *Goldberg v. Kelly* illustrated two important principles. First, as in *Sherbert v. Verner*, bureaucratic largess is constitutionalized in the sense that it cannot be withheld in the absence of some measure of procedural due process. Second, the case indicates that to the extent that one is dependent upon such largess, it cannot be terminated by the government without first making procedural due process protections available to the citizen-client of the administrative state.[8] This is a very long way from the doctrine of

[7]Citizens also have comprehensive equal protection rights in the allocation of largess. This was established at a relatively early date, perhaps because the doctrine of privilege did not logically preclude the requirement that benefits be distributed without regard to race. See *Mills v. Board of Education* (1939); *Alston v. School Board* (1940).

[8]More recently, a discussion has developed concerning the extent to which an entitlement to largess can be conditional upon a statutory limitation of procedural due process. See *Arnett v. Kennedy* (1974), where the issue was forcefully debated by the Supreme Court, which remained complexly divided on the matter.

privilege since the citizen-client still lacks a constitutional right to the largess itself. Indeed, Justice Black's dissenting observation was appropriate: "The procedure required today as a matter of constitutional law finds no precedent in our legal system" (277).

The constitutionalization of bureaucratic largess is a remarkable aspect of the judiciary's response to the rise of the administrative state. Though to some extent its origins rest in the evolution of concepts of due process and substantive constitutional rights, its ramifications reach to the heart of citizenship in the administrative state. Reich perceived this well before the constitutional changes under discussion became established doctrine:

> If the individual is to survive in a collective society, he must have protection against its ruthless pressures. There must be sanctuaries or enclaves where no majority can reach. To shelter the solitary human spirit does not merely make possible the fulfillment of individuals; it also gives society the power to change, to grow, and to regenerate, and hence to endure. These were the objects which property sought to achieve, and can no longer achieve. The challenge of the future will be to construct, for the society that is coming, institutions and laws to carry on this work. Just as the Homestead Act was a deliberate effort to foster individual values at an earlier time, so we must try to build an economic basis for liberty today—a Homestead Act for rootless twentieth century man. We must create a new property (1964:787).

The constitutionalization of bureaucratic largess is a major step toward the creation of a "new property." Like property itself, it cannot be denied to the individual without due process of law. Nor can its distribution be used to assault substantive constitutional rights. In this fashion, the judiciary has sought to harmonize the individual's dependence on the administrative state with the kind of political community anticipated by the Constitution.

C. The Citizen as Captive of the Administrative State   Perhaps the most direct judicial challenge to the rise of administrative power has occurred where individuals are involuntarily institutionalized by the government. Prison, mental hospitals, facilities for the retarded, and related types of institutions predate the rise of the administrative state. However, increasingly they are being assimilated into it, reflecting its concepts of organization and administrative thinking. Moreover, such units often provide more than institutionalization alone. For example, in the early 1970s, the Federal Bureau of Prisons contained a Community Services Division, responsible for overseeing work release, community treatment centers, drug abuse aftercare, jail inspectors, state and local consultative and training services, and coordination between corrections and probation and parole services (U.S. Government Organization Manual, 1972/73:290). Even less developed organizations of this type are in frequent interaction with other public agencies having related missions. Hence, such facilities now constitute a well-developed component of the administrative state in terms of personnel, budget, and mission. The institutionalized population has also grown in conjunction with this administrative evolution. In 1977 there were approximately 292,000 prisoners, 173,000 parolees, 415,600 persons confined to public mental hospitals, and about 150,000 in public facilities for the mentally retarded (U.S. Department of Commerce, 1979:194, 194, 118, 118).

Historically, the judiciary, perhaps reflecting the dominant societal attitude, showed little interest in those held in such institutions.[9] As Judge Bazelon pointed out, ". . . until recently, many areas, such as prisons, were regarded by the courts as involving 'mere housekeeping' matters and remained largely untouched by judicial review" (1976:101). A few cases are illustrative. In one case the censorship and the limitation of prisoners' correspondence were held to be "inherent incidents in the conduct of penal institutions" (*Lee v. Tahash*, 1965:971); in another, a complaint by Muslim prisoners unable to abide by their religion's dietary laws was dismissed as nonjustifiable on the grounds that ". . . courts will not interfere with matters of routine prison administration. . . ." (*Childs v. Pegelow*, 1963:490); and in a final example, prisoners' complaints regarding theft of personal property, insect contaminated food, and insufficient daily rations of water were considered not to "rise to a sufficient status of ill treatment to authorize judicial interference" (*Konigsberg v. Ciccone*, 1968:597–600).

During the first part of the 1970s, however, a significant shift in the judicial response to this aspect of the administrative state occurred. The precise reasons for a more activist judicial response to the problems of captives of the administrative state are difficult to identify. Certainly the expansion of individual's rights vis-à-vis ad-

---

[9]See generally, *Harvard Civil Liberties Law Review* (1977); see also *Yale Law Journal* (1975).

ministrators generally was a factor, as was greater concern with the right to treatment generally. The racial strife and protests of the 1960s may also have created greater concern with prison conditions. In addition, the expansion of the rights of those accused of crimes tended to direct attention to the rights of those convicted of crimes as well.

In any event, today the judicial response to the plight of the captives of the administrative state is characterized by the judges' willingness to confront administrators directly and essentially to engage in administrative activity to protect captives' constitutional rights. Two cases are illustrative of the general tendency.

Wyatt v. Stickney (1971) involved the constitutional rights of individuals confined to public mental hospitals and a facility for the retarded in Alabama. The court proceeded on the premise that "When patients are so [civilly] committed for treatment purposes they unquestionably have a constitutional right to receive such individual treatment as will give each of them a realistic opportunity to be cured or to improve his or her mental condition . . ." (784). Upon reviewing the abominable conditions in the facilities in question—under which four patients had died and one had been confined to a straight-jacket for nine years to prevent hand and finger sucking—the court allowed the hospital administrators six months during which to develop and implement proper standards for adequate mental care.

The administrators failed to accomplish this to the court's satisfaction and eventually the court promulgated its own standards and created Human Rights Committees to oversee their implementation. These standards were guided by the belief that three conditions had to be met for constitutionally adequate and effective treatment: 1) a humane psychological and physical environment, 2) qualified staff in sufficient numbers, and 3) individualized treatment plans. The extent to which the court assumed an administrative role was evident in its translation of these requirements into specific conditions.

Among the court ordered requirements were such elements as: no excessive medication, the patient's right to his/her own clothes, the right to physical exercise, no more than six patients per room, no single rooms with less than 100 square feet of space, at least one toilet per 8 patients and one shower per 15 patients, at least 10 square feet per patient in the dining facility, various staffing ratios per patient for professionals and other employees, and a temperature range between 68 degrees F. and 83 degrees F.

Hamilton v. Schiro (1970) serves to illustrate parallel developments concerning those confined to prisons. After reviewing prison conditions, the court concluded:

> Prison life inevitably involves some deprivation of rights, but the conditions of plaintiffs' confinement in Orleans Parish Prison so shock the conscience as a matter of elemental decency and are so much more cruel than is necessary to achieve a legitimate penal aim that such confinement constitutes cruel and unusual punishment in violation of the Eighth and Fourteenth Amendments . . ." (1010).

As in *Wyatt*, the court eventually ordered the implementation of various reforms that clearly brought it into the realm of administration. The most obvious instance of this was its directive that "The management and operation of the prison shall be improved immediately" (*Hamilton v. Landrieu*, 1972:550). A more direct challenge to the authority of the agents of the administrative state would be hard to imagine. The court also ordered that a total of 124 additional employees be hired, that various training programs be established, that prison officers be stationed in specific locations, and that there be better food, sanitation, and conditions generally. In all, the court mandated 54 changes necessary to bring the prison up to constitutional standards.

In sum, the conditions under which captives of the administrative state have sometimes been held have been so inhumane that the judiciary has abandoned its traditional posture of limiting its review and of granting great deference to administrative expertise and discretion. Instead, it has responded to this aspect of the administrative state by directly confronting administrative inadequacies and substituting administrative judgments of its own for those of administrators. In so doing, the courts have a major advantage over administrators in that they can present an ultimate choice to legislators and the electorate. As one court put it:

> Inadequate resources can never be adequate justification for the state's depriving any person of his constitutional rights. If the state cannot obtain the resources to detain persons awaiting trial in accordance with minimum constitutional standards, then the state simply will not be permitted to detain such persons (*Hamilton v. Love*, 1971:1194).

The courts themselves may also have a choice once they find a facility to be unconstitutional. They can order the administrators to develop a plan for reform that meets constitutional standards under threat of judicially ordered closure of the institution in question; or, they can develop a plan of their own as in the cases reviewed here. Neither course is without its dangers. The first is certain to engender outrage if, for instance, prisoners or the mentally ill are actually freed. As suggested earlier, the second involves a host of questions concerning judges' expertise, the effectiveness of their decrees, and the judiciary's legitimacy (Horowitz, 1977; Crampton, 1976; Chayes, 1976). To take a minor, yet extreme, example, it is a long way from the letter of the Constitution to the mandating of a specific constitutional temperature range in a public mental hospital. Yet, whatever one can say about the judiciary's changing role (Chayes, 1976; Horowitz, 1977; Crampton, 1976), it is beyond a doubt that its response to the plight of captives of the administrative state has been direct, extremely forceful, and a remarkable departure from traditional practices.

D. The Citizen as Antagonist of the Administrative State   The federal judiciary has responded to the rise of the administrative state by redefining individuals' rights as employees, clients, and captives of the contemporary version of that state. But, as suggested in the cases regarding the citizen as captive of the administrative state, these newly created rights are not necessarily self-enforcing. One means by which they can be enforced is for the judiciary to respond to suits by taking over the administration of a facility, as in *Wyatt* and *Hamilton*. Another is to allow individuals to sue administrators directly and personally for monetary damages for breaches of their constitutional rights. This not only enables the individual to initiate a direct mechanism for enforcing his/her rights vis-à-vis the administrative state; it also establishes a kind of accountability of administrators to the citizenry that is particularly well adapted to the administrative state since it does not depend on attenuated connections between the will of the electorate and the performance of bureaucrats.[10] Additionally, the judiciary has moved to reduce the barriers of "standing" facing citizen antagonists who seek to sue the administrative state. Indeed, the creation of these enforcement

---

[10]Smith and Hague (1971:27) observe that inevitably under traditional mechanisms "accountability gets lost in the shuffle somewhere in the middle ranges of bureaucracy." Mosher (1968), Fiorina (1977), Arnold (1979), Dodd and Schott (1979), Heclo (1977), Cronin (1975), and numerous others also find that traditional approaches to accountability depending upon a chain of relationships reaching from the electorate to the career bureaucrat are inadequate.

mechanisms provides a great deal of coherence to the judiciary's response to the rise of the administrative state.

The erosion of public administrators' official immunity from civil suits damages is a recent and far-reaching development. Though found nowhere in the Constitution itself, in 1896 the Supreme Court created such an immunity based on the rationale that:

> In exercising the functions of his office the head of an Executive Department, keeping within the limits of his authority, should not be under apprehension that the motives that control his official conduct may, at any time, become the subject of inquiry in a civil suit for damages. It would seriously cripple the proper and effective administration of public affairs as entrusted to the executive branch of the government, if he were subject to any such restraint (*Spalding v. Vilas*, 1896:498).

Department heads, of course, could be held accountable by the president and consequently the ruling was not a drastic blow to governmental accountability. However, in *Barr v. Matteo* (1959) the same principle was extended to career bureaucrats, who were afforded both legal and some measure of constitutional protections against dismissals. A plurality of the Supreme Court now subscribed to the premise that:

> To be sure, the occasions upon which the acts of the head of a department will be protected by the privilege are doubtless far greater than in the case of an officer with less sweeping functions. But it is because the higher the post, the broader the range of responsibilities and duties, and the wider the scope of discretion it entails. It is not the title of his office but the duties with which the particular officer sought to be made to respond in damages is entrusted—the relation of the act complained of to "matters committed by law to his control or supervision" . . . which must provide the guide in delineating the scope of the rule which clothes the official acts of the executive officer with immunity from civil defamation suits (573–4).

Based on this reasoning a host of public administrators were afforded immunity, including an acting director of an Office of Rent Stabilization (in *Barr*), a deputy U.S. Marshal, a district director and collection officer of the IRS, a claims representative of HEW, and a secret service agent (Davis, 1972:487).

In the two decades following *Barr*, the Supreme Court recognized the potential consequences of an absolute official immunity for public administrators and sought to redress the citizen's right to hold the administrative state accountable for its actions. That the Court was reacting precisely to the consequences of the rise of the administrative state is suggested by Justice Brennan's question in *Barr*, "Where does healthy administrative frankness and boldness shade into bureaucratic tyranny?" (590). Ultimately, the Court afforded the citizen-antagonist of the administrative state a new avenue for challenging its alleged unconstitutional abuses.

The standard of public administrator's official immunity was adjusted to protect the citizenry of the administrative state. Rather than an absolute immunity or even an immunity based on traditional concepts of good faith or the reasonability of an administrator's actions at the time they were taken, the Supreme Court has opted for a standard that requires public administrators to be fully cognizant of the constitutional rights of the individuals upon whom they act. In the context of school board members, this standard was articulated as follows:

> The official himself must be acting sincerely and with a belief that he is doing right, but an act violating a student's constitutional rights can be no more justified by ignorance or disregard of settled, indisputable law on the part of one entrusted with supervision of students' daily lives than by the presence of actual malice. . . .
> . . . [A] school board member is not immune from liability for damages . . . if he knew or reasonably should have known that the action he took within his sphere of official responsibility would violate the constitutional rights of the students affected, or if he took the action with the malicious intention to cause a deprivation of constitutional rights or other injury to the student (*Wood v. Strickland*, 1975: 321, 322).

Although there might be some rationale for limiting this standard to situations involving school children or extending it only to institutionalized populations, in *Butz v. Economou* (1978) the Supreme Court treated it as the proper standard of immunity for public administrators generally. However, in that case, the Court created an absolute immunity for public administrators exercising adjudicatory functions, such as hearing examiners, administrative law judges, and agency attorneys exercising "prosecutorial" functions. This limitation on the ability of the citizen-antagonist to hold the agents of the administrative state accountable was considered by the Court to follow directly from the absolute immunity enjoyed by judges and public prosecutors generally.

Civil suits for damages by citizen-antagonists of the administrative state against state and local officials for breach of constitutional rights are authorized by 42 USC 1983.[11] Where such rights are abridged pursuant to the policy of a political subdivision, it is now possible to sue the subdivision directly, and the latter can no longer raise a "qualified good faith immunity" (*Monell v. New York*, 1978; *Owen v. City of Independence*, 1980). In establishing this principle, the administrative state was very much on the Supreme Court's mind:

> The knowledge that a municipality will be liable for all of its injurious conduct, whether committed in good faith or not, should create an incentive for officials who may harbor doubts about the lawfulness of their intended actions to err on the side of protecting citizens' constitutional rights (*Owen v. City of Independence*, 1980:B1768).

In politically related developments, the Supreme Court created a new right for the citizen-antagonist to sue federal administrators for breaches of constitutional rights, even in the absence of statute explicitly authorizing such suits.

This right was first created for citizen-antagonists whose Fourth Amendment rights had been violated. In *Bivens v. Six Unknown Named Federal Narcotic Agents* (1971) the Supreme Court reasoned that expecting an individual whose Fourth Amendment rights were violated by federal agents to seek to recover them by bringing an action in tort under state law, the traditional remedy, was unrealistic in the contemporary administrative state:

> Respondents seek to treat the relationship between a citizen and a federal agent unconstitutionally exercising his authority as no different from the relationship between two private citizens. In so doing, they ignore the fact that power, once granted, does not disappear like a magic gift when it is wrongfully used. An agent acting—albeit unconstitutionally—in the name of the United States possesses far greater capacity for harm than an individual trespasser exercising no authority other than his own (392).

The possibility that such suits would be confined to Fourth Amendment rights was foreclosed by their authorization for breaches of the

---

[11]"Every person who, under color of any statute, ordinance, regulation, custom, usage, of any State or Territory, subjects or causes to be subjected, any citizen of the United States or other person within the jurisdiction thereof to the deprivation of any rights, privileges, or immunities secured by the Constitution and laws, shall be liable to the party injured in an action at law, suit in equity, or other proper proceeding for redress."

Fifth Amendment's equal protection aspects (*Davis v. Passman*, 1979) and for violations of the Eighth Amendment's prohibition against cruel and unusual punishment (*Carlson v. Green*, 1980). Suits of this nature permit the citizen-antagonist to have a jury trial and to seek punitive damages. Consequently, as the Supreme Court pointed out in *Carlson v. Green* (1980:B2033), ". . . the Bivens remedy, in addition to compensating victims, serves a deterrent purpose" that should reduce abuses of individuals' constitutional rights by administrative officials. Moreover, in *Butz*, the Court suggested that federal officials' immunity in such cases would be the same as that of state and local officials in suits under section 1983 because "the 'constitutional design' would be stood on its head if federal officials did not face at least the same liability as state officials guilty of the same constitutional transgression" (*Carlson v. Green*, 1980:B2034; interpreting *Butz v. Economou*, 1978).

In practice, the erosion of public administrators' official immunity can have profound effects on the administrative state. It provides the citizenry with a means of holding administrators accountable for breaches of their constitutional rights. But since "constitutional law," as Justice Powell observes, "is what the courts say it is . . . " (*Owen v. City of Independence*, 1980:B1787), the liability of administrators also encourages them to keep abreast of changing constitutional standards and interpretations. For an extreme example, if the temperature range mandated in *Wyatt* were not adhered to, it would theoretically present a breach of constitutional rights suitable for vindication through a suit for damages under Section 1983. Consequently, judicial decisions concerning individual rights must be integrated into administrative decision-making and action if administrators hope to minimize suits and judgments for damages. In this fashion, the judiciary has acted to enhance its participation in the administrative state and to infuse the administrative process with its constitutional values.

It should be noted briefly that the citizen's role as antagonist of the administrative state is not confined to suits for damages in connection with breaches of constitutional rights. It is also possible to challenge administrative policies and regulations on the grounds that they are illegal or unconstitutional. Here, though less clearly related to the judiciary's view of the rise of the administrative state, the courts have acted to facilitate suits by reducing the barriers presented by "standing."

Although Justice Douglas once admonished that "Generalizations about standing to sue are largely worthless as such" (*Association of Data Processing Service Organizations v. Camp*, 1970:151), a liberalizing trend does seem to have taken place. In *Flast v. Cohen* (1969), a 65 year barrier against federal taxpayer suits was substantially breached and in *U.S. v. Students Challenging Regulatory Agency Procedures (SCRAP)* (1973), the Court found standing on the most minimal of potential injuries. In summarizing these developments, Kenneth Culp Davis writes:

> Beginning in 1968 the Supreme Court has given the federal law of standing a new basic orientation. Many now have standing who were denied it before 1968. . . .
>
> The present law of standing differs no more than slightly, if it differs at all, from the simple proposition that one who is hurt by governmental action has standing to challenge it (Davis, 1972:72).

Thus, despite some exceptions (*U.S. v. Richardson*, 1974), it is now far easier for citizen-antagonists of the administrative state to challenge its actions, and, as noted earlier, the scope of judicial review in such cases appears to be growing wider. . . .

Bibliography

Alston v. School Board (1940). 112 F2d 992.

Arnett v. Kennedy (1974). 416 U.S. 134.

Arnold, R. Douglas (1979). *Congress and the Bureaucracy.* New Haven: Yale.

Association of Data Processing Service Organizations v. Camp (1970). 397 U.S. 150.

Bailey v. Richardson (1950). 182 F2d 46; affirmed by an equally divided Court, 341 U.S. 918 (1951).

Barr v. Matteo (1959). 360 U.S. 564.

Bazelon, David (1976). "The Impact of the Courts on Public Administration," *Indiana Law Journal*, 52: 101–110.

Bivens v. Six Unknown Named Federal Narcotics Agents (1971). 403 U.S. 388.

Board of Regents v. Roth (1972). 408 U.S. 564.

Branti v. Finkel (1980). Slip Opinion, No. 78-1654 (March 31).

Brooks v. School District (1959). 267 F2d 733.

Butz v. Economou (1978). 438 U.S. 504.

Carlson v. Green (1980). 40CCH S. Ct. Bull. B2026.

Chayes, A. (1976). "The Role of the Judiciary in a Public Law System," *Harvard Law Review*, 89: 1281–1316.

Childs v. Pegelow (1963). 321 F2d 487.

Commager, Henry Steele (1947). "Who is Loyal to America?" *Harper's Magazine*, 195: 193–199.

Crampton, Roger (1976). "Judicial Lawmaking and Administration in the Leviathan State," *Public Administration Review*, 36: 551–555.

Cronin, T. (1975). *The State of the Presidency.* Boston: Little, Brown.

Davis, Kenneth Culp (1972). *Administrative Law Text*, 3d ed. St. Paul: West Publishing.

Davis v. Passman (1979). 442 U.S. 228.

Dodd, Lawrence, and Richard Schott (1979). *Congress and the Administrative State.* New York: John Wiley and Sons.

Elrod v. Burns (1976). 427 U.S. 347.

Environmental Defense Fund v. Ruckelshaus (1971). 439 F2d 584.

Ethyl Corp. v. EPA (1976). 511 F2d 1.

Fiorina, Morris (1977). *Congress: Keystone of the Washington Establishment.* New Haven: Yale University Press.

Flast v. Cohen (1968). 392 U.S. 83.

Goldberg v. Kelly (1970). 397 U.S. 254.

Hamilton v. Landrieu (1972). 351 F. Supp. 549.

Hamilton v. Love (1971). 328 F. Supp. 1182.

Hamilton v. Schiro (1970). 338 F. Supp. 1016.

Harvard Civil Liberties Law Review (1977). "Confronting the Conditions of Confinement: An Expanded Role for Courts in Prison Reform," vol. 12: 367–404.

Heclo, Hugh (1977). *A Government of Strangers.* Washington: Brookings.

Hess, S. (1976). *Organizing the Presidency.* Washington: Brookings.

Horowitz, Donald (1977). *The Courts and Social Policy.* Washington: Brookings.

Hummel, Ralph (1977). *The Bureaucratic Experience.* New York: St. Martin's.

Humphrey's Executor v. U.S. (1935). 295 U.S. 602.

Jahoda, Marie (1955). "Morale in the Federal Service." *Annals of the American Academy of Political and Social Science*, 300: 110–113.

Kiiskila v. Nichols (1970). 433 F2d 745.

Konigsberg v. Ciccone (1968). 285 F. Supp. 585.

Lee v. Tahash (1965). 353 F2d 970.

Lowi, Theodore (1969). *The End of Liberalism.* New York: W. W. Norton.

Mills v. Board of Education (1939). 30 F. Supp. 245.

Monell v. New York (1978). 56 L. Ed. 2d 611.

Mosher, Frederick (1968). *Democracy and the Public Service.* New York: Oxford University Press.

Nachmias, David, and David H. Rosenbloom (1980). *Bureaucratic Government, USA.* New York: St. Martin's.

National Cable TV v. U.S. (1974). 415 U.S. 336.

Owen v. City of Independence (1980). 40 CCh. S. Ct. Bull. Bi738.

Pickering v. Board of Education (1968). 391 U.S. 563.

Reich, Charles (1964). "The New Property," *Yale Law Journal*, 73: 733–787.

Rosenbloom, David H. (1971). *Federal Service and the Constitution*. Ithaca: Cornell University Press.

Rosenbloom, David H. (1978). "The Burger Court and the Public Employee," *Southern Review of Public Administration* (September), 239–259.

Rossiter, Clinton, ed. (1961). *The Federalist Papers*. New York: The New American Library.

Schecter Poultry Corp. v. U.S. (1935). 295 U.S. 495.

Shapiro, Martin (1968). *The Supreme Court and Administrative Agencies*. New York: The Free Press.

Sherbert v. Verner (1963). 374 U.S. 398.

Smith, B., and D. Hague (1971). *The Dilemma of Accountability in Modern Government*. New York: St. Martin's.

Spady v. Mount Vernon (1974). 419 U.S. 983.

Spalding v. Vilas (1896). 161 U.S. 483.

Sugarman v. Dougall (1973). 413 U.S. 634.

U.S. Department of Commerce, Bureau of the Census (1979). *Statistical Abstract of the United States*. Washington: Government Printing Office.

U.S. Government Organization Manual, 1972/1973. Washington: National Archives of the United States.

U.S. v. Lovett (1946). 328 U.S. 303.

U.S. v. Richardson (1974). 418 U.S. 166.

U.S. v. SCRAP (1973). 412 U.S. 669.

U.S. v. Southwestern Cable (1968). 392 U.S. 157.

Van Alstyne, W. (1968). "The Demise of the Right-Privilege Distinction in Constitutional Law." *Harvard Law Review*, 81: 1439–1464.

Weber, Max (1958). *Essays in Sociology*. Trans. and ed. by H. H. Gerth and C. W. Mills. New York: Oxford University Press.

Wilson, James Q. (1975). "The Rise of the Bureaucratic State," *The Public Interest*, Fall: 56–76.

Wood v. Strickland (1975). 420 U.S. 308.

Wyatt v. Stickney (1971). 325 F. Supp. 781; 334 F. Supp. 387 (1972); *Wyatt v. Anderholt*, 503 F2d 1305 (1974).

Wyman v. James (1971). 400 U.S. 309.

Yale Law Journal (1975). "The Wyatt Case: Implementation of a Judicial Decree Ordering Institutional Change," vol. 84: 1338–1379.

Yarmolinsky, Adam (1955). *Case Studies in Personnel Security*. Washington: Bureau of National Affairs.

V

The Public Response to Bureaucracy

Since World War II Americans have come to depend more and more on both the services that bureaucracies provide and the regulations they enforce. Simply by leaving largely intact the New Deal programs it had inherited, the Eisenhower administration legitimized these programs as ongoing governmental commitments in the United States. Then in the 1960s Lyndon Johnson's Great Society programs introduced a host of new governmental roles in this country, expanding services for the needy and broadening regulatory activity to achieve social as well as economic goals. Inevitably, this growth of government activity brought on an expansion of bureaucracy.

However, although the American people have thus become more dependent on bureaucracy for vital services and protective regulations, the general drift of public opinion in the 1970s and 1980s has been decisively antibureaucratic in character. Grass-roots disaffection with the cost of financing bureaucratic activities was dramatically symbolized by the events described by David O. Sears and Jack Citrin in "Tax Revolt: Proposition 13 in California and Its Aftermath." Proposition 13 was an initiative adopted in California to curb growth in property taxes. It won voter approval despite warnings from a variety of state and local officials that it would lead inevitably to cutbacks in public services.

The passage of Proposition 13 in California was followed by the enactment of similar measures in other states. Even more important, the strength of the grass-roots antagonism toward government spending that it demonstrated led politicians of both political parties to conclude that there had been a significant erosion in public support for any further expansion of governmental activities. At least in the civilian sector of government, bureaucracy thus found itself in retreat—dealing with cutbacks, reductions in force, and, in some instances, the outright elimination of long-established programs.

And yet Sears and Citrin also discovered in their investigation that even in those parts of the country where the tax revolt was strongest, the public still strongly supported the continuance of the government services it was already receiving— with the possible exception of welfare. So the paradox with which politicians were left to wrestle was that the public supported the continuance of a wide range of specific public services at the same time that it was voting for a substantial reduction in overall public expenditures.

Some resolution of this paradox is attempted by the authors of "Americans Love Their Bureaucrats." Americans, they contend, dislike bureaucrats in general but often take a much more favorable attitude toward the particular officials with whom they have face-to-face encounters. Consider, for example, these discrepancies, as reported by the authors:

> . . . stereotypes live long and die hard, and the image of the insolent bureaucrat and his inefficient organization survives *in spite* of people's experiences, not because of them. We found that our respondents consistently described their own encounters more positively than what they thought everyone else was getting. For example, 71 percent of all the clients said that their problems were taken care of, but only 30 percent think that government agencies do well at taking care of problems.

The unhappy fact that bureaucrats must thus confront is that their ability to do a good job in the eyes of those they serve does not necessarily improve the generally unfavorable public image of bureaucracy. At the same time, however, they can draw some comfort from the fact that this negative stereotype of bureaucracy does not prevent their clients from appreciating the services they do provide and praising the agency that provides them.

Critics of bureaucracy often contend that the way in which agencies respond to the public is characterized by a very obvious class bias. The rich and powerful are very well served when they deal with government, whereas impoverished citizens are neglected or treated very arbitrarily by the agencies with which they deal. This is the major theme that emerges in "Bureaucracy and the Lower Class" by Gideon Sjoberg, Richard A. Brymer, and Buford Farris.

As the authors point out, the lower-income citizen "lacks knowledge of the rules of the game." As compared to middle- or upper-class individuals, the client in a poverty area "stands in awe of bureaucratic regulations and frequently is unaware that he [or she] has a legal and moral claim to certain rights and privileges." Moreover, the impersonality of bureaucracy poses communication problems for the poor, whereas "middle-class persons are better able to relate to others within an impersonal context."

On the positive side, this article suggests that when disadvantaged citizens improve their use of political resources—by becoming better organized, better led, and more militant in expressing their grievances—the agencies on which they depend become much more sensitive to their needs and concerns when formulating policies or providing services. As the article says, "traditionally disadvantaged groups such as Negroes and Puerto Ricans" have now acquired sufficient political power in New York City to challenge and force the revision of certain practices and procedures carried on by the school system and other city agencies. Through aggressive political action, lower-income citizens can thus transform their status; instead of merely being acted upon by an administrative agency, they can significantly affect the way in which they are treated.[1]

[1]For a very interesting discussion of the different degrees of power Americans may have in dealing with bureaucracy, see Eugene Lewis, *American Politics in a Bureaucratic Age: Citizens, Constituents, Clients and Victims* (Cambridge: Winthrop, 1977).

16

Tax Revolt: Proposition 13 in California and Its Aftermath

DAVID O. SEARS
AND JACK CITRIN

The tax revolt in California was not an isolated event.* This is hardly surprising, for other states and nations also experienced many of the political, cultural, and economic changes that provided the background for the protests in California. The decline of public confidence in government's ability to solve pressing problems manifested itself throughout America and in most European countries.[1] So too did concern about the erosion of traditional values and communal institutions. And in the late 1970s, complaints that the reach of state activity had gone too far gained in political strength. In the economic realm, the impact of the world recession, to which California, in fact, was relatively immune, stretched governmental resources, while inflation boosted both income taxes and property taxes for most people.

The expansion of the welfare state in most Western countries throughout the 1950s and 1960s was smoothed by the sustained economic growth that simultaneously furnished governments with more

Reprinted by permission of the authors and publishers from *Tax Revolt: Something for Nothing in California*, Enlarged Edition, by David O. Sears and Jack Citrin, Cambridge, Mass.: Harvard University Press, Copyright © 1982, 1985 by the President and Fellows of Harvard College. Footnotes are renumbered.

*Editor's note: Proposition 13 was a ballot initiative passed in California in 1978 that drastically reduced and restricted the future growth of property taxes.

[1]For findings about Western Europe see S. Barnes et al., *Political Action: Mass Participation in Five Western Democracies* (Beverly Hills: Sage, 1979).

revenues at the same tax rates and raised the individual wage-earner's take-home pay.[2] In the 1970s, however, the costs of public policy rose at a much more rapid rate than the growth of the private economy. Whatever fiscal dividend the government enjoyed now came from inflation's pushing people into higher tax brackets rather than from real economic progress. Public spending increased steadily in all Western countries from 1970 to 1977, but real disposable income fell in at least one year in each of them.[3] In the absence of a shift in public tastes away from private consumption to government services, this reallocation of collective resources prepared the ground for diverse forms of resistance to taxes.

The rebellious response to the squeeze of rising taxes on stagnant income has taken several forms. An essentially private mode of the tax revolt is simply to evade or avoid taxes—either by cheating or by participating in an "underground" economy in which transactions are demonetized exchanges of personal services or conducted in cash at a reduced rate. Several scholars have argued that this kind of tax rebellion has been growing in recent years.[4] One collective mode of protest is the "populist insurgency" along the lines of Proposition 13, when resentment at the grass roots mobilizes for electoral action. Another is the "institutionalized austerity" of conservative administrations, such as Margaret Thatcher's or Ronald Reagan's, which convert mass protests against high taxes into official policy and broaden the objectives of the tax revolt to encompass an ideologically based reordering of governmental activities. An exhaustive survey of protests against taxes outside California is beyond the scope of this study, but a brief selective review of major developments on the American scene illustrates clearly that Proposition 13 was an aspect of a broader political phenomenon.

Other American States

The passage of Proposition 13 stimulated a rash of similar initiatives in other states. Throughout most of the country taxes and government spending had been rising, so it is easy to understand the onset

---

[2]See this discussion in R. Rose, "The Nature of the Challenge," in *Challenge to Governance*, ed. R. Rose (Beverly Hills: Sage, 1980).

[3]R. Rose and G. Peters, *Can Government Go Bankrupt?* (London: Macmillan, 1979).

[4]See R. Rose, "Ordinary People in Extraordinary Circumstances," in *Challenge to Governance*.

of the anti-government contagion. But it is hard to generalize about the results of these ballot measures.[5] . . . [T]he tax rebels succeeded in some states where the tax burden and government spending were relatively high—California in 1978 and 1979, Massachusetts in 1980—but there were losses in such states too, and victories where the level of taxes was below the national norm, as in Texas and Idaho. In Michigan, where the reliance on property taxes was relatively heavy, a Proposition 13-like measure to cut property taxes failed. But a Gann-like spending limit simultaneously passed, even though the overall level of taxes was moderate. In Colorado, however, even a moderate "spending cap" proposal failed in 1977.

. . . [T]he inflation of real estate values in the late 1970s was unusually severe in California, and . . . this produced the very high property taxes targeted by Proposition 13. Most other states did, however, share at least the shift in the overall property tax burden from business onto individual homeowners, and a variety of specific mechanisms were proposed to meet homeowners' complaints. For example, in addition to property tax cuts or limits, many states have legislated or are considering indexation of income taxes, "truth-in-taxation" procedures, property tax circuitbreakers, postponement of property taxes for senior citizens, and the functional reassignment of expenditures from local to state government. In addition to legislation, popular initiatives were a frequent response to rising taxes, especially in the western and mountain states where Populist and Progressive traditions have firmly implanted the institutions of direct democracy and the inclination to resort to them.

One tentative conclusion about the onset of grass-roots tax protests is that they occur when visible taxes rise rapidly *and* overall taxes are high.[6] It also appears that after voters impose far-reaching tax or spending cuts they adopt a wait-and-see attitude, as their concern about the delivery of services mounts. The cycle of anger-protest-caution observed in California has also been displayed in such dissimilar states as Connecticut, Colorado, and Michigan.[7] What

[5]See Chapter 2 [of Sears and Citrin, *Tax Revolt*] and *Intergovernmental Perspective* (Winter, 1979).

[6]The experience of California and Massachusetts, where the two most radical tax-cutting proposals passed, in particular, corroborates this conclusion of Wilensky's comparative studies of advanced industrial societies. See H. L. Wilensky, *The Welfare State and Equality* (Berkeley: University of California Press, 1975).

[7]For a good summary of the events in these states see R. Kuttner, *The Revolt of the Haves* (New York: Simon and Schuster, 1980).

seems clear too is that the dynamics of each election campaign and the way officials respond to public concern about taxes are important determinants of the outcomes of anti-public-sector referenda. This can be illustrated by a brief look at selected recent contests outside California.[8]

Idaho

Although Idaho's taxes ranked thirty-third in the nation in 1977, the Jarvisite approach to property tax reform found fertile soil there. State-ordered reassessments in several counties had resulted in increases of as much as 75 percent in the property tax bills of homeowners. Proposition 1, a Jarvis-Gann imitation limiting property taxes to 1 percent a year and restricting increases in assessments to 2 percent a year, qualified for the ballot with the largest total of signatures of any initiative in Idaho history.[9]

State action to alleviate the tax burden was belated and much less far-reaching than the initiative would provide. The rhetoric of the campaign and the alignment of forces in Idaho followed the California pattern. The pro-initiative arguments criticized bureaucracy, governmental waste, and the threat of high taxes to besieged homeowners. The opposition, led once again by the education lobby and public employee unions, warned of the threat to educational programs and the likelihood that other taxes would be raised should property taxes be cut so sharply. In Idaho, as in Oregon and Michigan, there was a tendency to downplay the general threat to public services; mindful of the California experience, the anti-initiative forces felt this scare tactic would be counterproductive.

As in California, the Idaho property tax initiative took an early lead in the polls and then slipped in popular favor. By late October, the *Boise Statesman* reported that among those who had decided to vote 34 percent were in favor and an equal proportion opposed. This galvanized the advocates of tax relief into a renewed effort in the media that emphasized how much property tax bills would rise

---

[8]This discussion of ballot measures and public opinion in states other than California relies heavily on R. Palaich, J. Kloss, and M. F. Williams, *Tax and Expenditure Limitation Referenda: An Analysis of Public Opinion, Voting Behavior, and Campaigns in Four States* (Denver: Education Commission of the States, 1980); and for Massachusetts on Kuttner, *Revolt of the Haves.*

[9]The increase in the burden of property taxes on homeowners was the result of a state supreme court decision in 1967 that forbade different assessment ratios for different types of property. This caused the familiar shift in the tax burden toward the individual homeowner—that is, toward voters.

should Proposition 1 fail. The fact that an earlier supreme court decision required homeowners' reassessments to "catch up to those of business" by 1977–1978 dramatized the growing tax burden; success at drawing attention to this led to a surge of anti-tax feeling in the late stages of the campaign, and the initiative ultimately won with 59 percent of the vote.

Massachusetts

The victory of a Jarvisite measure in liberal Massachusetts— Taxachusetts to some cynics—again shows how, as in California a decade or so earlier, political reform in the name of equality under the law can fuel the tax revolt. Although taxes were high in both California and Massachusetts, the distribution of the tax load was much more progressive in the former state. Massachusetts depended more heavily on the property tax so an individual's overall state and local tax rate tended to fall as income rose.[10] But as in California before the late 1960s, a "political" form of tax relief had traditionally eased discontent: local tax assessors usually assessed homes far below their actual market value.

Trouble began because some neighborhoods suffered as a result of this discretionary procedure. They sued for equity. In 1975 the state supreme court's Sudbury decision required the state to assess all properties at 100 percent of their market value. This set in motion what Kuttner describes as a tax revolt of the "left"—a homeowners' movement for relief that was aimed as much against the tax advantages of businesses as against government. In November 1978 the Classification Initiative qualified for the ballot, providing lower property tax assessments for homeowners than for business. At the behest of Mayor Kevin White, the organizers of this measure, Fair Share, received a million dollars from the city of Boston. The initiative passed easily.

But this populist victory was short-lived. In March 1979 the state supreme court ruled that business and residential property had to be assessed at the same rate. Massachusetts had shown no inclination to cut public services, so the demise of preferential assessments for homeowners set off a search for alternative sources of revenue. Efforts to impose new taxes on business failed to garner sufficient support, and as property taxes continued to rise Proposition 2½

---

[10]Kuttner, *Revolt of the Haves*, p. 310.

emerged. The initiative was so named because it provided that the property tax be limited to 2.5 percent of a property's market value and that the total annual growth of property tax levies be restricted to the same proportion. In addition, the state's high auto excise tax would be cut in half. Proposition 2½, unlike its local predecessor, the Classification Initiative, was not hostile to business. Like California's Proposition 13 it was a constitutional amendment that cut revenues drastically without indicating how they could be replaced. And Massachusetts had no state surplus to fall back on. Thus when the measure passed in November 1980, even as Ronald Reagan carried the only state that had gone for McGovern in 1972, the prognosis was clear. Massachusetts would have to impose new state taxes or else cut current levels of staff and services.

Michigan

In November 1978 Michigan had a complicated set of measures on the ballot related to limiting taxes and public spending. One proposal, sponsored by Robert Tisch, a little-known drain commissioner and the leader of a "people's organization" of local taxpayers' groups, was to slash property taxes by cutting assessments in half and limiting annual increases in assessment to 2.5 percent. Theoretically, the state could step in and replace these lost revenues, but this was thought to be politically unfeasible. Tisch's movement resembled Jarvis's in the early stages of the campaign over Proposition 13, but it never progressed in comparable fashion beyond that.

The more moderate Headlee Proposal was more directly designed to curtail public spending, and proposed that state revenues in Michigan be "capped" at 9.5 percent of personal income. Like California's Proposition 4, which was to pass a year later, this measure was an outgrowth of the activity of the National Tax Limitation Committee. Their guiding idea was not so much that government is bad per se but rather that any further growth in the public sector would be excessive. A precursor of the Headlee amendment had been defeated in 1976; this time its backers assuaged the fears of the pro-public-sector elements by raising the allowable limit of revenues and by including a limit on local taxes to prevent the shift of taxes from the state to the localities. Opposition to Headlee among elected officials and major interest groups was muted, in part because it was viewed as a "responsible" alternative to the Jarvis-like Tisch amendment.

Polls showed that voters believed that the Tisch amendment would be more effective than Headlee in reducing their overall tax burden. But Tisch was also perceived as more likely to reduce revenues available for services, particularly the local schools. This concern became the focus of the opposition's campaign. Without a charismatic leader, a reassessment mess, or a supreme court decision to help, and facing a well-prepared alternative measure to act as a lightning rod for discontent, the Tisch amendment failed by a 63 percent to 37 percent margin. Headlee passed with 52 percent of the vote.

Oregon

In Oregon, both a Jarvis-Gann facsimile (Ballot Measure 6) and an establishment alternative (Ballot Measure 11) were on the ballot in November 1978. At first it appeared that the California scenario would be replayed. With Howard Jarvis on hand, Ballot Measure 6 qualified for the ballot soon after Proposition 13's victory and held a wide early lead in the polls. Oregon's counterpart to Jarvis, Jimmy Dale Wittenburg, proposed to cut property taxes by 40 percent, and the same anti-government, anti-spending themes evoked by Jarvis characterized his campaign. The Democratic governor and legislature, backed by a coalition of teachers and other public-employee organizations, proposed an alternative consisting of a one-year freeze on assessed values, a state rebate of up to $1500 of property taxes, and a limit to the allowable increase in state spending. Renters were also guaranteed a rebate. After some hesitation, the Republican candidate for governor endorsed the more radical plan, and the partisan battle lines were drawn.

Property taxes had grown in Oregon along with rising real estate values, but overall taxes were below the national norm, in part because there was no state sales tax.[11] As this campaign progressed, the "people's proposal" lost ground to the "establishment" alternative, but ultimately neither measure passed. Concern over the availability of government services and the recognition, as in Michigan, that there was no California-like state surplus to compensate for the loss of property tax revenues seemingly prevailed over the desire to cut taxes. As in California, the defeat of the more moderate tax reform suggests that once two such measures are portrayed as antagonists people find it hard to vote for both.

[11]Palaich et al., *Tax and Expenditure Limitation Referenda*, p. 43.

Overview

To recapitulate, inflation, a rise in the property tax burden of homeowners, judicial decisions that are less sensitive to homeowners' plights than to ensuring equal treatment under the tax laws, and legislative delay, are the ingredients of explosive protests against the growing size and cost of the public sector. Yet despite the intensity of public concern about high taxes, drastic remedies are not always adopted. The tax revolt has not swept all before it. Jarvis-like amendments won in Idaho and Massachusetts but lost in Michigan and Oregon. They lost in part because people also continue to want government to provide a high level of service, and in part because political elites, like college adminstrators a decade earlier, are learning how to cope with rebellious constituents. With the example of California's failure to sidetrack Jarvis-Gann in mind, they attempt to provide some tax relief to head off more far-reaching reforms, and they avoid the doomsday predictions that seem to anger voters rather than intimidate them. Local factors such as the nature of tax laws and assessment practices, the availability of mechanisms to alleviate painful tax increases, partisan infighting, and intangible elements of campaigning are important influences on the outcomes of anti-tax referenda. These shape public perceptions of the need for a proposed tax cut, the likelihood of obtaining it, and the consequences of implementing it.

Despite the differences in the fiscal climate of states in which tax and spending limitation referenda have recently occurred and their varied outcomes, the pattern of public opinion in these diverse locales is strikingly similar. To be sure, inconsistencies in the timing of polls and the wording of questions make precise comparisons difficult. And there are inevitable differences in the absolute level of discontent expressed. For instance, during the peak years of recent protest, 1977–78, voters in western states were more likely than their counterparts elsewhere to single out the property tax as particularly burdensome.[12] In Idaho a survey at the time of the vote on Proposition 1 found that 76 percent felt that taxes were too high relative to their ability to pay.[13] Before the vote on Proposition 13 the California Poll found that 62 percent of Californians felt that property taxes were unfairly high, whereas a Florida Poll conducted in 1979

[12]Advisory Commission on InterGovernmental Relations, *Changing Public Attitudes on Government and Taxes* (Washington, D.C., 1978).

[13]Palaich et al., *Tax and Expenditure Limitation Referenda*, p. 50.

reported that only 27 percent of that state's residents felt that way. Parenthetically, there is little variation among states in the degree of antipathy to the federal tax burden.[14]

What is even more regular from state to state is the persistent support for continued government services. In Michigan, for example, people expressed a preference for maintaining or increasing government services in every area of policy except welfare. Local expenditures, which the Tisch amendment addressed, were more popular than programs paid for by the state, whose expenditures the Headlee amendment sought to control. And a substantial minority of Michigan's voters said they would be willing to pay more in taxes for the services they desired. For example, 38 percent reported a desire for more spending on local schools and 32 percent of this group were willing to bear a heavier tax load for this purpose. At a more general level, on the eve of the vote on Tisch and Headlee a majority of Michigan's residents said they preferred the status quo to either a reduction or an increase in *both* spending and taxes.[15] And the smattering of data available from other state polls shows a similar preference for maintaining existing levels of state services, which, it should be remembered, had been growing in the 1970s.

Anti-government sentiments were also widespread outside California. The pervasiveness of political cynicism in Massachusetts is legendary. In Idaho a November 1978 poll found that 83 percent of the public believed "government wastes a lot of our tax money."[16] In Florida a year later, only 27 percent felt that the government could be trusted to do what is right most of the time.[17] In sum, the combination of beliefs we found to be most prevalent in California reappeared in states with widely varying fiscal and political conditions: taxes were too high, public spending was excessive, and government was wasteful and inefficient, but the flow of public services should continue at least at their current level.

Nor was California unusual in the nature of the demographic, political, or attitudinal factors that accounted for support for anti-

[14]See P. A. Beck and T. Dye, "Sources of Public Opinion on Taxes" (manuscript, Florida State University, 1980).

[15]P. Courant, E. M. Gramlich, and D. L. Rubinfeld, "The Tax Limitation Movement: Conservative Drift or the Search for a Free Lunch," Institute of Public Policy Studies Paper no. 141 (Ann Arbor: University of Michigan, 1979).

[16]Palaich et al., *Tax and Expenditure Limitation Referenda*, p. 50.

[17]Beck and Dye, "Sources of Public Opinion," p. 22.

tax or anti-spending measures. Opinions about the tax burden and preferences for public spending correlate in the predicted fashion. In Michigan, Oregon, and Idaho, surveys indicated a crude rationality among voters; that is, their choices tended to conform to their preferences about the impact of a ballot measure on their tax bills and the supply of services.[18] Beliefs that the government was wasteful were also associated with support for the tax revolt in these states.

With some departures, other findings are similar to our own. A high level of education tended to reduce support for the Jarvis-like property tax reforms proposed in Michigan, Oregon, and Idaho, but not for the Gann-like Headlee amendment or Ballot Measure 11, Oregon's establishment alternative.[19] Blacks were more likely to oppose the proposed tax cuts in other states. Income was positively associated with support for Headlee but not for Tisch in Michigan. Men were more likely than women to favor the more drastic initiatives in Oregon and Idaho, although this difference did not emerge in Michigan; Democrats were more likely to oppose the tax- or spending-limitation measures in every case except the Tisch proposal, whose following conformed most closely to the "middle mass" described by Wilensky.[20]

There are numerous other nuances we might note, but the thrust of the data is clear enough. Symbolic attitudes invariably play an important role, and self-interest tends to assume greater explanatory importance when a ballot measure provides a clear, calculable and substantial cash benefit. When respondents are asked about cutting taxes in the abstract or about a hypothetical proposal, the tendency of personal circumstances and social background to predict choices weakens, and responses are governed most heavily by symbolic predispositions of long standing.[21]

---

[18]See the summary in Palaich et al., *Tax and Expenditure Limitation Referenda*, p. 56.

[19]Ibid., pp. 20–23; and Courant et al., "The Tax Limitation Movement."

[20]See Wilensky, *The Welfare State and Equality*, ch. 1.

[21]This emerges clearly from an analysis of responses in a national survey conducted after the 1978 national elections by the University of Michigan's Center for Political Studies. Support for a measure like Proposition 13 "in your community" had no relationship to demographic variables at all: even blacks were as likely to support it. The only significant predictors were indicators of generalized malaise and mistrust of government. In the absence of a concrete measure whose costs and benefits are being debated, symbolic attitudes dominate completely.

The Tax Revolt Goes to Washington

At the national level, the opportunity for citizens to take direct electoral action on taxing and spending issues does not exist. But after the presidential election of 1980 the tax rebels enjoyed a much more potent weapon than the ability to mount initiative drives: the White House was in their corner. We have already noted that the Republican party had made cuts in the federal budget, reduced taxes, and made "smaller" government the centerpiece of their domestic political program. In Ronald Reagan these Jarvisite themes had an eloquent spokesman. . . . [S]urveys . . . show that public attitudes were favorable toward these elements of the president's program. The federal income tax was viewed as too high by more than 70 percent of the public in polls conducted at intervals throughout 1979 and 1980. Inflation was viewed as the most important national problem, and government spending was often regarded as its principal cause. Polls suggested that inflation was eroding expectations of personal financial progress and that people blamed "bracket creep" and the resultant rise in effective tax rates for the deterioration of their after-tax incomes.[22] Calls for a balanced federal budget won overwhelming approval in the polls, and this objective was given higher priority than a cut in taxes. Finally, perceptions of bureaucratic waste and governmental inefficiency showed no sign of slackening.

At the same time, there was little evidence as President Reagan took office that the public's preferences concerning the government's activities in the economic and social domains had substantially changed. Indeed, the available data consistently point to strong majorities for the maintenance or expansion of social security benefits, health care programs, aid to education, crime prevention, and even the problems of big cities.[23] There is no obvious mandate for the emasculation of the New Deal.

Although President Carter recognized the drift of public opinion about the size and cost of government and proposed substantial reductions in his last budget, it seems obvious that the Democratically controlled Congress throughout the 1970s was in feeling and action attached to the idea of expanding the scope of entitlements

[22]See "Why the Middle Class Supports Reagan," *U.S. News and World Report*, May 19, 1981.

[23]For a summary see J. Citrin, "The Changing American Electorate," in A. J. Meltsner, ed., *Politics and the Oval Office* (San Franciso: Institute for Contemporary Studies, 1981).

from government rather than curtailing the flow of benefits. How much President Reagan owed his electoral triumph to a shift toward conservatism among the public rather than to frustration and disappointment with the performance of the Carter regime, particularly in the realm of economic management, is still being debated. There can be no doubt, however, that President Reagan has taken the line that his election constituted a mandate for his program of tax and spending cuts. With the Republicans in control of the Senate, the renascent conservative coalition able to provide a majority in the House, and the liberal leadership of the Democrats in disarray, an unprecedented set of budgetary reductions and then major tax cuts were passed into law by August 1981. In both legislative battles, the Democratic opposition felt the need to present an alternative program tailored to fit the preferences of their own constituents. Even so, their program accepted the basic premises that cuts in taxes and public spending were imperative. To oppose the idea of cuts altogether was regarded as politically unfeasible.

This is not the place for a detailed description of the recently mandated cuts in federal spending and taxation. Our concern rather is the interplay between the president's proposals and mass opinion. It should be stressed that the Reagan administration's proposed cuts in government spending recognized the popularity of the so-called safety net programs: social security retirement benefits, veterans' compensation, Medicare benefits, supplemental security income for the disabled, and educational assistance for low-income families. This bow to political reality is conveniently part of the "supply-side" economic doctrine that the administration has adopted. This doctrine holds that the basic infrastructure of the welfare state is an entrenched feature of modern economies, and that under these circumstances, tamping down inflationary forces by reducing the overall level of economic activity is unlikely to work. People have access to a wide range of costly benefits and the budget deficit therefore widens rather than shrinks during recessions, further feeding inflation. The best that can be done, therefore, is to hold the flow of benefits to a reasonable level.

President Reagan's budget cuts therefore aimed mainly at the long list of entitlements provided by Congress in the 1970s, leaving the core of the New Deal and even some major elements of the Great Society, such as Head Start, relatively intact. A Harris Survey conducted in February 1981 showed that 81 percent approved of the president's call for a $41 billion cut in the federal budget. However, 92 percent favored the president's exemption of the safety net programs listed above from the budgetary axe, and majorities ranging from 74 percent to 59 percent approved reducing expenditures on welfare, free school lunches to children from families able to pay, food stamps, and unemployment compensation. Only the proposed cuts in federal aid to primary and secondary education, a program that benefits the middle class, and Medicaid were opposed by more than half of those polled. In sum, the president's initial program of budgetary reductions was tailored to fit the contours of public preferences on government spending. By demanding a single vote on the entire package rather than accepting a series of votes on separate expenditure programs, the president also made the level of spending per se the salient issue. And on this there is no mistaking the massive symbolic attachment to cutting back government. The polls did record doubts about whether the impact of the budgetary cuts would fall equitably, but these voices were overwhelmed by the pervasive agreement that government spending should be limited.

Somewhat ironically, in view of the evidence of sustained antagonism toward high taxes, many observers believed the president's proposed reduction of individual income taxes by 30 percent over a three-year-period would have a more difficult time in Congress. . . . Nevertheless, the president ultimately had his way. At the national level of American politics the tax revolt is no longer an opposition movement seeking change; at least temporarily, its central tenets have redefined the political status quo.

A Successful Protest

In American politics, Proposition 13 stands out as a watershed event whose national repercussions amount to a reversal in the direction of domestic public policy. President Reagan's program places economic growth at the top of the nation's priorities and shifts the balance of responsibility for individual welfare away from the state toward private institutions. His message to the public is, "Ask not what your government can do for you. Ask what you can do for yourself."

In California, the tax revolt began as a grass-roots protest against the cost of programs which had grown over the years partly because of pressures from the less well-off segments of the electorate.

Now the institutions of direct democracy have forced political elites to attend to a different set of popular grievances, if only in self-protection.

The victory of Proposition 13 legitimized Jarvis's credo as majoritarian sentiment. To propose new activities for government and to impose new taxes, even on the wealthy or on corporations, was, in the new political climate, to flout the popular will. The Republican party seized on the opportunity to expand its national following, and the mass upheaval that Jarvis had sparked became institutionalized. With the liberal political forces that had dominated American politics since 1932 in silent retreat, the populist hostility toward large institutions was harnessed to conservative policies favorable to business interests.

Proposition 13 therefore was successful on several fronts. It did achieve its overt purpose, providing property owners in California with a sizeable reduction in their taxes. Before the passage of Proposition 13, the per capita burden of state and local taxes in California ranked behind only Alaska, New York, and Wyoming. But by 1980, it had fallen to twenty-second among the fifty states. As we have shown, the electorate is now generally satisfied with the state's property tax structure, indicating that substantive reforms can defuse public anger. The symbolic outcry against the government's size and insensitivity to popular needs also has had tangible results. The growth of public spending has been slowed and legislators are now keenly attuned to the ebb and flow of concerns about high taxes and can be expected to act quickly to head off accumulating resentments. The initiative process remains as a potential outlet for popular frustrations, however, and as familiarity with the sophisticated new techniques for soliciting signatures and financial support spreads, we must anticipate new efforts on the part of citizen groups to change the ground rules for fiscal policy in California.

The Fiscal Crunch

While property owners continue to enjoy the benefits of Proposition 13, state and local officials are now confronting a gloomy fiscal future. The state's surplus has run out, and the 1981–1982 state budget reflected the reduced revenues available to state and local governments. Indeed, in early October 1981 Governor Brown was forced by the lack of state funds to order an additional 2 percent cut in the expenditures of all state agencies. He warned of the need to raise local fees and hinted at the possibility of amending the state's constitution to allow a split roll that would tax owners of business property at a higher rate than homeowners.

Thus a wide variety of interest groups, public employees, welfare recipients, school officials, and so on, are starting to squabble over a smaller fiscal pie. And as the impact of budget cuts at both the federal and state levels, and the redistribution of the tax burden, become clear, it is likely that conflicts will intensify among groups that have gained and groups that have suffered, and that cracks will appear in the consensual support for the prevailing anti-government mood.

Social Conflict in the Tax Revolt

Although our analysis emphasized the mass character of the protests against high taxes and government spending and the absence of strong differences in social background between those who supported and opposed the tax revolt, some elements of class politics do appear. In California, the amount of money one expected to gain from a proposed tax cut was an important factor in determining how one voted. And on balance support for the tax revolt rose steadily with income. Moreover, although corporate interests were sometimes cautious about supporting anti-tax referenda and for the most part opposed Proposition 13, it is clear that the main beneficiaries of the recent changes in the state and national tax structure have been business and the relatively wealthy. The tax revolt thus is likely to redistribute income upward.

In California, Proposition 13 is a catalyst for several conflicts of interest. The continuing shift in the share of the local property tax burden away from owners of commercial property toward homeowners is one source of future controversy. Without a surplus in the state treasury, there is no avoiding the incompatibility between the public's desire to maintain extensive government services and its unwillingness to provide additional revenues. In this fiscal crunch the revival of proposals to increase taxes on business and to institute the split roll is predictable, particularly since these taxes are more likely to win popular endorsement than are levies that fall on individuals. For example, the California Poll conducted in February 1980 found that two-thirds of the public favored increasing taxes on business property and corporate income if Proposition 9 had passed and the loss in revenue threatened services. Less than 15 percent preferred cutting education, health, or emergency services to imposing these new taxes. . . .

The demands of public employees are another source of potential political turmoil. Understandably, public employees resist the layoffs that result from cuts in public spending. More important perhaps is that in seeking increased pay and benefits, government workers are now contending for a share of a fixed, if not shrinking, pie. Throughout the 1970s the salaries of public employees rose more rapidly than salaries in the private sector; a highly mobilized bloc of voters, public employees also obtained generous retirement and other fringe benefits. Today, however, public employees are at a double disadvantage. Public opinion is hostile to their claims; as the California Tax Revolt Survey showed, there is widespread sentiment that government workers are overpaid. And political leaders are far less sympathetic, if not out of conviction, as in the cases of Ronald Reagan and Jerry Brown, then out of necessity. And with the normal budgetary process closed as an avenue for achieving their demands, it is to be expected that public employees will resort to "industrial" action. The wave of strikes among teachers, firemen, police, and other public employees that has followed in the wake of the tax revolt is likely to continue. Such strikes appear to be very unpopular, even among unionized workers in the private sector. This cleavage between the taxpayers in the private sector, whether they have white-collar or blue-collar occupations, on the one hand, and the tax-receiving employees in the public sector on the other hand, was already evident in our analysis of support for Proposition 13. This may well become a dominant line of division in American politics in the coming years.

As this suggests, we should expect sharpened conflict between the clienteles of government programs and the taxpayers who support reduced public spending. While it is too early to gauge the full impact of the tax revolt on the provision of public services, either in California or nationally, there is no doubt that the next several years will witness reductions in transfer payments and in programs varying from inoculations to basic scientific research. Moreover, the fact that public revenues and expenditures are shrinking simultaneously at local, state, and national levels is bound to tighten the fiscal vise for the public sector. In the absence of a major upsurge in the private economy, those dependent on the state for their economic well-being are bound to suffer some personal deprivation. Most experts agree that the state surplus has run out. And as cuts in services have to be made, the recent political successes of conservatives in local, state, and national elections make it likely that these cuts will fall most heavily on economically disadvantaged groups. In Los Angeles County, for example, the Board of Supervisors has reacted to a diminution of state aid by closing regional health centers and pharmacies that served ghetto residents.

How much the "truly needy" are affected will doubtless be established soon enough. That the upper middle class will survive the loss of low-interest loans to their college-student offspring is certain. But it is also clear that the low-income and black citizens who have been heavy consumers of government services will be deprived of some assistance. Blacks have consistently opposed the tax revolt, viewing government as the principal agency of their collective economic and social progress. To a considerable extent, the proliferation of government programs in the middle and late 1960s was a reaction to black demands, sometimes expressed in violent protests such as the Watts riot. Racial polarization leading to similar outbreaks may be an unfortunate consequence of the tax revolt, particularly should the promised economic recovery not occur. For blacks are on the disadvantaged side of each cleavage engendered by fiscal limitation: they are more likely to be renters, public employees, and recipients of government services.

The tax revolt is likely to have unfortunate symbolic as well as practical effects upon the black community. Blacks are, not surprisingly, quite sensitive to the political winds as they blow from the white majority. Many blacks expected that one of the major consequences of the ghetto riots would be more attention from whites to blacks' problems. And they hoped it would be sympathetic attention.[24] In retrospect, it seems to us that such attention was indeed one of the major consequences of the riots, though clearly interwoven with fear, anger, and other less sympathetic feelings. Many of the civil rights gains of the past decade, especially those carried out by governmental institutions, began as responses to such events. And those gains had great symbolic as well as practical value, as expressions of whites' concern for blacks. However blacks have sensed a fading momentum behind such efforts, not without some reason. We

[24] D. O. Sears and J. B. McConahay, *The Politics of Violence: The New Urban Blacks and the Watts Riot* (Boston: Houghton Mifflin, 1973).

find symbolic racism to be a major factor in whites' support for the tax revolt. Should this finding be replicated in other research on other political choices being made by whites, it would bode ill for race relations, and for continued progress toward a more racially egalitarian society, at least in the near future.

Whither the Tax Revolt?

Any assessment of the staying power of the tax revolt must at this stage be somewhat speculative. The historical forces underlying the steady growth of government in advanced industrial societies are strong. Whether the constraints imposed by the recent fiscal reforms are more than a temporary check probably depends in large part on whether ideological changes take place to overcome the demographic push toward more public spending on old age pensions and health care.

The tax revolt also expressed a negative reaction against social and cultural changes that had been endorsed if not always promoted by liberal governments. The unsettling changes in race relations, the declining role of institutional religion, the increased permissiveness of personal behavior, and the challenge to traditional patterns of family that the feminist movement posed are an important part of the background to the electoral changes of recent years. The sense that things had gone too far, that freedom had become license, that government had overstepped its bounds in regulating economic and social relationships ran deep among supporters of the tax revolt and President Reagan. The impulse to call a halt and revive traditional values, including patriotism, broadened the base of the tax revolt and provided much of its fervor. The combination of economic discontent and cultural revivalism interrupted the long era of liberal political dominance in America. But it should be noted that belief in the traditional virtues of frugality and individual effort are weakened in the younger cohorts of the population.[25] So demographic trends, at least, are unlikely to reinforce the recent move to the political right.

Whether the events of 1978–1980 signal the beginning of a long period in which government no longer grows must depend on the interplay of events with popular values. There is as yet no compelling evidence of a slackening in the public's attachment to the govern-

[25]D. Yankelovich, *The New Morality: A Profile of American Youth in the 70's* (New York: McGraw-Hill, 1974).

ment programs that make up the welfare state. Indeed, a CBS/New York Times Poll conducted in June 1981 found that 66 percent of the public favored increasing social security taxes if necessary to keep the social security system solvent. This is not to underplay the ability of political leadership to reshape public opinion, but merely to repeat that enduring public preferences place political limits on the pace and extent of fiscal retrenchment.

A subject that still requires investigation is the degree to which people's expectations about their economic circumstances are changing and the influence of such expectations on attitudes toward government. The prolonged economic difficulties of the late 1970s seem to have spread pessimism about the future. Respondents are now telling polltakers that they expect their children to have a harder time economically than they themselves have had; for example, to be less likely to own a home.[26] Earlier we reported the somewhat puzzling finding that worries about inflation and pessimism about the economy had no appreciable influence on attitudes toward the tax revolt. It is unclear whether, when people revise their long-run economic expectations downward, they want more or less governmental activity on their behalf. Should a prolonged period of sluggish economic growth limit chances for upward mobility, demands that the government expand its activities to redistribute income and soften the blow of macroeconomic misfortune may well increase.

Longer-term demographic changes may also influence the demand for public services. As middle-class white parents become a smaller portion of the electorate, the constituency for increased spending on public education may weaken. At the same time, the aging of the population is a major potential force in favor of increased government spending on both social security and health care. The net result of these changes varies from one level of government to another, but on balance they suggest that the current pattern of preferences for government activity will persist.

The Tax Revolt
and American Political Culture

The recent tax revolt, particularly in its national incarnation, exemplifies a number of features that have historically distinguished American political culture from those of other countries. Most ob-

---

[26]See "Opinion Roundup" in *Public Opinion*, 4, no. 2 (1981).

viously, the size of the public sector . . . , as measured by the proportion of the gross national product that is accounted for by public expenditures, is much smaller in America than in other industrialized countries. The tax revolt aims at keeping this so. Americans seemingly expect fewer entitlements from government than do their European counterparts. This is true even among the lower-class clienteles of the public sector, who also have a lesser symbolic attachment to class-oriented ideologies and a lower rate of political participation.

The popular disdain for public officials that contributed to the success of the tax revolt has been an important aspect of American political life from the very beginning. The nation's political tradition legitimates attacks against authority, whereas those defending the growth of the public sector lack equivalent institutionalized symbolic support to draw upon.

The fragility of political party organizations, particularly in California, has often made established programs vulnerable to sudden upheavals in the public mood. In the absence of organized channels of political communication and persuasion, political leaders are less able to contain expressions of discontent. The Townsend plan for the elderly in the 1930s and the temperance movement are but two examples of single-issue protest movements whose appeals drew adherents over the opposition of both established parties. The availability of the initiative process clearly enhances the political reach of fringe elements. And the expanded role of the mass media in transmitting political information also tends to inflate the impact of dramatic events.

Finally, one can see in the ideological defense of the tax revolt, particularly as articulated by President Reagan, an attempt to reassert the validity of the ethos of economic individualism that is a predominant element in the historical political culture in this country. Restricting the growth of government, in the president's view, is an essential step toward restoring the virtue of Americans and the power of America. In broad perspective, then, the tax revolt is a challenge to recent political history, in which the growth of government was a deeply embedded and rarely challenged aspect of public policy.

At the more mundane level of the costs and benefits of government, the questions of what services to supply and how to pay for them, the issues the tax revolt raises are permanent dilemmas in political life. Recent events have altered the political tide on these matters and elicited new conflicts. These promise to be intense; not only are there differences in interest and ideology among groups, but, as we have tried to show, there are often competing impulses within the same individual.

Underneath the illusion that we can get something for nothing lies the reality that there is no such thing as a free lunch. Voters in California, indeed all American citizens and politicians, are going to have to face up to this. Since we have become habituated to the steady growth of government, to expecting government to do more, adjustment to an era of fiscal limitation cannot be easy. Is the American pie now limited? And if it is, how is it to be divided? The tax revolt has posed these questions. The struggle over the answers is the political agenda for the 1980s.

17

Americans Love Their Bureaucrats

ROBERT L. KAHN,
BARBARA A. GUTEK,
EUGENIA BARTON,
AND DANIEL KATZ

Bureaucrats have had a bad press. The vision is of a petty tyrant who wraps the cloak of office around inadequate shoulders, dominates those below him, and crouches sheepishly before those above him. That image has been with us a long time; centuries ago, Hamlet counted "the insolence of office" among his list of reasons not to be. Even princes fume at bureaucrats.

The insolence of office reaches its heights in societies more stratified and repressive than ours, in which little men with big titles wield power by whim. But the United States runs on bureaucracy too. Increasingly we depend on goods and services provided by organizations rather than by our own efforts, the family group, or trade and barter.

It turns out, however, that for all the snickering at the stereotype, Americans like the bureaucrats they deal with pretty well. They aren't so sure about *other* bureaucrats and they take a dim view of bureaucrats in general, but their own experiences are far from the picture of pettiness and inefficiency that we have come to assume is real.

The typical bureaucratic encounter is an exchange between strangers, one who needs and one who grants. On one side of the desk sits the applicant, with all of the individual feelings, experiences and peculiarities that have brought him there. On the other side sits the agent of the organization, who acts to determine the validity of the request, to decide whether the person is entitled to service. The agent-bureaucrat is not supposed to bring his or her own idiosyncracies to bear on the decision; sympathy or antipathy for the applicant should not make a difference.

Their conversation is likely to be brief, and the encounter ends with a decision or a referral. At best, the exchange is competent and professional, at worst frustrating and dehumanized. In either case, the outcome is more likely to be determined by organizational policy than by the desires of either participant.

The quality of our lives and the satisfaction or frustration of our basic needs now depend considerably on the results of such encounters—in work, medical care, welfare, retirement, and many other essential areas. Accordingly, we decided to evaluate the quality of bureaucracy in America. We purposely chose organizations that provide services rather than products because it is more difficult to evaluate them. It is easier to identify shoddy goods than sloppy service, to protest against tangible, tinsel Corvairs than against pomposity and pettiness, inefficiency and red tape.

Yet measuring the quality of service is essential if we are to understand modern bureaucracy, especially when the agency in question represents the government. Government agencies are the sole providers of some services; dissatisfied customers can't complain by shopping elsewhere. The worker who is out of a job and seeks employment, the retired worker who wants social-security payments, the divorced mother who needs aid for her young children must all deal with a single supplier.

Bureaucracies Without Baksheesh

Philosopher Abe Kaplan once warned eager social scientists that if you can measure it, that ain't it. But we set out to pin down Americans' experiences with government bureaucracies as best we could. The quality of the encounters, the rules that govern them, and the concrete results for the persons involved provide, together, a good social indicator for a community or an entire society. For example, in some times and climes, the client must go outside the formal rules of the exchange; he or she may have to offer bribes, *baksheesh*, to the bureaucrat. The game often depends on having, and mentioning, friends in high places. In some yet-to-be-constructed Utopia it may be sufficient for the client only to describe the need or problem.

Thus we can characterize bureaucratic episodes in terms of promptness or delay, openness or secretiveness of decision-making, right or denial of appeal, adequacy of service, and so on. In the worst of all possible bureaucracies, incompetent agents make secret decisions during long and lazy afternoons, and ultimately grant your request only if they like your looks. Fortunately, we're not that bad off, even though on some days it may seem so.

Our work is based on a representative sample of 1,431 American adults, and so is descriptive of the quality of service that Americans as a whole feel they are getting. We asked them to describe their experiences with seven common but serious problems that government bureaucracies service: employment, job training, compensation for accidents and injuries at work, unemployment compensation, medical and hospital care, public assistance, and retirement benefits.

Specifically, our survey of government services concentrated on the State Employment Services, Workmen's Compensation offices, Aid to Families With Dependent Children, and the Social Security Administration. The State Employment Services aid people who are seeking jobs, and pay unemployment compensation to those out of work. They also administer most job-training programs, such as the Job Corps and the Neighborhood Youth Corps.

Welfare services (also called public assistance) are usually administered by local agencies under state guidelines. There are separate rules, regulations, and offices for the blind, the disabled, the elderly poor, and for poor families with dependent children. Government hospital and medical benefits are handled primarily through the Medicare and Medicaid programs, which may be separate offices or part of the Social Security Administration. Finally, retirement benefits are of course provided through the SSA, and to a lesser extent by the Veterans' Administration.

We asked respondents what their own needs and problems were in regard to these agencies, whether they were satisfied or dissatisfied with the outcome of the encounter, and—in order to place their experiences in a larger social context—whether and how they supported the political system. And we asked about various aspects of the bureaucracy they dealt with—such as its efficiency, fairness, efforts to help.

A majority of Americans use the government services available to them. About 58 percent had contacted at least one agency; the two most popular services are unemployment compensation (26 per-

Services	Percent Having Problem	Percent Using Agency
Job Finding	33	24
Job Training	30	9
Workmen's Compensation	13	8
Unemployment Compensation	27	26
Public Assistance	12	12
Hospital/Medical Care	8	6
Retirement Benefits	19	15

cent) and job finding (24 percent). Only eight percent had received workmen's compensation, and only six percent had sought government medical and hospital care.

Not everyone who needs a service is getting it, however. The most significant discrepancy is in job training: 30 percent of the respondents said they could use such training but only nine percent have in fact gotten it. We also found a gap between the number of people who need help in finding a job (33 percent) and those who have gone to an agency to get that help (24 percent).

Different agencies, of course, cater to different clients, but in general more men than women use these services, especially the four related to work. Women outnumbered men only in applying for public assistance (e.g., Aid to Dependent Children). Blacks were one third as likely as whites to have sought retirement benefits but twice as likely to have sought help in job finding and job training from the State Employment Services, the Job Corps, and other such agencies. Public assistance and government medical aid predominantly serve people who are low in income, education, and occupational status. But overall, these factors—race, education, age and income—were only partially able to explain who uses government services and who does not. Most of us get to one or another of these bureaucracies sometime in our lives.

Getting the Horse to Water

American bureaucracy apparently faces problems not only in helping people once they come in for service, but in getting them to come in at all. Among those who reported specific problems that the government might solve, many never found their way to the right agency and some had no idea an agency could help them. For example, of people who had been injured or disabled on the job, 41 percent did not seek workmen's compensation and almost half of that number did not know that workmen's compensation exists. Of the people who had problems finding a job but did not use any of the government job-finding services, over one fourth (28 percent) did not know such agencies could help them. And over half (55 percent) of the people who needed government hospital and medical care and did not get it, did not know where to get it. Worst of all, 70 percent of those who needed job training did not find any government agency to provide it, and half of them did not know one existed.

If the gloomy stereotype of the bureaucrat is true, we would expect people who have to deal with one frequently to give us muttered complaints about inefficiency, delay, hierarchy, pettiness, and surly officials. We didn't get many. Americans simply have had fewer experiences with the insolence of office than Hamlet did. Indeed, two thirds of them reported complete satisfaction with the way the office handled their problems, and more than four in 10 said they were *very* satisfied, thank you. Only 14 percent were very dissatisfied with the service they got.

True, there was the Michigan matron who said she was "treated like a convicted murderer" when she went to pay a traffic fine. "And it wasn't just me; they were treating everybody that way." And there was the middle-aged welfare recipient who demanded a job instead of public assistance: "They told me that if I made any more trouble my checks might just get lost." But most people had positive things to say. "They treated me very good; they seem to have a sincere interest," said a 45-year-old black woman. "I had an appointment with a nice lady and I got a favorable reply," reported a man seeking disability payments. "They were cooperative, nice, no trouble," said an elderly woman seeking old-age assistance.

Are these numbers good or bad? We can look at all the satisfied customers and interpret the results positively, or we can worry about the dissatisfied people. In the best of all bureaucracies, as with circuses, everyone goes away happy. Some agencies might propose a higher standard of satisfaction than, say, the 61 percent that welfare gets. One hundred percent might be impossible in this imperfect world, but 90 percent perfection is not an unreasonable standard.

| | Problem | | | | | | | |
Rating	Job Finding	Job Training	Workmen's Compensation	Unemployment Compensation	Welfare	Hospital/Medical	Retirement	Total
Very satisfied	35	51	53	35	27	49	64	43
Fairly well satisfied	26	23	23	36	34	9	24	26
Somewhat dissatisfied	16	19	5	14	18	24	4	13
Very dissatisfied	20	6	10	12	10	18	3	14

| | Problem | | | | | | | |
Rating	Job Finding	Job Training	Workmen's Compensation	Unemployment Compensation	Welfare	Hospital/Medical	Retirement	Total
More than had to	12	25	25	4	11	20	26	16
About right	57	57	15	71	59	49	61	57
Less than should have	16	8	3	13	21	13	5	12
No effort at all	12	8	13	8	7	18	1	9

Satisfaction with Services

To see which services get the best marks, we compared satisfaction across agencies. Americans are happiest about social security: 88 percent were satisfied with the way their retirement problems are handled. But they are least content about the quality of medical and hospital care; only 58 percent had positive experiences. There is probably an objective reason for this difference. Social Security offices have a simpler, or at least better defined, problem to handle than health services; they know who their clients are and they have made determined efforts to reach retirees. They administer a clearer program than health services do, with specifications for who is entitled to aid that their many branch offices can easily follow.

To probe beyond general feelings of satisfaction or displeasure with bureaucracies, we took the stereotype apart and asked about its specific elements. We asked people to describe their most important experience with a service agency, and went on to find out whether the problem was solved, how favorably the client evaluated the procedures for a solution, and how fair he or she considered the treatment. About one fifth thought that their problems were not taken care of by the office they sought, a fairly low failure rate considering the difficult nature of some of their problems and the limitations under which some agencies must operate.

Procedures

Americans apparently will tolerate great quantities of red tape before they complain about it. They don't *enjoy* the bureaucratic procedures that agencies require—filling out papers, making appointments, delay—but most don't complain, either. They simply describe the procedures in neutral tones. Three agencies, however, provoked some negative reactions; complaints about procedures outweighed satisfaction by three to one for Workmen's Compensation and welfare; and medical and hospital services brought out more nays than ayes, by two to one.

Finding the Right Official

We asked: "Was it hard to find an office or official who could handle your problem?" Over all, only 12 percent said yes, but again the agencies differed. A mere five percent had trouble finding the right person in retirement agencies, but almost a third did in medical services and welfare. These two bureaucracies consistently get low ratings, which is less a result of the kind of problems they handle than of the policies by which they are governed.

Agency Efforts to Help

Contrary to our image of the lazy bureaucrat who won't lift one finger more than necessary to help a client, many Americans think that their bureaucrats are doing a splendid job. As a Kentucky veteran said, describing his efforts to arrange early retirement, "they're friendly—do anything they can for you." Some 57 percent thought that the agency people made the right amount of effort to help them, and another 16 percent said they helped *more than they had to*. Only 12 percent said that the agency people expended less effort than they should have, and only nine percent said *no effort at all*. Retirement services win again, with one out of four people commending their bureaucrats for doing more than they needed to do, and only six percent criticizing them on this score at all. The worst bureaucracies were the medical services, whose people made no effort to help at all, according to 18 percent of those they treated.

Efficiency

Surely, we thought, efficient Americans, who complain about delays at traffic lights, will complain about the glacierlike speed of bureaucracies. Most of them don't. Young people were less favorable than others, but on the whole only one respondent in 10 found the agency he or she dealt with to be very inefficient, and an equal number said "rather inefficient." In contrast, the great majority said that their problems were handled quickly and efficiently. As a Detroit respondent put it, "they're *very* efficient. I had to show evidence and the man took care of it."

| | Ethnic Group | | |
Satisfaction	White	Black	Other
Very satisfied	45	32	31
Fairly well satisfied	26	24	28
Somewhat dissatisfied	12	20	14
Very dissatisfied	12	19	22

Fairness of Treatment

Nor do Americans worry about *baksheesh* or favoritism or discrimination in the service they get. Only 13 percent, overall, believe they were treated unfairly, although the proportion rises to 18 percent among blacks and 21 percent among people under 30 years of age. Those most likely to report unfair treatment were clients of medical services (29 percent) and public assistance (23 percent); those least likely were applicants for retirement benefits (five percent) and workmen's compensation (five percent).

Possibility of Appeal

We asked: "Was there someone at a higher level in the office to whom you could appeal for help if things were not working out all right?" Most (47 percent) said yes, and only 14 percent felt that there was no appeal. But a large minority simply did not know, and even fewer people had actually attempted to appeal a decision. Retirement services got the fewest appeals (eight percent) and public assistance the most appeals (31 percent).

Who Is Happiest

We considered a number of factors that might influence how people view the bureaucratic encounter: age, race, sex, income, education and occupation. Age and race were the only ones that made a consistent difference in satisfaction with bureaucracy. That is, as age increases, so does satisfaction: 27 percent of those under 30, for example, were extremely satisfied with their experiences, compared to 60 percent of people over 70. Older groups rarely expressed strong dissatisfaction, but one fourth of the young people did. It may be that younger people expect more—not only in relation to government services, but of everything. Or it may be the kind of agency that different age groups encounter: older people are more likely to be dealing with social security, young people with employment problems.

Fewer blacks than whites reported being very satisfied (32 percent to 45 percent), which is related less to discrimination at the agency than to the kinds of problems the two groups have. Blacks seek help much more frequently for finding jobs, job training and welfare—a fact which reflects discrimination in other times and places.

Taken all together, these demographic factors did not do much to explain why some who seek government services are more satisfied than others. This is good news. It means that these bureaucracies are not discriminating in the service they provide according to the personal characteristics of the client. It means that some social groups are not getting special attention at the expense of others. Any society that aspires to equal treatment for its citizens must hope that their satisfactions and grievances with government services are a result of administrative problems, for which there are administrative solutions. Our research suggests that this is the case for most American bureaucracies. Some, like retirement and workmen's compensation, are working efficiently and fairly for almost all of their clients—of whatever race or age or sex. Others, like medical care and public assistance, are administered more clumsily, provoking complaints among a good minority of clients—of whatever race or age or sex.

The Stereotype Survives

Americans, then, have tackled the great bureaucratic beast, and found it not such a dragon after all. But stereotypes live long and die hard, and the image of the insolent bureaucrat and his inefficient organization survives *in spite* of people's experiences, not because of them. We found that our respondents consistently described their own encounters more positively than what they thought everyone else was getting. For example, 71 percent of all the clients said that their problems were taken care of, but only 30 percent think that government agencies do well at taking care of problems. Eighty percent said that they were treated fairly, but only 42 percent think that government agencies treat most people fairly. Almost eight in 10 believe that they were treated considerately, but only half that number think that government agencies are generally considerate.

In other words, most Americans do not let their experiences affect their stereotypes; it is apparently much easier to decide that their experiences represent an exception to the rule. People who have had *bad* experiences, however, are likely to bring their general perceptions into line with their encounters. Those who report unfair treatment, for instance, tend to think that everyone else is getting unfair treatment too.

In order to get an idea of whether people place their experiences with bureaucracy in a larger political framework, we asked

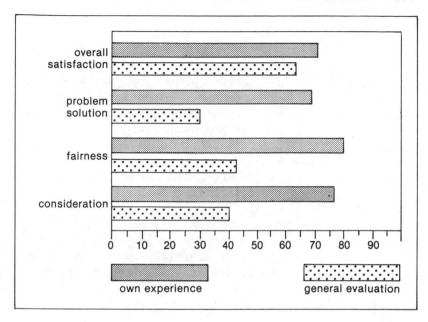

them questions about national Government ("the people in Washington"), and about the symbols of national identity and unity (feelings of patriotism, the flag, the national anthem).

Love That Flag, Doubt That Congress

Most Americans have a disjointed set of political attitudes. They have become increasingly more cynical and negative about the national leadership; trust in Government has gone down, skepticism about Government decisions has gone up. But they still maintain substantial emotional involvement in our national symbols: they think the schools put too little emphasis on patriotism; they think everyone should stand for the national anthem; they love the flag. In short, people are positive about their direct experiences and about the most general patriotic ideals; but they are critical of government agencies generally and politicians in particular.

We find this lack of connection disturbing. If people do not link their own experiences with governmental services to their ideals of public bureaucracies, they can be supportive at one level and destructive at another. The formulation of public policy requires generalized statements of program objectives, which in turn determine many specifics of how a given program will operate. But if policy and practice are not linked, neither can influence and improve the other. The majority of Americans do not see how policies relate to their own experiences with government agencies. The policy-makers remain aloof in Washington, remote and probably crooked, and Americans doubt their goals and programs.

People's current frustrations about the growing problems of unemployment, inflation, and shortages can be channeled in two ways. The one would be demagogic and populist, directed against incumbent scoundrels, using slogans and stereotypes. The other would be aimed at structural reform and policy change—attacking the issues, not merely the scoundrels. Our findings suggest that people respond realistically to their own experiences, but that they do not carry that realism to more general issues, with a resulting inconsistency of belief. Unless people get more involved with policy reform and bridge that inconsistency, we can expect that they will accept populist dogma far sooner than programs based on sweet reason.

18

Bureaucracy and the Lower Class

GIDEON SJOBERG, RICHARD A. BRYMER, AND BUFORD FARRIS

. . . Sociologists have devoted little attention, on either the community or national level, to the impact of bureaucracy upon the stratification system. Yet our experience, based on research among lower-class Mexican-Americans in San Antonio, points to the critical role of bureaucratic organizations in sustaining social stratification. Sociologists frequently compare lower- and middle-class culture patterns, but they fail to recognize that bureaucratic systems are the key medium through which the middle class maintains its advantaged position vis-à-vis the lower class.

Our analysis of the effect of the client-centered bureaucracy upon the lower class is cast in rather theoretical terms. However, illustrative materials from our research project and the writings of other scholars indicate the kinds of data that support our generalizations. After delineating the main elements of the bureaucratic model, we discuss the lower class from the perspective of the bureaucratic system and then bureaucracy from the viewpoint of the lower class. These materials set the stage for a consideration of various emergent organizational and political patterns in American society.

From Gideon Sjoberg, Richard A. Brymer, and Buford Farris, "Bureaucracy and the Lower Class," reprinted by permission of the authors and the publisher from *Sociology and Social Research* 50 (April 1966):325–337. Footnotes are renumbered.

The Nature of Bureaucracy

In the post–World War II era various sociologists[1] have questioned the utility of Weber's analysis of bureaucracy. Nevertheless, sociologists continue to assume that bureaucracy (as conceived by Weber) is positively associated with the continued development of an advanced industrial-urban order and that this bureaucracy is more or less inevitable.

Modern bureaucracies lay heavy stress upon rationality and efficiency. In order to attain these ends, men are called upon to work within a hierarchical system, with well-defined lines of authority, and within a differentiated social setting, with an elaborate division of labor that stresses the specialization of function. This hierarchy and division of labor are, in turn, sustained through a complex set of formalized rules which are to be administered in a highly impersonal and standardized manner. There is considerable centralization of authority, and as one moves from top to bottom there is greater specialization of function and adherence to the rules.

What is not as clearly recognized is that efficiency and rationality are predicated upon an explicit statement of the organization's goals. Only when an end is clearly stated can one determine the most efficient means for its attainment. Thus, because the corporate structure has had an explicit goal (i.e., profit), it has been quite successful in measuring the efficiency of its programs (i.e., means).

The corporate system has been the model that other bureaucracies have emulated. As a result, there has been considerable concern with efficiency within, say, the federal government. McNamara's reorganization of the U.S. Defense Department in the 1960s is a case in point. It is significant that McNamara . . . [drew] heavily upon the work of Hitch and McKean[2] in developing his program, for Hitch and McKean argue that organizational goals must be spelled out in rather concrete terms in order to measure the effectiveness of various programs. An understanding of the interrelationships among measurement, objectification of goals, and efficiency and rationality

---

[1]Peter Blau, *The Dynamics of Bureaucracy*, rev. ed. (Chicago: University of Chicago Press, 1963); and Alvin Gouldner, *Patterns of Industrial Bureaucracy* (New York: The Free Press, 1965).

[2]Charles J. Hitch and Roland N. McKean, *The Economics of Defense in the Nuclear Age* (Cambridge, Mass.: Harvard University Press, 1960).

is essential if we are to assess the impact of bureaucratic structures upon the lower class.

Orientations of Bureaucracies Towards the Lower Class

Bureaucratic organizations frequently reinforce the class structure of the community and the nation through their staffing procedures. When a bureaucracy serves both upper- and lower-class groups, as does the school, the poorly qualified teachers tend to drift into lower-class neighborhoods, or, as frequently occurs, beginning teachers are placed in "hardship" districts, and then the most capable move up and out into upper-status school districts where higher salaries and superior working conditions usually prevail. Thus, the advancement of lower-class children is impeded not only because of their cultural background but because of the poor quality of their teachers.

In welfare bureaucracies, social workers have struggled to escape from their traditional identification with the poor, either by redefining their functions in order to serve middle-class clients or by moving away from clients into administrative posts. Once again, evidence suggests that the lower class comes to be served by the least qualified personnel.

In addition to staffing arrangements, the bureaucracy's method of selecting clients reinforces the class system. At this point we must remember that bureaucracies are under constant pressure to define their goals so that the efficiency of their programs can be measured. But unlike corporate systems, client-centered bureaucracies experience grave difficulties in specifying their goals and evaluating their efficiency. The client-centered bureaucracies meet the demands placed upon them through the use of simplified operational definitions. Universities, for instance, do not judge their effectiveness in terms of producing "educated men" but according to the ratings of their students on national tests, the number of students who gain special awards, etc. These operational criteria reflect the orientation or view of persons in positions of authority within the bureaucracy and the broader society. In turn, these criteria become the basis for the selection of clients. Through this procedure, a bureaucratic organization can ensure its success, and it can more readily demonstrate to the power structure that the community or society is "getting something for its money." The bureaucracy's success is likely to lead to an increase in funds and expanded activities. It follows that client-centered bureaucracies often find it advantageous to avoid lower-class clients who are likely to handicap the organization in the attainment of its goals.[3]

Several illustrations should clarify our argument. The federal Job Corps program has been viewed as one means for alleviating the unemployment problem among youth, especially those in the lower class. This program has sought to train disadvantaged youths in various occupational skills. The success of the Job Corps is apparently to be evaluated according to the number of trainees who enter the industrial labor force. Consequently, the organization has sought to select those youths who have internalized some of the middle-class norms of upward mobility and who are likely to succeed in the occupational system. The Job Corps bypasses many persons who in theory stand in greatest need of assistance; for example, potential "troublemakers"—young men with criminal records—are not accepted as trainees. Because of this selection process the Job Corps leadership will likely be able to claim success and to convince Congressmen that the program should be continued and perhaps broadened.

A more subtle form of client selection can be found in child guidance clinics. Here clients are often accepted in terms of their "receptivity" to therapy.[4] However, this criterion favors those persons who have been socialized into the middle-class value orientation held by, for example, the clinic staff and the social groups who pay the bill. The poor, especially the families from ethnic groups within the lower class, who according to the ideal norms of these agencies should receive the greatest amount of attention, are quietly shunted aside. Moreover, one study has indicated a positive association between the social status of the client and the social status of the professional worker handling the case in the agency.[5]

The procedures by which school systems cope with their clients are perhaps central to understanding the community and national

[3]See, e.g., Martin Rein, "The Strange Case of Public Dependency," *Transaction* 2 (March–April 1965):16–23.

[4]Based on the personal observations of Buford Farris who, as a social worker, has had extensive contact with these agencies.

[5]Raymond G. Hunt, Orville Gurrslin, and Jack L. Roach, "Social Status and Psychiatric Service in a Child Guidance Clinic," *American Sociological Review* 23 (February 1958):81–83.

class system, for the educational variable is becoming increasingly significant in sustaining or advancing one's status. At this point we are concerned with the differential treatment of clients by the organization once they have been accepted.

School systems frequently employ IQ tests and similar instruments in their evaluation of pupils. These tests, however, have been constructed in such a manner that they articulate with the values, beliefs, and knowledge of the middle class and the demands of the power elements of the society. That these tests are used to make early judgments on the ability of pupils serves to support the existing class system. Lower-class pupils often come to be defined as "dull," and, through a kind of self-fulfilling prophecy, this definition of the situation structures the students' future career. In fact, school counselors frequently interpret test scores according to their middle-class expectations; they, therefore, tend to discourage lower-class pupils from attending college even when their scores are relatively high.[6]

It is significant that the New York City school system has been forced to abandon the use of IQ tests.[7] It appears that the traditionally disadvantaged groups such as Negroes and Puerto Ricans have attained sufficient political power to challenge those methods that the school bureaucracy has used for determining success, methods that have been oriented to middle-class rather than lower-class norms.

Bureaucratized school systems place the lower-class clients at a disadvantage in still other ways. Various types of standardization or categorization, which are a product of middle-class expectations and which are viewed as essential for maintaining efficiency, limit the school's ability to adjust to the "needs" of lower-class pupils. We know of a special class, for example, that was established for the purpose of teaching lower-class and problem children, but in which the rules demanded that the teacher follow the same teaching plan employed in other classes in the school.

Actually, bureaucratic structures socialize the incumbents of roles in such a manner that they are frequently incapable of under-

---

[6]Aaron Cirourel and John I. Kitsuse, *The Educational Decision-Makers* (Indianapolis: Bobbs-Merrill Co., 1963). For a general discussion of the bureaucratization of the school system see Dean Harper, "The Growth of Bureaucracy in School Systems," *American Journal of Economics and Sociology* 23 (July 1965):261–271.

[7]Fred M. Hechinger, "I.Q. Test Ban," *The New York Times*, March 8, 1964, Section E, p. 7; Fred H. Hechinger, "Testing at Issue," *The New York Times*, November 1, 1964, Section E, p. 9.

standing the world-view of the lower-class client. Discussions of the bureaucratic personality, such as those by Merton and Presthus,[8] have given but scant attention to the difficulty of the bureaucrat's taking the role of the lower-class other. For as a result of his role commitment, the bureaucrat tends to impose his own expectations and interpretations of reality upon the client. He often comes to view the norms of the system as invariant. And bureaucrats in the lower echelons, those who have the greatest amount of contact with lower-class clients, are also the most bound by the rules. Faced with recalcitrant clients or clients having divergent value orientations, the typical office holder will say in effect, "If only clients would act properly, everything would be all right, and we could get on with our work."

The bureaucrat, oriented as he is to the middle- or upper-class life styles, usually lacks knowledge about the lower-class client's subculture. Moreover, he finds it difficult to step outside his formalized role. If he seeks to take the role of the client—in the sense of understanding the latter's belief and value system—he will ultimately have to challenge or at least question some of the rules that govern the operation of the system of which he is a part. For if he understands why clients act the way they do, he is likely to recognize that they have valid reasons for objecting to his conception of reality or, more specifically, to some of the bureaucratic regulations. Consequently, bureaucratic organizations tend to penalize those of their members who "overidentify" with clients.

Social workers who overidentify with their clients or teachers who overidentify with their students are considered to be indulging in nonprofessional action. Such action, so the reasoning runs, makes it impossible for the professional to adhere to the ideal norms of universalism and objectivity and thus to assist his clients effectively. Professional norms such as these reinforce those bureaucratic norms that impose barriers upon the lower-class person's advancement in the social order.

The controls exerted by the bureaucrats over members of the lower class are intensified because the office holders are constantly called upon to normalize and stabilize the system with an eye to maintaining the proper public image. One means of stabilizing and

[8]Robert K. Merton, *Social Theory and Social Structure*, rev. ed. (New York: The Free Press, 1957), pp. 195–206; and Robert Presthus, *The Organizational Society* (New York: Vintage Books, 1965).

rationalizing the system's performance is to work within the context of established rules or categories. But to cope really effectively with such deviants as juvenile delinquents, the schools would have to alter radically their time-honored categories. Our experience suggests, however, that school systems stifle the grievances of deviant or lower-class groups, for these grievances, at least implicitly, challenge the bureaucratic norms that are supported by the groups that determine public policy.

The general insensitivity of bureaucracies to lower-class persons and their problems is highlighted in the "custodial function" adopted by many mental hospitals and even slum schools.[9] Because the bureaucracy's normative system runs counter (or at best ignores) the norms and values of the lower class, a minimum of attention is given to socializing clients into the bureaucratic—or broader societal—norms. Bureaucratic systems adjust to this situation through the caretaker function.

Orientations of the Lower Class Towards Bureaucracies

Just as significant as the bureaucrat's orientation towards the lower class is the latter's orientation towards the bureaucracy. Our investigations, particularly depth interviews of Mexican-American families in San Antonio, support the conclusion of other social scientists—that members of the lower class encounter serious difficulties when they attempt to understand or to cope with the normative order of bureaucratic systems.

First and foremost, the lower-class person simply lacks knowledge of the rules of the game. Middle-class persons generally learn how to manipulate bureaucratic rules to their advantage and even to acquire special "favors" by working through the "private" or "backstage" (as opposed to the "public") sector of the bureaucratic organization. Middle-class parents teach by example as they intervene with various officials—e.g., the police or school teachers—to protect the family's social position in the community. In contrast, the lower-class person stands in awe of bureaucratic regulations and

---

[9]See, e.g., Ivan C. Belknap, *Human Problems of a State Mental Hospital* (New York: McGraw-Hill Book Co., 1956); Fred M. Hechinger, "Poor Marks for Slum Schools," *The New York Times*, December 12, 1965, Section E, p. 9; Kenneth Clark, *Dark Ghetto* (New York: Harper and Row, 1965), chap. 6.

frequently is unaware that he has a legal and moral claim to certain rights and privileges. More often, however, it is the lack of knowledge of the system's technicalities and backstage regions that is responsible for the lower-class person's inability to manipulate a bureaucratic system to his advantage.

We mentioned earlier that in its lower echelons the bureaucracy is highly specialized and governed by numerous regulations. Therefore, the lower-class person, whose knowledge of the system is least adequate, must interact with the very officials who are most constrained by the formal rules. This situation is complicated by the fact that the problems the lower-class person faces are difficult to treat in isolation. The lack of steady employment, of education, and of medical care, for example, interlock in complex ways. Yet, the lower-class client encounters officials who examine only one facet of his difficulties and who, in the ideal, treat all cases in a similar fashion. After one agency (or official) has dealt with the special problem assigned it, the client is then referred to another agency which will consider another facet of the situation. It follows that no official is able to view the lower-class client as a whole person, and thus he is unable to point up to the client how he might use his strengths to overcome his weaknesses.

Middle-class persons, on the other hand, are in a position to deal with higher-status officeholders, who are less encumbered by the rules and thus can examine their clients' problems in holistic terms. Delinquents from middle-class homes, for instance, are more apt than those from lower-class surroundings to be judged by officials according to their overall performance—both past and present.

The cleavage between modern bureaucracies and the lower class is intensified by various cultural differences. Gans,[10] for example, has found that lower-class persons typically relate to one another in a personal manner. Middle-class persons are better able to relate to others within an impersonal context. Thus, members of the lower class face a greater gulf when they attempt to communicate with middle-class bureaucrats who ideally must administer rules accordingly to impersonal, universalistic norms.

This divergence between the lower class and bureaucratic officialdom in patterns of social interaction simply makes it more difficult for a lower-class person to acquire knowledge of how the system

---

[10]Herbert Gans, *The Urban Villagers* (New York: The Free Press, 1965).

operates. It is not surprising that under these circumstances members of the lower class often experience a sense of powerlessness or alienation. This alienation in turn reinforces and is reinforced by the sense of fatalism that is an integral part of "the culture of poverty."[11] That is, those who live in the world of the lower class account for events in the social sphere in terms of spiritual forces, chance, luck, and the like; they have little or no sense of control over their own destiny.

Because bureaucratic officials find it difficult to understand the perspective of lower-class clients and because lower-class persons must increasingly cope with highly specialized and technically oriented systems, the social distance between the bureaucratically skilled members of American society and some elements of the lower class may well be increasing rather than decreasing.[12] A kind of "circular causation," in Myrdal's terms,[13] is at work, as various social forces tend to exaggerate the schism between at least some sectors of the lower class and the upper socioeconomic groups who control the bureaucratic organizations.

Organization Implications

The dilemmas of client-centered bureaucracies which deal with lower-class persons are reflected in a variety of programs designed to eliminate poverty, juvenile delinquency, and other social problems. By examining these programs we can clarify some of the relationships between bureaucracy and the lower class discussed above and can bring to light other issues as well.

There have been two broad strategies for resolving the problems faced by the lower class on the national, state, and local levels. The dominant strategy emphasizes increased bureaucratization. The second approach, of theoretical rather than practical import at the present time, calls for a fundamental restructuring of client-centered bureaucracies.

[11]See, e.g., various essays in Frank Riessman, Jerome Cohen, and Arthur Pearl (Eds.), *Mental Health of the Poor* (New York: The Free Press, 1964).

[12]U.S. Bureau of the Census, *Current Population Reprint Series P-60. No. 47, Income in 1964 of Families and Persons in the United States* (Washington, D.C.: Government Printing Office, 1965).

[13]Gunnar Myrdal, *Economic Theory and Under-Developed Regions* (London: Gerald Duckworth and Co., 1957), pp. 16–20.

1. The primary means of overcoming the problems that have been associated with the lower class has been more and more bureaucracy. This pattern has taken two forms.

    a. The social problems of the lower class that have resisted solution (in terms of the values and beliefs of the dominant groups in society) are to be resolved through expansion of existing bureaucratic structures or the addition of new ones. This has been the main thrust of most legislation on both the national and the state levels since the 1930s. The programs initiated during the New Deal era have reached their fruition in President Johnson's "Great Society." In one sense the problems generated by bureaucracy are to be met by more bureaucracy.

       The efforts to resolve social problems through bureaucratization have proliferated in the nongovernmental sector as well. For example, some programs—e.g., the YMCA Detached Workers Program in Chicago[14]—seek to combat delinquency among lower-class groups by fitting youth into an organizational apparatus.

       The sociologist Glazer[15] views this organizational revolution as the basis of the new utopia. It is the model towards which men should strive. He, like many other sociologists, considers an industrial-urban order to be equivalent with a bureaucratic social order.

    b. A small group of persons believe that the problems of the lower class require a counter-organizational solution. The Mobilization for Youth program in New York—as it has been interpreted by some social workers—is an instructive case in point.[16] Here a number of social workers, perhaps as a reaction to their traditional overidentification with middle-class norms, have been attempting to organize the poor in order to counter the problems generated by entrenched bureaucracies. In theory the new bureaucratic systems should side with the poor against the established bureaucracies which are controlled by the upper socioeconomic groups.

[14]Charles N. Cooper, "The Chicago YMCA Detached Workers: Current Status of an Action Program," paper presented at a joint session of the annual meeting of the Society for the Study of Social Problems and American Sociological Association, Los Angeles, California, August 1963.

[15]Nathan Glazer, "The Good Society," *Commentary* 36 (September 1963):226–234.

[16]See, e.g., Charles F. Grosser, "Community Development Programs Serving the Urban Poor," *Social Work* 10 (July 1965):15–21.

2. Along with this trend towards bureaucratization, there have been increased efforts to remake bureaucratic structures or to create nonbureaucratic systems in order to attain certain ends.[17]

   a. Although the therapeutic community in the mental health field has not been specifically designed for lower-class clients, this development has been spurred by the sociological descriptions of custodial hospitals that have cared for lower-class patients. These highly bureaucratized systems have fallen far short of their stated goals; indeed, they have done much to stifle communication between therapists and patients.[18] The therapeutic community, which in extreme form calls for a complete breakdown of status barriers between therapist and patient, has thus emerged as a new organizational form in order to further the treatment of patients.

      Somewhat similar communities have emerged in other areas as well. The Provo Experiment[19] with juvenile delinquents has displayed some of the characteristics of the therapeutic community. In at least the early stages of their contacts with delinquents, the workers in this project have placed considerable reliance upon informal groups (in sharp contrast to, say, the bureaucratized reformatory) as a mechanism for revising the delinquent's orientation.

   b. In a similar vein, there have been efforts to set up organizations along collegial lines. Some writers, like Litwak, seem to regard this type of system as a "professional bureaucracy."[20] But if we take the Weberian model as our starting point, the very notion of a professional bureaucracy is a contradiction of terms. The collegial organization and the bureaucratic system are built on divergent principles. The former stresses, for example, equality among officeholders and the need for generalists rather than specialists. The generalist, unencumbered by highly formalized rules, can view clients in holistic terms and thus examine their weaknesses relative to their strengths. There emerges here a type of rationality that is not encompassed by

---

[17]There has been considerable interest in reorganizing corporate bureaucracy in recent years, but this material does not bear directly upon the problems at hand.

[18]See, e.g., Belknap, *op. cit.*

[19]LaMar T. Empey and Jerome Rabow, "The Provo Experiment in Delinquency Prevention," *American Sociological Review* 26 (October 1961):679–695.

[20]Eugene Litwak, "Models of Bureaucracy Which Permit Conflict," *American Journal of Sociology* 57 (September 1961):177–184.

Weber's notions of "formal rationality" (typical of bureaucratic systems) and "substantive rationality" (typical of traditional paternalistic systems).[21]

Some mental hospitals are apparently being built along collegial lines—as a compromise between a bureaucratic system and a therapeutic community.[22] Our experience in a neighborhood agency indicates that a collegial organization is necessary if social workers are to function as "mediators" between divergent class elements.[23] Workers within a bureaucratic welfare agency, as depicted by Wilensky and Lebeaux,[24] must take the class structure (as defined by the upper socioeconomic groups) as their frame of reference. Because bureaucratic functionaries find it difficult to understand the role orientations of lower-class others, they cannot mediate effectively between elements of different social classes.

Overall, the trends in the development of nonbureaucratic organizations suggest a close association between the system's internal structure and its relationships with clients. These trends also support our contention that bureaucratic systems have not been successful in working with lower-class clients.

Political Implications

The tensions generated by the bureaucratic solution to current social problems are highlighted by the efforts to resolve the difficulties encountered by the Negro lower class. The debate generated by the "Moynihan Report" is of special theoretical interest.[25] (This Report,

[21]*From Max Weber*, trans. and ed. by H. H. Gerth and C. Wright Mills (New York: Oxford University Press, 1946).

[22]Research being carried out by James Otis Smith, J. Kenneth Benson and Gideon Sjoberg as part of the Timberlawn Foundation Research Project, Dallas, Texas, will bear directly upon this issue.

[23]Gideon Sjoberg, "The Rise of the 'Mediator Society'," Presidential address delivered at the annual meeting of the Southwestern Sociological Association, Dallas, Texas, March 1964, examines the overall role of mediators in modern society.

[24]Harold L. Wilensky and Charles N. Lebeaux, *Industrial Society and Social Welfare* (New York: The Free Press, 1965), pp. 238–240.

[25]U.S. Department of Labor, *The Case for National Action* (Washington, D.C.: Government Printing Office, 1965). For reactions to this essay see: "The Negro Family: Visceral Reaction," *Newsweek* 60 (December 6, 1965):38–40, and John Herbers, "Moynihan Hopeful U.S. Will Adopt a Policy of Promoting Family Stability," *The New York Times*, December 12, 1965, p. 74.

issued by the U.S. Department of Labor, was written by Daniel P. Moynihan, although he is not formally listed as author.) Moynihan argues that the family structure of the lower-class Negro—which is mother-dominated and highly unstable by societal standards—must be revised if Negroes are to adapt to the industrial-urban order or the bureaucratic school systems, economic organizations, etc.

Elements of the Negro leadership have sharply attacked the Moynihan Report. They believe that instead of restructuring the lower-class Negro family we must remake modern bureaucratic systems so that these will be more responsive to the "needs" of the Negro lower class.

Moynihan's position is in keeping with that of many sociologists who accept present-day structural arrangements as more or less inevitable. Sociologists often argue that social problems arise because lower-class individuals or families are committed to sociocultural patterns that make it difficult for them to accommodate to the demands of industrial-urban organizations. Although some scholars have analyzed the dysfunctions of bureaucratic systems,[26] they rarely, if ever, assume that basic structural reorganization is necessary or possible. But the Weberian model may not be a rational or efficient organization for coping with many of the problems that have emerged (and will emerge) in an advanced industrial order where the problems of production have been resolved and the issues dealt with by client-centered organizations loom increasingly larger.

Sociologists must reexamine their basic premises if they are to grasp the nature of current social trends. For one thing, politics in a post-welfare, advanced industrial-urban order may become oriented around pro-bureaucratic and anti-bureaucratic ideologies. The rumblings of minorities (including some intellectuals in England, the United States, and Sweden) suggest that this type of political struggle may be in the offing. It is of interest, for example, that in the United States elements of the New Left—e.g., Students for a Democratic Society—share a common "devil"—the bureaucratic system—with elements of the right wing. We would hypothesize that some relationship exists between these ideological concerns and the problems of client-centered bureaucracies. Certainly, these developments are worthy of serious sociological investigation—and before, not after, the fact.

[26]See, e.g., Harry Cohen, *The Demonics of Bureaucracy* (Ames: Iowa State University Press, 1965).

Conclusions

Evidence indicates that modern bureaucracies, especially client-centered ones, stand between lower-class and upper-status (particularly middle-class) persons. These groups do not encounter one another within a vacuum but rather within an organizational, bureaucratic context. Even when they meet in relatively informal situations, the bureaucratic orientation of the middle-class person structures his response to the lower-class individual. It is through their positions in the key bureaucracies that the higher-status groups maintain their social advantages and even at times foster bureaucratic procedures that impede the advancement of lower-class persons into positions of privilege. While our illustrative data are limited to the United States, many of our generalizations seem to hold for other industrial-urban orders as well. . . .

VI

Framing Public Policy: The Bureaucratic Role

Bureaucratic organizations can affect the character and direction of national policy through either of two main avenues. First, a bureaucratic organization can influence, if not actually shape, the broad policies the government adopts to deal with specific problems that arise in either the domestic environment or the international arena. And second, after a policy is agreed upon, it is usually a bureaucratic organization that is charged with carrying it out—so as to ensure that the policy achieves its desired effects. The articles in this section focus on the bureaucratic role in policy formulation; the process by which policies are implemented is examined in Section VII.

I

James Fesler's "Policymaking at the Top of Bureaucracy" draws our attention to the fact that U.S. bureaucracies differ from similar organizations in other advanced industrial societies in one salient respect. The number of political appointees in the upper echelons of bureaucracy has been growing much more rapidly in the United States than in other democratic states. Executive policymaking in this country is thus a process in which top bureaucrats share power with a variety of presidential appointees from the outside world. In such an organizational setting, senior career officials can easily find themselves occupying a back seat when major policy decisions are being made.

The American way of policymaking is also characterized by

frequent power struggles among political appointees. White House aides compete with cabinet officials for control over key decisions, and departmental officials in turn vie with one another for ascendancy in this policymaking system. But one view that most of these political appointees share is a strong distrust of career bureaucrats. Hence, as Fesler notes, senior career officials in many policy areas are allowed far less input into major decisions than their experience and ability may warrant. This problem was aggravated recently by a change brought about by passage of the Civil Service Reform Act of 1978: the establishment of the Senior Executive Service (SES), which gives the president greater control over assignments of senior career personnel.[1]

II

Nowhere in the structure of U.S. bureaucracy is the dominance of political appointees over bureaucrats more pronounced than in the area of foreign policy. Here, as Bert Rockman points out in "America's Two Departments of State," the "irregulars" (outsiders holding temporary posts in the government) have been at the center of policymaking in foreign affairs during the last twenty-five years, while the "regulars" (career diplomatic officials) have been at its periphery. Rockman traces the ascendancy of the "irregulars"—or "in-and-outers," as Richard Neustadt once called them[2]—to the fact that they have had such a large presence on the staff of the National Security Council, an agency that recent presidents regard as a more responsive and pliable instrument than the State Department, and thus better suited to helping the president achieve mastery over the foreign policy agenda.

What is most striking in Rockman's and other accounts of the role of U.S. bureaucracy in foreign affairs is the extraordinary passivity of the career bureaucrats who constitute the foreign service officer corps. These career officials are more adept at reacting to than at initiating policy proposals. Their chief role

---

[1] The Reagan administration has made good use of the SES system to strengthen its control over executive policymaking. See Dick Kirschten, "Administration Using Carter-Era Reform to Manipulate the Levers of Government," *National Journal* 9 (April 1983), 732–736.

[2] See Richard E. Neustadt, "White House and Whitehall," *The Public Interest* No. 2 (Winter 1966), 55–69, a trail-breaking analysis of the subject.

seems to be to criticize the innovations proposed by the
"irregulars." As a result, the initiative in policymaking shifts to
these outsiders, who become the major architects of policy
changes. Presidents come to distrust the career foreign policy
bureaucracy, partly perhaps because it seems to lack imagination,
but partly also because it is committed not so much to White
House goals as to its own professional norms and perspectives. The
president and the State Department thus tend to drift apart, and
in the United States a foreign policy bureaucracy that is without
access to the president is without access to power.

However, such passivity is by no means universal among U.S.
bureaucrats. On the domestic side of the policy spectrum,
professional bureaucrats are often very active in implementing and
defending the policy goals their agency has been set up to pursue.
In "The Art of Cooptation: Advisory Councils in Social Security,"
Martha Derthick examines an administrative agency in which
career officials have been anything but bashful about exerting
influence over their organization's policy decisions. At the core of
policymaking in social security are "a small number of program
executives" who are concerned more with the development and
protection of the social security system than with the fortunes of
the president or the political party temporarily in power. These
program executives have shaped the course of the social security
system from its inception in 1935 down to the present time.
Presidential appointees, whether Democrat or Republican, have
simply ratified policy changes initiated by the agency's career
personnel.

Derthick provides an illuminating analysis of the way in
which these program executives solidified their power even while
seeming to be sharing it. The citizens advisory councils that have
long been a part of the social security network were set up to
provide an avenue through which the public could effect changes
in social security law. However, agency executives were able to
utilize these councils for their own purposes by exerting behind-
the-scenes influence over their policy recommendations. They did
this by placing social security personnel in a dominant position on
each advisory council's staff and by selecting people for council
membership who were basically in sympathy with their own
objectives. "Typically," Derthick writes, "advisory council reports
paved the way for the program executives' own current

recommendations." What this case clearly reveals is the skill with which bureaucrats can use the forms of democracy to conceal their own dominance over policy development.

III

However skillful they may be in advancing or protecting their own power, bureaucrats do not by themselves control any area of national policy in the United States. When power is distributed in the pluralistic manner that is characteristic of this country, bureaucrats must ally themselves with other centers of influence if their policy views are to gain ascendancy. They must get the White House on board their policy bandwagon, build alliances within Congress or with outside groups, or mobilize public opinion through the press. If the measures they wish to see adopted represent a radical departure from existing practice, bureaucrats must build very formidable coalitions to overcome the inertia that characteristically sustains the status quo in policy as in other matters.

In "Bureaucratic Coalition Building," Leon Sigal discusses some of the means bureaucrats use to develop coalitions in support of the policies they favor. One of their strategies is to leak information to the press in order to mobilize public opinion behind their point of view when a policy dispute is taking place within the executive branch. "The volume of detailed information on the inner workings of the U.S. government in the press astonishes, and occasionally dismays, foreign observers," Sigal writes. This flow of information in large part reflects coalition-building efforts on the part of executive officials.

The target of some of the information released by bureaucratic organizations is the White House itself. Sigal quotes John Kenneth Galbraith, a former ambassador to India, as saying that he "found it easier to bring my views to bear on the President of the United States by way of *The Washington Post* and its New Delhi correspondent than by way of the State Department." Other times the information is directed toward Congress. Pentagon officials may try to muster congressional support for the use of military force abroad by publicizing "secret" intelligence information about threatening developments in, for example, the Caribbean.

Of course the public itself is the favorite target of all these bureaucratic disclosures. If the indignation of the public can be aroused, the White House and Congress may be forced into policy decisions they would otherwise be reluctant to make. Thus, the efforts of bureaucrats to gain public support may ultimately be designed to win over Congress or the president to their point of view.

19

Policymaking
at the Top
of Bureaucracy

JAMES W. FESLER

The exceptional nature of the American governmental system has attracted many interpreters, some grandly addressing the whole complexity, others focusing on particular sectors of the system. Our concern here is the sector in which the president, political executives, and career executives interact in the formulation of policy initiatives and in responding to policy decisions. The character of this sector is unique to the United States. In a major study of bureaucrats and politicians in seven Western democracies, the authors frequently interrupt their main course of cross-national generalization to acknowledge "American exceptionalism" and "the American aberration."[1]

Though our focus is on only one part of the whole system, that part is remarkably interactive with other elements of the system, most prominently Congress, interest groups, communications media, public opinion, and the courts. Even within this sector the dynamics of interactions among officials with different capabilities and time frames, and the dynamics energized by competing values—the free market and government intervention, politics and neutral competence, innovation and continuity, for instance—are so complex as to

From James W. Fesler, "Politics, Policy, and Bureaucracy at the Top," *Annals of The Academy of Political and Social Science*, Vol. 466 (March 1983), pp. 24–37, 39–40. Copyright © 1983 by The Academy of Political and Social Science. Reprinted by permission of Sage Publications, Inc. Footnotes are renumbered.

[1]Joel D. Aberbach, Robert D. Putnam, and Bert A. Rockman, *Bureaucrats and Politicians in Western Democracies* (Cambridge, MA: Harvard University Press, 1981).

have uncertain outcomes. It is not clear whether and when these dynamics work synergistically to effect forward movement, are so constructively conflictual as to assure prudence, or immobilize government when action is needed.

At the Top

The upper reaches of the executive branch are a curious mélange. They include roughly 9000 officials: about 100 in the White House and other parts of the Executive Office of the President; about 700 cabinet and subcabinet posts, commissionerships, and bureau chiefships filled by presidential appointment, usually with the advice and consent of the Senate; some 7000 members of the Senior Executive Service, of whom 700 are political appointees and 6300 are senior civil servants; and about 1200 scientists and other specialists without managerial responsibilities.[2] Altogether these top officials amount to four-tenths of one percent of total federal civilian employment.

Except immediately under the cabinet, no line can be drawn across the executive branch, or across a single department, above which all senior officials are political executives and below which all are civil-service careerists. By law, some bureau chiefs are presidential appointees confirmed by the Senate, some are noncareer appointees of a cabinet member, and some are career appointees. A further complexity is that some civil-service careerists accept appointment as political executives, though until recently they thereby lost civil-service status, including tenure.

The United States outdoes all other modern democracies in its provision for change when party control of the executive branch shifts. About 1600 higher positions are filled by political appointment. This contrasts with the approximately 100 top officials in Britain and 360 in France—though 85 percent of France's are drawn from the civil service—that a new administration is entitled to choose afresh. In a typical American department, the secretary, deputy and under secretaries, assistant and deputy assistant secretaries, administrators of large aggregates, chiefs of several bureaus, and regional

[2]U.S. House Committee on Post Office and Civil Service, *United States Government Policy and Supporting Positions*, 96th Cong., 2nd sess., 18 November 1980 (Washington, DC: Government Printing Office, 1980); "The Pick of the Plums," *National Journal*, 12:I (29 Nov. 1980), Special Insert. The Senior Executive Service, with an authorized strength of 8500, is not fully staffed.

directors are replaced by a new set of officials. In the Department of Commerce, 93 high political incumbents can be displaced; in the Department of Agriculture, 65.

For three decades the number of politically filled posts has increased. This occurred partly by interposition of new layers of political appointees and partly by multiplication of executives' staff assistants. But existing positions were also shifted from the career service to political appointment; examples are departments' assistant secretaries for administration and regional directors. If political executives are the principal means by which a president and a department head can grasp control of the bureaucracy and institute changes in policy and program, the United States has abundantly provided for it.

The President's Entourage

Nearest the president are the White House staff and the agencies housed in the Executive Office of the President, especially the mostly career-staffed Office of Management and Budget (OMB). Between them one might expect a happy melding of short-term political and long-term careerist points of view in service of the president's policy and management responsibilities.

The White House Staff

Every president needs near him a few intimate advisers who are politically astute and personally loyal. He turns to those with whom he has been closely associated in the campaigns for nomination and election and to friends in his home state. The problem that arises is twofold. One is that his closest advisers are often poorly qualified for the responsible governmental roles in which they are suddenly cast, roles that have become magnified by the centripetal pull of policy and short-term decision making to the White House and by the president's delegation of the tangle of domestic affairs to his aides as he increasingly becomes absorbed in foreign affairs.

The other form of the problem is extension downward in White House staffing of the same recruitment criteria, except for prior intimacy with the president: personal loyalty, campaign service, and congruence of substantive policy views, if any, with those voiced in the election campaign. In 1981, runs one report, "with few exceptions, the professionals on the policy development staff were active in Reagan's 1980 campaign for the presidency." Two of them, in their mid-twenties, had been campaign speech writers.[3] In the Carter administration, the then associate OMB director recalls, "OMB felt that the Domestic Policy Staff was too pervasive, too concerned with short-term political considerations and that some of its junior people were not too capable."[4]

Characterizations of the presidential assistants constituting the White House staff vary more in tone than in essentials. One, kinder than most, reads, "They tend to be young, highly intelligent, and unashamedly on the make. They take chances, they cut corners, and unlike most politicians they sometimes have a little spontaneity and irreverence left in them. This accounts for much of their charm and most of their problems."[5] The words are from Patrick Anderson's study of assistants serving presidents from Roosevelt to Johnson. Characterizations of assistants to Nixon, Ford, Carter, and Reagan have a darker cast.

Efforts to strengthen the president by furnishing him with a staff of several hundred creates more problems than it solves. The White House itself becomes a complex, layered bureaucracy that is difficult to manage. The number of aides with the ready access to the president that propinquity promotes reduces his opportunities for conferring with cabinet members and seeking counsel from knowledgeable persons outside the government. The number, energy, and policy-area assignments of lower-level aides draw business to the White House that might well be left to cabinet departments. Such aides' intrusiveness into departmental affairs often bypasses department heads, thus weakening the prestige of those on whom the president depends for departmental management. The policy-formation process is slowed and complicated by in-house clearance procedures

[3]Dick Kirschten, "Reagan Sings of Cabinet Government, and Anderson Leads the Chorus," *National Journal*, 13:824–27, 827, 824 (9 May 1981). In 1982, Martin Anderson's resignation as director of the staff was accepted.

[4]W. Bowman Cutter, quoted in Dick Kirschten, "Decision Making in the White House: How Well Does It Serve the President?" *National Journal*, 14:584–89, 588 (3 Apr. 1982).

[5]Patrick Anderson, *The President's Men: White House Assistants of Franklin D. Roosevelt . . . Lyndon Johnson* (Garden City, NY: Doubleday, Anchor Books, 1969), p. 469. In the 1976 campaign, Anderson was a speech writer for Jimmy Carter; he declined appointment to the White House staff.

and by substantive and personal controversies among aides.[6] The White House contribution, then, becomes not the comprehensive, long-range view of policy and honest brokering of conflicting departmental advocacy positions, but often a poorly coordinated battle for the president's mind among his own assistants. . . .

Cabinet Members

The initial selection of members of the cabinet receives more personal attention by the president-elect than that of any other set of political executives, save his few top aides. Recent presidents have had such confidence in those they select as to assert an intention to institute cabinet government, meaning reliance on cabinet members for counsel and for the staffing and running of their departments.

Cabinet members are an abler lot than the conspicuous exceptions lead us to believe. Many have achieved distinction in their careers and, for good or ill, are members of the establishment. Eisenhower appointed nine millionaires and Reagan at least eight. Carter's 1977 cabinet included five members with Ph.D.s and five who were lawyers.[7] Most have had federal government experience. From 1953 to 1976, this was true of 55 percent of the initial appointees and of 85 percent of replacement appointees.[8] They often are generalists who have served in other cabinet posts, at the subcabinet level in the same or other departments, or as top presidential aides. Early exemplars of the pattern are George Marshall, Dean Acheson, Robert Lovett, Averell Harriman, and Douglas Dillon. Later ones are Elliot Richardson, James Schlesinger, Cyrus Vance, Harold Brown, Joseph Califano, Alexander Haig, Caspar Weinberger, and George Shultz. Many are highly qualified, whether by pub-

---

[6]"The Carter decision loop covered well over a dozen separate offices within the White House; the process could take several weeks to complete, and it often generated considerable conflict." Paul C. Light, *The President's Agenda: Domestic Policy Choice from Kennedy to Carter* (Baltimore: Johns Hopkins University Press, 1982), p. 55.

[7]Nelson Polsby, "Presidential Cabinet Making: Lessons for the Political System," *Political Science Quarterly*, 93:15–25 (Spring 1978); "Financial Reports Show that 10 Members of Cabinet Are Worth $1 Million or More," AP dispatch in *New York Times*, 26 Jan. 1981, p. A24. Our text's count excludes cabinet members without departmental portfolios.

[8]James J. Best, "Presidential Cabinet Appointments: 1953–1976," *Presidential Studies Quarterly*, 11:62–66, 65 (Winter 1981).

lic or private experience, for the processes of advocacy, negotiation, and compromise that are at the heart of governmental policymaking—lawyers more so, corporate executives and academics somewhat less so, the few ideologues not at all.

However able and experienced they are, the president's early promise of cabinet government soon evaporates. Why should this be so? A too easy explanation, favored by White House aides, is that cabinet members "marry the natives"; each, headquartered in his department, is captured by the bureaucracy and by the clientele groups in the department's immediate environment. Responsiveness to the president, and to his aides, lapses.

An explanation that receives too little attention is that each cabinet member, as department head, is obligated to see to the faithful execution of the laws that fall within his department's jurisdiction. In most of its statutes, Congress vests authority directly in departments and their heads, not in the president. A department head is bound to resist White House aides' urging that he neglect or distort any of his principal statutory responsibilities. Should he not resist, he will alienate his career executives and will have to answer to clientele groups, congressional committees, and the courts.

A political element helps to poison the well. Though the president may initially promise cabinet members free hands in filling their subcabinet and other executive posts, this commitment eventually yields to the White House staff's insistence on clearance of nominees and, often, appointment of candidates centrally identified and preferred.

A variety of factors set cabinet members and White House aides on a collision course. In addition to those mentioned, petty and not-so-petty behaviors play their part. Cabinet members' access to the president is denied, White House aides fail to return cabinet members' telephone calls, and deliberate slights of protocol signal that individual members are out of favor. President Carter's purge of his cabinet in 1979 focused on those who had incurred White House aides' displeasure.

Joseph Califano quotes from his exit interview with Carter: "'Your performance as Secretary has been outstanding,' the President said. 'You have put the Department in better shape than it has ever been before. You've been the best Secretary of HEW. . . . The problem is the friction with the White House staff. The same qualities and drive and managerial ability that make you such a superb Secretary create problems with the White House staff.' "[9] The secretary must have sensed an odd reversal of role, for in the Johnson White House, "serving as the chief expediter for an impatient and demanding President, Califano made many enemies," some among cabinet members. "Time and again . . . Califano fought to impose Johnson's interests over the narrower interests of the departments of government."[10]

Whether by their own or the president's choice, cabinet members' median term since World War II has been barely more than two years. Over one-fifth of the secretaries were in place for less than 11 months.[11] From 1953 through 1976, there were 5 presidents, but 12 secretaries of commerce, 11 secretaries of HEW, 10 attorneys general, 9 secretaries of labor and of the treasury, and 8 secretaries of defense.[12]

Brevity of tenure, perhaps because it is not anticipated, does not deflect cabinet members from according highest priority to the making and influencing of policy. This is no doubt appropriate, but there is a price to pay. Many give very low priority to departmental management, which is the key to assuring responsiveness and effectiveness of the bureaucracy. This is as true of able corporate executives as of their colleagues from other walks of life. Secretary of the Treasury Michael Blumenthal, formerly head of the Bendix Corporation, made the point: "You learn very quickly that you do not go down in history as a good or bad Secretary in terms of how well you ran the place, whether you're a good administrator or not. You're perceived to be a good Secretary in terms of whether the policies for which you are responsible are adjudged successful or not. . . . But that's not true in a company. In a company it's how well you run the place."[13]

[9]Joseph A. Califano, Jr., *Governing America: An Insider's Report from the White House and the Cabinet* (New York: Simon & Schuster, 1981), pp. 434–35.

[10]Anderson, *The President's Men*, pp. 443, 446.

[11]G. Calvin Mackenzie, *The Politics of Presidential Appointments* (New York: Free Press, 1981), p. 7. The period covered was 1945–77; in 1979, President Carter replaced five cabinet members.

[12]Best, "Presidential Cabinet Appointments," p. 63.

[13]W. Michael Blumenthal, "Candid Reflections of a Businessman in Washington," *Fortune*, 99(2):36ff., 39 (Jan. 1979).

Political Executives

Below cabinet members and other major agencies' heads are most of the 1600 political executives. A president intent on effecting change within the executive branch normally transmits his intentions through these appointees and, at least in theory, should be able to rely on them for vigorous translation of intentions into action. Yet the multiplicity, qualifications, and tenure of political executives probably hamper the effecting of change more than does any obduracy of the permanent bureaucracy.

Numbers

The large number of political appointments available guarantees that errors of choice will be made, and the earlier the more. In the 10-week post-election rush, self-nomination, others' recommendations, the old-boy network, the BOGSAT technique ("a bunch of guys sitting around a table"), and a variety of other means provide the large pool of candidates and the disorderly modes of selection.

The numbers also account for how deeply political appointments extend into the bowels of departmental administration. The proliferation of subcabinet posts, strictly defined, affords one clue. These positions—of under secretary, deputy under secretary, and assistant secretary—increased from 55 in 1950 to 84 in 1960, 113 in 1970, and 145 in 1978.[14] The secretary may have as many as 15 politically appointed assistants attached to his own office, and the subcabinet officials may average two such assistants apiece.[15] Below the subcabinet level are a number of political appointees with such titles as deputy assistant secretary, bureau chief, deputy bureau chief, and regional director.[16]

The large number of political executives and their penetration

[14]Thomas P. Murphy, Donald E. Nuechterlein, and Ronald J. Stupak, *Inside the Bureaucracy: The View from the Assistant Secretary's Desk* (Boulder, CO: Westview Press, 1978), pp. 5–6.

[15]Based on the Interior Department's management pattern, as charted in Hugh Heclo, *A Government of Strangers: Executive Politics in Washington* (Washington, DC: Brookings Institution, 1977), p. 58.

[16]In 1977, political appointees in the Department of Health, Education and Welfare included 13 deputy assistant secretaries, 12 bureau chiefs, 10 deputy bureau chiefs, and 10 regional directors. James W. Fesler, *Public Administration: Theory and Practice* (Englewood Cliffs, NJ: Prentice-Hall, 1980), pp. 135–36.

of departments, bureaus, and the field service distance able careerists from the centers of decision making. Their rich potential remains untapped, especially in the early period when the administration's and departments' major policy proposals are formulated.

Qualifications

By most standard criteria, especially educational level and subject-matter knowledge relevant to their particular program-area responsibilities, political executives are a well-qualified elite. Three other criteria concern us here. These are partisan and policy compatibility with the president, governmental experience, and capacity to manage large organizations.

Political executives are less partisan than their designation suggests. From 1961 to 1978, members of the president's party averaged only 58 percent among the four administrations' sets of political appointees, with a range of 47 percent under Johnson to 65 percent under Nixon. Within cabinet departments, two-thirds of the political appointees, on average, belonged to the president's party, with State and Defense on the low side (44 and 47 percent) and Housing and Urban Development and Agriculture (89 and 86 percent) on the high side.[17]

Old images of party patronage have largely ceased to reflect reality. White House personnel staffs try to deflect partisan pressures by rewarding large financial contributors and taking care of defeated candidates for electoral office by minor, though sometimes major, ambassadorships; membership in multimember bodies—regulatory boards and commissions, presidential advisory commissions, and departmental advisory committees—and invitations to White House galas for foreign dignitaries.

The politics of policy, if not of party, plays a large role in recruitment. This politics takes two forms: loyalty to the president and his policies throughout his term, including the possibility of his changing course, and inflexible loyalty to particular policies, most of them compatible with the president's campaign rhetoric but selectively erosive during his term. The second kind of loyalty can turn antipresidential. Initial selection of subcabinet and subordinate ex-

---

[17]Calculated from tables in Roger G. Brown, "Party and Bureaucracy: From Kennedy to Reagan," *Political Science Quarterly*, 97:279–94, 283, 285 (Summer 1982). These and related data in the text partly reflect the promotion of civil servants to political-executive posts, especially in the last half of a president's term.

ecutives depends heavily on nominations and recommendations from the economic and professional communities interested in particular programs. A number of those chosen are likely to be drawn from interest groups, single-cause movements, conservative or liberal think tanks, and congressional staff members who share the president's initial orientation. Many such are advocates, with agendas of their own. There is little assurance that such political appointees will flexibly respond to the president's initiatives for change rather than firmly adhere to their convictions, constituencies, political patrons. Yet they are arrayed in many layers between the good to be done, as the president perceives it, and those who can do it, the career executives in closest touch with implementation.

Advocates, it is true, have a strong impulse to innovate, whether to turn the clock forward or backward. But innovations can be good or bad, well timed or ill timed, contributors or embarrassments to a larger strategy of change. Advocacy-oriented political executives are not the president's men and women. They march to a different drummer.

Prior experience in the federal government is a criterion closely linked to political executives' performance. Looking back, former appointees confess that they were poorly prepared for the Washington setting of interest groups, congressional committees, the White House staff, the goldfish-bowl exposure to the media, the budget process, and the permanent bureaucracy. In 1970 over two-thirds of presidential and two-fifths of departmental political appointees had less than two years of federal government experience.[18] Another two-fifths of the departmentally appointed political officials had over 10 years of federal experience and, like the top civil servants, were better prepared. Hugh Heclo notes the anomaly, that "unlike the situation in most private organizations, in the U.S. executive branch those in the top positions of formal authority [that is, presidential appointees] are likely to be substantially less familiar with their working environment than both their civil service and political subordinates."[19]

Capability for the management of large organizations or for

---

[18]Heclo, *A Government of Strangers*, p. 101 (drawing on a study by Joel D. Aberbach). The year 1970 may seem unrepresentative, as the Nixon administration had followed almost a decade of Democratic administrations. However, experienced Eisenhower executives had aged no more than 10 years in the decade.
[19]Ibid.

operating in them is a third criterion of executives' effectiveness. Few of the political executives who are lawyers or who are recruited from universities and research institutes, interest-group organizations, congressional staffs, and small business firms have had experience that prepares them for running a bureau of 5000 employees, let alone for operating in one of the cabinet departments, which range from 15,000 to one million employees. Sometimes, as Dean Acheson and George W. Ball have noted, even the head of a major corporation may have served only an ornamental function there and can do no more in government.[20]

Tenure

Independently of other attributes, the brief tenure of political executives suffices to explain the marginality of their impact. In the period of 1960 to 1972, over half of the under secretaries and assistant secretaries moved out within less than two years, including a fifth who left in less than one year.[21] How much time does a new political executive need to achieve effectiveness? Maurice Stans, former secretary of commerce, said, "A business executive needs at least two years to become effective in government, to understand the intricacies of his programs, and to make beneficial changes."[22]

Rapid turnover not only reduces individual effectiveness, it impairs three relationships that are at the heart of the administration's effectiveness. First, it complicates a department head's effort to establish teamwork among his principal subordinates, for they are ever changing. Second, rapid turnover near the top recurrently breaks up interdepartmental networks of political executives sharing concern with, and perhaps having divergent views on, particular policy and program areas extending across several departments. For these, especially, there need to be what Heclo terms "relationships of confi-

---

[20]Both write acidly about Edward R. Stettinius, who had been vice-president of General Motors and chairman of the board of United States Steel. Between 1939 and 1945, he served as a defense production official, land-lease administrator, under secretary of state, and secretary of state. Dean Acheson, *Present at the Creation: My Years in the State Department* (New York: W. W. Norton, 1969), pp. 88–91; and George W. Ball, *The Past Has Another Pattern: Memoirs* (New York: W. W. Norton, 1982), pp. 29–30.

[21]Arch Patton, "Government's Revolving Door," *Business Week*, Sept. 1973, pp. 12–13.

[22]Quoted, ibid., p. 12. The same estimate is made in Frederick V. Malek, *Washington's Hidden Tragedy* (New York: Macmillan, 1978), p. 49.

dence and trust."[23] The chemistry involved in these interpersonal relations takes time to develop and is upset if new elements are constantly being introduced. Third, top civil servants' relations with political superiors that are here today and gone tomorrow cannot faithfully follow copybook maxims. Some careerists, if called on, will patiently tutor one after another political executive to speed his learning process. Others, particularly those in charge of bureaus and programs, will take protective measures to minimize the damage an ill-prepared and very temporary political executive can do.

Political executives share a number of attributes that limit their effectiveness as the president's agents of change. Their number is too large. Partisanship is too weak to make them a cohesive group. In its place is the politics of policy. For some this means a commitment to support the president and, so, to adapt flexibly to his changing policy agenda and priorities. But for many it means tenacious devotion to particular program areas and particular policies, whether or not they comport with the president's strategic emphases. Too few political executives have prior governmental experience; fewer know how to run a large organization well. Finally, political appointees' stay is short and their comings and goings erratic.

Career Executives

Recent presidents campaigned against the bureaucracy and complained during their terms of the unresponsiveness of the bureaucracy. Most political appointees enter office with a stereotypical view of bureaucrats. This inhibits their seeking a collaborative relation with those best informed on departmental programs and best prepared to warn inexperienced superiors of minefields in the surrounding terrain. The three elements of the president's and political executives' stance are an assumption that the bureaucracy is swollen, a doubt of careerists' competence, and an expectation of their unresponsiveness to the administration in power. The first is quickly disposed of. For three decades the number of federal civilian employees has been substantially stable, in contrast to increases in the nation's population, its employed labor force, and the range of governmental responsibilities.

Doubt of careerists' competence is ill founded. Elmer Staats,

---

[23]Heclo, *A Government of Strangers*, p. 158 and passim.

after a distinguished career in politically appointive posts, said on ending his term as the comptroller general of the United States that ever since World War II days, "I have worked with business people who have been in the government. . . . And I have yet to find a single one of those business executives after their experience here who doesn't go out and have nothing but praise for the calibre and the hard work of the people in the government."[24] And Alan K. Campbell, an executive vice-president of ARA Services, Inc.—and earlier a Carter appointee—reports that "the quality of top managers I knew in the federal government . . . is every bit as high as we have at ARA; and on the whole, the people at ARA are paid from 1½ to 3 times more than their public sector counterparts."[25]

An expectation that the bureaucracy will be unresponsive to the administration in power is too simplistic to fit comfortably with the complexity of factors determining senior civil servants' behavior. Top careerists are remarkably diverse in ideological orientation and in party identification. On a scale of attitudes ranging from state intervention to free enterprise, Joel D. Aberbach and his colleagues found that their sample of such American careerists was "more heterogeneous than any of the European bureaucratic samples." The basic picture is a distribution of attitudes that is not only wide but substantially congruent with the distribution pattern in Congress.[26]

Party affiliations of careerists are weaker predictors of behavior. In social-service agencies in 1970, "even Republican administrators . . . were not wholly sympathetic to the social service retrenchments sought by the Nixon administration."[27] Sample surveys in 1970 and 1976 found that top careerists were 47 percent Democratic (38 percent in 1976), 36 percent Independent (48 percent in 1976), and 17 percent Republican (16 percent in 1976). Using different tests of Independents' leanings, the surveyors drew different

[24]Transcript, *The MacNeil/Lehrer Report: Elmer Staats Interview*, 6 Mar. 1981, pp. 6–7.

[25]Alan K. Campbell, in a symposium, "The Public Service as Institution," *Public Administration Review*, 42:304–20, 315 (July–Aug. 1982).

[26]Aberbach, Putnam, and Rockman, *Bureaucrats and Politicians*, pp. 122, 124–25. On congruence with Congress, see Joel D. Aberbach and Bert A. Rockman, "The Overlapping Worlds of American Federal Executives and Congressmen," *British Journal of Political Science*, 7:38 (Jan. 1967), Table 6.

[27]Joel D. Aberbach and Bert A. Rockman, "Clashing Beliefs Within the Executive Branch: The Nixon Administration Bureaucracy," *American Political Science Review*, 70:456–68, 467 (June 1976).

conclusions. For 1970, Joel Aberbach and Bert Rockman held that "the belief that a Republican administration does not have natural political allies within the federal bureaucracy seems well-justified."[28] For 1976, Richard Cole and David Caputo believed that "Independents and party identifiers combined assure either a Republican or a Democratic president substantial support at the senior career levels of the federal bureaucracy."[29]

Beyond ideologies and party affiliations, and often overriding them, is another attitudinal orientation. Most careerists perceive their role as one entailing the obligation to serve loyally the people's choice as president. Because senior careerists have served through several changes in administration, this is a well-internalized commitment. It is qualified, to be sure, by resistance to illegality, a resistance that served the nation well in the Watergate era.

This basic commitment, however, can be attenuated by another attitude toward role performance. Typically, senior civil servants identify with their agency and its responsibilities. Their finding fulfillment in achieving the purposes of statutes entrusted to them, instead of being passively neutral, generally strengthens the faithful execution of the laws. But it lures some into bureaucratic politics—protection of the agency's turf, development of a degree of autonomy, and mobilization of allies in Congress and clientele groups.

How responsive careerists are to presidential policy shifts is a complex product of ideologies, party affiliations, the civil-service doctrine of loyalty to the incumbent president, and devotion to particular programs and agencies. The relative weights of these factors vary with circumstances. The most negative reactions can be expected when the president orders termination of an agency or of well-established programs, reduction of funds, or slashing of staff. Yet when, by President Reagan's order, the Community Services Administration, an antipoverty agency, was dismantled in three months, the agency director reports, "The career service had demonstrated in a dramatic way the best of professional integrity in executing a difficult assignment most of them opposed." It shows, he adds, that

---

[28]Ibid., p. 458.
[29]Richard L. Cole and David A. Caputo, "Presidential Control of the Senior Civil Service: Assessing the Strategies of the Nixon Years," *American Political Science Review*, 73:399–413, 412 (June 1979).

"the mythology of an untrustworthy bureaucracy poised to undermine a policy with which it disagreed was simply not true."[30]

The Shared World of Political and Career Executives

Though political and career executives differ in important regards, the considerable degree of congruence of orientations permits expectation that they might harmoniously collaborate in their shared world. The recent institution of the Senior Executive Service is designed to facilitate such collaboration. Yet careerists' morale has fallen to perhaps its lowest point, and their career paths often poorly prepare them for engagement in the fashioning of broad policy.

Some Congruent Orientations

Political executives and top careerists have a good deal in common. Both groups are highly educated; more than half the members of each hold graduate or professional degrees. However, more of the senior civil servants, 40 percent, majored in technology and natural science; only 10 percent of political executives did so. Members of the two groups do not differ substantially in the proportions that see their role, or roles, as that of advocate, legalist, broker, trustee, facilitator, policymaker, or ombudsman. The civil servants, though, are twice as likely as political executives to have a technician-role focus, and half as likely to have a partisan-role focus. Their external activities disclose a common pattern: nearly two-thirds of each group have regular contacts with members of Congress; over 90 percent of each have regular contacts with representatives of clientele groups. Internally, not surprisingly, political executives have about twice as much contact with their department heads as do senior civil servants.[31] But, if not surprising, it indicates exclusion or filtering of counsel from members of the permanent government.

Top careerists share political executives' frustrations with bu-

<hr/>

[30]Dwight Ink, "CSA Closedown—A Myth Challenged," *Bureaucrat*, 11:39–43, 39, 43 (Summer 1982).

[31]Aberbach, Putnam, and Rockman, *Bureaucrats and Politicians*, pp. 52, 94, 230–31, 234; Aberbach and Rockman, "The Overlapping Worlds," p. 28. On meagerness of bureau chiefs' contacts with department heads, see Herbert Kaufman, *The Administrative Behavior of Federal Bureau Chiefs* (Washington, DC: Brookings Institution, 1981), pp. 59–62, 184–90.

reaucratic obstacles to effective performance, particularly the pervasiveness of red tape and the constricting personnel system. At least two-thirds of those sampled in 1981 answered no when asked whether "the administrative support systems" provide a pool of qualified professional and managerial talent to hire from, make it easy to hire employees, or make it easy to fire or to apply lesser sanctions against poorly performing employees.[32]

Finally, the infiltration of political-executive ranks by career civil servants fosters congruence of outlook with those continuing in civil-service status. Former careerists filled 25 percent of assistant secretaryships in the 1933–61 period—an average for the three presidencies. In the mid-1970s they held nearly half of such posts, and in 1978, under Carter, 61 percent.[33] Below the assistant secretaries, Heclo reports, "one-third to one-half of the noncareer . . . posts . . . are usually filled by career civil servants."[34] In the period Heclo deals with, such cooptation by the incumbent administration required sacrifice of civil-service status and possible dismissal from government service by the next administration. This has changed.

The Senior Executive Service

The 1978 Civil Service Reform Act pooled most political executives and top career executives in a Senior Executive Service (SES). The service currently includes about 7000 executives, 90 percent of them careerists and 10 percent political appointees. This is a specified governmentwide ratio; within it an individual agency's political appointees may rise as high as 25 percent. Except for presidential appointees requiring senatorial confirmation, or requiring White House clearance, a department head freely chooses political appointees who meet his previously established qualification standards. In making career appointments to the SES, he must adhere to competitive merit principles.

The key feature is the new flexibility with which the department head can assign and reassign SES members, whether political or career, to particular positions. Only two restrictions apply. A careerist is protected against involuntary reassignment for the first 120

[32]Thomas D. Lynch and Gerald T. Gabris, "Obstacles to Effective Management," *Bureaucrat*, 10:8–14, 9–10 (Spring 1981).

[33]Murphy, Nuechterlein, and Stupak, *Inside the Bureaucracy*, pp. 7, 195.

[34]Heclo, *A Government of Strangers*, p. 131.

days after appointment of a new department head, or of a political executive with reassignment authority. And in about 45 percent of the positions, the department head can assign and reassign only careerists, not political appointees. These are posts reserved for civil servants "to ensure impartiality, or the public's confidence in the impartiality of the Government," as the statute phrases it.[35]

These necessary protections accounted for, the system is one in which the department head can assemble his large management team, mixing political and career executives as suits his purpose. Additionally, advised by performance-review boards, he can at any time remove from SES a career member rated "less than fully successful."

Morale

The Senior Executive Service had a troubled start.[36] Pay was a major problem. Though the Reform Act directs the president to establish SES pay levels, Congress later set a pay ceiling that in 1982 put 84 percent of SES members at the same pay, $6000 below the president's top pay level. The performance awards and substantial bonuses for abler SES careerists, provided in the act, were also later curtailed. The most basic problem was eased when, at the end of 1982, Congress authorized pay increases of up to 15 percent for some 32,000 senior government employees.

For nonpay reasons, too, the morale of SES career members fell to a lamentably low point. They tired of being flayed as bureaucrats by a succession of recent administrations. They believed that "the quality of political leadership in the agencies has been declining" in the last several years, so that "career staffs are being directed by persons who are simply not capable of providing the kind of leadership and guidance that the programs of agencies and the public deserve."[37] They were disturbed by political executives' short time frames. In 1981 over three-fifths of top careerists sampled said that rapid turnover of political appointees made long-term planning difficult, and that such appointees focus on short-term projects "nearly all the time" or "rather often."[38] And, rightly or wrongly, they re-

---

[35]*U.S. Code*, Title V, secs. 3395, 3132 (b).

[36]Panel on the Public Service, National Academy of Public Administration, *The Senior Executive Service: An Interim Report, October 1981* (Washington, DC: National Academy of Public Administration, 1981).

[37]Ibid., pp. 34–35.

[38]Lynch and Gabris, "Obstacles to Effective Management," pp. 9–10.

acted negatively to the reversal of programs by foxes in the chicken coop.

Whatever the causes, an alarming exodus of top careerists occurred. About 1600 career executives left the federal service between July 1979 and June 1981. In 1981 about 95 percent of the most experienced senior careerists, those eligible for voluntary retirement at ages 55 to 59, with 30 years' service, were deciding to leave, compared to about 18 percent in 1978.[39]

Career Paths

Two features of the careers of senior civil servants weaken their potential contribution to high-level policymaking and management. Most were initially recruited in their twenties and thirties as specialists—scientists, engineers, economists, and the like. What they know about public affairs and the management of large organizations must, therefore, be haphazardly acquired as they move forward in their careers. The second career feature is confinement of most of their experience to one agency. The two specializations, by discipline and by agency, reinforce each other. Top careerists, therefore, have depth of expertness but not the breadth of training and experience that in other countries produces generalist administrators. For the same reasons, many American senior civil servants develop a myopic loyalty to particular agencies and programs.

These disabilities are not necessarily compensated for by political executives. Many of them qualify for particular political positions because their professional specialties and private-sector activities closely relate to the programs they are to administer. Though this may make for some congruence of outlook with that of top careerists, it also imposes blinders that remove much of the world from their field of vision.

Policymaking Problems

Formation and effectuation of an administration's policies are plagued by two major problems. One is the counterpull of centrif-

---

[39]Annette Gaul, "Why Do Executives Leave the Federal Service?" *Management* (published by the U.S. Office of Personnel Management), 2:13–15 (Fall 1981); William J. Lanouette, "SES—From Civil Service Showpiece to Incipient Failure in Two Years," *National Journal*, 13:1296 (18 July 1981).

ugal and centripetal forces. The other is the prevalence of short time perspectives.

Centrifugal and Centripetal Forces

The multiplication of governmental responsibilities has generated a geometrical growth of interrelations among programs and among departments. Whether the focus is on reduction of poverty, environmental protection, or foreign policy, the range of relevant factors and of concerned departments casts a shadow of quaintness on classic organizational doctrines of compartmentalization of authority and responsibility. Everything seems to be connected with everything else. Yet centrifugal forces create narrowly oriented, substantially autonomous policy communities in the governmental system.

George P. Shultz and Kenneth W. Dam, before becoming the secretary and deputy secretary of state, wrote of the costs of such partitioning: "In a balkanized executive branch, policymaking is necessarily a piecemeal affair; policymakers are under the constraint that they are not permitted to view problems whole."[40] Many share their concern that "the trend of events is toward greater fragmentation" and inveigh against iron triangles—enduring alliances of bureau, relevant congressional committees, and special-interest groups concerned with the bureau's programs. Joseph Califano believes that "the severest threat to governing for all the people" comes from the pernicious fact that "we have institutionalized, in law and bureaucracy, single-interest organizations that can accede only in the narrow interest and are incapable of adjudicating in the national interest." "We must," he says, "have people and institutions . . . that will render national policy more than the sum of the atomistic interests. We must design bureaucratic structures that permit and encourage top government officials to assess special interests, rather than pander to them."[41] . . .

Time Perspectives

George W. Ball, the under secretary of state under Kennedy, recalls, "When one tried to point out the long-range implications of

---

[40]George P. Shultz and Kenneth W. Dam, *Economic Policy Beyond the Headlines* (New York: W. W. Norton, 1977), p. 173.

[41]Califano, *Governing America*, pp. 451, 452. "Government by advocacy" (Shultz and Dam's term) has invaded the White House itself. Charged with "public liaison" are assistants and deputy assistants to the president for the elderly, youth, women, consumers, Hispanics, Blacks, the Jewish community, and other groups.

a current problem or how it meshed or collided with other major national interests, Kennedy would often say, politely but impatiently, 'Let's not worry about five years from now, what do we do tomorrow?' "[42] This attitude pervades the White House staff, is less operative among cabinet members and their deputy and under secretaries, gets strongly reinforced among assistant secretaries and other political executives, and is the despair of career civil servants. Systemic factors, not personal quirkiness, account for its prevalence.

The president's major opportunity for formulating his major policies with an expectation of favorable congressional action falls in the period between the popular election and the end of his first six months in office. He can, or does, claim a mandate for change, his public-approval ratings quickly register 70 percent or so, Congress grants a honeymoon period, the president can usually focus on domestic rather than principally foreign policies, and his cabinet members are not yet alienated by the White House staff.

Most presidents seize the opportunity offered. They initiate more requests for legislation in the first than in any later year. If wise, they act early in that year, for, Paul C. Light reports, 72 percent of requests introduced in January to March of the first year are eventually enacted, but only 25 percent of third- and fourth-quarter requests are so successful.[43]

The period of greatest opportunity is also the period when the administration may be least capable of carefully fashioning a policy program. Legislative proposals advanced in the first three months are largely products of the campaign staff and pro tem transition advisers. Though the cabinet is completed in December, appointment of subcabinet and other political executives stretches through several months. The permanent bureaucracy is not fully available in the preinaugural period. After the inauguration the bureaucracy is not trusted. So the new administration deprives itself of data, expertness, sophisticated understanding of the Washington environment, and longer time perspectives, all of which could strengthen the policy-formation process.

Coming elections, congressional and presidential, soon cast their shadows. That, together with the president's increasing absorption in foreign affairs, explains why, as John Helmer writes, "for only one year, the first for a one-term president, can it be said that he has

[42]Ball, *The Past Has Another Pattern*, p. 167.
[43]Light, *The President's Agenda*, pp. 44–45. See p. 42 for comparison of the number of the first and later years' requests.

time and some political incentive to consider longer-term problems and to make decisions and commitments whose results may not be immediately apparent."[44] In the second year, seeking to minimize loss of his party's congressional seats, he and his aides prefer initiatives with quick impact. The presidential reelection campaign begins in the third year and becomes all-important in the fourth year. Furthermore, neither Congress nor foreign governments welcome major policy proposals for which negotiation must bridge the current and a possibly different successor administration.

The irony is that by the second half of the presidential term, the administration has become better equipped to formulate long-range policies. The White House usually has achieved a clearer structure and more orderly processes, though it may have increased friction with cabinet members. Half the initial political appointees have left their posts and replacements have been more prudently chosen, often by promotion or transfer of able and responsive political executives and by promotion of careerists.[45] Continuing political executives have acquired Washington experience, discovered that civil servants are colleagues, not enemies, and learned that the designing of policies needs to take account of their implementability.[46] Regrettably, these resources cannot be exploited in a period dominated by short time perspectives.

A Modest Proposal

Deficiencies in the making and implementing of policy at the top levels of the executive branch derive from many sources. Some of the most basic lie outside the scope of this article. Within our framework one thing is clear: exhorting officials to behave differently than they do is profitless unless incentives are created that will alter their behavior. That daunting task might be circumvented by changing the mix of top executives.

[44]John Helmer, "The Presidential Office: Velvet Fist in an Iron Glove," in *The Illusion of Presidential Government*, eds. Hugh Heclo and Lester M. Salamon (Boulder, CO: Westview Press, for the National Academy of Public Administration, 1981), pp. 78–79.

[45]This staffing strategy partly reflects reluctance of persons in the private sector to accept appointments in the terminal years or months of an administration.

[46]However, negative factors are the fall in the president's public-approval ratings, the shift of his personal energies to foreign affairs, and, consequently, substantial delegation of domestic affairs to his aides.

Reducing the number of political executives would permit greater care in their selection and would open opportunities for experienced careerists, with their longer time perspectives, to contribute to the design and implementation of programs that embody the administration's innovative policies. Surprisingly, this is strongly advocated by President Nixon's top political recruiter. Frederick Malek writes,

> The solution to problems of rigidity and resistance to change in government is *not* to increase the number of appointive positions at the top, as so many politicians are wont to do. . . . An optimum balance between the number of career and noncareer appointments . . . should be struck in favor of fewer political appointees, not more. In many cases, the effectiveness of an agency would be improved and political appointments would be reduced by roughly 25 percent if line positions beneath the assistant secretary level were reserved for career officials.[47]

If his prescription were followed, top careerists would play a more significant role, one that is common in Europe and one that would bolster their morale and reduce the rate of prime-age resignations and retirements.

James L. Sundquist compared the policymaking capacity of the United States with that of five Western European countries that successfully developed and applied policies to influence the regional distribution of their populations—largely a matter of incentives for private investment in declining areas and disincentives for investment in regions growing too rapidly. By 1970 the United States had a clear national policy, in principle. It was embraced in both major parties' platforms, was frequently set forth by President Nixon, and was partially reflected in two congressional statutes. But, in contrast to European countries, "the institutional structure in the United States did not respond to the political directives."[48] Why not?

Among several reasons, Sundquist emphasizes the "gulf between the career bureaucracy, which was familiar with the data and had some degree of competence to analyze it, and the [White House] staff advisers who had responsibility for developing policy recom-

[47]Malek, *Washington's Hidden Tragedy*, pp. 102–3.
[48]James L. Sundquist, "A Comparison of Policy-Making Capacity in the United States and Five European Countries: The Case of Population Distribution," in *Population Policy Analysis*, eds. Michael E. Kraft and Mark Schneider (Lexington, MA: D. C. Heath, 1978), pp. 67–80, 71.

mendations." In Europe a typical participant "was at the same time the long-time career civil servant and the respected policy adviser." In the United States, "many of the most competent and ambitious of the career officials—the kind that rise to the top in European civil services—find themselves excluded from the inner policy-making circles, or subordinated to younger, less experienced political appointees, and so depart. The capability of the career service is reduced, which leads to pressures for further politicization, in a vicious circle."[49] . . .

From 1953 on, says Sundquist, "no administration devoted any appreciable attention to training and developing a new generation of career managers, or even seemed to care."[50] The reason is a familiar one. This requires a long time perspective and yields no credit for an administration in its short life.

---

[49]Ibid., p. 73. The theme is more fully developed in James L. Sundquist, "Jimmy Carter as Public Administrator: An Appraisal at Mid-Term," *Public Administration Review*, 39:3–11, 6–8 (Jan.–Feb. 1979).

[50]Sundquist, "Jimmy Carter as Public Administrator," p. 8.

20
America's Two Departments of State

BERT A. ROCKMAN

The United States possesses two foreign ministers within the same government: the one who heads the Department of State, and the one who is the assistant to the president for national security affairs. The former heads a classically contoured bureaucracy. Proximate to him are appointed officials, often with substantial foreign policy experience. At greater distance is a corps of professional foreign service officers (FSOs). Beneath the national security assistant, on the other hand, is a smaller professional staff of somewhat variable size (ranging in recent times from about three dozen to slightly over 50) whose members typically are drawn from universities, other agencies, and research institutes.

This latter group—the National Security Council staff—is the institutional embodiment of White House aspirations for imposing foreign policy coordination. Its "director," the president's assistant

From Bert A. Rockman, "America's *Departments* of State: Irregular and Regular Syndromes of Policy Making," reprinted by permission of the author and the American Political Science Association from *The American Political Science Review* 75 (December 1981):911–927. Table is renumbered.

Author's note: Christine Dodson, former staff secretary to the National Security Council, and Phyllis Kaminsky, NSC information officer, responded kindly to my requests for documentation. I am especially grateful to Cole Blasier, Paul Hammond, and Robert Putnam with whom I have had extensive discussions regarding ideas presented here. All three combine ideas with experience in the foreign policy and national security areas. In the spirit of the "irregular," they encouraged me to pursue my ideas; in the spirit of the "regular," they doused many of them, perhaps too few. They, of course, bear no responsibility for the contents of the article. I am enormously indebted also to one anonymous reviewer of an earlier rendition of this manuscript for efforts beyond the call of duty. If not all of his suggestions are incorporated here, they were all carefully considered, and my conclusion almost always was, "He's right about that."

for national security affairs, in recent years has come to be seen as the president's personal foreign policy spokesman as well as an influential molder, and sometime executor, of his policy choices. Though, at least publicly, the overt role of the president's national security assistant has been diminished in the Reagan administration relative to the prominence it attained during the Nixon and Carter presidencies, a common perception is that, since the Kennedy administration, policy power has drifted steadily from the State Department to the president's team of foreign policy advisers (Campbell, 1971; George, 1972a; Destler, 1972a, 1972b, 1980; Allison and Szanton, 1976). If perceptions govern, this alone may constitute sufficient evidence of such a drift. Beyond perception, however, there is unmistakable evidence of growth in the role of the national security assistant (who postdates the founding of the National Security Council itself), and in the size and character of the NSC staff. Since McGeorge Bundy's incumbency, and especially because of the Kissinger and Brzezinski periods, the assistant to the president for national security affairs has become a visible public figure in his own right (Destler, 1980, pp. 84–85). In general, his role has evolved from one of coordinating clearance across departments to one of policy adviser. Similarly, the NSC staff itself has grown greatly, boosted especially during the Nixon administration. It is less and less composed of graying and grayish anonymous career foreign service officers, and more and more composed of foreign policy intellectuals and prospective high-fliers, many of whom are drawn from America's leading universities.

I do not mean to imply that the presidential foreign policy apparatus and the State Department always or even usually clash, nor that they have wholly overlapping functions. Nonetheless, it is clear that the NSC, at least in form, is today something far beyond what it was in Truman's time or in Eisenhower's. To some degree Truman, protecting what he believed to be his prerogatives, held the then-nascent National Security Council at arm's length as an advisory forum. Eisenhower, on the other hand, employed it frequently as a collegial body, one whose statutory members and staff were also, in some measure, representatives of their departments (Hammond, 1960, pp. 905–10; Falk, 1964, pp. 424–25). Since then, the role and character of the NSC staff, and especially that of the national security assistant, have mutated. This evolution into a role not originally envisioned for the NSC or the then special assistant (executive secretary in Truman's time) has notable consequences for policy making.

Even within the constricted sphere of executive forces on policy making, the foreign policy process involves a complex of actors and not merely a bilateral relationship between the NSC and the State Department. Although the State Department's position has been most eroded by the policy role of the NSC, neither it nor the NSC is a monolithic force. The national security assistant and the NSC staff are *not* the same actors, nor necessarily of common mind. Similar cautions are even more necessary to describe relationships between the secretary of state and the foreign service professionals of the State Department. A significant difference in intraorganizational relationships, however, is that the national security assistant to some extent selects his own staff, whereas the secretary of state has a department to manage and an established subculture that exists well below the level of those whom he selects. If the NSC staff is more nearly the creation of the national security assistant, the secretary of state, unless he divorces himself from the department, is more likely to be seen as its creation. This difference provides one of these actors with considerable strategic advantages in influencing the views and decisions of presidents.

As clearly as this somewhat ambiguous distinction permits, the NSC (and the national security assistant) and the State Department (though not necessarily the secretary) have come to embody, respectively, the differing commitments given to the roles of "irregulars" (those not bound to a career service) and of "regulars" (members of a career service) in the policy process. The correlation is quite far from unity, of course. There are mixes of personnel and outlooks within each organizational setting, but there are characteristically different career lines and perspectives as well. Above all, each setting provides for different roles. The operational responsibilities of the State Department give it the advantages of detailed knowledge and experience, and the political disadvantage of lacking an integrated world view. The NSC, on the other hand, is less constrained by the existence of operational responsibilities, by distance between it and the president, or by the communications complications typical of large hierarchically structured organizations. Its sterling political assets, however, are offset in some measure by the disadvantages of removal from day-to-day detail and highly specialized expertise. The differences between these organizational settings, to be sure, are quite significant. The NSC is a fast track. In contrast, the State Department can be a ponderously slow escalator. One setting is oriented to solving problems, the other to raising them. One is more oriented to attaining a bottom line, the other to journeying down a bottomless pit. In sum, the presidential foreign policy apparatus largely exhibits the advantages and disadvantages of an organ that is staffed to some degree by irregulars, and which is not charged with line functions. The State Department, in the main, illustrates the advantages and disadvantages of a hierarchically structured organization responsible for implementation, and which, therefore, tends to have a regular's orientation. . . .

The Quest for Policy Integration

The growth of coordinative institutions in modern governments and the growth in importance of irregular staffers in government are not the same thing, but they are traceable to the same sources, namely, the need to compensate for the inadequacies of traditional ministries in absorbing the policy agendas and perspectives of the central decision-making authority within the executive. The massive expansion of policy agendas themselves—"overload," as Klein and Lewis (1977, p. 2) call this phenomenon—is the signal cause of efforts to overcome the parochialness of the ministries and their civil servants. Problems of assimilation clearly have multiplied as governments pursue more and more complex, frequently conflicting objectives (Rose, 1976a; Neustadt, 1954). The forms taken by these coordinative mechanisms have varied across both political systems and policy arenas. The extent to which they have been composed of irregulars has similarly varied.

The more feeble the gravitational pull of directional authority in government, the more necessary it becomes to institutionalize coordinative functions. In Britain, the relatively strong pull of cabinet government, and the doctrine of ministerial responsibility, means that the interface of politics and policy often takes place within the ministries themselves. There, irregulars are usually planted directly in the ministries. In the Federal Republic of Germany, the gravitational pull of cabinet government is substantially weaker, and the activism of the *Bundeskanzleramt* (the Chancellery) is greater than that of the British Cabinet Office (Dyson, 1974, pp. 361–62). In the case of the United States where the gravitational pull of political forces is exceedingly weak, mechanisms to achieve policy integration abound not only in the Executive Office of the President, but even throughout Congress. The development of these mechanisms throughout the EOP is particularly intriguing in view of the fact that the American line departments are already well saturated with officials whose political pedigrees have been carefully checked out. American administration, as is well known, is laden with irregulars at some depth beneath the cabinet secretary, yet even this has often been considered insufficient to attain presidential control and integration over policy (Nathan, 1975; Heclo, 1975).

This, of course, brings us to the central issue, which is whether the quest for policy integration, defined as comprehensive control over vital policy objectives, can accommodate expertise defined in terms of specialized knowledge. The dilemma, as Paul Hammond once observed, is this (1960, p. 910):

> While the mind of one man may be the most effective instrument for devising diplomatic moves and strategic maneuvers and for infusing . . . creative purpose, its product is bound to be insufficient to meet the needs of the vast organizational structures . . . which are the instruments of foreign policy.

The growth of integrative machinery has brought to the fore officials who sometimes differ from their counterparts in the operating agencies.[1] At least as important, though, is that they are provided substantial policy-influencing opportunities without equivalent operational responsibility. To the extent that "central" staff agencies have challenged more traditional bureaucratic sources of policy, they have merely reflected the perplexing problems that nearly all modern democratic governments face in both integrating and controlling policy objectives, and in rendering them politically acceptable.

From these more general observations, I wish to take up the special case of the National Security Council and the assistant to the president for national security affairs as a remarkable example of how the facilitating function evolved into far more heady activities. This evolution also starkly illustrates the advantage of a staff agency at the expense of the traditional operating agencies. Put another way,

---

[1]Campbell and Szablowski (1979) note, for instance, that senior officials in the Canadian central coordinating agencies differ from the main-line civil servants in the traditional line ministries in that they are more likely to have entered laterally rather than to have moved upward through the civil service system.

it reflects the advantages that "irregulars" often have over "regulars."

From Manager to Competing Secretary of State

From its inception in 1947, the National Security Council was designed to be a high-level policy review committee rather than a strictly staff operation (Sapin, 1967, p. 84). As a mechanism for arriving at major policy decisions, however, a support staff quickly emerged underneath the statutory membership of the NSC. Indeed, until the Eisenhower administration came into power in 1953, there was no overall coordinator who had immediate access to the president. In 1953, however, Eisenhower appointed a special assistant to the president for national security affairs whose responsibilities, among others, entailed playing an executive director's role with the NSC staff. An indication of how far the function of the president's national security assistant, and that of the NSC staff as well, has diverged from the original coordinating and facilitating function is the fact that it takes a monumental effort to recall who these presidential assistants were.[2]

Why has the national security assistant and the NSC staff moved from this relatively modest, if necessary, role to one which frequently has vied with the secretary of state and the State Department for foreign policy-making influence? At the outset of the Carter administration, for example, a sympathetic article referred to the NSC staff as the "other cabinet" (Berry and Kyle, 1977). There are numerous answers to this question, of course. At bottom, though, the "many" reasons are made particularly compelling by the peculiar political culture of Washington politics—an inheritance in part of extravagant institutional disaggregation.

It is true, of course, that whatever clout the national security assistant has exists only at the sufferance of the president (Art, 1973; Destler, 1977). Presidents can make or break the role of their national security assistants as policy advocates. They *can* minimize the

---

[2]From earliest to latest in the Eisenhower administration, they were Robert Cutler, Dillon Anderson, and Gordon Gray. During the Truman administration there were two executive secretaries of the NSC. Each, Sidney Souers and James Lay, reflected the "neutral competence" ideal.

visibility of their assistant; they *can* play down the substantive functions of the NSC staff relative to the State Department, for example. There are obvious manipulables in the relationship between America's "second State Department" and the White House, but the norms that have been established now seem firm in spite of the present and perhaps momentary diminution of the NSC role in the Reagan administration. The tendency to shift from central clearance to central direction has helped give the NSC apparatus and, above all, a policy-advocating national security assistant, an unusually important role. In the Reagan administration, Richard Allen has proclaimed his role model to be that of Eisenhower's anonymous special assistant, Gordon Gray. But Allen's own prior roles largely have been advocacy and advisory ones, rather than managerial or facilitative ones (Smith, 1981).

Overload as an Explanation

Understandably, the National Security Act of 1947 which set up the National Security Council was enacted at the beginning of America's postwar eminence as the leading Western power. The role of global power with far-reaching responsibilities produces a busy agenda, and the busier that agenda the more the management of policy and of advice becomes important. According to a relatively recent report prepared for the president, there have been at least 65 studies of the U.S. foreign policy machinery since 1951 (*National Security Policy Integration*, 1979, p. 49). This abundance of studies bears witness to the great diversity of actors with some share of the foreign policy pie, to continuing problems of coordination between them, and to their reputed lack of responsiveness to the president. How, under these circumstances, is a president to make decisions without some final filter that reduces unmanageable complexity to at least endurable perplexity?

Undoubtedly, in an age of instant communication, some of the present NSC apparatus would have had to have been invented did it not already exist. Working out statements with counterparts in the Elysée, the Chancellery, or 10 Downing Street before the principals are themselves engaged is the kind of task that may need to be located close to the head of government. However, the enhanced role of the national security assistant over the past two decades (Destler, 1980) makes it unlikely that these tasks are sufficient to satisfy policy drives created by recent organizational practices.

Institutional and Organizational Explanations

"Overload" explains the existence of coordinative mechanisms such as the NSC. It does not, however, explain the transformation of a once-anonymous role with a small staff to a prominent contender for policy-making power in foreign affairs.

Because government in Washington is as unplanned as the society it governs, criticisms of the foreign policy-making machinery overwhelmingly recommend organizational reforms (Campbell, 1971; Destler, 1972b; Allison and Szanton, 1976). As with virtually all governmental activity in the United States, fragmentation also characterizes the process of foreign policy decision making. Centrifugal tendencies begin at the top levels of American government, induced in part by the absence of effective mechanisms for cabinet decision making.[3] Lack of clarity at the top molds bureaucratic tendencies below. Thus, while the problems of bureaucratic politics exist everywhere, they are made more obvious by unclear boundaries of authority, by the fractionation of power centers, and by the ready availability of the press as a resource in policy struggles. Contemporary Washington epitomizes these conditions. It is not difficult, therefore, to find targets for reform.

Despite repeated calls for its resuscitation, the cabinet is to the functioning of American government what the appendix is to human physiology. It's there, but no one is quite sure why. Whatever initial presidential intentions may be, presidents soon learn that cabinet meetings are mainly for public relations benefits rather than for decision making. They also learn another lesson of particular importance in Washington, namely, that the probability of leaks to the press which may foreclose presidential options is geometrically expanded by the number of participants involved. Later I will discuss how an "information-leaky" environment, unique to Washington among world capitals, estranges presidents from their cabinet departments. For now it is useful merely to indicate that the extreme splintering of responsibilities means that presidents with innovative

---

[3]This, of course, is a by-product of the presidential system. Ironically, the Eberstadt Report which set forth the rationale for the National Security Act and, thus, the NSC, apparently was motivated by a desire to create a high level British type cabinet committee. As Hammond notes (1960, p. 899): "The Eberstadt Report assumed that the proposed National Security Council could be a kind of war cabinet in which the responsibilities of the President could be vested. . . . The premise arose . . . out of an inclination to modify the Presidency as an institution."

intentions will be desirous of centralizing in the White House that which is otherwise uncontrollable or unresponsive to them.

All leaders are apt to demand more responsiveness than they can or even ought to get. But American presidents crave responsiveness in part because so little is obviously available to them. Large organizations, and especially those that are highly professionalized, develop definable subcultures and resist intrusions from inexpert outsiders. Regardless of what it is that presidents order the first time, there is a strong tendency for them to be served fudge—or jelly, to employ the culinary metaphor used by President Kennedy. While this frustration is not peculiar to the foreign policy and national security agencies, foreign policy matters are often far more central to what it is a president, or a prime minister for that matter, must attend to (Rose, 1976b, pp. 255–56; 1980, pp. 35–38). Typically, too, there is less legislative direction of the foreign policy organs than of departments having primarily domestic responsibilities or impacts.

Among the agencies involved with foreign policy, moreover, the State Department largely deals with political analysis, impressionistic evidence, and judgment. Since politicians who become presidents are likely to defer to no one when it comes to making what are essentially political judgments, the vulnerability of the State Department becomes apparent. It is not only that the department moves slowly that frustrates presidents; it is often the message that it delivers that leads them to despair (Silberman, 1979).

In addition to its distance from the White House, a problem which to some extent affects all line departments, the culture and technology of the State Department are also factors in its organizational disadvantage. These factors interact with, indeed greatly exacerbate, its distance problem. The State Department is a regular organization *par excellence* with a highly developed professional subculture. The stock in trade of the regular foreign service officers, granted individual differences among them, is a large supply of cold water with which to dash ideas that emanate elsewhere or which challenge prevailing professional perspectives. In the words of one sympathetic observer:

> The most useful service that a senior State Department official can perform in a policy-making role is to douse the facile enthusiasms of administration "activists" in the cold water of reality. But most of them bring so little energy and skill to this task that they merely project an image of negativism (Maechling, 1976, pp. 11–12).

Put somewhat more generally, "Political appointees seem to want to accomplish goals quickly while careerists opt to accomplish things carefully" (Murphy et al., 1978, p. 181).

As a citadel of foreign service professionalism, the State Department is an inhospitable refuge for ideas and initiatives blown in from the cold. "It's all been tried before" is a refrain that may characterize the responses of professional bureaucrats whatever their substantive craft, but it is one that is at the heart of the department's perceived unresponsiveness.

Ironically, in this light, the professional subculture of the foreign service, as some have noted, ill prepares foreign service officers for the rough-and-tumble of bureaucratic politics (Destler, 1972b, pp. 164–66; Maechling, 1976, pp. 10–12; and even Silberman, 1979). Indeed, the recruitment of FSOs traditionally has made them America's closest facsimile of the British administrative class (Seidman, 1980, pp. 144–47). This is manifest also in operating style, a style characterized as one of "alert passivity" (Allison and Szanton, 1976, p. 126). While American bureaucrats in the domestic departments readily adopt the role of advocate to a far greater extent than their European peers (Aberbach, Putnam and Rockman, 1981, pp. 94–98), FSOs tend to be more like British bureaucrats, defusing programmatic advocacy so as to maintain the flexibility necessary to deal with the differing priorities imposed by new leaders. Unlike their colleagues in the domestic departments, officials in State lack domestic constituencies to help them weather episodic storms. In addition, the foreign service is oriented to serving abroad. The cost of this absorption is a lack of sophisticated political understanding of the policy-making machinery. In a system in which boundaries of authority are remarkably inexact, FSOs tend to lack both skills and bases for effective bureaucratic infighting—a considerable disadvantage.

As noted, the modal technology of the State Department is soft and impressionistic, and thus endlessly vulnerable. This helps to explain why the State Department is especially apt to be victimized. For as a former department official comments:

> New presidents and their staffs soon start to search for opportunities for leadership, areas in which to demonstrate that the President is on top of things and making policy. When this game is played, the loser is almost invariably the State Department and not, for example, the

Pentagon. . . . To do more than scratch the surface of a few front page military issues would require a much larger White House staff than any President would want to contemplate. Foreign policy, on the other hand, is largely a matter of words, and the President and his staffers can step in at any time and put the words together themselves (Gelb, 1980, p. 35).

Once the staff has been constructed to oversee policy proposals, the next step toward advocacy seems nearly ineluctable unless the president is fully and unequivocally committed *in combination* to the secretary of state as the principal foreign policy maker *and* the State Department institutionally as the principal source of foreign policy advice—a combination that almost necessarily eliminates skilled policy entrepreneurs such as Henry Kissinger from the role. Why this combination of conditions is first unlikely to happen, but difficult to sustain if it does, is the question that needs to be addressed. To do so requires an exploration of the Washington political culture.

The Political Culture of Washington as an Explanation

To explain the transformation of the NSC from a central clearance mechanism and a long-range policy planning one to an active center of policy making requires a focus on institutional and organizational features such as those we have just discussed. Yet the peculiar climate that pervades government in Washington helps to explain these institutional and organizational operations. For the distinguishing characteristic of government in Washington is its near-indistinguishability from politics in Washington. While politics in the capitals of all democratic states mixes together a variety of interests—partisan, pressure-group, bureaucratic, regional, and so forth—the absence of party as a solvent magnifies the importance of other interests. Above all, the overtness of the bureaucratic power struggle is likely to be in inverse proportion to the intensity and clarity of the partisan struggle.

Confronted with singular responsibility and inconstant support, presidents are often driven to managerial aspirations over "their" branch of the government. Sooner or later they sense that at best they are confronted with inertia, at worst, opposition. Rarely can they rely consistently upon their party for support, especially if they are Democrats; rarely too can they assume that their cabinets are composed of officials who are not essentially departmental emissaries. Cabinet ministers everywhere, of course, are departmental ambassadors to the cabinet. All ministers find it convenient, if not necessary, at some time to promote departmental agendas pushed from below. The late R. H. S. Crossman's assertion that "the Minister is there to present the departmental case" is universally true (1972, p. 61), yet he also observes that an American cabinet is only that—an aggregation of departmental heads (p. 67).

The basic themes of American governmental institutions are distrust and disaggregation. Together, they fuel suspicion. Presidents often come to divide the world into "us" and "them." "They" typically cannot be relied upon. "They" will be seen as torpid, bureaucratically self-interested, and often uncommitted or skeptical of presidential initiatives. Above all, "they" will be seen as an uncontrollable source of hemorrhaging to the press.

Unmediated by any tradition of, or basis for, a cabinet team, distance defines "us" and "them." There are always winners and losers in executive politics everywhere, but the more ambiguous the boundaries of authority, the less clear the adjusting mechanisms by which the winners and losers are determined, and the more pervasive the involvement of the media in policy struggles (a largely American phenomenon), the more ferocious the struggle. Under these conditions, the department heads will tend to lose ground to the White House, because whatever advantages in autonomy distance permits, the more obvious are the disadvantages in accessibility.

Washington is a capital as obviously open as Moscow is obviously closed. The intimate involvement of the prestige press in internecine executive policy debates is legendary. Little remains confidential in Washington for very long, at least insofar as the exposure of confidentiality can assist any of the policy contestants. The lifelines connecting presidents to the cabinet departments are longer and perceived to be more porous than those that link presidents to the Executive Office. This perception undoubtedly is fortified by the belief that under most circumstances cabinet secretaries would as soon push their departmental perspectives or even their own special agendas than those of the White House. The secretary of state is not immune from this. Despite the "inner" role of the secretary of state (Cronin, 1975, pp. 190–92), *to the extent that he is perceived within the White House as someone who presses the interests and perspectives of the foreign service regulars, he is apt to be written off as one of "them."* The case of William Rogers is instructive in this regard, and even more so is that of Cyrus Vance, who began in office with strong presidential support for his power stakes.

Although one must beware of self-serving tales that dribble *ex post facto* to the prestige American press from disgruntled ex-officials, the evidence, however partial it may be, is that leaks to the press are more likely to be blamed on the cabinet departments than on the executive office staff itself. A report in the *Washington Post*, for instance, indicates that after President Carter severely chastised noncareer and career State Department officials in early 1979 for suspected press leaks regarding policy toward Iran, Secretary Vance pressed upon him the view that the State Department was being unfairly singled out as a source of leaks that were regularly occurring everywhere, especially from within the NSC staff. The president's response, according to the report, was to meet with his national security assistant and several of his senior staff members and request them to smooth their relations with their counterparts at the State Department (Armstrong, 1980). To officials at State, the president threatened; to NSC officials, the president cajoled. "Us" versus "them," in other words, was not unique to the Nixon administration (Aberbach and Rockman, 1976).

The isolation of presidents from their cabinet departments, the absence of a common point of meaningful political aggregation—all of this within the information-leaky environment peculiar to Washington among world capitals—is a ready stimulant to the "us" versus "them" outlook that commonly develops in the White House, and in the departments as well. Distance and distrust are promoted on both ends of the tether line connecting departments to the White House. Departmental frustrations are often exacerbated by presidential distrust of bureaucratic institutions in an antibureaucratic culture. American politicians who enter through the gates of the White House have neither learned to endure the frustrations that arise through a slow and steady apprenticeship in party politics such as is found in Britain, nor to appreciate by virtue of living in their midst the skills and qualities that professional civil servants bring to government.

Because it contains memory traces from the past, bureaucracy is the enemy of novelty. Memory imposes constraint, while presidents typically want to make their mark as innovators.[4] Presidential frustrations derive, therefore, from the incapacity of large organizations to be immediately responsive to presidential wishes, and from the tendency of such organizations to protect their interests and core technologies from presidential intrusion. On the other hand, departmental frustrations arise when departments become the victims of imagined nonresponsiveness to presidents, as related in a recently revised version of the trade, proposed by the Soviets during the 1962 Cuban missile crisis, of American Jupiter missile bases in Turkey for those installed by the Soviets in Cuba.[5]

Thus far, I have outlined generally why presidents in America tend toward White House centrism—that is, why they seek to build a policy-making apparatus around them rather than relying exclusively upon the cabinet departments. I have not attempted to explain exhaustively this drive toward centrism, nor its ebbs and flows across particular administrations. My concern is with the trend line rather than the perturbations within it. Some aspects of the drive toward centrism are undoubtedly largely idiosyncratic, having to do with particular presidential styles and personalities within administrations. There are some reasons too that are probably universal, for example, the growth of technological capacity for central control, and some that are speculative, for example, hypothesized imperatives of leaders to try to exert control over policy without comprehending the mechanics—to reach, in other words, a bottom line without much concern for the algorithm. Of the reasons I explicitly cite, however, one—the increased agenda of governments—can be found in all modern democracies, and has resulted in efforts to devise

[4]A recent study of organizational memory development among three EOP agencies, for example, finds that the NSC consistently has the least cross-administration continuity as measured by several indicators (Covington, 1981). The author of this report concludes that organizational continuity reflects presidential detachment, whereas lack of memory reflects intense presidential interest.

[5]As Barton J. Bernstein (1980, p. 103 n.) observes from his study of recently declassified materials regarding this episode:

> A chief executive may often express preferences (not orders) for policies, and [then] he may sincerely reinterpret them as *orders* when his own inaction leaves him woefully unprepared in a crisis. In this way, a president can place blame on a subordinate, and other aides who listen to his charges tend to believe that the president actually issued an order, and not simply stated a wish or a hope.

For a general review of this incident, see Bernstein (1980), and also Hafner (1977).

coordinative machinery. The other reasons I have identified are more system-specific, and are rooted in institutional and cultural considerations. A dispersed policy universe generates needs for greater centrism. The weaker the pull of political gravity, the more the emphasis upon central staffing. Thus, according to one report, the load on central staff personnel in the EOP (at least during the Carter presidency) is immense when compared with staff counterparts in other nations (Campbell, 1980, p. 22). This apparently reflects White House obsessions for detailed policy control in an environment in which such control is as elusive as it is expected.

Foreign Policy by Irregulars: White House and Departmental Settings

The conditions that make American presidents turn to staff at the White House rather than bureaucrats, or even their appointees in the departments, undoubtedly characterize all policy sectors. Departmental appointees who have strong links to the career subcultures within their departments are often viewed with suspicion at the White House. They will be seen as advocates of parochial interests. Officials at the White House want presidential objectives to be "rationally" managed. Officials in the departments, on the other hand, want "rational" policies as they define them. This difference in perspective exists everywhere, and is by no means a peculiar characteristic of White House–State Department relations. What is peculiar about this particular relationship, however, is the extent to which the foreign service regulars are cut adrift from other sources of support in the political system and within their own department. Unlike their counterparts in the domestic agencies, they have no statutory-based standards to apply, only their judgments and knowledge to rely on. Unlike analysts in the domestic agencies, and in other national security agencies such as the Defense Department and CIA, their "data" are contained in imprints rather than print-outs.

Thus, at least since Dean Acheson's stewardship, most secretaries of state who wielded great influence (Dulles, Rusk under Johnson, and Kissinger) traveled light—in other words, without much departmental baggage. Strong secretaries often have been strong precisely because they ignored the department. When secretaries of state are perceived as representing departmental perspectives, they become especially vulnerable to competing sources of influence—most particularly from within the White House. Why?

One must begin with the fact that foreign policy is a *high-priority* item. By its importance, its capacity to push other items on the agenda to a lesser place, foreign policy, though not equally appetizing to all presidents, becomes the main course of the presidential meal. The extent to which foreign policy is a focal point of attention, of course, depends on the extent to which any nation is deeply involved and committed as an actor in world affairs. And that, understandably, is related to a nation's capacities for such involvement.

Crises especially lend themselves to central direction. Foreign policy is often nothing but crises—either reacting to them or creating them. Filled with crisis and presumed to be of first-order importance, foreign affairs are, in fact, glamorous. Much more than apparently intractable or technically complex domestic problems, foreign affairs often seem to be contests of will—games against other players rather than games against nature.

In such games, regular bureaucrats are unlikely to be key players. Their instincts are to think small, to think incrementally, and to see the world in not highly manipulable terms. The glitter that presidents often see in foreign policy is at odds with the cautious instincts of the professional service entrusted to deal with it. Unattached to specific operational responsibilities and accessible to the White House, the NSC can take on the qualities of a think-tank unencumbered by the more limited visions that flow from the State Department itself. Moreover, the NSC, like any staff organization, is far more readily adapted to the changing foreign policy themes of presidents than a line bureaucracy such as the State Department. State is, of course, highly adaptable to modulated swings in policy, but not to strong oscillations. Organizational memory and bureaucratic inertia preclude it from reinventing the world every four years.

This particular difference in settings—White House staff versus line bureaucracy—also implies a difference in styles of policy analysis. One setting is accessible to power, the other more remote. One is especially attractive to the ambitious and purposive, the other to the cautious and balanced. One setting is tailored for "in-and-outers" and "high-fliers" borrowed from other agencies, while the other is meant for "long-haulers." One effect of this difference in settings is that even though the NSC staff is not overwhelmingly composed of academic figures, more NSC staffers are apt to be academics than their counterparts at state. For example, a study of senior foreign service officers indicates that fewer than 8 percent are Ph.D.s (Mennis, 1971, p. 71), while 58 percent of the NSC staff with which Zbigniew Brzezinski began were holders of the Ph.D. degree,[6] as are 43 percent of the present staff. Such differences do not reflect merely ephemeral circumstance. The Reagan NSC also represents a mixture of scholars and government career officers with Washington experience (Smith, 1981). And as Destler describes the NSC staff under Presidents Kennedy and Nixon: "The typical staff members were not too different from the Kennedy period—relatively young, mobile, aggressive men, combining substantial background in the substance of foreign affairs with primary allegiance to the White House" (1972b, p. 123).

In other words, there is a correlation between background and organizational setting even though it is quite far from perfect. Backgrounds, of course, are only frail indicators of differences in syndromes of policy thought, and such differences need not imply substantive disagreement. Nonetheless, the correlation implies that the White House miniature of the State Department is more innovative than the real one at Foggy Bottom, more aggressive, and also more enthusiastic for White House policy directions.

The NSC staff and the national security assistant, of course, may conflict (as may the regulars in the State Department and their noncareer superiors). There have been notable clashes in the past, especially in the immediate aftermath of the American incursion into Cambodia in 1970 during the Vietnam engagement. The national security assistant and the NSC staff are not necessarily in agreement upon substance, but their *forma mentis* are likely to differ from those of their State Department counterparts. If presidents are served amorphous goo from the State Department bureaucracy (which they often see as representing other nations' interests to Washington), they may be provided with clear-headed principles from their in-house foreign policy advisers. Concerned with direction and results, presidents are usually predisposed to cut through the rigidities of complex bureaucratic systems and the cautions of the foreign policy regulars. In this, of course, lies the potential for isolating policy advice from

[6]Compiled from data in Berry and Kyle (1977).

implementation. Going through the bureaucracy often means spinning wheels, but ignoring the bureaucracy poses the prospect of personalizing policy rather than institutionalizing it. In this latter course, there is, to be sure, less wheel-spinning but there is, at least in the long run, also more spinning of castles in the air.

Finally, the soft technology of foreign relations means that it is just precisely the kind of thing that politicians think they are better qualified for than anyone else (Merton, 1968, p. 265). A former non-career ambassador writes, for instance: "The average American has a sounder instinctive grasp of the basic dynamics of foreign policy than he does of domestic macro-economics. . . . Common sense— the sum of personal experience—will take one further in the realm of foreign policy than in macro-economics" (Silberman, 1979, pp. 879–80). Because little seems mystical or technical about foreign policy to presidents, reliance upon cumbersome bureaucratic machinery seems unnecessary. In most instances, presidents like to be directly engaged with foreign policy because it is more glamorous and central to their historical ambitions, less dependent upon congressional approval, and because it activates their "head of state" role (and in the event of possible military involvement, their "commander-in-chief" one also). In contrast to the trench warfare and haggling involved with domestic policy formulation, foreign policy making tends to promote self-esteem and presidential prestige. With all of these possibilities, it is improbable, therefore, that presidents want the powers of foreign policy making to be distant from them. Usually, they want it close to them. Presidents need to legitimate White House centrism, then, by investing it in a flexible staff operation headed by an unattached foreign policy "expert." These specific reasons, encapsulated within the more general determinants already discussed, have led the White House Department of State to loom as a contender for policy-making influence with the "cabinet" Department of State.

Irregular and Regular Syndromes

. . . Beginning with a broad distinction between irregular staff and regular bureaucratic settings, Table 1 sketches some of the important respects in which these settings differ. These differences point to modal variations in function, in vantage point, in personnel, and in orientations to policy. In the analysis that follows, however, I start

TABLE 1   *Differences between Irregular Central Staff Settings and Regular Bureaucratic Settings in Foreign Policy Making*

	Irregular Staff Settings	Regular Bureaucratic Settings
Typical Responsibilities	Coordinating functions which provide breadth and integrative perspectives, and foster coherence	Implementing functions which provide detailed knowledge and particularistic perspectives, and foster local rationality
Location Relative to Decisional Authority	Proximate to political authority, therefore perceived as "Us"	Distant from political authority, therefore perceived as "Them"
Type of Personnel	Irregulars and regular "floaters" with few organizational commitments	A mix of irregulars and regulars toward the top, with regulars with long-term organizational commitments at the core
Typical Policy-Making Styles	Activists Theorists Conceptualizers Deductivists "Simplifiers"	Skeptics Specialists Inductivists "Complexifiers"
Dominant Policy Implications	Directive and thematic, initiatory and bold	Cautious and nonthematic, incrementalist and narrow-gauged
Resulting Policy Problems	Superficiality	Particularism

Source: Created by the author.

with differences between personnel, work back to settings, and then to forms of policy thinking.

How do irregulars differ from regulars? First, irregulars are more likely to be charged with coordinating functions (policy planning, for instance) than are regulars even when they are each engaged in departmental responsibilities. These functions provide the irregular with greater breadth and the capacity to see a more integrated policy picture, but one limited in depth. On the other hand, the regular is located so as to see detail but is less able or likely to see beyond it. These structural features also lead to different interpretations of rationality. The irregular is apt to define rationality as coherence from the vantage point of policy management. The regular, however, is apt to see rationality in terms of informed policy making.

Free of operational responsibilities, irregulars are apt to be conceptualizing and deductive (more "theoretical" or "ideological") in policy thinking than are foreign policy regulars. Intimate detailed knowledge possessed by the regular tends to induce skepticism toward ideas that are abstract and aesthetically interesting. As the regular sees him, the irregular is a simplifier with tendencies toward an excess of imagination and a scarcity of discriminating judgment. Irregulars are rarely lacking in expertise; but their possibilities for thought are distanced from the immediacy of operational problems. Whether by role difference, by recruitment path, or by their interactive effects, the irregular is more disposed to theoretical thought than the regular. Theories are the precursors of activism for they simplify reality sufficiently to permit general, though not necessarily operational, plans of action. The inductivism that is more characteristic of the regulars leads them often toward perceiving complication; it leads them frequently to be skeptical about generalized schemes of action; often it leads them into paralysis. It is both the virtue and the liability of the regular's "hands-on" involvement that he will be predisposed to illustrate the invalidity of proposals and the assumptions they are based on than to advance alternative solutions. After all, it is normally the regular who has to live with the consequences of "rashness."

Ideas and skepticism, while polar intellectual traits, are nonetheless each valuable ones. Large bureaucracies are the wellspring of skepticism and the depressant of ideas. This bureaucratic characteristic flows from the inertia associated with established routines as well as from the concreteness of the regular official's world. Met daily, concreteness and detail induce awareness of complexity. It is this awareness of complexity that ironically is at the heart of the State Department's self-perception as a protector of real long-term interests (Gelb, 1980, p. 34).

Given their natural proclivities, regular bureaucrats are apt to be oriented to the long term within their specialized realms, and likely to be skeptical of overarching themes. This characteristic is not especially attractive to presidents whose "common-sense" approaches to foreign policy often coincide with what is also politically supportable. Being policy generalists, presidents tend to be impatient with "can't-doers," failing to understand or appreciate the skepticism of the foreign policy regulars. From the presidential vantage point, sober thoughts are mere fudge, and skepticism rarely accords with presidents' political needs. Unattached foreign policy "experts," on the other hand, can articulate ideas and push proposals unencumbered by bureaucratic constraints or operational responsibilities. This gives them an obvious advantage over those representing the particularizers in the foreign policy bureaucracy. As for the secretary of state, his advisory and policy-making roles will likely be as large as his distance from the department is great.

There are dangers in the detachment of policy advice and policy influence from operational responsibilities. The triumph of theory over fact is obviously troubling. If regulars, by their skepticism (and probably also their convenience) tend toward incrementalist thinking, it is also true that, at least in the short run, no one ever died of incrementalism. Still, the failure to produce and institutionalize policy integration can be a long-term carcinogenic agent. For politics contoured only by those with operational attachments are likely to suffer from deficiencies of imagination. . . .

Conclusion

Presidents ultimately determine foreign policy. Whatever system of advice and decision making exists can exist only with the president's approval. It is within the range of presidential discretion to permit the national security assistant to become a leading contestant for foreign policy influence. Similarly, it is within the scope of presidential judgment to permit the national security assistant to appear as the chief foreign policy representative for their administrations. Nixon and Carter did permit these things; indeed, they encouraged them, though for different reasons. Thus far, the Reagan model (if there is one) has resulted in decreased visibility for the national security assistant. The NSC professional staff, however, is no smaller than it was during the Carter administration, and at least one report indicates a more direct White House staff involvement monitoring operations through the NSC machinery (Evans and Novak, 1981). Additionally, somewhat reminiscent of Nixon's "administrative presidency" model, a loyal operative has been slipped into the deputy secretary's role at State. In the last 14 months of the Ford administration, the role of the national security assistant and, to a modest degree, that of the NSC veered closer to the Eisenhower model of a dominant secretary of state and a "neutral competent" national security assistant (Brent Scowcroft). The reason for this, however, now seems clear. Ford's secretary of state, Henry Kissinger, was his leading foreign policy spokesman and leading foreign policy maker, yet not really his foreign minister. To be both foreign minister (representing departmental perspectives) and leading foreign policy maker has within it increasingly the seeds of an insoluble role conflict.

Presidents vary, of course, in their ideas as to how foreign policy making ought to be organized, what they want from it, and how much weight is given at least at the outset to the values of harmony and diversity. The difficulty lies in isolating which aspects of their variability will lead to a heightened emphasis upon staff irregulars, and how they will be used. Similar results, as the disparate cases of Nixon and Carter indicate, may flow from different organizational modes. While each held widely different models of the policy-shaping process in foreign affairs, each also further enlarged the role of the NSC as a policy mechanism. Early on, Nixon seemed to prefer policy to be shaped at the White House, and as much as possible to skirt around the bureaucracy. Carter's organization, on the other hand, seemed to exaggerate Alexander George's ideal of multiple advocacy except, quite importantly, that Zbigniew Brzezinski was meant to be an advocate and not just a mediator. Different intentions seem to have produced fairly similar results—a highly visible national security assistant and a "competing" State Department.

The variability of presidents notwithstanding, the overall thrust since Eisenhower seems fairly clear: more White House centrism in foreign policy making, and an enlarged NSC role. Presidential variability tells us a lot about form—the particular uses of the NSC mechanism and of the national security assistant—but it does not tell us why the NSC today looks so different from the NSC of 25 years ago, nor does it tell us why the national security assistant has so often been a primary policy maker. While the water has both risen and receded, the watermark is a good bit higher now than it was then.

To explain this trend toward centrism, and thus the importance of policy irregulars, my analysis focuses upon a theory of government—a theme somewhat broader than its specific target. . . . From the hyperpoliticized ambience of American government the role needs of foreign policy contestants are shaped. Institutional fragmentation and weak parties not only beget one another, they also promote a level of bureaucratic politics of unusual intensity—grist for the mill of a highly inquisitive press.

No wonder presidents find their political and policy needs better served from within the White House. From this vantage point, the departments sooner or later are perceived as representing or pursuing interests that are not those of the president. This is especially so for the State Department because it is frequently seen as representing interests of other countries. With virtually no domestic constituencies and reflecting a subculture that, much like the British civil service, emphasizes "neutral competence" and balance, the foreign service regulars in the State Department are singularly disadvantaged. The steamy adversarial climate of Washington's executive politics does not nourish such values. The White House and often department heads are anxious for "movement," and unreceptive to "let's wait a moment." In the long run, the danger in any such setting is that the tools of central clearance will metamorphose into mechanisms for central dominance.

In sum, the reasons why America has . . . competing State Department[s] turn out to be both excruciatingly complex and yet remarkably simple. [The] simplicity lies in the structure of antagonistic forces given form by the American Constitution. [The] complexities lie in the conditions—the importance of foreign policy, the role of the media, the burgeoning of policy intellectuals—that have since ripened.

The problem of reconciling "the persistent dilemmas of unity and diversity" (Fenno, 1975, p. 339) remains to be solved as much in the foreign policy sphere as in the domestic one, especially as the distinction between these arenas erodes. In unity lies strategic direction and clarity, but also the dangers of a monocled vision. In diversity lies sensitivity to implementation and to nuance, but also the dangers of producing least common denominators. Ironically, during the Eisenhower presidency when the NSC performed most nearly like a cabinet committee producing consensus from diversity, it was criticized for the ambiguities remaining in its products (Destler, 1977, pp. 152–53). If not a fudge factory, it was at least a fudge shop.

Each president to some extent will develop mechanisms that suit him best. Among other things, the policy system established will reflect the idiosyncracies of interpersonal chemistry. Each, though, has inherited an in-house foreign policy apparatus defined in the last

20 years more by how it has been used than by its original statutory rationale. How that apparatus will evolve cannot be foretold with preciseness. But how and why it has evolved from its inception to its present state is a saga that should be of as much interest to students of American government as to those of foreign policy.

References

Aberbach, Joel D., Robert D. Putnam, and Bert A. Rockman (1981). *Bureaucrats and Politicians in Western Democracies*. Cambridge, Mass.: Harvard University Press.

Aberbach, Joel D., and Bert A. Rockman (1976). "Clashing Beliefs within the Executive Branch: The Nixon Administration Bureaucracy." *American Political Science Review* 70: 456–68.

Allison, Graham (1980). "An Executive Cabinet." *Society:* 17, July/August, 41–47.

———, and Peter Szanton (1976). *Remaking Foreign Policy.* New York: Basic Books.

Armstrong, Scott (1980). "Carter Given Oaths on 'Leaks,'" *Washington Post,* 16 July 1980, pp. A1, A4.

Art, Robert J. (1973). "Bureaucratic Politics and American Foreign Policy: A Critique." *Policy Sciences* 4: 467–90.

Bernstein, Barton, J. (1980). "The Cuban Missile Crisis: Trading the Jupiters in Turkey?" *Political Science Quarterly* 95: 97–126.

Berry, F. Clifton, Jr., and Deborah Kyle (1977). "The 'Other Cabinet': The National Security Council Staff." *Armed Forces Journal* 114 (July): 12–20.

Campbell, Colin (1980). "The President's Advisory System under Carter: From Spokes in a Wheel to Wagons in a Circle." Presented at the annual meeting of the American Political Science Association, Washington, D.C.

———, and George J. Szablowski (1979). *The Superbureaucrats: Structure and Behaviour in Central Agencies.* Toronto: Macmillan of Canada.

Campbell, John Franklin (1971). *The Foreign Affairs Fudge Factory.* New York: Basic Books.

Covington, Cary R. (1981). "Presidential Memory Development in Three Presidential Agencies." Presented at the annual meeting of the Midwest Political Science Association, Cincinnati.

Cronin, Thomas E. (1975). *The State of the Presidency.* Boston: Little, Brown.

Crossman, R. H. S. (1972). *The Myths of Cabinet Government.* Cambridge, Mass.: Harvard University Press.

Destler, I. M. (1980). "A Job That Doesn't Work." *Foreign Policy* 38: 80–88.

——— (1977). "National Security Advice to U.S. Presidents: Some Lessons From Thirty Years." *World Politics* 29: 143–76.

——— (1972a). "Making Foreign Policy: Comment." *American Political Science Review* 66: 786–90.

——— (1972b). *Presidents, Bureaucrats, and Foreign Policy: The Politics of Organizational Reform*. Princeton, N.J.: Princeton University Press.

Dyson, K. H. F. (1974). "Planning and the Federal Chancellor's Office in the West German Federal Government." *Political Studies* 21: 348–62.

Evans, Rowland, and Robert Novak (1981). "The Education of Al Haig." *Washington Post*, 1 May 1981, p. A19.

Falk, Stanley L. (1964). "The National Security Council under Truman, Eisenhower, and Kennedy." *Political Science Quarterly* 79:403–34.

Fenno, Richard F., Jr. (1975). "The President's Cabinet." In Aaron Wildavsky (ed.), *Perspectives on the Presidency*. Boston: Little, Brown.

Gelb, Leslie H. (1980). "Muskie and Brzezinski: The Struggle over Foreign Policy." *New York Times Magazine*, 20 July 1980, pp. 26–40.

George, Alexander L. (1972a). "The Case for Multiple Advocacy in Making Foreign Policy." *American Political Science Review* 66: 751–85.

——— (1972b). "Making Foreign Policy: Rejoinder." *American Political Science Review* 66: 791–95.

Hafner, Donald L. (1977). "Bureaucratic Politics and 'Those Frigging Missiles': JFK, Cuba and U.S. Missiles in Turkey." *Orbis* 21: 307–32.

Hammond, Paul Y. (1960). "The National Security Council as a Device for Interdepartmental Coordination: An Interpretation and Appraisal." *American Political Science Review* 54: 899–910.

Heclo, Hugh (1975). "OMB and the Presidency: The Problem of 'Neutral Competence.' " *The Public Interest* 38 (Winter): 80–98.

Klein, Rudolf, and Janet Lewis (1977). "Advice and Dissent in British Government: The Case of the Special Advisers." *Policy and Politics* 6: 1–25.

Maechling, Charles, Jr. (1976). "Foreign Policy-Makers: The Weakest Link?" *Virginia Quarterly Review* 52: 1–23.

McGregor, Eugene B., Jr. (1974). "Politics and the Career Mobility of Bureaucrats." *American Political Science Review* 68: 18–26.

Mennis, Bernard (1971). *American Foreign Policy Officials: Who They Are and What They Believe Regarding International Politics*. Columbus: Ohio State University Press.

Merton, Robert K. (1968). "Role of the Intellectual in Public Bureaucracy." In R. K. Merton, *Social Theory and Social Structure*. New York: The Free Press.

Murphy, Thomas P., Donald E. Nuechterlein, and Ronald J. Stupak (1978). *Inside the Bureaucracy: The View from the Assistant Secretary's Desk*. Boulder, Colo.: Westview.

Nathan, Richard P. (1975). *The Plot that Failed: Nixon and the Administrative Presidency*. New York: John Wiley.

National Security Policy Integration (1979). Report of a Study Requested by the President under the Auspices of the President's Reorganization Project. Washington, D.C.: Government Printing Office.

Neustadt, Richard E. (1954). "Presidency and Legislation: The Growth of Central Clearance." *American Political Science Review* 48: 641–71.

———— (1980). *Presidential Power: The Politics of Leadership from FDR to Carter.* New York: John Wiley.

Rose, Richard (1976a). *Managing Presidential Objectives.* New York: Free Press.

———— (1976b). "On the Priorities of Government: A Developmental Analysis of Public Policies." *European Journal of Political Research* 4: 247–89.

———— (1980). "Government against Sub-governments: A European Perspective on Washington." In Richard Rose and Ezra Suleiman (eds.), *Presidents and Prime Ministers: Giving Direction to Government.* Washington, D.C.: American Enterprise Institute.

Sapin, Burton M. (1967). *The Making of United States Foreign Policy.* New York: Praeger.

Sayre, Wallace S. (1964). "Bureaucracies: Some Contrasts in Systems." *Indian Journal of Public Administration* 10: 219–29.

Seidman, Harold (1980). *Politics, Position, and Power: The Dynamics of Federal Organization.* New York: Oxford University Press.

Silberman, Laurence H. (1979). "Toward Presidential Control of the State Department." *Foreign Affairs* 57: 872–93.

Smith, Hedrick (1981). "A Scaled-Down Version of Security Adviser's Task." *New York Times*, 4 March 1981, p. A2.

Stanley, David T., Dean E. Mann, and Jameson W. Doig (1967). *Men Who Govern: A Biographical Profile of American Federal Executives.* Washington, D.C.: Brookings Institution.

21

The Art of Cooptation: Advisory Councils in Social Security

MARTHA DERTHICK

. . . The pattern [of social security politics has been] one of constricted participation. At the core of policymaking were a small number of highly expert program executives and a small number of congressional committee members some of whom in time became expert themselves. If political executives, holders of high office inside the government, could not find places in this proprietary network, it would be surprising to find that appointees to advisory councils could.

And yet they have. The student of social security policymaking soon learns that he is expected by program executives and close observers of social security affairs to take citizen advisory councils seriously, as places where important decisions are made.

Citizen advisory councils have been created for social security intermittently since the start of the program, and in 1956 were prescribed by statute. Here as elsewhere in the federal executive branch, which contained over 1,200 such committees and councils in 1973, they are a familiar form.[1] Probably more in social security than in other programs, they are also regarded as significant. The most important of them in the past have been integral to policymaking, and

From Martha Derthick, *Policymaking for Social Security*. Washington, D.C., The Brookings Institution, 1979, pp. 89–109. Reprinted with the permission of the author and the publisher. Footnotes are renumbered.

[1]*Federal Advisory Committees: Second Annual Report of the President Covering Calendar Year 1973* (GPO, 1974), pp. 1–3.

their deliberations constituted a useful, possibly vital, stage in achieving consensus on major measures. Before both the 1939 and 1950 amendments, they functioned much like precongressional legislatures, representative bodies in which the major affected interests reached agreement about significant policy proposals. Nonetheless, it would not be accurate to see the councils as consisting of outsiders who successfully staked out a policymaking role independent of other policymakers. More accurately, the advisory council became for the SSA's executives a convenient mechanism of "cooptation"—in Selznick's classic definition, "the process of absorbing new elements into the leadership or policy-determining structure of an organization as a means of averting threats to its stability or existence."[2] Though the councils were discontinuous—each one was created anew—their leadership was continuous. A few individuals served time after time, developed their own strong sense of proprietorship in the program, and were absorbed into the structure of policymaking. Through them, and through the SSA leadership's influence on the councils' deliberations, the councils as a whole were absorbed too.

Origin and Structure

Program executives did not initially conceive of the advisory council as an instrument of cooptation. Arthur Altmeyer, as chairman of the Social Security Board, did not want to create the first council. It was thrust upon him in 1937 by the chief Republican critic of the program on Capitol Hill, Senator Arthur H. Vandenberg.

Perhaps it was the recollection of experience in 1934 that made Altmeyer wary. There had been an advisory council to the Committee on Economic Security then, and it had not worked well. It was quite large. Some of the members were highly opinionated. The CES staff was so engrossed in its own work that it did not know what to do with a group of advisors, and the council was assembled so late—just two weeks before the deadline for the committee's report to the President—that even the pretense of meaningful advisory participation was impossible to sustain. The members concluded that they were being used, and they rebelled. In all, it was not an experience that Altmeyer would have cared to repeat, but when Van-

[2]Philip Selznick, *TVA and the Grass Roots: A Study in the Sociology of Formal Organization* (University of California Press, 1949), p. 13.

denberg insisted in a Finance Committee hearing that an outside group be formed, Altmeyer could not get out of it.

If nothing else, the partisan and critical context of Vandenberg's proposal would have made Altmeyer reluctant. Urged on by leaders of the insurance industry, Vandenberg was conducting a fervent campaign against the accumulation of a large reserve fund, which conservatives feared would encourage government profligacy and undermine private investment opportunities. He had introduced a concurrent resolution calling on the Social Security Board to prepare a plan to abandon the huge reserve, and the Finance Committee was holding hearings on this resolution. Altmeyer agreed that the board would make a study, but Vandenberg was not satisfied with this. "With great respect to the Social Security Board," he said, "I am not willing to leave the investigation solely with them, because I think it is prejudiced in favor of the existing system."[3] He proposed that Congress make its own study. Thus trapped, Altmeyer agreed to the creation of an advisory committee that would be responsible jointly to the Finance Committee and to the Social Security Board. The appointment of the council was announced in May by Senator Pat Harrison, Finance Committee chairman, and Altmeyer, but Altmeyer was still reluctant to proceed. By September the council still had not met and Altmeyer was unsure whether it should. He solicited President Roosevelt's advice on the point and was told to go ahead.

Altmeyer need not have been so anxious. Before very long the twenty-five-member council was agreeing to nearly all of the SSB's proposals for change in the 1935 law, including the very significant recommendation that monthly benefits be paid to surviving dependents of deceased workers. Marion B. Folsom, who was one of the representatives of business on the council, recalled the experience:

> Now, if you had taken a vote on this council when we started in, I bet you would have found about two to one against survivors' benefits. Before we got through, we were all for it. You see, we met with the social security people. They sat in on all our discussions, so everybody came out all together on the thing. When we got through, we were pretty well unanimous on it. . . . That really was an educational process—that committee.[4]

[3] *Reserves under Federal Old-Age Benefit Plan—Social Security Act*, Hearing before the Senate Committee on Finance, 75 Cong. 1 sess. (GPO, 1937), p. 22.
[4] Interview with Marion B. Folsom, Oral History Collection, Columbia University (1965–68), pp. 116–17, 205. (Hereafter Folsom, OHC.)

This second and far more favorable experience with an advisory council showed the leaders of the Social Security Administration that the form need not be feared—could, in fact, be quite useful—and in 1947 they urged the Senate Committee on Finance to create a council again. The social security payroll tax was scheduled to rise from 1 percent to 2.5 percent (for both employers and employees) in 1948, but the SSA leaders were sure that Congress would postpone the increase as it had always done before. Rather than try to prevent the freeze on the rate, SSA executives and their allies in organized labor elected to accept it but simultaneously to ask the Finance Committee for a new advisory council. They approached Senator Vandenberg with the idea, and Senators Eugene Millikin and Walter F. George, the ranking members of the committee, introduced the necessary resolution, which authorized the committee to create an advisory council to study coverage, benefits, taxes, and all other aspects of social security. Congress was Republican at the time, and Senator Millikin, as the committee's Republican leader, took charge of constituting the council in consultation with Senator George.

That the council of 1947–48 was created under Republican auspices increased the frustration of partisan critics of social security when this council too endorsed the social insurance program and called for enlargement along traditional lines. In the House in 1949, Representative Carl T. Curtis filed a minority report in the Ways and Means Committee that criticized social insurance comprehensively and concluded with a critique of the advisory council in particular. Because they were important people, Curtis said, the members had been too busy to make an independent study and almost inevitably accepted the proposals of the Social Security Administration. Curtis called for a study by persons who could work full time for several months and be wholly independent of the administration.[5]

The third in this series of advisory groups alarmed the SSA leadership, for it was created by a Republican administration at a time when the political environment in general was more threatening than ever before. For a brief time, the advisory group itself seemed a threat.

In the fall of 1952, soon after the election of President Eisenhower, the U.S. Chamber of Commerce issued a policy declaration

---

[5]*Social Security Act Amendments of 1949*, H. Rept. 1300, 81 Cong. 1 sess. (GPO, 1949), p. 184.

that the SSA leaders took to be a fundamental attack on their program. It called for covering all of the aged and for pay-as-you-go financing. The SSA interpreted this as a repudiation of contributory, wage-related social insurance. Program executives feared that an incoming Republican administration, in combination with a Republican Congress, might be receptive to this proposal from a conservative source, and this fear intensified momentarily when the new FSA administrator, Oveta Culp Hobby, began meeting informally with a five-member advisory group of whom three had been members of the Chamber of Commerce committee on social security policy. Partisans of social security labeled it "the Hobby lobby."

In response to criticism from organized labor, Mrs. Hobby promptly enlarged her "lobby" into a conventionally representative group. Seven members were added, including two members each from organized labor and organized agriculture, and this enlarged committee, meeting in the spring of 1953, followed its predecessors down the path of uncritical support for the established program. It declined to consider the Chamber's plan, which was tantamount to opposing it. Its own report consisted of a series of recommendations for increased coverage, steps on which Republicans and Democrats, business and labor, could agree. That was the one kind of expansion that conservatives wished to push farther and faster than liberals. It was an easy thing to get agreement on, even in a time of political turbulence.

Once again, the staff work was done by SSA. Roswell B. Perkins, a young Republican lawyer who entered the Hobby administration with an assignment to work on social security, later recalled that the consultants' advisory report was "a straight SSA report . . . just churned up right out of Ball's boys."[6]

Mrs. Hobby's consultants were the last advisory group to be assembled ad hoc. The Social Security Act amendments of 1956 formalized the councils by providing that they should be created periodically. The first statutory council was to be appointed in 1957, and succeeding ones were to be set up in advance of each scheduled tax increase. This provision was added, it appears, at the request of the AFL-CIO, which may well have concluded after the experience of 1953 that it was risky to leave too much to chance and the dis-

[6]Interview with Roswell B. Perkins, Oral History Collection, Columbia University (1968), pp. 139–41. (Hereafter Perkins, OHC.)

cretion of the secretary of health, education, and welfare. The law
provided that the commissioner of social security should serve as
chairman of the advisory council, and that twelve other persons
should represent employers and employees in equal numbers and self-
employed persons and the public, a composition that of itself gave
partisans of the program an influential if not dominant position.
. . .

The statutory councils, like their less formal predecessors, ap-
plauded the program and attested to its financial soundness. "[The]
almost universal acceptance of this program of social insurance is
well deserved," the 1957–59 council said. "The Council finds that
the present method of financing . . . is sound, practical, and appropriate for this program."[7] The council of 1963–65 endorsed the extension of social insurance to cover medical costs of the elderly and
disabled. The council of 1969–71 helped lay the basis for a 20 percent
benefit increase in 1972 by endorsing a change in actuarial techniques.

This brief history poses an obvious puzzle. The six advisory
groups between 1937 and 1971 were strikingly different in their
origins and strikingly similar in their results. The first one was inspired by Congress, even if it was technically a joint executive-
legislative creature. The second was created by Congress though inspired by executives behind the scenes. The third was created by the
administration acting alone. The last three were appointed by the
executive (the secretary of HEW) according to statutory prescription.
The second, third, fourth, and sixth councils began under Republican auspices. So did the first, if Vandenberg is regarded as its orig-
inator. Only one—the council of 1963–65—was unequivocally the
creature of a Democratic administration. Yet they all approved the
program fundamentally. None ever produced a substantial, significant critique of it. Most called for major expansion.

Relations with the SSA

Robert Myers, as chief actuary of the SSA, stood always a bit apart
from the other program executives, privately not altogether of the

[7]*Financing Old-Age, Survivors, and Disability Insurance: A Report of the Advisory Council on Social Security Financing* (Washington, D.C.: the Council, 1959),
pp. 2–3.

faith, and one sign of Myers's detachment was his assessment of the advisory councils. "They were biased," he told an interviewer in 1967. The membership was "always selected so that you include a majority of the people who are going to think the way you want them to think." In Myers's opinion, the councils ought to contain "people on all sides of the fence," including the side that favored a need-based, means-tested form of assistance to the aged.[8]

Opinion in the councils was of course not completely uniform, but differences were confined within a spectrum defined by acceptance of social insurance as a general approach to aiding dependent persons. "I have long been a strong supporter of the principles that have been incorporated in our social security program," Reinhard Hohaus, an insurance company executive, wrote in 1965, in a separate statement that questioned the arguments for medicare. This was typical of advisory council dissents; it was a dissent at the margins. Hohaus questioned only the proposed expansion to include health insurance and not the basic principles.[9]

The councils were ordinarily composed of three groups—representatives of labor, of business, and of "the public." For various reasons . . . , organized labor generally supported the social security program uncritically. Businessmen were a more likely source of dissent, except that the businessmen who served on advisory councils were in general distinguished by their relative liberalism. They were the statesmen of the corporate world, businessmen with a social conscience, whose own corporations (for example, General Electric, Eastman Kodak) had been leaders in the development of pension plans. The public members were typically university professors with an interest in social insurance. In 1963–65, when the subject of health insurance was to be considered, the medical profession was represented by the president of the National Medical Association, an organization of black physicians, and not by the American Medical Association, which was implacably hostile to government health insurance.

Even when the SSA executives did not, as in 1937, directly participate in constituting the councils, they suggested names informally

[8]Interview with Robert J. Myers, Oral History Collection, Columbia University (1963), pp. 67–68. (Hereafter Myers, OHC.)

[9]*The Status of the Social Security Program and Recommendations for Its Improvement: Report of the Advisory Council on Social Security* (Washington, D.C.: the Council, 1965), pp. 93–94.

to the appointing authorities in Congress or the HEW secretary's office. They knew who their friends were, and their friends identified potential friends. Thus, for example, in finding businessmen to serve on the councils, Altmeyer consulted Folsom, a reliably sympathetic business executive whose identification with the social security program dated from service on the advisory council of 1935. Without any prompting from SSA executives, organized labor could be counted on to insist on membership in advisory groups. Nelson Cruikshank of the AFL-CIO recalled for an interviewer how Senator Millikin had been importuned privately to include labor representatives in the council of 1947–48, through a plumbers' union official who had belonged to the legislature in Colorado, Millikin's home state.[10] In 1953 labor pressured Mrs. Hobby publicly to expand her consultants' group. After 1956, of course, labor was guaranteed representation by statute, and labor representation of itself guaranteed a solid bloc of support for the program within the advisory councils.

With the exception of the council of 1947–48, the advisory councils were always staffed by the SSA. Altmeyer, Cohen, and others attended the meetings of the council of 1937–39, and the headquarters organization prepared proposals, supporting technical data, and legislative drafts. "It is essential," Cohen later wrote, "that such a council be given adequate technical assistance, not only so that it can do a good job but in order that it will not set up a separate staff by itself."[11] The SSA served the councils with its customary energy and competence. (The technique, so it seemed to the heretical Myers, was to "flood them with material that they can't possibly read, and then they're so embarrassed that they haven't read it all that they don't dare speak too much because somebody is going to say, 'Oh, didn't you read this?' ")[12] Being amply served by the SSA, advisory councils had no motive to look elsewhere for staff assistance unless for independent expertise.[13]

[10]Interview with Nelson H. Cruikshank, Oral History Collection, Columbia University (1967), p. 39. (Hereafter Cruikshank, OHC.)

[11]Wilbur J. Cohen to M. S. Pitzele, August 28, 1941 (File 025 Federal Security Agency, R. G. 47, SSA Central Files 1935–1947, Box 15, National Archives).

[12]Myers, OHC, p. 62.

[13]See the comments of the chairman of the 1974–75 advisory council, W. Allen Wallis, in *Financing the Social Security System*, Hearings before the Subcommittee on Social Security of the House Committee on Ways and Means, 94 Cong. 1 sess. (GPO, 1975), p. 104.

Senator Millikin appears to have sought independent expertise in 1947. The charter of the 1947–48 council authorized it to appoint its own staff, as well as to request assistance from the executive branch. The result of Millikin's interest in being served by "outsiders" was the hiring of Robert Ball as staff director. Ball by then had had seven years of experience in the SSA, but had left it in 1946 to give training in social welfare and public administration to state and federal officials under the auspices of the American Council on Education. Several other members of his small staff in 1947–48 had had experience in the SSA, and his executive assistant was on detail from the agency. When Representative Carl Curtis charged that the advisory council had lacked independent expertise, Millikin replied that it was impossible to obtain. "The cold fact of the matter is that the basic information is alone in the possession of the Social Security Administration," he told Curtis. "There is no private actuary for any insurance company, including the biggest, that can give you the complete picture on this subject. . . . I spent a whole summer working on that problem, sweating here in Washington when I did not have sense enough to stay in the Senate Office Building, trying to find those kinds of people, and I finally—by the admission of the people in private business—had to give up the job because those people were not available. They did not have them."[14] Through the ubiquitous Cohen, the SSA kept informed of the council's work, and it performed staff assistance for the labor members. When one business member prepared a statement in favor of holding the line on the wage base, Cohen drafted a statement for the labor members in support of a big increase. When the same business member prepared a statement opposing a disability insurance program, Cohen supplied the labor members with a statement in support of one.[15] Thus, even when the SSA was not actually in charge of staff work for the councils, it was very influential indirectly.

As Cohen was the central figure in the SSA's relations with Congress, Ball was for some years central to relations with the ad-

[14]*Social Security Revision*, Hearings before the Senate Committee on Finance, 81 Cong. 2 sess. (GPO, 1950), pt. 3, pp. 1953–54.
[15]A. J. Altmeyer to Nelson H. Cruikshank, February 19, 1948, and enclosure (File 025 Social Security, acc. no. 62A-82, R. G. 47, Box 26, Washington National Records Center. Suitland, Md.); and route slip, Wilbur J. Cohen to AJA [Arthur J. Altmeyer], no date [1948], and enclosure (File 025 Advisory Council 1948, acc. no. 56-A533, R. G. 47, Box 6, Washington National Records Center, Suitland, Md.).

visory councils. Ball, Charles Schottland once remarked in admiration, was a "terrific teacher."[16] On the subject of social insurance, he was also a very experienced one by 1947. He had entered the SSB in 1939 as a field representative, moved two years later to the central office to do research, and soon after that to the training office, where he taught the principles of social insurance to new employees. It fitted him well for his later work of teaching social insurance to secretaries of HEW, congressmen, and advisory councils. He was always clear, patient, knowledgeable, and very good at laying out the alternatives and explaining their implications. He was also self-restrained rather than opinionated and aggressive—in other words, the kind of teacher who helps his students reach their own conclusions, or at least to leave the classroom believing that they have. Marion Folsom, who observed him in 1947–48 and in later councils after he became deputy director of the Bureau of Old Age and Social Insurance and then commissioner of social security, told an interviewer, "He's very impartial. He'd generally say, 'It's up to you.' He'd have all the facts and everything, but he wouldn't try to impose his own views on us."[17] . . .

In the advisory councils, as in the congressional committees, there was also "the other Bob," as Eveline Burns called him—Myers, the chief actuary, who provided cost estimates.[18] Myers would tell the councils, as he would tell congressmen, what various proposals for changing the program would cost, and the councils, like Congress, would make choices secure and self-satisfied in the knowledge that they had taken costs into account after hearing from a competent technician.

Because they served as staff to the councils, SSA officials were in a position to influence their agendas. Sometimes they had an interest in keeping the agenda narrow, as in 1953, when they wished to discourage consideration of the fundamental criticism raised by the Chamber of Commerce and Representative Carl Curtis, and sometimes they wished to broaden it, as in 1937, when Vandenberg wanted to talk about keeping taxes low and reducing the reserve fund, whereas Altmeyer wanted to talk about adding new types of

[16]Interview with Charles J. Schottland, Oral History Collection, Columbia University (1965), p. 82.

[17]Folsom, OHC, p. 120.

[18]Interview with Eveline M. Burns, Oral History Collection, Columbia University (1965), pp. 99–100.

protection. The 1937–39 council had its agenda laid out in the original announcement of the council's formation. What the advisory council was to study, such as the advisability of commencing monthly benefit payments sooner than 1942 and extending benefits to survivors of deceased workers, turned out to be a fairly good guide to what the group would recommend. And what it was to study was outlined by the Social Security Board.

If the membership of the councils could be limited to persons who were in general supporters of the program, and if staff assistance could be limited to persons drawn directly or indirectly from the SSA, and if the councils' agenda could be limited to topics the SSA's leaders judged to be timely, there was not much danger that these groups of outsiders would get out of control and produce unwanted recommendations. The SSA's techniques of influence minimized the risks associated with admitting such a group to a role in policymaking. Furthermore, whatever risks there were diminished with time. It was unlikely that a part-time group of citizens, however distinguished or independent, would question what was firmly established and widely accepted. Social security executives, watching one after another of these groups assemble, were never entirely sure that they would not do something quixotic. "I must say I never worked with any council without feeling that it might go off the deep end with inconsistent and peculiar recommendations," Robert Ball recalled.[19] But they never did.

The Councils' Functions

From the perspective of a thoroughly experienced insider, the advisory councils served two main functions. Princeton's J. Douglas Brown, who served on all of them between 1935 and 1972 but the informal Hobby lobby, came to see them as an instrument of executive-legislative relations and independent legitimators of major policy decisions. For so important a program, he argued, the ordinary processes of executive presentation and congressional hearings were insufficient. Something more was needed to supplement the deliberations of congressional committees that were overburdened and an administration in which outsiders, including Congress, were

---

[19]From tape-recorded comments addressed to the author by Robert M. Ball, May 6, 1978. (Hereafter Ball transcript.)

bound to suspect bias.[20] He also believed that the councils improved the depth and objectivity of deliberation and that this reassured the public, especially in regard to the fiscal soundness of the program. "I would say . . . it is the strength and prestige of the general conclusions that have influence," he told an interviewer. "A group, including people from industry, public, labor, and all the rest, has come to these conclusions after months of discussion and having every possible source of information . . . so that the ordinary industrialist, or ordinary labor leader, the ordinary member of the public could say, 'Well, those fellows have put a hell of a lot of time into it, and I guess they can't be too far wrong.' "[21]

Leaders of the SSA, from their different but hardly more detached perspective, came to view the councils as important for rather different reasons. Asked to evaluate the councils, Altmeyer stressed their representative role. "They do give you the opportunity to understand what the reaction is of interested groups."[22] Robert Ball's interpretation was similar. He suggested that policy for social security historically had emerged from areas of agreement between business and labor. The advisory councils discovered and defined these areas.[23] From the perspective of program executives, then, the usefulness of the councils lay primarily in their serving as a channel of communication with salient interests and a medium through which differing interests could be reconciled.

These differing interpretations express different emphases only. The three roles—link between the executive and legislative branches, independent legitimator of policy choices, reconciler of competing interests—were not mutually exclusive. I suggest, however, an interpretation of the councils somewhat different from any of them, though compounded of their elements.

In my view the councils evolved into a distinctive form well suited to the practice of program-oriented policymaking. Constituted in representative fashion, so that various interests could be spoken for, they nonetheless functioned so as to foster program-serving attitudes and choices. The councils did serve to legitimate social security policy, but they were not strictly independent legitimators, for

[20]J. Douglas Brown, *An American Philosophy of Social Security: Evolution and Issues* (Princeton University Press, 1972), p. 44. Interview with J. Douglas Brown, Oral History Collection, Columbia University (1965), p. 73. (Hereafter Brown, OHC.)
[21]Ibid., p. 147.
[22]Interview with Arthur J. Altmeyer, Oral History Collection, Columbia University (1967), p. 80. (Hereafter Altmeyer, OHC.)
[23]Interview with the author, February 2, 1976.

they developed their own corporate pride and sense of proprietorship. That they were influenced by the SSA is only part of the explanation for their lack of detachment. Beyond that, a group dynamic was at work. Having a life of their own, the councils acquired their own particular stake in maintaining and enlarging the social security program.

"We're trustees, you see," Brown once remarked of the councils, whose function was to prevent anyone, including the federal government, from "fooling with the system."[24] This choice of language, like that of Ways and Means Committee members, who also thought of themselves as "trustees," suggests something of how the advisory councils conceived of their task. In the councils, the "we" consisted of a core of leading members who returned to service again and again—Brown, of course, who served five times; Nelson Cruikshank, from organized labor, who served four times of the six; and Marion Folsom, representing business, who served on three councils, participated informally in the Hobby lobby, and could not serve in 1957 only because he was then secretary of HEW. Reinhard A. Hohaus, an actuary of the Metropolitan Life Insurance Company, was another veteran—he chaired Mrs. Hobby's group, served twice thereafter, and before that had served as an adviser to the actuary's office and to the council of 1937–39—but as a member of the insurance industry he was always a bit suspect to program executives and did not become an insider in quite the same sense. The triumvirate of Brown, Cruikshank, and Folsom reflected the tripartite composition of the councils—"public," labor, and business—and each informally led his respective subgroup, tutoring those newcomers who needed initiation into the principles of the social security program.[25] This relieved SSA executives of much of the burden of guiding the

---

[24]Brown, OHC, p. 89.

[25]Brown told an interviewer:

May I just say this? It sounds awfully smug, but there were three of us who have sort of followed through: Marion Folsom, as an industrial member, . . . Nelson Cruikshank on the labor side, and myself. The three of us have appeared repeatedly on advisory councils. So in a way it was fortunate that we were on three sides, so to speak. We'd each help educate our own side. Nelson time and again would have to explain to [Emil] Rieve of the textile workers why this would have to work the way it did or some other trade unionist. Marion would quietly in a very calm way explain to some industrial member why this wouldn't work. Now, with the public members, since I was the old hand, they'd often listen to me. I had one public member this time who said, "Doug, whenever you are in favor of something, I'll go along with you."

I said, "Don't do it unless you really think it out." "Oh, no. That's all right. You've been at it longer." (Brown, OHC, pp. 81–82.)

councils in acceptable directions. With reliable leaders present in the councils, SSA officials could confine themselves to staff functions and minimize the risks of intrusion. Brown, who was certainly no cynic about such matters, perceived the SSA's interest in having familiar hands at the helm. "I think Bob Ball and the secretary . . . purposely did that," he remarked, to explain the presence of himself and the other old hands in the council of 1963–65.[26] . . .

Under Brown's leadership, and with SSA officials as staff, the advisory councils became a means of drawing interest group representatives into program-oriented policymaking. Through the councils, interest group leaders learned the rationale for the principal features of the social security program, participated in the decisions concerning it (albeit advisory, not authoritative, decisions), and in some measure became program leaders too. If, for example, one were to characterize Cruikshank's career in a phrase, it would be hard to know whether to call him a leader in social security or a leader of organized labor; the identification with the program rivaled identification with an organization. Insofar as interest group representatives developed allegiance to the program, they moderated group claims that were in conflict with program principles. Pressures from their constituencies were countered with pressures from fellow program leaders, and, in the actual deliberations of the councils, the latter became more compelling.

Having "learned" program principles through the medium of the councils, business and labor leaders could in turn be expected to convey them to their constituencies; and some, as prominent and influential individuals in their own right, could also be expected to enter positions of social or political leadership, where their acquired expertise in social security would be an asset to the program. Such expertise could of itself constitute a qualification for office, as it did for Folsom, the most prominent council member and program partisan to turn into a holder of high office. Secretary of HEW between 1955 and 1958, Folsom before that was under secretary of the treasury in the Eisenhower administration. Mrs. Hobby, who was a complete novice in social security, called on him for advice, and SSA leaders, who had no confidence in the incoming Republicans generally but much confidence in Folsom, turned to him for support. On his last day in office as social security commissioner, Altmeyer

[26]Ibid., p. 84.

saw Folsom to say goodbye and urge him to take part in the Eisenhower administration's discussions of social security.[27] Folsom's marginal position—as a high-ranking executive in a Republican administration, trusted by other political executives, yet a partisan of the social security program and trusted by program executives—was good for the program at a potentially troublesome time, though it proved to be hard on Folsom. Roswell Perkins, in his recollections for an interviewer, remembered that Folsom as secretary had "tortured himself for weeks" over the administration's position on covering disability, and only "with considerable emotional difficulty" decided that he must oppose cash disability benefits.[28]

That the councils helped to indoctrinate outsiders does not gainsay their usefulness also in bringing outside reactions to bear on the proposed next moves of the Social Security Administration. Communication did run in both directions. Within the limits of the agenda, which took the basic program as given, the SSA's solicitation of advice and opinion was often genuine enough. The dialogue among interests that normally develops when Congress considers legislation was anticipated and in some measure preempted by deliberations of the advisory councils. However, to the extent that consensus was reached within the councils, their effect was to constrict rather than expand the policymaking arena. The interplay of interests took place within a narrow, relatively controlled forum, to which program executives had ready access.

That the advisory councils were dominated by supporters of the program in combination with the SSA staff meant that service on them could be frustrating for someone who stood outside the consensus. Charles A. Siegfried, who was vice chairman of the board of the Metropolitan Life Insurance Company, found the 1969–71 advisory council a "dismal experience" and filed a dissenting statement.[29] He sensed that the chairman, who was a former secretary

[27]Arthur J. Altmeyer, *The Formative Years of Social Security* (University of Wisconsin Press, 1966), pp. 214–15.

[28]Perkins, OHC, p. 28. Ball commented as follows: "My belief is that Folsom was directed to oppose cash disability benefits. All during this period he was talking to me about possible entering-wedge type proposals, age sixty for the disabled and so on." Ball transcript.

[29]Both the business members and the labor members filed dissents to this report. The 1969–71 council was more than usually divided, perhaps because it was the first in which the business and labor representatives were nominated by business and labor organizations. Representative Thomas B. Curtis, an outspoken conservative Republican, had charged in 1963 that the newly named council was stacked by the admin-

of HEW, was leading the group toward predetermined results with the support of Commissioner Ball. From this and other experience, he concluded that policymaking for social security was concentrated heavily in the hands of an expert few within the government, and that the councils reinforced the domination of the inner group rather than dispersing power.[30]

Cooptation of outsiders is likely to have a price even under conditions favorable to the coopting organization, and SSA officials did not always get exactly what they wanted from the advisory councils. In 1937–39 they had hoped that the council would endorse a disability program, but it did no more than agree in principle that disability benefits were socially desirable. In 1947–48 a clear majority favored disability benefits, but only after so compromising the recommendation that Cohen was very upset by the outcome. Cruikshank later said that he learned from this experience the danger of premature compromise.[31] The proponents had given in and given in until the recommendation was very narrow, and then the two dissenters proceeded to dissent anyway. One of the most important recommendations of the 1947–48 advisory council—that an "increment" for each year of work under social security be dropped from the benefit schedule—had been opposed by Altmeyer and Cohen. It is hard to judge how costly such defeats were to the SSA. Administrators were not bound by the advisory councils' recommendations. From

---

istration and was just " 'window dressing' for things some of the Social Security staff want put into law." Two years later the law was changed to provide that members of the councils should represent *organizations* of employers and employees as well as the self-employed and the general public; in response, the secretary of HEW solicited nominations from leading business and labor organizations and made his selections from among them. Another change in the law eliminated the provision that the social security commissioner serve as council chairman. Close observers of the councils believe that these changes have increased their independence somewhat. They may also produce tension between the organizations that nominate council members and the secretaries of HEW who name them. For example, when the 1974–75 council was named, the Nixon administration's secretary of HEW, Caspar W. Weinberger, rejected some of the AFL-CIO's nominees, whereupon the AFL-CIO leadership boycotted the council. The only labor members whom the Nixon administration could induce to serve on the council were relatively obscure members of the building trades and teamsters unions. Curtis's criticisms appear in the *Congressional Record* (May 23, 1963), p. 9246, and *Congressional Record* (September 17, 1963), pp. 17309–11.

[30]Interview with the author, November 3, 1976; Society of Actuaries, *Transactions*, vol. 22, pt. 2 (1970), p. D508.

[31]Cruikshank, OHC, p. 104.

the SSA's point of view, advisory council support for its own proposals was highly desirable but not essential. "We would have made exactly the same proposals even if . . . there'd been no advisory council," Altmeyer said, recalling the legislation of 1939.[32] And when an advisory council did diverge from the SSA leadership (as did that of 1948 in proposing to eliminate the increment), it was not necessarily to the political detriment of the program. Because dropping the increment meant lower costs in the long run, it made possible a major increase in benefits in the short run, a trade that enabled the advisory council to present a nearly unanimous report and that also proved highly popular in Congress. Robert Ball's service as director of this council, far from putting him seriously at odds with the leadership of the program, marked his emergence as a member of it.

Congress, of course, was no more bound by the recommendations of the advisory councils than was the administration. The council's recommendation for a disability insurance program in 1948, though much too weak to satisfy Cohen, was too strong to get through the Senate Finance Committee, which rejected it in favor of grants-in-aid to the states for relief of the disabled. Congress did not uncritically accept advice even from the early councils that were its own creatures, and much of the advice that it did accept was obviously congenial. This was advice that called for paying benefits sooner and more broadly in the short run.

Nevertheless, leaders of the SSA believed that the councils were quite helpful in producing legislation, particularly the crucial amendments of 1939 and 1950. By arriving at a consensus among representatives of disparate groups, the councils performed a useful service for a Congress that was still groping its way with an unfamiliar program. Thus when a dissident council member, Walter D. Fuller, suggested to the Ways and Means Committee that the 1937–39 council had compromised to such an extent that its report could not be of much use, committee member Jere Cooper received this observation with skepticism. In a congressman's eyes, it was precisely the compromises that gave the report its value:

> MR. FULLER. . . . Based on a year and a half experience with the Social Security Advisory Council . . . my own personal belief is you gentlemen would get greater help if you had one committee of employers,

[32]Altmeyer, OHC, p. 78.

let us say, one committee of representative labor and perhaps a third committee of the so-called public, and let each of them make their own report. I think in that way you might get a more complete statement and you could judge. . . . The difficulty with a [council] like this is you are bound to compromise your position.

MR. COOPER. Just on that point, from a practical standpoint, . . . suppose we follow up the suggestion just made. . . . Then instead of the whole council being under the necessity of making a compromise and reaching some common level, they would just pass the responsibility to us to do the same thing, would they not?

MR. FULLER. That is true, and I think that is where it ought to be.[33]

Also, the working of the councils created a supply of highly credible individual witnesses, the council leaders, on whom Congress could rely for well-informed, presumably expert, advice. In 1939 both Brown and Folsom testified at length. As individual witnesses, members did not necessarily support everything that was in the council reports, but in general the weight of their testimony supported both the reports and the administration's bills, with which the reports closely corresponded.

As congressmen improved their understanding of the new program, they became less dependent on outside opinion. The diffidence of 1939 eventually gave way to the mastery of Wilbur Mills. Probably no subsequent council was more important than that of 1937–39, which offered solicited advice to a Congress puzzled and divided over the issue of financing and unable as yet to get any guidance from the most comforting and credible witness of all: experience. Besides developing its own expertise in the person of Mills, the Ways and Means Committee in time developed intimate working relations with SSA officials, and after these routines were worked out, advisory councils receded to the periphery of policymaking. Once a link between executive and legislature, by the early 1960s they were more of an appendage.

Still, the councils remained potentially useful to program executives as a channel for putting items on the legislative agenda in a legitimized form that congressmen could not readily ignore and might, at their discretion, make use of. By endorsing significant changes in actuarial and financing techniques, the 1969–71 advisory council laid the basis for the 20 percent benefit increase of 1972,

[33]*Social Security*, Hearings before the House Committee on Ways and Means, 76 Cong. 1 sess. (GPO, 1939), vol. 3, pp. 2083–84.

which was one of the foundations of the modern program. Mills, who took the initiative in proposing the big increase, was responding to the political situation created by the appearance of the council's report, which defined political opportunities in a new way. In justifying his response to this new situation, Mills made a point of citing the expert authority of the advisory council.[34]

Advisory councils composed of "outsiders" reinforced rather than compromised the program-oriented character of policymaking. The outsiders tended to become insiders as they were drawn into the councils' deliberations; a few who served time and again became in effect members of the proprietary inner family. Leadership, membership, staffing, and the definition of the agenda all combined to preclude consideration of alternatives that were in conflict with program maintenance, and to assure recommendations falling within a range that program executives would find acceptable. Typically, advisory council reports paved the way for the program executives' own current recommendations.

[34]*Congressional Record* (February 23, 1972), p. 5270.

each other for actions but rely on different constituencies for support. This condition virtually eliminates the possibility that major policy change will percolate up through the bureaucracy rather than drip down from the top. It makes White House involvement in multibureau policy innovation almost mandatory. The dominant strategy for policy innovation is then to get the President "signed on" as a precondition for moving the rest of the government.

Moreover, career patterns in Washington are more strongly related to personal policy preferences than in London. American officials frequently enter government service out of a substantive interest in policy and a desire to play a role, rather than in search of a high-status profession. Once in government service, they often find that the right policy commitments can speed advancement. Policy can make a difference to the careers of permanent officials. Autonomous ladders of promotion nurture departmentalism. The fact that each military service has its own career line, for instance, may strengthen an officer's resolve to defend a service goal against the other services, and helps explain the volume of press maneuvers in interservice rivalries. The ambitious, whether in-and-outer or career bureaucrat, come to have a sizeable stake in outcomes. This puts the cost of unauthorized disclosure at a discount to officials.

Consequently, strategies for career advancement make it feasible for U.S. officials to go over the heads of their department secretaries to achieve their policy goals. Strategies for policy innovation make it necessary to use the press to do so.

A second reason for the extensive use of press maneuvers in Washington is that the network for circulating information inside the American government is inadequate to the task. In this respect Whitehall presents a striking contrast to the vast size, geographic diffuseness, and insularity of Washington bureaus. In 1968, when the Administrative Grades of the British civil service totaled some 2,700, equivalent grades in the American government had fifty times that number.[4] Scattered throughout the capital, various bureaus tend to interact primarily at rather senior levels. Departments in London, by comparison, link up formally through an extensive network of interdepartmental committees and informally through the "old boy net," the clubs, the luncheon, the weekend in the country. The Brit-

[4]Great Britain, Parliamentary Papers, *Reports*, Cmnd. 3638, June 1968, "The Civil Service," I, p. 97, 147.

ish Establishment simply has no Washington peer. Under their circumstances, using the press to circulate information is less imperative.

The contrast between Great Britain and the United States suggests that officials give a lot of information to reporters in order to disseminate it in and around Washington, especially to other officials in the Executive Branch and the Congress, in order to affect policy outcomes. Cataloguing the purposes of press maneuvers offers additional evidence for this proposition. It also throws light on the ways in which information is disclosed.

Informational Press Maneuvers

Informational press maneuvers seek to influence the outcome of a decision by changing the information on which it is predicated. The condition which makes possible the success of such maneuvers is the uncertainty endemic to all governmental systems. Uncertainty in the minds of all political men about the nature of the reality they confront permits alternative formulations of the "meaning" of events and issues to coexist. It allows everyone to have within himself "his own special world." Like a Pirandello play, much of politics consists of conflict among actors, each of whom seeks to gain acceptance for his own definition of reality, his own version of the facts. From the ideologue at the barricades of eighteenth century Paris to the bureaucrat in the corridors of present-day Washington, all political actors have sought to shape each others' perceptions of events and issues as a means of achieving their goals.

Conflict over the meaning of reality implies disagreement on the criteria for evaluating specific bits of information. Much information, then, is unknowable, in the sense that there is no agreement on its meaning. The extent of the unknowable puts a premium on the unknown—information whose significance would be clear to all if it became available. If such a piece of information were common knowledge, moreover, it might favor one side or another in a policy debate. That side has a stake in planting it in the news, giving it currency throughout Washington, and focusing the attention of other officials on it in order to make it the basis of their actions.

Officials monitor the press for information about their external environment, particularly about the world and public opinion. Their reliance on the press gives other officials a stake in manipulating what information they get through the news.

Information About the World

A classic illustration of officials' use of the press to disseminate information that implied acceptance of their policy preferences occurred during the Formosa Straits crisis of 1954–55. Gradual redefinition of the Eisenhower Administration's China policy produced a spate of stories with contradictory assessments of Chinese intentions. *The New York Times* of March 26, 1955, ran a three-column right-hand lead headlined, "U.S. Expects Chinese Reds to Attack Isles in April; Weighs All-Out Defense." Under it defense correspondent Anthony Leviero reported a "significant change" in American planning, grounded "in the belief Red China will begin its campaign to capture Quemoy and Matsu about the middle of April."[5] Leviero pictured military advisers as urging the President to intervene on an "all-out" basis in the event of attack. Three days later in the same position on page one the *Times* ran another three-column headline, "Eisenhower Sees No War Now Over Chinese Isles." Again failing to identify his source by name, White House reporter Bill Lawrence wrote,

> The President did not like stories published over the weekend that said his military advisers were satisfied that such attacks might begin by mid-April. . . . The White House believes it is aware of the source of these stories and treats them as "parochial," representing the view of only one man or one service. . . . One statement published last weekend was that the President was being urged to use atomic weapons, if necessary, to destroy Red China's industrial potential and thus end its expansionist tendencies. This view did not please the President either.[6]

What Chinese leaders could have taken for a veiled threat turned out to be a figment of a split developing within the Joint Chiefs of Staff over employment of tactical nuclear weapons in defense of the offshore islands. The first story originated from a background dinner addressed by Chief of Naval Operations Robert B. Carney, who was pushing his analysis of Chinese intentions. At that time the United States had no means other than nuclear for blunting a potential invasion. If his definition of the situation were to prevail, then Admiral Carney might succeed in committing the Administration to the use of tactical nuclears in the present situation—a policy pre-

[5] *The New York Times*, March 26, 1955, p. 1.
[6] *The New York Times*, March 29, 1955, pp. 1–2.

cedent that would be difficult to overturn in any future confrontation. White House press secretary James Hagerty was the source of
the second briefing. President Eisenhower makes its purpose plain in
his notes:

> Lately there has been a very definite feeling among the members
> of the Cabinet, often openly expressed, that within a month we will
> actually be fighting in the Formosa Straits. It is, of course, entirely
> possible that this is true, because the Red Chinese appear to be com-
> pletely reckless, arrogant, possibly overconfident, and completely in-
> different as to human losses.
>
> Nevertheless, I believe hostilities are not so imminent as is in-
> dicated by the forebodings of a number of my associates. It is clear
> that this gloomy outlook has been communicated to others because a
> number of articles in the papers state that the Administration is rather
> expecting hostilities within a month.[7]

The need to pass information via the press becomes particularly
acute in the field. As John Kenneth Galbraith, one-time Ambassador
to India, attests in the affidavit filed in U.S. *v.* Ellsberg, "I found it
easier to bring my views to bear on the President of the United States
by way of *The Washington Post* and its New Delhi correspondent
than by way of the State Department."[8]

Information About Public Opinion

Especially important among the imponderables in the official's
calculus is the state of public opinion. What the public—or some key
segment of it—wants is the subject of considerable argument in most
official debates. Molding other officials' perceptions of public opinion in order to affect governmental outcomes can involve several different uses of the news. The news itself may influence public opinion
and, thus indirectly, the perceptions that officials have of it. Moreover, what news stories say about public opinion can directly affect
officials' perceptions. Finally, because of the difficulty of ascertain-
ing public opinion on any given issue, officials rely on the opinions
of commentators and editorial writers for a "quick reading of the
public mind." As a consequence, the press not only shapes and rep-

[7]Dwight D. Eisenhower, *Mandate for Change* (New York: Doubleday, 1963),
pp. 478–479. Further details are in Sherman Adams, *Firsthand Report* (New York:
Harper, 1961), p. 133.
[8]John Kenneth Galbraith, affidavit filed in *U.S. v. Ellsberg*, quoted in *The
Washington Post*, June 26, 1972, p. A-15.

resents public opinion but also *is* public opinion in the eyes of officials. Stimulating public reaction, disclosing poll results, and trying to persuade opinion-makers in the press are all commonplace in an effort to impress other officials that the public favors a particular course of action during the formative states of policy development.

Senior officials float trial balloons for the purpose of testing public and Congressional sentiment on a policy issue before committing themselves overtly to a stand. While the Kennedy Administration was drafting the Civil Rights Act of 1965, for instance, a Justice Department aide recalls that "Administration spokesmen—though generally careful not to be identified by name or even by agency—kept key reporters rather fully advised on Administration thinking." In particular, Deputy Attorney General Nicholas Katzenbach served as a major source for stories by *New York Times* reporter Anthony Lewis during the period.[9]

Inside Dope

Given their uncertainty about the world outside, officials inside the government often take their cues on what policy stand to adopt from other officials around them. Their need to adjust themselves in relation to other officials often indicates their analyses of the external environment, not the reverse. Even when their policy preferences do rest on their understanding of the world outside, translating these preferences into governmental action requires a thorough grasp of the world inside the government. In particular, officials need to know what their boss wants, who has power, and "who's got the action."

What the Boss Wants   Officials at all levels of government depend to some extent upon their immediate superiors for career advancement. Giving the boss what he wants, or at least avoiding the appearance of insubordination, is a bureaucratic way of life. Conversely, the boss has an interest in letting subordinates know what he wants.

Because of his constitutional authority, if not his power, the President is the senior official whose preferences matter most to bureaucrats. Not many bureaucrats work for the President, but many

---

[9]David Filvaroff, "Origins of the Civil Rights Act" (mimeo.), Institute of Politics, Kennedy School of Government, Harvard University, pp. 16–17.

have to pay attention to him. The importance of the President's preferences gives rise to a variety of maneuvers.

1. *Issuing a 'hunting license.'* To obtain the outcome he desires from the policy process, a President first must find subordinates who want to do what he wants and then enable them to begin work. What they require of him is a "hunting license," a mandate to act in his behalf, to invoke his name in order to persuade reluctant colleagues to go along. Publicity implies commitment. It means alerting outsiders with a stake in having that commitment kept. It means putting his reputation on the line.

But public commitments run the risk of premature opposition, of foreclosing options, and sometimes even of successful defiance from below. A prudent President may prefer to avoid locking himself in. Harry Truman, in defending his ban on direct quotation of Presidential press conferences, stated it this way:

> The idea of a press conference is to find out what the President thinks about pending matters, but it must be obvious that he should not be quoted directly on every question. That could often change an answer from an expression of opinion to a final commitment. This would serve no useful purpose, for in order to avoid commitment on matters still pending, the President would be reluctant to answer or even suggest a clue that might reveal his line of thought.[10]

To the extent that he dare not offer formal commitment to a course of action, a President must resort to veiled indications, which, while making commitment more ambiguous and hence subject to avoidance, provide minimal license for action to those who want to act. When Lyndon Johnson, for example, wanted to curb State Department promotion of the multilateral force (MLF) in December 1964, he not only had a memorandum to that effect drafted for circulation within the government, but also showed a copy of it to James Reston of the *Times*, who published selections practically verbatim in a right-hand lead on December 21.[11] Unlike an internal memorandum with limited circulation inside the Executive Branch, a press clipping could be cited as proof of the President's wishes by opponents of the MLF on both sides of the Potomac and the Atlantic.

[10]Truman, *Memoirs, I: Year of Decisions* (New York: Signet, 1955), p. 61.
[11]*The New York Times*, December 21, 1964, p. 1. Further details are in Philip Geyelin, *Lyndon B. Johnson and the World* (New York: Praeger, 1966), pp. 174–176.

2. *Eliciting commitment from above.* Mirroring the need of a senior official to demonstrate commitment in order for subordinates to act is the desire of the subordinate to elicit that commitment. The news thus serves as a means of communicating upward instead of down. Thus, the "theologians" in the State Department, pressing for the MLF, succeeded in inserting a line into a speech President Kennedy delivered to the Canadian parliament in May 1961 that the United States was looking toward "the possibility of eventually establishing a NATO seaborne force which would be truly multilateral in ownership and control, if this should be desired and found feasible by our allies. . . . "[12] In briefings for the press, they saw to it that this line was not ignored, thereby giving themselves a go-ahead to sell their plans abroad.

Subordinates can also prod their boss by making information public which makes it harder for him not to act. In the months prior to Diem's overthrow, for instance, many "inspired" stories emanating from Saigon signified the outbreak of a long-simmering attempt to reform the South Vietnamese regime. Upon taking over as ambassador in Saigon, Henry Cabot Lodge began feeding stories to American correspondents there, among them David Halberstam of the *Times* and Neil Sheehan of Associated Press, in part to push Diem into instituting reforms and in part to prod Washington into withholding support from the regime if Diem remained unmoved. "The leak," argued Lodge, "is the prerogative of the ambassador. It is one of my weapons for doing this job."[13] It is also in the arsenal of staff members on Capitol Hill trying to get reluctant Congressmen or committees to take action.[14]

3. *Announcing a decision.* Announcing a decision can influence subordinates' behavior even more than publicizing a tentative policy preference. Publicity may not guarantee their compliance, but it greatly enhances the prospects. A President often finds it effective to tell the press what he has decided in order to ensure that officials get the word quickly, and to tell them openly through press confer-

---

[12]U.S., Department of State, *Bulletin* 44, 1145 (June 5, 1961): 841.

[13]John Mecklin, *Mission in Torment* (Garden City, N.Y.: Doubleday, 1965), p. 223. Cf., Roger Hilsman, *To Move a Nation* (Garden City, N.Y.: Doubleday, 1967), p. 514.

[14]Clark Mollenhoff, *Washington Cover-up* (New York: Doubleday, 1962), pp. 116–119.

ences and press releases in order to demonstrate that his mind is made up. Such disclosures are quite often part of a formal governmental decision.

Because publicity makes execution more likely, officials whose policy goals are advanced have an incentive to put Presidential decisions on the record. They sometimes plant questions at press conferences to that end, as in the case of President Johnson's appointment of Nicholas Katzenbach to be Under Secretary of State in 1966.[15]

4. *Promulgating a policy preference as if it were a decision.* Issuing hunting licenses and announcing decisions to get subordinates moving are maneuvers available to senior officials other than the President. Some actions, however, he and he alone can authorize. The need for Presidential authorization gives rise to a maneuver which a politically independent senior official may attempt, which is to promulgate policy on his own initiative as if it were the product of Presidential decision in the hope that he won't be reversed. General Douglas MacArthur frequently indulged in such tactics. On one occasion, when he became impatient with Washington's hesitancy in getting negotiations on a peace treaty underway with Japan, he called a press conference in Tokyo and, to the dismay of officials back home, simply announced, "The time has now approached that we must talk peace with Japan."[16] On another, he publicly called for enemy surrender in Korea at the very time the Truman Administration was seeking to negotiate a ceasefire.[17] It was this act that precipitated the General's dismissal.

Enjoying the President's support can facilitate such maneuvers. As Ambassador to India, John Kenneth Galbraith was in this position:

> I had a huge press conference at which I announced the changes which I am hoping to put into effect in our technical assistance program—concentration on fewer fields, on fewer agricultural institutions, with fewer people in New Delhi. I needed some news and one of the best ways of getting the policy is to proclaim it. Washington

[15]Hugh Sidey, *A Very Personal Presidency* (New York: Atheneum, 1968), pp. 188–189.
[16]Martin E. Weinstein, *Japan's Postwar Defense Policy, 1947–1968* (New York: Columbia University Press, 1971), p. 14.
[17]Neustadt, *Presidential Power*, p. 20.

will be surprised and may wonder which part of the bureaucracy there authorized the change. However, no one will challenge it.[18]

When the President's stand is unclear, interpreting his words for reporters on a not-for-attribution basis may accomplish similar ends. After President Johnson's speech of March 31, 1968 announcing that he would not seek reelection, Defense Secretary Clark Clifford did just that in imposing limits on American involvement in Vietnam and trying to reverse the policy of escalation. Justifying his actions in the President's own words and implying that they represented Administration policy, Clifford unilaterally set a ceiling of 549,500 on U.S. forces in South Vietnam. He publicly refuted arguments for a resumption of the bombing in North Vietnam north of the Twentieth Parallel. Again and again he sounded optimistic notes about the peace talks being conducted in Paris. "[W]hile scrupulously refraining from burrowing under the ground on which the President presently stood," writes an aide, "Clark Clifford consistently and skillfully moved in public to occupy the ground the President had not yet reached."[19] Like the young women who send premature wedding announcements to society editors, officials can sometimes use the news successfully to create a fait accompli.

Who Has Power   Power, like beauty, is in the eye of the beholder. Presidential power, as Neustadt employs this concept, depends crucially on the perceptions of other players in the political system.[20] It rests ultimately on the expectations of those upon whom he must rely for execution of his decisions that unacceptable costs will accrue to them if they fail to comply with his wishes. Estimations of his will and skill in getting others to do what he wants them to do, his "professional reputation," are important to any official, not just the President. Officials' assertions to reporters about their success in having their way, their intimations about their closeness to the President, and their revelations to show they are in the know involve more than egomania; they are the building blocks of reputation.

In 1934, for instance, President Franklin Rosevelt appointed

---

[18]John Kenneth Galbraith, *Ambassador's Journal* (Boston: Houghton Mifflin, 1969), pp. 206–207. Copyright © 1969 by John Kenneth Galbraith. Reprinted by permission of Houghton Mifflin Company. Cf., pp. 328–351.

[19]Phil G. Goulding, *Confirm or Deny* (New York: Harper and Row, 1970), p. 329.

[20]Neustadt, *Presidential Power*, chap. 4.

Donald Richberg to chair both the Executive Council and the National Emergency Council, two Cabinet-level committees dealing with domestic affairs. When the two bodies were consolidated in October, *The New York Times* carried a story describing Richberg as the Assistant President and bearing the headline, "Richberg Put Over Cabinet in New Emergency Council . . . Now No. 1 Man."[21] According to Interior Secretary Harold Ickes, many attributed the *Times* piece to Richberg's staff.[22] The President sought to allay Cabinet pique by dismissing Richberg as no more than "an exalted messenger boy." He had his press secretary get in touch with *Times* correspondent Arthur Krock and tell him "that this kind of thing is not only a lie but that it is a deception and a fraud on the public."[23]

Palace politics can be endlessly intriguing. As George Reedy, who worked in the Johnson White House, writes,

> The inexperienced courtier may make the mistake of using his press contacts . . . to secure favorable mention of his name in public. But the wilier practitioners of the art of palace knife-fighting take a different tack. They seek to feature their competitors' names in a context which will displease the man who holds the real power. The reverse-thrust technique is somewhat more complex than it appears at first glance. It is not inconceivable, for example, that a newspaper story speculating on the promotion of an assistant to higher office may be the death knell of that assistant's government career.[24]

Presidents can conspire, too. While assuming public responsibility for the Bay of Pigs debacle, for instance, President Kennedy privately put the blame on the Joint Chiefs of Staff, who had given *pro forma* endorsement to the CIA plan. *Times* columnist Arthur Krock recalls, "The President said he had 'lost confidence' in the Chiefs of Staff. When I asked him if I could publish that on my own responsibility, he agreed."[25]

[21]Arthur Schlesinger, Jr., *The Coming of the New Deal* (Boston: Houghton Mifflin, 1958), p. 546.
[22]*The Secret Diary of Harold L. Ickes* (New York: Simon and Schuster, 1954), Vol. I, pp. 220–221.
[23]Schlesinger, *The Coming of the New Deal*, p. 546.
[24]George Reedy, *The Twilight of the Presidency* (New York: World, 1970), pp. 90–91.
[25]Arthur Krock, *Memoirs* (New York: Funk and Wagnalls, 1968), p. 371.

'Who's Got the Action' Decisions within the government do not occur at random. Constitutional and legal authority and custom all structure who may take action, attend meetings, even read internal documents. Often, where officials look for clear lines of responsibility they find only ambiguity. Charters are then a matter of choice. This is frequently the case inside the White House. Whenever an issue comes up for decision, the President delegates to one of his staff the task of channeling information and options to him. Knowing "who's got the action" is a prerequisite for exerting influence over a President's decision.

If they want to solicit information and options—and it is not always the case—those who have got the action must publicize the fact. They may do so through the press. In announcing his appointment of McGeorge Bundy as Special Assistant for National Security Affairs, for example, President-elect Kennedy simply issued a press release detailing the responsibilities of the new post.[26] Promulgating job description by press release has its limitations, however. A companion press release abolishing the Operations Control Board of the National Security Council did not delegate to the Secretary of State the legal authority he required in order to control operations. The press release did not supersede a standing executive order, and could be ignored by other agencies.[27]

Other Maneuvers in the Press

There is more to politics than persuasion. Besides manipulating the information upon which decisions are premised, officials use the press to alter the ways in which decisions are made.

1. *Getting other officials involved.* On many issues, law and custom mandate who must become involved in a policy dispute. On most issues for most officials, however, involvement is a matter of choice. Fighting losing battles does not enhance a bureaucrat's reputation. Even fighting winning battles depletes time and energy, resources not without limit. Press maneuvers can be employed to get officials into the game, or to keep them on the sidelines. What observers may mistake for a trial balloon is frequently a premature disclosure of a policy option—or a deliberately distorted version of it—

---

[26]Henry Jackson (ed.), *The National Security Council* (New York: Praeger, 1965), pp. 302–303.
[27]Ibid., pp. 304–305.

designed to kill it off by arousing opponents before the arguments in its favor are fully articulated or its potential supporters mobilized.

A 1958 attempt to transfer a team of rocket experts led by Wernher von Braun from the Army to the newly chartered National Aeronautics and Space Administration prompted just such a disclosure. Under the terms of the chartering legislation no Congressional assent would be required if the transfer took place before January 1. Anticipating that White House approval for the shift would come the next morning and aware of the protective attitudes that Congressional committees adopt towards agencies in their purview, the director of the Army program, General John B. Medaris, plotted his strategy. He ruled out a direct appeal to the President over the heads of immediate superiors: "If we had done so, discipline would have demanded that the offender be sacrificed, regardless of the justice of his cause." Instead, he reasoned,

> I had one particular friend in the press, whom I had found over the years to be honest, reliable, objective, patriotic, and thoroughly dependable. He was Mark Watson of *The Baltimore Sun*. . . . I laid the whole situation before Mark and asked his opinion. If he had told me it should be let alone, I would have heeded his advice. However, he too recognized the gravity and essential unfairness of the situation, and agreed that the only proper thing to do was to make sure that the President knew that this was a highly controversial matter.[28] Almost immediately press representatives began to call the White House for comment. In other places, the press sought out important members of Congress and asked their views. Some of these Congressmen sent messages to the White House and at least one prominent Senator dispatched a telegram. Our point was made.[29]

2. *Obtaining a change of venue.* Instead of holding a hearing in order to influence a decision to be made elsewhere, the committee could have gone further and introduced legislation to bar the transfer. Such action entails more than merely getting other officials involved. It moves the locus of decision-making out of the Executive Branch up to Capitol Hill, where it is susceptible to an entirely different array of procedures, pressures, and personalities. More generally, officials losing a fight in one decision-making arena, say, inside

---

[28]John B. Medaris, *Countdown for Decision* (New York: G. P. Putnam's Sons, 1960), p. 246.
[29]Ibid., p. 247.

their own department, attempt to shift it to another, most often the White House or Capitol Hill, by publicizing their plight. This maneuver is especially prevalent during budget preparation at the Defense Department when cutbacks in procurement are at issue. Whenever agreement is unattainable within the Defense Department, the Office of Secretary of Defense may raise the issue in the White House, whereupon the military service may seek to reinstate the cut before a Congressional committee. The Navy adopted this maneuver in 1949 after President Truman backed Defense Secretary Louis Johnson's rejection of a new aircraft carrier requested in its 1950 budget submission. Once the hearings began, the Navy launched a campaign of disclosures, the so-called "revolt of the admirals" inspired by Admiral Arleigh Burke, to win approval for its program.[30]

3. *Changing the rules of the game.* Many procedures followed in the policy process are not codified and hence are subject to alteration. But changes in the rules of the game can stimulate intense opposition among officials normally not inclined to talk to reporters. The internal deliberations of the Supreme Court, for instance, are almost never made public. Traditionally, too, the Chief Justice assigns the task of writing the opinion of the Court only in cases when he votes with the majority. When his view is in the minority, he routinely allows the senior Justice on the majority to make the assignment. When Chief Justice Warren Burger reversed this tradition in 1972, a law clerk disclosed the change to a *Washington Post* reporter covering the Court.[31] The breach of silence seemed symbolically equivalent both as a break with the Court's past rules of the game and [as] a threat to the traditional process of obtaining an internal consensus.

4. *Triggering outside intervention.* Many agencies have constituencies vitally interested in a narrow range of issues which officials can mobilize in a policy fight. To trigger intervention by those outside the U.S. government, officials pass the word to reporters, particularly those in the trade press and on specialized journals.

In the foreign policy area, officials of foreign governments are important outsiders capable of intervening in behalf of their allies

---

[30]Walter Millis, *Arms and the State* (New York: The Twentieth Century Fund, 1958), pp. 241–242. Cf., Jack Raymond, *Power at the Pentagon* (New York: Harper & Row, 1964), pp. 198–201.

[31]*The Washington Post*, July 4, 1972, p. 1.

inside Washington. When foreigners are the target, officials must be circumspect in disclosing information, lest they leave themselves open to the charge of damaging national security. In March 1961, for example, a task force headed by former Secretary of State Dean Acheson proposed strengthening NATO's conventional forces to meet a conventional attack in Europe with a purely conventional response, a shift away from reliance on U.S. Air Force bombers. When Secretary of State Rusk sent a memorandum to Secretary of Defense McNamara discussing changes in NATO deployments, Air Force officers disclosed a distorted version of the memorandum, one calculated to upset already uneasy Europeans.[32]

5. *Wooing allies for the future.* The readiness of allies outside the government to intervene is a negotiable asset in policy disputes. Publicizing who won and who lost and assessing blame by letting onlookers know that he has "fought the good fight" and his opponents have not helps an official to woo allies for the future and alienate the affections of rivals' constituencies. A spate of self-serving disclosures after the Cuban missile crisis in 1963 came from a variety of insiders claiming responsibility for the outcome and trying to show the proper mix of toughness and restraint. During the crisis preparations for the aftermath had proceeded *pari passu* with debate on the options. Even after the President had decided on a blockade, the Joint Chiefs of Staff continued to push for either an air strike or an invasion. "It was clear," says Roger Hilsman, "that some of the memoranda being written were not so much to present this or that case to the President—since he had already heard them all—but to build a record. If something went wrong, many of these papers would obviously begin to leak."[33]

6. *Keeping reporters obligated.* Reporters are themselves important allies. Their favorable treatment of information can aid an official's cause at some future date. Dispensing "exclusives" to a reporter increases the likelihood of such treatment because the exclusive, or "scoop," the story he and only he obtains, enhances a reporter's reputation among his colleagues. One man's leak is the other's exclusive. Keeping reporters in their debt is a subsidiary motivation in most officials' disclosures.

[32] *The New York Times*, March 24, 1968, p. 9. Cf., Hilsman, *To Move a Nation*, p. 8.
[33] Hilsman, *To Move a Nation*, p. 205.

How Information Makes the News

Instrumental concerns dominate the relations of the men who govern with the men who write about them. These relations are a reflection of operating need. That need is not idiosyncratic but organizational in origin. It is intrinsic to the policy process in Washington and elsewhere. Officials have incentives to tell reporters what they want them to know and nothing more.

From the array of purposes elaborated above, it is clear that the incentives are more varied and more compelling in Washington than in London. The American governmental system gives greater scope to the tactical use of the press than does the British system.

Another inference from the catalogue of press maneuvers is that the way information gets to reporters is a function of its purpose. News management encompasses more than just keeping secrets a secret. Officials want to disclose the information they want, when they want, and in the way they want. Getting out the message they want to deliver to the audience they want to reach poses two choices: where to put the message and how to get it there.

The Medium for the Message

The target audience for many press maneuvers is not the general public, but attentive elites in and around Washington, especially bureaucrats and Congressmen. That audience pays more attention to newspapers than to other media. The evening news shows on network television may provide the general public with the latest word on public affairs, but work schedules effectively impose a blackout for officials. A handful of them receive news summaries prepared by their staffs, more listen to the radio while driving to and from work, but the vast majority get their news from newspapers. In Washington . . . , nearly everybody reads the *Post* and the *Times*.

Two other characteristics of newspapers as a medium, permanence and precision, make them more effective than television for transmitting intragovernmental messages. The words are there on paper to be shown to others, filed away and retrieved. As for precision, reportorial inaccuracy may matter less than audience misperception.

Most important of all in favor of using newspapers over television is the accessibility of newspapermen to many officials. Not all the news media position their reporters where officials can get at them. Television newsmen cover few beats around Washington. They tend to operate like general assignment reporters, responding to news initially reported by the wire services or other news organizations. Moreover, the "newshole," the time or space available for news stories, imposes far greater restriction on television than on newspapers. Only a handful of senior officials can get coverage for what they have to say; lesser functionaries must get to a newspaperman if they are to make the news.

Alternative Channels to the Press: To Leak or Not to Leak

How the official gets word to reporters also depends on who he, the official, is. Three routine channels exist: the press release, the press conference, and the background briefing. Use of these channels, though, is virtually the exclusive prerogative of senior officials and public information officers. Lesser officials can issue their own press release or hold their own press conference and get reporters to pay attention to them only if they intend to quit, and doing so may well be tantamount to retirement. Instead, they must resort to a fourth channel, the leak.

A leak, as used here, differs in three respects from a background briefing. First, the official deals with reporters as individuals, never in a group. Most often, he discloses his information on an exclusive basis. Secondly, the contact is nonroutine and initiated by the official. Some background briefings are held on a regular basis at the instigation of the reporters themselves, meeting as a group over breakfast or dinner. Above all, cloaking the identity of the source of the information and even obscuring the fact that it became available through a leak are critical to tactical success. This is not always the case with backgrounders, as evidenced by many of Henry Kissinger's sessions in the Nixon Administration or the weekly backgrounders by Secretaries McNamara and Rusk in the Johnson Administration. Officials will adopt the expedients of embargoing what they say until they can establish an alibi by leaving town or employing an intermediary such as a friendly Congressman or a Ralph Nader to reach reporters discreetly.

Senior officials, too, find it essential to leak information to the press. When they are at odds with the Administration, few care to risk open insubordination. From Douglas MacArthur to Walter Hickel, the precedents are all too clear. The fear of reprisal forces official opposition underground. Dissenters must leak; they dare not do otherwise.

Even when he is hewing to the Administration line, a senior official can see advantages in using a covert channel to get information to reporters. In informational press maneuvers, he faces three operating dilemmas.

First is his desire to shape the context in which other officials and the public view an issue without revealing that he is doing so and thereby prejudicing his audience against the effort. What might smack of partisan arguments coming from an official's own lips may seem like disinterested observations in a newsman's story.

Second is the dilemma inherent in having to address a multiplicity of audiences simultaneously—wanting to tell one audience what he knows the other will not like to hear him say.

Third is the dilemma of policy innovation: the incompatibility between providing firm commitments to subordinates as a stimulus to change and avoiding such commitments lest they foreclose his options.

The frequency with which these dilemmas recur in policy-making explains the heavy traffic in covert channels by senior officials acting in accordance with Administration policy. As a consequence, most unattributed disclosures in the news are not leaks from below deck, but semaphore signals from the bridge.

The Struggle to Control Disclosures

The threat of leaks invites retaliation. Every recent President has tried to shut off the flow of disclosures. But as one aide to President Johnson puts it, "Of course, the people at 1600 Pennsylvania Avenue are not really worried about all leaks—only those that originate outside the White House."[34] In a broader sense, officials at the top of every government agency try to centralize control over the disclosure of information as a means of determining policy outcomes. It is through the efforts of most senior officials to exercise this control—and of

[34]George E. Reedy, "Moynihan's Scholarly Tantrum," *More* 1, 1 (September 1971): 6.

subordinates to circumvent it—that newsmaking has its most profound impact on the policy process.

Superiors have introduced a variety of tactics in order to seal leaks.

They have tried jawboning. President Eisenhower once confided in a Congressman the steps he intended to take to achieve a no-leak administration. Word quickly passed to columnist Arthur Krock, who commented, "The fact that this report of the President's attitude is in itself a leak suggests how difficult of attainment the goal will be."[35] They also have taken reprisals against reporters who accept information from dissident subordinates. They have withheld favors ranging from exclusives to admittance to briefings. They have criticized offenders and complained to their editors. They have harassed them with FBI investigations.[36]

They have sought to monitor contacts by requiring subordinates either to obtain prior permission to talk to newsmen or to report all conversations at which public information personnel are not present.[37] They have circulated memoranda warning dissidents to keep their expressions of opposition within proper channels, with the usual result of having their own memoranda leak to the press.[38] They have required advance clearance for texts of any public statements.[39]

They have singled out offenders as object lessons for their colleagues. Prosecuting them for violation of criminal statutes or imposing administrative sanction is unnecessary. A simple notation in personnel files can suffice to retard advancement. This seems to have occurred in the case of two Air Force officers suspected of leaking the Rusk-McNamara memorandum on NATO deployments.[40] Dismissals are rare but not unknown. General Douglas MacArthur and Dean Acheson are among those fired for unauthorized disclosures.[41]

But more subtle pressures are the rule. Calling in the FBI to

[35]Arthur Krock, *In the Nation* (New York: McGraw-Hill, 1966), p. 219.

[36]Hanson W. Baldwin, "Managed News: Our Peacetime Censorship," *Atlantic Monthly*, 211, 4 (April 1963): 54. Cf., Alsop and Alsop, *The Reporter's Trade*, pp. 64–68; *The Washington Post*, July 9, 1971, p. A–1.

[37]U.S., Congress, House, Committee on Government Operations, Hearings, Government Information Plans and Policies, 88th Cong., 1st Sess., 1963, pp. 105–107, 122–124. Cf., *The Washington Post*, November 5, 1971, p. A–2.

[38]*The New York Times*, November 22, 1971, p. 1. Cf., Samuel P. Huntington, *The Common Defense* (New York: Columbia University Press, 1961), p. 305.

[39]Truman, *Memoirs, II: Years of Trial and Hope*, p. 167, 383. Cf., Raymond, *Power at the Pentagon*, pp. 176–181.

[40]*The New York Times*, March 24, 1968, p. 9.

[41]Neustadt, *Presidential Power*, p. 20n. Schlesinger, *The Coming of the New Deal*, p. 242.

track down the source of a leak, sometimes by means of lie detectors, can have a quieting effect.[42] A "persistent if less visible source of restraint" is described by ex-ambassador John Kenneth Galbraith:

> Anything that comes in over the press wires is scrutinized by the score or more people in Washington who are concerned in one capacity or other with that country. There is not much that will not strike someone as out of line even when the location of the line is known only to God. . . . This alert officer then tucks the clipping or tape in his pocket and at the next meeting with his Assistant Secretary, says, "Did you see, sir, what came out of Phnom Penh yesterday? Going a little far I think. . . . " In all organizations the cultivation of executive vanity is a considerable industry. The State Department is up to average. Officials are rather easily persuaded that their prerogatives are being prejudiced. Out goes a telegram of warning, "We note with some concern. . . . "[43]

Admonitions have little force without the threat of harsher reprisal to come, and in some circumstances that threat is not compelling. Sometimes commitment to a cause can overcome fear of the consequences. In 1934 a fight raged within the Agricultural Adjustment Administration over whether or not to permit collusion among firms in order to raise farm prices. The A.A.A.'s legal staff opposed the codes on antitrust grounds. One attorney explains his decision to disclose an economist's report critical of a meat-packing code which was awaiting final approval:

> I went right over to talk to Justice Brandeis about it and he said that if I thought it was worth my job to stop the code, why, go right ahead. He pointed out that if I did it, I would then automatically have to expect to be fired. But if I was willing to let the job go, why then, I might just as well do it if the code was that important. Well, at that time I didn't have to worry about the job so I went back to the department and gave [the Associated Press] the report.[44]

[42]Theodore C. Sorensen, *Kennedy* (New York: Harper and Row, 1965), p. 314. Cf., *The New York Times*, September 3–4, 1971, p. 1.

[43]John Kenneth Galbraith, "Why Diplomats Clam Up," in Louis Lyons (Ed.), *Reporting the News* (Cambridge: The Belknap Press of Harvard University, 1965), p. 377.

[44]William H. Riker, "The Firing of Pat Jackson," Inter-University Case Program No. 1 (mimeo.), pp. 7–8.

Even the risk of dismissal fails to hold a man like this in thrall. Strong beliefs brace weak knees. For the in-and-outer with a constituency back in the corporate or academic world, moreover, losing a job may mean gaining a reputation for taking righteous stands.

Other times, immediate superiors can shield career officials against reprisals from above. It was not until a year after the dropping of the code that the attorney lost his job. By then, the pro-code faction had gained the upper hand inside the A.A.A., and this disclosure along with others served as the pretext for purging the legal staff. Sympathetic superiors can provide protection from lesser sanctions as well. A few years after they were reprimanded, the two Air Force officers accused of leaking the Rusk-McNamara memorandum were publicly cleared by the Air Force General Nathan F. Twining, then chairman of the Joint Chiefs of Staff.[45] Even when formal charges are brought, a plea of overzealousness can mitigate punishment if the right man makes the appeal. In 1957 the Army court-martialed Colonel John C. Nickerson, Jr., for disclosing classified information about the Jupiter missile. The man in charge of the Army missile program, Dr. Wernher von Braun, testified in his behalf,

> The Jupiter involves several hundred million dollars of the taxpayer's money. One hundred percent security would mean no information for the public, no money for the Army, no Jupiter. . . . The ideal thing would be 100 percent security and all the money you want. But the world is not built that way. The Army has got to play the same game as the Air Force and the Navy.[46]

Despite a guilty plea, Nickerson got off lightly. As these cases suggest, being on the right side in a policy dispute affords protection from retaliation to subordinates.

It is the threat to restrict access to the "inner councils" that most inhibits talkative subordinates, particularly those most ardently committed to their policy preferences. Other sanctions have little demonstrable effect on officials, whether in-and-outers or career bureaucrats, so long as the danger to their careers seems remote. Exclusion, however, is a penalty at once easy for superiors to impose and hard for subordinates to bear. It is thus a common practice.

---

[45]*The New York Times*, March 24, 1968, p. 9.
[46]*The New York Times*, June 27, 1957, p. 8. Cf., Michael H. Armacost, *The Politics of Weapons Innovation* (New York: Columbia University Press, 1969), pp. 125–128; and Medaris, *Countdown for Decision*, pp. 124–133.

Among those excluded from Nixon Administration councils is the State Department. Secretary of State William P. Rogers himself had to pay a steep price for admission. "I had to pledge to the President personally that there would be no leaks from our department on the Peking and Moscow trips and the shift in monetary policy," Rogers acknowledges. "We had favored all these actions, but it would have been difficult to keep the secret if it had been known by more than a few. After the announcements were made, many of the people here were, of course, disappointed that they didn't know of them in advance. . . . But I breathed a sigh of relief when we passed the test of silence. That was what really counted."[47]

There is nothing unique about the Nixon Administration's attempts to exclude dissidents. Under President Johnson, the arena for many key decisions on the Vietnam War was a weekly luncheon attended by a handful of senior officials. "The Tuesday luncheons were where the really important issues regarding Vietnam were discussed in great detail," recalls Secretary of State Dean Rusk. "We were always talking about ways and things to do with the bombing. This was where the real decisions were made. And everyone there knew how to keep his mouth shut."[48] Among those kept out for most of 1965 was Vice President Hubert Humphrey.[49] In the Kennedy Administration, the barring of staff subordinates from the deliberations of ExCom during the first week of the Cuban missile crisis was aimed at sealing off potential leaks.[50]

The workings of the classification system can best be understood in terms of the bureaucratic politics of public disclosure. What began as a way of keeping information out of the hands of enemies abroad has become primarily a way of keeping it away from rivals at home. The apparatus for circulating information internally to those subordinates with a need to know can readily be used to cut off those whom senior officials feel a need to exclude. By routing

[47]Milton Viorst, "William Rogers Thinks Like Richard Nixon," *The New York Times*, February 27, 1972, Section VI, p. 30.

[48]John B. Henry, II, "March 1968: Continuity or Change?" (Senior thesis, Harvard University, Department of Government, April 1971).

[49]*The New York Times*, April 17, 1966, Section IV, p. 3.

[50]Schlesinger, *A Thousand Days*, p. 802. Also, the Kennedy, Johnson, and Nixon Administrations have all excluded intelligence panels like the Office of National Estimates from advance knowledge of sensitive options under consideration by the President for fear of leaks. [Chester L. Cooper, "The C.I.A. and Decision-Making," *Foreign Affairs* 50, 2 (January 1972): 225.]

documents around them, by barring them from crucial meetings, and by avoiding substantive discussions in their presence, senior officials can keep troublesome subordinates in the dark. Decision-making is moved out of the back room into the closet.

Both the quest for secrecy and the need for disclosure are intrinsic to a governmental process in which the test of a good policy is the support it can muster and maintain in and out of Washington. Disclosures are essential to win policy fights. The basic issue is who should control them. Any system that allocates this control to a small number of high officials gives those officials substantial influence over the outcomes of the policy process, influence which others in the government are bound to resist.

VII

Implementing Public Policy: Bureaucratic Problems

Much of the criticism leveled at bureaucracy in recent years has focused on what are seen as deficiencies in implementation. National policies initiated with high hopes and great fanfare have come to grief, allegedly because the organizations given responsibility for carrying them out have not been up to the job. This at least is the allegation frequently made by members of Congress and the White House staff, who of course have a vested interest in shifting the blame for failure from the policies they initiated to the bureaucrats who were unable to carry them out. It is equally possible that those policies were so poorly designed in the first place that they could not have been successfully implemented by any bureaucratic organization now in existence or capable of being devised.

But although some of the faultfinding can be dismissed as mere scapegoating by politicians trying to conceal their own shortcomings, there is clearly more to it than that. Large bureaucracies are indeed unwieldy and clumsy instruments for the achievement of social or economic objectives. And the policies they are charged with administering may not actually be appropriate solutions for the problems they address. Knowing the right course to take is as difficult in governmental decision-making as it is in personal decision-making. Some policies may actually compound the problems they are designed to solve. Moreover, as discussed on pp. 45–46, domestic programs in the United States are commonly implemented through a system of intergovernmental administration involving two and sometimes three levels of government. When policy is carried out through such a complex organizational network, unintended and even disastrous consequences are sometimes unavoidable.

I

In "Problems in Bureaucratic Communications," George Edwards calls attention to another obstacle to successful bureaucratic implementation: communication problems. When the top executives of an organization are obliged to transmit their orders through an elaborate bureaucratic structure, the chance is very great that messages will be distorted or misinterpreted. If the orders are too vague, they may encourage subordinates to go off in a variety of directions of their own choosing; if they are too specific, they may tie the hands of subordinates, who need to be free to adapt general directives to particular circumstances if their efforts are to be successful.

Also, because bureaucracies are very hierarchically structured organizations, it is difficult for their executives to get accurate information on what is happening in the field, where the impact of what an agency is doing is being felt, so that they can determine whether the organization is actually achieving its goals or merely spinning its wheels. Communication blockages may interfere with moving information up the chain of command, as well as transmitting policy directives from headquarters to the field. These problems have not been eliminated by the great advances that have been made in communication technology during recent years, although obviously these advances have made it easier for executives to transmit orders to their subordinates and to monitor compliance with these directives after they have been issued.

From the point of view of the public at large, the chief obstacle to satisfactory bureaucratic performance is the red tape that so often accompanies the administration of government programs. In "Red Tape: An Incurable Malady," Herbert Kaufman examines some of the reasons why there is so much public resentment against the elaborate bureaucratic procedures and requirements generally labeled red tape. Individuals who must deal with bureaucratic procedures regard them as time-consuming and expensive, diverting their own and their organizations' resources from more productive activity. In some cases, these bureaucratic procedures require private citizens and organizations to perform what seems to be contradictory actions— for example, to be nondiscriminatory in their hiring practices and yet keep very careful records of their employees' racial or ethnic characteristics.

Moreover, much of this regulatory rigmarole either is obsolete or does not apply to the person or organization at which it is directed. Even worse, it is imposed in behalf of programs that are widely considered ineffective—regulatory programs, for example, that are not achieving the consumer protection goals for which they were established. What is most often resented about such red tape is the delay it often entails, since in many instances the delay puts a heavy economic or psychological burden on a private citizen or organization waiting for the government to make a decision. Although, as Kaufman notes, red tape can often be explained or even defended as a necessary means of ensuring that government officials make the right decisions, its prevalence in organizational decision-making contributes heavily to the low regard in which bureaucratic performance is generally held.

II

In recent years some of the most severe criticism leveled at bureaucratic failures in implementation has been directed at the War on Poverty programs that were put in place during the Johnson administration in the 1960s. Neoconservatives use the disappointing experience with some of these programs to make the case that well-intentioned policies designed to help the poor seldom achieve a beneficial effect. Indeed, some neoconservatives argue that the way in which bureaucrats administer such programs often aggravates the problems they are designed to remedy.

However, in "Conquering Space and Poverty: Implementation as Success and Failure," Paul Schulman offers alternative explanations for the fact that the War on Poverty fell short of meeting the fond expectations of its sponsors. One factor to which he attaches particular importance is the government's failure to make an adequate commitment of fiscal resources to the antipoverty battle. In contrast, the space program won generous financial support at its inception as well as greatly increased funding in the years immediately thereafter—a much higher level of spending than the government provided for the antipoverty program.

Certain kinds of programs, Schulman argues, can only succeed if they are undertaken on a very large scale. In the case of programs devoted to such causes as space exploration, war on poverty, and urban transit, half-measures are doomed to failure from the outset. Thus a program like the War on Poverty may fail not because of any lack of skill on the part of the bureaucratic organization charged with implementing it, but because this organization is denied the necessary level of funding.

Criticism of the way in which bureaucratic organizations carry out public policy also focuses on the fact that a variety of agencies often seem to be doing the same or very similar things. It is commonly charged that such duplication and overlap represent a wasteful expenditure of public funds and often force private citizens and organizations to deal with a half-dozen government agencies that are working on the same problem. It is worth noting that such organizational redundancy tends to be tolerated in areas like national defense, where a consensus exists that the activities being carried on are essential to the national interest, but comes under bitter attack when it occurs in, for example, welfare programs, which enjoy much less public support and are even regarded by some as representing illegitimate governmental functions.

In Martin Landau's view, there is more to be said for such organizational redundancy than meets the eye. In "Redundancy, Rationality, and the Problem of Duplication and Overlap," he contends that such redundancy should be regarded not as a vice but as a virtue, since a governmental goal is more likely to be reached if a group of agencies rather than a single agency is relied on to achieve a particular result. What we need in public administration, Landau argues, is a system of organizations for delivering services or performing other tasks that is more reliable than any of its parts. Such a system is only attainable if we accept organizational redundancy as a principal feature. Paradoxically, however, the goal of all reorganization programs in the national government has always been to reduce or eliminate redundancy wherever possible. We pursue this goal in spite of the fact that any success we have in developing an administrative system that is "perfect" from the point of view of organization theory may increase the likelihood of failure in implementation, which is so often the source of public criticism of bureaucratic performance today.

23

Problems in Bureaucratic Communications

GEORGE C. EDWARDS, III

The first requirement for effective policy implementation is that those who are to implement a decision must know what they are supposed to do. Policy decisions and implementation orders must be transmitted to the appropriate personnel before they can be followed. Naturally, these communications need to be accurate, and they must be accurately perceived by implementors. Many obstacles lie in the path of the transmission of implementation communications, however, and these obstacles may hinder policy implementation, as we shall see below.

If policies are to be implemented properly, implementation directives must not only be received, but they must also be clear. If they are not, implementors will be confused about what they should do, and they will have discretion to impose their own views on the implementation of policies, views that may be different from those of their superiors. In . . . this chapter, the problems created by lack of clarity in implementation instructions are examined and explanations of why this ambiguity occurs are presented. . . .

Transmission

Before people can implement a decision, they must be aware that the decision has been made and an order to implement it issued. This

Excerpted by permission from *Implementing Public Policy* by George C. Edwards, III, pp. 17–21, 25–39. Copyright 1980 by Congressional Quarterly, Inc. Footnotes are renumbered.

is not always as straightforward a process as it may seem. Ignorance or misunderstanding of decisions frequently occurs. One of the numerous obstacles to transmitting implementation instructions is the disagreement of implementors with them. Disagreement over policies can lead to either outright blockage or distortion of communications as implementors exercise their inevitable discretion in handling general decisions and orders. Similar problems of distortion may arise as information passes through multiple layers of the bureaucratic hierarchy. The use of indirect means of communication and the absence of established channels of communication may also distort implementation instructions. Finally, the reception of communications may be hindered by implementors' selective perception and disinclination to know about a policy's requirements. Sometimes implementors attempt to ignore the obvious and try to guess at the "true" meaning of communications. As we illustrate the impact of these obstacles on effective communication, we will also see their consequences for policy implementation.

Executive Branch

Although most executive branches have highly developed lines of communication throughout the bureaucracy, this does not guarantee that communications will be transmitted successfully. The Bay of Pigs fiasco illustrates this point.

On April 17, 1961, a force of 1,200 Cuban refugees—recruited, trained, and supplied by the U.S. Central Intelligence Agency (CIA)—landed 90 miles south of Havana with the announced goal of overthrowing the communist-oriented regime of Fidel Castro. Within three days the "invasion" had been crushed, inflicting a disastrous blow to American prestige, not to mention that of the new president, John F. Kennedy. The CIA never told the leader of the brigade sent to invade Cuba that the president had ordered the soldiers to go to the mountains and fight a guerrilla war if the invasion failed. The CIA disregarded the president's order, which it thought might weaken the brigade's resolve to fight or encourage the brigade to go to the mountains too quickly.[1]

Sometimes aides and other officials ignore executive directives with which they disagree primarily to avoid embarrassment for their

---

[1]Haynes Johnson, *The Bay of Pigs* (New York: W. W. Norton & Co., 1964), pp. 68–69, 86, 224.

chief. Such orders are generally given in anger and without proper consultation. Our best examples come from the White House. After President Johnson had made the decision not to run for a second term, he fired an assistant secretary of agriculture for his support of Robert Kennedy's candidacy for the presidency. That evening Joseph Califano, one of Johnson's aides, told the resigning official to forget the whole thing.[2] President Kennedy once called Newton Minow, the chairman of the Federal Communications Commission, and told him to "do something" about the Huntley-Brinkley NBC nightly news, which had carried a long speech attacking the president. Fortunately, Minow did nothing.[3]

President Nixon especially liked to let off steam by issuing outrageous orders. At one time he instructed Secretary of State William Rogers to "fire everybody in Laos." He often told aides to "go after" reporters and once ordered that all reporters be barred from Air Force One. He also directed that a 24-hour surveillance be kept on a dissenting senator and that all State Department employees be administered lie detector tests to stop leaks. These and similar outbursts were ignored by H. R. Haldeman and other aides close to Nixon. They knew the president would view things differently when he calmed down.[4]

Disregard of directives given in anger, unlike other barriers to effective communication, usually have benefited presidents. Their close associates have provided them safe outlets for their frustrations and protected them from their worst instincts. One might even argue that President Nixon would have been better served if Haldeman had not been so responsive to his desires for political intelligence during the 1972 presidential campaign. It was this demand that led to Watergate.

In most instances, implementors have considerable discretion in interpreting their superiors' decisions and orders. Orders from the top are rarely specific. Personnel at each rung in the bureaucratic

---

[2]Joseph A. Califano, Jr., *A Presidential Nation* (New York: W. W. Norton & Co., 1975), pp. 44–45.

[3]David Wise, *The Politics of Lying: Government Deception, Secrecy, and Power* (New York: Vintage Books, 1973), pp. 370–371.

[4]William Safire, *Before the Fall: An Inside View of the Pre-Watergate White House* (New York: Doubleday & Co., 1975), pp. 112–113, 285–287, 353, 556–557; H. R. Haldeman, *The Ends of Power* (New York: Times Books, 1978), pp. 58–59, 111–112, 185–187; Raymond Price, *With Nixon* (New York: Viking Press, 1977), p. 29.

ladder must use their judgment to expand and develop them. Obviously, this process invites distortion of communications, and the further down in the bureaucracy implementation directives go, the greater the potential for distortion. Moreover, . . . subordinates do not always interpret the communications of superiors in a way that advances the goals of the original decisionmakers. Bureaucrats often use their discretion to further their personal interests and those of their agencies.[5] Interest groups also take advantage of the discretion granted bureaucrats by pushing for their own demands at intermediate and low decisionmaking levels.

It is for these reasons that observers of the federal bureaucracy often recommend that presidents and other high officials make every attempt to commit their directives to writing (in detail where possible), use personalized communications where appropriate, and show persistence in attempting to convey accurately their orders to those who actually implement policies.[6]

President Dwight Eisenhower liked to have National Security Council decisions announced at the council's meetings so that those who were to implement them (at least those at the top of the hierarchy) got the word in his presence. Political scientist Fred Greenstein points out that Eisenhower's "great personal effectiveness in face-to-face settings spurred identification with his purpose."[7] To reduce transmission problems, former CIA Director William Colby recommends that the president meet regularly with the CIA chief so the latter can keep in tune with the president's concerns regarding intelligence.[8]

[5]See, for example, George C. Edwards III and Ira Sharkansky, *The Policy Predicament: Making and Implementing Public Policy* (San Francisco: W. H. Freeman, 1978), chapter 5; Carl E. Van Horn, "Implementing CETA" (Paper delivered at the annual meeting of the Midwest Political Science Association, Chicago, Illinois, April-May 1976), p. 26.

[6]Hugh Heclo, *A Government of Strangers* (Washington, D.C.: Brookings Institution, 1977), pp. 206–207; Robert R. Sullivan, "The Role of the Presidency in Shaping Lower Level Policy-Making Processes," *Polity* 3 (Winter 1970): 211–212; Victor A. Thompson, *Modern Organization* (New York: Alfred A. Knopf, 1961), pp. 138–139; and Frederic V. Malek, *Washington's Hidden Tragedy: The Failure to Make Government Work* (New York: Free Press, 1978), p. 98.

[7]Fred I. Greenstein, "Presidential Activism Eisenhower Style: A Reassessment Based on Archival Evidence" (Paper delivered at the annual meeting of the Midwest Political Science Association, Chicago, Illinois, April 1979), p. 9.

[8]William Colby, *Honorable Men: My Life in the CIA* (New York: Simon & Schuster, 1978), p. 374.

In general, the more decentralized the implementation of a public policy, the less likely that it will be transmitted to its ultimate implementors accurately. Decentralization usually means that a decision must be communicated through several levels of authority before it reaches those who will carry it out. The more steps a communication must traverse from its original source, the weaker the signal that is ultimately received will be.[9] A president can tell a secretary of state to go to another country and deliver a policy pronouncement to its prime minister, or the Supreme Court can order a state legislature to be reapportioned, with little concern that their messages will not be accurately transmitted. But they cannot have the same confidence about messages aimed at caseworkers in a city welfare office or police officers walking their beats. The distance between the original source of the communication and the implementors is too great.

Many laws are implemented by persons in the private sector. Laws requiring gas station owners to sell gas on certain days to only certain motor vehicles (such as those with odd-numbered license plates) are a good example. While simple and highly visible policies such as this one may be easily transmitted through the press or by mailings, most policies implemented by the private sector are more complex and less visible. Thus, the transmission of these policy directives is more problematical.

According to one study, many realtors know little about open housing laws that prohibit discrimination in the sale or rental of housing.[10] Similarly, thousands of loan officers in banks, stores, and automobile dealerships are uninformed concerning consumer credit laws. The vastness of the credit bureaucracy causes problems in disseminating information to the public. Borrowers as well as lenders need to be aware of the law so that they will know if they have been denied credit illegally and what their legal remedies are.[11] Since most Americans use credit, the number of people involved in the transmission of credit information numbers into the tens of millions. Because the number of people is so great and the information is rel-

[9]See, for example, Daniel Katz and Robert L. Kahn, *The Social Psychology of Organizations* (New York: John Wiley & Sons, 1966), pp. 236–238.

[10]Alan H. Schechter, "Impacts of Open Housing Laws on Suburban Realtors," *Urban Affairs Quarterly* 8 (June 1973): 452.

[11]Joel F. Handler, *Social Movements and the Legal System: A Theory of Law Reform and Social Change* (New York: Academic Press, 1978).

atively complex for the average person, we cannot assume that it is accurately transmitted to the typical consumer.

At times, executives and their staff prefer *not* to transmit policy directives personally; they would rather get others to do their communications for them. President Johnson wanted Secretary of the Treasury Henry Fowler to apply "jawboning," or powerful persuasion, to try to lower interest rates. Because Fowler opposed such efforts, Johnson decided not to communicate his wishes to the secretary directly. Instead he called House Banking Committee Chairman Wright Patman, a supporter of "jawboning," and asked him to pressure Fowler.[12] Any time a step is added to the chain of communication, the potential for distortion is increased. Those who speak for others will have their own styles, their own views, and their own motivations. Not even presidents can depend upon other people to transmit directives exactly as they would desire.

In 1971 President Nixon employed a roundabout means of communication in an attempt to make the Federal Reserve Board more responsive to his wishes. He had aide Charles Colson leak to the press a "shot across the bow" of Arthur Burns, the board's chairman. The story was that the president's advisers were urging him to increase the size of the board—a threat to Burns—and that Burns was hypocritically asking for a raise while opposing raises for other federal employees. The fact that neither of these points was true (the president later had to deny them) undoubtedly influenced Nixon's choice of transmission channels.[13]

The technique of communicating indirectly through the press is a common one at all levels of government. Communicating through leaks in the press, however, invites even more message distortion than communicating through another individual. The press is under no obligation to aid the official providing the leak. It may alter the message to serve its own purposes, or it may distort the communication inadvertently. Moreover, because this mode of communication is so indirect, there is no guarantee that those at whom a message is aimed will receive it at all. Nor can the sender ensure that the recipient will understand the message's significance, even if it is received. Messages communicated through the press are usually nebulous to protect the

[12]Califano, *A Presidential Nation*, p. 207.
[13]Safire, *Before the Fall*, pp. 429–436.

sender's identity. If senders did not wish to remain anonymous, they would not use the press in the first place.

Some officials do not have personalities well suited to direct communication. According to former White House chief of staff H. R. Haldeman, Nixon attacked problems or persons from the side, often through subordinates when the "victim" was not looking.[14] Nixon aide William Safire adds that the president was reluctant to get on the phone and issue an order himself because he wanted to avoid the possibility of rejection.[15] . . .

Reception of Communications

As we noted earlier, the reception of messages by implementors is just as vital to implementation as relaying them. Selective perception, i.e., screening out information that is contrary to one's existing values and beliefs, can hinder public officials' understanding of the content of policies. Although the Supreme Court in 1962 prohibited religious exercises, even voluntary ones, in public schools, some local elites selectively perceived that the ruling referred only to mandatory prayers. Since they did not coerce anyone in their schools to participate in religious exercises, they disregarded the Court's decision. Most of them could not believe that the activities in their schools could be unconstitutional. Coupled with this selective perception was a disinclination to know about what "obviously doesn't affect us."[16]

In such situations officials may be unaware of court decisions that affect them. This is what one scholar found in his study of the communication of Supreme Court decisions on criminal rights. Prosecutors, defenders, judges, and police chiefs in small towns in Illinois and Massachusetts were often ignorant of the Court's decisions.[17] Another author found that even the most professional police departments he examined were unaware of information regarding their responsibilities for implementing decisions.[18] Two researchers dis-

[14]Haldeman, *Ends of Power*, p. 56.

[15]Safire, *Before the Fall*, pp. 619–620.

[16]Kenneth M. Dolbeare and Philip E. Hammond, *The School Prayer Decisions* (Chicago, Ill.: The University of Chicago Press, 1971).

[17]Stephen L. Wasby, *Small Town Police and the Supreme Court: Hearing the Word* (Lexington, Mass.: Lexington Books, 1976).

[18]Neal A. Milner, *The Court and Local Law Enforcement: The Impact of Miranda* (Beverly Hills, Cal.: Sage Publications, 1971).

covered a similar lack of understanding of Supreme Court decisions on prayers in the public schools among teachers, principals, school board members, and, to a lesser extent, school superintendents in the midwestern cities they studied. They also found a state deputy attorney general for education affairs who was ignorant of crucial decisions.[19]

Bureaucrats, in their efforts to interpret directives, are often guided by innuendos about policy directions and personnel and by the refusal of superiors to talk to certain people. In an attempt to determine what their superiors "really" intended, they may discount what seem to be clear proclamations.[20] For example, the attitudes of central administrators toward innovations in education provide a signal to participants in these projects "as to how seriously to take project goals and how hard they should work to achieve them."[21]

Clarity

If policies are to be implemented as those who enacted them intended, implementation directives must not only be received, but must also be clear. Often the instructions transmitted to implementors are vague and do not specify when or how a program is to be carried out. Lack of clarity provides implementors with leeway to give new meaning to policies, meaning that sometimes is contrary to the original intention of the law. This section begins with a discussion of the obstacles to effective implementation created by vague laws. We then discuss efforts to reduce implementors' discretion. The implementation difficulties created by ambiguous court decisions are also examined in this section. Ambiguity does not always hinder implementation, however. As we shall see, implementors need flexibility and can be hampered by overly specific instructions.

There are numerous reasons for lack of clarity in implementation directives. Among the factors we consider are the complexity of public policies, the desire not to irritate segments of the public, a lack of consensus on the goals of a policy, the problems in starting

---

[19]Dolbeare and Hammond, *School Prayer Decisions*, pp. 52, 75, 78, 79 and 83.

[20]Heclo, *Government of Strangers*, pp. 206–207.

[21]Milbrey W. McLaughlin, "Implementation as Mutual Adaptation: Change in Classroom Organization," in *Social Program Implementation*, eds. Walter Williams and Richard F. Elmore (New York: Academic Press, 1976), p. 170.

up a new policy, avoiding accountability for policies, and the nature of judicial decisionmaking.

Vague Laws

The phrase "maximum feasible participation" in the Economic Opportunity Act of 1964 was intended by those who drafted the act to mean that only citizens excluded from the political process were to receive benefits from the law. This original interpretation, however, was never clearly stated. The people running local community action programs interpreted the phrase to mean involving the poor in running the programs and in political activism, and they acted on the basis of this interpretation. The misunderstanding of "maximum feasible participation" was compounded by the fact that few persons in the administration or Congress knew what the architects of the policy intended the phrase to mean.[22]

Many federal programs provide grants to lower level jurisdictions, but the laws are frequently vague, contributing to a less-than-effective supervision of the expenditure of the funds. Title I of the Elementary and Secondary Education Act of 1965 established a program of grants to state education departments and through them to local school districts. The funds were intended to meet the "special needs of educationally deprived children"—not to supplant already existing resources reserved for the educationally deprived. The act, however, did not specify clearly who the "educationally deprived" were or what an acceptable program to meet their needs was. Many thought the law was intended to be a *general* aid bill under another name.

The U.S. Office of Education's initial guidelines on the expenditure of these funds by local school districts reflected this ambiguity. No wonder many local education agencies also viewed the funds as general aid and often spent them for materials or services that did not help educationally deprived children! It took several years for the Office of Education to tighten its regulations constraining local education agencies' allocation of Title I funds.[23] When it

[22]Daniel P. Moynihan, *Maximum Feasible Misunderstanding* (New York: Free Press, 1969), p. 87. See also John C. Donovan, *The Politics of Poverty*, 2d ed. (Indianapolis: The Bobbs-Merrill Co., 1973), p. 40; and James L. Sundquist, ed., *On Fighting Poverty* (New York: Basic Books, 1969), p. 29.

[23]Floyd E. Stoner, "Federal Auditors as Regulators: The Case of Title I of ESEA," in *The Policy Cycle*, eds. Judith V. May and Aaron B. Wildavsky (Beverly

did this, the federal funds did go to aid disadvantaged children more than in other federally funded education programs.[24]

Title V of the Elementary and Secondary Education Act was designed to "strengthen" state departments of education and improve educational programs. But "strengthen" is an ambiguous term and the relationships between educational programs and improved performance is not well understood. Moreover, the law contained no objective criteria by which to judge projects and did not tell the state departments how they ought to change. Consequently, little change has taken place.[25]

The Department of Health, Education and Welfare (HEW) and one of its subdivisions, the U.S. Office of Education, also had problems implementing Title VI of the 1964 Civil Rights Act. (As of May 7, 1980, all of HEW's educational programs were transferred to the new cabinet-level Department of Education.) The 1964 Civil Rights Act, which prohibited the provision of federal funds to programs that discriminated against citizens on the basis of race, color, or national origin, did not have a clear legislative history to provide explicit direction for administrators. Neither did the White House give implementors much help. HEW's guidelines regarding funding for school districts were considered insufficient at the Office of Education, which developed its own directives. Moreover, HEW did little to develop information programs to help communities understand federal policies.

Often the dissemination of information that occurred was the

Hills, Calif.: Sage Publications, 1978), pp. 202–204, 206, 208; Stoner, "Implementation of Federal Education Policy: Defining the Situation in Cities and Small Towns" (Paper delivered at the annual meeting of the Midwest Political Science Association, Chicago, Illinois, May 1975), pp. 8–9; Stephen K. Bailey and Edith K. Mosher, *ESEA: The Office of Education Administers a Law* (Syracuse, N.Y.: Syracuse University Press, 1968), p. 103; John F. Hughes and Anne O. Hughes, *Equal Education* (Bloomington, Ind.: Indiana University Press, 1972), pp. 33, 47, 50; and Milbrey W. McLaughlin, *Evaluation and Reform: The Elementary and Secondary Education Act of 1976/Title I* (Cambridge, Mass.: Ballinger Publishing Co., 1975), p. 18.

[24]Joel S. Berke and Michael W. Kirst, "Intergovernmental Relations: Conclusions and Recommendations," in *Federal Aid to Education: Who Benefits? Who Governs?*, eds. Joel S. Berke and Michael W. Kirst (Lexington, Mass.: Lexington, 1972), p. 401. For other examples of USOE guidelines confusing state and local education agencies, see p. 378.

[25]Jerome T. Murphy, *State Education Agencies and Discretionary Funds* (Lexington, Mass.: D.C. Heath & Co., 1971), pp. 8, 21–22, 25.

result of activities by the U.S. Commission on Civil Rights or private groups—institutions without program implementation responsibilities. Understandably, school officials in the South were uncertain about the procedures by which their compliance with Title VI would be reviewed. They were not alone in their confusion. Even Office of Education staff members were unable to use their agency's guidelines to evaluate compliance efforts.[26] When HEW finally developed specific administrative standards for determining compliance with the law, progress on school desegregation accelerated. The more precise were desegregation guidelines, the more desegregation took place.[27]

In 1966 Congress passed the Demonstration Cities and Metropolitan Development Act. The purpose of the Model Cities program, as the act came to be known, was to help revitalize America's urban areas. The act called for innovation, coordination, and citizen participation, but these vague terms were not clearly defined. Officials at the Department of Housing and Urban Development (HUD) who had to implement the law were uncertain what their goals should be. Furthermore, Congress showed little interest in the specifics of future guidelines when it passed the policy, and it did not follow up on the program carefully once it was under way.

Like the legislative branch, the executive branch paid little attention to the process of developing guidelines for the Model Cities program. The White House was more interested in which cities were selected for participation and in trying to obtain the cooperation of other departments whose support the new policy required. Under these conditions, it is no wonder that the guidelines sent from HUD's central office to regional officials were vague and often increased rather than reduced confusion at the local level.[28]

Let us examine the requirement that there be citizen participation in Model Cities projects. As two authors concluded, "It was

[26]Beryl A. Radin, *Implementation, Change, and the Federal Bureaucracy* (New York: Teachers' College Press, 1977), pp. 92, 103–105, 108–109, 134, 160–161.

[27]Harrell R. Rodgers, Jr. and Charles S. Bullock III, *Law and Social Change: Civil Rights Laws and Their Consequences* (New York: McGraw-Hill Book Co., 1972), p. 199. See also Charles S. Bullock III, "The Office for Civil Rights and Implementation of Desegregation Programs in Public Schools," *Policy Studies Journal* 8 (Special Issue No. 2, 1980): 606–607.

[28]Lawrence D. Brown and Bernard J. Frieden, "Guidelines and Goals in the Model Cities Program," *Policy Sciences* 7 (December 1976): 459–461, 470, 487. See also Judson L. James, "Federalism and the Model Cities Experiment," *Publius* 2 (Spring 1972): 69–94.

one thing for HUD to insist upon an 'organizational structure' for participation, but quite another to decide what kind of structure met the intent of the guidelines."[29] Did HUD expect cities to establish separate citizen boards? If so, what did "separate" mean? Was the citizen organization supposed to be subordinate or equal to the city government? If cities had a veto power over Community Development Agency (CDA) actions, did this include the comprehensive plan as a whole, individual projects, specific decisions within the projects, or all, some, or none of these?

Lower level officials faced similar problems in interpreting the national policy directive that citizen representatives be "acceptable" to residents of the model neighborhood. They were not told how to evaluate the "acceptability" of citizen leaders chosen by elections in which a turnout of more than 20 percent of the eligible voters was unusual. Nor did their instructions include information on what election techniques, such as mass meetings, literature, and television announcements, should be required to promote acceptability. They also faced, without higher level guidance, the question of what electoral units within a neighborhood were legitimate if various ethnic, racial, religious, and other interests were to feel represented adequately on the citizen boards.

The central office of HUD had endorsed the principle that citizens were to have staff and technical assistance made available to them, but the application of this guideline was not easy. It was not clear who might make legitimate claims on the staff's time or to whom the staff was directly accountable. How large should the staff be? What should its members be paid? Who should control the hiring of the staff? How should the staff be deployed? Should the citizen staff consult and share information with the CDA staff? Could the CDA head use the citizen staff? The unanswered questions were numerous. It is worth noting that Model Cities was relatively *precise* for an urban program.[30]

The provisions of the 1972 Water Pollution Control Act Amendments were very detailed, but the law still left room for considerable elaboration through administrative rulings and regula-

---

[29]Brown and Frieden, "Guidelines and Goals," pp. 470–471.
[30]Ibid. See also Rufus P. Browning, Dale Rodgers Marshall, and David H. Tabb, "Implementation and Political Change: Sources of Local Variations in Federal Social Programs," *Policy Studies Journal* 8 (Special Issue No. 2, 1980): 616–632.

tions. Federal officials in the Environmental Protection Agency (EPA) had substantial leeway in its implementation as they defined such phrases as "best practicable control technology currently available" and the "best available technology economically achievable" for controlling water pollution.[31]

A key aspect of the legislative intent of the act was set forth in Section 208, which contained detailed provisions regarding planning water pollution control. A subsection of Section 303 provided for a continuous planning process and required states to submit plans for this process. Congress was less interested in Section 303 than in Section 208, and the EPA was told to give Section 303 secondary priority. Nevertheless, the EPA made this subsection "the keystone of their entire water management and planning strategy." This originally obscure clause, according to one authority, became the primary tool for the implementation of the act. Moreover, EPA's interpretation of the clause expanded the authority the subsection originally delegated to the agency. Conversely, the implementation of Section 208 was delayed as long as possible by the EPA, despite Congress' great interest in its being rapidly and effectively implemented.[32]

The EPA's implementation of state program grants also resulted in a considerable change from the intent of Congress. It tried, in effect, to change one categorical grant program into four or five and thus give Washington maximum flexibility to reallocate funds where it felt the need was greatest. It did this by adding criteria that state programs must meet in order to receive grants, criteria that were not included in the act.[33]

This is not the only example of implementing agencies finding leeway in legislation designed to protect the environment. Following passage of the National Environmental Policy Act in 1969, the Army Corps of Engineers ordered its officials to prepare environmental impact statements for all its projects. The Soil Conservation Service (SCS) in the Department of Agriculture, interpreting the same law, mandated that environmental impact statements be prepared only

[31]Harvey Lieber, *Federalism and Clean Waters: The 1972 Water Pollution Control Act* (Lexington, Mass.: Lexington Books, 1975), pp. 95, 195; Robert J. Rauch, "The Federal Water Pollution Control Act Amendments of 1972: Ambiguity as a Control Device," *Harvard Journal of Legislation* 10 (June 1973): 572–585.

[32]Lieber, *Federalism and Clean Waters*, pp. 100–105.

[33]Ibid., p. 110.

for all *pending* projects. The Corps followed the law's intention to involve the public in a two-way communication on its projects. The SCS only instituted a one-way public information program and consulted with interested parties to a lesser degree. The Corps also took a much speedier and more aggressive role in demanding balanced environmental impact statements and providing detailed guidelines for their preparation. In short, the Army Corps of Engineers and the Soil Conservation Service interpreted the law differently. The Army Corps of Engineers saw the National Environmental Policy Act as a new mandate. The Corps' decisions and decisionmaking procedures reflected this mandate. The Soil Conservation Service, at least for four years, misinterpreted the same law as a reiteration of its existing policies and procedures. The SCS thus saw little need for change.[34]

While the two agencies interpreted the new law differently in the ways mentioned above, their leaders also shared certain interpretations—incorrect ones—and communicated these to their subordinates. Both centered their attention on environmental impact statements and disregarded, for the most part, other provisions of the law. Although those who wrote the law intended to emphasize policy goals, the agencies that implemented the act were preoccupied with its procedural requirements. The Corps and the Soil Conservation Service failed to develop guidelines concerning the achievement of such goals as stewardship for future generations, achieving the widest possible range of beneficial uses of the environment without degradation, maximizing the recycling of depletable resources, enhancing the quality of renewable resources, preserving diversity and the national heritage, and achieving balance between population and resource use.[35]

We should not be overly critical of these two agencies. The language of the act was vague, providing little direction on how to strike a balance between environmental goals and "other essential considerations of national policy." The act did not specify the "appropriate weight" to be given environmental impacts in reaching decisions.

[34]Richard N. L. Andrews, *Environmental Policy and Administrative Change* (Lexington, Mass.: Lexington Books, 1976), pp. 100–103, 131.

[35]Ibid., pp. 133–134. Daniel Mazmanian has informed me in personal correspondence that the Corps developed guidelines requiring the *assessment* of a broad range of possible impacts of their projects.

Similarly, the act did not specify the number or types of alternatives to the typical projects that were to be considered.[36]

Unanticipated Change   Lack of clarity in policy may not only inhibit intended change; it also may lead to substantial unanticipated change. From 1962 through 1972 the Social Security Act provided open-ended grants-in-aid to the states for social services. However, neither the law nor the Department of Health, Education and Welfare, which administered the program, clearly defined "services." This imprecision became the basis for an unintended rapid growth in the funds expended for the program as states asked for larger and larger grants. Moreover, the states used most of the money to pay for services they already provided. The act turned out to be fiscal relief for the states, contrary to the intentions of both Congress and the president.[37]

It is difficult to enforce administrative controls without legislative underpinnings. The vague language of the act did not allow or encourage HEW or its regional offices to take firm stands against state abuses. The vagueness of the act also made administrators more vulnerable to political pressure from state officials for more funds for more uses.[38] Thus, there are times when officials may desire *less* discretion as they implement policy in order to provide themselves some protection in battles with special interests.[39]

Vague goals may lead officials to lose sight of the purpose of their implementation activity. In the words of Elliot Richardson, who has held several high federal executive positions:

[36]Richard A. Liroff, *A National Policy for the Environment: NEPA and Its Aftermath* (Bloomington, Ind.: Indiana University Press, 1976), pp. 84–87. For other examples of ambiguous policies, see Robert L. Butterworth, "The Arms Control Impact Statement: A Programmatic Assessment," *Policy Studies Journal* 8 (Autumn 1979): 82–83; Van Horn, "Implementing CETA," p. 26; Charles O. Jones, *Clean Air* (Pittsburgh: University of Pittsburgh Press, 1975), pp. 69, 133–134; Theodore R. Marmor, *The Politics of Medicare* (Chicago: Aldine, 1970), pp. 85–86; and Jeffrey L. Pressman and Aaron B. Wildavsky, *Implementation* (Berkeley, Cal.: University of California Press, 1973), p. 74.

[37]Martha Derthick, *Uncontrollable Spending for Social Services Grants* (Washington, D.C.: Brookings Institution, 1975).

[38]Ibid., pp. 13, 107.

[39]See Gary Orfield, *Congressional Power* (New York: Harcourt Brace Jovanovich, 1975), p. 168.

All too often uncertainty about objectives leads to a trap that might be called management by activity. This is a euphoric state of mind which equates more with better, which suggests that, as doing good things produces good results, doing twice as many good things will quite obviously produce twice as many good results. In other words, if you don't know where you're going, run faster.[40]

True Intentions   The potential for implementors to misunderstand their orders is great when they try to follow the "true" intentions of their superiors. According to former CIA Director William Colby, some people in the CIA took high-level "expressions of official hostility . . . as a suggestion, consent or even authority to mount operations aimed at assassinating Castro. . . . The ambiguity with which covert policy vis-à-vis Castro was stated in this period led to vigorous efforts to achieve what the policymakers were *thought* to have meant. [emphasis added]"[41]

During his tenure as CIA director, Richard Helms ordered the agency to turn its attention from the domestic antiwar movement to international terrorism, but this directive was misinterpreted by a few in the CIA to be a cover story for continued domestic action. As William Colby has written, "The habits and language of clandestinity can intoxicate even its own practitioners." For this reason, internal directives must be "crystal-clear and thorough, especially when the secrecy of the operation prohibits external oversight."[42]

Reducing Discretion

There are times, of course, when the guidelines legislatures provide to adminstrators are clear. A prime example of this is Social Security, a program in which eligibility requirements, size of benefit levels, and other considerations are precisely established. This provides a minimum of discretion to administrators. On the whole, their decisions are consistent and predictable. Satisfaction with the administration of Social Security is generally quite high.

The Voting Rights Act of 1965 reduced the discretion of local voting registrars by limiting the use of literacy tests or similar voter qualification devices. In some cases the administration of voting reg-

[40]Frederick V. Malek, *Washington's Hidden Tragedy*, p. 148.
[41]Colby, *Honorable Men*, pp. 213–214.
[42]Ibid., pp. 316–317.

istration was physically taken over by federal officials so that local officials could not inhibit voter registration. Another example of limiting implementors' discretion occurred in early 1973 when the Nixon administration issued new rules that restricted the way funds could be expended to aid the poor through social services. Funds could be used only for persons with specifically defined conditions of need and then only under a system of detailed accounting of the services provided. This was an attempt by the Nixon administration to restrict the options available to social workers.[43]

In response to the independent actions of U.S. attorneys around the country, the Justice Department produced a *U.S. Attorneys Manual* requiring advance approval for certain actions and allocating certain cases to the department itself. Specific forms and reports were also required, and many policies were outlined. Moreover, the manual established special department strike forces on crime, thereby removing various types of cases from the jurisdictions of some U.S. attorneys.[44]

Innovations in procedures are not always successful in constraining implementors. The National Environmental Policy Act requires agencies to produce environmental impact statements on their programs and to take environmental concerns into consideration in their implementation decisions. Yet . . . there is evidence that these statements have had limited impact on projects. In the case of the Army Corps of Engineers, the requirement to consider environmental concerns actually freed it somewhat from the tough and quantifiable criteria applied to projects by the Office of Management and Budget and allowed it to support projects in which the economic costs exceeded the benefits, but in which the environmental benefits, according to the Corps' calculations, made up the difference.[45]

It is generally easier to reduce the discretion of officials with orders to stop doing something than to start doing something. For example, an absolute ban on providing funds for abortions for poor women is more likely to be unambiguous and more likely to be noticed if it is violated than an order to begin implementing a new policy. The implementation of most policies, however, requires pos-

[43]Richard P. Nathan, "The 'Administrative Presidency'," *Public Interest* (Summer 1976): 47–48.
[44]James Eisenstein, *Counsel for the United States: U.S. Attorneys in the Political and Legal Systems* (Baltimore: Johns Hopkins University Press, 1978), pp. 88, 90.
[45]Andrews, *Environmental Policy*, p. 144.

itive actions—not prohibitions. Moreover, usually a series of positive actions extending over a long period of time and involving the technical expertise of numerous persons throughout a bureaucratic hierarchy is necessary to implement a policy. The complexity of such policymaking makes it very difficult to communicate and enforce rules that effectively reduce the discretion available to most policy implementors. . . .

Value of Flexibility

Vague policy decisions hinder effective implementation, but directives that are too specific may also adversely affect implementation. Implementors sometimes need the freedom to adapt policies to suit the situation at hand. The Rand Change Agent Study, an extensive evaluation of innovations in education, including many dealing with classroom organization, underscored the importance of adaptation in the implementation process:

> Because classroom organization projects require teachers to work out their own styles and classroom techniques within a broad philosophical framework, innovations of this type cannot be fully specified or packaged in advance. Thus, the very nature of these projects requires that implementation be a *mutually adaptive process*. Specific project goals and methods must be made concrete by the users themselves as they acquire the skills appropriate to the innovation.[46]

All of the successfully implemented projects the Rand team studied, even fairly straightforward technical projects, underwent mutual adaptation to some extent. Specifics evolved over time as modifications were made in the project designs and in the personnel and institutional settings of the implementors. The Rand researchers suggest that adaptation rather than standardization is the most realistic and fruitful objective for policymakers.[47] Similarly, in a study of federal education programs in six states, the authors concluded that "federal administrative practices which use one set of regulations to cover a variety of state practices are doomed, and . . . more flexible approaches are needed."[48]

One scholar has described the effective development of the Polaris missile system as one of "disciplined flexibility." This technique of implementation in the field of weapons development is not unlike

[46]McLaughlin, *Education and Reform*, p. 168.
[47]Ibid, pp. 169, 178–179.
[48]Berke and Kirst, "Intergovernmental Relations," p. 401.

mutual adaptation in the classroom. The technique is disciplined because of the physical constraints of submarines and the determination to meet accelerated deployment schedules. Flexibility is needed to avoid premature commitment to any particular performance goals. Guidelines evolved as the project's implementors proceeded through each step of the missile development process.[49]

A myriad of specific regulations can overwhelm and confuse personnel in the field and may make them reluctant to act for fear of breaking the rules. Strict guidelines may also induce a type of goal displacement in which lower level officials become more concerned with meeting specific requirements than with achieving the basic goals of the program. By rigidly adhering to the letter of a regulation, they may become so bogged down in red tape that the purpose of the rule is forgotten or defeated. Conversely, implementors sometimes ignore rigid legislative decisions. The Economic Development Administration, for example, attempted to circumvent at the regional level its own restrictions on making loans and formulated new and unsystematic criteria in Washington *after* it saw the applications for loans.[50]

At this point the already highly complex process of policy implementation becomes even more confusing. The choice of whether to guide implementors as much as possible or to build flexibility and adaptation into implementation is a difficult one to make. The evidence is mixed. The Rand researchers concluded that implementation directives should not be too specific, but other scholars have found that the lack of clarity surrounding innovations in education is a principal cause of implementation problems.[51]

While vague decisions can leave implementors confused or allow them to exercise their discretion contrary to the intent of a pol-

[49]Harvey M. Sapolsky, *The Polaris System Development: Bureaucratic and Programmatic Success in Government* (Cambridge, Mass.: Harvard University Press, 1972), p. 250. For other examples, see Helen Ingram, "The Political Rationality of Federal Air Pollution Legislation," in *Approaches to Controlling Air Pollution*, ed. Ann F. Friedlaender (Cambridge, Mass.: MIT Press, 1978), p. 41.

[50]Pressman and Wildavsky, *Implementation*, pp. 75–78.

[51]Neal Gross, Joseph B. Giacquinta, and Marilyn Bernstein, *Implementing Organizational Innovations: A Sociological Analysis of Planned Educational Change in Schools* (New York: Basic Books, 1971), pp. 123–129; and John Pincus, "Incentives for Innovation in Public Schools," in *Social Program Implementation*, Williams and Elmore, eds., p. 56.

icy, highly specific language can make it more difficult for officials in the field to adapt programs to the particular needs of states or localities. Decisionmakers must consider each implementation situation individually and be sensitive to the issues raised above.

Reasons for Lack of Clarity

Complexity of Policymaking The lack of clarity in many implementation orders can be attributed to several factors. Perhaps the most important is the sheer complexity of policymaking. Neither executives nor legislators have the time or expertise to develop and apply all the requisite details for implementing policy. They have to leave most (and sometimes all) of the details to subordinates. Former HEW Secretary Joseph Califano writes that when he was President Johnson's chief domestic policy aide he was unable to meet, consult, or guide more than one-third of the noncabinet agency and commission heads. Johnson saw even fewer.[52]

Police administrators often do not provide detailed policy guidelines on important matters to police officers. When should an officer intervene in a serious family dispute? When should firearms be used? Very little helpful direction is given to officers who must answer these questions. Although the inappropriate use of firearms by the police has been a cause of substantial conflict between citizens and the police in recent years, many police departments lack professional expertise and issue only very general statements, such as the following, to guide the discretion of police officers: "Firearms shall be used only in extreme cases, and in a manner consistent with the provisions of the state penal law." A police department relying upon such a vague guideline, unlike large departments that have supplemented state penal codes with detailed rules regarding the use of firearms, will be unlikely to have much success in controlling the exercise of officers' discretion.[53]

The federal government, like a local police department, has difficulty issuing specific, helpful directives. Regarding the community action programs of the war on poverty in the mid-1960s, one

[52]Califano, *A Presidential Nation*, p. 23.
[53]Jameson W. Doig, "Police Policy and Police Behavior: Patterns of Divergence," *Policy Studies Journal* 7 (Special Issue, 1978): 438.

authority has written, "The Government did not know what it was doing. It had a theory. Or, rather, a set of theories. Nothing more."[54] According to former Secretary Califano, "the basis of recommendations by an American cabinet officer . . . nearly resembles the intuitive judgment of a benevolent tribal chief in remote Africa."[55]

Implementation of Title I of the pathbreaking Elementary and Secondary Education Act of 1965 relied heavily upon "intuitive judgment." As one author has written, "No one really knew how to run a successful compensatory educational program."[56] Therefore, local school districts received little guidance on how to spend their funds. Likewise, Project Head Start was "undertaken with a hunch and a prayer," and local officials could proceed with their own ideas with little central guidance.[57]

Public Opposition   The desire to avoid alienating politically influential groups in the public may cause vague implementation directives. In "victimless crimes"—crimes in which there is no complainant, such as gambling, prostitution, and illegal drug use—the potential for policy discretion in arresting violators is greater than in other types of crimes. The police do not always enforce these laws strictly, and many people feel that police discretion is exercised arbitrarily, with some offenders punished and others left alone. Although the lack of both public support and police resources makes discretion in the enforcement of laws against victimless crimes inevitable, police executives are reluctant to issue directives to officers specifying the circumstances under which the laws will and will not be enforced.[58] Such rules could create obvious political problems for them. Thus, police on the beat are left on their own to make these important decisions about the use of the coercive power of government, and the implementation of these laws is widely criticized as unjust.[59]

[54]Moynihan, *Maximum Feasible Misunderstanding*, p. 170.

[55]Daniel P. Moynihan, *The Politics of a Guaranteed Income* (New York: Vintage Books, 1973), p. 240. See also the comments of former Price Commissioner C. Jackson Grayson in Theodore C. Sorensen, *Watchmen in the Night* (Cambridge, Mass.: MIT Press, 1975), p. 32.

[56]Alice M. Rivlin, *Systematic Thinking for Social Action* (Washington, D.C.: Brookings Institution, 1971), pp. 80.

[57]Ibid., p. 84.

[58]Doig, "Police Policy and Police Behavior," pp. 438–439.

[59]See Burton M. Atkins and Mark Pogrebin, eds., *The Invisible Justice System: Discretion and the Law* (Cincinnati: Anderson Publishing Co., 1978), Part II.

Competing Goals and the Need for Consensus Another cause of vagueness in implementation directives is the difficulty decision-makers have in reaching a consensus on goals. As we discussed earlier, for a decade the federal government provided funds to states for social services without defining what "services" meant. The states used the money for many purposes never intended by the president and Congress, and the program expanded way beyond all the expectations of the federal government as a result. The vagueness of the law was due in part to conflict within HEW between the Bureau of Family Services and other agencies, especially the Children's Bureau and the Office of Vocational Rehabilitation, over what constituted "services." Rather than alienate an agency, HEW chose to leave the term vaguely defined. In addition, members of Congress had conflicting intentions. The notion of funding services (rather than direct grants to individuals) appealed to conservatives as a method of saving money and decreasing dependency while it appealed to liberals as a way to help the poor and serve good purposes.[60]

The lack of clear policy goals is very common in America and occurs in all types of policies at all levels of government—from effluent limitations to block grants for community development, from the West Side Highway in New York City to the war in Vietnam, and from federal support for higher education to evaluation requirements for elementary and secondary education programs.[61]

In the United States we share wide agreement on the goals of avoidance of war, equal opportunity, and efficiency in government, but this consensus often dissolves when specific policy alternatives are under consideration. Disagreement over precise goals is inevitable in a large and diverse country in which people have different views of what government ought to do (such as the extent of its regulation of the economy), of what government can accomplish (such as the degree to which laws can alter racist behavior), and even of whether there is a problem in society that calls for any action at all

[60]Derthick, *Uncontrollable Spending*, pp. 9, 13.
[61]Rauch, "The Federal Water Pollution Control Act Amendments of 1972"; Regina Herzlinger, "Costs, Benefits, and the West Side Highway," *Public Interest* (Spring 1979): 84; Herbert Y. Schandler, *The Unmaking of a President: Lyndon Johnson and Vietnam* (Princeton, N.J.: Princeton University Press, 1977); Norman C. Thomas, *Education in National Politics* (New York: David McKay, 1975), p. 52; McLaughlin, *Evaluation and Reform*, p. 18; "HUD Authorization: House Panel Challenges Harris Move to Boost Block Grant Aid to Poor," *Congressional Quarterly Weekly Report*, June 3, 1978, p. 1398.

(such as the use of saccharin or fluorocarbons in aerosol sprays). Just think of the different goals that might be attributed to a policy to increase spending for education: improving character and moral values; changing the social structure by fostering mobility; freeing parents for work; developing greater student knowledge and skills; increasing staff and student productivity; equalizing opportunity for learning and livelihood; creating jobs for minority teachers; building healthier bodies through improved physical education facilities; producing a winning football team to boost school or civic pride; integrating public schools; and many more.[62]

Lyndon Johnson once said, "If the full implications of any bill were known before its enactment, it would never get passed."[63] Clearly, imprecise decisions make it easier for policymakers to develop and maintain winning decisional coalitions. Different people or groups can support the same policy for different reasons. Each may hold its own conception of the goal or goals the program is designed to achieve. Ambiguous goals also may make it less threatening for groups to be on the losing side of a policy conflict, and this may reduce the intensity of their opposition.

When it is difficult to agree on goals, policymakers often seek general improvements, having a better notion of what they want to escape than what they want to achieve. In the words of David Braybrooke and Charles Lindblom:

> Policy aims at suppressing vice even though virtue cannot be defined, let alone concretized as a goal; at attending to mental illness even though we are not sure what attitudes and behaviors are most healthy; at curbing the expansion of the Soviet Union even though we do not know what positive foreign policy objectives to set against the Kremlin's; at reducing the governmental inefficiencies even though we do not know what maximum level of competence we can reasonably expect; at eliminating inequities in the tax structure even though we do not agree on equity; at destroying slums even though we are

---

[62]For examples of the diverse foreign policy goals, see Morton H. Halperin, *Bureaucratic Politics and Foreign Policy* (Washington, D.C.: Brookings Institution, 1974), p. 78; and Robert L. Gallucci, *Neither Peace nor Honor* (Baltimore: Johns Hopkins University Press, 1975), pp. 47–54.

[63]Doris Kearns, *Lyndon Johnson and the American Dream* (New York: Harper & Row, 1976), p. 137.

uncertain about the kinds of homes and neighborhoods in which their occupants should live.[64]

As we have seen, the de-emphasis on goals serves useful purposes for policymakers interested in enacting policies into law. Another consequence of vague goals, however, is the lack of clarity in policies. Thus, while vague goals may make it easier to pass laws, they increase the chances of slippage in implementing them. . . .

[64]David Braybrooke and Charles E. Lindblom, *A Strategy of Decision: Policy Evaluation as a Social Process* (New York: Free Press, 1963), pp. 202–203.

24

Red Tape:
The Perpetual Irritant

HERBERT KAUFMAN

Once in a long while, a voice is raised in defense of red tape. Or at least in explanation of it.[1] These voices are almost never heard. They are drowned in an unceasing chorus of denunciation. Everybody seems to hate red tape.

I say "seems to" because the apparent unanimity conceals significant differences. One person's "red tape" may be another's treasured procedural safeguard. The term is applied to a bewildering variety of organizational practices and features.

Still, a common set of complaints is embedded in most definitions even though the complaints refer to different specific irritants. When people rail against red tape, they mean that they are subjected to too many constraints, that many of the constraints seem pointless, and that agencies seem to take forever to act. That is, we detest our *respective* forms of red tape, but for the same reasons.

From Herbert Kaufman, *Red Tape: Its Origins, Uses and Abuses*. Washington, D.C.: The Brookings Institution, 1977, pp. 4–22. Reprinted by permission of the author and the publisher. Footnotes are renumbered.

[1]For instance, Paul H. Appleby, *Big Democracy* (Knopf, 1945), chap. 6; Dwight Waldo, "Government by Procedure," in Fritz Morstein Marx, ed., *Elements of Public Administration* (Prentice-Hall, 1946); Alvin W. Gouldner, "Red Tape as a Social Problem," in Robert K. Merton and others, eds., *Reader in Bureaucracy* (Free Press, 1952).

One common theme that runs through all of these essays is the relativity of red tape. Appleby: "Red tape is that part of my business you don't know anything about" (p. 64). Waldo: "One man's red tape is another man's system" (p. 399). Gouldner: "red tape as a social problem cannot be explained unless the frame of reference employed by the individual who uses this label is understood" (p. 411).

Too Many Constraints

We all hate to be told we have to do something or may not do something. Even if we actually enjoy the compulsory tasks and dislike the forbidden ones, the command rankles. The element of compulsion itself is distasteful. And it is much worse if we are forced to do what we don't want to do, and are prohibited from doing what we profoundly want to do.

Today, you can hardly turn around without bumping into some federal restraint or requirement. It wasn't always so; there was a time you could embark on almost any venture without encountering a single federal constraint. Now, however, if you should take it into your head, say, to manufacture and market a new product, you would probably run into statutes and administrative regulations on labor relations, occupational safety, product safety, and air purity. Your advertising would probably fall within the jurisdiction of the Federal Trade Commission. The Department of Justice would be interested in your relations with your competitors. Should you want to raise capital by the sale of stock or bonds, you would fall under the Securities and Exchange Commission. You would need export licenses from the Department of Commerce to sell your product in some areas of the world. Federal prohibitions against race, age, and sex discrimination in hiring and promotion would apply to you. If you were to extend credit to your customers, you might fall under truth-in-lending laws. You would have to file sundry reports for tax, social security, pension, and census purposes. In some fields—communication, transportation, energy, insurance, and banking, for instance—restrictions and oversight are especially stringent. But firms of all kinds, large and small, are subject to diverse federal requirements. You can't just start and run a business without reference to federal specifications and officials.

Business is not the only activity affected this way. Labor unions, foundations, political parties, universities, lobbyists, and even farmers are similarly constrained. Every recipient of government subsidies, loans, and other forms of public assistance finds these benefits come with conditions and obligations that have to be satisfied. The government's reach is very long.

The sheer mass of binding official promulgations and interventions in the marketplace begins to be oppressive. The number seems to increase steadily. The media revel in embarrassing exposés. Although it is possible that this impression is engendered partly by the irritations of corresponding actions by state and local governments and the private sector of society, which are no less prolific,[2] the federal government, being the largest and most visible institution, attracts a disproportionate share of the venom. Many people seem to feel it is closing in on them from all sides, and it is to this sensation that they react when they excoriate red tape.

They are dismayed also because the torrent of requirements descending on them is too overwhelming for them to comply with. Conscientious, upright citizens are often distressed when they find themselves in violation of government directives, yet they simply cannot keep up with the flood. Said one desperate victim, "We have reached the saturation level, and each new law and each new agency at every level of government . . . is forcing decent citizens into involuntary noncompliance with the law. Now, this is tragic when upstanding honest citizens just can't comply with the laws."[3]

It is certainly undeniable that the output of the federal government is prodigious. Congress alone produces over a thousand printed pages of public laws in an average session. Federal courts routinely publish thousands of pages of decisions and opinions every year. The regulations of federal administrative agencies, including both draft and final forms, total more than 50,000 printed pages annually. One especially prolific agency was said to have issued enough documents to make a stack seventeen feet high.[4] Of course, there is substantial redundancy in this outpouring. Moreover, only a small percentage of it is likely to affect any given individual or organization. Still, it is easy to understand why red tape has become a matter for concern. The stream appears to be at flood stage and relentlessly rising.

Another indicator of its ostensible menace is the volume of material the federal government requires people to submit to it: the total number of submissions has been put at more than 2 billion a year, or nearly ten for each man, woman, and child in the country. Over 70 percent of these, it is true, are connected with taxes, chiefly for

[2]*Government Reports and Statistics*, S. Rept. 1616, 90:2 (Government Printing Office, 1968). On p. 37, the Senate Select Committee on Small Business concludes, "As for State and local government reporting, we can no longer close our eyes to the fact that it has become equally burdensome with the Federal system."

[3]*The Federal Paperwork Burden*, S. Rept. 93–125, 93:1 (GPO, 1973), p. 55.

[4]Ibid., p. 4.

internal revenue and social security, but this means the impact is extremely broad. Moreover, the remaining 600 million are highly diversified; indeed, the number of different forms authorized for distribution to the public by federal agencies exceeds five thousand.[5]

Many people are hard hit by these requirements. A "Mom and Pop" store with a gross annual income of less than $30,000 had to file tax forms fifty-two times a year. A firm with fewer than fifty employees had to prepare seventy-five or eighty submissions a year for various agencies.[6] A small securities broker-dealer sent thirty-eight submissions to seven different agencies in one year.[7] A plant employing seventy-five people had two of them working half time solely to draw up compulsory plans and reports; a company with a hundred employees made seventy filings or payments each year to the Internal Revenue Service alone; a small radio station assigned two employees full time for four months to supply all the information specified by the Federal Communications Commission for license renewal, and another reported that its application for renewal weighed forty-five pounds.[8] The chairman of the board of a large pharmaceutical firm claimed that his company prepared 27,000 government forms or reports a year at a cost of $5 million. ("We spend," he added, "more man-hours filling out government forms or reports than we do on research for cancer and heart disease combined.")[9] Even personal income tax forms, despite great progress in simplifying them, are now complicated enough to require a good deal of effort by most taxpayers and to have fostered numerous commercial services that help them with the tasks of computation and filing.

Nobody escapes. Each of us has his or her own complaint. Each hears similar complaints from others. Each realizes that his or her discontent, though it represents only an infinitesimal segment of the broad band of government activities, is part of a pattern too vast for one person to perceive. No wonder everybody begins to feel suffocated by red tape. The sheer magnitude of the government's de-

[5]Ibid., p. 2; *The Federal Paperwork Jungle,* H. Rept. 52, 89:1 (GPO, 1965), pp. 23 ff.

[6]*The Federal Paperwork Burden,* S. Rept. 93–125, pp. 8, 2.

[7]*The Federal Paperwork Burden,* Hearings before the Senate Subcommittee on Government Regulation of the Select Committee on Small Business, 92:2 (GPO, 1972), pt. 4, p. 1430.

[8]*The Federal Paperwork Burden,* S. Rept. 93–125, pp. 4, 5, 10.

[9]Richard D. Wood, "Paperwork, Paperwork," *Washington Post,* July 12, 1976.

mands and constraints, no matter how reasonable each of them is individually, guarantees this reaction.

"Pointless" Constraints

From the point of view of the individual citizen, however, they are *not* all reasonable. Some of them make no sense to the people who must comply with them. If people find self-evidently justified requirements intolerable when they become too numerous, imagine how they feel about requirements that seem pointless. It would not take many of these to discredit the whole body of government constraints.

Of course, what is pointless to one person may seem essential to another. Values and perspectives vary. Also, the reasons for any given program or policy may be persuasive, though not obvious; inadequate explanation may account for its ostensible pointlessness, or perhaps some critics fail to evaluate it carefully. Pointlessness is relative.

But it is people's *perceptions* of government constraints, not objective measures of reasonableness, that lead them to attack some constraints as red tape. With torrents of new promulgations pouring from government organs, if even a small proportion strike some people as senseless, the absolute number of the disaffected must be large. From all indications, that is exactly what happens.

"Irrelevant" Requirements

For example, many complaints about red tape come from critics who believe that they have been compelled to obey commands that should not apply to them and probably were never meant to. Thus the legislative counsel of the National Society of Public Accountants, testifying about some reports collected from businessmen by the Census Bureau, told a Senate subcommittee:

> The detailed complexity of some of the census economic forms has questionable value. . . . The compilation of a great mass of statistics has little value to the persons whom it was apparently meant to benefit. . . .
>
> Information, I must add, that in large part was supplied by the people who basically do not need it. In my own practice—and in this

I am experienced—I know of no business that uses any of the census statistics in any way, even though they must supply this information.[10]

Similarly, a small retailer stormed:

I have here a 32-page booklet, published by the Department of Labor, explaining what we must do to comply with the recent Occupational Safety and Health Act. It also contains copies of three new records we employers must maintain and then keep on hand for two years. I must sit down with these materials and figure out what I have to do to comply with this law, and then see to it that the requirements are carried out. Yet retailing isn't even a target industry of OSHA.[11]

To which a small New Hampshire manufacturer added:

OSHA was written for companies like Ford Motors which actually owns a huge hospital in Dearborn. The act was not written for my little company with a medicine cabinet containing a bottle of Mercurochrome and a bottle of aspirin.[12]

Testimony of this kind from a number of witnesses persuaded the Senate Select Committee on Small Business that

the Federal bureaucracy, the governmental units most removed from the people, fails to understand the circumstances or the need of the private citizens or the small business. . . . Bureaucrats, accustomed to dealing with situations of massive scale, find it virtually impossible to comprehend the stress their demands . . . place on the small firm.[13]

The problem of irrelevant requirements was said to be so pervasive as to arouse suspicions of a conspiracy:

Some small businessmen who make little or no use of officially compiled information, themselves, suspect that there exists an unholy alliance between Government and big business in these matters and that the information supplied by them to the Government is often used by market researchers, location specialists, and sales analysts of the large companies to the detriment of small business.[14]

[10] *The Federal Paperwork Burden*, Hearings, pt. 5, pp. 1953–54.
[11] *The Federal Paperwork Burden*, S. Rept. 93–125, p. 54.
[12] *The Federal Paperwork Burden*, Hearings, pt. 6, p. 2178.
[13] *The Federal Paperwork Burden*, Rept. 93–125, p. 3.
[14] *Government Reports and Statistics*, S. Rept. 1616, p. 2.

But it is not only small businessmen who object. The representative of the pharmaceutical manufacturer mentioned earlier observed,

> Our application to the FDA for a drug for treatment of arthritis consisted of 120,000 pages. . . . About 25 percent of these pages—or 30,000 of them—contained information that was important to the evaluation of the drug by FDA. The other 90,000 pages contained incredibly detailed records.[15]

Officials themselves concede the prevalence of wide disparities in viewpoint between themselves and the public. A group of high-level Washington administrators ("admirals and generals of the bureaucracy," they were called by a commentator) were brought to New York City to learn at first hand something about the life of the poor. Many of them were astonished. "Here we are in Washington passing on licenses for Con Ed," one of them said, "and we never think about how people like this are on the other end of the line." "We are too insulated in Washington," another remarked. "We don't realize what's going on out there in the country."[16]

"Out there in the country," countless Americans agree with them and disparage as useless and irrelevant many of the things the federal government requires and forbids.

Duplicative and Contradictory Requirements

Even when they acknowledge the usefulness and relevance of specific requirements and prohibitions, people are incensed at having to do the same thing many times for different agencies when it appears to them that once would be enough if the government were more efficient. Witnesses testifying at congressional hearings complained of this again and again. One observed,

> In the requirement of the reporting and process of compliance with the Equal Employment Opportunity requirements under the law . . . it seems to us that if we work for five or six agencies of the Government we should only have to . . . indicate that we are in compliance with the law one time. But by reason of the fact that the bureaucrats . . . in each agency want exactly the same thing, instead

---

[15]Wood, "Paperwork, Paperwork."
[16]Edith Evans Asbury, *New York Times*, October 16, 1975.

of filing once . . . we have to file as many different sets of these as [there are] different agencies.[17]

Another explained,

We are not unreasonable people in business. We realize that you have to have a record and you have to measure accomplishments and all of these things, but we do not believe that it takes the same record 10 different times to produce the results that are actually required by law.[18]

The congressional committee joined in wondering "why he must report similar information to several Federal agencies, and identical information to a federal and to a state agency," and concluded:

The form-maker, sitting in Washington surrounded by hundreds of other bureaucrats, does not comprehend the urgency of this man's point of view; the man is only being asked to spend a few hours filling out a form. What the bureaucrat fails to understand is that the few hours his agency requires multiplied by the requests of several other Federal agencies places an enormous strain on the resources of the small enterprise.[19]

Executing the same forms over and over is not only boring and, to the people who must complete them, a foolish result of poor management; it adds to expenses. Nobody knows exactly how general such duplication is, but the scale of government operations is so large that it apparently occurs frequently and casts a shadow on the need for most of the things the government does or demands.

Still more irritating from the point of view of the conscientiously law-abiding person, in government as well as in private life, are government requirements drawn in such a way that to obey one seems to lead to violations of the other. I say "seems to" advisedly. The apparent inconsistencies are often ambiguities rather than contradictions. But even ambiguities impose dilemmas and burdens on those who strive to comply; each individual must resolve for himself or herself uncertainties created by poor draftsmanship, inadvertent contradictions, or deliberate avoidance of hard choices on the part

[17] *The Federal Paperwork Burden*, S. Rept. 93–125, pp. 12–13.
[18] Ibid., p. 15.
[19] Ibid., pp. 4, 15.

of officials, and the most painstaking attempt to obey all provisions of all applicable sets of requirements meticulously may eventually be judged to have violated one or another.

For example, legislation protecting the right to privacy may conflict with the spirit, if not the letter, of the Freedom of Information Act. To take another case, one strategy for reducing racial discrimination is to prohibit inquiries about race on application forms of all kinds in both the private sector and in government, but another strategy is to require records on the treatment of minority applicants so that patterns of prejudice may be exposed and reversed; people can get caught between the two. A third illustration is the uncertain line between the expectation that career public servants will carry out the edicts of their political superiors without regard to their own predilections and the principle that duty requires them to disobey improper orders. These conflicting guidelines shift the difficulties of reconciliation from the promulgators of official policy to the individual private citizen or public employee without much guidance and with the possibility of punishment no matter what course is chosen. . . .

Inertia

Once requirements and practices are instituted, they tend to remain in force long after the conditions that spawned them have disappeared. A committee of the House of Representatives, reporting on federal paperwork requirements in 1965, commented on "obsolete and archaistic reports" and offered two illustrations. One was

> the Bureau of Customs forms for the entry and clearance of vessels at U.S. ports. As brought out in the subcommittee hearings, these forms have not changed to any great extent since 1790, and merchant vessels today are required to report on the number of guns mounted.[20]

The other was also a maritime example—the shipping articles that merchant seamen were required to sign before voyages, based on legislation of 1872 and 1873.[21] Among the articles was a Sunday food schedule as out of date as kerosene lanterns and buggy whips. All the same, the empty provisions were still solemnized a century later. . . .

[20]*The Federal Paperwork Jungle*, H. Rept. 52, pp. 30–31.
[21]Ibid.

Similarly, a single embarrassing incident may inspire practices that go on and on at great cost and minimal benefit. As a former director of the Bureau of the Budget put it,

> The public servant soon learns that successes rarely rate a headline, but governmental blunders are front page news. This recognition encourages the development of procedures designed less to achieve successes than to avoid blunders. Let it be discovered that the Army is buying widgets from private suppliers while the Navy is disposing of excess widgets at a lower price; the reporter will win a Pulitzer prize and the Army and Navy will establish procedures for liaison, review, and clearance which will prevent a recurrence and which will also introduce new delays and higher costs into the process of buying or selling anything. It may cost a hundred times more to prevent the occurrence of occasional widget episodes, but no one will complain.[22]

Presumably, federal administration is shot through with cases of this kind, though nobody can be sure. Nor, of course, can anybody certify that continuous review of government operations to get rid of such ludicrous requirements would not cost more than letting them remain on the books. The search for outmoded practices takes government time and money, yet old, unchanging procedures, once learned, are easily followed, and utterly obsolete ones are usually ignored by everyone. So the burden of correcting them may be greater than that of letting them linger. Whether or not the direct cost of eliminating them exceeds the direct cost of enduring them, however, there is no doubt that even occasional exposures of such anomalies bring discredit on the whole establishment. And when enough requirements are on the books, as in the federal government, elimination of these embarrassments is a virtual impossibility.

Programs That Fail

Nothing, however, is as likely to render requirements pointless, in the opinion of some of those who must comply with them and of neutral observers, as constraints that obviously do not produce the results proclaimed as justifications for them. Restrictions and burdens imposed for announced ends that are never attained are probably the hardest to bear.

[22]Kermit Gordon, "After Vietnam: Domestic Issues and Public Policies" (speech delivered to the Stanford Business Conference, San Francisco, February 19, 1969; processed).

Government regulation of business illustrates the point. Many regulatory programs originated in response to demands for government suppression of abuses, either actual or potential. The prices of products or services were seen as excessively high, the quality unfairly or dangerously low, the supply uncertain. Consumers of these goods and services, denied what they wanted in the marketplace, asked the government to intervene to prevent these deficiencies. Such intervention was accomplished by new legislation, new agencies, new regulations and orders and controls. These measures were deemed by their backers to be worth their cost because they would eliminate or reduce evils. Naturally, if the evils did not disappear, or if even worse evils took their place, the regulatory programs would make no sense.

Gradually, some observers began to suspect that the programs were falling far short of their proclaimed objectives, or even making things worse. In the first place, the observers noticed that the regulated interests often benefited more from regulation than consumers did. The interests were relieved of competition, yet the controls on them allegedly did not shore up quality or hold down prices in return for this security. In a free market, low-quality or overpriced practitioners or manufacturers, shorn of official protection, would presumably be forced to improve quality, lower prices, or go out of business. Regulation has therefore been given low grades by critics from all sectors of the political spectrum.[23]

In the second place, it has been said that regulatory officials acquire the same perspectives and values as the interests they regulate.[24] The two groups are in constant contact and thus become indistinguishable, especially since personnel move from one to the other freely. In any event, in the contest to exert influence on the regulators, consumers are ordinarily outclassed by the well-organized, well-

---

[23]See, for example, Edward F. Cox, Robert C. Fellmeth, and John E. Schulz, *"The Nader Report" on the Federal Trade Commission* (Baron, 1969); Louis M. Kohlmeier, Jr., *The Regulators* (Harper and Row, 1969).

[24]Roger G. Noll, *Reforming Regulation: An Evaluation of the Ash Council Proposals* (Brookings Institution, 1971), chap. 3, especially p. 31: "The preceding discussion of regulatory failures only summarizes a vast literature in which regulators are accused of being excessively concerned about the welfare of the regulated." See also the item on extensive interchange of personnel between regulatory agencies and regulated industries by David Burnham, *New York Times*, January 2, 1976.

heeled, well-informed, well-connected, continuously functioning, experienced producers. Furthermore, the incentive structure motivates the powerful more effectively than the weak; a regulatory decision meaning millions to a firm often costs individual consumers less than the cost of protesting it, so it would be irrational for individual consumers to fight even though the loss hurts them deeply. Adding to dissatisfaction is the ability of regulated interests to pass along to consumers their costs of exerting pressure and of fighting consumer suits. Under these conditions, ask the critics, how effective can regulation be?

Measures to nullify these biases have been adopted in many jurisdictions. These include limited bans on employment of regulatory staff by regulated industries, insulation of decisionmakers from pressure, and authorization of class-action suits. Nevertheless, complaints about the regulatory process continue, and some commentators have characterized it as largely symbolic, adopted for the purpose of quieting public discontent by a show of governmental action when those who adopt it know that the programs will be vitiated in practice.[25]

Indeed, regulatory bodies have even been called agents of the regulated rather than their masters. That is why regulated interests, once the bitterest foes of regulation, are now among the most ardent defenders of their regulatory agencies, and why some industries have actively sought to be placed under regulation. By the same token, consumer organizations are among the most vehement critics, claiming that consumers, the ostensible beneficiaries, have been victimized. Those who subscribe to this interpretation of regulation regard as pointless all the laws, regulations, hearings, procedural complications, administrative machinery, and other trappings of government control and oversight of business. In their eyes, the programs are failures, and the constraints associated with them are so much useless red tape.

Other constraints are derided as pointless not so much because they are turned to the advantage of the people they were supposed to restrain as because they are not one hundred percent effective. Take the procedures, described later, to ensure the integrity of gov-

[25]Murray Edelman, *The Symbolic Uses of Politics* (University of Illinois Press, 1967).

ernment funds, the impartiality of the civil service, and the fairness of government contracting. These impose burdens, inconveniences, and costs within the government and on all who deal with it. Yet scandals occur repeatedly. Not a year goes by without exposés of public officers and employees being deceived or bribed by unscrupulous citizens or taking advantage of their positions to enrich themselves. Political connections reputedly do no harm when one is trying to get ahead in government service. High officials have been lavishly entertained by major defense contractors. Corruption and favoritism persist despite layers of requirements, platoons of overseers, and convolutions of procedures intended to prevent them.

Of course, one might infer from the exposure and prosecution of such infractions that the system is working. But if you are incommoded by preventive measures that are repeatedly violated, you are more likely to see the measures as useless. When violators are able to penetrate the defenses yet honest people who would never think of defrauding the government or abusing their authority must go through all the rigamarole set up to thwart scoundrels, it is understandable that the honest people grow resentful. They would doubtless concede that some would-be violators are deterred by the safeguards. But to make large numbers suffer in order to reduce the percentage of noncompliance by a tiny fraction does not seem rational. "It usually doesn't pay," said one congressional witness, "to set up a system—any system—to make two percent of a group 'behave' at the expense of the other 98 percent."[26] Moreover, insult is added to injury; it appears to come observers that "the Government has a deep and abiding distrust of citizens generally" and "assumes every citizen is automatically a crook."[27] To people with this outlook, catching the handful of crooks does not prove that all the troublesome constraints designed to avert dishonesty justify all the machinery; rather, it proves that the machinery is not worth the hardships it inflicts on the innocent.

This skeptical view is not universally shared, but it has many adherents. And those who subscribe to it perceive government requirements in general as red tape. Government controls are seen not only as failing to work, but as inherently incapable of working. In this view, therefore, they are neither justified nor justifiable.

[26]*The Federal Paperwork Burden*, S. Rept. 93–125, p. 11.
[27]Ibid., p. 12.

Quagmire

Even programs considered successful in the long run, however, will be called red tape if they are also considered excessively slow in acting on pending matters. Such perceptions are relative, of course; people waiting for desperately needed financial assistance, for contracts that make the difference between profit and loss, or for licenses without which they may not do business are apt to believe that operations are much slower than uninvolved observers believe them to be, and certainly much slower than public servants toiling furiously against budgetary limitations and procedural constraints believe them to be. But large numbers of people are victims at one time or another of delays when they are impatient for action. Often, this being one of their few direct contacts with the government, they conclude that the whole system is bogged down.

Indeed, there are *always* people waiting for government action of some kind. Except in matters of law enforcement, government agencies ordinarily respond to applications and demands on them— and even in many law-enforcement cases, act on the complaint of an interested party. Individuals and organizations petition them for all sorts of things: licenses and permits, welfare benefits, subsidies, tax refunds, payments for goods or services rendered, pension benefits, insurance benefits, veterans' benefits, loans, and others. They also seek changes in standing rules and regulations, in procedures, and even in the location of field offices. Millions of decisions of these kinds are made routinely every day and apparently, despite the impatience of the petitioners, are made promptly enough to keep most people quiet, if not happy. Some, however, do become mired.

For example, it is not extraordinary for federal agencies to take two years to reach decisions. In one state, officials decided to forgo federal funds for an urgently needed highway because the two or three years required to get them meant that construction costs would meanwhile have increased more than the amount of the aid.[28] And extreme delays go far beyond this; the Food and Drug Administration took a decade to develop standards of identity for peanut butter,[29] and the Federal Communications Commission was warned by a federal court to pick up the pace of its proceedings after a case

---

[28]James Feron, *New York Times*, October 27, 1975.
[29]William F. Pedersen, Jr., "Formal Records and Informal Rule-making," *Yale Law Journal*, vol. 85 (November 1975), p. 44.

instituted ten years earlier came before the bench.[30] Some construction industry spokesmen charged that more than a decade often elapsed between the initial studies of a federal project and project authorization, and another five to ten years before project completion.[31] Extenuating circumstances account for these snail-paced proceedings, but explanations seldom overcome the negative image the delays engender. Explanations or no explanations, ten years are deemed too many by most observers; that to them is red tape under any circumstances.

Horror stories add to the negative impact. A United States congressman, for instance, publicly recorded one of those depressing tales that tarnish the reputation of the whole governmental process. A workingman was afflicted with severe mental illness and committed to a mental hospital. His parents, whom he helped support, applied for and received his disability benefits, part of which went to the hospital for his maintenance. After a while, he improved enough to win off-grounds parole, and he took a menial job. His parents, as required by law, notified the Social Security Administration, which promptly terminated the disability benefits (even though a nine-month trial period of continued benefits, to see if the insured really had overcome his handicap, would have been permissible under the law).

The young man proved unequal to the stress and returned to the hospital. His parents applied for reinstatement of benefits, but their application was denied, apparently in part because they were unable to get a supporting letter from the hospital physician, who feared it might be the basis of a suit against him. They filed an appeal. Nothing happened. According to them, they made repeated inquiries about the status of the appeal. Still nothing happened. The adverse initial decision left them unhappy, but at least they could take some action to have it reversed or modified; the delay on the appeal left them without benefits or formal recourse, an utterly frustrating position.

They therefore turned to the congressman for help, and in the spring of 1975 he assigned one of his caseworkers to assist them and

[30]Kenneth Culp Davis, *Administrative Law of the Seventies, Supplementing Administrative Law Treatise* (Lawyers Cooperative Publishing, 1976), p. 282.
[31]*The Federal Paperwork Burden*, S. Rept. 93–125, p. 14.

wrote personally to the Commissioner of Social Security. By the time October rolled around, the worker was still in the hospital, his parents were still without his disability benefits, and there was still no ruling on the appeal. "As of this date," the congressman fumed, "he still has not received a decision on his case: 1 year and 188 days after his case was opened." . . .

. . . [I]t was clearly a lamentable affair. And when it moved a U.S. congressman to air the situation in testimony before a congressional committee and in a major newspaper, it contributed to a hostile, scornful attitude toward government requirements on the part of a good many people. A few such cases from time to time can reinforce and spread the attitude. The belief that government is a quagmire of red tape is thus diffused throughout the society notwithstanding the possible unrepresentativeness of the individual cases underlying it.

25

Conquering Space
and Poverty:
Implementation as
Success and Failure

PAUL R. SCHULMAN

The Poverty Policy Start-up

The war on poverty began in a fashion not unlike the acceleration associated with manned space exploration—with an explicit Presidential mandate. On January 8, 1964, President Lyndon B. Johnson, in his first State of the Union address, announced to the nation: "This Administration today, here and now, declares unconditional war on poverty in America. I urge this Congress and all Americans to join with me in this effort." "Our aim," the President continued, "is not only to relieve the symptom of poverty, but to cure it, and above all, to prevent it."[1]

The President shortly after reinforced his "declaration of war" with a special message to Congress outlining the provisions of an Economic Opportunity Act. "I have called for a national war on poverty," Johnson reminded the Congress. "Our objective: total victory." The President described the act as a "total commitment by this President, and this Congress, and this nation, to pursue victory over the most ancient of mankind's enemies."[2]

Reprinted by permission of the publisher from Paul R. Schulman, *Large-Scale Policy Making*, pp. 78–95. Copyright 1980 by Elsevier Science Publishing Co., Inc. Tables are renumbered.

[1]*Public Papers of the Presidents, Lyndon B. Johnson, 1964* (Washington, DC: U.S. Government Printing Office, 1965), p. 114.
[2]Ibid., pp. 376, 380.

Again, as in the case of manned space exploration, it is instructive to review earlier efforts to cope with poverty problems prior to the casting of poverty policy in President Johnson's expansive terms. Prior to the Johnson commitment, little in the way of antipoverty policy was pursued among governmental agencies. To be sure, a patchwork of assorted public assistance and income support programs existed at federal and state governmental levels directed toward ameliorating the effects of poverty, but no public undertakings were directed toward systematically identifying and attacking the *causes* of poverty.[3] Indeed, much of the ancestry of the war on poverty lies in the private sector—in the "Grey Areas Program" of the Ford Foundation.

An experimental program of the late 1950s, the Grey Areas project was designed to effect slum rejuvenation in several major cities. It operated under the assumption that "rehabilitation of slum areas requires institutional changes including governmental reorganization."[4] In addition to the Ford Foundation, the President's Committee on Juvenile Delinquency and Youth Crime, formed in 1961, was also involved in antipoverty efforts—offering small grants to local communities for youth opportunity programs.

In these early days, antipoverty efforts lay essentially within the province of a technical elite of foundation officials, business leaders and social scientists, largely detached from formal policy-making institutions. In addition, unlike the case of manned space exploration, there did not exist a corpus of formal theory and research experience regarding poverty problems and their causal determinants. This is not to imply, however, as some have asserted, that there were no underlying theoretical persuasions surrounding the nature of antipoverty objectives. Peter Marris and Martin Rein in *Dilemmas of Social Reform* argue persuasively that an antipoverty "philosophy" did reside among many of the early antipoverty strategists.[5] There were several major ideas around which this philosophy coalesced:

> Poverty and delinquency were perpetuated by an inherited failure to respond, through ignorance, apathy and discouragement, to the de-

---

[3]Anderson, James E., Brady, David W., and Bullock, Charles, *Public Policy and Politics in America* (North Scituate, MA: Duxbury Press, 1978), p. 132.

[4]Levitan, Sar A., "The Design of Antipoverty Strategy," in *Aspects of Poverty*, edited by Ben B. Seligman (New York: Thomas Crowell, 1968), p. 252.

[5]See Marris, Peter and Rein, Martin, *Dilemmas of Social Reform: Poverty and Community Action in the United States* (New York: Atherton Press, 1967).

mands of urban civilization. The institutions of education and welfare had grown too insensitive and rigid to retrieve these failures, from a characteristic, morbid preoccupation with the maintenance of their organizational structure. The processes of assimilation were breaking down, and could only be repaired by an enlargement of opportunities. But this emancipation would only come about as the enabling institutions of assimilation—the schools, the welfare agencies, the vocational services—recognized their failure and became more imaginative, coherent, and responsive. The attack was directed at a self-protective hardening of middle-class American society, which at once neglected and condemned those it excluded.[6]

It was from this perspective that the Grey Areas program and many of the activities of the President's Committee were launched. It was also this persuasion that heavily influenced the architects of the war on poverty.

Early antipoverty efforts conducted during this period were oriented largely toward interruption of a perceived "cycle of poverty." This entailed vocational training and educational support for youth, job development and placement programs, as well as the provision of legal aid and other community services. Perhaps the most far-reaching dimension of early antipoverty strategy, however, was the stress on organizational reforms designed to upgrade community action. The community action commitment was derived from the idea that one of the major causal components associated with the cycle of poverty is a deficiency in political activity, efficacy and legitimacy on the part of the poor. Given the limited institutional base from which initial antipoverty efforts were launched, it was perceived as imperative that the poor develop their own independent political base from which to enlarge and safeguard poverty programs.

Community action, during this period, entailed the creation of local organizations that enlisted citizen participation in the drafting and submission of grant proposals for antipoverty aid. Community involvement from these earliest planning stages was considered a major safeguard against contamination of poverty efforts by hostile bureaucratic interests.

It is not appropriate here to describe in detail the design and practice of these early antipoverty programs. But it *is* important to evaluate these formative efforts from the standpoint of those thresh-

[6]Ibid., p. 53.

old problems in antipoverty objectives with which they were confronted. . . .

Basically, three major deficiencies beset antipoverty efforts during this period: an absence of political activation on the part of the poor; vastly inadequate organizational resources; and a lack of coherence in program application. From these deficiencies a variety of secondary dilemmas followed in turn.

Problems of Political Quiescence

Antipoverty policy in its early stages entailed the design and pursuit of projects directed toward a clientele singularly devoid of political energy.[7] Perhaps no other factor was as crucial to the pursuit of poverty policy in this early period as this. The absence of political mobilization on the part of the poor led first to an indifference and, later, to unreserved hostility from established political and bureaucratic interests. The absence of a politically articulate constituency left the reform projects of the Ford Foundation and the President's Committee in precarious institutional positions vis-à-vis these interests. This basic political insecurity was responsible for a multitude of specific problems in early antipoverty efforts.

One such problem involved the resistance of professional educators and school officials to provisions in many of the educational opportunity programs for the poor. These programs frequently sought to induce curricular and grading reforms, new teaching and counselling techniques, and even home visitation on the part of teachers.[8] Because of the novelty of these approaches, many educators were suspicious of their intent and resentful of perceived intrusions upon professional autonomy. Yet the lack of an institutional base from which to implement their programs forced early poverty officials to rely solely upon the cooperation of the schools—a requirement that necessitated delicate and complex negotiations, frequent delays and program compromises which led to highly uncertain implementation in the best of cases and subversion of intent in the worst.

Attempts at the selective mobilization of poverty clientele

[7] Economist Gunnar Myrdal has referred to America's poor as "the world's least revolutionary proletariat." See Myrdal, Gunnar, "The War on Poverty," in *New Perspectives on Poverty*, edited by Arthur B. Shostak and William Gomberg (Englewood Cliffs, NJ: Prentice-Hall, 1965), p. 122.

[8] Marris and Rein, op. cit., p. 59.

proved scarcely more successful. One such effort was made by the Mobilization for Youth project in New York City. Leaders of this project "recognized the limitations of cooperation, and used it [sic] to justify a more aggressive approach. Since Mobilization believed that the exercise of power would help the poor to overcome their apathy, it turned to the organization of pressure upon the schools."[9]

Yet the Mobilization project soon discovered itself to be in a position from which selective political pressure could not successfully be applied. The schools had the power to resist such pressure by employing a strategy termed by E. E. Schattschneider, the "socialization of conflict."[10] As Schattschneider asserts, "As likely as not, the audience determines the outcome of a fight."[11] By escalating the public scope of controversy, the schools were able to project their disputes with the Mobilization project into a political arena in which their resources were simply overwhelming. The schools, in other words, "could expose Mobilization to national attention. . . . Mobilization was not prepared to withstand an attack on this scale, and lacked a political constituency large enough to defend it."[12]

Here a major threshold problem is illustrated. The project was confronted with an *absence of middle ground* between total dependency upon school system cooperation (with its attendant threat of program distortion) and high level political conflict in which their limited constituency support was easily overwhelmed. "Mobilization for Youth found, then, that it could not pursue a militant strategy on its own terms, limiting the conflict to issues of its choosing. Any confrontation exposed it to the risk of an overwhelmingly virulent reaction, which it lacked the resources to withstand, while cooperation robbed it of the freedom to attempt any radical innovation."[13]

This dilemma encountered by the Mobilization project surrounded many of the other antipoverty programs of this period as well. With no activation on the part of the poor and no legitimate institutional base from which to gain policy compliance from established bureaucracies, the Grey Areas and President's Committee un-

[9]Ibid., p. 67.
[10]See Schattschneider, E. E., *The Semi-Sovereign People* (New York: Holt, Rinehart and Winston, 1960).
[11]Ibid., p. 2.
[12]Marris and Rein, op. cit., p. 69.
[13]Idem.

dertakings generally foundered. Most remained in inchoate and turbulent organizational states.

Problems in Resource Deficiency

A second major contributing factor to the effectiveness problems of these early antipoverty efforts was a deficiency in resources with which they were afflicted. The President's Committee appropriations ran from $6 to $8 million annually with less than $11 million available for project support in its first three years. The Ford Foundation, meanwhile, appropriated approximately $20 million all told to its Grey Areas and related programs.[14] These funds were limited in both amount and application. Most of the President's Committee's resources, for example, were directed toward planning grants substantially detached from the establishment of frameworks for program implementation and action. The Grey Areas project channeled its funds into only five major cities and the state of North Carolina.

Limited funding and commensurately small staffing undermined seriously the effectiveness of these early antipoverty undertakings. Moreover, the projects were consistently unable to generate the commitment of public resources at the local level—resources which were urgently needed to augment their own inadequate funding. The indifference of local communities left the projects not only undersupported, but also fragmented and isolated, without coordination with existing urban programs. As Marris and Rein assert: "In the end, cities seldom made any substantial contributions from their own resources . . . ; innovative ideas tended to relapse into conventional practice, or were simply ignored; undertakings were not honored; or programs which should have reinforced each other were, for administrative convenience, implemented without coordination."[15]

Problems of Coordination and Coherence

The coordination difficulties encountered in these early antipoverty programs are particularly significant insofar as thresholds in poverty objectives are concerned. As poverty-cycle theory asserted, the causal determinants of poverty were multiple and interrelated,

---

[14]Levitan, op. cit., p. 253, and Marris and Rein, op. cit., pp. 28–29.
[15]Marris and Rein, op. cit., p. 148.

requiring concerted attack on many fronts. Antipoverty policy architects were persuaded as to the necessity of this approach and entertained hopes that such a coordinated set of attacks could be designed. " 'We wanted to provide a framework,' as Lloyd Ohlin, consultant to the President's Committee, explained, 'where we could concentrate a whole series of programs together in the same area. This would show greater impact. We felt that the problem was not just one of providing new services here and there but of *trying to reach a new threshold* by an integrated approach [emphasis added].' "[16] It was just this aspiration that was not realized, indeed could not be realized, at the scale of these pioneering programs.

Many important aspects of the poverty "problems" addressed by these early efforts lay essentially outside the range of their possible impact. The job training and placement projects, for example, could only hope to be effective insofar as jobs were actually available in private sector industries and these industries were willing to hire the disadvantaged. The education projects depended upon the cooperation of educational bureaucracies which had few incentives and fewer guidelines under which to offer it. All of the poverty projects depended, in a larger sense, upon the performance of the American economy.

It was the growing realization of the need to gain some measure of control over many of these external poverty-influencing factors— the need for a concerted and comprehensive antipoverty approach— that was in large part responsible for the arousal of governmental interest in a war on poverty. One might, in fact, argue that it was the implicit recognition of scale requisites associated with antipoverty objectives that motivated governmental policy planners.[17] This recognition, heightened during the early days of the Kennedy administration, became a primary drive behind the early design of the war on poverty. As one analyst described it:

> The Kennedy piecemeal programs, built on those of his predecessors, were reaching toward the substratum of the population in which all the problems were concentrated but somehow not making contact,

[16]Ibid., p. 141.

[17]For a useful account of this formative period of the war on poverty, see James L. Sundquist, "Origins of the War on Poverty," in *On Fighting Poverty*, edited by James I. Sundquist (New York: Basic Books, 1969), pp. 3–33; and Levitan, Sar, *The Great Society's Poor Law* (Baltimore: Johns Hopkins Press, 1969).

not on a scale and with an impact that measured up to the bright promise of a new Frontier. The measures enacted, and those proposed, were dealing separately with such problems as slum housing, juvenile delinquency, unemployment, dependency and illiteracy but *they were separately inadequate* because they were striking only at some of the surface aspects of a bedrock problem, and that bedrock problem had to be identified and defined so that it could be attacked in a concerted, unified and innovative way.[18]

Related to this sense of inefficacy surrounding the evaluation of existing programs was a growing realization within the Kennedy administration that the "spillover" effects of technology and prosperity were in themselves insufficient to result in the eradication of poverty. Economic expansion, once presumed to be the best overall remedy for problems of poverty, came under increasingly critical scrutiny in the Kennedy administration insofar as its antipoverty powers were concerned. The Council of Economic Advisors, under the direction of Walter Heller, in May of 1963, communicated a report to the President, asserting a diminishing impact of economic growth upon the reduction of "poor" families (annual income below $3000) in the United States. The Council's analysis "showed that for the postwar period ending in the early 1960s economic growth had apparently become continuously less effective in reducing poverty, and that the incidence of poverty, although declining, was declining at an ever slower rate. . . ."[19]

President Kennedy, apparently persuaded by these arguments, directed the Council, the Budget Bureau and the Departments of Labor and Health, Education, and Welfare "to make the case for a major policy attack on poverty."[20]

The Design and Prosecution of the War on Poverty

It remained for President Lyndon B. Johnson to propose formally in 1964 the war on poverty program. The architects of this program, many of whom had participated in Grey Areas or President's Com-

---

[18]Sundquist, op. cit., p. 8.

[19]Kershaw, Joseph A., *Government Against Poverty* (Washington, DC: The Brookings Institution, 1970), p. 22.

[20]Plotnick, Robert D. and Skidmore, Felicity, *Progress Against Poverty* (New York: Academic Press, 1975), p. 3.

mittee projects, were sensitive to the scale dilemmas encountered in the earlier antipoverty efforts. Many scale requisites were directly addressed in the proposal to the Congress of the Economic Opportunity Act.

Recognition of the need for coordination and coherence in antipoverty programming, for example, was reflected in the proposed Office of Economic Opportunity—an independent agency within the Executive Office of the President, described as "a national headquarters for the war against poverty." In communicating the Economic Opportunity Act to Congress, President Johnson asserted that "I do not intend that the war against poverty become a series of uncoordinated and unrelated efforts—that it perish for lack of leadership and direction."[21]

Problems relating to political mobilization were attacked in the Economic Opportunity Act on two fronts. First, the Act proposed creation of the Community Action Program, designed to activate local citizens and the poor themselves (although in ways initially unspecified), on behalf of antipoverty programs. In addition, by asserting a Presidential commitment, the Johnson administration was in effect "nationalizing" the war—or, in Schattschneider's terms, enlarging the political arenas within which poverty programs could successfully compete.

Lastly, the antipoverty act addressed itself to the resource deficiencies encountered by earlier poverty efforts. President Johnson proposed the appropriation of $970 million to finance the war on poverty during fiscal year 1965 and called for the enlistment of thousands of antipoverty personnel.

Primarily, the EOA consisted of job training and education programs for youth, the Community Action Program, a volunteer project (VISTA), and rural and small business loans. With large Democratic majorities in both houses of Congress, the EOA was enacted substantially as President Johnson proposed it (with an $800 million appropriation for fiscal year 1965) after only a minimum legislative delay.

Policy Problems Relating to Scale

It is appropriate at this point to portray important contrasts between the prosecution of the war on poverty and the development

---

[21]*Public Papers of the Presidents, Lyndon B. Johnson, 1963–64*, p. 379.

of the space program in its post-legislative period. Although both undertakings had been launched under Presidential mandate and strong Congressional endorsement, dissimilarities between the two are evident at once.

The consolidation and integration of components of the two policies varied substantially. NASA, upon its formation, began to acquire control over major research and development projects of foreseeable consequence to manned space exploration. In poverty policy, however, a very different consolidation pattern developed. The Office of Economic Opportunity was never able to gain an effective integration among the major offenses of the war on poverty. Of the programs outlined in the Opportunity Act, only Community Action, the Job Corps, Vista and the Migrant Farm Workers programs fell under the direct jurisdiction of OEO. The Neighborhood Youth Corps was quickly placed under the management of the Department of Labor, the College Work Study and Work Experience programs fell to H.E.W., the Rural Loan and Small Business Development programs were delegated to the Department of Agriculture and Small Business Administration, respectively. These agencies were instructed to cooperate with the Director of OEO, and the delegated programs were financed through appropriations made to the Economic Opportunity Office, but in practice the coordination did not go smoothly. As one observer noted:

> [Throughout the history of the war on poverty] . . . the business of delegation has raised a number of questions. Not the least of these is who is responsible for a delegated program. It might seem clear that OEO's director should be responsible—it is his authorization by law and the funds are his by appropriation. But it is not that simple. While the director has to fit the delegated programs into the overall war against poverty, each agency administering a delegated program also has its own constituency to think of, and conflicts have never been far below the surface.[22]

Not only were there specific problems of coordination arising from the delegation of programs (and in this regard conflicts between OEO and the Department of Labor in connection with the Neighborhood Youth Corps were particularly acute) but the war on poverty as a policy lacked coherence on a much larger scale. The entire public assistance program of the Federal government and the Federal and

[22]Kershaw, *Government Against Poverty*, op. cit., pp. 152–153.

state unemployment compensation program were unincorporated into the framework of the war. These programs addressed large numbers of constituents identified as "poor" (and consequently claimed by OEO) and at the same time commanded enormous financial resources. In fiscal year 1965, the first year of OEO operation, Federal outlays for major public assistance programs alone amounted to $3.7 billion and these funds reached over 7 million recipients.[23] (Contrast this with OEO's appropriation for 1965 of $800 million.) These public assistance and unemployment compensation programs amounted to substantial interventions in the "poverty constituency" yet they were ungovernable in connection with antipoverty policy. Moreover, during the life of the war these programs were to grow and diversify at impressive rates, with public assistance expenditures (including newer medicare, medicaid and food stamp outlays) amounting to over $27 billion by 1973.[24] In the detachment of these programs from the framework of the war on poverty, a major source of problem-solving leverage was denied to poverty policy makers.

In short, the design of the war did not feature an administrative and programmatic cohesion at anywhere near the level attained in the space program. In fact, one antipoverty policy analyst has contended that "It is apparent from the legislative history of the Economic Opportunity Act that no overall rational plan dictated either the selection of programs to be included in the Act or their distribution between the new OEO and federal agencies already in the poverty business."[25]

A second important departure between the war and space program can be found in the rate of increase in budgetary allocations accorded to each. It is inappropriate to compare actual allocations to the two policies directly, as if poverty and space "dollars" were equivalent units, but it *is* useful to consider in each case the relationship between expenditures prior to policy acceleration (as a base)

---

[23]These figures include expenditures under the Aid to the Aged, Blind and Disabled as well as the Aid to Families with Dependent Children programs. See Schultze, Charles L. et al., *Setting National Priorities: The 1973 Budget* (Washington, DC: The Brookings Institution, 1972), p. 188.

[24]See Blechman, Barry M. et al., *Setting National Priorities: The 1975 Budget* (Washington, DC: The Brookings Institution, 1974), p. 168.

[25]Levitan, Sar A. and Davidson, Roger H., *Anti-Poverty Housekeeping: The Administration of the Economic Opportunity Act* (Ann Arbor: University of Michigan Press, 1968), p. 6.

and subsequent appropriations after Presidential commitment. It is also revealing to relate postcommitment expenditures to the *expectations* of support residing among policy makers themselves.

First, a brief reminiscence regarding space program growth. Table 1 displays rates of appropriations increase for NASA over each previous fiscal year during the period 1960–1966.

As can readily be discerned, the expansion of appropriations to the space program was very rapid—representing an immediate and sizeable series of dollar increases over those expenditures made prior to policy acceleration. Even before the lunar landing commitment, the formation of NASA itself in 1958 led to a 62 percent increase in research and development and research plant expenditures in the very next year.[26]

The war on poverty, despite its rhetorical presentation, experienced only a marginal build-up and expansion, particularly in relation to total expenditures for public assistance-oriented programs. Table 2 depicts OEO and antipoverty related expenditures during the 1965–1974 period. In addition, it displays the rates of increase in these funds during each fiscal year. No rate of increase is computed for FY 1966 as the 1965 appropriation was for a six-month period only. FY 1966 is the first full-year OEO appropriation.

Also revealing are comparisons between poverty program funds and amounts spent on low income and public assistance support.

TABLE 1 *Rates of Appropriation Increase—NASA (FY 1960–66)*[a]

Fiscal Year	Rate of Increase[b]
1960	58.4
1961	84.7
1962	88.9
1963	101.3
1964	38.8
1965	2.9
1966	1.4

[a]Compiled from data obtained from NASA, Program and Special Reports Division, Washington, D.C.
[b]Percentage of gain over previous fiscal year.

[26]See, for data regarding research expenditures over time, *Federal Funds for Research and Development and Other Scientific Activities*, National Science Foundation (Washington, DC: U.S. Government Printing Office, 1970), pp. 230–231.

TABLE 2   *OEO and Antipoverty-Related Expenditures: FY 1965–74*[a]

Fiscal Year	Expenditures ($ × 10⁶)	Percentage Increase Over Previous Fiscal Year
1965	737.0	———
1966	1403.6	———[b]
1967	1623.4	15
1968	1695.5	4
1969	1896.1	11
1970	1824.9	−3
1971	1286.6	−29
1972	681.2	−47
1973	465.4	−31
1974	328.5	−29

[a]Compiled from Plotnick, Robert and Skidmore, Felicity, *Progress Against Poverty* (New York: Academic Press, 1975), pp. 8–10.
[b]No percentage computed due to half-year appropriation in FY 1965.

These latter funds represent, in some respects, the "unincorporated resources" denied to the war on poverty: their proportion provides a sense of scale regarding poverty program expenditures. (See Table 3.)

As is suggested here, the resource scales of the war on poverty and space program varied considerably. The war was never funded at levels anticipated in line with its publicly asserted tasks nor was it able to gain any measure of incorporation or control over those programs that were accorded large appropriations and that directed them toward appropriate constituencies. Manned space exploration, in contrast, featured a coordinating agency (NASA) that gained jurisdiction over the majority of funds spent within a sustained period on space exploration research and hardware development. In fact, during its appropriations peak in 1966, NASA expenditures accounted for almost 37 percent of *all* research and development and R&D-plant funds spent throughout the entire Federal government.[27]

As is evident, the war on poverty was placed within an appropriations framework far different from that experienced by NASA. OEO was never able to attain the level of support required to mount an effective attack upon those thresholds associated with poverty pol-

[27]Idem.

TABLE 3 OEO and Antipoverty Expenditures vs. Federal Low-Income
and Public Assistance Expenditures[a]
(Selected Fiscal Years)

Fiscal Year	OEO and Antipoverty Expenditures[b]	Low-Income and Public Assistance[b]	% OEO vs. L.I.–P.A.
1970	1824.9	12,927	14
1973	465.4	20,945	2

[a]Includes unemployment compensation, AFDC, food stamp, medicaid programs, etc.; *excludes* social security, medicare and other retirement expenditures.
[b]In millions of dollars.

icy making. "Basic to all other problems [was] the lack of resources to do the job."[28]

Moreover, the rate of OEO's appropriations increase was never matched appropriately with poverty policy *expectations*. The promise of continuing and enlarging support, so important in the early stages of the space program, was significantly eroded within the framework of poverty program finance. At the outset of the war, expectations were high that a substantial enlargement of funds would take place in subsequent years—expectations held among policy makers and policy recipients alike. Yet clearly such increases did not occur. "Instead of expanding antipoverty programs, OEO in 1967 was fighting for its very life."[29] Important problems of management as well as substantial political turbulence were introduced into the poverty program because of its funding insecurities. As two poverty analysts contend:

> Of all OEO travails, those associated with funding were the most serious impediment to efficient and smooth operations. That there was not enough money to wage 'an unconditional war on poverty' needs no repetition; but the way Congress handled the annual OEO appropriations bears particular emphasis. . . . Even within the usual constraints of annual budgeting, Congress seemed to do its utmost to prevent orderly planning and administration of EOA efforts.[30]

Under these financial circumstances, many long-range planning efforts undertaken within the poverty agency had to be abandoned. In

[28]Kershaw, op. cit., p. 165.
[29]Levitan and Davidson, op. cit., p. 27.
[30]Ibid., p. 58.

addition, operating programs of the war also suffered considerably. Community action was one such program in particular.

> The growth and development of community action was stunted after its first year when, in December 1965, the White House imposed severe and unexpected budgetary limitations on domestic programs for the period beginning July 1, 1966. These limitations were made more severe the next year when Congress earmarked large portions of community action funds for specific programs. This double deceleration of the community action program was particularly painful because of disappointed expectations around the country, right down to the neighborhood level in city after city. The limitations also made it harder to recruit and retain capable local administrators and project directors, whose presence may turn out to be the single most important variable in the success of local programs.[31]

Budgetary stringency during the critical developmental period of the war not only undermined the evolution of poverty programs, it also placed these programs within much more turbulent political environments. "OEO found that it had created activities and expectations in more communities than it was able to persuade the Congress to finance during succeeding years, so that incipient programs were not funded and existing programs sometimes cut back."[32] The cutback of these programs aroused cynicism and antagonism toward OEO on the part of many of those who had become self-identified as war on poverty clientele. For many poverty projects, there was "little difficulty in evoking a response from the people they tried to serve: their most urgent and intractable problem was to satisfy the demand they raised."[33] Ultimately, some have contended, unfulfilled antipoverty expectations contributed to outbreaks of urban violence throughout the United States in the middle and late 1960s. In this connection, Detroit Mayor Jerome Cavanagh asserted after the July 1967 riots in his city: "What we've been doing, at the level we've been doing it, is almost worse than nothing at all. . . . We've raised expectations, but we haven't been able to deliver all we should have. . . . "[34]

[31]Wofford, John G., "The Politics of Local Responsibility: Administration of the Community Action Program," in *On Fighting Poverty*, edited by James L. Sundquist, p. 101.

[32]Yarmolinsky, Adam, "The Beginnings of OEO," in Sundquist, op. cit., p. 50.

[33]Marris and Rein, op. cit., p. 225.

[34]Cavanagh, Jerome P., as quoted in Kershaw, op. cit., p. 166.

Additional Poverty Program Deficiencies

Administrative consolidation and budgetary support are not the only points of departure between the space program and the war on poverty. The prosecution of the war never attained the degree of political independence and self-sufficiency evidenced by space exploration after the Kennedy lunar landing commitment. I have discussed earlier the importance to large-scale policy objectives of such independence. These objectives in their pursuit are highly vulnerable to the reduction and compromise processes associated with conventional political negotiation. Such processes are forces of disaggregation which threaten to push large-scale undertakings below one or more critical effectiveness thresholds.

In the case of antipoverty policy, a self-sustaining political foundation did not ensue from the Johnson mandate to end poverty. It is, in fact, very revealing to note how quickly the Johnson mandate *itself* eroded under the impact of political attack. As poverty programs began to confront established political interests and arouse new political activism among heretofore quiescent clienteles, a Presidential retrenchment began. "Less was heard of the 'War on Poverty' and more of the 'poverty program.' And the latter had a much narrower definition. . . . "[35] A Lyndon Johnson increasingly preoccupied with the conduct of another war—the war in Vietnam—had little interest in further association with a policy beset on all sides by political controversy.

For the poverty program, the Johnson mandate was in no sense the mobilizing and sustaining force that the Kennedy commitment proved to be in the case of manned space exploration. Indeed, "few would have dared predict on the midday in January 1964 when a new President declared 'unconditional war on poverty,' saying that the objective was 'total victory,' that in the months ahead the presidential resolve would diminish and withdraw, not all at once, but in numerous, painful, almost measureless ways."[36]

The consequences of this diminishing resolve were widely ramified throughout the poverty program. A direct effect was the increased vulnerability of the war on poverty to external intrusion and intervention. The Economic Opportunity Act itself was subject to

[35]Sundquist, op. cit., p. 31.
[36]Selover, William C., "The View from Capitol Hill: Harassment and Survival," in *On Fighting Poverty*, edited by James L. Sundquist, p. 185.

frequent Congressional amendment—altering the foundation upon which the war depended. Particularly vulnerable to legislative modification was the Community Action Program. Political turmoil engulfed community action projects at their outset with disputes centering around representation of the poor, the selection of objectives and the political independence of the projects from City Hall jurisdictions.[37] As a result of these antagonisms, important revisions were made in the operating guidelines of the community action program.

One such modification resulted from the well-publicized "Green amendment" to the Opportunity Act. This 1967 reform enabled city administrations "to assume sponsorship of Community Action Programs."[38] The Green amendment, coupled with internal executive directives from the Bureau of the Budget to OEO officials, placed community action more squarely within conventional urban institutional settings than antipoverty architects had originally intended. In addition, an earlier legislative action had an even more direct effect in undermining the independence of the community action program. In 1966, under pressure from many of the nation's mayors, Congress enacted the Model Cities program. This represented an alternative and competing approach to urban housing and antipoverty policy making. Termed a "mayor's program," Model Cities was directed at many of those same problems addressed by community action but was firmly under the control of local governments. Moreover, Model Cities by virtue of its administrative location within the Department of Housing and Urban Development represented yet another set of antipoverty resources detached from OEO jurisdiction and the framework of the war.

The Poverty War and the Welfare Establishment

Perhaps the most revealing illustration of the failure of the war on poverty to gain the degree of political self-sufficiency acquired by the space program is the "capture" of many antipoverty undertakings by established welfare personnel and institutions. One of the viewpoints, it will be recalled, taken to heart by many antipoverty policy architects was that professionalized bureaucracies in welfare and ed-

---

[37]For an interesting treatment of the controversy surrounding the Community Action Program, see Moynihan, Daniel P., *Maximum Feasible Misunderstanding* (New York: The Free Press, 1969).

[38]Plotnick and Skidmore, *Progress Against Poverty*, op. cit., p. 24.

ucation had lost both the sensitivity and flexibility to deal effectively with problems of the poor.

> OEO was at first conceived as independent of the "welfare professionals" who had traditionally dealt with the needy and the unskilled—educators, training specialists and social workers. However well-intentioned the traditional welfare programs had been, Shriver and many of his associates seemed to believe that they had stagnated in the hands of the professional associations and state agencies which controlled them. Moreover, these groups were accused of having 'captured' some bureaus in the Department of Health, Education and Welfare which were charged with implementing national programs.[39]

Early antagonisms erupted between these "welfare professionals" and poverty program officials as the latter attempted to assert and maintain their independence. Yet, ultimately, without adequate resources or a self-sustaining political base, major compromises had to be made in the conduct of the war to the power of established welfare interests. In its precarious political position, "OEO could not live without the welfare profession and . . . it soon realized this fact."[40]

Unlike the pursuit of space exploration, the war on poverty was never able to attain an organizational transcendence of those limiting factors associated with conventional policy compromise and competition. Yet these very limiting factors were perceived by many antipoverty policy makers to be *precisely at the heart of the poverty problem*. "Whether OEO liked it or not, existing organizational and personnel resources were firmly in the hands of the so-called professionals. Of necessity, OEO found many of its dollars going to the same interests which had been administering the traditional programs."[41]

The final set of jurisdictional battles lost by OEO were fought over control of its original set of core programs, and ultimately, over the agency's survival itself. Between 1965 and 1969, OEO lost no fewer than eight of its programs to rival cabinet departments and executive agencies. Some of the initial losses were major ones—Work Study, Adult Education, Head Start and Upward Bound programs transferred to H.E.W.; the Neighborhood Youth Corps and Job Corps

---

[39]Davidson and Levitan, op. cit., p. 45.
[40]Ibid., p. 46.
[41]Ibid., pp. 45–46.

to the Department of Labor.[42] The dissolution accelerated between 1971 and 1974, and in the latter year OEO itself was abolished by Congress, the war on poverty having long since been abandoned as a viable policy by the executive branch.

Antipoverty Policy: Performance and Factors of Scale

The inventory presented here of policy problems associated with the war on poverty is clearly not an evaluation of the *effects* of the war on the dimensions of American poverty. Such evaluations have proven extremely difficult despite intensive political and academic interest in them—just as evaluation has proven difficult in a variety of other policy areas.[43]

Statistical analyses reveal a significant drop in the number of American families living below "official" poverty income levels during the 1965–1968 period.[44] But beyond this evidence, assessments of the war are contradictory. There are no persuasively demonstrated causal linkages, for example, between this statistical decline and the war on poverty specifically. Many other public welfare-oriented programs were in operation during this same period. Moreover, two antipoverty analysts have contended in this connection that "the most effective antipoverty program of the 1960s was the Vietnam war."[45] (Also at issue in the evaluation of the poverty program is the contention that the number of families living in relative poverty has actually *increased* since 1968.)[46]

[42]For an account of this jurisdictional decay see James, Dorothy B., *Analyzing Poverty Policy* (Lexington, MA: Lexington Books, 1975).

[43]For a discussion of evaluation difficulties connected with the war, see Rossi, Peter, "Practice, Method and Theory in Evaluating Social Action Programs," in Sundquist, op. cit., pp. 217–234; and Williams, Walter and Evans, John W., The politics of evaluation: The case of head start, *Annals of the American Academy of Political and Social Science* 385 (September, 1969): 118–132.

[44]See Blechman, Barry M., et al., *Setting National Priorities: The 1975 Budget*, op. cit., p. 167; and Plotnick and Skidmore, op. cit., pp. 169–189. For a more general assertion of success regarding the war and other "Great Society" programs see Levitan, Sar and Taggart, Robert, *The Promise of Greatness* (Cambridge: Harvard University Press, 1976).

[45]Levitan, Sar and Mangum, Garth, Programs and priorities, *The Reporter* (September 7, 1967), p. 22.

[46]Plotnick and Skidmore, op. cit., p. 175.

For our purposes here, however, certain assessments of the war on poverty can be safely undertaken aside from these controversies. Clearly, the war has failed in its publicly stated objective of "total victory" in the elimination of American poverty. It has failed to live up to those expectations it aroused among its own clientele. The war has also failed to sustain itself as an ongoing public policy venture, as the elimination of many of its programs and the dissolution of OEO will attest.

Yet for all this, there is a failure associated with the war on poverty that is even more important from our standpoint. This is the failure of the poverty program in its operation and institutionalization *to reflect the theories and design of its architects.* Here, indeed, is the failure of a policy—large-scale in its objectives and design— to find accommodation in an appropriate political and organizational environment.

Antipoverty policy, in the eyes of its primary theoreticians and managers, was an enterprise with important requisites associated with its pursuit. Among these requisites were a political activation on the part of the poor; a substantial commitment of public resources for education and employment programs; and a detachment of these programs from unresponsive and self-serving welfare bureaucracies. As it turned out, these proved to be large-scale requisites; that is, they had to be provided at high levels or they simply could not be provided at all. Antipoverty policy requisites could not be attained in piecemeal fashion appropriate to conventional pluralist processes. Instead, they were beset by thresholds just as were those requisites associated with manned space exploration. In this case, however, these thresholds were never breached in the institutional expression of the policy. . . .

26

Redundancy, Rationality, and the Problem of Duplication and Overlap

MARTIN LANDAU

Not so long ago I experienced an emergency landing. We had been aloft only a short time when the pilot announced some mechanical failure. As we headed toward the nearest airport, the man behind me, no less frightened than I, said to his companion, "Here's where my luck runs out." A few minutes later we touched down to a safe landing amidst foam trucks and asbestos-clad fire fighters.

On the ground I ran into the pilot and asked him about the trouble. His response was vague, but he did indicate that something had been wrong with the rudder. How, then, was he able to direct and land the plane? He replied that the situation had not really been as ominous as it had seemed: the emergency routines we had followed were necessary precautions and he had been able to compensate for the impairment of the rudder by utilizing additional features of the aircraft. There were, he said, safety factors built into all planes.

Happily, such matters had not been left to chance, luck, as we say. For a commercial airliner is a very redundant system, a fact which accounts for its reliability of performance; a fact which also accounts for its adaptability.

Reprinted with permission from *Public Administration Review* (July/August 1969). © 1969 by The American Society for Public Administration, 1120 G Street, N.W., Washington, D.C. 20005. All rights reserved. Footnotes are renumbered.

A Paradox

The English language presents us with a striking curiosity. Its lexicons establish an instance of *redundancy* as a "liability" and yet it is precisely the liberal use of redundancy that provides linguistic expression with an extraordinary measure of "reliability."

The Definition

In the context of ordinary language, redundancy is said to exist whenever there is an excess or superfluity of anything. The excess may be of parts, of rules, of words, . . . of anything. *Excess*, as defined lexically, is something which is more than the normal, the required, the usual, the specified. It is useless, superfluous, needless— terms which are variously employed to define *redundancy*.

This linguistic habit directs a negative judgment. It points to features of a situation which are of no value, which are wasteful, which are bad. The force of this habit is immediately to be seen by noting that the synonyms for the adjective *excessive* are: immoderate, intemperate, inordinate, extravagant, exorbitant, and extreme. If we need a time scale here, we can note that excessive has been used to define redundancy for some 400 years.

Accordingly, to say of a person's speech that it is redundant is not to extend a compliment. To observe an excess of parts is to observe an unnecessary duplication which, almost automatically, is seen as waste. To confront an excess of rules is, naturally, to make unhappy contact with red tape. And so on. In each case, more than is necessary is apparent, a condition which is sometimes regarded as affluent but more often as profligate. It is rarely regarded as economic and even less often as efficient. Indeed, there are many who seem to make *zero redundancy* the measure of both economy and efficiency. And if this condition is not fully realizable in practice, it nevertheless stands as the optimal state to be attained.

So powerful is this convention, that when Harry Nyquist introduced "redundancy" as a technical term in information theory, it referred to the useless portions of a message—those which could be eliminated without any loss of information. Nyquist sought a non-redundant system, one which would permit the transmission of information with the absolutely minimal number of signs that could possibly be employed.[1] Today, however, this goal is no longer entertained. It has been set aside; not because it is impossible of achievement, but because its realization would, in fact, increase the probability of failure—of false, misleading, and distorted messages.

Public Administration and Redundancy

It is, however, the lexical evaluation of redundancy which prevails in public administration. Indeed, this view is to be seen as programmatic in such revitalization movements as Taylorism and scientific management. These demanded the wholesale removal of duplication and overlap as they pressed for "streamlined organizations" that would operate with the absolutely minimal number of units that could possibly be employed in the performance of a task. Zero redundancy constituted the measure of optimal efficiency and this ideal, fortified by a scarcity of resources and an abundance of precedent, has informed both the theory and practice of public administration since the earliest days of the reform movement. Now, of course, we possess new vocabularies, direct our attention to management control systems, and seize upon such new technologies as PPBS (Planning-Programming-Budgeting System). But our perspective remains fully as Utopian as it was a half-century ago.[2]

For the plain fact is that no amount of effort has yet been able to produce, even for limited time-spans, the precise mutually exclusive differentiation of activity that administrative integrationists long for. . . . In the last thirty years we have observed massive efforts to reduce duplication: we have moved from the radical reconstructions which followed upon the Roosevelt and Hoover commissions to the institution of continuous executive reorganization—only to find that duplication and overlap are as conspicuous today as they have ever been. . . .

. . . The removal of redundancy is rarely, if ever, challenged in the technology of public administration. It is an article of faith, a commanding precept: and if its injunctions cannot be followed today, one can always dream of tomorrow. Those controversies that

---

[1] J. R. Pierce, *Symbols, Signals and Noise* (New York: Harper & Row, 1961), pp. 35–39. Also, see chap. 7 and 8.

[2] Dwight Waldo, *The Administrative State* (New York: Ronald Press, 1948), pp. 37–38.

do arise generally concern the manner in which repair is to be effected and are not expressed any more differently than when Francis W. Coker cast a skeptical eye on the dogmas of administration. The doubts he raised turned on whether more might be accomplished through an incremental strategy than by a process of radical integration. But with respect to the need to "eliminate duplication and overlapping,"[3] he felt obliged to state, "No serious exception can be taken to this principle."[4]

In what follows, I shall exercise a theoretical option and take such exception. I cannot argue the case in full here, but I shall try to show that there are good grounds for suggesting that efforts to improve public administration by eliminating duplication and overlap would, if successful, produce just the opposite effect. That so many attempts have failed should perhaps alert us to what sociologists would call the "latent function" of this type of redundancy. This possibility alone is sufficient warrant for transforming a precept into a problem.

Redundancy and Error Suppression: Reliability

There is, however, an additional reason for doing so.

The reader will observe that the phenomenon of "duplication" is no longer left to chance in the study of language. Nor is it overlooked in the design of automobiles, computers, and aircraft; the latter are reliable to the extent that they are redundant—and we have all had occasion to note that a good deal of the controversy over "safe cars" has had to do with the introduction of this feature as a standard element of design, as with the dual braking system, for example. That is, there is now a developing theory of redundancy, and while it was originally conceived of in the domains of information science (including computer technology) and natural automata (neural networks), it appears to have very wide application. In many areas, therefore, "over-engineering," "reserve power," and "safety-factors" of all sorts need no longer be dealt with intuitively. . . .

In public administration the standard policy for improving the

[3]Once again this is a goal of the newly proposed "Hoover Commission"; see *Public Administration News*, August 1967, p. 2.
[4]"Dogmas of Administrative Reform," *The American Political Science Review* 16 (August 1922).

performance characteristics of an administrative agency has rested upon the classical axiom that the reliability and efficiency of an operating system, man or machine, is dependent on the reliability and efficiency of each of its parts, including linkages. Improvement, therefore, calls for a system to be broken down (decomposed or analyzed) into its most basic units, these to be worked on to the point of infallibility. So much success has attended this procedure, especially as regards machine-based systems, that it not only constitutes a sound problem-solving paradigm, but is often generalized into a good common-sense rule. About the only limitations which are imposed on its application are those which derive from market conditions, the law of diminishing returns, and the state of the art.

Yet it is doubtful that the risk of failure can be removed in this manner even in the most advanced technologies. No matter how much a part is perfected, there is always the chance that it will fail. In some cases, many in fact, this is a tolerable risk—the unit involved may not be a basic component and the consequences of failure may be minimal. But where a system is important, and where it is made dependent upon operating parts that are organized into a tight means-end chain, the problem becomes acute. In such systems, especially when large, there is a tendency for even minor errors to be so amplified along the length of the chain as to make the end-result quite unreliable. In formal organizations this tendency can be expressed in terms of "the absorption of uncertainty."[5] The failure, then, of a single part can mean the failure of the entire system: as when the breakdown of a switching circuit blacks out an entire region or the failure of a duty officer to heed radar readings permits a force of unidentified aircraft to attack Pearl Harbor with devastating success. The latter case, it will be recognized, constitutes a stark illustration of the uncertainty principle. Here it was not the *evidence* which was transmitted, only the *inferences*.[6] In complex and tightly ordered systems the cost of error can run very high.

This is the context in which the theory of redundancy bulks so large. For it sets aside the doctrine that ties the reliability of a system to the perfectibility of parts and thereby approaches the pragmatics of systems in action much more realistically. That is, it accepts the

[5]James G. March, Herbert A. Simon, and Harold Guetzkow, *Organizations* (New York: John Wiley, 1958), pp. 164–166. I am indebted to Aaron Wildavsky for this suggestion.
[6]*Ibid.*, p. 165.

inherent limitations of any organization by treating any and all parts, regardless of their degree of perfection,[7] as risky actors. The practical implications of this shift in orientation is immediately to be seen when the following question is asked: Is it possible to take a set of individually unreliable units and form them into a system "with any arbitrarily high reliability"?[8] Can we, in other words, build an organization that is more reliable than any of its parts?

The answer, *mirabile dictu*, is yes. In what is now a truly classical paper, Von Neumann demonstrated that it could be done by adding sufficient redundancy.[9] Developments in this domain move swiftly and where before we could only resort to an intuitive and rather pragmatic redundancy, there now exist powerful theorems which can be applied with far greater certainty and much less waste.[10] This, it can be said, is a cardinal feature of "systems analysis"—all too often overlooked.

The theory itself is a rather complicated set of formulations and it serves no purpose to dwell upon it in any great detail. Yet there is one theorem that must be indicated because of the profound effect it can have on organizational design: that the probability of failure in a system decreases exponentially as redundancy factors are increased. Increasing reliability in this manner, of course, raises the price to be paid and if fail-safe conditions are to be reached, the cost may be prohibitive. But an immediate corollary of the theorem eases this problem for it requires only arithmetic increases in redundancy to yield geometric increases in reliability. Costs may then be quite manageable.

[7]It is assumed, of course, that any component meets a specified standard of performance.

[8]Jagjit Singh, *Information Theory, Language and Cybernetics* (New York: Dover Publications, 1966), p. 173.

[9]John Von Neumann, "Probabilistic Logics and the Synthesis of Reliable Organizations from Unreliable Components," in C. E. Shannon and J. McCarthy (Eds.), *Automata Studies* (Princeton, N.J.: Princeton University Press, 1956). Also, see C. E. Shannon and W. Weaver, *The Mathematical Theory of Communication* (Urbana: University of Illinois Press, 1949). And see Pierce, *op. cit.*, chap. 8; Singh, *op. cit.*, chaps. 4 and 5; and Colin Cherry, *On Human Communication* (New York: Science Editions, 1961), chap. 5.

[10]W. H. Pierce, "Redundancy in Computers," *Scientific American* 210 (February 1964). Also, see W. S. McCulloch, "The Reliability of Biological Systems," in M. G. Yovitz and S. Cameron (Eds.), *Self-Organizing Systems* (New York: Pergamon Press, 1960); and Singh, *op. cit.*, chaps. 10–12. And see Robert Gordon, "Optimum Component Redundancy for Maximum System Reliability," *Operations Research* 5 (1957).

The application of this formula, however, depends upon the ability to construct a system so that it satisfies those conditions which permit the laws of probability to apply, in this case, the multiplication theorem or the product rule for independent events: alternatively, the failure of parts must be random and statistically independent (unrelated). In practical terms, therefore, a system must be so arranged that when parts fail, they do so unpredictably and in such manner *that they cannot and do not impair other parts,* as in the dual braking system of a car. If each braking assembly is not completely separated from the other, the redundancy is not waste, it becomes a very dangerous addition: when it fails it is likely (perhaps certain) to damage the other assembly. So much for a theorem which has to do with duplication. We turn now to "overlapping."

"Overlapping"

Generally employed to denote biological organisms (neural physiologies, in particular), "self-organizing systems" command fully as much attention in the study of redundancy as computing machines and communication networks. There is nothing surprising about this since the theory of redundancy is a theory of system reliability. And self-organizing systems exhibit a degree of reliability that is so far superior to anything we can build as to prompt theorists to suggest "that the richly redundant networks of biological organisms must have capabilities beyond anything our theories can yet explain."[11] In Von Neumann's phrasing, they "contain the necessary arrangements to diagnose errors as they occur, to readjust the organism so as to minimize the effects of errors, and finally to correct or to block permanently the faulty component." Error refers here to malfunction, and Von Neumann states that there is now little doubt that they are "able to operate even when malfunctions set in . . . [while] their subsequent tendency is to remove them."[12] Pierce adds that they are able to improve reliability when errors are common even as they improve their capabilities when errors are infrequent.[13]

[11]Pierce, "Redundancy in Computers," *op. cit.*, p. 112.
[12]John Von Neumann, "The General and Logical Theory of Automata," in James R. Newman, *The World of Mathematics* (New York: Simon and Schuster, 1956), IV, 2085–2086.
[13]Pierce, "Redundancy in Computers," *op. cit.*

Equipotentiality

How, precisely, this works remains an object of inquiry. But it seems clear that such systems possess a fantastic number of parallel hookups of many different types. McCulloch, in commenting on the reliability of biological organisms, speaks of redundancies of codes, of channels, of calculation, and of potential command, noting that each serves differently. "The reliability you can buy with redundancy of calculation cannot be bought with redundancy of code or channel."[14] To these we can add the property of "equipotentiality" which provides the system with an extraordinary adaptive power.

Equipotentiality, interestingly enough, is often referred to as "overlapping."[15] It denotes the tendency of neural networks to resist that kind of precise differentiation of function which is mutually exclusive. Even in the case of highly specialized subsystems the tendency is restricted but not lost. There appears to be some "overlap" at all times which enables residual parts or subsidiary centers to "take over," though somewhat less efficiently, the functions of those which have been damaged. It is this overlap[16] that permits the organism to exhibit a high degree of adaptability, i.e., to change its behavior in accordance with changes in stimuli.

Duplication and Overlap: Politics

And this is why it may be quite *irrational* to greet the appearance of duplication and overlap by automatically moving to excise and redefine. To unify the defense departments, or the several independent information-gathering services of the government, or the large number of agencies engaged in technical assistance, or the various antipoverty programs, or the miscellany of agencies concerned with transportation, or the great variety of federal, state, and local administrations that function in the same areas, may rob the system of its necessary supports. It can be hypothesized that it is precisely such redundancies that allow for the delicate process of mutual adjust-

[14]McCulloch, *op. cit.*, p. 265.

[15]Singh, *op. cit.*, pp. 246–247, 323.

[16]It is interesting to note that learning machines, machines which "interpret their environment," are built upon this principle. They are much more flexible than computers and "can rise to occasions not foreseen by programmed instructions." *Ibid.*, p. 225.

ment, of self-regulation, by means of which the whole system can sustain severe local injuries and still function creditably.

Hypothesis?—perhaps it is more than that. If, of course, "men were angels," the systems they constitute would be foolproof. But they are not; and this is the fact that stands at the foundation of the organization created in Philadelphia. For the charter of the national system is a patent illustration of redundancy. Look at it: separation of powers, federalism, checks and balances, concurrent powers, double legislatures, overlapping terms of office, the Bill of Rights, the veto, the override, judicial review, and a host of similar arrangements. Here is a system that cannot be described except in terms of duplication and overlap—of a redundancy of channel, code, calculation, and command.

These are the redundancies which prompt public administration theorists to regard this system as quite inefficient—if not irrational. Where they wish one unambiguous code, there are many and these are hardly unequivocal; where they seek a unity of command, there is a redundancy of command; and so on. As a decision system, the organization of government certainly appears to be inferior to that which underlies program budgeting—which is why we see an expressed longing for a "wholesale revision of the federal structure." After all, as some programmers see it, the objectives of the architects of the Constitution were as much political as economic, and their economics "had a philosophic rather than managerial or operational character. The decision-making structure came . . . under the influence of objectives other than rationality of choice."[17] And, as Smithies has noted, "It is fundamental to our culture that rational choice is better than irrational choice."[18] . . .

Auxiliary Precautions

The Constitution-makers, it appears, were eminently "rational." They chose wisely and they did so under hazardous conditions. They knew that they were "organizing" a system in the face of great uncertainty. We need not list the profound and abiding cleavages which existed nor the intense fears which were displayed:

[17]Roland N. McKean and Melvin Anshen, "Limitations, Risks and Problems," in David Novick (Ed.), *Program Budgeting* (Cambridge, Mass.: Harvard University Press, 1965), p. 287.

[18]Arthur Smithies, "Conceptual Framework for the Program Budget," *ibid.*, p. 24.

The Federalist alone makes this clear. But it also instructs that in fabricating the Constitution, the architects were ever mindful of the grave possibility of failure and sought a system which could perform in the face of error—which could manage to provide a stable set of decision rules for an exceedingly unstable circumstance. And they found their answer in Newton's Third Law.[19] Experience, Madison wrote, has taught mankind the necessity for *auxiliary precautions:* these were to be had "by so contriving the internal structure of government so that its several constituent parts, may by their mutual relations, be the means of keeping each other in their proper places."[20] The principle of action and reaction, of checks and balances, turns out to have been, in organization terms, the principle of interwoven and competing redundancies.

"That which is redundant is, to the extent that it is redundant, stable. It is therefore reliable."[21] One hundred and seventy-nine years have passed since the original design, and save for one massive failure, the system has withstood the severest of shocks—and may well continue to do so even in the face of today's unprecedented problems. We like to say that [it] is the oldest constitutional government in the world, yet it remains a novelty. It seems to have worked like a "self-organizing" system exhibiting both the performance reliability and adaptability that such systems display. Marked by a redundancy of law, of power and command, of structure and linkage—*the whole has appeared as more reliable than any of its parts.* Where one part has failed another has taken over, and even when duplicates were not there to be employed, the presence of equipotentiality, of overlapping functions, permitted the load to be assumed elsewhere, however imperfectly. Scholars have for years spoken of the "cyclical character" of intragovernmental arrangements, of a "pendulum of checks and balances," frequently pointing to this phenomenon as an adaptive response. The "uncertain content" (jurisdiction) of the various parts of government just will not allow it to sit still and the hyphenated phrases we are forced to use in describing government are indicative of the extent of its equipotentiality. Even when such reference is pejorative, as often happens in the instance of "judicial-

---

[19]Martin Landau, "On the Use of Metaphor in Political Analysis," *Social Research* 28 (Autumn 1961).

[20]*The Federalist*, No. 51, emphasis added; see also Nos. 47 and 48.

[21]McCulloch, *op. cit.*, p. 265.

legislation," such a concept points to an overlap which enables adaptation. *Baker v. Carr* is a recent illustration of this kind of self-regulation.[22] The boss, the historical master of an "invisible government," was a redundancy that developed to offset the failures of local government,[23] and this would not have been possible but for the redundancy of party. Senator Mike Mansfield, speaking on the floor of the Senate, warns his colleagues that if they do not act, other branches of government will:

> It is clear that when one road to this end fails, others will unfold as indeed they have unfolded. If the process is ignored in legislative channels, it will not necessarily be blocked in other channels—in the executive branch and in the courts.[24]

And the President has been severely criticized because he has radically curtailed the number of channels, formal and informal, that are employed for purposes of control. Richard Neustadt, after describing the extraordinary redundancy which marked FDR's administration, concludes the president cannot function effectively without competing information sources.[25] . . .

Public Administration

Not so for public administration, however. Its prevailing notions of organizational rationality are built upon contrary assumptions. Where the "rationality" of politics derives from the fact that a system can be more reliable (more responsive, more predictable) than any of its parts, public administration has postulated that a system can be no more than the sum of its parts: reliable components, thus, add up to a reliable system and *per contra*.

The logic of this position, to iterate, calls for each role to be perfected, each bureau to be exactly delimited, each linkage to articulate unfailingly, and each line of communition to be noiseless— all to produce one interlocking system, one means-end chain which

---

[22]See Martin Landau, "Baker v. Carr and the Ghost of Federalism," in G. Schubert (Ed.), *Reapportionment* (New York: Scribners, 1964).

[23]Robert K. Merton, "Manifest and Latent Function," in *Social Theory and Social Structure* (Glencoe, N.Y.: The Free Press, 1957).

[24]Quoted by Marquis Childs, *New York Post*, May 10, 1962.

[25]Richard E. Neustadt, *Presidential Power* (New York: John Wiley, 1960), chap. 7.

possesses the absolutely minimum number of links, and which culminates at a central control point. For the public administration rationalist, the optimal organization consists of units that are wholly compatible, precisely connected, fully determined, and, therefore, perfectly reliable. The model which represents this dream is that of a linear organization in which everything is arrayed in tandem.[26] It is as if the entire house is to be wired in series.

If the analogy holds, and it does to a considerable extent—especially as regards communication processes, organizational systems of this sort are a form of administrative *brinkmanship*. They are extraordinary gambles. When one bulb blows, everything goes. Ordering parts in series makes them so dependent upon each other that any single failure can break the system. It is the old story of "For want of a nail . . . the battle was lost." Other illustrations: each of us can supply any number of instances of rather serious disruptions because of a faulty part, a malfunctioning actor, a noisy channel. Serial arrangements have the property of intensifying error.

In fact, they may be conducive to error—and to all sorts of problems. For they presuppose the human actor is a linear element and can, therefore, produce outputs in proportion to inputs, and on schedule. There is no doubt, of course, that the human actor can perform "indifferently" over a very wide task environment and under very diverse conditions: otherwise, large-scale formal organization as we know it would not be able to maintain itself.[27] But we have come to learn, and at sad cost, that even if serial demands fall within an actor's "zone of acceptance," there are limits to his linearity. The strains imposed can be too much, the burden of error can be too great—in short, he can be overloaded. A ready resort to a "rational calculus," which places actors in serial interdependence on the assumption of linearity, courts trouble. As against optimum performance, it may beget even less than a satisfactory one. Indeed, it is more likely to breed a "resistance" which ultimately results in a sharply reduced zone of acceptance. And this reduction may be so severe as to constitute a direct challenge to organizational authority. In this circumstance, organizational expenditures to secure compli-

[26]James D. Thompson refers to this organizational pattern as the "long-linked technology" involving "serial interdependence," *Organizations in Action* (New York: McGraw Hill, 1967), pp. 18–19.

[27]*Ibid.*, pp. 105–106. Also, see Herbert Simon, *Administrative Behavior* (New York: Macmillan, 1947).

ance may be far more than the cost of parallel hookups which do not require perfectibility to increase reliability and which, thereby, reduce strain.

There are additional risks as well—not the least of which is an intensification of the "displacement of goals."[28] Because each part assumes so weighty a responsibility in the system, exacting controls are required. Rules, therefore, assume even more importance than they ordinarily do. And the more precise they are, the better the control. There is, then, an even greater possibility that strict and slavish adherence to regulations will obtain. The burden of error is sufficient to prompt a refusal to exercise discretion when an untoward situation arises. This holds *a fortiori* in a government organization which is bound by rules that have the force of law: for a mistake in interpretation may place action outside the limits of the rule and render it *ultra vires*. Under such strictures there will neither be the "taking advantage of a technicality" or of a "loophole"—and it is a practice such as this one which often constitutes an adaptive response to an urgent problem. . . .

There are, then, a number of decision systems,[29] each of which calls for a different organizational perspective. None, however, can do without redundancy. Whatever claims are made for programmed decisionmaking, it is to be recognized that if its organizational structure consisted only of the "absolutely minimal number of parts," error could not be detected. As against pragmatics and negotiation, there is little doubt that reliable performance requires lesser amounts of redundancy. But the task remains to learn to distinguish between inefficient redundancies and those that are constructive and reinforcing—and this includes the kind of knowledge which will permit the introduction of redundancies so that they can work to increase both reliability and adaptability. This task, needless to say, attends pragmatics and negotiation as well, for they are redundant by their nature.

[28]Robert Merton, "Bureaucratic Structure and Personality," in Merton *et al.*, (Eds.), *Reader in Bureaucracy* (Glencoe, N.Y.: The Free Press, 1952).
[29]The system of classification that I have employed is based upon James D. Thompson and Arthur Tuden, "Strategies, Structures, and Processes of Organizational Decision," in *Comparative Studies in Administration* (Pittsburgh, Pa.: University of Pittsburgh Press, 1959). My own explication of their formulations is to be found in "Decision Theory and Comparative Public Administration," *Comparative Political Studies*, Vol. 1 (July 1968).

A Final Note

The appearance, therefore, of duplication and overlap in administrative agencies is not necessarily a sign of waste and inefficiency. On the contrary, it is becoming increasingly evident that large-scale organizations function as self-organizing systems and tend to develop their own parallel circuits: not the least of which is the transformation of such "residual" parts as "informal groups," into constructive redundancies. Where we are sometimes prone to regard such groups as sources of pathology, they may be compensating for the deficiencies of the formal organization in the same way that the "boss" once did.

At one and the same time, thus, redundancy serves many vital functions in the conduct of public administration. It provides safety factors, permits flexible responses to anomalous situations and provides a creative potential for those who are able to see it. If there is no duplication, if there is no overlap, if there is no ambiguity, an organization will be able to neither suppress error nor generate alternate routes of action.[30] In short, it will be most unreliable and least flexible, sluggish, as we now say.

"Streamlining an agency," "consolidating similar functions," "eliminating duplication," and "commonality" are powerful slogans which possess an obvious appeal. But it is just possible that their achievement would deprive an agency of the properties it needs most—those which allow rules to be broken and units to operate defectively without doing critical injury to the agency as a whole. Accordingly, it would be far more constructive, even under conditions of scarcity, to lay aside easy slogans and turn attention to a principle which lessens risks without foreclosing opportunity.

[30]As an immediate illustration, an agency often encounters situations which require prompt and necessary action. Where rules duplicate and overlap, safety factors exist. If one set of rules fails or does not cover the situation, an alternate route can be found or rules can be stretched—broadly interpreted. The problem, again, is to eliminate an inefficient profusion and to provide efficient redundancy.

VIII

Improving Bureaucratic Performance: The Politics of Reform

Reform has a very lengthy history in the United States. Almost as long as we have had political institutions in this country, we have been trying to improve their performance. Reform movements have been at the root of many of the changes that have taken place in American society, as various groups sought to abolish slavery, emancipate women, protect the environment, and take a host of other actions to make this country into the Utopia many Americans felt it already was.

It is not surprising, therefore, that the history of bureaucracy in the United States has been very much affected by a recurring zeal for reform. It began in the late nineteenth century with a congressional drive to improve the efficiency of executive operations through reorganization. In the twentieth century, however, the presidency has spearheaded the movement for organizational reform. There has also been a long-standing effort to improve the effectiveness of the budgetary process in bureaucracy, either by securing better control over agency expenditures or by developing some means of appraising the practical results of these expenditures.

The interest that presidents have taken in administrative reform is understandable, since much of it has had the effect if not the intention of making the bureaucracy a better instrument for the achievement of White House purposes. The reorganization of the executive branch that took place after the report of the first Hoover Commission under Truman certainly helped the president to become in fact as well as in name the chief executive officer in the land. Likewise, the various reforms that have occurred in the area of budgeting in recent decades have given the White House a better handle on the expenditures of individual executive agencies. Recent White House interest in administrative reform may thus be said to have been of a very self-serving character.

I

Administrative reformers themselves have tended to ignore the political side effects of what they do. They see their work as being purely scientific in character—designed only to enhance the efficiency of bureaucracy. What proponents of reorganization generally believe is that there are certain fundamental management principles that must be followed if the executive branch is to operate with maximum efficiency, and that these principles can be appropriately applied in every administrative setting. Chief among these canons of management science is the need to centralize authority at the top of an executive agency, so that the organization's activities can be coordinated and duplication of effort eliminated through executive oversight. Another management dogma is the rule that similar governmental functions should be grouped together in a single department, enabling each major government organization to become a family of closely related activities.

But, as Harold Seidman suggests in "The Politics of Government Organization," attempts to put these administrative dogmas into practice may be strongly resisted by administrative agencies out of fear that such changes in the organizational status quo will threaten their power or even their survival. Moreover, the constituency groups they serve may see reorganization proposals as thinly disguised attempts to reduce their own access to the agency or their influence over its policies. Congressional committees that deal with an agency may also view reorganization as endangering their ability to influence its policies.

The fear of these various parties that administrative reorganization will adversely affect their interests is not necessarily well founded. Many of the expected consequences of administrative reorganization never occur. An administrative agency's power may not be greatly affected by a shift in its location within the executive branch, or in the scope of its activities. Its clientele's influence over its policies may not be appreciably diminished, and the agency may still defer to pressure from the same congressional committees. Still, changes in form can bring changes in substance, and an agency and its supporters are not entirely without grounds for believing that administrative reorganization may bring important shifts in the politics or policy of the agency.

In the area of fiscal administration, the belief that reform can rest on a solid scientific foundation has also been strongly held. In the 1960s fiscal reform efforts centered on PPBS, a planning-programming-budgeting system designed to enable administrative agencies to identify the least costly of the alternative strategies available for achieving their goals. Although it had some apparent success in the area of defense expenditures, PPBS faltered when it was applied to the domestic budget during President Lyndon Johnson's second term.[1] It was replaced as the dominant reform proposal in the 1970s by zero-based budgeting, a new managerial panacea that sought to make all agencies justify not only the additional funds they were requesting each fiscal year—so-called incremental budgeting—but also all the funds they were requesting for every activity they were carrying on.

In "Reforming the Budgetary Process," Aaron Wildavsky reminds us that no system of budgeting can be completely apolitical in character. Budget decisions inevitably generate consequences with political or policy implications. Changes made in the budgetary process in the name of increased productivity or efficiency cannot help but have side effects, or "externalities," as the economists call them. No scientific theory of budgeting can ignore the political choices involved in the preparation of a budget, choices deeply affected by the shifting weight of political influence in Congress and in the public at large, as well as by changes in popular conceptions of what it is important to spend money for. Budgeting, at least as it relates to the central issue of allocating expenditures among various competing public programs,

---

[1]For an account of the rise and fall of PPBS, see Allen Schick, "A Death in the Bureaucracy: The Demise of Federal PPB," *Public Administration Review* 33 (March/April 1973): 146–156.

is inextricably linked with both politics in the sense of power and politics in the sense of policy.

II

Although their proposals may have sometimes had stronger political implications than they recognized at the time, traditional administrative reformers were certainly far removed from the clash of liberal and conservative political ideologies that is at the center of current democratic politics. None of those early reformers would have seriously argued that administrative reorganization was necessary to save American democracy or that the preservation of freedom in this country required the establishment of a new budgetary system.

More recently, however, administrative reform has tended to be fueled by just such intense political passions. Liberals, for example, have been at the forefront of the movement launched in the postwar period against the growing tendency of administrative agencies to withhold information from the public. Such secrecy, they have charged, poses a threat to a fundamental value on which democracy is based—the right of citizens to determine what policies the government will pursue. This "open government" movement has been an important force behind the enactment of freedom-of-information statutes and other measures taken in recent years to restrict the ability of executive agencies to operate in secret.

"Executive Secrecy: Change and Continuity" discusses these achievements, but it also tries to show that bureaucrats themselves cannot be held entirely responsible for the growth of secrecy in U.S. government. The Watergate affair was a vivid demonstration of the degree to which presidents can resort to secrecy. The White House is often obsessed by the belief that rather than being too secretive, bureaucrats are much too prone to leak information to the outside world. And in the world outside government, administrative secrecy protects a variety of interests, such as the need of citizens for privacy regarding matters they are obliged to disclose to the government. Indeed, liberal reformers are faced with the fact that freedom-of-information statutes that open up the affairs of government to greater public scrutiny may jeopardize the personal privacy that is an equally important liberal value. So the task of liberal reformers with respect to administrative secrecy has proved to be far more difficult than they originally anticipated.

While liberal reformers have been seeking to make bureaucracy more responsive to public control, conservatives have been disturbed by what they regard as excessive power in the hands of bureaucrats, and the extent to which this power is used to regulate private behavior, especially in the economic sphere. This is not, of course, a new concern on the part of conservatives. From the beginning of this century conservatives have been alarmed by the growth of bureaucracy—the high cost of the services that bureaucrats are now responsible for providing as well as the burdens that their regulatory power imposes on private citizens. But in recent years this traditional conservative distaste for bureaucracy has taken on new life with the rise of the deregulatory movement, which has made successful efforts to reduce the power of regulatory bodies in U.S. politics. As Susan and Martin Tolchin reveal in their critical survey of deregulation, "The Rush to Deregulate," this movement has drawn strong support from both Democratic and Republican politicians. When it is seen as benefiting consumers, as in the case of airline deregulation, it has been supported by liberals as well as conservatives. Otherwise, liberals tend to be staunch supporters of administrative regulation, especially when they see it as advancing some socially desirable objective such as civil rights, environmental protection, or safety in the workplace.

In any case, administrative reform, which used to be at the periphery of public attention, has now moved very near to the center of the political stage. Once exclusively the concern of management types worried about the fact that government was not as efficient as it could be, or as the private sector appeared to be, administrative reform now preoccupies liberals worried about the possibility that the CIA may set up a government of its own, altogether free from public control, and conservatives who are equally apprehensive that the power of bureaucracy may be used to stifle the liberties of individual citizens.

27

The Politics of Government Organization

HAROLD SEIDMAN

. . . Organizational arrangements are not neutral. We do not organize in a vacuum. Organization is one way of expressing national commitment, influencing program direction, and ordering priorities. Organizational arrangements tend to give some interests and perspectives more effective access to those with decision-making authority, whether they be in the Congress or in the executive branch. As Richard Neustadt has pointed out: "In political government, the means can matter quite as much as the ends; they often matter more."[1]

Institutional location and environment, administrative arrangements and type of organization, can raise significant political questions concerning the distribution and balance of power between the executive branch and the Congress; the federal government and state and local governments; states and cities; the federal government and organized interest groups, particularly the principal beneficiaries of federal programs; and finally, among the components of the executive establishment itself, including the president's relationship to the departments and the bureaucracy.

If our democratic system is to be responsive to the needs of *all* our people, organization structure and administrative arrangements need to so balance the competing interests within given program areas that none is immune to public control and capable of excluding less powerful segments of our society from effective participation in the

From Harold Seidman, *Politics, Position, and Power: The Dynamics of Federal Organization*, Third Edition. Copyright © 1980 by Oxford University Press, Inc. Reprinted by permission.

[1]Richard E. Neustadt, *Presidential Power: The Politics of Leadership*, John Wiley & Sons, Inc., 1960, p. 47.

system and an equitable share of its benefits. Failure to maintain this balance has contributed to the present malaise.

President Eisenhower in his farewell address to the nation warned against "the acquisition of unwarranted influence, whether sought or unsought, by the military-industrial complex." Other complexes, notably the science-education and agricultural establishments, wield power equal to or exceeding that of the perhaps overly dramatized military-industrial combine. Scientific research is said to be the only pork barrel for which the pigs determine who gets the pork.

The political implications of organization structure were recognized as early as 1789 when the states endeavored to control the extension of federal power by limiting the creation of executive departments. In 1849 the bill to establish the Department of the Interior was opposed because "it meant the further extension of federal authority to the detriment of the states."[2] Opposition to the establishment of the Department of Education in the 1970's stemmed from much the same concern.

Application of "economy and efficiency" as the criteria for government organization can produce serious distortions, if political and environmental factors are ignored. It led the first Hoover Commission to proceed from the indisputable finding that the Farmers Home Administration's functions duplicated and overlapped those of the Farm Credit Administration and Agricultural Extension Service to the seemingly logical conclusion that the Administration ought to be liquidated and its functions divided between its two competitors. The conclusion was obviously faulty to anyone in the least familiar with the histories of the Farm Credit Administration and the Extension Service as creatures of the American Farm Bureau Federation and the most conservative elements in the agricultural community. The Farm Bureau was proud of its role in scuttling the Rural Resettlement Administration and Farm Security Administration, the immediate predecessors of the FHA.[3] If there were ever a case of letting the goats loose in the cabbage patch, this was it. The FHA was cre-

---

[2]Lloyd M. Short, *The Development of National Administrative Organization in the United States*, The Johns Hopkins Press, 1923, p. 89.

[3]For excellent analyses of the role played by the American Farm Bureau Federation in organizational politics see Sidney Baldwin, *Poverty and Politics*, University of North Carolina Press, 1968; Philip Selznick, *TVA and the Grass Roots*, University of California Press, 1949.

ated to furnish special assistance to farmers who constitute marginal risks and possess little political clout. Commissioners Acheson, Pollock, and Rowe observed in their dissent that "the purpose of the Farmers Home Administration is to make 'good' tenant farmers out of 'poor' tenant farmers, and not to restrict credit to 'good' tenant farmers who can probably obtain credit from other sources."[4]

Some now question whether the Farmers Home Administration or any other agency within a department so conceived and so organized as the Department of Agriculture can respond adequately to the needs of the rural poor in the South, most of whom are black. It was no coincidence that the 1968 Poor People's Campaign in Washington singled out the Department of Agriculture for special attention. The Citizens Board of Inquiry into Hunger and Malnutrition in the United States asserted that the Department of Agriculture and the congressional Agriculture committees are "dominated by a concern for maximizing agricultural income, especially within the big production categories. Other objectives always yield to this one . . . almost never does our agricultural policy take a direct concern with the interests of consumers."[5] The board proposed reorganization and removal of food programs from Agriculture's jurisdiction as the answer.

Powerful groups in the commercial banking, research, and educational communities regard overlapping and duplication not as vices, but as positive virtues. The American Bankers Association through the years has successfully blocked efforts to consolidate bank supervisory and examining functions in a single federal agency. The division of responsibility among the Comptroller of the Currency, the Federal Deposit Insurance Corporation, and the Federal Reserve Board is viewed by the ABA as "wholly in keeping with the broad principle that the success and strength of democracy in America is largely due to the sound safeguards afforded by the wisely conceived checks and balances which pervade our composite governmental system."[6] The system is defended because banks retain the option of

[4]The Commission on Organization of the Executive Branch of the Government, "Federal Business Enterprises," A Report to the Congress, March 1949, p. 102.

[5]Reprinted in hearings before the Subcommittee on Executive Reorganization of the Senate Committee on Government Operations on "Modernizing the Federal Government," January–May 1968, p. 355.

[6]American Bankers Association, "Reply to Questionnaire of U.S. Senate Committee on Banking and Currency," April 1941, p. 65.

changing their federal supervisors and thus gaining "some possible relief from unduly stringent examinations."[7]

Whatever advantages may have been gained by these "checks and balances" now appear to be more than offset by the loss of power within the councils of government. Without a single spokesman, the common interests of the commercial banks may be obscured in a chorus of discordant voices. This was a matter of little importance when most commercial banks enjoyed *de facto* monopolies and did not face competition from newly chartered commercial banks and an aggressive, politically wise savings and loan industry. The commercial banks are now in a position where they might be better served by organizational arrangements designed to stimulate and influence, not prevent, federal action. Unwillingness to abandon long cherished positions is not the exclusive disease of government bureaucracies.

Overlapping and duplication among federal agencies making research grants do not alarm scientists and educators. On the contrary, diversity in support is held essential to maximize the opportunities for obtaining federal funds and to minimize the dangers of federal control. The Committee on Science and Public Policy of the National Academy of Sciences strongly endorsed a "plural system" which has many roots for its authority "and many alternative administrative means of solving a given problem."[8]

Assignment of administrative jurisdiction can be a key factor in determining program direction and ultimate success or failure. Each agency has its own culture and internal set of loyalties and values which are likely to guide its actions and influence its policies. A number of satellites grow up and around and outside the institution and develop a mutual dependence. Private bureaucracies in Washington now almost completely parallel the public bureaucracies in those program areas where the federal government contracts for services, regulates private enterprise, or provides some form of financial assistance.

Shared loyalties and outlook knit together the institutional fabric. They are the foundation of those intangibles which make for institutional morale and pride. Without them, functions could not be decentralized and delegated with the confidence that policies will be administered consistently and uniformly. But because people be-

[7]*Ibid.*, p. 67.

[8]National Academy of Science, "Federal Support of Basic Research in Institutions of Higher Learning," Washington, D.C., 1964.

lieve what they are doing is important and the way they have been taught to do it is right, they are slow to accept change. Institutional responses are highly predictable, particularly to new ideas which conflict with institutional values and may pose a potential threat to organizational power and survival. Knowledgeable Budget Bureau officials once estimated that agency positions on any major policy issue can be forecast with nearly 100 percent accuracy, regardless of the administration in power.

There is an ever-present danger that innovative programs which challenge accepted norms, demand new skills and approaches, and create conflicts with agency constituencies will be assimilated into the "system" and their purposes muffled or distorted. One way to kill a program is to house it in a hostile or unsympathetic environment.

The Congress tacked a rider to the 1953 RFC Liquidation Act authorizing the president to designate an agency to make loans to public bodies for the construction or acquisition of public facilities.[9] Budget Bureau staff recommended that the Housing and Home Finance Agency be designated because its mission was most closely related to urban and community development, but the then budget director preferred Treasury "because it wouldn't make the loans." Treasury obviously would be less susceptible to pressure from state capitols and city halls and could be expected to apply strict banking criteria in reviewing loan applications. The final solution was not to make any designation. The Congress solved the problem by enacting legislation vesting program responsibility in the Housing and Home Finance Agency.

In their zeal to construct neat and uncluttered organization charts, professional reorganizers and reorganization commissions tend to downgrade, when they do not wholly ignore, environmental influences. Certainly, the poverty program would have been different, whether better or worse depends on one's point of view, if, as many advocated, responsibility at the outset had been given either to the Department of Health, Education, and Welfare or to the choice of the big-city mayors, the Department of Housing and Urban Development. Creation of a new agency is likely to present fewer problems than reform of an old one and enables the president and the Congress to finesse competing jurisdictional claims. Compromise ar-

[9]Reconstruction Finance Corporation Liquidation Act, 1953 (40 U.S.C. 459).

rangements are possible, and program seedlings under some circumstances can take root and grow within established departments if protected during the developmental period by a self-contained, relatively autonomous status.

Adherence to the principle of organization according to major purposes provides no automatic answers. Herbert Hoover would have resolved the problem by having the Congress define "major purpose" and then leaving it to the president to reorganize executive agencies in accordance with their purposes as set forth in law.[10] Granted that Mr. Hoover made this proposal in 1924, when federal programs were simple by today's standards, it is incredibly naïve.

Federal programs are likely to have multiple purposes. Disagreements as to priorities among diverse and sometimes conflicting objectives are a major source of current controversies. Is the major purpose of the food stamp program to dispose of surplus agricultural commodities or to feed the poor? Is mass transportation a transportation or an urban development program? Are school lunches a nutrition or an education function? Should the federal water pollution control program have as its principal objective health protection, or should it be concerned more broadly with the development of water resources?

Major purposes cannot be ascertained by scientific or economic analysis. Determination of major purpose represents a value judgment, and a transitory one at that. Thus President Nixon could argue in 1971 that the Department of Transportation "is now organized around methods and not around purposes," although transportation was assumed to be a major purpose when the department was established in 1966.[11] What is the secondary purpose for one, is a major purpose for another. To quote Miles's law: "Where one stands depends on where one sits."[12] Major purposes are not constants but variables shifting with the ebb and tide of our national needs and aspirations.

Debates about organizational type also may mask basic differences over strategy and objectives. Orthodox theory postulates that

[10]Library of Congress, *A Compilation of Basic Information on the Reorganization of the Executive Branch of the Government of the United States, 1912–1947* (Washington, D.C.: Government Printing Office, 1947), p. 1216.

[11]*Papers Relating to the President's Departmental Reorganization Program* (Washington, D.C.: Government Printing Office, 1972), pp. 14–15.

[12]Attributed to Rufus Miles, formerly assistant secretary for administration, Department of Health, Education and Welfare.

all federal agencies, with the possible exception of the independent regulatory commissions, be grouped under a limited number of single-headed executive departments and consequently ignores the other possible forms of organization. Except for the regulatory commissions and government corporations, the Hoover Commissions and President's Committee on Administrative Management took little interest in the typology of organization—a disinterest shared by most students of public administration.

The significance of institutional type has been underrated. . . . The differences among institutional types are more a matter of convention and tradition than legal prescriptions. Yet some have acquired a "mystique" which can profoundly influence public attitudes and executive and congressional behavior for good or ill. Institutional type can be crucial in determining who controls—the president, the Congress, or the so-called "special interests."

Institutional type, for example, was a major issue when Congress authorized the Marshall Plan. Republicans wanted the plan administered by a government corporation because by definition it would be more "businesslike."[13] A corporation would also make it more difficult for the State Department to meddle in the European recovery program. The compromise was to establish an independent agency outside the State Department and to authorize creation of a corporation, if and when needed.

Scientists devised a new government institution named a "foundation" when existing institutions would not support their postwar grand design of "science governed by scientists and paid for by the public."[14] The ostensible aim was to duplicate within the executive branch a typical university structure. Effective control over the proposed National Science Foundation was to be vested in a twenty-four-member National Science Board to be appointed by the president after giving due consideration to nominations submitted to him by the National Academy of Sciences, the Association of Land Grant Colleges and Universities, the National Association of State Universities, the Association of American Colleges, or by other scientific or educational institutions. The board would be required to meet only once a year. It would, in turn, select biennially from among its mem-

---

[13]House Select Committee on Foreign Aid, "Preliminary Report Eleven—Comparative Analysis of Suggested Plans of Foreign Aid," November 22, 1947.

[14]Daniel S. Greenberg, *The Politics of Pure Science*, The New American Library, Inc., 1967, p. 107.

bers a nine-member executive committee which would meet six times a year and exercise the board's powers. The foundation's full-time executive officer, a director, would be appointed by the executive committee unless the board chose to make the appointment itself.

A bill incorporating the scientists' proposal was enacted by the Congress but drew a strongly worded veto from President Truman.[15] Truman recognized that "the proposed National Science Foundation would be divorced from control by the people to an extent that implies a distinct lack of faith in the democratic process" and would deprive the president "of effective means for discharging his constitutional responsibility." He took particular exception to the provisions insulating the director from the president by two layers of part-time boards and warned that "if the principles of this bill were extended throughout the government, the result would be utter chaos." Truman's views only partially prevailed. The Congress deleted the most objectionable feature by making the foundation director a presidential appointee, but retained the basic structure desired by the science establishment.

Institutional advisory bodies often are as much of a potential threat to executive power as the National Science Foundation proposal, but they are far more difficult to combat. Creation of the National Security Council properly could be construed as a ploy by a Republican Congress to circumscribe a Democratic president's powers in areas where he was constitutionally supreme. Not only did the Congress designate those officials who were to "advise" the president in the exercise of his constitutional powers, but it also included the curious provision that other secretaries and undersecretaries of executive departments could be appointed council members only with the advice and consent of the Senate. Advice is potentially one of the most powerful weapons in the administrative arsenal.

Up to now we have been discussing mainly the strategic implications of executive branch organization. But power relationships are not always involved in organization decisions. The president, the Congress, and even outside groups may use organizational means to obtain some immediate tactical advantage.

Herbert Hoover himself was not above using organization for

[15]Harry S Truman, Memorandum of Disapproval of the National Foundation Bill (S.526), August 6, 1947.

tactical purposes. He claimed that he was "a much misunderstood man on this question of committees and commissions." According to Mr. Hoover,

> There is no more dangerous citizen than the person with a gift of gab, a crusading complex and a determination "to pass a law" as the antidote for all human ills. The most effective diversion of such an individual to constructive action and the greatest silencer on earth for foolishness is to associate him on research committee with a few persons who have a passion for truth, especially if they pay their own expenses. I can now disclose the secret that I created a dozen committees for that precise purpose.[16]

Presidents have continued to employ committees and commissions to capture and contain the opposition. Committees and commissions can also offer an immediate, visible response in times of national catastrophe, such as the assassinations of President Kennedy and Senator Kennedy or the Watts riot. Study commissions are employed as a kind of tranquilizer to quiet public and congressional agitation about such matters as pesticides, crime, and public scandals. Attention, it is hoped, will be diverted to other issues by the time the commissions report. A poem appearing in *Punch* some years ago put it very well:

> If you're pestered by critics and hounded by faction
> To take some precipitate, positive action,
> The proper procedure, to take my advice, is
> Appoint a commission and stave off the crisis.[17]

Prestigious commissions can also build public support for controversial courses of action. What is wanted is endorsement, not advice, although "run-away" commissions are not unknown. On sensitive issues such as congressional pay, where members of Congress are politically vulnerable, a commission report helps to take them off the hook. Both Presidents Kennedy and Johnson used commissions to support legislation to increase executive, congressional, and judicial salaries.[18]

---

[16]Herbert C. Hoover, *The Memoirs of Herbert Hoover: The Cabinet and the Presidency, 1920–1933*, The Macmillan Co., 1952, p. 281.

[17]Geoffrey Parsons, "Royal Commission," *Punch*, August 24, 1955. © *Punch*, London.

[18]For a perceptive analysis see Elizabeth D. Drew, "How to Govern (or Avoid It) by Commission," *Atlantic Monthly*, May 1968.

Interagency committees sometimes create an impression of neatness and order within the executive establishment, even when a president cannot or will not resolve the basic differences and jurisdictional conflicts. If differences surface publicly and become embarrassing to the administration, the president's reflex reaction is to appoint another committee or to reorganize existing committees. The pressure is almost overwhelming "to do something" which might do some good and certainly will do no harm. No president can confess that he is stumped by a problem.

Pressure for immediate, tangible answers to highly complex problems may result in reorganizations. President Eisenhower's first response to the national trauma caused by the Soviet Union's successful launching of Sputnik in 1957 was to appoint a special assistant to the president for Science and Technology and to transfer the Science Advisory Committee from the Office of Defense Mobilization to the White House office. Creation of the Department of Energy in 1977 was a response to the energy crisis caused by the 1973 oil embargo.

Reorganization may provide a convenient way to dump an unwanted official, particularly one with strong congressional or constituency ties. The maneuver is not always successful, as was seen with Secretary of State Dean Rusk's abortive plan to abolish the Department's Bureau of Security and Consular Affairs. Mr. Abba Schwartz's version of this incident is highly colored, but there is no question that Secretary Rusk's timing was influenced by his desire to shift Mr. Schwartz from the bureau directorship to another post. The Bureau of Security and Consular Affairs was the brainchild of Senator Joseph McCarthy, and the Bureau of the Budget had targeted it for reorganization long before Mr. Schwartz arrived on the scene.

Use of reorganization to bypass a troublesome committee or subcommittee chairman in the Congress can also be hazardous when it does not succeed. Transfer of civil defense activities from the Office of Civil and Defense Mobilization to the secretary of defense in 1961 was expected as an incidental benefit to remove the shelter program from the jurisdiction of an unfriendly appropriations subcommittee chairman.[19] Albert Thomas, however, had the power to retain jurisdiction to the great discomfiture of the civil defense officials.

Organization choices may be motivated almost entirely by a

[19]Executive Order No. 10952, July 20, 1961.

desire to exclude billions in expenditures from budget tabulations. The 1969 budget was the first to include trust funds and mixed-ownership government corporations in the administrative budget. President Eisenhower's 1955 proposal to create a Federal Highway Corporation for financing the construction of the National System of Interstate Highways was deliberately designed to keep the authorized payments of $25 billion out of the budget totals. The proposal was later abandoned when it was found that establishment of a highway trust fund could serve the same purpose. Conversion of the Federal National Mortgage Association from a wholly-owned to a mixed-ownership government corporation in 1954 also had as its principal appeal the appearance of a multi-billion-dollar budget reduction. When the ground rules were changed with the 1969 budget, legislation was enacted to turn the Federal National Mortgage Association into a "government sponsored private corporation" so as to keep its expenditures out of the budget.

To escape arbitrary and unrealistic ceilings on civilian personnel, federal agencies have been compelled to utilize so-called "nonprofit intermediaries" to carry out programs mandated by congressional enactments. The Labor Department's organizational choices were limited when it was allowed forty-nine full-time positions in order to design and implement a complex multi-million-dollar youth employment and training program.[20]

A new name and a new look may be necessary to save a program with little political appeal, particularly one which congressional supporters find difficult to sell to their constituents. At times reorganization supplies the rationale needed by members of Congress to explain their vote. The frequent reorganization and renaming of the foreign aid agency reflect efforts to bolster congressional support and to demonstrate presidential interest, rather than to introduce new policies and improve management. There have been no less than eight successive foreign aid agencies—from the Economic Cooperation Administration in 1948 to the Agency for International Development in 1961—until 1961 an average of a new agency less than every two years.[21]

For many, organization is a symbol. Federal councils on aging,

---

[20]National Academy of Public Administration, *Government Sponsored Non-Profits*, November 1978.

[21]Michael K. O'Leary, *The Politics of American Foreign Aid*, Atherton Press, 1967, p. 117.

mental retardation, physical fitness, consumers, and the arts, for example, are more important as evidence of national concern than as molders of federal policies.

Some seek the creation of new federal agencies or reorganizations to enhance their status in the outside community. The demand for an independent National Archives disassociated from the government's "housekeeper," the General Services Administration, in part stems from the archivists' desire to improve their standing as a scholarly profession. Several years ago the firemen's association sought Bureau of the Budget support for a Federal Fire Academy. While the academy was not perceived at the time as fulfilling any identifiable federal need, it would place firemen on a par with policemen, who had a federal "sponsor" in the Federal Bureau of Investigation, and thus strengthen their bargaining position in dealing with mayors and city councils.[22]

The Congress is highly skilled in the tactical uses of organization and reorganization. If you come from a district with a jet airport, establishment of an Office of Noise Abatement in the Department of Transportation has tremendous voter appeal. Even though there is doubt that a separate office could do much to reduce noise levels, at least it offers a place where members of Congress can send constituent complaints. While the administration was able to defeat an amendment to the Department of Transportation bill to create such an office on the valid grounds that aircraft noise was a research and development and traffic control problem, Secretary Alan Boyd later found it expedient to create an Office of Noise Abatement by administrative action. Members of Congress are more susceptible to pressures from sectional, economic, and professional interests than is the president, and these often become translated into organizational responses.

Economy and efficiency are demonstrably not the prime purposes of public administration. Even such a single-minded and zealous advocate of "efficiency" and "competency" in government as President Jimmy Carter has acknowledged:

> Nowhere in the Constitution of the United States, or the Declaration of Independence, or the Bill of Rights, or the Emancipation Proclamation, or the Old Testament or the New Testament, do you find the

---

[22]A National Academy for Fire Prevention and Control was authorized by the Federal Fire Prevention and Control Act of 1974.

words "economy" or "efficiency." Not that these words are unimportant. But you discover other words like honesty, integrity, fairness, liberty, justice, patriotism, compassion, love—and many others which describe what human beings ought to be. These are the same words which describe what a government of human beings ought to be.[23]

Supreme Court Justice Louis D. Brandeis emphasized that the "doctrine of separation of powers was adopted, not to promote efficiency but to preclude the exercise of arbitrary power."[24] The basic issues of federal organization and administration relate to power: who shall control it and to what ends?

The questions that now urgently confront us are as old as the Republic itself. How can we maintain a government structure and administrative system which reconcile liberty with justice and institutional and personal freedom with the general welfare?

What we are observing today are the strains and tensions inevitably produced by revolutionary changes in the federal government's role and its relationships to other levels of government, institutions of higher learning and other nonprofit institutions, and the private sector. Dividing lines have become increasingly blurred. It is no longer easy to determine where federal responsibilities end and those of state and local governments and private institutions begin. These changes began with the "New Deal" in the 1930's, but the most dramatic developments have occurred since 1961.

Organizational ills are not easily diagnosed. Organization problems are often merely symptoms of growing pains or more deep-seated organic disease. Institutions do not perform well when called upon to accomplish significant transformations in the economic and social structure of our society within a one- or two-year time frame. Yet this is exactly what we have done in the poverty and model cities programs. In piling one new program on top of another, we have tended to ignore the need to find or develop the necessary managerial capability at all levels of government and have overloaded the system.

Yardsticks for measuring organizational health are admittedly inadequate and may be misleading. Strong public and congressional criticism may reflect effective performance, not the reverse. Servile obedience to congressional and constituency pressures, or inaction,

---

[23]Jimmy Carter, *Why Not the Best?* Bantam Books, 1976, p. 132.
[24]Cited in Lewis Meriam and Lawrence F. Schmeckebier, *Reorganization of the National Government*, The Brookings Institution, 1939, p. 132.

may win more influential "friends" and supporters than would vigorous pursuit of the public interest.

Growth has been a factor. Expenditures for major social programs, such as health and education, now exceed $67 billion a year. Federal aid to state and local governments jumped from about $7 billion in 1961 to an estimated $82.9 billion in 1980. In the same period annual expenditures for research and development have increased from approximately $9 billion to between $31 and 32 billion.

As a percentage of Gross National Product, federal outlays for civilian programs rose from 1 percent or less in the 1920's to about 5 percent in immediate postwar years to 16 percent in fiscal 1980.[25]

These increases would not be significant if they represented in the main stepped-up spending for traditional programs (welfare payments, price supports, veterans benefits, public works, highway construction) which could be smoothly channeled through the comfortable time-worn, single-purpose, single-agency groove. But the new programs to combat poverty, air and water pollution, crime and urban blight rewrote the ground rules. Under these programs, the federal government directly participates in specific projects in states and communities and acts as a co-equal partner with state and local governments, either individually or as a member of joint federal-state organizations such as the Appalachia Regional Commission. These programs call for participation by many federal agencies and cut across established jurisdictional lines at all levels of government.

The Hoover Commission solution of "placing related functions cheek-by-jowl" so that "the overlaps can be eliminated, and of even greater importance coordinated policies can be developed" is not workable when you must combine the major purpose programs—health, education, manpower, housing—in alleviating the social and economic ills of a specific region, city, or neighborhood. We could regionalize the executive branch, as some have proposed, but members of Congress, governors, and mayors would be unwilling to accept such a concentration of power in any one federal agency. Such modest proposals as those to establish HUD "urban expediters" in key cities are viewed with suspicion. If one official could control the flow of federal funds into a region, that person would be in a position to dictate state and local policies.

Senator Robert Kennedy posed the fundamental question when

---

[25]The Budget of the United States for Fiscal Year 1980, p. 82.

he asked: "Do the agencies of Government have the will and determination and ability to form and carry out programs which cut across
departmental lines, which are tailored to no administrative convenience but the overriding need to get things done?"[26]

Straight lines of authority and accountability cannot be established in a nonhierarchical system. The federal government is compelled to rely increasingly for accomplishment of its goals on
cooperation by nonfederal institutions which are not legally responsible to the president and subject to his direction. Federal powers are
limited to those agreed upon and enumerated in negotiated contracts. Success of the foreign aid, energy, space and defense research
and development programs depends almost as much on performance
by contractors as by the government's own employees. About 80 percent of federal expenditures for research and development are made
through nonfederal institutions, under either grants or contracts.[27]
The government since 1948 has caused to be organized and wholly
financed a host of university- and industry-sponsored research centers and so-called nonprofit corporations for the sole purpose of providing services to the government. Legally these are private
organizations, but many, such as the Institute for Defense Analyses,
Aerospace Corporation, Urban Institute, Lincoln Laboratory, Pub-
lic/Private Ventures, and Oak Ridge National Laboratory, have more
in common with traditional government agencies than with private
institutions.

Fundamentalist dogmas were developed for a different universe—for the federal government as it existed in the 1920's and early
1930's. It was a time when Herbert Hoover could be told by one of
his predecessors as secretary of commerce that the "job would not
require more than two hours of work a day. Indeed that was all the
time that former secretaries devoted to it. Putting the fish to bed at
night and turning on the lights around the coast were possibly the
major concepts of the office."[28] In the 1920's the Department of
Commerce was engaged in what were then typical government services: collection and dissemination of statistics, preparation of charts
and maps, operation of lighthouses, issuance of patents, and licens-

[26]Senate Committee on Government Operations, hearings on "Federal Role in
Urban Affairs," 1967, p. 40.
[27]U.S. Bureau of the Budget, "Report to the President on Contracting for Research and Development," April 30, 1962.
[28]Hoover, *op. cit.*, p. 42.

ing, inspection, and regulation. Except for public works projects, timber, grazing and mineral rights, agricultural loans, and land permits, the federal government had little power to confer or withhold economic benefits. Federal intervention in the economy was indirect through economic regulation, the tariff, fiscal, monetary, and credit policies.

Government and business regarded each other as adversaries, not as potential partners. Theodore Roosevelt argued that establishment of a Department of Commerce would represent "an advance toward dealing with and exercising supervision over the whole subject of the great corporations doing an interstate business."[29] Roosevelt considered that the secretary's first duty would be to regulate commerce and industry, rather than to act as a spokesman for their interests.

The regulatory approach reached its high-water mark with the New Deal. To the Interstate Commerce Commission, Federal Trade Commission, and Federal Power Commission, there were added the Securities and Exchange Commission, Federal Communications Commission, Civil Aeronautics Board, U.S. Maritime Commission, and the National Labor Relations Board. As far as the regulated industries were concerned, except for maritime and aviation subsidies, the less the federal government did the better. Tactics were defensive and designed to weaken, capture, and control the regulators.

It is highly significant that in *Public Administration and the Public Interest*, which was published in 1936, and is a ground-breaking analysis of the role played by special interest groups in the administrative process, Pendleton Herring devotes 150 pages to the regulatory agencies and internal revenue and only 74 to the executive departments—State, Agriculture, Commerce, and Labor. The War, Navy, and Interior departments receive only passing mention.[30] If the book were written today, the emphasis would be reversed.

In the years since World War II, the federal table has become crowded with dependents, each clamoring to be fed and demanding the biggest slice of pie. Where before the federal government was tolerated as a nuisance or at best a marginal customer, major industries, universities, and other institutions have now come to depend on federal funds for survival.

[29]Library of Congress, *op. cit.*, pp. 1205–6.
[30]E. Pendleton Herring, *Public Administration and the Public Interest*, McGraw-Hill Book Co., 1936.

In contrast to the situation in World War II, and even that during the Korean War, a large share of defense production is performed by highly specialized defense contractors, many of whose products bear little resemblence to civilian items, and who have had little experience outside defense production. For many companies their only important customer is the United States government. Fifteen companies in 1968 derived more than half of their business from United States government contracts. For Lockheed Aircraft, McDonnell Douglas, AVCO, Newport News Shipbuilding, and Thiokol, government purchases accounted for more than 70 percent of sales.[31]

The federal government currently finances almost two thirds of university research and development programs. This money goes for basic research in such fields as chemistry, physics, biology, astronomy, materials, oceanography, and earth sciences.

States and cities see no solution to their critical financial problems other than more federal money. Federal aid has risen as a proportion of state and local expenditures from 12 percent in 1958 to 26.7 percent in 1978.

The federal government may not be loved, but its capacity to raise revenues is greatly envied. Industry interests, however, may go beyond money. Otto Klima, Jr., and Gibson Wolfe, for example, advocate one federal agency with overview and program responsibility for all of this nation's interests in the oceans primarily as a means of helping U.S. industry by providing it with better decisional criteria.[32]

Unlike the regulated industries, it is not enough for these federal dependents to maintain a strong defensive posture. Under our system of checks and balances, it is relatively easy to block action. It is far more difficult to persuade the executive branch and the Congress to do something, particularly when there are strong competing demands for limited resources. Offense demands a new team and a different strategy. Some industries, such as the railroads, have been penalized because they were too slow in getting their defensive team off the field.

Each of the dependents endeavors to manipulate the organization structure and assignment of program responsibilities so as to

[31]*Congressional Quarterly,* Special Report on "The Military-Industrial Complex," May 24, 1968.
[32]Otto Klima, Jr., and Gibson M. Wolfe, "The Oceans: Organizing for Action," *Harvard Business Review,* May–June 1968.

maximize its ability to obtain federal funds and to minimize federal interference in the allocation and use of funds. Scientists had these objectives in mind when they developed their original design for the National Science Foundation. Farm organizations were inspired by identical motives when they convinced President Eisenhower to support legislation which provided independent financing for the farm credit system and immunized it to effective federal control. Not all dependents have been as successful as the farm credit organizations in gaining the four freedoms: freedom from financial control by the Congress, freedom from independent audit by the comptroller general, freedom from budget review by the president, and freedom to use federal funds. But for many these freedoms remain the goals.

The struggle for power and position has contributed to fragmentation of the executive branch structure and the proliferation of categorical programs. By narrowing the constituency, agencies are made more susceptible to domination by their clientele groups and congressional committees.[33] Efforts to narrow the constituencies have been accompanied by demands for independent status or autonomy within the departmental structure.

Programs are packaged in such a way as to elicit congressional and clientele support. General programs have far less political appeal than specific programs. Support can be mobilized more readily for federal programs to combat heart disease, blindness, cancer, and mental illness than for such fields as microbiology or for general health programs. For this reason in 1955 the National Microbiological Institute was renamed the National Institute of Allergy and Infectious Diseases. As was explained at the time, the Institute had been handicapped in making its case to the Appropriations Committees because "no one ever died of microbiology."[34]

It would be a mistake to assume, however, that dependents always have the wisdom to know what is in their own best interests. The maritime unions have become so obsessed with the idea that an independent maritime agency would solve all of their problems that they have ignored the plain fact that any transportation agency outside the Department of Transportation would be in a very weak competitive position.

[33]For a brilliant analysis of the significance of constituencies see Grant McConnell, *Private Power and American Democracy*, Alfred A. Knopf, 1967.
[34]*The New York Times*, December 14, 1969.

We are faced with the strange paradox that the privilege of access to public funds is believed to carry with it the right to exercise public power, where the payment of large amounts in taxes does not. This thesis is expressed in such euphemisms as "decentralization," "grass-roots administration," and "freedom from politics." Thus Yale alumni were reassured that the university's independence has not been compromised by accepting federal money because "the men who fix the Government's policy in this respect are themselves university and college men. . . . "[35]

The issue of dependence vs. subservience is at the heart of our present dilemma. How can we reconcile a growing federal involvement in all aspects of our national life with the maintenance of deeply cherished pluralistic values? The typical answer is that offered by Alan Pifer, president of the Carnegie Corporation.[36] He proposed the creation of a federal center for higher education which would "depend heavily in all its activities on men and women co-opted from the colleges and universities *so that it is as much of higher education itself as it is of government*" (italics supplied).

Few would dispute that federal domination of science and education would be undesirable. Yet grave risks are run when public power is exercised by agricultural, scientific, and educational elites who are more concerned with advancing their own interests and the interests of the institutions they represent than the public interest. Serious distortions and inequities may occur in the allocation of funds among those eligible for assistance. Vested interests are created which are resistant to change and the reordering of priorities to meet new national needs.

As our one elected official, other than the vice president, with a national constituency, the president of the United States stands almost alone as a counterweight to these powerful centrifugal forces. Sometimes the executive branch takes on the appearance of an arena in which the chiefs of major and petty bureaucratic fiefdoms, supported by their auxiliaries in the Congress and their mercenaries in the outside community, are arrayed against the president in deadly combat.

Herbert Emmerich, a highly perceptive student of federal or-

[35]*Report of the Treasurer of Yale University for the Fiscal Year Ended June 30, 1967*, p. 18.
[36]Alan Pifer, Speech to the Association of American Colleges, January 16, 1968, reprinted in *Congressional Record*, May 1, 1968, p. E.3631.

ganization, has said: "The Presidency is the focal point of any study of reorganization. . . . The Presidency focuses the general interest as contrasted with the centrifugal forces in the Congress and the departments for the specialized interests of subject matter and of region."[37]

It is significant that the lasting contributions of the first Hoover Commission, the President's Committee on Administrative Management, and the earlier Taft Commission on Economy and Efficiency are to be found in their recommendations to strengthen the office of the presidency, not in the long-forgotten proposals for reshuffling agencies and providing more efficient and economical administration. Institutional type and organization structure are important because they can help or hinder the president in performing his pivotal role within our constitutional system.

Reorganization also can be exploited by the president to alter the delicate balance within our constitutional system by eliminating or eroding the checks and balances resulting from the distribution of power within the executive branch as well as among the three branches of government. Watergate and its attendant "horrors" raise fundamental and disturbing questions about the centralization of power in the White House, the fractionalization of presidential power among assistants to the president, and the division of responsibilities between the White House Office and the statutory agencies within the Executive Office of the President, the executive departments, and independent agencies. It is one thing to support and strengthen the president's capability to perform his pivotal role within the constitutional system. It is quite another to restructure the government so the president, in the words of Assistant to the President Bryce N. Harlow, "is running the whole government from the White House."[38]

[37]Herbert Emmerich, *Essays on Federal Reorganization*, University of Alabama Press, 1950, p. 7.
[38]Emmet J. Hughes, *The Living Presidency*, Coward, McCann & Geoghegan, Inc., 1973, p. 344.

28

Reforming the
Budgetary Process

AARON WILDAVSKY

A large part of the literature on budgeting in the United States is concerned with reform. The goals of the proposed reforms are couched in similar language—economy, efficiency, improvement, or just better budgeting. The President, the Congress and its committees, administrative agencies, even the interested citizenry are all to gain by some change in the way the budget is formulated, presented, or evaluated. There is little or no realization among the reformers, however, that any effective change in budgetary relationships must necessarily alter the outcomes of the budgetary process. Otherwise, why bother? Far from being a neutral matter of "better budgeting," proposed reforms inevitably contain important implications for the political system; that is, for the "who gets what" of governmental decisions. What are some of the major political implications of budgetary reform? We begin with the noblest vision of reform: the development of a normative theory of budgeting (stating what ought to be) that would provide the basis for allocating funds among competing activities.

In 1940, in what is still the best discussion of the subject, V. O. Key lamented "The Lack of a Budgetary Theory." He called for a theory that would help answer the basic question of budgeting on the expenditure side: "On what basis shall it be decided to allocate X dollars to Activity A instead of Activity B?"[1] Although several at-

From Aaron Wildavsky, *The Politics of the Budgetary Process* (Boston: Little, Brown and Co., 1984), 4th ed., pp. 127–144. Reprinted with the permission of the author and the publisher.

[1]V. O. Key, Jr., "The Lack of a Budgetary Theory," XXXIV *The American Political Science Review* (December 1940), pp. 1137–1144.

tempts have been made to meet this challenge,[2] not one has come close to succeeding. No progress has been made for the excellent reason that the task, as posed, is impossible to fulfill.[3] The search for an unrealizable goal indicates serious weaknesses in prevailing conceptions of the budget.

If a normative theory of budgeting is to be more than an academic exercise, it must actually guide the making of governmental decisions. The items of expenditures that are passed by Congress, enacted into law, and spent must in large measure conform to the theory if it is to have any practical effect. This is tantamount to prescribing that virtually all the activities of government be carried on according to the theory. For whatever the government does must be paid for from public funds; it is difficult to think of any policy that can be carried out without money.

The budget is the lifeblood of the government, the financial reflection of what the government does or intends to do. A theory that contains criteria for determining what ought to be in the budget is nothing less than a theory stating what the government ought to do. If we substitute the words "what the government ought to do" for the words "ought to be in the budget," it becomes clear that a normative theory of budgeting would be a comprehensive and specific political theory detailing what the government's activities ought to be at a particular time. A normative theory of budgeting, therefore, is utopian in the fullest sense of that word: its accomplishment and acceptance would mean the end of conflict over the government's role in society.

By suppressing dissent, totalitarian regimes enforce their normative theories of budgeting on others. Presumably, we reject this solution to the problem of conflict in society and insist on democratic procedures. How then arrive at a theory of budgeting that is something more than one man's preferences?

The crucial aspect of budgeting is whose preferences are to prevail in disputes about which activities are to be carried on and to

---

[2]Verne B. Lewis, "Toward a Theory of Budgeting," XII *Public Administration Review* (Winter 1952), pp. 42–54; "Symposium on Budget Theory," X *Public Administration Review* (Winter 1950), pp. 20–31; Arthur Smithies, *The Budgetary Process in the United States* (New York, 1955).

[3]Key, in fact, shies away from the implications of his question and indicates keen awareness of the political problems involved. But the question has been posed by subsequent authors largely as he framed it.

what degree, in the light of limited resources. The problem is not only "how shall budgetary benefits be maximized?" as if it made no difference who received them, but also "who shall receive budgetary benefits and how much?" One may purport to solve the problem of budgeting by proposing a normative theory (or a welfare function or a hierarchy of values) which specifies a method for maximizing returns for budgetary expenditures. In the absence of ability to impose a set of preferred polices on others, however, this solution breaks down. It amounts to no more than saying that if you can persuade others to agree with you, then you will have achieved agreement. Or it begs the question of what kind of policies will be fed into the scheme by assuming that these are agreed upon. Yet we hardly need argue that a state of universal agreement has not yet arisen.

Another way of avoiding the problem of budgeting is to treat society as a single organism with a consistent set of desires and a life of its own, much as a single consumer might be assumed to have a stable demand and indifference schedule. Instead of revenue being raised and the budget being spent by and for many individuals who may have their own preferences and feelings, as is surely the case, these process are treated, in effect, as if a single individual were the only one concerned. This approach avoids the central problems of social conflict, of somehow aggregating different preferences so that a decision may emerge. How can we compare the worth of expenditures for irrigation to certain farmers with the worth of widening a highway to motorists and the desirability of aiding old people to pay medical bills as against the degree of safety provided by an expanded defense program?

The process we have developed for dealing with interpersonal comparisons in government is not economic but political. Conflicts are resolved (under agreed-upon rules) by translating different preferences through the political system into units called votes or into types of authority like a veto power. There need not be (and there is not) full agreement on goals or the preferential weights to be accorded to different goals. Congressmen directly threaten, compromise, and trade favors in regard to policies in which values are implicitly weighted, and then agree to register the results according to the rules for tallying votes.

The burden of calculation is enormously reduced for three primary reasons: first, only the small number of alternatives politically feasible at any one time are considered; second, these policies in a democracy typically differ only in small increments from previous policies on which there is a store of relevant information; and, third, each participant may ordinarily assume that he need consider only his preferences and those of his powerful opponents since the American political system works to assure that every significant interest has representation at some key point. Since only a relatively few interest groups contend on any given issue and no single item is considered in conjunction with all others (because budgets are made in bits and pieces), a huge and confusing array of interests is not activated all at once.

In the American context, a typical result is that bargaining takes place among many dispersed centers of influence and that favors are swapped as in the case of log-rolling public-works appropriations. Since there is no group of men who can necessarily impose their preferences upon others within the American political system, special coalitions are formed to support or oppose specific policies. Support is sought in this system of fragmented power at numerous centers of influence—Congressional committees, the Congressional leadership, the President, the Budget Bureau, interdepartmental committees, departments, bureaus, private groups, and so on. Nowhere does a single authority have power to determine what is going to be in the budget.

The Politics in Budget Reform

The seeming irrationalities of a political system that does not provide for even formal consideration of the budget as a whole[4] (except by the President, who cannot control the final result) has led to many attacks and proposals for reform. The tradition of reform in America is a noble one, not easily to be denied. But in this case it is doomed to failure because it is aimed at the wrong target. If the present budgetary process is rightly or wrongly deemed unsatisfactory, then one must alter in some respect the political system of which the budget

---

[4]See Charles E. Lindblom, "The Science of 'Muddling Through,' " XIX *Public Administration Review* (Spring 1959), pp. 79–88, for a description and criticism of the comprehensive method. See also his "Decision-Making in Taxation and Expenditure," in National Bureau of Economic Research, *Public Finances: Needs, Sources, and Utilization* (Princeton, 1961), pp. 295–336, and his "Policy Analysis," XLVIII *American Economic Review* (June 1958), pp. 298–312. His recent book (with David Braybrooke), *A Strategy of Decision* (New York, 1963), contains the most extensive statement of his position.

is but an expression. It makes no sense to speak as if one could make drastic changes in budgeting without also altering the distribution of influence. But this task is inevitably so formidable (though the reformers are not directly conscious of it) that most adversaries prefer to speak of changing the budgetary process, as if by some subtle alchemy the intractable political element could be transformed into a more malleable substance.

The reader who objects to being taken thus far only to be told that the budget is inextricably linked to the political system would have a just complaint if the implications of this remark were recognized in the literature on budgeting. Since these implications have not been spelled out, it seems worthwhile to do so now. One implication is that by far the most significant way of influencing the budget is to introduce basic political changes (or to wait for secular changes like the growing industrialization of the South). Provide the President with more powers enabling him to control the votes of his party in Congress; enable a small group of Congressmen to command a majority of votes on all occasions so that they can push their program through. Then you will have exerted a profound influence on the content of the budget.

A second implication is that no significant change can be made in the budgetary process without affecting the political process. There would be no point in tinkering with the budgetary machinery if, at the end, the pattern of budgetary decisions was precisely the same as before. On the contrary, reform has little justification unless it results in different kinds of decisions and, when and if this has been accomplished, the play of political forces has necessarily been altered. Enabling some political forces to gain at the expense of others requires the explicit introduction and defense of value premises that are ordinarily missing from proposals for budgetary reform.

Since the budget represents conflicts over whose preferences shall prevail, the third implication is that one cannot speak of "better budgeting" without considering who benefits and who loses or demonstrating that no one loses. Just as the supposedly objective criterion of "efficiency" has been shown to have normative implications,[5] so a "better budget" may well be a cloak for hidden policy preferences. To propose that the President be given an item veto, for example, is

[5]Dwight Waldo, *The Administrative State* (New York, 1948); Herbert A. Simon, "The Criterion of Efficiency," in *Administrative Behavior*, 2nd edition (New York, 1957), pp. 172–197.

to attempt to increase the influence of the particular interests that gain superior access to the Chief Executive rather than, say, to the Congress. Only if one eliminates the element of conflict over expenditures, can it be assumed that a reform that enables an official to do a better job from his point of view is simply "good" without considering the policy implications for others.

A Typical Reform

Arthur Smithies may stand as a typical proponent of a typical reform. Identifying rationality with a comprehensive overview of the budget by a single person or group, Smithies despairs of the fragmented approach taken by Congress and proposes a remedy. He suggests that a Joint (Congressional) Budget Policy committee be formed and empowered to consider all proposals for revenue and expenditure in a single package and that their decisions be made binding by a concurrent resolution. And he presents his reform as a moderate proposal to improve the rationality of the budget process.[6] If the proposed Joint Committee were unable to secure the passage of its recommendations, as it would surely be, it would have gone to enormous trouble without accomplishing anything but a public revelation of futility. The impotence of the Joint Committee on the Legislative Budget,[7] the breakdown of the single Congressional attempt to develop a comprehensive legislative budget,[8] and the failure of Congressional attempts to control the Council of Economic Advisers[9]

---

[6]Smithies, *op. cit.*, pp. 192–193 ff. See also Jesse Burkhead, *Government Budgeting* (New York, 1956), for a useful historical account of proposals for reform.

[7]Avery Leiserson, "Coordination of Federal Budgetary and Appropriations Procedures Under the Legislative Reorganization Act of 1946," I *National Tax Journal* (June 1948), pp. 118–126.

[8]Robert Ash Wallace, "Congressional Control of the Budget," III *Midwest Journal of Political Science* (May 1959), pp. 151–167; Dalmas H. Nelson, "The Omnibus Appropriations Act of 1950," XV *Journal of Politics* (May 1953), pp. 274–288; Representative John Phillips, "The Hadacol of the Budget Makers," IV *National Tax Journal* (September 1951), pp. 255–268.

[9]Roy Blough, "The Role of the Economist in Federal Policy-Making," LI *University of Illinois Bulletin* (November 1953); Lester Seligman, "Presidential Leadership: The Inner Circle and Institutionalization," XVIII *Journal of Politics* (August 1956), pp. 410–426; Edwin G. Nourse, *Economics in the Public Service; Administrative Aspects of the Employment Act* (New York, 1953); Ronald C. Hood, "Reorganizing the Council of Economic Advisors," LXIX *Political Science Quarterly* (September 1954), pp. 413–437.

and the Budget Bureau,[10] all stem from the same cause. There is no cohesive group in Congress capable of using these devices to affect decision making by imposing its preferences on a majority of Congressmen. Smithies' budgetary reform presupposes a completely different political system from the one that exists in the United States. To be sure, there is a name for a committee that imposes its will on the legislature and tolerates no rival committees—it is called a Cabinet on the British model. In the guise of a procedural change in the preparation of the budget by Congress, Smithies is actually proposing a revolutionary move that would mean the virtual introduction of the British parliamentary system if it were successful.

Smithies (pp. 188–225) suggests that his proposals would be helpful to the President. But the membership of the Joint Committee would be made up largely of conservatives from safe districts, who are not dependent on the President, who come from a different constituency than he does, but with whom he must deal in order to get any money for his programs. Should the members of the Joint Committee ever be able to command a two-thirds vote of the Congress, they could virtually ignore the President in matters of domestic policy and run the executive branch so that it would be accountable only to them.

Program Budgeting Versus Traditional Budgeting

The basic idea behind program budgeting is that instead of presenting budgetary requests in the usual line-item form, which focuses on categories like supplies, maintenance, and personnel, the presentation is made in terms of the end-products, of program packages like public health or limited war or strategic retaliatory forces. The virtues of the program budget are said to be its usefulness in relating ends to means in a comprehensive fashion, the emphasis it puts upon the policy implications of budgeting, and the ease with which it permits consideration of the budget as a whole as each program com-

[10]Fritz Morstein Marx, "The Bureau of the Budget: Its Evolution and Present Role, II," XXXIX *The American Political Science Review* (October 1945), pp. 869–898; Richard Neustadt, "Presidency and Legislation: The Growth of Central Clearance," XLVIII *ibid.* (September 1954), pp. 641–671; Seligman, *op. cit.*

petes with every other for funds.[11] Interestingly enough, the distinguishing characteristics of the program procedure are precisely the reverse of those of the traditional practice. Federal budgeting today is incremental rather than comprehensive, calculated in bits and pieces rather than as a whole, and veils policy implications rather than emphasizing them.

This brief account will focus on three major consequences resulting from the differences in budgetary procedure. First, the traditional procedure increases agreement among the participants whereas the program device decreases it. Second, the program budgeting procedure increases the burden of calculation on the participants; the traditional method decreases it. And, third, the specific outcomes in the form of decisions are likely to be different.

The incremental, fragmented, non-programmatic, and sequential procedures of the present budgetary process aid in securing agreement and reducing the burden of calculation. It is much easier to agree on an addition or reduction of a few thousand or a million than to agree on whether a program is good in the abstract. It is much easier to agree on a small addition or decrease than to compare the worth of one program to that of all others. Conflict is reduced by an incremental approach because the area open to dispute is reduced. In much the same way the burden of calculation is eased because no one has to make all the calculations that would be involved in a comprehensive evaluation of all expenditures. Calculations are made sequentially, in small segments, by subcommittees, and are accepted by the Congress as a whole. Were each subcommittee to challenge the results of the others, conflict would be greatly exacerbated. Were each Congressman to fail to accept the decisions of the subcommittees most of the time there would be (assuming that time was available to make the necessary calculations) continual dis-

---

[11]On program budgeting see A. E. Buck, *Municipal Finance* (New York, 1926), and *Public Budgeting* (New York, 1929); The (Hoover) Commission on the Organization of the Executive Branch of the Government, *Budgeting and Accounting* (Washington, D.C., 1949); Arthur Smithies, *op. cit.*; Jesse Burkhead, *op. cit.*; Gladys Kammerer, *Program Budgeting: An Aid to Understanding* (Gainesville, Fla., 1959); Symposium, "Performance Budgeting: Has the Theory Worked?" XX *Public Administration Review* (Spring 1960), pp. 63–85; Stanley T. Gabis, *Mental Health and Financial Management: Some Dilemmas of Program Budgeting*, Public Administration Program, Department of Political Science Research Report, No. 3 (East Lansing, Mich., 1960).

agreement over most items instead of only a few as at present. Finally, agreement comes much more readily when the items in dispute can be treated as differences in dollars instead of basic differences in policy. Calculating budgets in monetary increments facilitates bargaining and logrolling. It becomes possible to swap an increase here for a decrease there or for an increase elsewhere without always having to consider the ultimate desirability of programs blatantly in competition.

Procedures that de-emphasize overt conflicts among competing programs also encourage secret deliberations, non-partisanship, and the recruitment of personnel who feel comfortable in sidestepping policy decisions most of the time. The prospects for agreement within the House Appropriations Committee are enhanced by closed hearings and mark-up sessions, and by a tradition against publicity. Were deliberations to take place in public—"open covenants openly arrived at"—committee members might find themselves accused of "selling out" as they made concessions. Willingness to compromise, to be flexible, is a quality sought in choosing members to serve on the appropriations committees.

Party ties might be disruptive of agreement if they focused attention on the policy differences between the two political persuasions. Instead, party differences are submerged during committee deliberations. Thus the usual process of taking something from a program here, adding to a program there, swapping this for that, can go on at the committee stage without having to take the kind of "yes" or "no" party positions that may be required at the voting stage on the floor.

Consider by contrast some likely consequence of program budgeting. The practice of focusing attention on programs means that policy implications can hardly be avoided. The gains and the losses for the interests involved become far more evident to all concerned.[12] Conflict is heightened by the stress on policy differences and increased still further by an in-built tendency to an all-or-nothing, "yes" or "no" response to the policy in dispute. The very concept

[12]Gabis, *op. cit.*, p. 46, writes that "under program budgeting the increase or decrease in the power and influence of each program would be spelled out in detail. It would be surprising if each addition or subtraction were not accompanied by a complicated process of maneuver and counter-maneuver among the affected program heads."

of program packages suggests that the policy in dispute is indivisible, that the appropriate response is to be for or against rather than bargaining for a little more or a little less. Logrolling and bargaining are hindered because it is much easier to trade increments conceived in monetary terms than it is to give in on basic policy differences. Problems of calculation are vastly increased by the necessity, if program budgeting is to have meaning, of evaluating the desirability of every program as compared to all others, instead of the traditional practice of considering budgets in relatively independent segments. Conflict would become much more prevalent as the specialist whose verdict was usually accepted in his limited sphere gave way to the generalist whose decisions were fought over by all his fellow legislators who could claim as much or (considering the staggering burden of calculation) as little competence as he. The Hobbesian war of all against all, though no doubt an exaggeration, is suggestive on this score.

I wish to make it clear that I am not saying that the traditional method of budgeting is good because it tends to reduce the amount of conflict. Many of us may well want more conflict in specific areas rather than less. What I am saying is that mitigation of conflict is a widely shared value in our society, and that we ought to realize that program budgeting is likely to affect that value.

The Program Budget
in the Department of Defense

By 1960 it had become clear that the major decisions of the Department of Defense revolved around the choice of hugely expensive weapons systems designed to accomplish the military missions of the nuclear era. In order to produce the data most relevant to the choice of alternative weapons systems, including the full cost of development, procurement, and maintenance, the Defense Department, under the aegis of Comptroller Charles J. Hitch, undertook the installation of a program budget. The nation's defense effort was categorized into seven basic programs—strategic retaliatory forces, continental air and missile defense forces, general purpose forces, airlift and sealift forces, special research and development, reserve and national guard forces, and general support—each composed of a number of program elements, such as Polaris submarines and Minuteman missiles, which were devoted to the accomplishment of a common military mission.[13] As it happened, the new program budget was used mainly for internal purposes; it was deemed desirable to present the defense budget to Congress by converting the program categories into the more traditional rubrics such as procurement, construction, and personnel. Although it might be good practice to use different kinds of budgets for internal and external purposes—or even to devise several different budget formulations for use by department officials—the installation of the program budget under these circumstances does raise interesting political problems that have largely been ignored in the debate over the superior efficiency of the old or new budget formulations.

Hearings before Senator Henry Jackson's Subcommittee on National Policy machinery in 1961,[14] in which program budgeting was discussed by knowledgeable participants, gives us an opportunity to suggest some of its likely policy implications. The hearings were held to help determine whether the newly installed program budget in the Defense Department was likely to have desirable consequences for defense policy.

Committee consultant Robert Tufts kept hammering away at the question of why the new program budget in defense would lead to different results than prior practice if the participants remained the same as they had in the past. Ultimately, Defense Department Comptroller Charles Hitch admitted that one difference would be that "Program decisions . . . are decisions of the sort which can only be made by the Secretary and, therefore, the role of the Secretary *and of the Secretary's advisers* will be greater" (italics supplied) (pp. 1031–32). The most significant result of the program budget may turn out to be the increased power it gives to the Secretary of Defense.

Former Comptroller Wilfred McNeil asserted that program packages

> would not be conducive to economy of force. . . . I would assume the number of destroyers in active service is probably around 225. I can assure you that if you broke that package up . . . budgetwise, and

---

[13]See Charles J. Hitch and Roland N. McKean, *The Economics of Defense in the Nuclear Age* (Cambridge, 1960), and Hitch's "Management of the Defense Dollar," XI *The Federal Accountant* (June 1962), pp. 33–44.

[14]*Jackson Subcommittee Hearings.*

allocated and assigned . . . separate groups of destroyers to the carrier force, to a possible convoy force, to an antisubmarine force, and to the various odd jobs they do, that you will find requirements above 225. . . . By budgeting for the maintenance of 225 destroyers and then thinking flexibly about their use, . . . you will find you don't need quite as many as you would if you divided them up in neat packages (p. 1066).

The point is that the way a budget is arranged suggests ways of thinking and comparison and that if you change the form you change the kinds of calculations and the probable outcomes.[15]

Senator Jackson chimed in with the observation that "What troubles me is that if . . . under the program package approach, the service finds that with the big increase occurring [say] . . . in the strategic striking force—other items are cut back, maybe they would be reluctant to push the newer and more costly programs that would tend to offset the so-called balance of forces within their own department." "All I can say," Hitch replied, "is that . . . under the program package procedures there is less chance of those cutbacks affecting the same service so that the tendency to hold back for this reason should be considerably less" (p. 1019). Perhaps. But if Hitch were correct, then inter-service rivalry would be increased and these severe conflicts might lead to similar difficulties. And if we take McNeil's hint and note that "almost the entire Army, with the exception of Air Defense, is in one grouping [program package]" (p. 1063), the Army would have to defend the strategic concept behind that program to the bitter end or else see the service disappear with a change in program.

Another kind of jurisdictional problem was brought up by Senator Jacob Javits. "If you [the Defense Department] are going to bring programs to the Appropriations Committee rather than the Armed

[15]In *Governing New York City*, Wallace Sayre and Herbert Kaufman show that "an almost incredibly detailed 'line item' budget, which the Budget Director has in fact prepared and of which only he and his staff are masters," is a potent factor in increasing that official's influence over budgetary decisions. They also observe that "Some of the city's most articulate interest groups have within the last decade found a weapon . . . by seizing upon a demand (widely supported by new budget doctrine in national, state, and local governments elsewhere) for a change . . . to a 'program' or 'performance' budget. This change would open up the budget process to more critical public scrutiny, increase the discretion of the Mayor and agency heads to make budget decisions, and restrict the opportunities of the Board of Estimate and the Budget Director to make their traditional detailed expenditure decisions." (New York, 1960), pp. 368–369.

Services Committees of the House and Senate," Javits asked, "do you think that we are going to have to do something about our congressional review of your programs . . . ? You are coming now with the basic program concept. When Congress approves your budget it approves the concept" (p. 1027). Speaking of program packages seems mild enough. But who is brave enough to tell the Armed Services Committees to abdicate their present responsibilities and powers?

The late Senator Mundt had his own worries. Although he was perfectly willing to accept the idea of program packages, he was disturbed by Budget Director David Bell's talk about country program packages in foreign aid budgeting.

> To me [Mundt declared] that opens up a Pandora's box of undesirable possibilities. I think if the word gets out that the U.S. Government, in its annual budgeting, is providing a country program . . . in Africa, Asia, and Latin America . . . that we are not too far away from the day when, in addition to the Appropriations Committees . . . listening to delegations from every one of our 50 States who come in for public works projects, we can anticipate we will have delegations from every one of 100 different countries (pp. 1150–51).

Whether or not program budgeting will lead to "better budgeting" in some sense is a moot point. (McNeil felt that those in authority might want to consider all sorts of packages at different times rather than being stuck with one in the budget. They might want to consider the portion of the effort allocated to offense as compared to defense of the United States, to look at the effort allocated to the defense of the fighting forces themselves in forward areas, and to group expenditures by geographic area to be defended and by proportion of defense effort going into research and testing versus actual procurement of military hardware [p. 1062]). What is clear is that the kind of categories used and the procedures of program budgeting are likely to have important consequences for our defense policies.

Efficiency

I do not mean to disparage in any way the important problem of efficiency, of finding ways to maximize budgetary benefits given a specified distribution of shares. In principle, there seems to be no reason why policy machinery could not be so arranged as to alter the ratio of inputs to outputs without changing the distribution of shares. One can imagine situations in which everyone benefits or where the losses suffered in one respect are made up by greater gains elsewhere. It may happen that such losses as do exist are not felt by the participants and they may be happy to make changes that increase their benefits. The inevitable lack of full information and the disinclination of participants to utilize their political resources to the fullest extent undoubtedly leave broad areas of inertia and inattention open for change. Thus, the "slack" in the system may leave considerable room for ingenuity and innovation in such areas as benefit cost analysis and the comparability and interrelatedness of public works without running into outstanding political difficulties or involving large changes in the system. Most practical budgeting may take place in a twilight zone between politics and efficiency. Without presenting a final opinion on this matter, it does seem to me that the problem of distributing shares has either been neglected entirely or has been confused with the problem of efficiency to the detriment of both concerns. . . .

Knowledge and Reform

Our concentration . . . on developing at least the rudiments of an adequate description of the national budgetary process is not meant to discourage concern with normative considerations or reforms. On the contrary, budgeting is worth studying from both standpoints. Surely, it is not too much to suggest that a lot of reform be preceded by a little knowledge. Until we develop a more adequate description of budgeting, until we know something about the "existential situation" in which the participants find themselves under our political system, proposals for major reform must be based on woefully inadequate understanding. A proposal which alters established relationships, which does not permit an agency to show certain programs in the most favorable light, which does not tell influential Congressmen what they want to know, which changes prevailing expectations about the behavior of key participants, or which leads to different kinds of calculations, would have many consequences no one is even able to guess at today. Of course, small, incremental changes proceeding in a pragmatic fashion of trial and error could proceed as before without benefit of theory; but this is not the kind of change with which the literature on budgeting is generally concerned. . . .

29

Executive Secrecy: Change and Continuity

FRANCIS E. ROURKE

Public interest in issues involving the reform of governmental operation or procedure has traditionally had a very short life span in American politics. As a general rule the public is not greatly interested in such questions and is aroused from its indifference only when scandalous misconduct by an officeholder is suddenly revealed. Dramatic exposure of wrongdoing usually does excite widespread public interest and, while it persists, the prospect for reform of the political process brightens if the wrongdoing can be linked to some basic defect in the system. But this support for change commonly recedes as the impact of the scandal wears off, and members of the public return to their customary private concerns. Relevant here is the model of an "issue-attention cycle" that Anthony Downs uses to suggest that reform is generally a transient phenomenon in a political system that is ordinarily quite resistant to change.[1]

The issue of secrecy, however, has proven extraordinarily durable in modern American politics. This may be because the media of communication themselves have a vested interest in the question of secrecy in government, and they are unwilling to allow it to recede from public attention. Moreover, public interest organizations like Common Cause have also taken a keen interest in the problem of secrecy in government. In this respect their behavior has been entirely consistent with that of reform groups which preceded them.

Adapted from Francis E. Rourke, "The United States," in Itzhak Galnoor (ed.), *Government Secrecy in Democracies* (New York: Harper Colophon Books, 1977), pp. 113–128. Copyright © 1977 by Itzhak Galnoor. Reprinted by permission of Harper and Row, Publishers.

[1]Anthony Downs, "Up and Down with Ecology—The 'Issue Attention' Cycle." *The Public Interest* 28 (Summer 1972):38–50.

It has long been characteristic of American reformers to put the cause of exposure at the top of their agenda.

With the events of Watergate providing dramatic proof of the reform belief that secrecy on the part of executive officials can be used to conceal criminal misconduct, the movement against secrecy in American government, already strong, has acquired extraordinary vitality. In this discussion we will look at some of the recent changes that have taken place in information policies and practices in the United States as a result of legislative and executive action. While these changes reflect the impact that traumatic events like Vietnam and Watergate have had upon the political consciousness of Americans, they stem also from underlying characteristics of political culture in the United States that were firmly established long before these contemporary developments occurred.

I. The Political Culture

While it is a very broad generalization that increasingly requires qualification, it is still true to say that the fundamental American political style is one of openness. Shils' description of the American political system as being based on "luxuriating publicity" remains close to the mark.[2] This is certainly true when the American system is viewed in comparison with other political systems around the world, where conventions of secrecy or privacy in governmental affairs are little questioned, and where strong legal penalties may be attached to the disclosure of information that executive officials wish to conceal.

However, the image of the United States as an open political system tends to change considerably if we look at it not from the vantage point of other societies with which it might be compared but from the perspective of its own internal development in the last three decades. Clearly, there has been a strong trend in American politics since World War II toward secrecy. It began most notably perhaps with the atom bomb—a development with awesome implications for modern life. Born in secrecy, the bomb was developed behind tight security precautions and then suddenly sprung on the world in August 1945.

---

[2]Edward A. Shils, *The Torment of Secrecy* (Glencoe, Ill.: The Free Press, 1956), pp. 37–44.

For the generation of political leaders that came to office after World War II, the atom bomb thus became a symbol of success through secrecy. The bomb was looked upon by many Americans as an extraordinary technological achievement because the United States actually was able to build such a weapon. It was also regarded as an achievement because the United States succeeded in ending World War II by using it. (So at least it seemed in the eyes of the public, although historians were later to dispute the point.) Out of that beginning there emerged a conviction that secrecy was an essential prerequisite for national security, and this view was to become firmly fixed as part of the dominant political consensus of the Cold War. The opposite viewpoint—that secrecy can sometimes be damaging to national security—was usually hard-pressed to make itself heard.

No institution has contributed more to the shift in the American perspective on secrecy than the presidency—the office chiefly responsible for the conduct of foreign affairs in the United States. Presidential ascendancy in American politics since World War II is linked in many ways to the growth of secrecy, and the defense of secrecy has thus become essential for American Presidents as a means of defending the power and prerogatives of their own office. Among the advantages the White House derives from secrecy is the fact that it enables a President to conceal disagreements within his official family, and thus present the public with an impressive even if spurious display of unity behind White House policies. Secrecy also adds to the mystery of the presidential office, helping to give it the air of authority on which it so often trades in American politics. The possession of secrets of state is another means by which Presidents exact awe and deference from their subjects.

So to the traditional American belief that openness on the part of government was essential to the successful functioning of democracy, there came to be added the idea that secrecy was indispensable for both the success of the nation's foreign policy and the effective operation of the central office of the political system—the presidency. As a result there exist in the United States today two cultures which exert sharply conflicting pressures on the development of political life. One is rooted in the tradition of openness, so dominant in the Progressive era in the early part of this century and so well expressed by Woodrow Wilson:

> I, for one, have the conviction that government ought to be all outside and no inside. I, for my part, believe that there ought to be no place where anything can be done that everybody does not know

about. . . . Everybody knows that corruption thrives in secret places, and avoids public places, and we believe it a fair presumption that secrecy means impropriety. . . . Government must, if it is to be pure and correct in its processes, be absolutely public in everything that affects it.[3]

This tradition of disclosure is sustained by a variety of powerful institutions in American society, especially Congress, the media of communication, and on occasion, the courts.

The other culture, which formed in the period immediately following World War II, defends and seeks to magnify the value of secrecy. Presiding over this culture of secrecy is the presidency, and it is buttressed by a variety of resourceful national security organizations from the Pentagon to the CIA. These institutions generate and exploit fears of the dire consequences that may ensue if the secrets of the United States are exposed to its enemies abroad, and they enjoy no small measure of public support in this endeavor.

Vietnam and Watergate have given new life to the traditional Wilsonian faith in publicity as the best remedy for the ills that may plague a democratic society. As a result, there has been a reinvigoration of the instruments and institutions of disclosure. But the culture of secrecy also remains intact—weak at the periphery, but strong at the core. Growing strain between these two divergent cultures of publicity and secrecy has generated recurrent crises in recent American politics over such matters as the Pentagon papers, the war in Vietnam, Watergate, and the operations of the CIA. Neither culture seems to be weakening appreciably, and conflict between them seems likely to be no less intense in the future than it has been in the past.

II. The Constitutional and Legal Background

Secrecy in the United States today is sustained by a wide and deeply rooted network of laws and constitutional practices. Perhaps the best known of the legal underpinnings on which it currently rests is executive privilege. Presidents have frequently invoked this concept in recent times to justify withholding information when they believed that its release would jeopardize national security or the ability of the White House to function effectively. The scope and constitutionality of the doctrine of executive privilege have often been challenged—most clearly and most notably by the Watergate special

---

[3]Woodrow Wilson, *The New Freedom*, edited with an introduction by William E. Leuchtenburg (Englewood Cliffs, N.J.: Prentice-Hall, 1961), pp. 76, 84.

prosecutor's office during its effort in 1973 and 1974 to gain access to tapes and documents withheld by the Nixon White House. But the decision of the Supreme Court in the Watergate case did seem to sustain the President's privilege to withhold information when he considers that its release would jeopardize national security, hamper him in his efforts to obtain candid advice, or have an otherwise damaging effect upon his ability to carry out his executive responsibilities.[4]

But while executive privilege has been at the forefront of public attention as a result of the frequent and sometimes searing confrontations it has triggered between Congress and the President since World War II, much of the secrecy that administrative officials practice in the United States rests on legal grounds other than executive privilege. This is necessarily so, since the courts have ruled that executive privilege belongs only to the President and cannot be claimed by any of his administrative subordinates as a prerogative of their offices.

There are, for example, more than 100 statutes enacted by Congress which either allow or require executive agencies to withhold information from the public. Much of this legislation is designed to protect what the legislature regards as rights of privacy on the part of either individuals or organizations. The material thus given statutory protection includes data in the personnel records of government employees, information submitted by citizens on their tax returns, and what business firms regard as trade secrets which would be very economically damaging for them to have disclosed. In enacting these statutes, Congress commonly seeks to protect not the secrets of bureaucracy but the privacy of nongovernmental groups and individuals.

Another major source of secrecy in the United States is the classification system under which information is given a security stamp by bureaucrats and withheld from disclosure. The legal basis for this system is a series of executive orders issued by modern Presidents, for example, Executive Order No. 11652 put into effect by President Nixon in 1972. These orders empower a variety of executive agencies

---

[4]*United States v. Nixon*, 94 S. Ct. 3090 (1974). However, the Court held that the privilege did not apply if the information requested was needed by the courts for the administration of justice. In effect, the Court ruled against President Nixon, while sustaining in large measure the doctrine of executive privilege. Hence, it can be said that while the President lost the case, the presidency won it.

and officials to put a secrecy stamp on documents which they believe would embarrass the United States or damage its security if exposed to public view.

Inevitably, bureaucratic caution and self-interest lead executive agencies to classify many more documents as secret than security interests actually require since the penalties attached to unauthorized disclosure may be severe, while overclassification is much less likely to be punished. In view of this skewed system of incentives, it is hardly surprising that bureaucrats should choose to conceal so much of the information placed under their jurisdiction.

Efforts to reform the classification system center on reducing the number of officials authorized to classify documents. The Interagency Classification Review Committee reported in 1975 that the number of persons holding classification authority had declined from 59,316 in June 1972 to 15,466 at the end of 1974. But the pace at which documents continue to be classified is phenomenal. In 1974 alone officials in the Defense Department classified 14,275 documents as top secret, 800,600 as secret, and 2.4 million as confidential. The Pentagon's way of declassifying many documents is to destroy them. The shredder has thus taken its place along with the classification stamp as a major instrument of concealment within the bureaucracy.

Perhaps the most ironic twist in the development of legislative protection for secrecy in the United States is the extent to which the Freedom of Information Act as enacted in 1966 and amended in 1974 was used to reinforce practices of secrecy in the United States. The act was designed to require executive agencies to furnish citizens and other interested parties outside of government with information they requested from the executive branch. If an agency proved unwilling to cooperate, these outside parties could obtain the assistance of the courts in getting access to the information they wanted. No legislation ever enacted in the United States represents a more comprehensive charter for disclosure than the Freedom of Information Act. The 1974 amendments even included provisions for penalizing officials who wrongfully withheld information.

As it turned out, however, the act also specified nine different categories of information that agencies could legitimately withhold from the public. These so-called exemptions from the act's preferred policy of disclosure represent a very formidable legal basis for the practice of secrecy by executive officials in the United States today.

For example, the first exemption permits agencies to keep information secret "in the interest of national defense and foreign policy." The third exemption allows them to withhold information that is "specifically exempted from disclosure by statute," thus reinforcing the statutory support Congress has already given to executive secrecy. The fifth exemption permits the withholding of interagency memoranda, while the seventh exempts "investigatory files compiled for law enforcement purposes." In total effect, these exemption clauses tend to strengthen patterns and powers of secrecy that already prevail within the bureaucracy.

III. The Politics of Information and Secrecy

On the surface there would appear to be few practices that more flagrantly contradict both the spirit and practice of democracy than the secrecy which has surrounded so many of the activities of American government in recent years. Democracy assumes that citizens can hold government officials accountable for what they do and can expel them from office when their policies do not meet with public approval. By shielding official action from public knowledge and review, secrecy makes such accountability impossible. Citizens can scarcely influence decisions they know nothing about. Where secrecy reigns, government officials are in a position to rule at virtually their own discretion.

Clearly, a practice which flies so directly in the face of democratic ideology and yet survives must have a very high degree of utility for the political system, or at least for major institutional clusters within the larger system. However incompatible secrecy may be with the norms of democracy, its prevalence and durability as a governmental practice suggests that it has become extremely functional for the operation of a wide range of institutions in American society.

1. The Executive

A large number of the major presidential decisions by which American political life has been shaped since World War II were made by Presidents operating in almost total secrecy. Witness, for example, the development of atomic weapons under Roosevelt, the conduct of U-2 flights over the Soviet Union during the Eisenhower years, the Cuban missile crisis in the Kennedy era, the planning for the escalation of American involvement in Vietnam under Johnson, and the Nixon rapprochement with Communist China in 1972. The withholding of information on these and many more such events testifies to the powerful role that secrecy has come to play in the conduct of the presidency in modern American politics.

In the past all American Presidents, beginning with George Washington, have had occasion to resort to secrecy. Every chief executive has been convinced of the necessity of maintaining his prerogative to withhold information, and each has been able to rely upon precedents set by his predecessors in doing so. This was true of Presidents like Thomas Jefferson, celebrated for his association with the ideals of liberal democracy, and of conservatives like William Howard Taft and Calvin Coolidge. However much they may have disagreed in other respects, Presidents have been united in this conviction that some measure of secrecy is essential for the conduct of White House business.

But even in the context of this historic tradition of presidential attachment to secrecy, Richard Nixon stands out in terms of the extraordinary salience the question of secrecy acquired during his years in office. In one way or another, the secrecy issue played a role in each of the major events of his administration: the conduct of the war in Vietnam; the negotiations with Hanoi, Peking, Moscow, and in the Middle East; the release of the Pentagon papers; and then ultimately and, from Nixon's perspective, disastrously, Watergate itself. Never before in American history had more continuous public attention been drawn to the issue of executive secrecy than during Nixon's five years in office.

Nixon was also distinctive because of the very great importance he placed upon secrecy as a prerequisite to effective governance. In part at least, this was a matter of necessity. The Watergate scandal triggered multiple demands for disclosure by the White House, and the President's inability to gratify these requests without incriminating himself led inevitably to a wide-ranging defense of confidentiality in the conduct of public affairs. In justifying its refusal to release Watergate-related materials, the White House resurrected all of the traditional arguments in favor of executive secrecy, including the need to guarantee candor in executive deliberations and to insure protection against the intelligence-gathering activities of potential adversaries abroad.

However much he was motivated by self-interest in this defense of secrecy, Nixon appears to have genuinely convinced himself of the linkage between secrecy and effective presidential performance. In speaking before the American prisoners of war who had returned from Vietnam in 1973, the President was quite explicit in linking what he felt were the great successes of his administration—including the return of the prisoners themselves—to the use of secrecy in diplomatic negotiations. "Had we not had secrecy," Nixon argued, "there would have been no China initiative, there would have been no limitation of arms for the Soviet Union and no summit, and had we not had that kind of security and that kind of secrecy that allowed for the kind of exchange that is essential, you men would still be in Hanoi rather than Washington today."

Unfortunately for Nixon, however, a preoccupation with secrecy could also be said to have played an equally large part in his administration's failures. Witness, for example, the decision to establish the "plumbers organization" in the White House to ferret out the secrets of Daniel Ellsberg, the man who had leaked the Pentagon papers to the press—a decision that led ultimately to the ill-fated burglary of Ellsberg's psychiatrist's office. Consider also the Watergate burglary itself—the surreptitious entry into the headquarters of the Democratic National Committee for the purpose of installing or removing eavesdropping equipment.

The costs of all these secretive ventures to the Nixon administration proved to be enormous. Moreover, these costs rose sharply as each stage of the Watergate drama unfolded—beginning with the original burglaries and culminating in White House claims of executive privilege in refusing to release evidence bearing on the affair—especially the celebrated tapes. The suspicion bred by each successive step in this continuing strategy of secrecy brought a precipitous decline in the President's standing in the eyes of both Congress and the public and led to his eventual resignation from office.

The ultimate irony of the Nixon years may well be the fact that a President so devoutly committed to the value of secrecy in the conduct of governmental affairs actually brought about a major swing toward disclosure on the part of Presidents. Future occupants of the White House are not likely to be favorably impressed by the results Nixon achieved through his use of secrecy. On the contrary, the Nixon precedent may actually serve to underline the advantages of openness as a presidential strategy in dealing with the public, the Congress, and the media. One of the first steps taken by President Jimmy Carter, winner of the first presidential election held in the wake of

Watergate, was to announce that he would conduct an "open" presidency—a pointed departure, at least in intention, from the strategy of secrecy that had led to Nixon's political demise.

2. Citizen Organizations and the Mass Media

Because of the creation of citizens organizations like John Gardner's Common Cause and the network of public interest groups under the direction of Ralph Nader, it is now possible to say that reform has become a permanent force in American politics. The establishment of these new public interest organizations means that the cause of governmental reform now has a continuing presence in Washington in the form of both an office and a staff of representatives who can buttonhole Congressmen or quickly organize an avalanche of telephone calls to their offices.

The power of such organizations has been reinforced greatly by the advent of the new media of communication, especially television, which make it possible for official misconduct to be given wide and instantaneous publicity throughout the country. In this way public indignation of great intensity can be aroused quickly, and, through a communications device like the telephone network of Common Cause, it can find rapid and effective political expression. Because of these developments, governmental reform now has a staying power it never before enjoyed in American politics, and when some governmental malfunction appears, the political system is subject to pressures for change it did not previously experience.

Linked together, as they often are, citizen organizations and the mass media represent major elements in what might be called the "antisecrecy" lobby in Washington—a lobby that has been working assiduously during the past decade to open up the processes of government to greater public scrutiny. The strategy of secrecy pursued by President Nixon during the Watergate affair greatly added to the strength of this antisecrecy lobby. Because of the success of its investigative reporting, the press emerged from Watergate with greatly enhanced authority as a fourth branch of government in the American political system, a branch charged with the task of exposing wrongdoing on the part of public officials. At the same time, public interest organizations have become much more aggressive in pushing for measures that would require greater publicity for executive deliberations and decisions.

But while the news media correctly regard themselves as being in the vanguard of the "freedom of information" movement in the United States—deeply hostile to all efforts on the part of government to interfere with the people's "right to know"—there are significant ways in which individual reporters benefit from executive secrecy and have on occasion been very supportive of it. Such secrecy gives some reporters an opportunity to publish information obtained from inside sources that would be of little value if it were freely available to the public at large. By sharing the fruits of their monopoly of information with selected reporters, government agencies can put themselves in a strong position to reward their friends and punish their enemies in the news media.

Newspaper columnists are particularly likely to acquire a stake in executive secrecy and become defenders of it.[5] The practice of their craft requires the preservation of privileged access to official sources. Disclosures that threaten the value of this access impair their ability to obtain inside information that is essential to maintain their reputation as pundits. A close relationship between secretive agencies like the CIA and friendly newspaper columnists is not uncommon in the United States. An agency that has secrecy as one of its distinguishing characteristics is in a very advantageous position to give a columnist preferred access to a story.[6] Thus, while executive secrecy often seems to create divergent interests on the part of government and the media, it is also a means through which segments of the press are linked to the government in a mutually advantageous exchange relationship. This may explain why a number of newspaper columnists were critical of President Carter's efforts to cut back on official secrecy.

3. Secrecy and the Private Sector

In their expanding assault upon secrecy in recent years, reformers have increasingly had private as well as public organizations as their target. The energy crisis that occurred in the winter of 1974 highlighted the power of private corporations over the development of public policy in the United States, since it quickly became clear

[5]For illustrations of such news media support for executive secrecy, see Francis E. Rourke, "Bureaucratic Secrecy and Its Constituents," *The Bureaucrat* 1 (Summer 1972):119–120.
[6]For an analysis of the role of such leaks in the relationship between executive agencies and the media, see Leon V. Sigal, *Reporters and Officials: The Organization and Politics of Newsmaking* (Lexington, Mass.: D. C. Heath, 1973), pp. 143–148.

that it was private oil companies which controlled most of the information available to the public on fuel supplies, and the ability of the Federal Energy Office to handle the crisis heavily depended upon the willingness of these companies to share this data with the government. For years reformers had been highly critical of secrecy when it was practiced by public agencies because of the danger it posed to the basic assumption of a democracy that the people control the government. The energy crisis made it abundantly clear that secrecy by private corporations could be no less threatening to the public's ability to exercise sovereignty over major policy decisions.

Sometimes secrecy can be linked together in the public and private spheres in ways that are mutually advantageous to organizations in both sectors of society, but highly detrimental to the rest of the country.[7] In 1972 a Federal Advisory Committee Act was passed in order to provide full publicity regarding the deliberations and decisions of outside advisory committees through which representatives of many powerful private corporations advise administrative agencies on their policies and decisions. The major purpose of this legislation was to prevent private organizations from wielding in secret an influence they would never be allowed to exercise in public or from joining together with government agencies in the covert development of policies harmful to the country. However, the new law did not succeed in opening up advisory committee meetings nearly as much as its sponsors had originally hoped, since executive agencies were quick to use certain of its provisions as a mandate for secrecy rather than publicity.

In any case, there are a host of groups in American society that have transactions with the government which they prefer remain unpublicized and a variety of statutes have been enacted to insure that these wishes are respected. Many of these transactions involve citizens reporting information to the government that they wish kept confidential, such as the personal history of an applicant for government employment or the economic status of a taxpayer. Some, of course, are much less innocent, such as the efforts of a private corporation like ITT to obtain a favorable settlement of an antitrust suit by the government or to influence American foreign policy in parts of the world like Chile where the company has a major financial

[7]See Mark V. Nadel, "Corporate Secrecy and Political Accountability," *Public Administration Review* 35 (January/February 1975):14–23.

stake. But whether the claim to privacy for any such transaction would meet with general public approval or not, the fact of the matter is that the secrecy which results springs in no small measure from the pressures of groups outside the governmental apparatus itself. An outside party supplies information to the government that he does not wish to have revealed to his neighbor or business competitor or seeks a favor that might not look very good in the cold light of public scrutiny.

4. The Congressional Role

On the surface, Congressmen in the United States are opposed to all executive efforts to withhold information from the public. Attacks on secrecy are a common feature of legislative life, and there have been major initiatives in Congress, including the Freedom of Information Act enacted in 1966 and amended in 1974, to curb excessive secrecy on the part of executive agencies.

And yet it needs to be remembered that while the collective attitude of Congress toward secrecy is one of hostility, individual Congressmen stand to gain a great deal from having privileged access to official information. Witness, for example, how much legislators may benefit from the opportunity afforded them by executive agencies to make public announcements about the establishment of new government programs or facilities in their districts. In disclosing such information, Congressmen can do a great deal to promote their visibility and stature in their own constituencies. They depend upon these information opportunities offered by the executive in much the same way as they once leaned upon executive patronage to nurse support in their own home districts.[8] As was true in the case of patronage, legislators are expected to return political support in exchange for these exclusive opportunities to disclose newsworthy items to the public.

Thus, while Congress has done a great deal to open up the affairs of bureaucracy to greater outside scrutiny (through the passage of legislation, the conduct of investigations, and relentless pressure for greater disclosure), individual legislators have also been willing to participate in the process of withholding information from the public when they are allowed to share in the secrets of the executive.

---

[8]See Stanley Kelley, Jr., "Patronage and Presidential Legislative Leadership," in Aaron Wildavsky (Ed.), *The Presidency* (Boston: Little, Brown and Co., 1969), p. 275.

The Pentagon and other national security agencies have recognized this legislative tendency to become more tolerant of executive secrecy when they are allowed to share in its benefits, and they have used it to build support among strategic groups like the Armed Services Committees in both the House and Senate.

IV. Reforming Government Secrecy

As the preceding discussion has shown, it is necessary to look at the entire political system in which executive agencies are linked in order to understand the strength and durability of secrecy in American government. Viewed from this systemic perspective, secrecy can be seen in its true colors—as a practice which serves a wealth of interests both inside and outside of government besides those of the executive officials. It is not only because of bureaucratic tenacity but also because a diverse range of institutions and groups in American society find secrecy useful that it has become so difficult to uproot secrecy through reform legislation.

Nonetheless, efforts to reform information policy and practices can be expected to continue in the United States. For while bureaucratic secrecy does serve the needs of a broad constellation of groups and organizations in the American political system, recent history clearly demonstrates that it is more easily put on the defensive in the United States than is the case in other parts of the world.

For one thing secrecy has less legitimacy as a governmental practice in the United States than in any other advanced industrial society with the possible exception of Sweden. This became very clear during the Watergate affair, when President Nixon tried unsuccessfully to justify his withholding of tapes and other information by claiming that such secrecy was essential to the effective functioning of the White House. His defense of secrecy on this ground seemed only to weaken his credibility and to further erode his standing in the public eye. In Britain, by way of contrast, a prime minister might very well have been able to persuade the public that such secrecy was necessary for the effective conduct of official business.[9]

A second distinctive attribute of American political culture is the fact that the network of organizations opposed to executive se-

[9]For a discussion of the role of secrecy in British culture, see James B. Christoph, "A Comparative View: Administrative Secrecy in Britain," *Public Administration Review* 35 (January/February 1975):23–32.

crecy is so much stronger in the United States than in other parts of the world. Congress has infinitely more leverage in ferreting out information from executive officials than legislative bodies elsewhere; the media enjoy a privileged position as a fourth branch of government they do not generally occupy in other political systems; and finally the extraordinarily tenacious and highly influential cluster of public interest groups opposed to secrecy finds no counterpart in countries other than the United States.

So while it may never be possible or desirable in the modern world to attain the "government in a goldfish bowl" toward which reformers often seem to be striving in the United States, it seems safe to say that secrecy will always be suspect in American politics, and that the recent events associated with Vietnam and Watergate will make it even more vulnerable to attack in the future than it has been in the past.

However, what the American experience with secrecy also suggests is the wide gap that exists between what reformers intend and what they achieve. Officials in the bureaucratic organizations whose information policies reform organizations are seeking to change have defenses in depth against altering procedural arrangements in which they have acquired a vested interest. They are very adept at transforming a mandate for change into a license to continue or even expand the secretive practices that are under attack. Thus, the Freedom of Information Act was the crowning achievement of reform efforts in the United States during the 1960s. By the 1970s it had become a prime target of the reform movement, as agencies proceeded to use minor provisions of the act which permitted withholding of information under certain very limited conditions as a broad charter for the preservation and even the expansion of secrecy.

30

The Rush to Deregulate

SUSAN J. TOLCHIN
AND MARTIN TOLCHIN

Few presidents have entered the White House with more well-defined or ambitious goals than those of Ronald Reagan. His objective was nothing less than a reversal of the direction of government, a repeal of much of the New Deal, a reduction in both the size and scope of government. A major part of that objective was the scaling back of the regulatory agencies, under the rubric of "getting the government off the backs of the people." But the prime targets were those agencies that sought to protect consumers and workers and to improve the air, water, and work place. They were the agencies, in effect, that tried to get industry off the backs of the people. President Reagan's antiregulatory stance was thus perceived as probusiness and antipublic, and fueled the fairness issue that was to haunt this presidency.

The new President lost little time converting his philosophy into reality. Nine days after his inauguration, he imposed a sixty-day freeze on all new regulations. A conservative, business-oriented politician, the new President placed a high priority on the dismantling of social regulations, which he considered excessive, inflationary, and counterproductive.[1]

He was familiar with the horror stories, and believed in a more laissez-faire approach to the problems of the environment and the work place; indeed, his replacement of Harry S Truman's portrait

[1]In addition to his business and acting background, Reagan also wrote a nationally syndicated column. See Ronald Reagan, "Nailing the Regulator," Special Weekly Column, King Features Syndicate, August 10, 1979.

in the White House with one of Calvin Coolidge said it all. Promising the American people speedy regulatory relief, he initiated the most comprehensive overhaul of the regulatory process in the history of the Republic. . . .

The key to Reagan's regulatory policy was a three-pronged attack, consisting of a regulatory rollback, budget cuts, and the appointment of key personnel dedicated to the Reagan philosophy of "getting the government off the backs of the people." Massive budget cuts left regulatory agencies bereft of resources, and struggling to maintain a minimum level of operation. Severe reductions in force (RIFs) curtailed their services and guaranteed that the agencies would need years, if not decades, to train the experts needed to do the job. Managers who remained faced a new set of bosses, Reagan appointees, who shared their President's commitment to reduce regulatory burdens and did not hesitate to quash regulations despite professional staff advice, or the number of years it took to develop those rules. "All of our appointees have religion," remarked James C. Miller III, a burly, fast-quipping former economics professor who headed the Office of Management and Budget (OMB) regulatory reform effort before going on to chair the Federal Trade Commission (FTC). "We want to make sure OSHA is no longer a four-letter word."

These changes, along with Reagan's Executive Order 12291— granting OMB superagency status over regulations and mandating economic analysis from the agencies—created a new regulatory landscape, a still life actually, with the presidential agencies fearful of issuing new regulations, or introducing too many new initiatives. White House regulatory policy also had a chilling effect on the "independent" regulatory agencies—the headless fourth branch of government, so called because they are technically accountable to Congress, which has traditionally ceded them wide discretion. Their discretion is limited, however, by the President's power to appoint the commissioners, and by the trend toward more direct White House intervention into their day-to-day policy activities. The independent agencies find themselves further constrained by the sensitivity of their leaders to public opinion, and by the winds of presidential and congressional change.[2]

---

[2]The regulatory agencies are divided into two basic categories: independent and executive branch agencies. Both types of agencies issue regulations, and share

Through its power to monitor the regulatory performance of the executive agencies, OMB kept the agencies so busy with requests for additional information that it held *de facto* control of their agendas as well as their output. After a while, OMB could relax, when it was evident the message had filtered down to the agency level. One midlevel management official at the Food and Drug Administration (FDA) described his agency's new approach by recalling a meeting held in the spring of 1981.

"We were meeting with the director of the Bureau of Drugs, on a drug we had been studying for over a year, and whose toxic effects included cancer and bladder trouble. The biggest concern from everyone was 'who's upset?'—meaning which industry would be upset. Everyone is extremely cautious about anything they let through that would upset industry. It's not that they're not proconsumer, but they're realists. They're sensitive to Reagan. They know he's there to represent business, and they're terrified. The result is that things are operating at a snail's pace. We're just doing busywork. Unless somebody's on our tail, like Ralph Nader, nothing gets

---

similar functions in terms of scope and power; indeed, the regulatory agencies issue more rulings than the courts and the legislature combined. The major difference is that the independent agencies are accountable primarily to Congress, while the executive branch agencies answer directly to the President. There are twenty-two independent agencies, among them: the Nuclear Regulatory Commission, the Federal Communications Commission, the Federal Trade Commission, the International Trade Commission, the Securities and Exchange Commission, the Interstate Commerce Commission, to name a few. They are headed by multimembered commissions, with the commissioners named by the President and submitted for congressional approval. In that way, the President shares power with Congress; his power limited by the fact that the terms of the commissioners do not run consecutively with the President's. The executive branch agencies are directly under White House control, although Congress through budgetary oversight can make an impact on their decisions. Executive branch regulatory agencies include the Occupational Safety and Health Administration, located in the Department of Labor; the Environmental Protection Agency, an executive agency headed by a subcabinet level administrator; the Army Corps of Engineers, in the Department of Defense; and the Social Security Administration, in the Department of Health and Human Services, to name several of the better known of the more than ninety executive agencies inside the executive branch that have been given the power by Congress to issue regulations ranging from strip mining to economic development. Some agencies find themselves in peculiar administrative arrangements that do not fit neatly into either of the two categories. The Federal Energy Regulatory Commission (FERC), for example, is an independent agency, but is located within an executive branch agency, the Department of Energy. An excellent source of reference on the regulatory agencies is the *Federal Regulatory Directory*, published annually by Congressional Quarterly Press.

done. The administration's point of view is that we're just slowing things down. We're just taking a closer look at everything. It's true these things are deadly or carcinogenic, but the economy's a mess and that takes precedence." . . .

Origins of Presidential Intervention

Andrew Jackson was the first President to argue that the President controls the actions of cabinet officers and agencies. Angered by the refusal of two consecutive Treasury Department secretaries to obey his orders to remove deposits from the Second Bank of the United States, Jackson fired them both, and announced that he would continue to hire and dismiss secretaries until he found one who would do his bidding. "A secretary," he said, "is merely an executive, an agent, a subordinate."[3]

Firing cabinet secretaries, however, represented a blunderbuss approach, surely not a viable management tool for the volume of regulation that had begun to surface by the early 1970s. Until that time, almost all regulations were issued by the independent agencies, and were primarily economic. The White House did not exert much influence, except through appointments to the commissions, and there is not much evidence to suggest that Presidents were able to make substantial inroads despite periodic attempts—including recommendations from various blue-ribbon panels—to bring these agencies closer to the executive branch. Moreover, there had not yet appeared any ground swell of concern on the part of interest groups, who had developed their own relationships with the agencies and

[3]Martin Tolchin, *New York Times*, January 17, 1979, pp. A1 and D17. Since Jackson, the President's power to fire and control officials in the administrative agencies has been considerably refined by Congress and the courts, both of which clearly differentiated between the executive branch and independent agencies. In *Myers v. United States*, 272 U.S. 52 (1926), for example, the Court ruled that the President could remove subordinate appointees without congressional consent, pointing out that as a postmaster, Myers clearly fell within the jurisdiction of the Chief Executive. Several years later, the Court clarified the difference in the removal power in *Humphrey's Executor v. United States*, 295 U.S. 602 (1935), which involved an independent regulatory commission, not under the direct control of the President. In this case, the Court ruled that the President did not have the right to remove without cause a member of the Federal Trade Commission, pointing out that Congress in granting rulemaking and adjudicatory powers to the FTC intended to insulate its decision makers from political interference.

saw regulation primarily in the context of their own individual transactions.

By 1970, it had become clear that regulation had a considerable social and economic impact on society, and that some form of centralized oversight was needed. It also became apparent that the agencies were unable to coordinate their efforts—particularly in the area of environmental regulation—and the call for presidential intervention took on a new sense of urgency.

Richard Nixon became the first President to introduce a formal management system into the regulatory arena, a process known as the Quality of Life (QOL) review. The review required all agencies involved in health, safety, or environmental regulation to advise all other affected agencies of all conceivable impacts of a proposed regulation—economic, intergovernmental, and environmental. Involving mostly Environmental Protection Agency (EPA) regulations, these comments were sent to other agencies like Commerce, Interior, and the Army Corps of Engineers, with OMB in the role of mediating interagency conflicts. Agencies could appeal OMB decisions to the head of OMB, and theoretically to the President, but according to James Tozzi, who then headed the Quality of Life program as chief of the environmental branch of OMB, this occurred "only once in a blue moon."

To Tozzi, who is now the deputy administrator for information and regulatory affairs at OMB, the "guts of the program" rested on a review process, a portent of things to come, that for the first time made agencies accountable to the President for their actions. Since most of the affected regulations were environmental, EPA became the agency most involved in QOL reviews and, in the process of going through those reviews, developed an analytical capability that many, including Tozzi, believed far superior to that of all the other agencies. As inflation began to rise, along with congressional pressure, President Gerald Ford redirected regulatory management from an environmental to an economic focus, a pattern that was to continue under President Carter. Ford's Economic Impact Statements (EIS) affected all agencies, and OMB's enforcement and coordinating role was replaced by the newly formed Council on Wage and Price Stability (COWPS). With COWPS in charge of compliance, OMB was virtually removed throughout the late 1970s from the nucleus of regulatory power until the Reagan administration resurrected the agency's earlier role and gave it primary responsibility for regulating the regulators.

With OMB on the periphery and no one technically in charge, it was easy to ignore prior executive orders in the period immediately following President Carter's election. Although OMB director Bert Lance pressed for the continuation of QOL review, he soon became preoccupied with his own problems, and the agencies quickly stepped in to fill the vacuum. With the agencies again in full ascendancy, presidential management fell by the wayside. Under pressure from one segment of the Carter campaign and from EPA staff members who opposed QOL reviews, the deputy director of EPA unilaterally canceled the reviews. During the next two years, presidential oversight was moderated, until members of the Council of Economic Advisers urged the President to renew efforts at regulatory management. "Lack of performance of the executive branch," remarked Tozzi, "was the best argument for oversight."

In quick succession, the Regulatory Council and the Regulatory Analysis Review Group (RARG) were formed in 1978, establishing the basis for what was to follow under Reagan. Despite the reluctance of Reagan appointees to acknowledge the Carter legacy, there is no question about its importance in laying the foundation for Reagan's more comprehensive program. Carter's efforts represented the first strong move by a President to intervene directly in the day-to-day operations of regulatory agencies. Other Presidents consistently made the effort to intervene in both executive and independent regulatory agencies, but not until President Carter was there such a blatant, concerted effort to manage the entire process. Previous attempts were academic exercises compared with Carter's efforts to apply his own political muscle to the problems of regulatory management. . . .

In a foreshadowing of Reagan's strategy, Carter relied on an executive order (EO 12044) promulgated in March 1978. The order focused on the economic impact of regulation and added a stronger role for the President in reducing its costs. The Carter administration was waging a losing battle against inflation, and the high cost of regulation was frequently cited as a major factor—another example of regulation as an all-purpose scapegoat. Under Carter's edict, all executive agencies were required to conduct economic analyses of their proposed regulations whenever those regulations appeared to have a substantial impact on the economy. A selected group of economic advisers, the Regulatory Analysis Review Group (RARG), then reviewed the most inflationary of the regulations—those costing industry more than $100 million a year—presumably with the intention of mitigating their impact.

By any name, RARG was there to modify regulations, to relax them, and ultimately to make them less expensive for the business community and, to a lesser extent, for states and localities. This practice of modifying the impact of proposed regulations through executive power turned out to be the crux of a controversy that plagued both Presidents Carter and Reagan in their efforts to establish a presidential beachhead in the regulatory arena.

Although the executive order formally assigned OMB to the task of reviewing these economic analyses, the agency at that time was too fragmented—"like the Balkans before World War I," one White House staff member explained—to take on such a politically sensitive task. Instead, extensive reviews of about six regulations a year were conducted by RARG, which included representatives of all cabinet departments (except State, Treasury, and Defense) and top officials from OMB, the EPA, and the White House Office of Science and Technology Policy. In actual fact, RARG was run by an executive committee, chaired by Charles L. Schultze, the original architect of RARG and chairman of the President's Council of Economic Advisers (CEA).[4] The bulk of the analytical staff work was undertaken by economists from the Council on Wage and Price Stability (COWPS). . . .

Clearly, RARG's existence depended almost entirely on President Carter's continuing personal interest and his willingness to exert political clout on its behalf. "The administration has found that the fact that RARG is there to monitor the quality of the analyses has helped to improve them," noted Charles Schultze in testimony before the Senate Judiciary Committee in May 1979. "This is especially true," he added, "because it is understood that the President personally authorized establishment of the program and is personally following its progress." In fact, White House aides sent the President a biweekly memo on the progress of the program.

Schultze's rule in the RARG process marked another turning point in presidential management of regulation: the ascendancy of

---

[4]Schultze, an economist from The Brookings Institution, was a well-known advocate of alternatives to regulation. His book, *The Public Use of Private Interest* (Washington: The Brookings Institution, 1977), is a classic in its field.

economists over lawyers. Shaped by their own discipline, White House economists did not even bother to conceal their disdain for what they considered rigid, legalistic approaches adopted by many of the agencies, especially when they encountered opposition. "The first time an agency is 'RARGed,' it is like a cold shower," reported one CEA staff member in the Carter administration. "Many have never done cost-benefit analysis and OSHA, for example, had, at most, one economist in the whole agency." . . .

For their part, critics feared the effects of the new supremacy of economists, who, they felt, were bound by their discipline into a new rigidity in which "sound analysis" was equated solely with economic analysis. Capitulating to the RARG standards of balancing costs against benefits meant viewing regulatory policy strictly through the context of White House economists, and in that framework, they predicted, cost factors would invariably take precedence over social concerns. No one knew where other forms of analysis—political, demographic, scientific—would fit into this scheme, although many guessed that it would not take long before health and safety standards would be sacrificed to the needs of cooling the economy. Still others warned that cost-benefit analysis was often misleading by failing to include the costs of inaction, in terms of increased illness, for example, with its related costs in lowered productivity and increased medical expenses. In a letter sent to President Carter in 1978, and cosigned by over thirty environmental, health, and labor groups, Richard Ayres of the Natural Resources Defense Council charged that White House regulatory oversight had become a "serious threat to the interests of millions of Americans" by substituting the judgment of CEA and COWPS "on questions of work place and environmental health and welfare for the technical and legal judgment of agencies that Congress has explicitly created and directed to make such decisions."

The Tightrope of Regulatory Management

As a management system, RARG incorporated many commendable features. But as a political institution, it raised two major issues, both of which remained to haunt the Reagan administration's program: the scope of the President's authority over regulatory decision making within the executive branch, and the compatibility of White House intervention with the requirements of the most comprehensive law governing the regulatory process, the Administrative Procedure Act. Through RARG and the executive order, President Carter hoped to establish hegemony over the regulatory actions of disparate agencies while allowing agency heads to retain the formal responsibility for making decisions. By adding another layer between himself and the agencies, the President hoped to shield himself from the responsibility for unpopular decisions. But there was no place to hide. Carter learned the hard way how costly these decisions could be. His experience with the cotton dust rule in May 1978, when he interceded directly to relax standards imposed by Secretary of Labor Ray Marshall (acting on the basis of proposals from OSHA) for maximum permissible levels of cotton dust in textile mills, touched off a storm of protest. The new standard came under intense criticism from labor unions, health groups, and industry—and, not surprisingly, most of the anger was aimed at Carter himself.[5] Carter faced similar criticisms when he tried to intervene in rule making on strip mining, following the passage of the Surface Mining Control and Reclamation Act. This time, two legal challenges were immediately initiated, both questioning the formulation of strip-mining regulations. Initially, environmentalists unsuccessfully sought an injunction to stop closed, off-the-record meetings between Charles Schultze and Secretary of the Interior Cecil Andrus. In a subsequent case that sounded what was to become a recurrent theme, the plaintiffs alleged that off-the-record consultations between CEA officials and Interior Department officials significantly affected the decision-making process.[6] Faced with litigation and political opposition, Carter never again directly intervened in a regulatory issue without covering his tracks.

President Carter's experience showed why previous Presidents had shunned blatant, overt intervention in the regulatory process, and had limited themselves to behind-the-scenes maneuvering. On the other hand, some argue, the President is ultimately praised or blamed for the decisions of the regulatory agencies, because the public does not make the fine distinctions between those agencies and

[5]The cotton dust case was later decided by the Supreme Court, which ruled in favor of the tighter standards advocated by OSHA, in *American Textile Manufacturers Institute v. Donovan*, 452 U.S. 490, 101 S. Ct. 2478, 69 L. Ed. 2d 185 (1981).

[6]*Natural Resources Defense Council et al. v. Schultze et al.*, U.S. District Court, D.C., Civil Action no. 79.

the President himself. That being the case, some believe that a President is in a no-win position and has little to lose in making his views public.

The issue, never clarified during the Carter years, continued to plague advocates of the Reagan executive order, with no legal resolution in sight. How far can the White House go to ensure that its policies are being carried out without violating the public comment provisions of the Administrative Procedure Act, which courts have interpreted as the prohibition of introducing new material in a regulatory proceeding after the public comment period has officially closed? Would not a President's intervention violate the prohibition against *ex parte* contacts—contacts made by private parties outside the official comment period? Or is it unfair to classify the White House as an outside party when it is communicating with its own executive branch?

Defenders of presidential intervention argued that RARG did not go far enough, that its interventions ceased at the close of the comment period, when its report was filed and made part of the public record. But those who worked in the White House admitted that the President really did intervene through his economic advisers, and actually set regulatory policy.

"The real oversight occurs when RARG hammers out its report," said economist Tom Hopkins, who then worked for COWPS and now occupies a similar position at OMB. "However, further intervention by presidential advisers, such as the CEA or COWPS chairman [as distinct from RARG], is possible after the comment period." . . .

Some of the problems encountered by RARG reflected recent political trends, while others originated in long-established patterns in national politics. Throughout its short tenure, for example, RARG confronted the problems of congressional oversight. The sponsors of some of the newer regulatory statutes maintained a proprietary interest in the administrative or enforcement policies developed under "their" programs. Former Senator Edmund Muskie (Democrat, Maine), one of the authors of the Clean Air Act and several clean water statutes, continued for almost a decade to display a keen interest in the activities of EPA, often defending the agency against pressures for compromise. With Congress having the last word at that time on the budgets and legislative authorizations (or restrictions) of the regulatory agencies, leading figures on congressional oversight committees were often more influential than the White House. Agency staff soon learned that lesson, often fleeing to congressional patrons for sympathy and support when they disapproved of the direction toward which they were being prodded by the President's staff.

That hard political reality often forced prior administrations to engage in quiet bargaining with congressional committee chairmen when they wanted to effect a change in regulatory policy or to develop a new rule along particular lines. These efforts were not always successful, but defeat at least could be accepted without public humiliation in most cases. In recent years, however, with the rising potency of single-interest advocates and their ready access to the media, disagreements over regulatory policy have suddenly flared up into heated public controversies. Today, the setting within which the White House operates is clearly more inflammatory, harsher, and more public than it used to be, with the President wedged between the proverbial rock and a hard place. When President Carter pressed EPA to pay closer attention to economic costs, he was branded an "enemy of the environment." When he promoted himself as an environmentalist, as he did many times, he was attacked for adding to the country's runaway inflation. Many critics at the time insisted that Carter himself compounded these problems with his antiseptic and apolitical style of leadership.

Taken together, these factors created a political climate that led agency leaders to scrupulously avoid antagonizing special interest groups or key figures in Congress while, at the same time, trying to meet the suggestions of the President's economists. But avoiding controvery did not seem to help: the criticism continued in the same whipsaw fashion. The government continued to be sued by the environmental groups, and agencies like OSHA and EPA were regularly attacked for overzealousness or for selling out. The intensity of the debate on all sides reflected people's awareness of the stakes involved: the lives of millions of citizens and their health, safety, and welfare were being weighed against billions of dollars in dwindling economic resources.

To its credit, the gist of Carter's program survived its political difficulties and marked a turning point in the history of presidential control over agency regulatory behavior. From that time on, as reflected in Reagan's reform plan, agencies began, on a routine basis, to introduce cost-benefit analyses into their decision-making activities. Although many seemed to adopt and exaggerate this method of analysis without the necessary modifications, it still represented an important step forward in introducing the awareness of cost factors to agencies that had previously ignored them.

The Reagan Juggernaut

Ronald Reagan undertook the role of an activist President, playing Henry V to Carter's Hamlet, with a love of political battle reminiscent of Franklin Roosevelt. Not for him the politics of ambivalence, or the legal niceties that called for at least an appearance of respect for the independence of the agencies. In short order, he sought to place the independent agencies as well as the executive agencies under his own executive order, yielding only when the legal obstacles became apparent. He then requested that the independent agencies "voluntarily" comply with the order.

The Reagan administration reaped the benefits of Carter's regulatory initiatives and learned from his mistakes. "We bulletproofed our executive order," said James C. Miller III, in the fall of 1981, referring to the legal protections of their program compared to the RARG. "RARG was an ordinary intervenor, with only a counseling capacity. RARG was analogous to someone writing an article for a professional journal, having to convince the editor it was worthwhile printing. Now we [OMB] are the editor; and we know we're being published. It's like being the editor of the *Federal Register*. Besides," he added, "our President is tough. Carter folded on his first big issue, cotton dust." . . .

No doubt, much of Reagan's success hinged on moving into the regulatory arena quickly, catching potential adversaries off guard, and insisting on White House hegemony over the process. Without this kind of mandate from the President, Miller was quick to point out, neither he nor other members of his team, whom he called the regulatory triumvirate, would have been able to push through their program. Lest they forget, all top members of the administration were constantly reminded of their mission, according to Miller, who said not a cabinet meeting went by without the President referring to "some regulatory horror story."

To ensure a substantial return on the enormous amount of political capital invested in this venture, the President put the full force of his office behind the reform effort. The White House task force responsible for implementing the executive order was represented on an operating level by Richard Williamson, assistant to the President for intergovernmental affairs; the Office of Management and Budget by James C. Miller III; and the Vice President by Boyden Gray. "Just like Meese, Baker, and Deaver were the Big Three, I called us the Little Three," quipped Miller.

As the formal leader of the task force, Vice President Bush kept a high profile on the subject of regulatory reform through his speeches and other well-publicized activities. OMB freely used the Vice President's influence to bring recalcitrant agency heads into line. One agency head called to tell Miller he wanted to go ahead anyway on a regulation that had been delayed by OMB. Miller said that was fine with him, but he would have to take it up with the Vice President. "I'm amazed at how fast the opposition withered," added Miller. . . .

The business community was assured in other ways as well that the Reagan administration meant to deliver regulatory relief by cutting red tape whenever possible. In a speech delivered to the Chamber of Commerce on April 10, 1981, Boyden Gray told businessmen not to be discouraged if they failed to get satisfaction from the agencies. That is what the White House is there for, he told them:

"If you go to the agency first, don't be too pessimistic if they can't solve the problem there. . . . That's what the task force is for.

"We had an example of that not too long ago. . . . We told the lawyers representing the individual companies and the trade associations involved to come back to us if they had a problem.

"Two weeks later they showed up and I asked if they had a problem. They said they did, and we made a couple of phone calls and straightened it out. We alerted the top people at the agency that there was a little hanky-panky going on at the bottom of the agency, and it was cleared up very rapidly. The system does work if you use it as sort of an appeal. You can act as a double check on the agency that you might encounter problems with."[7]

The informal system worked very well, downgrading the professional role of the agencies while increasing through White House intervention the influence of the special interests. But as with Carter's intervention through RARG, the Reagan administration

[7]"OMB: The Role of the Office of Management and Budget in Regulation," House Subcommittee on Oversight and Investigations, Committee on Energy and Commerce, June 19, 1981, p. 97.

needed some kind of legal foundation to add legitimacy to its regulatory maneuvers. It produced its own variation of RARG, through Executive Order 12291, issued February 17, 1981.

The executive order gave OMB the power to oversee all major regulations promulgated by the executive branch agencies, excluding the twenty-two independent agencies that are legally under the jurisdiction of Congress.[8] The order also imposed formal requirements on the agencies that would guarantee their submission to the President's program, in order to increase "agency accountability for regulatory actions," provide for "presidential oversight, minimize duplication and conflict of regulations, and ensure well-reasoned regulations."[9]

Heavy emphasis was placed on cost-benefit analysis, with informational requirements spelled out in great detail, directing agencies to develop new regulations involving the "least net cost to society." Agencies were discouraged from taking regulatory action at all unless the "potential benefits to society . . . outweigh the potential costs to society." Another requirement asked the agencies to "set regulatory priorities," taking into account the condition of particular industries affected by the regulation, as well as the "condition of the national economy." Additional requirements mandated that the agencies submit regulatory impact analyses justifying their finding that the benefits exceeded the costs; regulatory reviews establishing that a proposed regulation fell within the agency's legal authority; and regulatory agendas to be published twice a year, in October and April, containing a summary of each rule being considered.

On the process questions that had plagued Carter the most, the task force adopted a forceful political strategy, the only realistic option while the legal issue remained in limbo. The task force managed the secrecy and *ex parte* issues, for example, by assuming a Dr. Jekyll and Mr. Hyde posture that initially appeared to work well. On one level, the process seemed perfectly clear-cut, with everything aboveboard and on the record. Boyden Gray said he sent everyone who petitioned him on a regulatory issue straight to the agencies, where

[8]The administration asked the independent agencies to comply with the executive order voluntarily, but as of this writing only the Federal Trade Commission under the leadership of James Miller III indicated it would comply. As more Reagan appointees fill positions in the independent agencies, it would not be unreasonable to expect more agencies to join the FTC in submitting to the executive order.
[9]46 Fed. Reg. 13,193 (1981).

their complaints were immediately entered on the record. Answering critics who charged that this meant the business community could change any regulation by simply going through the backdoor at the White House, Gray countered by saying that he had made a special effort to contact groups on the other side of the fence: "We contacted the environmentalists; they hadn't contacted us." In stressing the importance of entering everything on the record, Gray added that he had once sent an "interested party" to an agency and the agency had failed to enter the material in the record; an oversight that was quickly corrected by the Vice President's office. . . .

Enter Mr. Hyde. The purity of the process all seems perfectly aboveboard until the role of OMB emerges. Although OMB was technically responsible for regulatory reform under Carter, the agency then was too ridden with internal strife to play any significant role. Its difficulties smoothed over, OMB today has assumed the role previously carved out by RARG and the President's economic advisers, intervening at all points in the regulatory process to ensure that the President's mandate is implemented. Its real goal, according to advocates of the process, is to eliminate the adversarial conflicts between business and government that have severely inhibited regulatory progress in the past. OMB can only do this by negotiating quietly, particularly at the beginning, as Boyden Gray explained, "before the train has left the station, when the polarizing begins—before the regs go to the *Federal Register.*"

The problem with OMB's efforts is that the benefits of public discussion, even when it turns into controversy, are neglected in the course of conducting business in secret. In order to avoid the inevitable controversies that surface following a proposed rule's publication in the *Federal Register,* the agency insists it must operate in private, and with a great deal of discretionary power. The architects of this process argue that if all meetings were open at every stage, the logistical difficulties would be insurmountable, not to mention the political problems. "I would have to summarize this conversation with you," explained Tozzi* during an interview in his office, to show the impossibility of an agency as small as OMB logging all meetings and conversations.

"There's no reason why OMB's contacts should be on the record; desk officers don't meet with outside parties," continued Boyden

---

*Editor's note: James Tozzi of OMB, a career civil servant.

Gray, who elaborated his analysis by analogizing OMB as an arm of the President. "It's not a theoretical matter. The public has no more right to know what a member of the President's staff says to an agency than a congressman who communicates privately with his staff. The Congress will never do it. Why should we?

"Also, it's a practical matter," he added. "You couldn't talk if you had to summarize everything. Why should the President be different?" And with echoes of the "happy family" theory, he said: "Besides, we're all one government." . . .

The Congressional Reaction

Even if 90 percent of the regulations passed OMB scrutiny unaltered, critics were still worried about the other 10 percent: troublesome regulations that were delayed by OMB, some never to see the light of day, unless a lawsuit or a newspaper story uncovered their existence. At this point, proving the disparities between what OMB said and what OMB did became easier, particularly to those attempting to follow up the progress of specific regulations. Fortunately, Congress does not for the most part operate in secret; its hearings and bill-drafting sessions are now conducted in public, a result of extending the principles of the sunshine laws to the legislature. It was through congressional oversight of this kind that OMB's regulatory activities were finally subjected to public scrutiny.

OMB maintained its right to secrecy before a congressional committee, the Subcommittee on Oversight and Investigations of the House Committee on Energy and Commerce, chaired by Rep. John Dingell, Democrat of Michigan. To obtain the most basic kinds of information, the committee was forced to subpoena OMB, going back repeatedly to the agency for basic data. OMB spokesmen claimed the agency did not keep logs of telephone calls or meetings, and that all business was conducted without much record keeping of any sort. The sketchy record finally compiled by the agency at the committee's request confirmed its suspicion that the mere fact that OMB was engaged in questioning a regulation struck sufficient terror in the hearts of the agencies to bury that regulation for good. "The record shows that from June to September 1981, seven regulations were returned to the agencies. Six were never resubmitted," said Patrick McLain, the committee staff member in charge of regulation. "What we want to know is how many regulations are never submitted at all?"

Regulations referred to by McLain included two Federal Aviation Administration (FAA) regulations, both affecting air safety and both involving minimal cost. The first dealt with the prohibition of hang gliders from airspace around airports, the second with blood alcohol rules for pilots. Since neither of these regulations imposed significant costs on industry, it was difficult to determine why OMB delayed them. OMB and White House sources refused to comment on specific regulations when questioned; they would comment only on the program as a whole. . . .

At an oversight hearing that June (1981), members of the Dingell committee tried to extract more information about OMB's activities. It soon became apparent, judging by the acerbic line of questioning, that the conflict represented a contest of power between the President and Congress, with allegiance to different political parties only an incidental factor. On what legal authority did witnesses James Miller and Boyden Gray base their effort to "hot-wire the regulatory proceedings at the agencies?" queried Rep. Albert Gore, Democrat of Tennessee.[10] Gore was followed by Rep. Mike Synar, Democrat of Oklahoma, who accused Miller and Gray of "stepping on some very serious constitutional questions" when they controlled "all these guys who are your 'hired guns' . . . circumventing the whole process of administering the law . . . and the prohibitions against *ex parte* communications."

Synar was especially concerned about the question of public access to the regulatory process, guaranteed by the Administrative Procedure Act, but under the new system dependent only on OMB's good will. "Do all people have the right to call you," he asked Boyden Gray, "or just a select group of people?" Can "my mom and dad who are upset about something call directly to you?" he asked. Miller and Gray both said "absolutely," although Gray added that he hoped Synar's mom and dad would go to the agencies first with their complaints. After later hearing Rep. Gore read the subpoenaed list of businesses, Synar concluded to the general amusement of those at-

---

[10]"OMB: The Role of the Office of Management and Budget in Regulation," House Subcommittee on Oversight and Investigations, Committee on Energy and Commerce, June 18, 1981, p. 103.

tending the hearing that "it does not look as if my mom and dad are getting in there."[11]

Miller denied categorically any correlation between OMB's meetings with corporate representatives and the withdrawal of specific regulations:

> MR. GORE: "You had a 20 minute meeting with the Chemical Manufacturers Association talking about regulatory relief a month before you asked to pull back the regulations on hazardous waste disposal, and you are telling me under oath that you did not even mention hazardous waste with the CMA?"
>
> MR. MILLER: "I am telling you, to the best of my recollection, that topic did not come up."
>
> MR. GORE: "What about February 18, 1981? You met with the American Mining Congress and discussed 'support for regulatory relief.' Isn't it more likely that you discussed their support for the postponement of the Interior Department's rule on extraction of coals, which has now been postponed indefinitely?"
>
> MR. MILLER: "I cannot recall that particular meeting."[12] . . .

Discontent was also growing in the Senate, even from those who supported an increase in presidential control over the regulatory process. Senator Carl Levin, Democrat of Michigan, after counting at least fifty-five regulations that failed to meet OMB's approval, called the process an "extraordinary but almost hidden centralization of power" that has "overturned some 35 years of practice under the Administrative Procedure Act." OMB's newly acquired power as superregulator, warned Levin, was "unchecked and unaccountable," subverting "Congress' appropriate oversight role," as well as the public's "basic right to petition government effectively."[13]

The tug of war between Congress and the President ultimately reached a draw. In the meantime, OMB moved quietly ahead, unafraid of what amounted to empty challenges that the superagency was privately displacing the authority, discretion, and expertise of the agencies. "It's some GS-12 budget examiner imposing his or her judgment on whether these rules were good or not," noted one critic, in an ironic reversal of previous accusations that midlevel bureaucrats were making high level policy through the regulatory process.

[11]Ibid., p. 105.
[12]Ibid., pp. 110–12.
[13]*Washington Post*, November 1, 1981, p. C7.

Only now those GS-12s come from OMB and act as representatives of the President.

"OMB needs to be the President's agent," countered Murray Weidenbaum, defending the agency. "It is the only agency with a broad array of concerns. If the U.S. Department of Agriculture could look at a farm bill from the point of view of the consumer, then I wouldn't have to get involved." But OMB also looks at the world through its own narrow perspective—fiscal policy. It is the government's fiscal watchdog, perforce not overly concerned with social needs such as public health and safety.

As yet, the question of OMB's legitimacy as a regulatory watchdog remains unresolved, although the legal and legislative foundations of the executive order have been reinforced through two laws preceding the order: the Regulatory Flexibility Act and the Paperwork Reduction Act.[14] The Paperwork Act gave OMB the power to pare down paperwork requirements, as well as other information-gathering burdens imposed by regulations; the Regulatory Flexibility Act, which mandated regulatory analysis in certain categories of rule making, supported OMB's efforts to impose cost-benefit analysis on the executive agencies.

To Reagan strategists, further affirmation for regulatory reform was indicated by a recent court of appeals decision, *Sierra Club v. Costle*.[15] This decision upheld the legality of "intra-executive contacts" between the President's staff and the agencies after the comment period had officially closed. Recognizing the need for the "President and his White House staff to monitor the consistency of executive agency regulations with administration policy," Judge Patricia Wald ruled that the government could not "function effectively or rationally if key executive policy makers were isolated from each other and from the Chief Executive."[16]

The *Sierra* case gave the Reagan "reform" effort a new lease on life, as well as increased legitimacy. Immediately following the decision, OMB director David Stockman distributed a memo declaring that OMB's procedures will be consistent with the "holding and policies" discussed in the *Sierra* case. In actuality, however, some

[14]Paperwork Reduction Act of 1980, Pub. L. No. 96-511, 44 U.S.C. et seq. (1980), and the Regulatory Flexibility Act, Pub. L. No. 96-354, 5 U.S.C. 601 et seq. (1980).

[15]*Sierra Club v. Costle*, 657 F. 2d 298 (D.C. Circ. 1981).

[16]Ibid., pp. 212–20.

legal scholars argue that OMB has gone beyond the legal limits of the *Sierra* decision, especially since the decision never "endorsed the principle of *secret* White House contacts with private parties or with agency officials."[17] During these secret meetings, OMB assumes the role of a "conduit contact," or a critical access point for outside pressure groups to influence the outcome of a rule-making proceeding, without the safeguard of a public record. The *Sierra* decision appears to indicate the reverse: "If oral communications are to be freely permitted after the close of the comment period, then at least some summary of them must be made in order to preserve the integrity of the rulemaking docket."[18] The court, in its landmark decision, did not bar oral communications between the White House and the agency, but it did rule that relevant communications be recorded so as not to violate the provisions of the agency's enabling legislation, which in the *Sierra* case specifically stated that any information affecting the final rule be placed "on the docket." . . .

OMB officials brushed off congressional oversight efforts as mere partisan harassment from a Democratic-controlled committee, noting it was time the White House made a permanent dent in the power of the congressional "barons" over the regulatory agencies. This was no mean feat, considering Congress's past power over the agencies, a relationship so strong it was termed the "iron triangle," a triad of interest groups, congressional committees, and the agencies, all revolving around their special issues—and all attempting to circumvent the White House. With OMB in control, these long-established patterns have receded, making it much more difficult for agency staff to flee to their congressional patrons for sympathy and support. . . .

In the final analysis, Reagan was able to finish what Carter had originally planned: the legitimization of OMB as a regulatory manager. Anchored with the full weight of the President's clout, OMB could exert a degree of control over the agencies never achieved by previous Presidents.[19] In return, the agency deflected most of the

[17]Nan Aron and Charles Ludlum, "Undermining Public Protections—The Reagan Administration Regulatory Program," Alliance for Justice, 1981.

[18]*Sierra*, p. 207.

[19]Although many previous presidents had tried. Proof of their efforts is the number of commissions created by the Chief Executive to study ways to bring the agencies more directly under presidential control, all under the rubric of administrative reorganization. See Herbert Kaufman, "Emerging Conflicts in the Doctrines of Public Administration," *American Political Science Review* 50 (December 1956): 1057–73.

inevitable controversy away from Reagan and onto a more diffuse target—a stroke of political acumen that made the regulatory reform program as effective as it was in terms of its own goals.

The new OMB also added another layer of bureaucracy to the already complex regulatory process—an ironic development in view of all the past criticism leveled at regulation for its delays and inordinate red tape. As OMB plunged deeper into the management of regulation, it added its own reams of red tape, this time delaying regulations indefinitely on the basis of cost criteria, in place of health and safety requirements.

In reality, OMB's capture of the regulatory process represented a victory for the President over the agencies. In the past, Presidents wielded substantial power over both executive branch and independent agencies. But this power was exercised through persuasion, budget, and appointments. Now there is a new twist: the White House, according itself new legitimacy through OMB, can control, discourage, or overturn agency actions that had previously served as a check on presidential power. . . .